Current Approaches to the Lexicon

A Selection of Papers Presented at the 18th LAUD Symposium, Duisburg, March 1993

DUISBURGER ARBEITEN ZUR SPRACH- UND KULTURWISSENSCHAFT

Duisburg Papers on Research in Language and Culture

Herausgegeben von
René Dirven, Martin Pütz und Siegfried Jäger

Band 24

PETER LANG
Frankfurt am Main · Berlin · Bern · New York · Paris · Wien

René Dirven
Johan Vanparys
(Eds.)

Current Approaches to the Lexicon

A Selection of Papers Presented at the 18th LAUD Symposium, Duisburg, March 1993

PETER LANG
Europäischer Verlag der Wissenschaften

Die Deutsche Bibliothek - CIP-Einheitsaufnahme

Current approaches to the lexicon : Duisburg, March 1993 / René Dirven & Johan Vanparys (eds.). - Frankfurt am Main ; Berlin ; Bern ; New York ; Paris ; Wien : Lang, 1995
(A selection of papers presented at the 18th LAUD symposium, Duisburg, March 1993)
(Duisburger Arbeiten zur Sprach- und Kulturwissenschaft ; Bd. 24)
ISBN 3-631-48756-8

NE: Dirven, René [Hrsg.]; 2. GT

ISSN 0934-3709
ISBN 3-631-48756-8

Printed in Germany 1 2 3 4 6 7

List of contributors

Angela ALBRECHT
Anglistik
Gerhard-Mercator Universität
Duisburg, Germany

Angeliki ATHANASIADOU
School of English
Aristotle University
Thessaloniki, Greece

Lut BATEN
Institute of Living Languages
Katholieke Universiteit Leuven
Leuven, Belgium

René DIRVEN
Anglistik
Gerhard-Mercator Universität
Duisburg, Germany

Jürgen HANDKE
Inst. f. Anglistik/Computerlinguistik
Phillips-Universität Marburg
Marburg/Lahn, Germany

Richard R. K. HARTMANN
University of Exeter
Exeter, Great Britain

Ulrike KAUNZNER
School of Translators
University of Bologna
Bologna, Italy

E. LANGE
Abteilung Fremdsprachen
Techn. Hochschule Köthen
Köthen, Germany

Nils LENKE
Computerlinguistik
Gerhard-Mercator Universität
Duisburg, Germany

Agnieszka LENKO
Institute of English Studies
University of Lodz
Lodz, Poland

Wolf-Andreas LIEBERT
Institut für deutsche Sprache
Mannheim, Germany

Leonhard LIPKA
Institut für englische Philologie
Universität München
München, Germany

Stefan MEHL
Computerlinguistik
Gerhard-Mercator Universität
Duisburg, Germany

Carol MYERS-SCOTTON
Linguistics Program
University of South Carolina
Columbia, U.S.A.

Monika SCHWARZ
Institut f. deutsche Sprache u. Lit.
Universität Köln
Köln, Germany

Dieter SEELBACH
Institut f. Allgem. Sprachwissensch.
Johannes-Gutenberg Universität
Mainz, Germany

Beate SEIDEL
Theoretische u. Angew. Linguistik
Universität Leipzig
Leipzig, Germany

Elżbieta TABAKOWSKA
Institute of English Studies
Jagiellonian University
Cracow, Poland

John R. TAYLOR
Linguistics Section
University of Otago
Otago, New Zealand

Friedrich UNGERER
Institut f. Anglistik/Amerik.
Universität Rostock
Rostock, Germany

Johan VANPARYS
Institute of Living Languages
Facultés Universitaires
Notre-Dame de la Paix
Namur, Belgium

Wim WAUMANS
Germanistik
Gerhard-Mercator Universität
Duisburg, Germany

Anna WIERZBICKA
Department of Linguistics
Australian National University
Canberra, Australia

Cornelia ZELINSKY-WIBBELT
Anglistik
Universität Hannover
Hannover, Germany

Contents

Introduction:
Coming to grips with the lexicon

Since the seventies, linguistics has witnessed a general trend away from focussing on syntax and sentence structures and towards a concentration on lexical items as the determining elements of grammatical processes. This lexical volte-face is not only the hall-mark of the lexicalist hypothesis or X-bar orientation in generative theorizing, but also of its antipode, the approach towards language in use and as part of cognition, known as "cognitive linguistics".

The purpose of the Duisburg University symposium on "The Lexicon" in 1993 was to take stock of the various current approaches to research on the lexicon. The present proceedings cannot, of course, give a complete picture of all the currently available approaches, but they may represent a fair cross-section of ongoing lexical research in the many areas of theoretical, descriptive, computational and/or applied linguistics. If a conference is viewed as a productive process, the product - made material here in the form of the proceedings - may be said to reside in a kind of *Gestalt*: it is not only the sum of these contributions and interactions, it also qualifies as a fragmentary survey of current trends in a given area of research. Though each contribution is the fruit of an individual effort, the total collection gives an overall portrait that reveals general tendencies within the discipline as a whole.

The structure of this volume represents one of the editors' own interpretation of this *Gestalt*. The five parts represent five interrelated paths to the same crucial phenomenon: the lexicon. It goes without saying that they are not mutually exclusive. The inclusion of a paper in a given part is not meant to deny its relevance to related parts. Books are linear phenomena, ideas are not. The first part consists of papers on the **structure and mental representation** of the lexicon. They share two properties. First, their principal orientation is theoretical. That is, the major purpose is to contribute to our understanding of the lexicon as such, rather than to describe particular lexical items or lexical fields (Part 2) or apply lexical theories to computational problems (Part 3), lexicographical practice (Part 4) or foreign-language learning (Part 5). Second, the authors claim the psychological validity of the models they propose. In the past, linguistics used to talk about the structure of the lexicon, while research on the way lexical items are stored in the mind, processed by it and retrieved from it was relegated to a separate discipline, i. e. psycholinguistics. Even a cursory glance at the table of contents of this volume (Part 1 and beyond!) indicates that the two areas are finally coming together. Linguistics is beginning to take into account the results obtained by psychologists and pycholinguists when they construct theories about the lexicon. The lexicon is increasingly equated with the mental lexicon. Correspondingly, (psycho)linguists use insights into the structure of the lexicon as a means to understand the processes taking place in the mind.

In his comparison of two cognitive theories about the structure of the lexicon that claim psychological validity, **J. R. Taylor** detects points of convergence and divergence. The basic issue has been with us since the early 20th century: the meaning of meaning. What do we know when we know a word? Or, what kind of knowledge is activated when we interpret a word-in-context? Taylor contrasts two similar approaches to these issues: the network model proposed by Langacker and the two-level model proposed by Bierwisch. Though both models claim psychological validity, they differ in their basic assumptions. Langacker radically equates meaning with (conventionalized) conceptualization: the lexicon is a conceptual encyclopedia. Bierwisch, on the other hand, distinguishes sharply between semantics and cognition, between lexicon and encyclopedia as two different levels. In other words, lexical knowledge is viewed as a self-contained module within cognition. After a meticulous comparison of both models, with the focus on the way they handle polysemy, Taylor lists a number of empirical issues to put both approaches to the test with regard to their psychological validity and concludes that the odds seem to be in favour of Langacker's model. But if the metatheoretical criterion "economy" receives priority, Bierwisch's two-level model seems to score better. In the network model, polysemy results in a proliferation of senses that seems (on the face of it) to run out of control. The two-level approach avoids this situation by positing a unitary meaning at the semantic level and relegating multiple senses to the non-linguistic, conceptual level. Here, two objections may be raised. The first is formulated by Taylor (this volume): economy may not be the appropriate criterion for settling empirical issues. Indeed, the principle "the shorter theory is the better one" can no longer be upheld from a cognitive point of view. The second objection comes from the hypothesis substantiated in the contribution by **C. Zelinsky-Wibbelt**: the flexibility of lexical categories is subject to cognitive restraints which guarantee that flexibility is not arbitrary. In other words, cognition has its own mechanisms to avoid the non-controllable escalation of senses, which eliminates the need for a special theoretical construct in the shape of a partition between semantics and cognition.

The relation between semantics and cognition is further explored from a psycholinguistic point of view by M. Schwarz and C. Myers-Scotton. I have already spelled out the fact that linguistics is increasingly beginning to equate the lexicon with the mental lexicon. If the distinction between linguistics and psycholinguistics can still be upheld, it is a matter of methodology rather than substance. Linguistics tends to reify the lexicon: it is approached as a static phenomenon, an object whose structure needs to be described. Psycholinguistics, on the other hand, deals with events, or processes. The basic issue is: what do we do when we use words? Quite interestingly, both approaches come to the same basic conclusion. **M. Schwarz** adduces experimental evidence about language processing to counter the traditional beliefs about the lexicon as a fully separate module within language and about language as a fully separate module within human cognition. Without explicitly referring to Langacker, she implicitly confirms his network model (as described by Taylor and Zelinsky-Wibbelt). Her notion "semi-module" should not be understood as suggesting that the lexicon would still be some sort of (semi-)separate compartment. Rather, it is meant to encapsulate the insight that semantic knowledge is a subset of conceptual knowledge, tied to phonological representation and syntactic structure, that lexicalizes specific parts of conceptual information. This account meshes perfectly with Langacker's claim that the lexicon is made up of conventionalized conceptual units.

If it is true that the lexicon were a separate compartment within language and that language is an autonomous component of human cognition, what would this entail for a bilingual person? Would he have two language systems, each with its own lexical module? Given the phenomenon of code-switching, this seems improbable. Indeed, aspects of two languages can be intertwined in one and the same utterance. If two languages can be activated at the same time, there is no point in positing two autonomous systems. In an extremely rich study of the mental lexicon in bilinguals, **C. Myers-Scotton** comes to the conclusion that bilinguals possess only one mental lexicon, with entries marked for either language.

The second part of this volume represents a number of **descriptive approaches** to the lexicon, thus necessarily involving a diverse array of subjects: cultural terms (A. Wierzbicka on the equivalents of *homeland* and *fatherland* in three languages), textual terms (B. Seidel on cohesion), speech-act terms (J. Vanparys on illocutionary verbs), grammatical terms (A. Athanasiadou & R. Dirven on conditionality), technical terms (E. Tabakowska on metaphor in computer science) and emotional terms (F. Ungerer).

Despite their diversity in subject matter and descriptive strategies, these contributions show a striking convergence in their basic assumptions. Indeed, none of the papers regards the lexicon as an isolated phenomenon. Each individual contribution represents an attempt to integrate the lexicon in the linguistic system (e.g. grammar, speech acts, text) or other aspects of cognition and human experience, thereby bearing witness to the fact that the rigid borderlines between the lexicon, grammar, cognition and other experiential factors are to a large extent artificial constructs invented for the sake of analytical convenience.

In "Lexicon as a key to history, culture and society", **A. Wierzbicka** examines in great detail the German, Polish and Russian equivalents of *homeland* and *fatherland*. A striking feature of her analysis is its encyclopedic orientation. As indicated in the title, the lexicon is seen as embodying historical, cultural and societal concepts and, as a result, lexical analysis encompasses these various encyclopedic dimensions, too. Since the lexicon thus qualifies as an integral facet of human cognition, an examination of concepts embodied in the lexicon provides a key to accessing these concepts. In a similar fashion, **J. Vanparys** advocates a lexical approach to speech acts. For decades, research in this field has been beset with a controversy regarding its proper object: either speech acts as universal categories, independent of the way they are grammaticalized or lexicalized in various languages, or else speech acts as culture-specific conventions embodied in the grammatical and lexical systems of individual languages. Like Wierzbicka, Vanparys takes the second position: if the lexicon is regarded as an integral facet of human cognition, it opens up a window through which culture-specific abstract concepts can be inspected. Another abstract domain that offers a strong challenge to analysts is the one involving emotions. In line with Wierzbicka and Vanparys, **F. Ungerer** equates lexical analysis with conceptual analysis. Given the abstract nature of the domain under investigation, metaphor and metonymy play a pivotal role: emotions are commonly experienced and, consequently, coded in terms of more concrete phenomena, such as their physiological effects. Cognition, metaphor and culture-specific factors also converge in **E. Tabakowska**'s study of the Polish equivalents of English computer terms. This contrastive analysis reveals that some metaphors are so deeply rooted in human experience that they are easily translated from one language/culture to another, whereas other metaphorical expressions are either rendered literally or else replaced by new metaphors in the target language/culture.

The interface between the lexicon and other aspects of linguistic organization is examined by **A. Athanasiadou & R. Dirven** (conditionals) and by B. Seidel (text structure). Again, the lexicon is integrated in a wider whole, this time the linguistic system as such: Athanasisadou & Dirven's basic working hypothesis is that "the strict separation of lexis and grammar is one of the many false dichotomies of structuralist and generative theories. In a cognitive-linguistic view there is a principled reluctance to draw such artifical dividing lines or to accept autonomous modules for each of the so-called levels of linguistic organization". This hypothesis is corroborated by an in-depth analysis of conjunctions related to conditionality and neighbouring conceptual domains. These conjunctions turn out to be situated in the twilight zone between the cores of lexicon and grammar. The relationship between lexicon and textual structure is explored by **B. Seidel** on an empirical basis. Again, the aim is "to investigate a particular linguistic aspect without risking an isolated interpretation of the results", in an attempt to "relate the semantic systematicity of the lexicon and cohesive relations in a text to its textual meaning patterns".

The maturity of a research paradigm can be measured to some extent by its potential for application. The collection of papers in this volume dealing with current approaches to the lexicon in computer linguistics, lexicography and foreign-language learning certainly reveals that the recent "revival" of the lexicon is bearing fruit.

Within the diverse array of **computational approaches**, the contribution by **J. Handke** addressess a crucial issue: how can we apply our present knowledge about the structure of the mental lexicon to enhance the functionality of machine-readable lexicons? In other words, what can machines learn from the mind? The answer depends on the extent to which computers can mirror the structure of the mind. A computer program has the shape of an algorithm that triggers operations on data. There was a time, not more than 30 years ago, when linguists believed that language was structured along the same lines: a strict division of labour between grammar (rules, operations) and lexicon (lists, data), accompanied by an algorithmic conception of grammar. This view, which sparked a great deal of optimism in the early days of computational linguistics, has now turned out to be untenable, so that one cannot expect artificial intelligence to replicate human cognition. Consequently, Handke's conclusion is a realistic one: although insights into cognitive principles may help the computational linguist in a number of isolated areas, "a direct conversion of natural techniques to develop an artifical mechanism may turn out to be impossible ... and undesirable". Similar questions are raised in Zelinsky-Wibbelt's paper, although approached in very tentative terms. The author claims that the quality of computational systems of natural language can be improved by exploiting cognitive principles, but a fully self-reflexive computational system will always remain an illusion and therefore a machine will never replace natural language discourse.

Though the goal pursued by **S. Mehl** is quite different, some parallels become apparent on closer inspection. The research question can be stated as follows: can a computer program be devised to extract semantic relationships (e.g. locating subordinates of the same superordinate term and pinpointing the *differentiae*) from lexical entries available in an electronic version of a traditional dictionary? The complexity of the issue resides in the fact that the definitions in such a dictionary are phrased in (a highly conventionalized variant of) natural language, which does not obey the structural dictates required by a computer database. The ultimate issue comes down to the possibility of natural language processing. It turns out that even such highly conventionalized utterances as dictionary definitions are hard to interpret by means of a computer algorithm. Mehl's conclusion is equally realistic as Handke's: though "extracting semantic relations promises to lead to interesting results, ... the difficulties should not be underestimated".

As already mentioned above, for years linguists have worked on the assumption that lexicon and grammar qualify as two separate modules within the linguistic system, an illusion that has been shattered by the cognitive revolution. Interestingly, techniques in computer programming have undergone a similar evolution. Until the mid-seventies, programming languages made a sharp distinction between data and operations (e.g. procedures and functions). This counter-intuitive division of labour has now been abandoned in favour of object-oriented programming, where data and operations are encapsulated in one type of structure, viz. objects. These facilitate the programmer's work to a great extent, since they mirror more adequately the world that a program tries to model. If this world is a lexicon, it should not come as a major surprise that object-oriented database management systems are more successful than their predecessors, as demonstrated by **N. Lenke, S. Dreckmann & R. Heinze.**

The paper by **D. Seelbach** examines an issue that has already come up several times: the interface between lexicon and grammar. His argument in favour of incorporating multi-word expressions in databases for computer-assisted translation and computer-assisted language learning and the way he analyses them mesh perfectly with the basic tenets of cognitive grammar: a language is made up of symbolic linguistic units, lexical and grammatical (depending on their degree of abstraction), with varying degrees of complexity. Even a complex expression, that is one made up of several component units, may be stored in memory as a single unit. The phrases examined by Seelbach clearly indicate that the borderline between grammar and lexicon is indeed a fuzzy one: they instantiate schemas with limited productivity. In other words, they can be understood only if one invokes rules *and* lists.

The **dictionary** qualifies as the most visible and best-known result of research on the lexicon. Outsiders even tend to equate linguistics with dictionary and grammar writing. What they are unaware of is the theoretical background, the "lexicology" behind lexicographic practice. Lexicologists are mainly concerned with the construction of theories about the lexicon and their application to rather small sets of lexical items, which often results in lengthy descriptions, understandable only to specialists. Lexicographers, on the other hand, have to cope with huge quantities of items and the requirement of conciseness. Another factor they have to take into account is user-friendliness. Consequently, the insights gained by lexicological research do not always easily translate into lexicographic practice. This tension between lexicology and lexicography, theoretical reflection and practice, is described by **L. Lipka**, who comes to the conclusion that lexicographic practice taking place independently of lexicological theory "produces most impressive descriptions of the language", but still he argues in favour of "more co-operation between linguists, lexicologists and lexicographers". A number of case studies show how linguistic concepts like categorization (fuzziness, prototype organization), lexical fields and metaphor are reflected in lexicographical practice. The encyclopedic conception of the lexicon manifests itself in a discussion on the function of supportive illustrations.

One type of dictionary, the one designed for learners of a foreign language, is examined by **R. R. K. Hartmann**. Despite the stream of pedagogical dictionaries that have become available since the publication of Hornby's *Oxford Advanced Learner's Dictionary*, Hartmann, too, observes a tension between theory and practice: "the dictionary is still an underused tool in language learning and an underresearched topic in applied linguistics". The core of his contribution consists in a long list of desiderata concerning research and practice, leading to the conclusion that "the field of pedagogical lexicography is there to be developed, and this development is likely to succeed better if we can encourage intensive interaction between language teachers, teacher trainers, dictionary makers, publishers and academic dictionary researchers".

W. Lange, too, focuses on foreign-language learning, more particularly in the field of English for science and technology. The specificity of specialist discourse poses particular problems that are well-documented but turn out to be hard to overcome: in the sector of language for specific purposes, "demand is high. Its realisation is utopian for the time being, the means are not there". The role of language in scientific research is also investigated by **W. A. Liebert**, in a contribution on the role of metaphor in analogical reasoning, that is problem-solving in one domain on the basis of perceived similarities with another domain. Two basic claims are made. First, awareness of one's own cognitive models can render one's problem-solving strategies more effective. Second, such an insight can be achieved on the basis of a lexicon of the metaphors one uses in one's problem-solving activities.

The final part of this volume is devoted to **pedagogical approaches to the lexicon**. All contributions deal with the application of electronic media in the area of foreign-language learning. **L. Baten & J. Vanparys** have developed a computer program to learn words-in-context, based on the notion of 'pregnant contexts', i.e. a set of rich, self-explanatory contexts illustrating the meaning(s) of words. This project is being developed into a more global project, encompassing some of the original key-concepts, but enlarging them to other cognitive aspects of the lexicon, such as prototypes and polysemy, the role of word-lists and thematic fields. These are explored in greater detail by **R. Dirven, A. Albrecht and W. Waumans**. Their paper clearly bears witness to the fact that insights from cognitive semantics are finding their way into computer-assisted language learning. Given the diverse array of computer programs that have become available for foreign-language learning, the paper by **A. Lenko** is a welcome contribution. It proposes a typology of programs, pointing out the strengths and some weaknesses of each type. **U. Kaunzner**, finally, proposes an original solution for an old problem in foreign-language learning: the difficulties encountered in listening comprehension and consequently also in lexical acquisition by adult learners. As late starters, they are bound to fail to perceive certain acoustic features of the target language, since the typical fluency patterns and frequencies used by different languages are less accessible for ears that have only been exposed to the typical frequency distribution used in the learner's own native language. The proposed solution derives from independent research on speech perception and is based on exercises with the so-called "electronic ear", an electronic device designed to direct the learner's attention towards the problematic frequency band of the target language and to "open" him up to it.

To conclude, the volume as a whole offers a rich picture of current linguistic research on one of the most crucial aspects of linguistic structure and language use. Moreover, it ranges over the whole spectrum of ongoing lexical research, from theoretical reflection via descriptive endeavours to practical applications and may thus contribute to a better understanding of the field as a whole.

Johan Vanparys

Part I

Structure and mental representation of the lexicon

Approaches to word meaning: The network model (Langacker) and the two-level model (Bierwisch) in comparison

John R. Taylor

1. Introduction

In this paper I compare two approaches to the study of word meaning, and make some proposals for their evaluation. The approaches under consideration are the "network model", due to Ronald Langacker, and the "two-level model" of Manfred Bierwisch.

Langacker[1] regards it as a normal state of affairs that lexical units - especially frequently used lexical units - are polysemous, i.e. exhibit a range of established, yet interrelated senses (whence the term "network model"). Each of the established senses is characterised "encyclopedically", relative to one or more cognitive domains, i.e. knowledge structures of varying degrees of complexity and sophistication. The network model - or variants of it - has been employed by Brugman (1988), Herskovits (1986), Lakoff (1987), Schulze (1991), and others.

In contrast, Bierwisch[2] makes a clean distinction between a word's purely linguistic meaning, and the interpretation that a word may have relative to conceptual knowledge; the term "two-level"[3] alludes precisely to this distinction between a linguistic-semantic level of meaning, and an essentially non-linguistic, conceptual level of interpretation. On the two-level model, polysemy tends to be seen as a consequence of alternative conceptual interpretations of a unitary semantic representation. The two-level model has been adopted by a number of linguists, especially in German-speaking countries, including Herweg (1988), Lang (1990, 1991), and Wunderlich (1991, 1993).

There are several reasons why I have selected just these two approaches for comparison. From the above brief remarks, it will be apparent that in spite of fundamental differences, the two approaches do address much the same kinds of issues. Foremost amongst these are the questions - central to any study of word meaning - of meaning variation, and of the role of conceptual, or encyclopedic knowledge in the determination of meaning. A more immediate reason is that some adherents of the two-level model have themselves invited the comparison, in that in various places they have polemically distanced themselves from Langacker's approach.[4]

Taking a wider perspective, the two approaches invite comparison in that they both have been dubbed, by their progenitors and adherents, as "cognitive linguistic" approaches.

Cognitive linguistics, broadly understood, is characterised by commitment to the thesis that language is a mental, i.e. cognitive phenomenon (Schwarz 1992:36). The goal of linguistic analysis is a descriptively adequate account, not only of language behaviour, but of the mental states and processes that cause the behaviour. A grammar is meant, quite literally, as a model, or hypothesis, of what a person who knows a language actually knows, and of what a speaker or listener actually does when speaking and listening.

The cognitive commitment, as just outlined, is highly programmatic and does not, of itself, dictate a specific research strategy. The approaches of Langacker and Bierwisch invite comparison precisely because they represent very different implementations of the cognitive commitment.

Broadly speaking, the approach of Langacker, Lakoff, etc. has been to constrain linguistic description by psychological considerations. Lakoff (1987), for example, has appealed to prototype categorisation - a phenomenon independently established by Rosch (1978) - in his analysis of a wide range of linguistic phenomena; whilst Langacker motivates his Cognitive Grammar largely by appeal to what one might call "common sense psychology" - aspects of mental experience that are said to be "mostly self-evident" (Langacker 1987:99), and presumably readily accessible to conscious introspection. It is on the basis of "common sense psychology" that Langacker rejects many features of the contemporary linguistic landscape, such as mathematical-logical formalism as a model of linguistic semantics, and the idea that there might be layers of abstract structure hidden beneath the overt linguistic form of an utterance.

An alternative approach - implemented by Chomsky, Bierwisch, and others - has been to use linguistic analyses as input to the construction of hypotheses about cognition. Consider the issues of autonomy and modularity, i.e. the notion that a person's linguistic competence is independent of other cognitive abilities, and that linguistic competence itself is the product of an interaction of a number of autonomous modules. Autonomy and modularity did not have the status of independently discovered facts of cognition, around which linguistic theories were built, nor can the issues be appraised by appeal to common sense intuitions. Autonomy and modularity are hypotheses, put forward, by linguists, to explain linguistic phenomena, as these have been analysed within certain linguistic theories.

In spite, then, of their commitment to cognitive realism, cognitive linguists have made incompatible assumptions about the mental representation and processing of language. Of course, cognitive linguists are, first and foremost, linguists, not cognitive scientists. Linguistic theories, even cognitive linguistic theories, tend to be evaluated, first and foremost, by linguistic criteria: explanatory power (with respect to linguistic data, in all their variety and complexity), as well as economy, explicitness, and internal consistency. But if appeal to cognitive realism is not to be completely vacuous, it is essential to consider ways in which conflicting cognitive linguistic analyses might, after all, be validated.

2. Meaning variation and encyclopedic knowledge

Let us begin by looking at the two issues mentioned earlier, i.e. meaning variation, and the role of encyclopedic knowledge in the determination of meaning.

It is commonplace that a word can denote different kinds of entities, or different kinds of states of affairs, according to the context in which it is used. To put it another way: Depending on context, the word may make different contributions to the truth conditions of the sentences in which it occurs. The phenomenon is ubiquitous, and could be illustrated on just about any item randomly selected from the dictionary. Below are some examples, mostly taken (slightly adapted) from the two-level literature.

(1) a. *John left the University at 4 pm yesterday*
b. *John left the University in 1980*
c. *John left the University a short time ago*
(Cf. Bierwisch & Schreuder 1992:31)

(2) a. *John is in the telephone booth*
b. *John is in the telephone book*
(Cf. Langacker 1990a:189)

(3) a. *the water in the vase*
b. *the crack in the vase*
c. *the flowers in the vase*
(Cf. Herweg 1988:15 *et passim*)

(4) a. *She ran round the lake*
b. *She swam round the lake*
(Cf. Wunderlich 1993:127)

(5) a. *Sam opened the window*
b. *Sam painted the window*
c. *The surgeon opened the wound*
(Cf. Searle 1983:145)

On its normal interpretation, (1a) means that John moved away from the university building, or campus, while (1b) means that John severed a relation of association with the university, e.g. he graduated, or resigned his position. Both readings are available for (1c), whereby *a short time ago* can invoke different time scales: "not many minutes/hours ago" vs. "not many months/years ago". Note in particular that the two readings of *university* (building vs. institution) co-vary with two readings of *leave* (move away from vs. sever a relation with). We could even say that *John* has slightly different readings. (1a) is about John *qua* physical object, whereas (1b) is about John *qua* rational being.

Different readings of *John* are also evinced by (2). (2a) is about the physical person, while in (2b) *John* denotes a printed representation of John's name, address, and telephone number.

Different *in*-relations are documented in (3). In (3a), the water is located in a hollow internal region of the vase, while in (3b) the crack is located in the material substance of the vase. (3c) is different yet again, in that the flowers are not just located with respect to the vase, they are supported, or held in position, in virtue of the containment of the lower part of their stems in the hollow region of the vase. Different readings of a prepositional phrase - *round the lake* - are also at issue in (4).

The contrasts in (5) are perhaps more subtle. A moment's thought, however, shows that what is opened, in *open the window*, is different from what is painted, in *paint the window*; also that the activity of opening a window is different in kind from opening a wound. You do not, for example, open a window by making incisions in it with a scalpel!

These few examples only scratch the surface of the phenomenon of meaning variation, even with respect to the words that have been discussed. On the basis of even these few examples, however, we may make the following observation.

This is that the interpretation of a sentence is rather closely tied up with encyclopedic, or conceptual knowledge, for example, knowledge of what water, cracks, vases, lakes, windows, wounds etc. actually are. If you run round the lake, then, obviously, the route that you take is external to the boundary of the lake. But given what we know of lakes and swimming, if you swim round the lake, your path has got to be internal to the boundary of the lake. And given what we know about windows, it is evident that when you open a window the part of the window that you manoeuvre is a different part from the one which you paint when you paint a window. Sometimes, quite extensive background knowledge is invoked. Consider the interpretations of (1). We know that the kinds of relation that a person may have with a university - as a student, or as an employee - are typically fairly long-term, measured in years and months, while a person's physical presence in a building is typically a matter of hours and minutes. The more coarse-grained temporal phrase (*in 1980*) is therefore more suited to relations of association with an institution, while the more fine-grained phrase (*at 4 o'clock yesterday*) is more appropriate when speaking about a person's physical presence in a building.

The role of encyclopedic knowledge may go further, in that it may enable us to draw various inferences from an expression. In (3a) and (3c), for example, we would infer that the vase was in its canonical position, while in (3b) the vase could be in any position whatsoever. We infer from (1b) that John used to be associated with the University in the capacity of a student or employee (though not in the capacity of a sponsor or benefactor). No such inference may be drawn from (1a). John could have been a member of the general public, who had taken a short cut by walking through the University premises.

That the interpretation of an expression is typically tied up with conceptual knowledge is, I take it, uncontroversial. But the above examples raise two further issues, whose treatment is by no means so straightforward.

The first concerns the possibility, and desirability, of a unified treatment of meaning variation, as exhibited in (1) - (5). For example, we might want to say that the two readings of *round* in (4) are not only mutually incompatible, they are sufficiently different to justify, perhaps, a claim that *round* is polysemous between "external to boundary of landmark entity" and "internal to boundary of landmark entity". With respect to (1), one might want to say that (1b) exemplifies the "basic" meaning of *university* ("kind of educational institution"), while (1a) exemplifies a metonymic extension of this basic sense ("building in which the institution is housed"). On the other hand, few people, I imagine, would want to say that *window* is polysemous between "movable panel" and "frame".[5] An even clearer case is *a short time ago*, which is simply indeterminate with respect to different time scales. With regard to the uses of *in* in (3) the situation is perhaps less clear. Do we want to say that *in* has only a general meaning "containment", or do we want to recognise distinct senses of *in*: "containment in hollow internal region", "containment in material substance", and "support by partial containment"?

Our answers to these questions will depend crucially on our approach to the second issue. To understand an expression, a person needs to draw, not only on encyclopedic knowledge, but also on knowledge of the language in which the expression is encoded. Our concern here is with just one aspect of a person's language knowledge - knowledge of the meanings of the words of which an expression is composed. But what does a person who "knows the meanings of the words" actually know? Does knowing the meaning of (say) the verb *(to) open* involve knowing the kinds of activities one performs when one opens entities of various kinds (windows, wounds, not to mention books, parcels, penknives, and bank accounts)? This would be Langacker's position, and it is one which could entail a high degree of polysemy in the mental lexicon. Alternatively, is this kind of encyclopedic knowledge only supplied in the act of interpreting the word in context, the word meaning itself being underdetermined with respect to its possible interpretations in different kinds of context? This would be Bierwisch's position, which would tend to severely limit polysemy in the mental lexicon, and treat instances of meaning variation as effects of conceptual interpretation.

3. Langacker's "encyclopedic" approach to word meaning

Let us first look at Langacker's approach. For Langacker, no principled distinction is drawn, or drawable, between "linguistic semantics" and "encyclopedic knowledge". Meaning, quite simply, is equated with conceptualisation. A word gets its semantic value by the relation of a profile to a base. The profile is what a word designates - the conceptual entity it refers to - while the base (or "base of predication") is the context necessary for the conceptualisation of the profile. *Radius* and *hypotenuse* both designate a line segment. Yet the two words are not synonymous, and both differ in meaning from *line*. Crucially, *radius* presupposes (has as its base) the conception of a circle (as well as other geometrical concepts), whilst *hypotenuse* presupposes the conception of a right-angled triangle. Divorced from knowledge of circles and right-angled triangles, the semantic values of *radius* and *hypotenuse* would be vacuous.

The base of predication is in principle open-ended, in that it may comprise everything a person knows about the concept. This is not to say that all such knowledge is equally central, or intrinsic to the concept, nor that each facet of conceptual knowledge is always relevant to each use of the word. In fact, variations in the relevance of a domain is one important way in which Langacker's semantic theory is able to account for some of the meaning variation in (1) - (5). In *swim round the lake*, the notion of a lake as an expanse of water is clearly very prominent, whilst in *run round the lake* the lake may be conceptualised simply as a bounded region. Likewise, *water in the vase* and *flowers in the vase* activate knowledge of the function of vases, whilst *crack in the vase* activates knowledge that vases are typically made of fragile material.

Different contexts may also cause shifts in the profile of a linguistic unit. Cruse (1986:52-3) speaks of "contextual modulation", while Langacker (1990a) handles these effects by means of the notion of "active zone". *Window* profiles an entity of a certain shape, function, manner of construction, etc., against background knowledge pertaining to buildings, their ventilation, illumination, etc. In different contexts, different facets of the profile may be involved in a predication. In *paint a window*, only the wood or metallic portion is involved, in *break a window*, only the glass portion is affected, and so on. More dramatic variations in active zone go under the traditional name of metonymy. Such is the case of *university*. On different occasions of its use, the word could profile the institution (*He works in the University*), the daily activities in the institution (*He's bored with the University*), the people associated with the institution (*The University protested*), the building (*We live near the University*), and so on.

Langacker's encyclopedic approach allows for the possibility that a word may have a one-off interpretation, as determined by the unique circumstances of its use in a context. In contrast with the two-level approach, however, the network model also allows for the possibility that a contextually-determined interpretation may become entrenched, or "routinised", for a speaker, leading to the establishment of a separate sense for the word. The process, clearly, is a gradual one. Consequently, meaning variation due to shifts in active zone and full-fledged polysemy are end-points on a continuum, rather than fully distinct phenomena.

It is worth mentioning (and on this point also Langacker's Cognitive Grammar differs substantially from Bierwisch's approach) that while word meanings, for Langacker, are cognitively complex (in the sense that they invoke many facets of a person's encyclopedic knowledge), they are not strictly compositional, in the sense that they are products of conceptually simpler elements (Langacker 1987:21-2). Bierwisch (1981:344, 1983:90), for example, decomposes the transitive predicates *melt* and *wake up* into structures that contain the primitive element CAUSE. On an encyclopedic approach, it is certainly allowed that some predicates may be construed, by speakers of a language, as similar, in various respects, to other predicates; also, that these perceived similarities may have important consequences for linguistic usage. *Melting the ice* may be perceived as similar, in certain ways, to *boiling the water, killing the fly, waking up Eva*, and even *teaching the students*. One might even say that the similarity involves the notion of "causation". But this is a very different matter to incorporating a semantic primitive, such as CAUSE, into the semantic entries for *melt, boil*, etc. At the very least, "cause" would itself be construed, within Langacker's approach, as a highly differentiated, and cognitively complex notion, characterised against a number of cognitive domains (purposeful activity, rational explanation, etc.).[6]

4. Bierwisch's two-level model

Whereas Langacker integrates encyclopedic knowledge into the lexicon, Bierwisch insists on the need to make a clean distinction between a purely linguistic level of meaning, and a non-linguistic level of conceptual representation. The distinction is justified on various grounds. It is claimed, for example, that an identification of linguistic-semantic knowledge with conceptual knowledge would make the factually incorrect prediction of a pre-established congruence between conceptualisations and semantic structures (Bierwisch & Schreuder 1992:28).[7] It is pointed out (p. 31), further, that a person may have various kinds of knowledge that in no way impinge on the semantic system of his language; thus, what I know of a certain John is irrelevant to the linguistic meaning of *John*, which is merely to refer to a person who is called "John". On the other hand, linguistic expressions may have interpretations that are clearly not part of their purely linguistic meaning. *A short time ago*, in (1c), illustrates the phenomenon. Bierwisch & Schreuder (1992:32) cite, as further examples, the context-determined interpretations of possessives (*my chair*) and deictics (*over there*). Further arguments for the two levels are based on theory-internal and metatheoretical considerations. Thus Herweg (1988:66) points out that a separation of semantic and conceptual principles leads to greater economy in the mental lexicon; lexical entries do not become "unnötig komplex" (p. 55); and rampant polysemy ("Polysemie-Inflation", p. 55) is avoided.

The separation of the levels is closely bound up with the thesis of modularity, according to which a person's linguistic knowledge constitutes an encapsulated mental module, independent of other skills and knowledge. Given such a conception of linguistic competence, it is necessary to posit a bridge, or interface, which links the linguistic system to the conceptual system. The semantic level serves just this function, in that the semantic entry for a lexical item points in two directions. On the one hand, the entry contains specifications which permit the item to enter into syntagmatic relations with other items. The entry also contains specifications which make it possible for the word to identify conceptual units at the conceptual level.

In order for a semantic entry to fulfil this dual function, Bierwisch proposes semantic representations which decompose a word's meaning into predicate-argument format. On the one hand, the predicate-argument structure determines the combinatorial possibilities of the lexical item (i.e. its valence potential). The semantic representation also contains open variables. These are parameters whose values can be fixed at the conceptual level, as determined by context. The semantic entry thereby specifies "sets of conditions for the identification of conceptual elements" (Lang 1991:146).

To see how this works, let us look at a couple of examples from the two-level literature. Consider, first, Bierwisch's account of words like *university, school, museum*. For these kinds of words, Bierwisch (1983:86) suggested semantic entries of the following general format.

(6) ^X [PURPOSE[X, W]]

PURPOSE has the status of a semantic primitive. The value of W varies according to lexical item, and serves to identity a conceptually complex unit (akin, perhaps, to the domain-based knowledge of Langacker's model). For *university*, one might suggest something like the following.

(7) ^X [PURPOSE[X, W] & ADVANCED STUDY AND TEACHING[W]]

The value of X is determined only at the conceptual level. To this end, Bierwisch proposed an inventory of functions, of the following kind:

(8) a. ^X [INSTITUTION[X] & PURPOSE[X, W]]
b. ^X [BUILDING[X] & PURPOSE[X, W]]

The effect of these functions is to assign to X in (6) the value "institution" or "building". The unitary semantic representation of *university* thus comes to be interpreted, on the conceptual level, as a kind of institution, or as a kind of building.[8] Bierwisch therefore denies that *university* in (1) is polysemous, neither does his account involve reference to metonymy. Both the institution and the building readings of the word are derived, by analogous means, from the same semantic entry.

As already noted, a general feature of the two-level approach is that it seeks to relegate polysemy, or much of what passes as polysemy, to the conceptual level, where unitary semantic representations are mapped into conceptual interpretations. Consider, for example, Herweg's account of the preposition *in*. He (1988:74) suggests the following semantic entry:

(9) ^Y ^X [LOC [X, PLACE [Y]]]

According to (9), the location of X (the located object, or trajector) is PLACE [Y], where PLACE [Y] is defined as the space that Y (the reference, or landmark object) occupies. Note especially that (9) is neutral with respect to the different readings in (3), i.e. with respect to whether X is located in a hollow region defined by the exterior sides of Y (*the water in the vase*), whether X is contained in the material substance of Y (*the crack in the vase*), or whether X is held in position by partial containment in Y (*the flowers in the vase*). These different possibilities are therefore not part of the semantic meaning of *in*. How *in* is interpreted, in a given context, depends on conceptual knowledge of the topological properties of the objects X and Y - cf. Lang's (1990) "object schemata" - and on our knowledge of the typical configuration of objects with respect to each other.[9]

In a similar spirit, Wunderlich (1993) proposed the following unitary semantic entry for the German preposition *um* "round".

(10) ^Y ^X [LOC[X, EXT[Y]] & ENCL[D[X], Y]]

According to this formula, the trajector entity X is located in a region external to Y, also D[X], i.e. a closed line that encircles X, encloses Y.

That *um*, like *round*, can, in apparent contradiction to (10), denote a path interior to the reference object (cf. *She swam round the lake*), is explained by Wunderlich in terms of a shift of conceptual focus. The device is similar, perhaps, to Langacker's notion of active zone, with the difference that for Wunderlich focus shift is a conceptual, not a linguistic-semantic phenomenon. Thus, if you run round the lake, you adopt an external perspective on the lake, such that (10) applies unproblematically. But if you are swimming round the lake, you adopt a different perspective, whereby the lake is conceptualised as the interior, central region of the lake. Your swimming is thus located in the shallow edge of the lake, external to this central region, again fully in accord with (10).

Wunderlich outlines some further principles of conceptual interpretation, whereby *um* (the principles would apply equally to English *round*) can denote only partial encirclement (*go round the corner*), and avoidance (*drive round the obstacle*). In brief, Wunderlich sees no reason to regard *um* as polysemous at all, on the semantic level.

5. Polysemy vs. unitary meanings

There is a long and important tradition in twentieth century linguistics which is highly sceptical of polysemy. In proclaiming, as a "heuristic principle", that different readings of a word are to be covered as much as possible by unitary semantic representations, Bierwisch (1983:76) and Wunderlich (1991:593) are merely restating the structuralist Saussurian doctrine of "one form - one meaning" (cf. Jakobson 1936, García 1991). Indeed, sympathisers with the two-level approach have seen its treatment of polysemy as a major strength of the approach.[10] Furthermore, they have explicitly contrasted the parsimony of the two-level approach with the rampant polysemy tolerated by "prototype semantics", as represented by the work of Lakoff, Langacker, Herskovits, etc.[11]

It needs to be borne in mind, however, that the possibility of a monosemous representation obviously depends on the facts of the case.

On the one hand, there are homophones like *bank*, which uncontroversially do need more than one entry in the lexicon. The same, presumably, goes for words like *board*. It is easy to see, if prompted, how the senses "food" (as in *board and lodging*) and "group of people" (*board of directors*) might be related to the sense "plank of wood", in virtue of the use of the plank of wood as the top of a table, at which people ate, or around which people sat (the senses, that is, would be related by metonymy). But what once, perhaps, may have been one-off extensions of a unitary meaning, have now acquired the status of independent senses, which the modern speaker, under normal circumstances, probably does not perceive as being related at all.

In contrast, there are items like the preposition *in*, discussed earlier, where it might well be plausible, at a certain level of analysis, to bring the different readings exemplified in (3) under a single common denominator ("containment"). The possibility of such an analysis, however, by no means entails that the more specific readings of *in* are not stored, by speakers of English, in the mental lexicon. (I return to this point later.)

The really problematic cases for the monosemy-polysemy issue are lexical items whose different readings are related, in a fairly transparent manner, and for which it might even be possible to identify a common semantic core, but whose different readings are significantly richer in semantic content than any putative unitary meaning. Furthermore, the specificity of the different readings goes beyond what might be determined by context. For an example, we need go no further than the verb *leave*. The verb exhibits a wide range of contextual variants. Here are some possibilities:

(11) a. *He stood up and left the room*
b. *He left home when he was 16*
c. *He left the communist party*
d. *If you leave your things on the floor, they'll get trodden on*
e. *I left my briefcase in the car*
f. *He left all this work for me to do*
g. *There's no money left* ("it's all been spent")
h. *He left his books to the library* ("bequeathed")
i. *He left a wife and two children* ("was survived by")
j. *Where did I leave my car-keys?*
k. *He left the door open* ("didn't close it")
l. *He ate the potatoes, but left the peas* ("didn't eat")
m. *Leave it alone* ("don't touch it")
n. *Leave me alone* ("don't disturb me")

The various uses of the verb cluster in three groups:

(i) Firstly, there is the sense already exemplified in (1a), i.e. "move away from", as in *leave the room*.
(i') On a metaphorical construal of motion, *leave* can denote the severing, or termination of a relation: *leave the communist party*. Note that in some cases the literal and metaphorical senses may both be present; the one, in fact, entails the other. If you *leave home at 16*, you both move away from, and sever a relation with, your parents' home.
(ii) A second group of uses have the sense "not to take (some object, or possession) with one (when one moves away from a place)": *I left my briefcase in the car*. The senses "bequeath" (11h) and "be survived by" (11i) reflect a metaphorical construal of death as a departure.
(ii') I may fail to take something with me either intentionally, or out of forgetfulness, or carelessness. In the latter case, *leave* acquires the nuance "mislay" (*Where did I leave my car-keys?*).

(iii) As a generalisation of (ii), *leave* can have the sense "not to do something (to some entity) that one might have been expected to do", where the nature of the omitted activity is determined by context: *leave the door open* (instead of closing it), *leave the tap running, leave the light on, leave it to me* (instead of doing it yourself). A situation is "left" as it is, it is not interfered with. Hence the readings "not to touch" (*Leave it alone!*), or "not to disturb" (*Leave me alone!*).

Consider now the possibility of bringing these (obviously related) senses under a single common denominator. On the one hand, all the variants do involve the notion of "lack of contact", or "lack of involvement", either in a spatial or a more abstract domain. But to postulate, say, "not to have contact with" as the unitary entry for *leave* would miss the distinctive contribution of *leave* in many contexts. The first group of senses involve lack of contact as the result of movement away from some place or region, while the third group denote lack of contact (or lack of involvement) as the consequence of a failure to interact with an entity. Alternatively, we could regard the first group as a special instance of "fail to do something (that one might have been expected to do)". This approach would miss the essential fact that whereas the omitted activity in *leave the peas* ("not to eat", "not to cook", "not to plant", etc.) can be specified only relative to a context, the interpretation of *leave the room* ("not to remain in the room") is very specific, regardless of context. In brief, the proposed unitary representations would fail utterly as a basis for predicting the diverse readings of the verb.

A final comment on these examples. The very possibility of relating the different uses of *leave* rests on the availability of conceptual knowledge, regarding, for example, the fact that people normally take certain of their possessions with them when they move around, that failure to take certain things with you may be analogous to a failure to turn off a light or to close a door. In other words, the examples provide compelling evidence of the inseparability of conceptual and linguistic-semantic knowledge.

6. The network model

Langacker (1988a:133-140) proposes that the different senses of a lexical item may be linked by two kinds of relation; recursive application of these relations can give rise to networks of considerable complexity:

(i) The first kind of relation is the relation of extension. Sense [B] is an extension of sense [A] if [B] is perceived to be similar, in some respects, to [A]. Similarity may be based on many factors. Certain specifications associated with [A] may be relaxed in [B]; [B] may be related metaphorically or metonymically to [A]; or [A] and [B] may be related in virtue of the fact that each instantiates a more schematic sense [C].

(ii) The second is the relation of instantiation or, conversely, schematicity. Sense [A] instantiates sense [C], or sense [C] is schematic for sense [A], if [A] is specified in more detail than [C].

These relations are pictured in Figure 1, where a broken line represents a relation of extension, a solid line a relation of instantiation. To illustrate on the example of *leave*: The sense "not to do something (which one might have been expected to do)" is schematic for the readings "not to close" (as in *leave the door open*) and "not to switch off" (as in *leave the light on*). "Not to close" and "not to switch off" are related through similarity - whereby the similarity plausibly resides in the presence of the more abstract schema. Note that in this particular case there may be no reason to attribute priority to either of the senses "not to close" and "not to switch off". But other examples are more clearly directional. The sense "move away from" (*leave the room*) is plausibly regarded as the source for the metaphorical "sever a relationship" (*leave the communist party*), while both senses could be brought under the more schematic sense "distance oneself from", unspecified with respect to the domain of instantiation (space vs. social institutions).

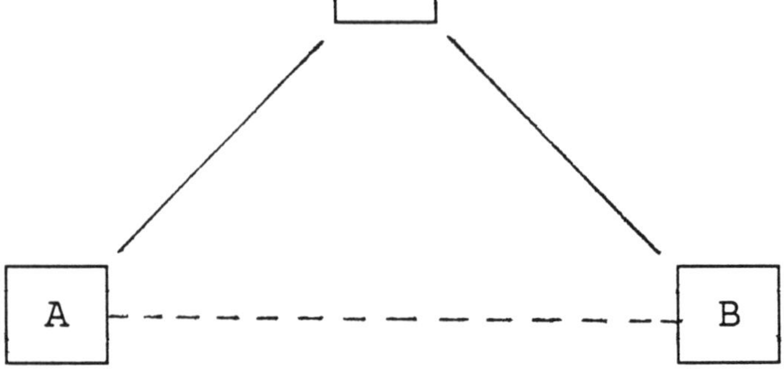

Figure 1. Network relations

Some observations on the network model:

(a) Content of the nodes
Recall that for Langacker, meanings are conceptualisations, which are characterised encyclopedically. This goes for the more schematic, higher level nodes as much as for the more specific, lower level nodes. The mere fact that a conceptualisation is vague, or underdetermined with respect to detail, by no means conflicts with the encyclopedic nature of semantic representations. It is perfectly possible to entertain a vague conceptualisation, e.g. of a relation of containment, which is underdetermined with respect to the shape, material substance, density, boundedness, relative size, etc., of the containing and contained entities.

(b) Possibility of a "superschema"
The network model certainly foresees the possibility of a "superschema" - a single node which is schematic for all the more specific uses of a lexical item. As already noted, the uses of *in* exemplified in (3) could well be brought under a single schematic node "containment" (construed, possibly, in image-schematic terms, cf. Johnson 1987). The network model and two-level model differ, however, in various respects. A first difference has to do with the cognitive status of the unitary representation. On the network model, a schema and its instantiations differ only in richness of detail, while on the two-level model the unitary representation is a different kind of entity from its more specific elaborations, i.e. it is a linguistic-semantic entity, while its elaborations are essentially non-linguistic, conceptual entities. A second difference concerns processing mechanisms. On the two-level model, the interpretation of an expression emerges through the interaction of the unitary semantic representation with conceptual information, relative to a context. Word meanings must therefore be accessed at the unitary semantic level. If it were allowed that specific interpretations of a lexical item could be stored and accessed, the two-level model would be indistinguishable from the network model! The network model, namely, foresees the possibility that an expression may be understood through accessing of more specific representations, without regard for the superschema. Indeed, a network which lacks a superschema still constitutes a coherent and operationally viable category.

(c) Conventionality
A related issue is that a network may embody a high degree of conventionality. Even though it might be possible to postulate very general, schematic representations for (some) word meanings, a person may still

have to learn which instantiations of the schema are sanctioned in the language. The schema does not of itself "generate", or "make available" to the language user the full range of possible instantiations. It is, for example, a matter of linguistic convention that in English you book a seat *on* a plane, not *in* a plane, contrary to what one might expect, given only the most schematic characterisations of *in* and *on*. *On a plane* instantiates a "local schema", which sanctions the use of *on* with respect to conveyance by scheduled means of transportation: *on a plane, on a bus, on an ocean liner*, but *in a car, in a taxi, in a rowing-boat*.

(d) Number of senses
The claim that a word is polysemous raises questions concerning the number of different senses, and the criteria by which these are established and demarcated. The two-level approach seeks to by-pass these questions by maintaining that (barring obvious cases of homonymy) each word has only one entry in the lexicon. The network model, on the other hand, suggests that the number of distinct senses of a word might not be determinable in principle (cf. Geeraerts 1994). The number of meanings that one recognises will depend on the schematicity, or, alternatively, the delicacy of one's analysis, whereby a more schematic analysis is in principle no more (or less) "correct" than a more delicate analysis; each in fact is needed as a complement to the other (Geeraerts 1992).

(e) Psychological reality of the network
A network is meant to have psychological reality, i.e. it is meant to capture aspects of a speaker's knowledge of a word's meaning. This raises the question of how the structure of a network, with respect to the identity and the content of the nodes, may be empirically determined.

The issue has been subject to relatively little investigation. As it is, published network structures appear to have been constructed largely on the basis of their authors' intuitions. That different linguists can have somewhat different intuitions is readily apparent from a comparison of Figures 2 and 3. These figures (taken, incidentally, from the same collected volume) purport to represent the structure of the same lexical item, American English *run*. While Langacker's proposal is less detailed than Tuggy's, and although Tuggy fails to indicate relations of extension, and in spite of substantial agreement on "central" aspects of the network, there are also some significant differences between the proposals. Even allowing for the possibility, fully recognised by Langacker (1987: 376), that two speakers of a language - in this case Messrs. Langacker

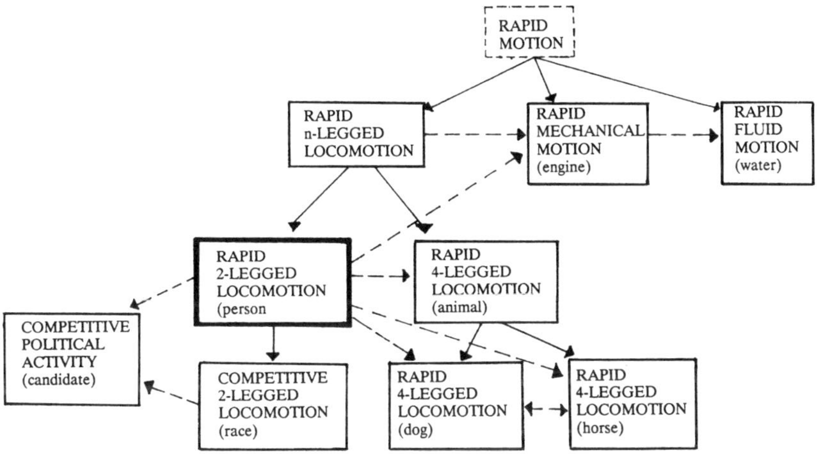

Figure 2. A network for *run* (Langacker 1988a:135, reproduced with permission)

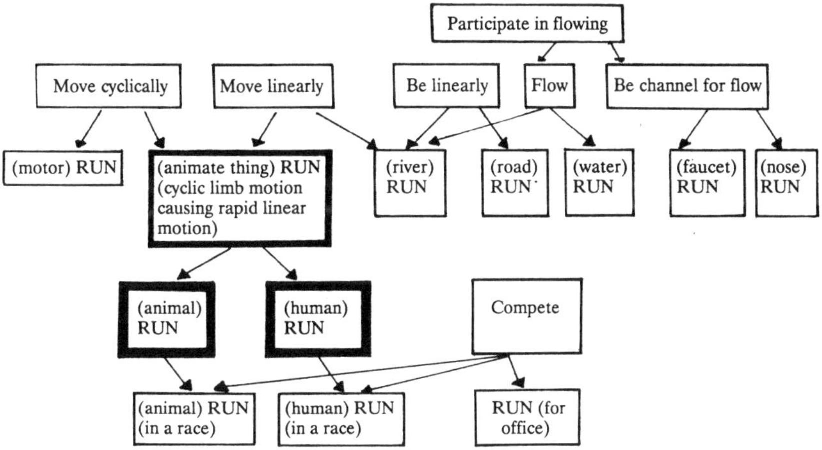

Figure 3. A network for *run*
(Tuggy 1988:588, reproduced with permission)

and Tuggy - need not share exactly the same mental representations of the words in their language, these examples do point to the need for empirical justification of network structures.

One strategy might be to build on the established fact that speakers of a language are able to make quite reliable judgements on the perceived degree of similarity between different senses of a word (Durkin & Manning 1989). Schulze (1991), in his investigation of the preposition *(a)round*, has subjected similarity judgements to hierarchical cluster analysis, the results of which may be used to confirm a network structure. Some further aspects of psychological reality are discussed below.

(f) Prototypes

Not all the nodes in a network are equally salient. (In Figures 2 and 3, highly salient nodes are represented by heavy boxes, lack of salience by broken boxes.) Salience can be characterised in terms of accessibility. Amongst the behavioural correlates of accessibility is the probability that a person, when required to cite an instance of a lexical item, will construct a sentence which instantiates the most easily accessible node. The most salient node in the network may be regarded as the prototype, or prototypical sense of the lexical item (cf. Williams 1992).

(g) Point of access

Whereas the prototype, by definition, is the node that is activated in a neutral, or zero context, specific usage events may require other nodes to be accessed. A general problem, here, concerns the level of schematicity at which meanings are processed. Take the example of *running tap*. Is this expression understood with reference to a rather specific sense of *run* - the sense associated specifically with taps - or is a more schematic sense activated (Tuggy's "be channel for flow", or even "participate in flowing"), of which *running tap* is an instance? The answer to this question bears not only on the network model, but also on an evaluation of the two-level and other monosemous approaches. For, as already pointed out, the two-level model predicts that word meanings will always be accessed at the most schematic level.

7. Concluding remarks

The above discussion of the network model has raised a number of empirical issues, concerning the shape of a network, the "depth" of a network, and the point of access into the network. I want to conclude by considering some further issues that might bear on an evaluation of the network model vis-à-vis the two-level approach. The following remarks will be brief and schematic, and are meant more as suggestions for further research, than as a conclusive evaluation.

(a) Acquisition

Langacker's cognitive grammar and Bierwisch's two-level approach are both meant as psychologically real models of the competence of a mature native speaker. But as Chomsky has taught us, an account of competence is incomplete without a proposal for how this competence could be plausibly acquired by the language learner. On Langacker's model, acquisition would entail the gradual "growth" - both horizonally and vertically - of a network, on the basis of an ever widening data base of usage events, and the child's increasingly sophisticated conceptual knowledge. For the two-level model, the central issue would be the acquisition - again, on the basis of exposure to specific usage instances, in interaction with the child's cognitive development - of unitary semantic representations, and of the principles by which the range of conceptual variants can be generated. Although a good deal of research on the acquisition of word meanings does seem broadly compatible with the network model, there have, to my knowledge, been no acquisition studies carried out explicitly within the framework of the model, neither have the implications of Langacker's Cognitive Grammar for acquisition ever been spelled out. Concerning the two-level model, some very general issues are discussed in Bierwisch (1981). What is lacking is a sufficiently explicit statement of the implications of the model, which would permit non-trivial predictions on the course of acquisition to be formulated.

(b) Language change

Another requirement on any linguistic theory is that it must be able to accommodate known facts of language change. On the network model, semantic change can be straightforwardly represented by the addition of nodes to the network (as well as, of course, by the loss of nodes), and shifts in salience within the network, resulting, possibly, in the emergence of new prototypes. Much of the detailed work on diachronic semantics (e.g. by lexicographers and philologists) does seem broadly compatible with this approach. Indeed, several studies (e.g. Geeraerts 1983; Winters 1989) explicitly invoke a prototype model. With regards to the two-level model, no proposals have been made, to my knowledge, for the treatment of diachronic change. Whether the two-level model can offer insightful accounts therefore remains open.

One important issue would concern the emergence of conventionalised metaphorical senses. These often have to be seen as extensions, not of a highly schematic sense, but of a rather specific reading. This fact in turn suggests that specific readings must enjoy a stable representation in the mental lexicon. For example: *Get round a person* ("manipulate") and *get round a problem* ("overcome") exemplify (slightly different) metaphorical extensions of the spatial sense illustrated in *drive round an obstacle* ("avoid by tracing a roughly semi-circular path"). Even if we accept Wunderlich's claim that the reading of *drive round an obstacle* has the status of a conceptual interpretation of the formula in (10), the metaphorical expressions cannot be derived directly from (10), and cannot therefore be seen as conceptual interpretations of (10).

(c) Cross-language differences
It is commonplace that a word in one language rarely has exactly the same range of uses as a word in another language, even in a historically closely related language. (Consider, for example, how the different uses of *leave* in (11) might be rendered in other languages.) The only partial overlap between word uses in different languages is easily accommodated on the network model. The situation could, however, be problematic for the two-level model, in that semantic representations would have to be sufficiently similar so as to determine the overlapping uses, whilst at the same time distinct in just those respects that concern divergent uses.

(d) Flexibility
The network model implies that learning the meaning of a word could be a lengthy, even a life-long process, whilst on the two-level model the learning of (the linguistically relevant aspects of) a word's meaning is finalised once the word's semantic representation enters the mental lexicon, presumably at a fairly early stage in a person's life. Some might find the notion of life-long language learning unacceptable, and thus be inclined to favour the two-level approach. I would see things differently. We can observe, almost on a day-to-day basis, how familiar words get used in new ways, in response to new demands that are placed on a speaker's linguistic resources. At the same time, familiar usage patterns may get dated, and gradually fall into disuse. The very flexibility of the network model is surely to be seen a major empirical strength (Geeraerts 1985). And there is a further aspect. This is that the learning process need not be identical for each speaker in a linguistic community. Again - and this is especially true with respect to the lexicon - it is a common observation that speakers of the "same" language often do differ in the details of their linguistic knowledge.

There are many other areas of investigation where predictions of the network model and the two-level model might be put to the test - areas such as language loss and language pathology, also foreign language learning, in both controlled and naturalistic settings, in addition to the possibility of psycholinguistic study of lexical access. The issues, I would like to stress again, are empirical. What does a person who knows the meaning of a word actually know? Which aspects of this knowledge are activated in acts of speaking and hearing? And how are these aspects processed? Unitary semantic representations (to the extent that these can be postulated at all) may be economical, a division of labour between linguistic and conceptual knowledge may be descriptively elegant, while the network model may be messy. But economy, tidiness, and descriptive elegance may not be the appropriate criteria for settling empirical issues.

Notes

1. For an exposition of Langacker's Cognitive Grammar, see Langacker (1987, 1991). A brief presentation of Langacker's view of word meaning may be found in Langacker (1988b).
2. The two-level model is presented in Bierwisch (1981, 1983); for a recent statement, see Bierwisch & Schreuder (1992). The most extensive implementation of the model is in Bierwisch & Lang (1989). For a critical discussion of some aspects of the model, see Taylor (1992, 1994).
3. The term has been popularised especially by Lang, e.g. Lang (1990, 1991). Bierwisch himself has not used the term.
4. See, e.g. Lang (1991:145); Herweg (1988:53ff *et passim*); Wunderlich (1993:111).
5. Lakoff (1987: 416), though, does seem to regard "opening in a wall" and "glass-filled frame" as polysemes of *window*.
6. See Dirven (to appear) for a study of the differentiation of the concept "cause", as this is expressed by prepositional phrases in English, German, and Dutch.
7. Note that Langacker's theory does not entail such a pre-established congruence between linguistic meanings and conceptualisations. Langacker (1990b:109) characterises semantic structure as conventionalised conceptual structure. That is to say, conceptualisations typically need to be shaped so as to conform with the semantic resources made available by a given language.
8. Actually, the application of the functions in (8) to the formula in (7) is far from unproblematic. It may make sense to say that a university *qua* institution has purpose W. But the building does not have purpose W, its purpose, rather, is to house the institution that has purpose W. The "conceptual interpretations" of (7) are thus compromised, not only by the fact that the building sense is derivative on the institution sense, but also by the fact that the semantic primitive PURPOSE itself turns out to have context-conditioned interpretations - to be, if one will, polysemous!

9. Conventional expectations may, of course, be overridden. Consider *the splinter in my hand* (cf. Herweg 1988:75). Although this expression would normally be taken to refer to the splinter in the flesh of my hand, given conceptual knowledge that a hand may be "cupped", and may thus define a hollow containing region, the expression may also denote the splinter that I am holding in my hand.
10. See the references in footnote 4.
11. The term "prototype semantics" is actually rather misleading, at least with respect to Langacker. This is not to deny that the notion of prototype does play a crucial role in Langacker's Cognitive Grammar, or that his network model can tolerate a large amount of polysemy.

Acknowledgement

The financial assistance of the Centre for Science Development (HSRC, South Africa) towards this research is hereby acknowledged. Opinions expressed and conclusions arrived at are those of the author and are not necessarily to be attributed to the Centre of Science Development.

References

Bierwisch, M.
1981 Basic issues in the development of word meaning. In: Deutsch, W. (ed.). *The Child's Construction of Language*. London: Academic Press, pp. 341-387.
1983 Semantische und konzeptuelle Repräsentation lexikalischer Einheiten. In: Růžička, R. & W. Motsch (ed.). *Untersuchungen zur Semantik* (studia grammatica XXII). Berlin: Akademie-Verlag, pp. 61-99.
Bierwisch, M. & E. Lang
1989 *Dimensional Adjectives: Grammatical Structure and Conceptual Interpretation*. Berlin: Springer.
Bierwisch, M. & R. Schreuder
1992 "From concepts to lexical items". *Cognition* 42:23-60.
Brugman, C.
1988 *The Story of Over: Polysemy, Semantics, and the Structure of the Lexicon*. New York: Garland.
Cruse, D. A.
1986 *Lexical Semantics*. Cambridge: Cambridge University Press.
Dirven, R.
to appear The construal of cause: The case of cause prepositions. In: Taylor, J. & R. R. MacLaury (eds.). *Language and the Construal of the World: Approaches to Cognition in Linguistics and Anthropology*. Berlin: Mouton de Gruyter.
Durkin, K. & J. Manning
1989 "Polysemy and the subjective lexicon: Semantic relatedness and the salience of intraword senses". *Journal of Psycholinguistic Research* 18:577-612.

García, E.
1991 Grasping the nettle: Variation as proof of invariance. In: Waugh, L. & S. Rudy (eds.). *New Vistas in Grammar: Invariance and Variation.* Amsterdam: Benjamins, pp. 33-59.

Geeraerts, D.
1983 "Prototype theory and diachronic semantics: A case study". *Indogermanische Forschungen* 88:1-32.
1985 Cognitive restrictions on the structure of semantic change. In: Fisiak, J. (ed.). *Historical Semantics.* Berlin: Mouton de Gruyter, pp. 127-153.
1992 "The semantic structure of Dutch *over*". *Leuvense Bijdragen* 81:205-230.
1994 "Vagueness's puzzles, polysemy's vagaries". *Cognitive Linguistics* 4:223-272.

Herskovits, A.
1986 *Language and Spatial Cognition: An Interdisciplinary Study of the Prepositions in English.* Cambridge: Cambridge University Press.

Herweg, M.
1988 *Zur Semantik einiger lokaler Präpositionen des Deutschen: Überlegungen zur Theorie der lexikalischen Semantik am Beispiel von "in", "an", "bei" und "auf".* (LILOG-Report 21). Stuttgart: IBM Deutschland.

Jakobson, R.
1936 Beitrag zur allgemeinen Kasuslehre: Gesamtbedeutungen der russischen Kasus. In: *Selected Writings*, Vol. 2 [1971]. The Hague: Mouton.

Johnson, M.
1987 *The Body in the Mind: The Bodily Basis of Meaning, Imagination, and Reason.* Chicago: University of Chicago Press.

Lakoff, G.
1987 *Women, Fire, and Dangerous Things: What Categories Reveal About the Mind.* Chicago: University of Chicago Press.

Lang, E.
1990 "Primary perceptual space and inherent proportion schema: Two interacting categorization grids underlying the conceptualization of spatial objects". *Journal of Semantics* 7:121-141.
1991 A two-level approach to projective prepositions. In: Rauh, G. (ed.). *Approaches to Prepositions.* Tübingen: Narr, pp. 127-167.

Langacker, R.
1987 *Foundations of Cognitive Grammar*, Vol. 1. Stanford: Stanford University Press.
1988a A usage-based model. In: Rudzka-Ostyn, B. (ed.). *Topics in Cognitive Linguistics.* Amsterdam: Benjamins, pp. 127-161.
1988b A view of linguistic semantics. In: Rudzka-Ostyn, B. (ed.). *Topics in Cognitive Linguistics.* Amsterdam: Benjamins, pp. 49-90.
1990 Active zones. In: *Concept, Image, and Symbol: The Cognitive Basis of Grammar.* Berlin: Mouton de Gruyter, pp. 189-201.
1991 *Foundations of Cognitive Grammar*, Vol. 2. Stanford: Stanford University Press.

Rosch, E.
1978 Principles of categorization. In: Rosch, E. & B. Lloyd (eds.). *Cognition and Categorization.* Hillsdale: Erlbaum, pp. 27-48.

Schulze, R.
1991 Getting round to (a)round: Towards the description and analysis of a "spatial" predicate. In: Rauh, G. (ed.). *Approaches to Prepositions.* Tübingen: Narr, pp. 253-274.

Schwarz, M.
1992 *Einführung in die Kognitive Linguistik.* Tübingen: Franke.

Searle, J.
1983 *Intentionality: An Essay in the Philosophy of Mind.* Cambridge: Cambridge University Press.

Taylor, J.
1992 "How many meanings does a word have?" *SPIL* 25:133-168.
1994 The "two-level approach" to meaning. *Linguistische Berichte* 149:3-26.

Tuggy, D.
1988 Náhuatl causitive/applicatives in Cognitive Grammar. In: Rudzka-Ostyn, B. (ed.). *Topics in Cognitive Linguistics.* Amsterdam: Benjamins, pp. 587-618.

Williams, J. N.
1992 "Processing polysemous words in context: Evidence for interrelated meanings." *Journal of Psycholinguistic Research* 21:193-218.

Winters, M.
1989 "Diachronic prototype theory: On the evolution of the French subjunctive." *Linguistics* 27:703-730.

Wunderlich, D.
1991 "How do prepositional semantics fit into compositional syntax and semantics." *Linguistics* 29:591-621.
1993 "On German *um*: Semantic and conceptual aspects". *Linguistics* 31:111-133.

Insights from categorization for a mental model of lexicalization[1]

Cornelia Zelinsky-Wibbelt

0. Introduction

Recently interest in lexical semantics has also taken hold within computational linguistics. The *ambiguity* vs. *vagueness* of lexical meanings and their *dynamic* use are central topics of discussion about how natural language processing (NLP) systems can achieve what native speakers seem to learn without difficulty. The meaning of a word differs from one usage event to another. The contextual framing of senses is potentially infinite, and all attempts towards objectivizing the process of word sense distinction have failed so far (Geeraerts 1993). Lexicalization seems to be a transitory phenomenon to the lexicographer, and not operationalizable to its very end. Yet speakers seem to be perfectly capable of communicating the nuances of their cognitive construals, of whatever complexity these contextual elaborations may be. Speakers handle the variation of information by mental *categorization*, i.e. by learning to ignore the contextually varying information as being irrelevant. However, categorization occurs also by *flexible use*, i.e. by stretching the boundaries of mental categories in an infinite potential of possible contexts. Speakers handle this flexibility by virtue of their knowledge about the *tolerance* range of each category. In natural language discourse, speakers are constrained by this tolerance range in relation to the specific situation when negotiating their mental "computations" to achieve sufficiently compatible semantic representations in complex cooperative social interactions. These complex interactions result in multiple adjustments of mental conceptualizations to the particular discourse requirements. This cognitive behaviour is indispensable, since it guarantees *economy* and *structure* in information processing. Its importation into NLP, however, poses a non-trivial problem, since as yet, no NLP system has available any social relations which it can make use of in linguistic discourse to achieve agreement or to overcome inconsistencies. In NL discourse, it is only by way of intricate and well learned social interactions that speakers can immediately understand and also eventually accept novel senses. It is not our intention to simulate the mental process of categorization. Instead, we intend to exploit cognitive principles and operations to improve the quality of NLP by making it *in part* more natural. A simulation is logically excluded by the never achievable goal of a fully self-reflexive computational system. We can only implement aspects of self-reference.

We assume a mental lexicon as one pole of the knowledge representation system pertaining to a language. In this lexicon speakers store their knowledge about the commonalities of the uses of each word. Or, in more abstract terms, one might reasonably suppose that speakers store their knowledge about the denotation functions of words in terms of semantically constant properties, which they have abstracted from their contextually varying conceptualizations. It is this knowledge or mental lexicon which establishes a major condition for understanding natural languages. We call this component in understanding *mental lexicalization*, because of the continuous change of lexical structures in accordance with the requirements of the speaker's environment. Lexicalization must at least consist in

- the *recognition* of a linguistic item as a previously occurring and more or less conventionalized one; this consists in the mental instantiation of a type concept by evaluating a token;
- the *creation of novel senses* by semantic extension. This is not predictable in the strong sense, since the emergence of novel senses depends on many conditions, most importantly on the situation giving rise to it. Nevertheless, semantic extension always occurs by way of exploiting certain well-known structures of our knowledge about language use. In this sense semantic extension during lexicalization by the creation of novel senses is indeed predictable. And it is for the same reason that speakers can immediately understand the creation of novel senses.

If we consider drastic cases of metonymy such as the subject NP in the following sentence uttered by a waiter in a restaurant

(1) *The beefsteak has ordered another mineral water.*

the immense opportunities that speakers have as to the contextual framing of word senses by virtue of their contextual indexicality become obvious. Now the subject of (1) does not provide a conventionalized sense, but this is purely contextually tuned. This is one instance of the general difference between indexically and conventionally achieved reference, which is sometimes blurred, for instance by situation semantics (Franks & Braisby 1990).

Speakers successfully interpret (1) by instantiating their schematic knowledge of the restaurant scene and thereby relate the conventional sense of *beefsteak* to the most likely agent of *order*, which is missing in this *ad-hoc* metonymy, mentally reconstruing something like the following paraphrase:

(2) *The customer who has ordered the beefsteak*

In order to be cooperative (Grice 1978) it is a major objective of speakers to rapidly reconstrue the missing information. This reconstrual is an intentional inference in (1), which contains a non-conventionalized metonymy. If we want to import this obviously economical cognitive ability into NLP we have to start with recognizing the *structure* in terms of metonymies and metaphors lying behind these at the same time *flexible* and *economical* ways of information processing.

Metonymical language use is one way of providing *partial information* in discourse and it is thus an instance of economy. Speakers easily access new occurrences of partial information by mentally complementing the missing linguistic items, called the *closure phenomenon* by Langacker (1987:106). If a particular expression conveying partial information becomes established, however, the closure phenomenon becomes a conventionalized cognitive routine, and speakers are no longer aware of the partiality or discrepancy of information. Instead, the meaning of the missing linguistic item becomes lexicalized with the linguistic item, to which the missing information is functionally related. The interpretation of partial information in NLP necessitates rich inference mechanisms, which take hold of the complex interactions between the components of the cognitive web as well as the negotiations between speakers.

In the following fairly conventionalized metonymies taken from Pustejovsky (1991) the object NPs *the beer* and *the cigarette* do not refer to the CONSUMABLE object itself, but to the not overtly expressed ACTIVITY of consuming the object, paraphrasable by *to finish drinking the beer*:[2]

(3) *I need time to finish the beer/cigarette.*

This ACTIVITY, which may be implied in objects, states, and relations, is compatible to Langacker's schematically characterized landmarks of intransitive verbs. Langacker (1987:232) considers verbal predicates to be conceptually dependent on some landmark, even if the latter is not elaborated by an object.

In (4a) *film*, in accordance with the ACTIVITY verb *enjoy*, refers to the ACTIVITY of watching the film, whereas in (4b) *film* evokes the concept of the SEMIOTIC OBJECT itself. The latter sense establishes the bounding point, the RESULT of the ACTIVITY of watching the film in accordance with the evaluation by the STATIVE adjective *informative:*

(4) a. *John enjoyed the film.*
b. *The film was indeed informative.*

While (3) and (4) are compatible with (1) as semantic extensions which speakers have originally created in accordance with their mentally construed discourse models by following the metonymical PART-WHOLE rule from whole to part, the difference consists in the novelty and thus in the speaker's intentional mental construal of the meaning of (1) in comparison to the conventionality and thus automatic construal of the meaning of (3) and (4).

Langacker (1991:170ff and 1993:29ff) considers *ad-hoc* metonymies as one of many instances of *reference-point* constructions, in which entities located in the same region by virtue of their functional relationships can be used to refer to each other. Langacker (1993:30) explains the speaker's capability of predicting reference-point relationships along the paradigmatic dimension by a mentally salient association between the entity, normally designated by the expression and the actually intended referent. The metonymy in (1) may be resolved by Langacker's POSSESSOR-POSSESSED rule, in which a HUMAN referent is the most salient one, preferred over other relations, such as the metonymic PART-WHOLE relations or the metaphorical CONCRETE-ABSTRACT relations.

The syntagmatic relationships involved in these cognitive construals motivate Dirven (1993b) to call this type of metonymy *linear metonymy*. Pustejovsky (e.g. Pustejovsky 1991) uses the term *logical metonymy*, because it arises from partial language use, in that the argument which is logically required is substituted and semantically absorbed by its own argument. We consider Pustejovsky's characterization "logical" to be a misleading concept, without being further constrained as belonging to higher-order logic, which we strongly believe to be non-monotonic in view of the highly complex way of reasoning required for the understanding of novel metonymies.

Obviously, speakers are able to understand novel linguistic items by exploiting knowledge resources they already have. As to the representation of this knowledge different, but related proposals have been made in the seventies, which originated primarily in Cognitive Science, i.e. in Artificial Intelligence (Minsky 1975) and Cognitive Linguistics (Lakoff & Johnson 1980). These authors use the term *frame* to refer to the schematic structures that speakers have abstracted from previous experience of objects, attributes, and situations. This frame representation is stored in memory and instantiated by compatible discourse situations to compare and thereby adapt it to the currently experienced situation. Formally speaking, a frame consists of attribute-value pairs, where values can be assigned by default assumptions. Applied to the representation of concepts, frames render a number of slots; for instance the frame related to the lexical item *cat* may have slots for the superordinate concept, for the typical behaviour of cats, etc. These, however, are highly abstract generalizations, which in many cases allow for exceptions. The straightforward matching of actually processed discourse situations with frame representations was therefore disproved by psycholinguistic evidence for a number of reasons. First of all, more than one frame may be evoked in a specific discourse situation, the frames then in part competing or overlapping so that the speaker has to select the situationally coherent parts. Secondly, the speaker has to make more or less strong adjustments of his frames, concerning their coherence with the current situation. Discourse Representation Theory (DRT) has refined the static frame conception in more dynamic terms. Speakers mentally construe a discourse model for each scene which is the topic of a conversation they take part in. The discourse model consists of the discourse referents which correspond to the parts of the scene and their relations. Now, in addition to these relations, speakers relate the explicitly mentioned discourse referents to the not explicitly mentioned background referents, which are part of the speaker's general encyclopedic knowledge of discourse situations. They test these relations as to situational relevance and consistency within the discourse model so far construed. Finally speakers select the most suitable background referents. Now, returning to (1), *beefsteak* cannot be assigned a discourse referent directly, as by relying on general encyclopedic knowledge no unification with the predicate *order* is possible. The discourse model would be completed at this stage of the dicourse, by taking the agent, namely the customer, as the most likely background referent related to *beefsteak* within this discourse model, and by unifying its semantic representation into the empty slot of the semantic representation of *beefsteak*. We take this discourse model to be a mental model (Johnson-Laird 1983), in which the speaker construes all relevant relations which are part of his encyclopedic knowledge. Propositions being the representations more directly related to linguistic utterances are construed especially for them by the speaker's extraction of those parts from the mental model which on the listerner's side necessitate to infer the missing parts. What exactly the speaker extracts from his mental model to transform it into the propositional representation depends on his own knowledge and on his assumptions concerning the listener's knowledge, as well as on the context and the earlier stages of the discourse (Langacker 1987:65).

The necessity to consider the speaker's mental construal of a discourse model in computational processing suggests the inadequacy of Pustejowsky's term "logical metonymy". Take for instance the following examples:

(5) *I need time to finish the beefsteak.*

(6) *I need time to finish the swimming pool.*

In (5) *finish* is ambiguous with respect to finish eating or finish grilling, depending on whether the conversation takes place in a dining room or in a restaurant, or in a kitchen. (6) is ambiguous with respect to many activities, which one can imagine to do with a swimming pool, one can fill it, clean it, empty it, or repair it, each of these activities being related to a different situation.

Thirdly, the inadequacy of assuming a purely static frame conception is shown by variations of mental models not only across situations, but also across speakers, who continuously have to negotiate their mentally construed discourse models. Partee (1972) claims that, dependent on the type of discourse, definite noun phrases are semantically underdetermined as to their "degree of identification". This is for instance the case with texts written for a broader readership, where the writer has to presuppose different portions of background knowledge. But also in rather specific discourse situations with more intimate discourse partners static frames do not apply in a straightforward way. The intended referent of *ad-hoc* metonymies cannot be identified "logically", but only in terms of degrees, these depending on the reader's judgement of what is relevant for the understanding of the whole discourse. This derives from his general encyclopedic knowledge as well as from his previous knowledge of the discourse referents.

Aside from focussing on the processing of partial information these introductory examples focus on central problems of lexical semantics, namely on the distinction between *polysemy* and *vagueness*. Is polysemy a case of lexical ambiguity or rather a case of lexical vagueness and contextual differentiation? Or do we have both lexical ambiguity and lexical vagueness, depending on the semantic function of the respective lexical item? These fundamental questions have important bearings on computational processing:

What should count as a lexicalized sense of a word and what should be inferred by contextual cues?

Recently, prototype semantics has come to recognize the importance of differentiating between conceptual structures of different lexical categories, such as between those of nominal predications occurring in locational domains on the one hand, and the relational predications of verbs, adjectives and prepositions occurring in configurational domains on the other hand (Croft 1991, Kleiber 1990). Langacker (1987:63) defines a noun to denote a region in some domain, this region consisting of interconnections between its parts. Therefore, in most cases nominal predications are lexically polysemous, because they denote a region in some natural or socio-cultural domain, which may be split up into contiguous, but related areas as in (7), called *conjunctive metonymy* by Dirven (1993b:7):

(7) *school, university, church, post*

Each of these nouns may be used to refer to the CONCRETE BUILDING, the INSTITUTION or the ACTIVITY which the members of the institution pursue in the building.

In contrast to this, verbs, adjectives, and prepositions are conceptually dependent, that is, the elaboration of their meaning does not rest on some lexicalized denotation function as with nouns, but is configurated by being related to different semantic functions on the syntagmatic level: for instance, the preposition *in* may have a vast number of different senses, depending on the semantics of the noun phrases it relates, to name only a few: *biscuits in the box, the bird in the tree, smoke in the air, a hole in the tissue.* Analogously, the meaning of adjectives configurates in dependence of the meaning of the noun or verb to which it attributes a particular quality. This is most obvious with dimensional adjectives, and there has been extensive discussion about the configuration of their Gestalt in terms of ORIENTATION, DIMENSIONALITY, SPATIAL, or TEMPORAL EXTENSION as in *long grass, long legs, a long queue, a fast typist, a fast trip* (Lang 1989, Vandeloise 1993, Vandeloise 1988, Dirven & Taylor 1988).

Irrespective of this obviously differing behaviour of lexical categories, however, the contrasting paradigm of the two-level approach to lexical semantics, introduced by Bierwisch (1989) and Lang (1989), would calculate some common socio-cultural intersection as the supercategory on the first, linguistic-semantic level from this conjunction of senses to be spelled out only on the subsequently processed, conceptual level. The prototype paradigm, however, has abundantly illustrated the general impossibility of assuming such common denominators, because a socio-cultural or natural field is not necessarily structured by way of one common resemblance between all senses; rather these are related in terms of family resemblances (e.g. Lakoff 1987; for the comparison of the two approaches to lexical semantics see also Taylor this volume and Zelinsky-Wibbelt 1993a). All examples illustrate productive sense relations predominantly arising in socio-cultural fields. The examples evidence what is now generally recognized in lexical semantics: the semantic part of the lexicon is highly structured and this gives us a means of predicting novel semantic extensions of word senses in certain degrees of probability.

For a computational interpretation of these conventionalized as well as novel metonymies we classify lexical items according to these relations, thus reducing redundancy and predicting the creation of novel senses; this prediction, however, would have to make use of human logic on which the mental model construal relies, and which very much seems to work in a non-monotonic way (Morreau 1988).

1. Structural types and their processing

We will approach the issues raised in the introduction by developing a provisional computational model of lexical processing using structured *semantic types* (Pollard & Sag 1987). These types correspond to regular, i.e. highly frequent polysemy relations, such as the PRODUCT-PRODUCER relation realized by the proper nouns *Mercedes-Benz* or *Big Mac.* Lexical units are semantically classified according to these *productive types of lexicalization patterns* consisting of an ordered set of senses. Thus a more *economical* lexicon will be achieved by abandoning unnecessary redundancy, i.e. recurrent listing of the same semantic pattern of senses with different lexical units. Instead, we make use of these analogical polysemies by expressing them in one general type with which all items exploiting the respective type are associated (Boguraev & Pustejovsky 1990, Briscoe, Copestake & Boguraev 1990, Brown & Nirenburg 1990). By means of their productivity these types should at the same time improve the *flexible and creative use of the lexicon*: semantic extensions to novel, unforeseen senses may then be interpreted by analogy with productive semantic types induced from their conventionalized exploitations. Of course each prediction is tested against the elaboration in actual usage patterns by speakers and computational systems respectively before being integrated.

The immediate understanding of a word's novel senses by native speakers motivates us to introduce flexibility and creativity in terms of analogical reasoning into computational lexicology. Therefore our feature types should reflect mental categorization (Dijk & Kintsch 1983, Garnham 1989, Whitney 1987, Strohner 1991). To achieve compatible economy in computational information processing, our lexical types represent word senses systemically, i.e. we rely on systems theory, thereby providing for interactive processing, i.e. the features as categorial components of senses are assigned values by recursive, functional analysis, in which all compatible components are related among one another as well as to their relevant context. This is carried on until an integrated, coherent structure evolves in the absence of irresolvable conflicts. The systemic representation of types consists of *hierarchically structured features*, which are *schematically* and *prototypically* organized, that is, dependent on their contextual functionality, semantic abstractions may consist in a generalization over different contextual functions in the vertical dimension of the hierarchy or in a prototype establishing the central tendency of usage along the horizontal dimension of the type hierarchy, where *inter-sense structure relations* between two or more senses correspond to polysemy relations; *intra-sense structure relations* constrain the possible category structure of one and the same sense. For instance a sense cannot fulfil two disjoint determiner functions at the same time, such as a SORTAL function, provided by the nominals *kind, type, sort, way, manner, fashion,* and a MENSURAL function, provided by conventionalized scales such as *kg, km, second, minute, hour.* These constraints, however, have no analytical value in Katz's sense (Katz 1972), i.e. we foresee mechanisms for overriding them in marginal situations.

Our systemic representation includes the *holistic* representation and processing: At the periphery categories may merge into each other, and disambiguation may only be achieved by resolving the relevant contextual relationships. This is evidenced by many antonymous pairs of values, such as the nouns *research* and *electronics* denoting regions in the ABSTRACT domain, for which the MASS/COUNT distinction is even more difficult to draw, i.e. to conceptually reconstrue for explanatory purposes, than for the CONCRETE domain. Existing lexicons categorize them as denoting a MASS concept (Sinclair 1989). But does this category apply on all occasions of use, or may we also use these nouns as referring to a COUNT, i.e. BOUNDED concept in marked situations, which would then obligatorily require the definite NP in English as in the following sentence, in which, by TEMPORAL delimitation a specific part of the UNBOUNDED concept normally associated with the noun *research* becomes individuated:

(8) *The research I am doing at the moment is not being funded.*

The open structure of categories thus implies the open structure of the lexicon, the components and relations of which change in accordance with the requirements of the continuously changing world.

Since it is well-known that lexical polysemy patterns are not predictable in the strong sense, because they are not exploited with complete regularity (Lehrer 1991, Dirven 1993a), it is a major objective of the model to achieve just the adequate level of economy, i.e. not to abandon the necessary redundancy or idiosyncracy, while still exploiting efficient structure and dynamic use. In accordance with this the parts of a type do not apply necessarily to tokens, but only with a certain probability. These probabilities imply the degree by which the respective semantic structure is related to its context. As the calculation of contextual applicability values suffers from a combination of well-known grammatical theories with statistical methods (Resnik 1992:418, Schabes 1992, Yarowsky 1992), the achievement of this combination is a priority objective of the model.

The importance of introducing structure and dynamics into computational lexicology follows from the inefficiencies of existing lexicons, which in general can be characterized as lacking generalization and flexibility (Boguraev & Pustejovsky 1990, Brown & Nirenburg 1990, Weischedel & Ramshaw 1987):

- A computationally processed word sense and its dominating phrase, clause, or sentence cannot be evaluated if it is not foreseen in the lexicon. An exhaustive listing of all senses of a word is impossible, as the lexicon is continuously changing. As traditional lexicons are not organized according to general semantic patterns, they lack the possibility of analogically processing unforeseen word senses.
- Word senses as *unordered sets* are inefficient, as they result in massive overgeneration both in analysis and synthesis. Instead, an empirically based preference system, which may be defeated by contextual cues, would exclude many senses right from the beginning.
- The selection of the adequate sense is often impossible, because the feature which is to unify with the selectional restriction is not within the range of the available context. This problem arises, because computational systems predominantly and exclusively rely on propositional representations. The additional construal of a mental model of the discourse situation is indispensable, because this would provide features to select the situationally coherent sense.
- An inefficient, mentally unnatural selection process makes computing time rise enormously.

2. Mental categorization into types

2.1. Flexibility and economy in categorization

The information provided to speakers by perceived reality is notoriously variegated. We have illustrated in the introduction that speakers have immense possibilities of processing and storing the bulk of information in economical ways. Prototype semantics assumes that humans abstract certain prototypical categories as relatively constant mental representations into which they continuously classify their environment (Rosch & Lloyd 1978). Corresponding to best exemplars of the category these provide a central tendency for application. The conceptual representation of a bird for instance consists of the properties of its *prototypical*, i.e. its most representative instance, which may be a sparrow in a certain natural environment. When evaluating less representative instances of a category, speakers can adapt the prototypical representations to these by transformations, shifts, specializations, and other mental reorganizations. Thus there is a continuous decrease from the centre of a category structure towards its periphery as to its tendency of application. The *flexible* mental processing of this structure establishes the *economy* of language use (Geeraerts 1988):

- *The flexibility of categorization* implies the continuous extension of concepts at their borders, by which ever more tokens may be subsumed under the same type. Speakers extend or transform categories by stretching their boundaries or shifting a category to adapt or approximate their mental abstractions in terms of categories to the affordances[3] of their continuously changing environment.
- Inspite of its continuous change, *categorization by extension* is also economical by reducing the immensely variegated information to conventionalized semantic types.

Another instance of economy is provided by the hypothesis of meaning dominance. Simpson (1981) and Glucksberg (1986) have found evidence for the psycholinguistic hypothesis that the semantic structure pertaining to a word has a dominant sense, which is generally preferred over other senses in mental processing. Thus for a significant period of time and for a significant speech community it is legitimate to assume a dominant sense as establishing the default within an ordered set of polysemy relations corresponding to decreasing typicality. This dominant sense, however, has the status of a hypothesis as a result of a high frequency of usage, which may prove to be invalid in certain less frequent, less expected discourse situations, which provide contextual information to defeat the dominant sense.

The hypothesis of meaning dominance establishes a refinement of prototype semantics, in that it is no longer the typicality structure of single senses, but also the typicality structure of polysemy patterns that are under investigation.

2.2. The systemic nature of categorization

In this section we want to elucidate the relation between lexical structures and dynamic processing. We will illustrate the speaker's linguistic performance of basic semantic *lexicalization patterns* in specific situational contexts. By doing this we distinguish with Langacker (Langacker 1987:73ff) between the paradigmatic *schematic* level, which one may conceive of as vertical in a hierarchical representation, and the *syntagmatic* level, which one may conceive of as the horizontal sequence of linguistic items. It is at the syntagmatic level, that, by means of composition, smaller linguistically manifested components are sequentially integrated into larger composite structures. The semantic well-formedness of each composite structure depends on the compatibility of the components' schematic meaning, i.e. on their *valency relations* (Langacker 1987:277). Thus, whereas at the syntagmatic level composition is the crucial function, it is categorization as the elaboration of semantic content at the schematic level. *Categorization*, however, also occurs along the horizontal dimension of a hierarchy. Along the vertical dimension it consists in the *specialization* into more fine-grained categories by mentally processing the surrounding information on the one hand, and in the *generalization* into more coarse-grained categories by way of abstracting from incompatibilities between categorized instances on the more fine-grained level, on the other hand. Categorization by *semantic extension* occurs both along the schematic and the syntagmatic dimension by widening the semantic paradigm corresponding to a word and by relaxing its contextual requirements, respectively. Hand in hand with both the vertical and horizontal extensions, the prediction of novel structures is a crucial function. In these terms the functions of composition and categorization will be used for dynamic lexical processing in economical and flexible ways. Below we will apply this mutual interaction between categorization and composition to the mental processing of the polysemous senses of *to leave.*

In accordance with our systemic and holistic view semantic categories do not establish primitives, as they are systemically organized in that their meaningful function derives from the relations to all other units of meaning within the conceptual encyclopedia. Or in more concrete terms, their meaning consists in their position within the cognitive grid. At the same time these relations determine the function of a semantic category in terms of its linguistic manifestation (Langacker 1987). Therefore the abstraction of a semantic category is not motivated without accounting for its systemic nature. This means that we do not abstract a semantic category in isolation, but that this goes hand in hand with modelling an overall semantic category network. Semantic categories establish an ordered set related by *hierarchy*, *disjunction*, and *conjunction*. In this system, constraints and inheritance mechanisms are easily expressed. The systemic nature of an evaluated word sense is then represented by the position of its partial structure within the overall potential structure of word meaning. Efficient processes occurring in mental categorization can operate on this conceptual type hierarchy:

- Specialization in the vertical dimension of the type hierarchy and extension in the horizontal dimension as the unification of partial information with complete information (Briscoe, Copestake & Boguraev 1990) are foreseen as natural processes. A special case of this is the relation between translational equivalents of different languages with differing semantic extensions.
- Hierarchy is related to usage probability: a higher degree of conceptual schematization relates to higher usage probabiltiy, whereas a higher degree of specialization relates to lower probability, but to a higher degree of informativity (Wu 1990:416).
- Polysemy relations between senses of a word may be represented by disjunctively related specializations of the same supercategory. Thus disjunction may represent how two related senses contrast in one category or how they complement each other. Overlapping sets of features represent the commonalities existing between polysemous senses. Let us illustrate the disjoint and overlapping sets of features with Taylor's example of *leave* (in this volume) taken from Bierwisch & Schreuder (1992), which we repeat here for the convenience of the reader:

(9) *a. John left the University at 4 pm yesterday.*
b. John left the University in 1980.
c. John left the University a short time ago.

In (9a) *leave* is used in the CONCRETE sense, predicating John's physical motion from the university building; in (9b) *leave* predicates an ABSTRACT motion as a CONVENTION in the SOCIAL domain, while in (9c) *leave* remains ambiguous with respect to both readings. Thus we may represent this metaphorical extension by the following feature sets, where brackets are meant to indicate the hierarchical relationship resulting in different levels of schematicity:

*leave*1	*leave*2
TEMPORAL EXTENSION	TEMPORAL EXTENSION
(BOUNDED (ACHIEVEMENT))	(BOUNDED (ACHIEVEMENT))
MOTION	MOTION
CONCRETE	ABSTRACT
	SOCIAL (CONVENTION)

This representation illustrates the overlapping set of features consisting in the same TEMPORAL EXTENSION of both senses as well as in the additional specification as a MOTION, whereas the disjoint CONCRETE and ABSTRACT domains explain the difference between the senses.

Now one may question whether one should assume two senses of *leave* in the lexicon, or whether one should assume the common features as disposition with this and compatible verbs in the lexicon, since verbs are conceptually dependent on some trajector and some landmark, having some configurational potential with respect to them, which is elaborated by the actually used trajector and landmark. This is exactly how the Bierwisch and Lang paradigm settles the case. Taylor also notes that the CONCRETE vs. INSTITUTION reading of *university* co-varies with the physical vs. abstract, rational reading of *John.* We would say that at a higher level of schematicity the trajector and landmark of *leave* unify, at a lower level of schematicity, however, they are disjoint, as indicated by the following representation:

*university*1	*university*2
ABSTRACT (SOCIAL (INSTITUTION))	CONCRETE
COLLECTION	INDIVIDUAL
SOCIAL INSTITUTION	PLACE

*John*1	*John*2
ANIMATE (HUMAN(MALE))	ANIMATE (HUMAN(MALE))
PHYSICAL	VOLITIONAL
INDIVIDUAL	INDIVIDUAL
CONCRETE	ABSTRACT (SOCIAL (GROUP MEMBER))

From the view of prototype semantics, however, the variation and co-variation indicated by the feature sets associated with *university, John*, and *leave* explain the family relationships existing between the senses of each word. We understand the "family of concepts" adhering to a word in the original sense which was introduced by Wittgenstein (Wittgenstein 1953). Wittgenstein's essential point was that a family of concepts does not necessarily have a common semantic denominator. Concerning the mental processing of *leave* we extend Lakoff's idea that verbs in general have a dominant aspectual profile. Another thing which is mentally dominant is that the elaboration of the aspectual profile is also provided by the action of a MOTION predicated by *leave*. We assume that the direction of the original metaphorical extension from the CONCRETE to the ABSTRACT domain is still mentally relevant to speakers when locating the sense of *leave*. Therefore we take it that on the syntagmatic level the conjunctive metonymies of *university* and *John* respectively provide the relevant components that, by way of testing the lexically assumed default sense of *leave,* and if necessary by shifting to the metaphorical sense to test this in turn, achieve the contextually coherent location of the senses of *leave.*

- The hierarchical relations between categories may help to resolve referential ambiguities, for instance between "given" and "new" (Gawronska-Werngen 1990 and Fargues & Perrin 1990). In the following example it may be inferred from the hyponomy relation existing between *pet and cat,* that *cat* refers to a discourse object already introduced, consequently designated by a definite NP, which is usually used to indicate the "given" in English:

(10) *We have bought a pet. The cat is more often indoors than outdoors.*

This information may be crucial, when translating from a language making poor use of articles.

- Constraints and inheritance mechanisms may be expressed easily.
- The projection of metonymy relations based on semantic types may be done with more expressive force.

2.2.1. Systemic categorization and economical information processing

Let us briefly illustrate now, how the three relations of hierarchy, disjunction, and conjunction become cognitively significant during mental processing.

Hierarchy is the specialization relation by which conceptualization occurs with the contextually adequate degree of granularity. Sometimes senses establishing metonymically related specializations may be left schematically underdetermined, i.e. vague, because the categorizing components are missing on the syntagmatic level. Thus the noun *cover* in the sentence

(11) *He forgot the cover of the book.*

is schematically indeterminate with respect to the CONCRETE or SEMIOTIC reading. We may mentally resolve the vagueness in two alternate ways:

(12) a. *He forgot to bring the cover of the book with him.*
b. *He forgot what the cover of the book looked like.*

What is interesting with this example, in particular with respect to the topics of economy and flexibility being in the foreground of this paper, is, that it doesn't work very well in German and Dutch, but according to English native speakers is perfectly possible in English.

Disjunction captures the fact that of two alternate specializations only one can apply, as in (12) where in (12a) and (12b) the senses of *cover* are disjoint specializations.

Conjunction captures the fact that several semantic domains as components together compose the structure of one sense. Again, the schematicity of the conjunction may vary, in that one or more components may become more prominent than the others by being highlighted by other components along the horizontal dimension. This is the TEMPORAL domain of the composite meaning of *research* in (13), the SPATIAL domain in (14), whereas the SPATIAL and TEMPORAL domain are equally prominent in (15). The possibility of locating the concept associated with the noun *research* in both the SPATIAL and TEMPORAL domain at the same time derives from the conjunctive relationship between the two domains, which therefore both apply, although with different prominence rendered by the context:

(13) *In Europe research in linguistics always lags behind the US.*

(14) *Linguistic research in Saarbrücken is strongly computationally oriented.*

(15) *Many people ignore the progress in research.*

Beyond this, our systemic analysis into components implies also holism, in that none of the three relations holds necessarily, but only in relation to the environment of the respective utterance.

2.2.2. Systemic categorisation and polysemization

We distinguish word senses by *basic cognitive domains* (Langacker 1987:147ff). These are basic, because they establish mentally irreducible units of meaning and because they are necessary for the schematic elaboration as well as for the syntagmatic composition of all higher-order conceptual structures. It follows from our systemic and holistic approach that these basic domains are not primitives. They comprise universal principles of *Gestalt* and function, such as dimensionality, outer and inner bounding, time, and space. These basic domains universally determine how speakers perceive and conceive of their environment, although they are distributed differently in different languages. In particular, polysemes as related senses of a word are to be distinguished and related by these basic cognitive domains and their prototypical organization of cognitive domains gives rise to the above mentioned sense dominance (Glucksberg 1986, Simpson 1981). If we come back to the example of *leave* given above in (9), we can reasonably assume that the CONCRETE SPATIAL MOTION sense is the dominant sense at least in ordinary language use. On the other hand it is also a question, whether we can claim a dominant sense of *university* to exist in ordinary language use, i.e. whether the original sense of ACTIVITY is still preferred over the CONCRETE PLACE and INSTITUTION senses of school, or whether the preference order has been reversed, or even whether we may not assume any order at all among the senses, their usage probabilities being of equal strength. The latter may in fact be true, as the functionality of this very large vocabulary paradigm is so differently distributed over the individuals of one and the same speech community, depending on whether they work at the university, at school, at the post, or at any other institution.

Specific domains establish another reason for polysemization, such as the noun *window,* which fulfills different functional requirements in the domain of BUILDINGS and COMPUTATIONAL TOOLS, respectively. These fine-grained distinctions, however, are not in the foreground of this paper.

3. From continuous to discrete structures

Creativity and flexibility are functional means of processing language which give rise to the continuum of linguistic structure. This structural continuity has been evidenced abundantly by cognitive linguistics. For instance the qualitatively different components of grammar and lexicon establish two poles of a continuum. This is illustrated by dubious cases, multi-word units such as idioms being a case in point, as their meaning is in part composed out of the literal meanings of their components, which in this respect have a compositional function (Gibbs 1991). In other respects these multi-word units, however, may behave like single words, for instance for co-referentially or in translation:

(16) *It is as easy as falling off a log!*
--->
Dies ist eine kinderleichte Sache!
'This is a child-light matter.'

Here the multi-word idiom behaves like a single verb, if one considers the comparative reference made by *it* as well as the translation into the single word *kinderleicht* in German; with this idiom, however, the speaker may still become aware of how the individual words contribute to the meaning of the whole idiom.

Cognitive semantics intends to account for the relation between the functional variations of meanings across usage events and their internal representation in terms of the speaker's knowledge of conventionalized rules. Meanings are not considered as being fixed a priori, but as being construed by flexible negotiation between speakers and their interpretations in complex communicative situations. This linguistic behaviour gives rise to the continuity of reference. Thus contrary to the folk view of communication in terms of the *container metaphor* words do not function as *static containers* for meaning, but they are *dynamically processed* by speakers, who for economical reasons have the possibility of adapting their conceptual categories to the specific affordances of their environment. From this perspective the distinction between system and environment is not an absolute one. Also, the distinction between polysemy, vagueness and indeterminacy cannot be drawn irrespectively of the particular purpose, discourse domain, and application which word sense distinctions should serve (Geeraerts 1993).

By the functional interactions during linguistic processing old structural relations are reorganized. It is this flexibility and creation of ever new semantic content which is the motivation and the delight of communication. Flexibility and creativity, however, are also an indispensable necessity, as they result from the speakers' ever new creation of perspectives on and purposes for their utterances. If speakers were constrained in conveying what is contained in a container, they would be constrained accordingly in their construals of thoughts, theories, in the solution of new problems, in short, speakers would be unable to fulfil any abstract, creative activities, which is an indispensable requirement in our rapidly changing world.

We adopt Langacker's formalized model to tackle the problem of how to achieve discrete structures by proceeding from the *structural continuum of the linguistic encyclopedia*. According to this image linguistic structure and function are characterized in four respects:

1. By relying on *systemicism* the structural representation embodies the *systemic* nature of semantic categorization in the sense of systems theory. By means of their interrelations components are progressively integrated into composite structures, where the relation to the situative environment effects the uniqueness of each sense pertaining to a composite structure, this fact ruling out the strict version of the principle of compositionality.
2. By residing in *interactionism* linguistic meaning is processed as part of some broader cognitive routine which reflects the overall interaction of speakers with their environment. The assumption of any autonomous linguistic-semantic processing becomes inefficient and superfluous. This interactive view is in line with psychological results, which have repeatedly corroborated the assumption that speakers do not mentally run through neatly distinguishable stages.
3. By relying on *symbolicism* grammar is assumed to be symbolic in principle; every distinction in form reflects a distinction in our conceptualization of the world, although the motivation for formal distinctions may fade with time.

From these basic hypotheses a broad notion of *compositionality* and *context* follow: Only by evaluating the overall context, comprising socio-cultural and psychological interactions between speakers in specific situations, can linguistic descriptions account for the complexity of the cognitive construals in communication, of which flexibility and creativity as well as the mental closure of partial information are outstanding complex problem solving activities. The emergence of novel word senses can only be evaluated in accordance with productive lexical patterns fitting in with the respective discourse situation by relying on all relevant components of the conceptual encyclopedia.

The relational and relative nature of word meaning on the one hand, but the methodological requirement of discrete senses on the other hand suggest the compromised image of the lexicon functioning as "bridge-head" within this encyclopedia (Strohner 1991), which, by relating to all knowledge resources can be moved in many directions of the system and its environment.

4. Finally, by relying on *holism* the continuity of reference is taken care of: language cannot be explained as a static structure, but only as a dynamic activity, with variations between the states out of which the activity is construed. The sum of these variations defines the range of plasticity of a category's periphery.

4. The contextual processing of word senses

It follows from the prerequisites given in the previous section that word senses only come to life by the mental activity which speakers pursue in order to process utterances (Barsalou 1987, Langacker 1987). Speakers achieve this during the semantic evaluation of an utterance by way of comparing an actually occurring token of a lexical item to a mentally stored type. These types are mental abstractions of previously experienced contextually processed word senses in terms of *schemata* and *prototypes*. These function as hypotheses, which are continuously tested against new experiences. With the assumption of the encyclopedic, i.e. purely conceptual representation and processing of linguistic knowledge, a purely schematic representation of lexical meaning would not satisfy the communicative requirements in terms of flexibility and creativity. The exclusive use of schemata often has proved these to be too coarse-grained and rigid for economical and creative information processing. In particular, inferences must be drawn in sufficiently flexible ways, which are often blocked by the exclusive reliance on schemata (Whitney 1987, Thorndyke & Yekovich 1980).

The interpretation or production of a linguistic utterance results from using known structures on the one hand, of whatever complexity their combination or reorganization may be; on the other hand utterances are processed by relating the assumed knowledge to the specific discourse situation. In Langacker's terminology meaning and utterances are "computed", not "generated" (Langacker 1987:439ff, 1991:529ff). The term "computation" is meant to grasp better the claim of cognitive grammar that language is not generated by means of purely linguistic skills, but rather "computed" in common with and in a way compatible with other cognitive abilities. We totally agree that the terminological distinction based on the drastically diverging theoretical assumptions about strictly modular, i.e. purely linguistic processing by way of generation on the one hand, and interactive cognitive processing on the other hand by computation with the construal of linguistic meaning as one major byproduct is of crucial importance. But this should not end up in a terminological dispute.

Yet, we differ from Langacker's claim that language is non-generative in consideration of its creativity and exceptions (Langacker 1987:63ff). As may be observed in language development, exceptions often become regularized and novel creations become easily conventionalized by their perfectly fitting into existing rule schemes. Also, speakers have rules for exceptions, which is evidenced by errors made by analogy to exceptions (Garman 1990:246ff). Moreover, exceptions may be accounted for by the prototype model, at least by a combination of etymology and synchronic relevance. And it seems very likely that rules in non-monotonic logic correspond to the prototype account for exceptional language use. The use of non-monotonic procedures, however, has to be constrained by cognitive principles as far as possible. We live in a specific world and interact in natural situations so that we can exclude the claim of situation semantics that in principle every semantic aspect associated with a word may be defeated (Franks & Braisby 1990). By not constraining our possible conceptualizations, massive overgeneration will be achieved instead of disambiguation. We rather constrain our lexical theory in accordance with the centre-periphery model and assumptions about the speaker's mental model construals of possible discourse situations. Following this, we assume conventions, which we believe to constrain speakers in their mental conceptualizations and in their usages of words within their natural and socio-cultural environment as well as in accordance with the respective communicative requirements in fairly non-arbitrary terms, at least for a certain period of time. Langacker also mentions the importance of these situational constraints, which are necessary knowledge resources for performing the problem-solving activity of creating and understanding novel expressions or meanings (Langacker 1987:65), so that we take it that his resistance to the generativity of language springs from the mainstream generative grammar conception, in which social negotiations as well as mental model construals do not play a part in the generation of utterances.

The centre-periphery model may be related to the psycholinguistically evidenced existence of relatively constant *context-independent* knowledge about word meanings, the rest being *context-dependent* (Barsalou 1987), i.e. fairly unpredictable without reference to context. Context-independent knowledge has developed from context-dependent knowledge by a high frequency of usage. Through time, however, even context-independent properties may change as the consequence of a significant frequency of new pragmatic relations pertaining to the respective word.

The way in which this distinction between context-independent and context-dependent knowledge is theoretically and empirically exploited has important consequences for the philosophy of linguistic theories. Atomistic theories, such as the two-level approach of Bierwisch (1989) and Lang (1989) assume that the interpretation of word meanings proceeds in two or more subsequent stages: from the interpretation of context-independent "semantic" or "linguistic" information to the interpretation of contextual information, which is considered to rely on "non-linguistic", conceptual world knowledge. In contrast to this, holistic and systemic theories assume context-dependent and context-independent information to interact closely during the whole process of interpretation. Categorization also proceeds across levels of processing and consists of a complex web of components. The crucial difference, however, is that we deny the strictly sequential fashion of information-processing, with a strict difference between levels. Rather, we assume in accordance with psycholinguistic observations (Hirst 1988, Prather & Swinney 1988) that information-processing is only a weakly sequential and a highly complex process, in which all levels and components interact in top-down and bottom-up as well as forward and backward directed processes, which are highly recursive. Due to its economical principles, information-processing is also not strictly interactive. Methodologically, the distinction between context-dependent and context-independent knowledge ultimately rests on hypotheses about how lexical knowledge is processed: how it is selected, specialized, complemented, shifted, or defeated in accordance with contextual information.

In the remaining sections of this paper we will discuss these processes and their impact on lexical representation from our systemic and holistic view.

4.1. Contextual functions

Proceeding from our hypotheses about the dynamic nature of word senses, we distinguish major contextual functions by which word senses are identified. These have implications on our lexical types and their contextual processing. The contextual processing consists in the *selection, configuration, shift, modulation, highlighting, extension*, or *inference* of senses by the operation of comparison. Which procedure is chosen in this contextual evaluation in order to determine the sense of a specific lexical item depends on its function within the information structure of an utterance. According to Langacker (Langacker 1987) the information structure of an utterance is achieved by a predication, where the predicate is conceptually dependent on the foregrounding and backgrounding of the parts of an utterance, i.e. its meaning is lexically indeterminate. It was for linguistic reasons that Langacker introduced the terms of *trajector* (TR) and *landmark* (LM), where the foreground is normally designated by the TR, and the background by the LM. Although having a far wider range of application, the TR typically corresponds to the subject and the LM to the object of a phrase or sentence. In sketching the functionally determined constitution of senses we proceed from the traditional concept of a phrase, which is controlled by a predicate associated with the typical meaning of its syntactic class (Croft 1991); this optimal form-meaning relationship of the controller, however, may be modified, where the modifiers of the predicate are in a preference relationship, thus effecting the decreasing typicality of the controlling predicate.

- *Contextual selection* of alternate, equally valid polysemes of a lexical unit presupposes a type associated with *disjunctively related senses*. A nice example is the polysemy type of *school*[4], for which the context may select at least the senses located in the CONCRETE BUILDING domain, in the ABSTRACT INSTITUTION domain, or in the TEMPORAL domain respectively:

  (17) *You can enter the school through the back door.*

  (18) *The school is famous for its teachers.*

(19) *In principle, school starts at 8.00.*

In (17) the TR is the agent's physical motion expressed by the relation between subject and verb. This can only move into the CONCRETE BUILDING, which provides the LM. This sense has originally arisen by way of metonymical extension from the teachers' activity of teaching, who in (18) by their quality of teaching contribute to the reputation of the institution, to the PLACE where teaching and learning takes place (Onions 1973).[5] In (18) the evaluation in ABSTRACT quality space functions as LM with respect to which only the ABSTRACT INSTITUTION may be evaluated as TR. In (19) a point in time functions as LM from which the predicated process starts and in parallel with which the duration of the PROCESS sense of *school* extends as the TR. We assume no conventionalized dominance relation existing between the senses, because synchronically we may rather observe a high social and situational flexibility in either direction.
The computational processing of this kind of polysemy pattern requires the respective lexical item to be associated with a type consisting of an unordered set of senses, which are in disjunctive relationship, i.e. they are not organized in a typicality space which might reflect their original semantic extension, but nowadays rather reflect their equally obligatory functions related to the semantic field of institutionalized teaching.

- *Contextual configuration* presupposes a *schematic* disposition in the lexicon. A schema is a generalization over several contextually induced specializations. If an instance (I) is categorized by comparison with a schema (S), S as a generalization over different specializations must always be implied in I, so that $I \subset S$ must hold. A case in point are DIMENSIONAL adjectives, which, as relational predications, are conceptually dependent on their nominal trajectors (Langacker 1987, Vandeloise 1993). As defendants of schema theory, Bierwisch (1989) and Lang (1989) consider this conceptual dependence as parametric knowledge on the linguistic level and the instantiation and specification of this parametrization as occurring on the conceptual level, which is processed after the linguistic level. We assume nominals to unify the relevant dimensional extension of the entity referred to into the dimensional disposition of the adjective. Dependent on the perspective induced by the situation of discourse, the mentally relevant shape of the referred entity may correspond to its whole or to a part of its extension. A proposition is the minimal context for the configuration of the adjective's meaning (Pustejovsky 1991:413), as in the following translationally relevant distinctions:

(20) *Der große Stuhl steht vor dem Klavier.*
--- >
The big chair is standing in front of the piano.

(21) *Diese Wohnung ist größer als die alte.*
--- >
This flat is larger than the old one.

(22) *Er hat sich große Mühe bei der Fertigstellung gegeben.*
--- >
He took great pains to finish it.

The relevant dimensions of a noun's meaning are conceptualized by projection in accordance with the context of discourse. Lexically a noun is associated with the maximal dimensionality of its denotation. As the conceptualization of an entity's dimensionality in the spatial or temporal domain is highly dependent on the speaker's perspective in the respective discourse situation, we do not consider the maximal dimensionality of an entity to establish a prototypical one, but instead it corresponds to what speakers conceive of as their "actual" Gestalt. This actual Gestalt is then projected to the contextually relevant dimensions by imposing "on them some extrinsic set of coordinates" (Langacker 1987:153). This projected part then establishes what Langacker (1987:273) calls the *active zone* of the referent. In (20) no projection occurs, THREE-DIMENSIONAL space provides the actual Gestalt within this context of discourse. In (21) the projection is achieved by the discourse topic of comparing the extension of flats, which is typically conceived in terms of the TWO-DIMENSIONAL AREA which one can furnish. The conceptualization of a TWO-DIMENSIONAL positive extension is preferentially designated by the adjective *large* in British English (otherwise, i.e. when talking about the VERTICAL, ONE-DIMENSIONAL extension of flats, the adjective *hoch* would be used in German; and situations in which one would talk about the volume of flats in terms of cubic metres are very special and marked, i.e. for ordinary language use the THREE-DIMENSIONAL sense is not foreseen). In (22) the noun *pains* is rather intrinsically calibrated in a locational domain: it is a MASS term predicating an EMOTION, the referent of which is located in ABSTRACT QUALITY space. This triggers the configuration of the German adjective's meaning *groß* as ABSTRACT, and with this meaning German *groß* preferentially translates into British English *great*.

- Contextual configuration applies in a similar fashion to adjectives, which are lexically vague with respect to their scalar realization. This operation also works on the lexical representation of *groß* in (20), (21), and (22). The extension predicated by SCALAR adjectives is contextually graded in dependence of the spatial extension referred to by the noun (Pustejovsky 1991 for examples of SCALAR adjectives in the temporal domain).
  The computational implementation of relational predications and their contextual configuration during processing establishes a major problem arising from the as yet sentence-bound processing. Whereas the proposition is the minimal context for the configuration of a relational predication, which is fortunately provided within the sentence in (20), (21), and (22), the maximal context may well be a whole paragraph.[6]
- *Contextual shift* occurs, when the context introduces a marked perspective. By this a dominant sense is projected to a non-typical sense. The psychological hypothesis of *meaning dominance* supports this contextual function (Glucksberg 1986). Within the graded applicability space (Rosch & Lloyd 1978) the dominant sense establishes the default, which applies in the absence of contextually conflicting conditions, such as the ordinary sense of *window* still dominating the one used in the computer world. When speakers evaluate the meaning of a lexical item occurring as a token in some utterance, a comparison to a mentally stored prototype would have to meet the following conditions: an instance (I) must approximate the prototype (P) or match it in the ideal case, i.e. a relation $P \geq I$ (P is more typical than/exactly as typical as I) must be computable by speakers in accordance with the typicality values of P and I (Langacker 1987:371ff). The prototype is related to a chain of senses with decreasing usage probability, due to its conventionality. If the evaluation by comparison with the dominant sense has failed, speakers mentally shift to decreasingly less typical senses in their semantic evaluation. Let us now, for methodological reasons, refine our concept of central meaning (Langacker 1987:159ff). The first criterion for a lexical item's centrality is *conventionality*, defined as its regular use by a significant part of a speech community. Second, *genericity*, defined as the degree of schematic elaboration, determines the semantic centrality of a sense: the more coarse-grained a

semantic property is, the more it is apt to become accepted as being mentally central; the more specific it is, the more it tends to be shared only by a small number of specialized speakers. Third, it is *intrinsicness*, the degree of mental internalization, which determines centrality. The more *decontextualized* a sense may be mentally processed, i.e. the less context is needed to categorize an instance, the more intrinsic the relation between the lexical unit and its meaning, i.e. the more context-independent this relation has become and for the time being this relation then dominates the chain of senses. While this relatively intrinsic sense then may be conceptualized relatively free of context, mental shifting through the chain of senses requires increasingly more context. For instance there are nouns which, if decontextualized, are mentally assumed to denote an UNBOUNDED MASS concept with relative intrinsicness. These nouns, however, may be semantically modified[7] as in (23), where what we normally conceive of as UNBOUNDED becomes BOUNDED by the CONTAINER function of *cup* to the specific quantity it contains:

(23) *The water in the cup is dirty.*

Finally *uniqueness*, the notion of being more "necessary" in the weak sense for some category to apply, determines centrality.
In (24) the verbal predicate is conceptually dependent on a FLUID LM and changes the normally COMPACT constitution of butter accordingly:

(24) *pour butter over the steak*

It is the specific discourse situation in which this unusual constitution of *butter* has to be mentally construed in order to be unified with the activity predicated by the verb *pour.* This is the activity of causing some substance to flow downwards like a liquid in a continuous stream.[8]
To illustrate that even fairly extreme exceptions may be rule-governed and fit into the prototype model, consider the HOMOGENEOUS MASS concepts corresponding to the English nouns *grain* and *hair,* which only under pragmatically extremely marked conditions may be used to refer to a HETEROGENEOUS concept. We normally abstract away from from the discrete, but compatible members of the COLLECTION. For instance the use of the cardinal phrase in the NP *10,000 grains per kg* results in the conceptualiza-

tions of discrete grains, which corresponds to HETEROGENEITY and individuation which may, as in our example, take a determiner phrase (Wierzbicka 1985:335). Or one could count a person's hairs per square cm, and as a result state the number of hairs, such as *you have only got 20 hairs on this square cm!*[9]

In accordance with these hypotheses about mental processing regular contextual shifts operate on an ordered set of default values. The default values corresponding to the senses of a word are neither necessary nor sufficient applicability conditions; context is equally important and may defeat the default assumptions in marked grammatical constructions or discourse situations, these reflecting the decreasing typicality of the nominal's meaning.

- *Contextual modulation* and *contextual highlighting* hold the referent constant. The former is an optional amplification of a sense by a non-conflicting predication, as by the INTENSIFIERS in (25) and (26):

(25) *an exciting adventure*

(26) *a complicated confusion*

Contextual highlighting consists in the general foregrounding and backgrounding of the conjunctively related semantic components of one sense. *Summer* as one period within the annual seasons provides a temporal LM for the location of the ACTIVITY referred to by *accident* in (27), hence the temporal domain of *summer* is foregrounded. In contrast to this the LM in (28) elaborates the QUALITY domain of TEMPERATURE with respect to which the referent of *summer* is located with its temperature in the foreground:

(27) *The accident happened last summer.*

(28) *Last summer was extremely hot.*

The coherence of discourse is achieved when several reference relations establish a coherent integrated system (Strohner 1991). This construal results from the interactive, recursive processing of contextual and lexical functions, if contextual selection, shift, or configuration apply. If contextual modulation or highlighting occur, however, no recursion is performed, as this does not affect the conceptualization of the referent but only enhances its active zone.

Thus in the computational processing of contextual modulation the nominal's sense is located in the quality space provided by the LM, which in (25) and in (26) is elaborated by the adjectives. Similarly, contextual highlighting is a case of differing enhancement of the semantic components which in common characterize a lexical item's sense. The computational achievement of this differing conceptual enhancement and granularity of the same referent is a natural process foreseen by our conceptual type hierarchy.

- We call *contextual inference* what Pustejovsky deals with under the term *coercion*. We prefer not to use Pustejovsky's term, as it suggests something like complete arbitrariness (although this is not how it is explained in Pustejovsky (1991); discussions with colleagues, however, have shown that this explanation of the mechanism somehow gets lost behind the negative force of the term "coercion". We now close our presentation by returning to the example with which we started:

(29) *The beefsteak has ordered another mineral water.*

This is an instance of non-conventionalized metonymy, whose intended referent may only be inferred by uncovering the VOLITIONAL agent on which the ACTIVITY predicated by *order* is conceptually dependent. This occurs by applying the metonymical POSSESSOR POSSESSED rule within the mental construal of the discourse model. An inference from PART to WHOLE results, namely from the partial and marked information provided by the conventionalized referent of *beefsteak*, to the customer as the consumer of the beefsteak figuring out as the most typical agent of the ACTIVITY of *order*.

In a similar fashion we must handle non-conventionalized metonymies in computational processing: a coherent structure of partial or incoherent information can only be obtained if the conflicting values of otherwise not to be related functions are overridden by inserting and thereby integrating a function, which by its typical fit into the mental model of the discourse situation reconciles the conflicting components.

5. Conclusions

Now that we have come back to the example with which we started, we can verify and extend our hypotheses: speakers indeed have immense opportunities in their flexible usages of words, but still there are predictable cognitive constraints, which reside in our mental representations of possible lexicalizations and discourse situations, intentions and registers, as well as presuppositions in terms of general and conversational knowledge, which the speaker expects on the listener's sides. These constraints may evoke the acceptability and eventually sanction the conventionality of novel linguistic items: at a specific point in time and dependent on communicative intentions our cognitive constraints guarantee that flexibility is not completely arbitrary. Instead, by its relative systematicity, flexibility guarantees understanding. And finally, by its very existence, flexibility enables speakers to understand and control their enormously variegated and ever changing environment. Our objective with this analysis of speakers' mental performance with contextually embedded lexical senses was to open windows for introducing compatible mechanisms into the computational processing of word senses.

It is the relation between conventionality and flexibility within one language which yields the language-specific structure and processing of the lexicon and thereby the indeterminateness of translation between different natural languages. We have described the relation between language-specific lexicalization patterns in finer detail elsewhere (Zelinsky-Wibbelt 1991, Zelinsky-Wibbelt 1993b, Zelinsky-Wibbelt 1994). We have refrained from dealing extensively with the topic in this paper, as we are not quite as pessimistic with respect to the indeterminateness of translation as Quine (1959) and leave a more sophisticated approximation towards an operationalization of the translation relation for semanticists continuing to deal with this question in the future.

Notes

1. I would like to thank Leila Behrens, Stephan Busemann, René Dirven, Johann Haller, Carlos Inchaurralde, Ian Pratt, and Robert Spence for giving me helpful comments on earlier versions of this paper. Special thanks are due to John Taylor and Robert Spence for doing the proof-reading so promptly.
2. A marked or less normal situation could be thought of, for instance with a barkeeper drawing beer, which is presumably performed by fewer people than the activity of drinking beer. Equally, the activity of rolling a cigarette may be assumed to occur less frequently with cigarettes than smoking them in general.
3. Cf. Gibson (1979) for the creation of this ecological term.
4. which has been abundantly discussed by the Bierwisch/Lang (1989) paradigm.

5. It is probably for this reason that with many institutions, such as *factory, ministry, garage* the PROCESS sense has not become conventionalized. Even with *university* it works well in English, but not in German.
6. In Zelinsky-Wibbelt 1993b the complexity of the sentence-bound configuration of relational predications is implemented in finer detail with prepositions.
7. By this we mean functionally related linguistic items which have an impact on the default sense (Zelinsky-Wibbelt 1990 and Zelinsky-Wibbelt 1994).
8. These are close paraphrases of the definitions given in the Advanced Learner's Dictionary as well as in the Longman's Dictionary.
9. Cf. Zelinsky-Wibbelt 1994, which is devoted to a detailed analysis of the mental shifting between the BOUNDED and UNBOUNDED pole.

References

Barsalou, L. W.
1987 The instability of graded structure: Implications for the nature of concepts. In: Neisser, U. (ed.). *Concepts and Conceptual Development: Ecological and Intellectual Factors in Categorization.* Cambridge: Cambridge University Press.

Berlin,B., D. E. Breedlove & P. H. Raven
1974 *Principles of Tzeltal Plant Classification.* New York: Academic.

Bierwisch, M.
1989 The semantics of gradation. In: Bierwisch, M. & E. Lang. *Dimensional Adjectives. Grammatical Structure and Conceptual Interpretation.* Berlin: Springer-Verlag.

Bierwisch, M. & R. Schreuder
1992 "From concepts to lexical items." *Cognition* 42:23-60.

Boguraev, B. & J. Pustejovsky
1990 Lexical ambiguity and the role of knowledge representation in lexicon design. *Proceedings of the 13th International Conference on Computational Linguistics.* Helsinki, Vol. 2

Briscoe,T., A. Copestake & B. Boguraev
1990 Enjoy the paper: lexical semantics via lexicology. In: *Proceedings of the 13th International Conference on Computational Linguistics*, Vol. 2. Helsinki.

Brown & S. Nirenburg
1990 Human-computer interaction for semantic disambiguation. In: *Proceedings of the 13th International Conference on Computational Linguistics*, Vol. 3. Helsinki.

Croft, W.
1991 *Syntactic Categories and Grammatical Relations: The Cognitive Organization of Information.* Chicago: Chicago University Press.

van Dijk, T. A. & W. Kintsch
1983 *Strategies of Discourse Comprehension.* London: Academic Press.

Dirven, R.
1993a Dividing up physical and mental space into conceptual categories by means of English prepositions. In: Zelinsky-Wibbelt, C. (ed.). *The Semantics of Prepositions: From Mental Processing to Natural Language Processing.* Berlin: Mouton de Gruyter.

1993b "Metonymy and metaphor: Different mental strategies of conceptualisation." *Leuvense Bijdragen* 82:1-28.

Dirven, R. & J. Taylor
1988 The conceptualisation of vertical space in English: The case of *tall*. In: Rudzka-Ostyn, B. (ed.). *Topics in Cognitive Linguistics*. Amsterdam/Philadelphia: Benjamins.

Fargues, J. & A. Perrin
1990 Synthesizing a large concept hierarchy from French hyperonyms. In: *Proceedings of the 13th International Conference on Computational Linguistics*, Vol. 2. Helsinki.

Franks, B. & N. Braisby
1990 *Sense Generation or How to Make the Mental Lexicon Flexible*. Research Paper EUCCS/RP-39, Centre for Cognitive Science, University of Edinburgh.

Garman, M.
1990 *Psycholinguistics*. Cambridge: Cambridge University Press.

Garnham, A.
1989 Inference in language understanding: What, when, why and how. In: Dietrich, R. & C. F. Graumann (eds.). *Language Processing in Social Context*. Amsterdam: North-Holland, pp. 153-172.

Gawronska-Werngen, B.
1990 Translation great problem - on the problem of inserting articles when translating from Russian into Swedish. In: *Proceedings of the 13th International Conference on Computational Linguistics*, Vol. 2. Helsinki.

Geeraerts, D.
1988 Where does prototypicality come from? In: Rudzka-Ostyn, B. (ed.). *Topics in Cognitive Linguistics*. Amsterdam/Philadelphia: Benjamins.
1993 "Vagueness's puzzles, polysemy's vagaries". *Cognitive Linguistics* 4(3):223-272.

Gibbs, R. W.
1991 "Psycholinguistic studies on the conceptual basis of idiomaticity." *Cognitive Linguistics* 1(4):417-451.

Gibson, J. J.
1979 *The Ecological Approach to Visual Perception*. Boston: Houghton Mifflin.

Glucksberg, S.
1986 How people use context to resolve ambiguity: Implications for an interactive model of language understanding. In: Kurcz, I., G. W. Shugar & J. H. Danks (eds.). *Knowledge and Language*. Amsterdam: North Holland, pp. 303-325.

Grice, H. P.
1978 Further notes on logic and conversation. In: Cole, P. (ed.). *Syntax and Semantics*, Vol. 3. *Speech acts*. New York: Academic Press, pp. 41-58.

Hirst, G.
1988 "Semantic interpretation and ambiguity." *Artificial Intelligence* 34:131-177.

Johnson-Laird, P. N.
1983 *Mental Models: Towards a Cognitive Science of Language, Inference and Consciousness*. Cambridge: Cambridge University Press.
1987 "The mental representation of the meaning of words." *Cognition 25:189-211.*

Katz, J.
1972 *Semantic Theory*. New York: Harper.

Kleiber, G.
1990 *La Sémantique du Prototype. Catégories et Sens Lexical.* Paris: Presses Universitaires de France.

Lakoff, G.
1987 *Women, Fire, and Dangerous Things: What Categories Reveal about the Mind.* Chicago: University of Chicago Press.

Lakoff, J. & M. Johnson
1980 *Metaphors we Live by.* Chicago: University of Chicago Press.

Lang, E.
1989 The semantics of dimensional designation of spatial objects. In: Bierwisch, M. & E. Lang (eds.). *Dimensional Adjectives. Grammatical Structure and Conceptual Interpretation.* Berlin: Springer-Verlag.

Langacker, R.
1987 *Foundations of Cognitive Grammar. Theoretical Prerequisites*, Vol. 1. Stanford: Stanford University Press.
1991 *Foundations of Cognitive Grammar. Practical Applications*, Vol. 2. Stanford: Stanford University Press.
1993 "Reference-point constructions." *Cognitive Linguistics* 4(1):1-38.

Lehrer, A.
1991 "Polysemy, conventionality, and the structure of the lexicon." *Cognitive Linguistics* 1-2:207-246.

Lowie, A. P. (ed.)
1989 *Oxford Advanced Learner's Dictionary of Current English.* Fourth Edition. Oxford: Oxford University Press.

Minsky, M.
1975 A framework for representing knowledge. In: Winston, P. H. (ed.). *The Psychology of Computer Vision.* New York: McGraw-Hill.

Morreau, M.
1988 Default formalisms in generics: a consumer report. In: Krifka (ed.). *Genericity in Natural Language. Proceedings of the 1988 Tübingen Conference.* Tübingen: SNS-Bericht, pp. 88-42.

Onions, C.T. (ed.)
1973 *The Shorter Oxford English Dictionary on Historical Principles.* Prepared by Little, W., H. W. Fowler & J. Coulson, 3rd ed. with etymologies revised by G. W. S. Friedrichsen. Oxford: Clarendon Press.

Partee, B.
1972 Opacity, coreference, and pronouns. In: Davidson, D. & G. Harman (eds.). *Semantics of Natural Language.* Dordrecht: Reidel Publishing Company, pp. 415-441.

Pollard, C. & I. A. Sag
1987 *Information-based Syntax and Semantics.* CSLI, Lecture Notes Number 13. Chicago: Chicago University Press.

Prather, P. A. & D. A. Swinney
1988 Lexical processing and ambiguity resolution: An autonomous process in an interactive box. In: Small, S. L., G. W. Cottrell & M. K. Tanenhaus (eds.). *Lexical Ambiguity Resolution: Perspectives from Psycholinguistics, Neuropsychology, and Artificial Intelligence.* San Mateo, Ca.: Morgan Kaufmann, pp. 289-310.

Pustejovsky, J.
1991 "The generative lexicon." *Computational Linguistics* 17(4):409-441.

Quine, W.
1959 Meaning and translation. In: Brower, R. A. (ed.). *On Translation.* Cambridge, Mass.: Havard University Press.

Resnik, P.
1992 Left-corner parsing and psychological plausibility. In: *Proceedings of the 15th International Conference on Computational Linguistics*, Vol. 1:191-197. Nantes.

Rosch, E. & B. B. Lloyd
1978 *Cognition and Categorization*. Hillsdale, N.J.: Erlbaum.

Schabes, Y.
1992 "Stochastic lexicalized tree-adjoining grammars." *Proceedings of the 15th International Conference on Computational Linguistics,* Vol 2. Nantes, pp. 425-431.

Simpson, G. B.
1981 "Meaning dominance and semantic context in the process of lexical ambiguity." *Journal of Verbal Learning and Verbal Behavior* 20:120-136.

Sinclair, I. (ed.)
1989 *Cobuild English Learner's Dictionary*. London: Collins.

Strohner, H.
1991 *Textverstehen. Kognitive und kommunikative Grundlagen der Sprachverarbeitung.* Opladen: Westdeutscher Verlag.

Thorndyke, P. W. & F. R. Yekovich
1980 "A critic of schema-based theories of human story memory." *Poetics 9:23-49.*

Vandeloise, C.
1988 Length, width, and potential passing. In: Rudzka-Ostyn, B. (ed.). *Topics in Cognitive Linguistics.* Amsterdam/Philadelphia: Benjamins.
1993 The role of resistance in the meaning of thickness. *Leuvense Bijdragen* 82:29-47.

Vendler, Z.
1967 *Linguistics in Philosophy*. London: Cornell University Press.

Weischedel, R. M. & L. A. Ramshaw
1987 Reflections on the knowledge necessary to parse ill-formed input. In: Nirenburg, S. (ed.). *Machine Translation: Theoretical and Methodological Issues.* Cambridge: Cambridge University Press.

Whitney, P.
1987 Psychological theories and elaborative inferences: Implications for schema-theoretic views of comprehension. *Reading Research Quarterly* 22:299-310.

Wittgenstein, L.
1953 *Philosophical Investigations*. Oxford: Blackwell.

Wierzbicka, A.
1985 *Lexicography and Conceptual Analysis.* Karoma Publishers: Ann Arbor.

Wu, D.
1990 Probabilistic unification-based integration of syntactic and semantic preferences for nominal compounds. In: *Proceedings of the 13th International Conference on Computational Linguistics,* Vol. 2. Helsinki.

Yarowsky, D.
1992 Word sense disambiguation using statistical models of Roget's categories trained on large corpora. *Proceedings of the 15th International Conference on Computational Linguistics,* Vol 2. Nantes, pp. 454-460.

Zelinsky-Wibbelt, C.
1990 The semantic representation of spatial configurations: A conceptual motivation for generation in machine translation. In: *Proceedings of the 13th International Conference on Computational Linguistics.* Helsinki, pp. 299-303.

1991 "Token reference vs. type reference: implications for machine translation." *Machine Translation. Eurotra Special Issue 1.*

1993a Introduction. In: Zelinsky-Wibbelt, C. (ed.). *The Semantics of Prepositions: From Mental Processing to Natural Language Processing.* Berlin: Mouton de Gruyter.

1993b Interpreting and translating prepositions: A cognitively based formalization. In: Zelinsky-Wibbelt, C. (ed.). *The Semantics of Prepositions: From Mental Processing to Natural Language Processing.* Berlin: Mouton de Gruyter.

1994 Reference as a universal cognitive process: A contrastive study of article use. In: Geiger, R. (ed.). *Reference in Multidisciplinary Perspective: Philosophical Object, Cognitive Subject, Intersubjective Process.* Hildesheim: Olms. Now available as: EUROTRA-D WORKING PAPER 21.

Accessing semantic information in memory: The mental lexicon as a semi-module

Monika Schwarz

The central topic of this paper is the activation of semantic information in the mental lexicon. More precisely, I want to concentrate on the question in what way semantic information is connected to non-verbal, modality-specific knowledge structure in long term memory (LTM) and in how far semantic information can be activated by non-verbal input. Many linguists consider the lexicon to be a separate, encapsulated module within the language module. Results from on-line studies on lexical comprehension and neuropsychological evidence from aphasic patients, however, indicate that semantic memory cannot totally be separated from our other knowledge systems.

1. The mental lexicon as a knowledge system in LTM

It is generally assumed that human cognition consists of many different systems which are responsible for the storage and reception of different types of information coming from different sensory modalities (tactile, motoric, visual, verbal, etc). One of the most difficult problems of cognitive science is to answer the question in what way these different knowledge systems interact. The mental lexicon is a system in our long term memory (LTM), where all our knowledge about the words of our language(s) is stored. This mental dictionary consists of a huge amount of lexical entries which combine phonological, syntactical, and semantic representations. These representations form the structural basis of language understanding and language production. In language processing the units of the mental lexicon are activated in order to build up meaningful cognitive structures. Research on the structure of LTM has shown that there are different principles along which the mental lexicon is organised (see Aitchison 1987). There is empirical evidence (e.g. the tip-of-the-tongue-phenomena (TOT) and speech errors in spontaneous speech which are based on formal similarity) that phonological representations and semantic representations can be accessed independently from each other. In this paper I will concentrate on the semantic information stored in the mental lexicon. Within this realm I deal only with concrete nouns.

2. Lexicon research within cognitive linguistics

The general theoretical framework here is that of cognitive linguistics (understood as a branch of cognitive science). The interesting questions of this approach concern the nature of our mental knowledge about language, how we represent this knowledge in memory, and how we put this knowledge to use. Thus, cognitive linguistics concentrates not only on the language system but also on the language processor (Schwarz 1992a).

Aspects of these phenomena are not easy to handle. Most of our mental representations and processes are unconscious and hence outside of the realm of our introspective faculty. In cognitive linguistics, the database therefore is expanded to include information on natural language understanding and brain research to account for how knowledge is stored and accessed in the lexicon.

According to this conception of linguistics, the theoretical constructs of linguistic theory should be taken as denoting real mental entities. Mentalism in generative grammar is a theoretical point of view which does not influence the methods used to analyse the nature of language; in cognitive linguistics mentalism is also a methodological approach. Thus, the main constraint for a theory within cognitive linguistics is that it should be compatible with empirical data.

3. The issue of modularity: the lexicon as a module?

The main assumption of cognitive scientists is that the human mind can best be described as a system of modules. Some evidence from neuroscience, especially from aphasiology, supports the idea of an overall modular organisation: a lot of dissociations between different mental functions have been observed, i.e. one mental faculty can be disturbed while another faculty will still work properly (Blumstein 1988, Shallice 1988). Language is regarded as an autonomous system which is governed by language-specific principles. The modular conception is being challenged by scientists working within a more holistic framework (such as Lakoff 1987, Taylor 1989). The holistic approach claims that natural language is an open cognitive system that interacts with general mental activities. If we take a look at the neuronal architecture of the human brain, we see a great amount of uniform patterns and a lot of interconnectiveness. At first sight, this makes the idea of strict modularity unlikely, at least at the neurophysiological level. However, it is important to point out that considering the brain as the physical substrate of cognition does not necessarily mean that all mental behavior can be reduced to neural mechanisms or can be explained in biological terms. The mental level displays characteristics which do not appear at the neurophysiological level (Lycan 1990). In the case of the mind/brain we do not simply have a micro- and a macrolevel, but a much more complex correspondence between sublevels, different layers of structural representation. Although most cortical regions of the brain are connected with each other by nerve fibers, clinical and neurolinguistic studies of aphasic patients have shown that there are much more selective impairments of cognitive functions than global impairments (see Ellis & Young 1990, Kelter 1990). Thus, interconnectivity at the neuronal level does not exclude modularity at the mental level. The current view of human brain organization supports the theory of discrete, relatively independent cognitive subsystems (see Schwarz 1992a, b).

What exactly is a module? A module forms a relatively autonomous knowledge domain for processing a particular type of information with only limited access to other types of information. According to Fodor (1983) a module is an input system which possesses the following properties: it is domain-specific, informationally encapsulated, mandatory, and it is represented in a specific area of the brain. There seem to exist modular systems in our cognition like visual perception and syntax which are distinct, autonomous knowledge and processing systems, relatively immune to contextual information, fixed to specific neuronal regions in the human brain (Fanselow & Felix 1987; for an alternative account see Taylor 1989).

Does the semantic part of the mental lexicon exhibit the same modular properties?

4. Semantic knowledge in the human brain

As far as the fixed neuronal representation is concerned, semantic knowledge obviously is represented and distributed in the brain much more diffusely than formal knowledge structure. Studies on aphasic patients have shown that the left hemisphere is dominant for language. Semantic impairments, however, can occur not only if the left hemisphere is damaged (which is the case for syntactic impairments) but also after lesions in the right hemisphere. Even damages of subcortical regions can lead to semantic impairments. In cortical dementias syntactic abilities usually are preserved, whereas the semantic faculty is often impaired. Recent clinical observations have shown that syntactic and semantic deficits are clearly dissociable in different aphasia types. An important question, however, is whether syntactic and semantic knowledge can be described as totally independent from each other in a linguistic theory (if we consider that in lexical items semantic and syntactic representations are often interrelated). Thus, the syntax/semantics-interface remains an issue to be further clarified.

Generally, the right hemisphere plays the dominant role in perceptuo-spatial functioning in all sensory modalities. But a growing body of evidence has shown that the right hemisphere also has some competence for the semantic processing of concrete words (Yoanette *et al.* 1990). This might be due to the fact that the referents of concrete nouns can be experienced through several sense modalities and therefore are not as specifically localised as abstract words which are known only through the verbal channel. Further neuropsychological observations indicate that semantics cannot be totally isolated from our general conceptual capacities: Aphasic patients with semantic impairment very often show impairments in conceptual representation as well (Kelter 1990). This, too, supports the view of the broader neural representation of semantic knowledge.

5. Semantic knowledge and conceptual knowledge

It is still a matter of intensive discussion whether word meanings and concepts (which constitute our general world knowledge) are identical. The question at issue is whether it is possible to draw a strict boundary between semantic knowledge and general world knowledge. So far there has been no satisfying account on this problem. I will take the following point of view: Although semantic knowledge and conceptual knowledge are closely interrelated, they are not identical. Conceptual knowledge undeniably constitutes the basis for the development of our semantic knowledge system: Children acquire word meanings by mapping formal representations on conceptual information units. Meanings, in this respect, are conceptual units bound to language-specific representations. According to this, no sharp boundary can be drawn between lexical semantic information and the more general knowledge of the world. Yet, there is no 1:1-relationship between concepts and meanings. For both adults and children concepts which are not connected to phonological or orthographic representations form lexical gaps. The meaning of a word is overlapping with the concept to a large extent (but not necessarily totally, the overall concept may extend the range of the word meaning). In the case of synonymy we have different lexical units denoting the same concept.

Semantic knowledge is bound to phonological representation and syntactic structure, thus governed by language-specific principles. Semantic knowledge, then, is a modality-specific subset of conceptual knowledge that lexicalises specific parts of conceptual information (Schwarz 1992b). Therefore, we find different lexicalisations of conceptual units in different languages. Consider, for instance, the well-known case that in German there is only one lexical item *Straße* for a specific conceptual pattern whereas in English it is differentiated between *road* and *street*. The underlying conceptual unit or pattern is the same. The difference lies in the specific selection of conceptual information which is bound to the verbal representation(s) in the lexical unit(s).

6. Empirical evidence for multi-modal access: Activating semantic representations through non-verbal processing routes

I will turn now to the question whether the modality-specific semantic representations are accessed only from verbal input. Is there only one processing channel through which we can activate semantic information? Or can semantic knowledge be accessed by different (tactile/perceptual/motoric) processing routes?

Semantic memory can best be described as a huge network in which word meanings are represented as units which are related to each other by specific relations. A very important concept in research on semantic memory is that of spreading activation. If units are connected in the mental lexicon, activation can spread from the activated unit to other connected units. This aspect of lexical processing has been investigated in numerous priming experiments. In priming experiments subjects are presented with a word. The task is to read as quickly as possible the word or to decide whether it is actually a word or just a string of letters. Shortly before this (target) word is shown, another word, the so-called prime is presented. So the prime could be *nurse* and the target *hospital*. In those priming tests it has been found that the reaction or lexical decision time is shorter when the prime word is related to the target word (Vanderwart 1984, Aitchison 1987). This priming effect is generally explained by assuming the process of spreading activation in the mental lexicon. The pre-activation of connected units is responsible for the mentioned facilitation in priming tests.

The process which activates representations in the mental lexicon is usually referred to as lexical access. In lexical access the information of the lexical entry which is activated through a specific word becomes available. For spoken and written words, this process has been shown to be relatively independent of contextual factors. Thus, an ambiguous word like *bug* always activates both its meanings at the level of the mental lexicon, regardless of the context (Swinney 1979). This process, of course, is unconscious. In this respect, lexical access is autonomous and mandatory. Post-lexical processing, then, takes contextual factors into account (Schwarz 1993).
Only recently, however, Shillcock & Bard (1993) could show that the lexical access system is permeable to contextual information in the case of closed-class words. They demonstrated in two cross-modal priming experiments that lexical access is affected by contextual information in the case of those closed-class-words like *can* or *would* which are homophonous with open-class-words. When *would* is heard in context, subjects do not access *wood*. These results suggest that modularity is not a matter of general cognitive architecture in the sense of Fodor (1983) but rather a matter of local processing efficiency.

Now I turn to the question whether lexical access is domain-specific. There are two kinds of evidence which support the assumption that semantic knowledge is connected to other processing domains: data from aphasic patients and data from on-line processing studies.

Many aphasic patients show a dissociation between different processing systems. The verbal processing channel can be disturbed while other processing channels are intact. Within linguistic processing, specific impairments of semantic processing may occur. Some aphasic patients are left with severe naming difficulties. Evidence for functionally separate, yet interrelated subsystems comes from modality-specific naming difficulties. Characteristic for these syndromes is that naming from one modality is impaired (Shallice 1988, Ellis & Young 1990).

In optic aphasia, for instance, visually presented objects cannot be named, but the same objects can be named if touched. So if the patient touches the object he/she cannnot name, he/she has access to the lexical entry. The syndrome is not a loss of the names of the objects or a deficit in the mental store. The aphasics are able to identify visually presented objects by demonstrating use. Hence, the impairment lies in the transmission of information from the visual system to the verbal system. In tactile aphasia, complementary results can be found: naming from touch is impaired, whereas visual naming abilities are preserved. Some aphasics are not able to access lexical entries via the verbal processing channel (both phonological and orthographic input are disturbed). If, however, they are presented with a picture of the referent the word denotes, they are able to retrieve the semantic information from the mental lexicon and to name the object.

The second line of evidence comes from priming tests in on-line processing with normal adults: A lot of experiments have shown that priming with associated pictures is as facilitating as priming with associated words. A picture of a flower can produce a priming effect for a word like *rose* (Vanderwart 1984). This means that semantic information can be activated directly by information from non-verbal perceptual input. Further support for this assumption comes from priming experiments which show that specific semantic information dealing with perceptual aspects (shape, form, colour, etc.) can be triggered by modality-specific processing systems (Schreuder & Flores d'Arcais 1989).

This explanation does not claim that hearing the word *rose* and seeing (the picture of) a rose leads to the same mental representation in memory. While some scientists argue that all knowledge units are represented at the conceptual level in a single modality-unspecific (amodal) format, others claim that there are separate systems for verbal, visual, and other sensory modalities. At present, this issue is still a matter of much debate, but a growing body of evidence supports the idea that there are both modality-unspecific representations and different modality-specific knowledge structures in our LTM (Engelkamp & Zimmer 1985).

Obviously, information in semantic memory can be accessed through different input channels. Since it is possible to access lexical entries from visual perceptual and tactile input there must be dynamic connections or processing routes between word nodes (for concrete referents) and other knowledge representations. Lexical access of semantic units is not restricted to the verbal input. Thus, the semantic part of the mental lexicon is not an informationally encapsulated and impenetrable module, but a knowledge system which is connected with other cognitive processing domains. In this respect, semantic memory is not a tight module, but rather some kind of a semi-module (Shallice 1988, Schwarz 1992b). As a first approximation, a semi-module can be described as a processing domain of our cognition which is functionally isolable as a specific subsystem, yet permeable to input from different knowledge systems. The most relevant and efficient input for the operations at the level of semantic memory is the verbal input. Hence, damage to this processing channel leads to the severest impairments. There are, of course, a lot of questions still left open. Although the existence of cross-modal priming provides support for the semi-modularity of the mental lexicon, it is still necessary to explain in more detail how the different subsystems of cognition interact in language processing.

Consequently, the issue of neuropsychological data deserves much more attention within cognitive linguistics.

7. Summary

The question at issue has been whether the semantic part of the mental lexicon has the status of a module which is informationally encapsulated and can be accessed only through the verbal input channel. Although lexical access seems to be mandatory and relatively independent from contextual factors, it is not domain-specific. Results from neuropsychological research show that there are dynamic connections between the semantic representations of concrete words in the mental lexicon and other knowledge systems in our LTM. These observations lead to the assumption that the mental lexicon can best be described as a semi-module.

Note

This research has been supported by the German Research Foundation (DFG).

References

Aitchison, J.
1987 *Words in the Mind: An Introduction to the Mental Lexicon.* Oxford: Blackwell.

Blumstein, S.
1988 Neurolinguistics: An overview of language-brain relations in aphasia. In: Newmeyer, F. (ed.). *Linguistics: The Cambridge Survey*, Vol. I-IV. Cambridge: Cambridge University Press, pp. 210-236.

Ellis, A. & A. Young
1990 *Einführung in die kognitive Neuropsychologie.* Bern: Huber.

Engelkamp, J. & H. D. Zimmer
1985 "Motor programs and their relation to semantic memory". *The German Journal of Psychology* 3:239-254.

Fanselow, G. & S. Felix
1987 *Sprachtheorie.* Tübingen: Francke (UTB 1441).

Fodor, J. A.
1983 *The Modularity of Mind. An Essay on Faculty Psychology.* Cambridge, Mass.: The MIT Press.

Kelter, S.
1990 *Aphasien. Hirnorganisch bedingte Sprachstörungen und kognitive Wissenschaft.* Stuttgart: Kohlhammer.
Lakoff, G.
1987 *Women, Fire, and Dangerous Things. What Categories Reveal About the Mind.* Chicago: The University of Chicago Press.
Lycan, W. G. (ed.)
1990 *Mind and Cognition. A Reader.* Oxford: Blackwell.
Schreuder, R. & G. B. Flores d'Arcais
1989 Psycholinguistic issues in the lexical representation of meaning. In: Marslen-Wilson, W. (ed.). *Lexical Representations and Processes.* Cambridge, Mass.: Bradford MIT Press, pp. 409-436.
Schwarz, M.
1992a *Einführung in die kognitive Linguistik.* Tübingen: Francke (UTB 1636).
1992b *Kognitive Semantiktheorie und neuropsychologische Realität. Repräsentationale und prozedurale Aspekte der semantischen Kompetenz.* Tübingen: Niemeyer (LA 273).
1993 "Retrieving semantic information from the mental lexicon". Paper presented at the 3rd International Cognitive Linguistics Conference, Leuven. Submitted for publication.
Shallice, T.
1988 *From Neuropsychology to Mental Structure.* Cambridge:Cambridge University Press.
Shillcock, R. & E. Gurman Bard
1993 "Restricting modularity in the lexical access of closed class words. *Would* does not prime *timber*". Centre for Cognitive Science, Edinburgh. Paper submitted for publication.
Taylor, J.
1989 *Linguistic Categorization. Prototypes in Linguistic Theory.* Oxford: Clarendon Press.
Vanderwart, M.
1984 "Priming by pictures in lexical decision". *Journal of Verbal Learning and Verbal Behavior* 16: 683-692.
Yoanette, Y., P. Goulet & D. Hannequin
1990 *Right Hemisphere and Verbal Communication.* New York: Springer.

Language processing and the mental lexicon in bilinguals

Carol Myers-Scotton

1. Introduction

This paper presents some hypotheses about the nature of the mental lexicon and the language production process, with special reference to bilinguals. The major data source comes from naturally-occurring codeswitching, supplemented by some data from second language attrition in children and from the study of aphasics. Codeswitching (CS) is generally defined as the use of two or more linguistic varieties in the same conversation. Here, only *intrasentential* CS between languages will be considered since intersentential switching tells us little special about language production processes. Further, CS is more narrowly defined here as the alternation by *proficient* bilinguals of two or more languages. While it may be impossible to define *proficient* with true precision, one can say that proficient bilinguals typically can produce monolingual, well-formed sentences in either language, even if they show more ability in one language than the other. Thus, here is what CS is *not*: (1) It is not the speech of second language learners, aiming to speak a single target language, but who miss that target because they have not yet mastered its structures. Such speakers show interference from another language - typically their first language, as well as other acquisitional/developmental phenomena characteristic of neither L_1 or L_2 (first or second language), for example, calquing. (2) CS also is not the speech of persons who are in the process of losing a language, often their first language. Such persons, frequently immigrants, can no longer speak the target language without introducing constituents or grammatical morphemes from another language in their repertoire which they now speak more fluently than the target. (3) CS also is not the use of grammatical patterns or semantic distinctions from language B in language A if the patterns are filled with morphemes from language A. In sum, then, intrasentential CS consists of sentences containing morphemes from two or more languages.[1]

Sentences from intrasentential CS may include three different types of structural patterns:

(i) ML + EL Constituents (mixed constituents). That is, a constituent consists of morphemes from both languages, one of which is called the *Matrix Language* (ML) and the other the *Embedded Language* (EL). Such constituents typically consist of only singly-occurring lexemes from the Embedded Language, inserted in a morphosyntactic frame supplied by the Matrix Language. See *leo si-ku-come* 'today I didn't come' in example (1).

(ii) Matrix Language Islands. A constituent is entirely in the Matrix Language, and is well-formed according to the grammar of that language. See *ana bagi nešri* 'I wanted to buy' in example (2).

(iii) Embedded Language Islands. Again, a constituent is entirely in a single language, this time the Embedded Language, meeting that language's requirements for well-formedness. See *voor de auto* 'for the car' in example (2).

(1) *Leo si-ku-COME na BOOKS zangu.*
today 1S/NEG-PAST/NEG-come with my
'Today I didn't come with my books.'
(Swahili/English Myers-Scotton 1993b:80)

(2) *...WET JE WEL, VIND IK LEUK, u kont ana*
know you well find I nice, and I was I
baga nešri dik S-SMURFEN VOOR DE AUTO
wanting I buy those the-smurfs for the car
'...you know, I like that [,] and I wanted to buy those smurfs for the car.'
(Moroccan Arabic/Dutch Nortier 1990:216)

This paper deals with three different organizational levels within bilingual cognitive structure and speech production. First, it considers some issues regarding the nature of entries in the bilingual mental lexicon. The mental lexicon is the speaker's internal representation of knowledge about forms which occur in surface structures. Such knowledge has to do with the phonology, syntax, and semantics of forms. The mental lexicon is made up of abstract entries called *lemmas* (cf. Levelt 1989). Lemmas include abstract information at two levels, the semantic and pragmatic level (Lexical-Conceptual Structure) and what is realized as the surface morphosyntactic level (Predicate-Argument Structure) (cf. Rappaport & Levin 1988, Talmy 1985).

Lemmas also include the sociolinguistic and pragmatic information which is critical to a speaker's selecting one lemma rather than another; for example, choosing between the lemmas which project the lexemes *maybe* and *perhaps* could be considered a sociolinguistic decision, based on the desired degree of formality. Much CS occurs because a speaker wishes, whether at a conscious or unconscious level, to convey one socio-psychological stance rather than another (cf. Myers-Scotton 1993a on the social motivations of CS). Thus, the claim here is that CS has its first causes at the conceptual level, as does monolingual speech - that is, before lemmas are selected.

A single mental lexicon is hypothesized for bilinguals; this is a rather non-controversial claim. (For example, de Bot 1992 reaches a similar conclusion). Note, however, that the argument here is that this lexicon does not contain lexemes as such, but rather more abstract elements, lemmas. Each lemma is tagged for a specific language and supports the realization of an actual lexeme at the surface level. In addition to socio-pragmatic intentional meaning, each lemma consists of subcategorization frames; these enable lemmas to "call" certain morphosyntactic procedures in the language production *formulator*. The formulator is a sort of "control central" in actual on-line production. While lemmas contain socio-pragmatic and semantic information, the directions they send to the formulator include only morphosyntactic information. Grammatical encoding in the formulator is followed by phonological encoding. (According to Levelt (1989), abstract phonological codes are retrieved from the mental lexicon, with each lemma "pointing to" its own code. This is called its *lexeme*, i.e. word form.) See Figure 1 for my sketch of the model of language production postulated here.

Conceptual Level:	Speaker's intentions regarding referential information and socio-pragmatic messages
Functional Level:	Select lemmas from Mental Lexicon (Congruent with intentions) Lemmas send directions to the formulator (regarding morphosyntactic procedures) *(Result: basic sentential frame is set)*
Positional Level:	Select phonological representations *(Result: lexemes are realized)* Direct positioning of lexemes

Figure 1. Model of language production

Is some overlap between the lemmas of language A and B possible? The answer is "yes" in the same sense that some overlap between languages is possible, if overlap is conceptualized abstractly as *congruence*. Congruence refers to matches between the lemmas at the two levels mentioned above (Lexical-Conceptual and Predicate-Argument Structures); these refer to subcategorization frames and the morphosyntactic procedures which lemmas call. This view, then, means that a language is not thought of so much as a set of lexical items and a finite grammar, but as a set of lemmas and the rule-governed apparatus which they call for their instantiation. This makes the conception of what is "language" an open one: if the minimal requirements of a certain lemma-based constituent frame are met, various lexical items can be plugged into that frame. Empirical support for this claim comes from intrasentential CS, since - as will become clear - constituents of morphemes from two languages consist of a frame supplied by one language, but with content morphemes called by the lemmas from two or even more languages.

Second, the paper considers relations across morphosyntactic procedures contained in the formulator. Lemmas from the mental lexicon activate specific sets of morphosyntactic procedures in the formulator. Because speech production is so rapid and fluent, psycholinguists propose that these procedures must involve parallel processing, but with one procedure blind to the workings of another. In fact, CS data provide empirical evidence for such parallel processing and blindness, a form of modularity.

Third, the paper discusses connections between lemmas (in the mental lexicon) and the lexemes (the actual word forms realized at the surface or positional level). As I use the term, lemmas underlie both word stems and affixes. For bilinguals, CS data provide evidence that their two languages are not equally "in control" of the selection of word forms. That is, while both languages are turned "on" all the time, one language has greater input in the resulting string in bilingual speech production.

2. The matrix language frame model

This section gives a brief sketch of the CS model followed here, the Matrix Language Frame Model.[2] This model receives motivation from several psycholinguistic sources regarding the distinction between what I will call *system* and *content* morphemes. These are discussed below.

Motivation for this distinction comes from speech error analysis (e.g. Fromkin 1973, 1980); hypotheses of the accessing of so-called closed vs. open class items at different points in the speech production process (e.g.

Garrett 1975, 1990); evidence from so-called "agrammatic" speech by aphasics and their responses to experimental tasks (Heeschen & Kolk 1985, Friederici *et al.* 1991); as well as differential loss of system vs. content morphemes in child language attrition of a second language (Kuhberg 1992). Other aspects of the model receive motivation from psycholinguistic experiments about the unequal role of the languages involved in bilingual production, such as the "base language effect" (Grosjean *et al.*, e.g. Grosjean 1988) or Green's (1986) ideas about unequal activation of languages in bilinguals. Finally, the model receives important motivation for the "top down" view of CS which it takes from Levelt's (1989, 1992) model of language production.

The Matrix Language Frame Model of CS is structured on two related hierarchies. The first involves the unequal division of labor between the two languages involved in CS, as well as in other forms of language production involving two or more languages. One language is more central in sentential frame-building. This language is called the Matrix Language while the more secondary language is called the Embedded Language.

The Matrix Language can be recognized as the "unmarked or expected choice" for the interaction type represented by the conversation containing the CS being studied. However, when the unmarked discourse mode itself *is* CS, that is, when switching back and forth between languages is the usual mode of a given group of speakers, then the Matrix Language cannot be identified with the unmarked choice. This is because both languages are, to some extent, even if not equally, unmarked. For this reason, as well as because of the gradiency of the concept of "unmarked choice", the Matrix Language must be identified by the convergence of more objectively based measures: (i) the Matrix Language is the language of relatively greater morpheme frequency, if a discourse sample of two or more sentences involving CS are studied. (ii) The Matrix Language is the language which the subjects engaged in CS will identify themselves as the "main language" being used. Kamwangamalu and Lee 1991 demonstrated that speakers formed a consensus in identifying the Matrix Language for Chinese/English CS in Singapore. (iii) Finally, the Matrix Language is the language which projects the sentential frame in CS utterances. This claim is operationalized by the Matrix Language and Blocking Hypotheses of the model, as will become clearer.

The second hierarchy which figures in structuring CS utterances involves the distinction between *content* and *system morphemes*. Note that it is not that system morphemes are members of "systems" and content morphemes are not, or that content morphemes have "content" and all system morphemes do not. Rather, *system morphemes* are so called because they are part of the grammatical system of the language; their primary function is to express relationships between words or at the discourse level - at the same time as they are more or less contentful. *Content morphemes* primarily express semantic content.

Recognizing the distinction between content and system morphemes is important because of its consequences for the appearance of Embedded Language material in intrasentential CS. "Syntactically relevant" Embedded Language system morphemes (i.e. morphemes with syntactic relations external to their heads) may occur only in Embedded Language islands (i.e. constituents entirely in the Embedded Language) and *never* occur in ML + EL constituents.

Prototypical content morphemes are nouns, descriptive adjectives, and most verbs. The primary formal feature of content morphemes is a plus setting as thematic role assigners or receivers. Prototypical system morphemes are quantifiers, specifiers, and inflectional affixes. The primary feature of system morphemes is that they are categories which pick out individuals or events across variables. More formally, one can say that system morphemes have a plus setting for the feature [Quantification].

Categories with a minus setting for [Quantification] are potential thematic role assigners or receivers. If they actually assign or receive thematic role, they are content morphemes. Thus, as thematic role receivers, all nouns and descriptive adjectives are content morphemes. For the same reason, free-form pronouns are content morphemes, except for dummy pronouns, since they do not receive thematic role (e.g. *il* in *il fait chaud* "it is warm" in French). Because they assign thematic roles, most verbs (but not the copula) and some prepositions are content morphemes.[3]

Note that what is a content morpheme in one language may have a counterpart in another language which is not. This is especially true regarding pronouns. Free-form pronouns behave like nouns syntactically, receiving thematic roles. In contrast, clitics, which are structurally-assigned, are system morphemes (e.g. French *je-*, *tu-*, etc.).

2.1. Hypotheses in the MLF model

Three main hypotheses structure the Matrix Language Frame Model.

2.1.1. The matrix language hypothesis

The Matrix Language determines the morphosyntax of ML + EL constituents (i.e. mixed constituents). Two testable principles follow from this hypothesis:

2.1.1.1. The morpheme order principle:

In mixed constituents, surface morpheme order must not violate that of the Matrix Language.

2.1.1.2. The system morpheme principle

In ML + EL constituents, all "syntactically relevant" system morphemes come only from the Matrix Language.

Because the main goal of this paper is not to explicate the Matrix Language Frame Model, but rather to discuss the implications of the model and the CS data which it explains for the organization of the lexicon and speech production processes in bilinguals, only a very few examples will be cited to support the Morpheme Order and the System Morpheme Principles. Note that upper-case is used for Embedded Language material in the examples.

(3) *Ku-Lilongwe, ndi-ka-kahla ma-WEEK-S a-wiri*
at Lilongue 1S-FUT-stay Cl.6/PL-week-PL Cl.6-two
'I will stay two weeks at Lilongwe.'
(Chewa/English Simango, personal communication, cited in Myers-Scotton 1993b:190)

First, note that the nominal modifier (*a-wiri*) "two" follows its head noun (*ma-week-s*), according to the morpheme order requirements for NPs of Chewa, which is the Matrix Language. The English order for NPs, of course, is the reverse. While this form shows a plural marker from both Chewa (*ma-* for class 6, which is a plural class) and English (*-s*), only the Chewa system morpheme for plural is "syntactically active". This is clear from the fact that it governs agreement (from class 6) on the modifier of the noun (i.e. on *a-wiri*). Finally, note that the verb inflections, the clitic for first person singular and the tense marker, which are system morphemes, of course, are from Chewa.

Example (4) also supports both the Morpheme Order Principle and the System Morpheme Principle. Note that the verb final morpheme order of Turkish, the Matrix Language, is followed. Regarding system morphemes, note that the plural marker on the Dutch noun *klant* "customer" comes from Turkish, as does the progressive marker on the Turkish verb *yap* for "do".

(4)	*Turkler alsa*	*KLANT-lar*	*WEGJAGEN*	*yap-iyor*
		customer-PL	chase	do-PROG

'Turks chase away customers.'
(Turkish/Dutch Boeschoten 1991:90)

This example is interesting for another reason. It shows a common strategy in diverse language pairs: a *do* verb from the Matrix Language carries any necessary verbal inflections, but it is used with a *bare form* from the Embedded Language. A bare form is a well-formed word in the Embedded Language, occurring in an ML + EL constituent without the Matrix Language system morpheme which would make the constituent well-formed in the Matrix Language. The bare form from Dutch, *wegjagen*, is a non-finite verb form, in this case an infinitive. Such a strategy avoids the occurrence of Embedded Language system morphemes on an Embedded Language verb. Such *do* verb examples are discussed further when the nature of the bilingual lexicon is raised.

(Both the Morpheme Order Principle and the System Morpheme Principle are exceptionally robust across data sets. For example, in the 40 naturally-occurring conversations including Swahili/English CS which I studied from Nairobi, only one counter-example to the System Morpheme Principle occurs. The data include many opportunities for counter-examples; for example, there are 91 finite Embedded Language (that is, English) verb stems, but all are inflected with Swahili system morphemes, as the principle predicts. Also, there are 55 instances of the noun compound construction, N "of" N, in which one of the nouns is from the Matrix Language (Swahili) and the other from the Embedded Language (English). In all cases, the Swahili morpheme for "of" (*-a*) appears, properly prefixed so that it agrees with the preceding noun (e.g. *uncle wa city*; *plan za Saturday*). Thus, the English morpheme conveying "of" never appears in such constructions.)

To summarize to this point, to call ML + EL constituents "mixed" obscures their highly systematic nature. They regularly consist of a Matrix Language morphosyntactic frame (system morphemes and morpheme order) into which content morphemes (or internal Embedded Language islands) are inserted. That is, this evidence leads us to claim that in bilingual speech, the constituent frame is constructed by higher-order procedures called by only the Matrix Language. Either Matrix Language or Embedded Language lemmas may call the procedures which will insert Matrix Language or Embedded Language content morphemes respectively into the frame. Yet, only Embedded Language lemmas which pass the Blocking Filter are possible. This filter is now discussed.

2.1.2. The blocking hypothesis

A Blocking Filter blocks Embedded Language lemmas which would call Embedded Language content morphemes in mixed constituents if these lemmas are not congruent with a Matrix Language counterpart in the following ways:

(a) Even if the Embedded Language realizes a given grammatical category as a content morpheme, if it is a system morpheme in the Matrix Language, its lemma may not be selected.

(b) The same filter still blocks an Embedded Language lemma calling an Embedded Language content morpheme which has a Matrix Language content morpheme counterpart *if* it is not congruent with its Matrix Language counterpart in terms of thematic role assignment properties. This is discussed further below.

(c) Finally, blocking occurs if the Embedded Language content morpheme and its Matrix Language counterpart are not congruent in terms of thematic role at the discourse level, i.e. one morpheme may have the discourse role TOPIC while its counterpart in the other language does not (cf. Jake 1994).

Consider, for example, (5).

(5) *Sawa tu.* *Labda YOU WILL HAVE TO BRING IT*
ok just perhaps
AT MY HOME. u-let-e *BEFORE kesho jioni.*
2S-bring-SUBJUNC tomorrow evening
'Ok. Perhaps you will have to bring it at my home. You should bring [it] before tomorrow evening.'
(Swahili/English Myers-Scotton 1993b:124)

This is one of only two cases in a Swahili/English CS corpus of about 20 hours of conversation in which an English preposition appears in a mixed constituent (*before kesho jioni*). While Swahili has very few prepositions, it happens to have a counterpart to *before*, which is *kabla + ya.* Both lexemes (*before* and *kabla*) are content morphemes. This speaker could have selected either morpheme. That one is called rather than the other implies that differences in semantic fields and socio-pragmatic features are salient in the lemma selection process at the conceptual level. These types of saliency are very abstractly-based, I argue; it is at this level that congruency is checked, and it is only "played out" at the surface level, where they are reflected in the choice of the lexeme *before* rather than *kabla ya*.[4]

Next, an example of non-congruence between Swahili and English is considered, also involving prepositions, but depending on the thematic role assignment projected by the Matrix Language verb.

(6) a. **Ni-ka-mw-ambia* *a-ni-p-e* *ruhusa*
I-CONSEC-him-tell he-me-give-should permission
ni-end-e *ni-ka-CHECK* *FOR wewe.*
I-go-should I-CONSEC-check for you
b. *Ni-ka-mw-ambia* *a-ni-p-e* *ruhusa*
ni-end-e *ni-ka-*CHECK FOR YOU.
'And I told him that he should give me permission so that I go and check for you.'
(Swahili/English Myers-Scotton 1993b:124)

Example (6b) with *for you* as an Embedded Language island actually occurs, while (6a) with *for wewe* does not. The problem here is not with lack of congruence between *you* and *wewe*, but because of differences in thematic role assignment. In Swahili, the thematic role of beneficiary is assigned by means of a clitic in the verbal assembly, not via a prepositional phrase, as it is done in English (i.e. *for you*). That is, a constituent consisting of an English preposition and an emphatic Swahili pronoun (*for wewe*) does not satisfy Swahili specifications for a Predicate-Argument Structure which includes "beneficiary", and such a constituent would be under Swahili control (since Swahili, as the Matrix Language, frames ML + EL constituents). The only way, therefore, to involve English in encoding the meaning "for you" is to produce an Embedded Language island (*for you*), as in (6b).

2.1.3. The embedded language island hypothesis

This hypothesis is a corollary to both the Matrix Language Hypothesis and the Blocking Hypothesis, since it specifies what happens to Embedded Language material disallowed under those hypotheses. Recall that Embedded Language islands consist only of Embedded Language morphemes which are not simply contiguous, but form constituents (that is, they show internal structural dependency relations). The Embedded Language Hypothesis proposes that such islands appear under one of two ways:

(a) An Embedded Language lemma, as the head of a constituent, is selected to satisfy directions from the conceptual structure, whatever their basis (for example, for socio-pragmatic reasons, an Embedded Language realization of a certain concept is preferred). In turn, this lemma activates Embedded Language morphosyntactic procedures in the formulator such that the higher-order procedure with S as its head, which is under Matrix Language control in intrasentential CS, is inhibited. The result is a constituent entirely in the Embedded Language.

(b) There is a "misfiring" in the formulator. An Embedded Language lemma for one of the system morphemes with its own lemma entry (e.g. lexicalized quantifying expressions, such as *all* in English), or an Embedded Language lemma calling an Embedded Language content morpheme not congruent with a Matrix Language counterpart, is accessed. Checking procedures in the formulator respond to the Embedded Language lemma, again closing down certain higher-order procedures under Matrix Language control, and setting in motion Embedded Language morphosyntactic procedures in the formulator. These procedures accept only Embedded Language material.[5]

Note that many Embedded Language islands which occur under option (a) above are either very formulaic (e.g. *from time to time*) and/or are constituents which are peripheral to the arguments of the verb (e.g. many are time adjuncts, such as *at the weekend*).

3. The matrix language frame model and other bilingual speech production

3.1. Child second language attrition

The above sketch gives prototypical examples of intrasentential CS and shows how the Matrix Language Frame Model explains their occurrence. The concepts in this model also explain other language data involving two languages, for example, the attrition of a second language in children. Kuhberg (1992) studied the loss of German by two young Turkish girls who returned to an all-Turkish milieu after spending their first years in Germany. Over the period of more than a year (15 to 20 months), Kohberg was the only one who carried on German conversations with these children. Gradually, their knowledge of German was diminished.

What is interesting is that this loss follows the principles of the Matrix Language Frame Model. At first, the girls spoke only German with the researcher. At the next stage, however, they began CS to Turkish content morphemes. Gradually, they replaced German system morphemes with Turkish system morphemes and Turkish morpheme order. See examples (7) and (8). This indicated, in terms of the model, that they were "turning over" their Matrix Language from German to Turkish. At the end of the observation period, the girls used little German, mainly content morphemes.

(7)	*EIS-*	*- ci-*	*-ya*
	ice cream-agentive	derivation-motion	towards
	'To the ice cream man'		

(8) *die Kind Hund-u ali-yor*
the child dog take-PROG
'the child is taking the dog'
NOT: die Kind aliyor Hundu
(Turkish/German Kuhberg 1992:149)

3.2. Aphasic speech

Similarly, the system vs. content morpheme distinction can explain certain aspects of the language behavior of aphasics. Given what is known about aphasics, especially those with Broca's aphasia, the model would predict that aphasics would show less loss for content morphemes than for system morphemes. This prediction is supported. For example, Nespoulous *et al.* (cited in Friederici *et al.* 1991) report that French agrammatic aphasics are more likely to produce those French pronominal forms which are content morphemes than those which are system morphemes (i.e. clitics).

4. Lemma specification

The basic premises in this argument should now be clear. The two main premises are that the Matrix Language and the Embedded Language have unequal roles in bilingual speech production, and that there is good reason to claim that system vs. content morphemes are differently accessed in either monolingual or bilingual speech. We can now consider the implications regarding the nature of the bilingual lexicon and bilingual language production of viewing actual CS examples in terms of these premises.

First, we consider lemma specification. Bilingual production, such as CS, provides strong empirical evidence for four conclusions about the nature of lemma entries.

4.1. Differential access of content and system morphemes

Clearly, the data indicate that system and content morphemes are accessed differently. Earlier evidence from speech error data and the study of speech in aphasics show that the two types of morphemes seem to have different retrieval histories; that is, the two types of morphemes may be slotted into the sentential frame at different steps. In most speech errors involving the exchange of content morphemes within a sentence (see example (9) and (10)), the system morphemes which "go with" the content morphemes do not move with them, but stay in their correct frame positions, indicating some difference in their status in the sentential frame.

(9) *We'll sit around the song and sing fire-s*
(target: we'll sit around the fire and sing songs)
(Garrett 1990:159)

(10) *The flood was road-ed*
(target: the road was flooded)
(Stemberger 1985:162)

Further, the fact that only Matrix Language system morphemes may appear in ML + EL (mixed) constituents in CS is evidence that a Blocking Filter (in the mental lexicon or in the formulator?) must be able to recognize which language the lemmas projecting system morphemes come from, since it allows only Matrix Language system morphemes to appear. This claim supports the earlier hypothesis that there is a common mental lexicon in bilinguals, but with lemmas tagged specifically for language.

When the evidence from CS and second language attrition is added to the speech error evidence, we have strong evidence that these two types of morphemes have different types of lemma entries in the mental lexicon, although specific details must await further psycholinguistic research.

4.2. The nature of lemma entries for nouns

One issue among psycholinguists and linguists is what types of entries there are for heads (e.g. nouns and verbs) and their affixes or morphophonemically attached specifiers. That is, do such heads have a separate entry or are they part of lemmas which also include their affixes? There is reason to argue that the types of entries may vary according to the language type and also according to whether a specifier shows morphophonemic attachment to a noun. Some linguists, such as Hankamer (1989), have argued against any "Full Listing Hypothesis" for an agglutinative language such as Turkish. Basically, such a hypothesis claims that a lexical entry includes representations of morphological structure so that affixed forms of the entry are accessed via the entry for the root. Of course in certain agglutinative languages, words consist of roots plus many affixes. The evidence from CS involving agglutinative languages, such as Bantu languages, is that their noun and verb roots have separate lemma entries from the affixes which accompany the surface realization of a noun or verb in monolingual speech. The evidence is the frequency with which such languages - when they are the Matrix Language in CS - accept a nominal or verb root from the Embedded Language. Recall, for example, *si-ku-come* "I didn't come" *(1SNEG-PAST/NEG-come)* in example (1) from Swahili/English CS. The same is true of other agglutinative languages around the world; Eliasson (1989) reports similar forms from Maori/English CS in New Zealand and they are found in Turkish/Dutch or Turkish/German CS in Europe. (For example, in Bantu languages, one would postulate a lemma for a noun stem and then separate lemmas which support noun class prefixes and include [+ or - plurality] as well. An obligatory morphosyntactic procedure would require that a noun class-marking lemma be accessed along with a noun stem lemma).

At the same time, some system morphemes may be entered in the same lemma entry with their heads. This is likely to be the case in German and Dutch, for example, regarding the plural system morpheme. Because plural forms in these languages are not predictable in any productive sense unless one knows the word class of the noun, each plural form has to be acquired on its own. For this reason, one would posit separate lemmas for the noun stem (= singular form) and for the plural form (= noun stem + plural suffix). There is some evidence for this claim from Moroccan Arabic/Dutch CS (Nortier 1990); in this corpus Dutch is the Embedded Language, but Dutch nouns often appear in their plural form. The situation is somewhat complicated by the fact that these nouns do not receive Arabic plural marking as well and therefore are considered as "bare forms" from the point of view of Arabic, the Matrix Language.[6]

Also, in various "Pennsylvania Dutch" corpora of German/English CS data showing convergence and/or CS (e.g. Enninger 1980), English nouns which are intended to be plural invariably appear with the English *-s* marking plurality. Since most English plural formations are regular (i.e. unlike the German case), it seems likely that English has a lemma for "noun stem" and a separate lemma for "plural" (although it also would have lemmas *including* plural for such English plurals as *mice*, which are not predictable in a productive sense).

Since German is the Matrix Language in the Pennsylvania Dutch case, what is postulated to happen is the following: the German lemma (consisting of noun stem + plural) accepts the English lemma (consisting only of noun stem) as a congruent match (because they generally match in regard to Lexical-Conceptual Structure and Predicate-Argument Structure). At the same time, the German lemma's activation is such that the English plural lemma is also called as part of the match, since the German lemma being matched also includes the specification "plural".

A scenario for English noun stem lemmas, as contrasting with that for German, also receives support from evidence on CS between English and various Bantu languages. Recall *book-s z-angu* "books my" in example (1) as well as *ma-week-s a-wiri* "weeks two" in example (3). In neither case, is the English plural suffix "syntactically active". In *book-s z-angu* the form which the modifier takes indicates it comes from Swahili class 10; that is, the prefix *z-* is obligatory with modifiers from this class. *Book-s* itself shows no overt Swahili class prefix, it is true, but the presence of *z-angu* implicates class 10 and, for nouns, class 10 may show a zero allomorph for the noun class prefix; this class prefix also marks plurality. In the *ma-week-s a-wiri* example, we have already remarked that clearly the prefix from Chewa class 6 (*ma-*) is the syntactically active one, not the English plural suffix; this is evidenced by the class 6 prefix which it governs on the number for two (*a-wiri*).

A motivation for the scenario postulated above is this: English plural suffixes do not *always* appear in Bantu languages/English CS: their incidence varies from language to language, although it is much higher in CS forms than it is with established loan words from English (cf. Bernsten 1990 on Shona/English) Now, if the English plural suffix *always* appeared in such CS forms, one would want to argue that the Bantu lemma for noun stem and the Bantu lemma for noun class plural (two different lemmas) are congruent with one lemma in English (that which includes the noun stem and the plural suffix). Rather, the fact that the English plural suffix does not always appear is evidence *instead* that both English and Bantu languages require two lemmas to support the concept "noun + plural". This does not mean, however, that the Bantu lemma supporting "plural" is totally congruent with the English lemma for "plural", since the Bantu noun class prefix encodes more information than just plurality). Note that the Bantu prefix is always obligatory; noun stems never appear on their own.

In order to explain the instances of "double morphology" involving plurals in Bantu/English CS data, the following scenario is postulated: the surface form *Bantu noun class prefix + English noun stem + English suffix* is the result of a "misfiring" in the formulator. What "should" occur is *Bantu noun class prefix + English noun stem*, since the Bantu language is the Matrix Language and the model predicts it will supply the system morpheme indicating plurality, which is what is contained in the Bantu noun class prefix. But there is a "misfiring" of sorts, resulting in the presence as well as *English plural suffix*. Recall such forms only occur *in some cases*; this is the reason a "misfiring" is posited.[7]

Figure 2 provides a schematic representation of hypothesized lemma status and congruence relations in German and English and Bantu languages and English. Note how German differs from English in its lemma entries, with Germany having a separate lemma entry for "noun singular" and another for "noun plural".

Lemma	*Lemma*	*Lemma*	*Lemma(s)*
German		*Bantu*	
Nstem	Nstem + PL	Nstem	Noun Class Prefix-S Noun Class Prefix-PL
English		*English*	
Nstem	PL	Nstem	PL

Figure 2. Lemma status and congruence relations

4.3. The nature of lemma entries and verbs

CS data also indicate that two types of closely related verb forms may come from two different lemmas. Evidence for this argument comes from two sources in CS data. First, consider examples (11a) and (11b):

(11) a. *a-li-kuwa* *ha-zi-buy* *hi-zo,*
3S-PAST-be 3S/NEG-Cl.10 OBJ-buy Cl.10 DEM
a-li-kuwa *a-na-kuwa* *OFFERED* *tu*
3S-PAST-be 3S-NON-PRES-be just
'He didn't buy those, he was just offered.'
(Swahili/English Myers-Scotton 1993b:115)

(11) b. *Noch* *schlimmer,* *wenne* *de* *CLIENT* *RECALÉ* *wurd*
even worse when DET client fail COP
am *PERMIS*
in the test...
'Even worse, when the learner is failed in the test...'
(Alsatian/French Gardner-Chloros 1991:216)

In these cases, a participial form from the Embedded Language appears, functioning as an adjectival complement after a Matrix Language form of the copula. In the one case, the participle is from English (*offered* in (11a)) and in the other it is from French (*recalé* in (11b)). In neither case does there seem to be any reason to consider the suffix marking the form as a participle to be syntactically active. Accordingly, it is argued that the entire form (verb root and participial affix) is accessed as a single form. If this claim holds, then one would want to argue that there are separate lemmas in the mental lexicon for finite verb stems and then for those verbal forms which sometimes function as adjectives (participles) and for those which sometimes function as nouns (infinitives). Lemmas supporting participles and infinitives would contain, in addition, to the verb stem, the relevant affix marking the verb form as a participle or as an infinitive (i.e. there would be separate lemmas for PRESENT PARTICIPLE, PAST PARTICIPLE, and INFINITIVE in addition to FINITE VERB STEM).

CS data suggest this may be the case in French and English for both participial and infinitival forms. The lemma supporting the English INFINITIVE, however, is different from the one supporting the French INFINITIVE. The English lemma contains directions "calling" or "not calling" the lemma supporting the English infinitival marker *to* (as in *to go)*, while the French lemma offers no choice; the French infinitival marker must be called (e.g. *all-er* "to go"). That there is this difference in infinitival lemmas is evidenced by the fact that English infinitival lexemes appear in CS data without *to* (when English is the Embedded Language), but French infinitival lexemes do not. Also, in monolingual English, sentences containing an infinitive, but without *to*, are well-formed.[8]

Reinforcement for the argument that Germanic participial and infinitival forms are called by different lemmas from those for finite verb stems comes from the existence of "double" participial forms in the languages today. That is, a formerly irregular verb (with an irregular past participial form) may now have a regularized past participial form. Dirven (personal communication) points out *slyp, geslypt* in Afrikaans for "grind, ground, ground", which has a regularized past participial today (cf. Dutch *slypen, sleep, geslepen* "grind"). Meanwhile, its former irregular past participial still exists as a "double", functioning as an adjective with a meaning involving metaphorical extension: *geslepe* "shrewd". And in English, there are a number of formerly irregular verbs which now have regular past participial forms, such as *mold, molded, molded*, but with the former past participial form retained as an adjective *molten* as in *molten iron*.

4.4. *Other connections between lemmas and lexemes*

Finally, consider what aphasic data imply about which lemmas are "intact" in aphasics and therefore how the production of aphasics can be better explained. For example, rather than producing an inflected verb form, a German aphasic has been recorded as producing such an utterance as (12b);

(12) a. *X trinkt gerne Bier*
drink-3S gladly beer
'He likes to drink beer'
b. *X gerne Bier trink-en*
gladly beer drink-INF
(Heeshen & Kolk 1988:300)

Students of aphasia have explained such utterances which lack system morphemes in verb forms as the result of a "processing difficulty". Instead, in the language production model motivated by CS data, these deficits can be explained more explicitly by arguing that there is a loss of a category in the mental lexicon, not just a processing difficulty. Recall above it was suggested that there are multiple lemmas in the mental lexicon for verbs, one for the lemma supporting finite verbs and others for participles and infinitives. To explain example (12), one would argue that the aphasic has lost those verbal lemmas which include the grammatical category INFL in their specification (INFL, of course, supports the tense and aspect verbal affixes). That is, he has lost the lemma calling a finite verb. Meanwhile, the aphasic producing *drink-en* still has the lemma supporting this morphologically complex lexeme, which includes the infinitival suffix, a system morpheme. This suffix is part of the lemma entry, and is available at D-structure, not assigned at S-structure.

5. Morphosyntactic procedures in the formulator

5.1. The matrix language sets the frame

The Japanese/English CS examples in (13a) and (13b) provide evidence about the relative relationship of the Matrix Language and the Embedded Language in sending directions to the formulator. (13a) is not attested, but (13b), which does not include a lexeme for *from*, occurs. The lemmas supporting the idea of "graduate" in Japanese and English have similar enough Lexical-Conceptual Structures for there to be sufficient congruence, but they have different Predicate-Argument Structures. In English, the lemma supporting *graduate* results in a surface form of *verb + particle* (resulting in a prepositional phrase) while its Japanese counterpart does not take a prepositional phrase, but rather only a direct object.

If the Embedded Language lemma supporting *graduate* were the one calling morphosyntactic procedures in the formulator for ML + EL constituents, then a sentence such as (13a) should be possible, since the system morpheme for *from* comes from Japanese, and only the content morpheme *graduate* comes from English (i.e. meeting other provisions of the Matrix Language Frame Model). Since (13a) is not attested but (13b) is, such evidence supports the hypothesis that the Matrix Language (Japanese here) is the only one sending morphosyntactic directions of any kind to the formulator when ML + EL constituents are being constructed - even though Embedded Language lemmas can support content morphemes in these constituents (*graduate* here).

(13) a. **Watashi wa Waseda kara* GRADUATE *shimashita*
1S TOP from did
b. *Watashi wa Waseda-(o)* GRADUATE *shimashita*
1S TOP ACCUS did
'I graduated from Waseda [University].'
(Japanese/English Azuma 1991:97-98)

5.2. *Modularity in production*

As indicated above, the examples showing "double morphology" (plural affixes from both languages) also reveal something about the workings of the formulator.

(14)	*...dzi-mwe*	*dze-nguva*	*ti-nenge*
	Cl.10-some	Cl.10-time	1PL-PROGR
	ti-chi-ita	*ma-GAME-S*	*panze...*
	1PL-FUT-do	Cl.6-	outside

'Sometimes we will be doing games outside...'
(Shona/English Myers-Scotton 1993b:132)

The very fact that "double morphology" can occur is evidence that there are parallel processes in the formulator which are not in touch with each other. Certainly, the Shona-based morphosyntactic procedure which takes directions from the Shona noun class lemma (which calls for a prefix indicating noun class/plurality) does not recognize that the noun stem from English is also receiving a plural marker from a different procedure activated by a different source, the English lemma for plurality. The result is a "misfiring" in the system. The formulator receives directions from two different sources for plurality and "misfires" by allowing both system morphemes to surface, although only the Bantu prefix is "syntactically relevant" (as discussed above under (3)). Such data as "double morphology" provide evidence that at least some morphosyntactic procedures in the formulator operate separately from each other.

5.3. *How internal embedded language islands are under matrix language control*

In addition, consider the surface form of what are called internal Embedded Language islands in the Matrix Language Frame Model. While many Embedded Language islands are attached constituents, there also are Embedded Language islands which are *within* a larger mixed constituent. Example (15) contains several Embedded Language islands in a Matrix Language frame.

(15)	*...ja*	*ni*	*w*	*kant*	*dak*	*LA*	*SEMAINE*	*djal*
	I	mean	and	it	was	that-the	week	where
	tajzawlu			*LES PERMIS.*				
	they take away			the driving licenses				

'...I mean, and it was that-the week where they take away the driving licenses.'
(Moroccan Arabic/Fr. Bentahila & Davies 1992:449)

Both *la semaine* "the week" and *les permis* "the driving licenses" are Embedded Language islands. That is, they are well-formed according to French grammatical constraints; thus, it is no surprise that the determiners, which are system morphemes, are from French, not from Arabic. The one island of interest here is *la semaine*. While it is well-formed in French, it is within a larger NP constituent for which the Matrix Language projects the frame, according to the Matrix Language Hypothesis. And this argument is supported by the data. For a noun phrase introduced by *dak* to be well-formed in Arabic, it must be followed by a determiner, not just by a noun. Thus, while **dak semaine* would not be predicted (since it doesn't conform to the Arabic specifications for this frame), *dak* plus *la semaine* does meet the specifications.

Contrastive evidence from other data sets involving French as an Embedded Language lead to the argument that while the island must be well-formed in the Embedded Language, this is not enough.[9] Rather, its particular form is governed by the constituent frame projected by the Matrix Language. In Wolof/French CS and in Lingala/French CS, such internal Embedded Language islands as *la semaine* (consisting of a DET + Noun) do not occur. The argument here is that in these cases the Matrix Language frame does not call for a determiner in this position or a morphophonemically-attached determiner, such as one finds in either Arabic or French. That is, while Wolof does have determiners, they follow their nominal heads (16a). Thus, while a mixed constituent in Wolof/French may well include a French noun (16b) those including internal Embedded Language islands of a French DET + Noun do not occur.

(16) a. *doom bi* 'child the', *kawar bi* 'hair the'
(Swigart 1992:166)
b. *appartements yi* 'apartments the'
*les appartements
(Swigart 1993, personal communication)

In contrast to Wolof, Lingala has no determiners; but like Wolof, it does not project an NP frame which will accommodate a French DET + N. Thus, (17a) is found, but (17b) is unacceptable:

(17) a. *Kindumba e-za-li* PUNITION *te*
prostitution it-PRES-be punishment NEG
'Prostitution is not a punishment.'
b. **Kindumba e-za-li* LA PUNITION *te*
(Lingala/French Kamwangamalu 1989:118-9)

Further evidence that an internal Embedded Language island must meet the specifications of the Matrix Language frame for the constituent comes from Moroccan Arabic/Dutch CS. In this case, Nortier (1990) reports many instances of "bare nouns" from Dutch, the Embedded Language in mixed constituents framed by Arabic (although there were also some examples which met the Arabic specifications of two determiners, but these were always both from Arabic, as in (18b)). The absence of Dutch internal islands to satisfy the "two-determiner requirement" and the presence instead of many "bare nouns" from Dutch with no determiners at all can be explained in this way: While Dutch has determiners which precede their nouns, they are not morphophonemically attached, as they are in both French and Arabic. Therefore, the Arabic frame does not accept them, *even* as part of internal Embedded Language islands. When there is only such partial congruence at Predicate-Argument Structure as is found in the Arabic/Dutch case, accessing "bare forms" from the Embedded Language is a compromise strategy. Jake and Myers-Scotton (1993) treat such forms further.

(18) a. Note: obligatory second determiner missing
wahed ø VERANTWOORDELIJKHEID
that responsibility
b. Note: obligatory second determiner present
wahed l- GESPREK
that the conversation
(Nortier 1990:147)

Finally, another example shows how the Matrix Language frame governs into an internal Embedded Language island. The Matrix Language in (19) is Turkish and therefore both instances of a Dutch ADJ + N may be considered Embedded Language islands. But note that the island in (19a) contains an overt agreement suffix on the adjective *blond* while the one in (19b) does not. In Dutch, definite NPs including a noun from the neuter class take *-e* as an agreement (AGR) suffix on their adjectives; however, indefinite NPs (as in 19b) in this class show a zero AGR suffix on adjectives. It seems clear here that whether the Dutch NP is considered definite or indefinite is controlled by a higher-level *Matrix*

Language procedure, expressed on the surface by the appearance of either "definite" or "indefinite" Turkish specifier lexemes. That is, the Matrix Language "control" over this Dutch NP (i.e. the internal Embedded Language island) is at the level of N" (N double bar).

(19) a. *ø BLONDE-E MEISJE afstudere yapti*
DET blond girl get-degree do-PRET
'That blond girl got [her] degree.'
b. *ENGELS-i birtane BLOND-ø MEISJE -dan*
English-ACCUS a blond girl -ABL
ali-you-dun
take-IMPERF-2S
'You got the English [lessons] from a blond girl.'
(Turkish/Dutch Backus 1989, cited Boeschoten 1991:91)

6. Conclusion

In conclusion, then, this paper has demonstrated how bilingual speech data, but especially CS data, provide empirical evidence for certain specifications about the mental lexicon and the language production process in bilinguals. In brief, the general conclusions supported are these:

(i) The bilingual's languages may both be "on" at the same time, but they are never equally activated at the same time. The evidence is that one language, called the Matrix Language here, sets the morphosyntactic frame in bilingual speech production.

(ii) The bilingual's mental lexicon includes lemmas which are from both languages known, but specifically tagged for their language - or, one can say that they are tagged to call specific morphosyntactic procedures and that the bundle of lemmas similarly tagged make up a language.

(iii) Bilinguals can access lemmas from whatever language is the Embedded Language in a conversation involving CS. However, these lemmas must pass the Blocking Filter of the Matrix Language in the language production formulator; that is, they must be congruent with Matrix Language counterparts in various ways related to both Lexical-Conceptual and Predicate-Argument Structure.

Abbreviations

1PL	1st person plural
1S	1st person
2S	2nd person
3S	3rd person
ABL	absolutive case
ACCUS	accusative case
AGR	agreement
Cl	noun class
CONSEC	consecutive tense
COP	copula
CS	codeswitching
DEM	demonstrative
DET	determiner
EL	embedded language
FUT	future tense
IMPERF	imperfective aspect
INF	infinitive
INFL	inflection
ML	matrix language
N	noun
N"	N double bar
NEG	negative
NON-PRES	non-present tense
NP	noun phrase
OBJ	object
PAST	past tense
PL	plural
PRES	present tense
PRET	preterit tense
PROG	progressive aspect
SUBJUNC	subjunctive mood
TOP	topic

Notes

1. I stress that most instances of CS are *not* the result of a speaker's "psycholinguistic need" to switch from one language to the other because of insufficient knowledge of the language in which the speaker has been proceeding. Rather, CS is better thought of as *skilled performance*

which conveys a social message (cf. Gumperz 1982, Myers-Scotton 1993a).

2. While phonological procedures are part of language production and therefore CS, of course, the basic mechanisms of CS seem to be morphosyntactic in nature and the motivations for which mechanisms are activated are even more abstract, involving crucially thematic role consideration, for example. These, therefore, are what concern us in this paper.
3. I favor a "prototype model" regarding the system:content morpheme distinction; that is, not all morphemes are equally "central" in their memberships as either system or content morphemes. Thus, I concur with this statement which Taylor (1989:196) makes for all formal elements in linguistic description: "Grammatical categories have a prototype structure, with central members sharing a range of both syntactic and semantic attributes. Failure of an item to exhibit some of these attributes does not of itself preclude membership." True, Taylor does refer to "borderline cases", but this is in discussing the word:clitic:affix distinction. Since the system:content morpheme distinction has nothing to do with whether a form is a word, Taylor's "borderline cases" are not relevant here.
4. These differences may involve semantic field. For example, while *kabla ya* means "before", it is derived from *kabili*, meaning "be in front", and therefore in the judgment of the speaker may retain more of a locative sense than *before* in English. Or, differences may involve socio-pragmatic features, such as the association of keeping appointments at set times with the culture of native English speakers as opposed to Swahili speakers. Thus, the choice to use the English word for the concept "before" referring to time may suggest "the need for punctuality" more than the Swahili word.
5. Hesitation phenomena precede some Embedded Language islands; this is implicational evidence that a "misfiring" has occurred.
6. Arabic, of course, has "broken" or ablaut plurals, which are lexically-specified; how such a plural formation would apply to Embedded Language nouns is an issue which has not been studied.
7. Jake (personal communication) suggests that variability in the occurrence of the English plural suffix may have something to do with syllable structure specifications of the Matrix Language. Some researchers suggest that there are two different ways of processing plurals in English: (a) add the plural affix to the noun stem, the approach supported for English by the codeswitching data, or (b) access the plural from one lemma (e.g. *books* as coming from a single lemma), as I have argued is the case for German and Dutch. Dirven (personal communication) has suggested that accepting the argument that, indeed, English has two different strategies for plural processing would "simplify" the necessary argument for cases of "double plurals" in codeswitching data, as discussed under 4.2. That is, if there are two ways to access English plural forms, there is even more potential for "double morphology" to occur, whether involving a "misfiring" or not.
8. For example, in English a sentence such as *Let him go* is well-formed, yet the infinitive is not marked by *to*.
9. This argument goes beyond Myers-Scotton (1993b).

References

Azuma, S.
1991 *Processing and Intrasentential Code-switching.* PHD thesis. University of Texas-Austin.

Backus, A.
1992 *Patterns of Language Mixing: A Study of Turkish-Dutch Bilingualism.* Wiesbaden: Otto Harrassowitz. (MA thesis 1989, University of Tilburg).

Bentahila, A. & E. E. Davies
1992 Code-switching and language dominance. In: Jackson Harris, R. (ed.). *Cognitive Processing in Bilinguals.* Amsterdam: Elsevier, pp. 443-458.

Bernsten, J.
1990 *The Integration of English Loans in Shona: Social Correlates and Linguistic Consequences.* PHD thesis. Michigan State University.

Bickmore, L. S.
1985 *Hausa-English Code-switching.* MA thesis. Los Angeles: University of California.

Boeschoten, H.
1991 Asymmetrical code-switching in immigrant communities. *Papers for the Workshop on Constraints, Conditions, and Models.* Strasbourg: European Science Foundation, pp. 85-100.

Bokamba, E. G.
1988 "Code-mixing, language variation, and linguistic theory: Evidence from Bantu languages". *Lingua* 76:21-62.

De Bot, K.
1992 "A bilingual production model: Levelt's *Speaking* model adapted". *Applied Linguistics* 13:1-24.

Dirven, R.
1993 Personal communication.

Eliasson, S.
1989 English-Maori language contact: Code-switching and the free-morpheme constraint. *Reports from Uppsala University, Dept. of Linguistics* 18:1-28.

Enninger, W.
1980 Syntactic convergence in a stable triglossia plus trilingualism situation in Kent Country, Delaware, US. In: Nelde, P. (ed.). *Sprachkontakt und Sprachkonflikt.* Wiesbaden: Franz Steiner, pp. 343-350.

Friederici, A., J. Weissenborn & M. Kail
1991 "Pronoun Comprehension in Aphasia: A Comparison of Three Languages". *Brain and Language* 41:289-310.

Fromkin, V. (ed.)
1973 *Speech Errors as Linguistic Evidence.* The Hague: Mouton.

Gardner-Chloros, P.
1991 *Language Selection and Switching in Strasbourg.* Oxford: Oxford University Press.

Garrett, M. F.
1975 The analysis of sentence production. In: Bower, G. H. (ed.). *Psychology of Learning and Motivation* 9:133-177.
1990 Sentence processing. In: Osherson, D. & H. Lasnik (eds.). *An Invitation to Cognitive Science*, Vol. 1. Cambridge MA: MIT Press, pp. 133-175.

Green, D. W.
1986 "Control, activation, and resource: A framework and a model for the control of speech in bilinguals". *Brain and Language* 27:210-223.

Grosjean, F.
1988 "Exploring the recognition of guest words in bilingual speech". *Language and Cognitive Progress* 3:233-274.
Gumperz, J. J.
1982 *Discourse Strategies*. Cambridge: Cambridge University Press.
Hankamer, J.
1989 Morphological parsing and the lexicon. In: Marlsen-Wilson, W. D. (ed.). *Lexical Representation and Process*. Cambridge MA: MIT Press, pp. 392-408.
Heeschen, C. & H. Kolk
1988 "Agrammatism and Paragrammatism". *Aphasiology* 2:299-302.
Jake, J. L.
1994 "Intrasentential Codeswitching and Pronouns: On the Categorial Status of Functional Elements". *Linguistics* 32: 271-298.
1993 Personal Communication.
Jake, J. L. & C. Myers-Scotton
1993 *Congruency in Codeswitching and the Nature of Lexical Entries*. MS.
Kamwangamalu, N. M.
1989 *Code-mixing across Languages: Structure, Function, and Constraints*. PHD dissertation. University of Illinois (Urbana).
Kamwangamalu, N. M. & Cher-Leng Lee
1991 *"Mixers* and *Mixing*: English across cultures". *World Englishes* 10:247-261.
Kuhberg, H.
1992 "Longitudinal L_2-attrition versus L_2-acquisition, in three Turkish children - empirical findings". *Second Language Research* 8:138-154.
Levelt, W. J. M.
1989 *Speaking, from Intention to Articulation*. Cambridge MA: MIT Press.
1992 "Accessing words in speech production: stages, processes, and representations". *Cognition* 42:1-22.
Myers-Scotton, C.
1992 "Constructing the frame in intrasentential codeswitching". *Multilingua* 11:101-127.
1993a *Social Motivations for Codeswitching: Evidence from Africa*. Oxford: Oxford University Press.
1993b *Duelling Languages: Grammatical Structure in Codeswitching*. Oxford: Oxford University Press.
Nepoulous, J.-L., A. R. Lecours, M. Puel, D. Lafond, A. Lemay, M. Puel, Y. Joanette, F. Cot & A. Rascol
No date (Cited in Friederici, A. *et al.* 1991). In: *Protocole Montréal-Toulouse d'Examen Linguistique de L'aphasie*. Montréal: Didier.
Nortier, J.
1990 *Dutch-Moroccan Arabic Code Switching*. Dordrecht: Foris.
Rappaport, M. & B. Levin
1988 What to do with theta roles. In: Wilkins, W. (ed.). *Syntax and Semantics, Vol. 21: Thematic Relations*. New York: Academic Press, pp. 7-36.
Simango, S. R.
1992 Personal Communication.
Stemberger, J. P.
1985 An interactive activation model of language production. In: Ellis, A. W. (ed.). *Progress in the Psychology of Language*. Norwood: Erlbaum, pp. 143-186.

Swigart, L.
1992 *Practice and Perception: Language Use and Attitudes in Dakar*. PHD dissertation. University of Washington.
1993 Personal Communication.

Talmy, L.
1985 Lexicalization patterns: Semantic structure in lexical form. In: Shopen, T. (ed.). *Language Typology and Syntactic Descriptions*, Vol. 3. New York: Cambridge University Press, pp. 57-149.

Taylor, J. R.
1989 *Linguistic Categorization*. Oxford: Oxford University Press.

Part II

Description of the lexicon

Lexicon as a key to history, culture, and society 'Homeland' and 'Fatherland' in German, Polish and Russian

Anna Wierzbicka

0. Introduction

There are three kinds of concepts: universal, unique, and intermediate. Universal concepts are shared by all human groups and in all probability are innate. Unique concepts belong to a single human group (usually, a single language community) and reflect this group's unique experience and way of life. Intermediate concepts may be more or less wide-spread across cultures and reflect certain commonalities of human experience; or they may be characteristic of a certain geographic and/or cultural area, in which case they are likely to reflect commonalities of experience and way of life based on contact.

The set of universal human concepts, which has emerged from an extensive empirical study of a wide range of languages, undertaken over more than two decades by the author and colleagues, includes the following elements (cf. Goddard & Wierzbicka (eds.) 1994):

[substantives] I, YOU, SOMEONE, SOMETHING, PEOPLE;
[determiners, quantifiers] THIS, THE SAME, OTHER, ONE, TWO, SOME, MUCH/MANY, LITTLE/FEW, ALL;
[mental predicates] KNOW, WANT, THINK, FEEL, HEAR;
[speech] SAY;
[actions, event, movement] DO, HAPPEN, MOVE;
[evaluators] GOOD, BAD;
[descriptors] BIG, SMALL;
[space] WHERE, SIDE, INSIDE, FAR, NEAR, ABOVE, UNDER;
[time] WHEN, AFTER, BEFORE, A LONG TIME, A SHORT TIME;
[taxonomy, partonymy] KIND OF, PART OF;
[intensifier] VERY, MORE;
[similarity] LIKE;
[clause linkers] IF, IF ... WOULD, BECAUSE;
[clause operators] NOT, MAYBE;
[metapredicate] CAN;

Quite apart from their inherent interest as building blocks of human thought, the universal concepts (lexicalized in all the languages of the world) have the practical value of being able to serve as the basis of a natural semantic metalanguage, in terms of which all other human concepts, including those which are uniquely culture-specific, can be described and compared (cf. Wierzbicka 1991a, b, and 1992).

I will illustrate this general proposition by analyzing and comparing three key words of modern German and Polish: *Heimat, Vaterland*, and *ojczyzna*. For comparison, I will also include a cursory discussion of the Russian word *rodina*.

Since many languages, especially European languages, have words denoting a person's native country, the concepts enbodied in these words may be assumed to transcend language boundaries. In fact, however, words which appear to match in this way often differ from one another in particularly telling ways, offering valuable insight into different national traditions and historical experiences. The German words *Heimat* and *Vaterland*, the Polish word *ojczyzna*, and the Russian word *rodina*, are good cases in point.

Despite the immense complexity of these concepts, which are laden with cultural significance, in analyzing them I will rely almost exclusively on simple, universal concepts such as "I", "people", "something", "part", "good", "think", "want", and "feel". I will, however, make three exceptions, by using, in addition to universals, the following three words: *country, born*, and *child*. These words, too, can be defined in terms of the universals, but to do so within the explications of such complex cultural concepts as *Heimat, Vaterland, ojczyzna*, and *rodina* would be confusing and counter-productive.

1. Heimat ("native country", "home country", "homeland", "home places")

Heimat is one of the most important words in the German lexicon, which "has the resonance of what Raymond Williams called a "key word". Like his key words *industry, democracy, class, art*, and *culture*, *Heimat* came into its current usage at a certain juncture in German history and has remained in both an everyday and a more formally argumentative vocabulary ever since." (Applegate 1990:6).

There is an extensive literature on the concept of *Heimat*, which, for reasons of space, I could not possibly try to survey here. But what is particularly interesting about the long history of *Heimat*, is that despite its extensive use and manipulation in the Nazi-propaganda and its resulting "corruption" (Applegate 1990:4), *Heimat* survived the Nazi era, losing nothing of its emotive, social, and political power in German life. The little vignette from a civic gathering in the area of Pfalz in 1946 offered by Applegate illustrates this point very vividly:

> The new Landrat (...) pledged himself to "restor[ing] the well-being and future of the Heimat" in a spirit of forgiveness, repeating the word *Heimat* twelve times in a speech of five minutes. He concluded with a plea for "all of us to put our work at the service of the higher ideals of the people and the Heimat." The final speech of the evening was an emotional affirmation of Heimat on the basis of German collective life. (1990:242)

Speaking of the word *Heimat* as something that gave coherence and purpose to the manifold activities which shaped the sense of distinctiveness and identity of the inhabitants of the area of Pfalz (in both the 19th and 20th century), Applegate (1990:3) writes (emphasizing the untranslatability of the German words quoted):

> The Pfalz was the homeland; the Pfalz was Heimat. Out of *Heimatliebe* [love for Heimat, A.W.] the Pfälzer undertook *Heimatpflege* [care for Heimat, A.W.] and thought *Heimatgedanken* [Heimat-thoughts, A. W.]. During his life, he might call himself a *Heimatkundler* ["Heimat-knower", A.W.] or simply a *Heimatler* ["Heimat-devotee", "Heimat-man", A. W.], and after his death his obituary would praise him for having truly loved his *Heimat*.

Given the crucial importance of the concept of "Heimat" in German culture, it would seem obvious that it is an important task of interpretive semantics to explicate its meaning, and to show what exactly is unique about it, and how it differs from its closest counterparts in other languages. But it has often been asserted that this task is simply not feasible. To quote Applegate once more:

> The term *Heimat*, one could argue, has entered into so many different discussions in such diverse areas of German society that it would be a great mistake to search for a solitary meaning, a single truth beyond all the white noise. And yet the ubiquity of the term and the deep emotionality of its appeal have proven irresistible temptations to interpreters in search of an essence for which *Heimat* is an expression. Their results have not always been enlightening. (1990:4)

Applegate herself was clearly wary of all the past and ongoing efforts to capture the meaning of *Heimat* in something resembling a definition, and she decided instead to devote a book to the study of this elusive word. ("Instead of generating more definitions for a word that has collected so many, this study will investigate the history of the word itself, which in the case of *Heimat* means the history of a certain way of talking and thinking about German society and Germanness.", p. 6).

I agree that *Heimat* deserves a book-length study, or indeed a number of book-length studies. But it also deserves a definition, and if tangible changes in the meaning of this word can be documented, then it needs more than one definition. In what follows, I will propose, and try to briefly justify, a definition for the modern usage, exemplified in the two quotes:

> Heimat ist ja nicht nur dieses Stück Land mit seiner Enge und Abgeschlossenheit, dieser kleine und übersehbare Gegensatz von Welt und Ferne und Leben. Die Ströme und Bäche sind Heimat, die durchs Land gehen, die Wolken sind Heimat, wenn sie darüber hinziehen, und die Sterne [...] gehören dazu. (Rainer Maria Rilke 1903:100, *SWV*, p. 595, quoted in Fullerborn 1992:100.)
> 'Heimat isn't merely this piece of land with its narrowness and seclusion, this small and surveyable antithesis of the world and distance and life. The streams and brooks are Heimat, the ones that move through the land, the clouds are Heimat, when they spread over and above it, and the stars (...) are part of it.'

> Von meinem Schreibtisch blicke ich über den Rhein in meine Heimat, das Elsaß, und wenn ich hinüberfahre, zücke ich an der Grenze, die seit 1918 wieder der Rhein bildet, einen französischen Paß (René Schickele, *Himmlische Landschaft* (1933); quoted in Storck (1992:106)).
> 'From my desk I look across the Rhine into my Heimat, the Alsace, and when I drive over there, I pull out a French passport at the border, which is again the Rhine since 1918.'

Trying to account for all the different aspects of *Heimat*, I would propose the following (tentative) explication of this complex concept:

Heimat
(a) a place
(b) I was born in this place
(c) there are many places in this place
(d) when I was a child, I was like a part of these places
(e) I felt something good when I was like a part of these places
(f) I felt that nothing bad could happen to me
(g) I can't feel like this in any other places
(h) because of this, when I think of these places I feel something good
(i)   I think something like this when I think of these places:
(j)   these places are not like any other places
(k)   I was like a part of these places once
(l) I can't be like a part of any other places

(m)? (I know: some other people think the same when they think of these places)
(n)? ([think these people feel the same when they think of these places)
(o)? (when I think of these people, I feel something good)

Component (a) indicates that *Heimat* is a "place" - not necessarily a "country", as, for example, *Vaterland, ojczyzna* (Polish) or *rodina* (Russian), to be discussed below, but simply "place". It is not a small place like a garden or even a village; there are many places in this place (component c); but it is small enough to have a human measure, so that a person, and indeed a child, can not only be aware of these many places but feel like a part of them.

Component (b) ("I was born in this place") may be questioned on the basis of various personal statements by people who were raised, but not born, in what they regard as their "Heimat". For example, Iring Fetscher regards Dresden as his "Heimat" although he was born, he says, in Württemberg:

> Ich kann mich noch ganz gut daran erinnern, daß ich als etwa Vierzehnjähriger das Aufsatzthema gestellt bekam: "Kann denn Großstadt Heimat sein?" "Denn" ließ auf eine womöglich negative Antwort schließen. Ich entschloß mich aber - aus Überzeugung - die Frage mit "ja" zu beantworten. Die Kunst- und Barockstadt Dresden mit ihren engen Gassen und verlockenden Antiquariaten war für mich - auch wenn ich, in Württemberg geboren, von zwei süddeutschen Eltern stammend, in Dresden nur "aufgewachsen" war - Heimat. (Fetscher 1992:17)
> 'I still remember clearly, when I was fourteen, having to write an essay on the topic: "Can a large city ever be Heimat?" "Ever" seemed to prompt a negative answer. Nevertheless, I decided - from conviction - to answer the question with "yes". The baroque city Dresden with its narrow lanes and alluring second-hand bookshops was for me - even if I, born in Württemberg, of South German parentage, had only "grown up" in Dresden - Heimat.'

But although statements of this kind are quite common, arguably they are based on a metaphorical extension - perhaps for Fetscher, Dresden was LIKE *Heimat* (even though it is a big city and even though he wasn't born in it); subjectively, for him Dresden was what "Heimat" was for other people. If a big city could normally be seen as someone's *Heimat* in the literal sense of the word, school essays topics' raising such a possibility for discussion would not be set.

It is of course possible for people to develop "Heimatgefühle", "Heimatfeelings", in places other than those where they were born, as one can develop "maternal feelings" for people who are not our children, but this means that one can develop for a new place feelings LIKE those normally associated with a *Heimat*, not that the new place becomes the *Heimat* (in a literal sense of the word).

One must agree with Fetscher, nonetheless, that the link between *Heimat* and childhood is stronger and more important than that between Heimat and a mere birthplace; and in particular, that *Heimat* suggests something like nostalgia for childhood and for the special, unrecoverable, happiness which can be associated with it.

> Freilich gilt das nur für die, denen ein günstiges Schicksal ein Mindestmaß von kindlicher Geborgenheit und Heimat zuteil werden ließ.
> 'Of course this can only be applied to those whom a favourable destiny granted a minimum of security and Heimat as a child.'

In the explication proposed here the special links between "Heimat" and childhood are reflected not only in the component (d) "when I was a child, I was like a part of these places", but also in the evocation of childhood happiness in (e) ("I felt something good when I was in these places"), and in the nostalgic components (g) and (l) ("I can't feel like this in other places", "I can't be like a part of any other places"); and also in the causal link between one's love for one's Heimat and the childhood connection (component (h): "because of this, when I think of these places, I feel something good"). Component (f) seeks to capture the idea that in one's *Heimat* one feels *"geborgen"*, that is, roughly speaking, safe (like in one's mother's arms).[1]

The idea of childhood "belonging" associated with *Heimat* is reflected in the components (d) and (k) ("... I was like a part of these places"), and the notion that *Heimat* referred to "something lost" and "only available to the memory" (debated, for example, by Heinrich Böll, Günther Grass, and Norbert Blüm, among others, in the 1970 Hessen radio discussion, related by Applegate 1990:4-5), corresponds to the components (g) and (i): "I can't feel like this in other places", and "I can't be like a part of any other places".

But the nostalgic ring of *Heimat* doesn't have to be interpreted exclusively in terms of childhood. The quote from Rilke adduced above is very characteristic in this respect, with its triple contrast between *Heimat* and *Leben* ("life", which takes us away from childhood in time), *Ferne* ("far-away-ness", distance, being far away from familiar places to which one once belonged), and *Welt* ("the world", that is, abstract social and political entities which come to replace the emotional security of one's local community).

Applegate (1990:11) is no doubt right when she points out that "in reality, of course, Heimat's nostalgic evocation of a closed and close-knit community reflected its replacement by these larger and less personal forms of political and territorial belonging"; in other words, in linking the modern concept of "Heimat" with the changes in the German national consciousness brought about by the formal unification of Germany in 1871 under Prussian leadership. The very fact that the word *Heimat* preserved its key position in the German cultural lexicon, beside the "larger" concept of "Vaterland" ("fatherland", to be discussed below), supports the claim implicit in the title of Applegate's book *A Nation of Provincials: The German Idea of Heimat*, and gives credence to statements such as the following:

> The idea of Heimat potentially embraced all of Germany, from its individual parts to its newly constituted whole. It offered Germans a way to reconcile a heritage of localized political traditions with the ideal of a single, transcendent nationality. Heimat was both the beloved local places and the beloved nation; it was a comfortably flexible and inclusive homeland, embracing all localities alike. (p. 11).
>
> For the incomplete nation of 1871, the invented traditions of the Heimat bridged the gap between national aspiration and provincial reality. These efforts [towards national integration on the basis of regionalism, A.W.] might be called federalist, in the sense that Heimat enthusiasts celebrated German diversity. They supported national cohesion without necessarily showing any enthusiasms for its symbols or for its agents, Prussia and the national government. (p. 13).

Unlike *Vaterland* (to be discussed below), *Heimat* does not refer to a nation, but arguably, its perspective is not purely individual either; perhaps the warm glow of this word ("Bei dem Wort Heimat wird uns allemal warm ums Herz", "the word *Heimat* gives us always a warm feeling in the heart", Fetscher 1992:15) extends in some way to the people who share our *Heimat* with us. To canvass this possibility, I have tentatively included in the explication of *Heimat* three additional components - (l), (m), and (n), for further consideration.

The widening of the use of *Heimat* after 1871 did not necessarily mean a semantic change. Applegate's (1990:13) observation that "the evolution of Heimat as a concept followed the shifting hierarchies of belonging, from hometown to territorial state to nation" can be accepted as a comment about changes in the sociopolitical psychology rather than in the semantic structure of Heimat. Common twentieth century uses of *Heimat*, such as that in the "Russland Lager-Lied" (a song of German captives in a Russian camp, dating from 1945 or later) seem quite compatible with the explication proposed here:

> Und wir ale hir in Rusland haben eine Bitren Schmerz
> und wir dachten oft in Stielen es zereist unz nur das Herz
> den die Mutter in der Heimadt Vater und Bruder an der Front

> und wir sind so arm aleine unter dem ferlassen Folk (quoted in Greverus 1972:452; spelling as in the original).
> 'And we all here in Russia have a bitter pain, and we often thought that it would tear our hearts, our mothers in the homeland (*Heimat*), fathers and brothers on the front, and we are so miserable alone among this abandoned people.'

It is interesting to note in this connection that it is the word *Heimat*, not *Vaterland*, which typically occurs in the songs of captivity, whereas in the "fighting songs", as well as the "corporation songs" (Burschenlieder), it is typically the word *Vaterland*, to which we will turn next.

2. Vaterland

2.1. Introduction

Vaterland (roughly, "fatherland") has been for a long time another extremely important word in the German lexicon. The fact that the Grimms' (1877) *Deutsches Wörterbuch* (German dictionary) lists as many as thirty compounds (and derivates) built upon this word provides telling evidence for this. A volume of German poems and songs (Harzmann 1930, henceforth referred to as "H") contains several dozen examples.

Characteristically, *Vaterland* occurs twice in the German national anthem:

> Einigkeit und Recht und Freiheit
> Für das deutsche Vaterland!
> (...)
> Blüh im Glanze dieses Glückes
> Blühe deutsches Vaterland!
>
> 'Unity and justice and freedom
> for the German Fatherland!
> (...)
> Blossom in the brilliance of this happiness
> Blossom German Fatherland!'

The Grimm dictionary offers the following definition: "Land, worin mein Vater lebte, als welchen Landesangehörigen ich mich betrachte; oft zusammenfallend mit Geburtsland, doch ist dies nicht nötig." 'The country where my father lived as the country to which I believe I belong; often coincides with the country of birth, but this is not essential.'

The more recent Brockhaus Wahrig dictionary (Deutsches Wörterbuch 1981) gives the following: "Land, in dem man geboren und/oder aufgewachsen ist, Heimat(land)" 'country where one was born and/or where one grew up, one's "Heimat", the country which is one's Heimat'; and Duden (1972): "Land, aus dem man stammt, zu dessen Volk, Nation man gehört, dem man sich zugehörig fühlt, Land als Heimat eines Volkes" 'the country from which one originates, to whose people, nation one belongs, where one feels one belongs, the country therefore as Heimat of a people.'

All these definitions contain useful elements, but none provides an adequate explication.

2.2. *Vaterland as a superordinate entity*

To begin with, let me adduce two classic quotes from early nineteenth century poetry, one from Ernst Moritz Arndt's famous poem "Was ist des Deutschen Vaterland?" and one from Heinrich von Kleist's "Catechism of a German":

> Was ist des Deutschen Vaterland?
> Ist's Preußenland, ist's Schwabenland?
> Ist's, wo am Rhein die Rebe blüht?
> Ist's, wo am Belt die Möwe zieht?
> Oh, nein, nein, nein!
> Sein Vaterland muß größer sein! (Arndt)
>
> 'Which is the Fatherland of the German?
> Is it Prussia, is it Swabia?
> Is it where the vines grow on the Rhine?
> Is it where seagull roves the Belt?
> Oh, no, no, no!
> His Fatherland must be bigger than this!'
>
> Frage: Sprich, Kind, wer bist Du?
> Antwort: Ich bin ein Deutscher.
> Frage: Ein Deutscher. Du scherzest. Du bist in Meißen geboren.
> Antwort: Ich bin in Meißen geboren, und das Land, dem Meißen angehört, heißt Sachsen, aber mein Vaterland, das Land, dem

Sachsen angehört, ist Deutschland, und dein Sohn, mein Vater, ist ein Deutscher. (Kleist)

'Question: Speak, child, who are you?
Answer: I am a German.
Question: A German. You are joking. You were born in Meissen.
Answer: I was born in Meissen, and the country, to which Meissen belongs, is Saxony, but my Fatherland, the country to which Saxony belongs, is Germany, and your son, my father, is a German.'

As these quotes suggest, *Vaterland* - in contrast to *Heimat* - referred from early on to a country, seen at least implicitly against the background of other countries (there are many different *Länder*, 'countries', and one of these *Länder* is one's *Vaterland*).

The psychological size of a *Vaterland*, then, was from the start much larger than that of a *Heimat*: if for *Heimat*, the point of reference, and standard of size, was provided by individual human experience, *Vaterland* could include many *Heimat*-s, because its implicit point of reference was not experiential but political, with a particular emphasis on the unity of a large abstract entity, seen against the background of a number of smaller local entities (as made clear in Kleist's "Catechism of a German" or in Arndt's poem).

These considerations lead us to the following initial (highly incomplete) explication:

Vaterland
a country
I am like a part of this country
there are many places in this country
these places are like one big thing

2.3. *High regard, love, and pride*

From early on, one's *Vaterland* was a country to which one felt one "belonged", a country which one loved, and a country which one held in high regard. Both the love and the high regard for the Vaterland are clearly reflected in Klopstock's (1770) "Vaterlandslied":

... Ich bin ein deutsches Mädchen! Mein gutes, edles, stolzes Herz / schlägt laut empor / Beim Süssen Namen Vaterland! So schlägt

mir einst beim Namen / Des Jüngling's nur, der stolz wie ich / Aufs Vaterland / Gut, edel ist, und Deutscher ist!
(quoted in Greverus 1972:291).

'... I am a German girl! My good, noble, proud heart / beats loudly / at the sweet name Fatherland! It once beat this way at the name / of the young man, who, like I, is proud of / the Fatherland / he is good, noble, and a German!'

The common compound *Vaterlandsliebe* 'love for the Vaterland' supports the emotional component of this word, as do recurring phrases such as *das liebe Vaterland* 'the beloved Vaterland' and *das teure Vaterland*, 'the dear Vaterland' (e.g. "ein dreifach Hoch dem lieben Vaterlande", Engelhardt 1818, Harzmann 1930:51, 'three cheers for the dear Fatherland'), and recurring oaths promising faithful love, e.g.:

Treue Liebe bis zum Grabe
Schwör ich dir mit Herz und Hand
Was ich bin und was ich habe
Dank ich dir, mein Vaterland

'Faithful love to the grave,
This I swear to you with my heart and hand
What I am and what I have
I must thank you for, my Fatherland'

Among the frequently declared "good feelings" for the *Vaterland* the most common ones are love, devotion, pride, high regard, honour, "fire" (burning love), gratitude, filial piety, and religious devotion. The words which most frequently recur in combination with *Vaterland* are *Liebe* 'love', *Ehre* 'honour', Stolz 'proud', *ergeben* 'devoted', *Dank* 'thanks', *heilige* 'holy', 'sacred', *Glut* 'burning in the heart' and *heil*! 'hail'. Some examples:

Ehre des Vaterlandes Fahnen
(Bardill 1820;, H. 18)
'Honour to the flags of the Fatherland'

Heil dir, mein Vaterland!
(J. L. Haupt, H. 57)
'Hail to thee, my Fatherland!'

Wir schwören neu mit Herz und Hand:
Kein Drohen soll, kein Gleissen,
Die Glut für Recht und Vaterland
Uns aus dem Herzen reissen.
(Heinrich von Treitschke, H. 209)
'We swear anew with heart and hand:
No threats, no glittering promises, can
Purge the fervour for justice and Fatherland
From our hearts.'

The expression of love and *Ehre* for the Vaterland is habitually linked with praise, with the *Vaterland* being described as the best country, the most beautiful one, a great one, and ascribed majesty and "highness":

... des Vaterlandes Majestät!
(E. A. Arndt 1915)
'... the Fatherland's majesty!'

Das höchste, was wir kennen, ist teutsches Vaterland
(Karl Reh 1815, H. 67)
'The highest thing that we know is the German Fatherland'

Nicht mit dem Schläger in der Hand (...)
Dient ihr dem grossen Vaterland ...
(Christoph Schneider 1867, H. 332)
'It is not with the sword in the hand (...)
that you serve the great Fatherland ...'

Und deine Kinder gingen Hand in Hand
Und machten dich zum größten Land auf Erden,
Wie du das beste bist, o Vaterland!
(Konrad Krez 1875, H. 200)
'And your children walked hand in hand
and made you the greatest country on earth,
just as you are the best, Fatherland!'

Mein heil'ges deutsches Vaterland!
(Walter Fler 1914, H. 372)
'My holy German Fatherland!'

The habitual praise of the *Vaterland* as a country exceptionally good, beautiful, virtuous, faithful, great, and generally uniquely praiseworthy, is well documented in the chapter on "Vaterlandspreis" in Greverus (1972).

On the basis of these considerations, we can expand our initial explication as follows:

Vaterland
a country
I am like a part of this country
there are many places in this country
these places are like one big thing
when I think of this country, I feel something good
I think very good things of this country
I think something like this when I think of this country:
  this country is not like any other country
  no other country is like this country

The combination of the two components "this country is not like any other country" and "no other country is like this country" may seem redundant, but I think it is probably needed to account for both the perceived "uniqueness" of the *Vaterland* and the ego's pride in it (and an apparent sense of superiority).

2.4. *Vaterland and nation*

Is *Vaterland* a country of birth?

As we saw earlier, the brothers Grimm's dictionary insists that one's *Vaterland* is not necessarily one's birth-country, and it is true that the word can be applied much more readily to people's "adopted" countries than *Heimat* or *homeland* can.[2] The fact that the Volga Germans (born in Russia) could readily refer to Germany as their *Vaterland* (though not their *Heimat*), too, suggests that *Vaterland* is not necessarily conceived of as the country of birth. In any case, it is certainly clear that *Vaterland* doesn't have, and has never had, the special sentimental link with childhood that *Heimat* does.

On the other hand, from early on *Vaterland* implied a link with other people "belonging" to the same country. In fact, Duden's quasi-definition of *Vaterland* as "Land als Heimat eines Volkes" (a country seen as the Heimat of a people) is correct, I think, in contrasting the individual perspective of *Heimat* with the collective perspective of *Vaterland*.

This collective perspective of *Vaterland* is linked with its emphasis on unity (against the background of diversity). The most characteristic and common collocation of *Vaterland* is *das deutsche Vaterland*, 'the German Vaterland'. Although the Polish word *ojczyzna* is also nation-oriented, it normally cannot be used in a similar collocation: *polska ojczyzna*, 'the Polish ojczyzna' (nor does the Russian word *rodina* occur in the collocation *russkaia rodina*, 'the Russian rodina'). The two first lines of the German national anthem, quoted earlier ("Einigkeit und Recht und Freiheit für das deutsche Vaterland") are very characteristic in the way they link the "Germanness" of the *Vaterland* with its unity (against the implicit diversity of the local *Heimat*-s, which are Prussian, Saxon, Swabian, or whatever). The phrase "das deutsche Vaterland" reflects both the collective, nation-oriented character of the concept 'Vaterland' and its emphasis on unity over and above diversity.

Trying to account for the collective, nation-oriented character of *Vaterland*, we may start by adding to our initial explication the following further components:

> many other people think the same when they think of this country
> these people feel the same when they think of this country
> all these people are like one thing
> I am part of this thing

Quotes such as the following ones support these components very clearly:

> Wir fühlen alle uns als Brüder
> Und drücken froh die Bruderhand,
> Denn wir sind einer Kette Glieder,
> Uns eint das deutsche Vaterland!
> (L. Mesunius 1859, H. 21,5)
> 'We all feel as brothers would
> and gladly squeeze the fraternal hand,
> Because we are the links on a chain,
> United by the German Fatherland!'

> Und wir haben alle ein Vaterland
> Dem wollen wir leben und sterben.
> (J. L. Haupt, H. 52)
> 'And we all have a Fatherland,
> for which we want to live and die.'

Was wir ersehnt, erstrebt seit langen Jahren:
Des deutschen Vaterlandes Einigkeit.
(Otto Haupt, H. 257)
'What we have long yearned and striven for:
The unity of the German Fatherland.'

Stets frei und einig erschaue
Das deutsche Vaterland!
(Richard Dehe 1907, H. 271)
'Always freely and unitedly look upon
the German Fatherland!'

An early example of a sentence equating 'Vaterland' with 'nation' is the following one:

es ist wahr, ich bin ein fürst wolbekannt
in deutscher nation, mein vaterlant.
(Schede, quoted in the Grimms' dictionary).
'It is true, l am a well-known prince in the German nation,
my Fatherland.'

The fact that the expression *Vaterlandsverräter* 'betrayer of the Vaterland', was in use in the first half of the nineteenth century, points in the same direction, as one betrays people rather than a place. For example, Heine wrote this in the preface to his poem "Deutschland, ein Wintermärchen" ('Germany, a wintertale'):

Ich höre schon ihre Bierstimmen: du lästerst sogar unsere Farben, Verräter des Vaterlands, Freund der Franzosen, denen du den freien Rhein abtreten willst!
'I can already hear their beer-voices: you even scoff at our colours, traitor of the Fatherland, friend of the French, for whom you will give up our free Rhine!'

2.5. *Duty and service*

Also linked with *Vaterland* from early on were ideas of duty, unconditional service, and obedience:

was Vaterlandspflicht fordert, kann der Ehre nicht schwer sein.
(Dyana Sore 5, 333, quoted in the Grimms' dictionary).

'what the duty towards the Vaterland demands, cannot be a burden for the honour.'

Nineteenth century German poetry offers plentiful examples of sentences where *Vaterland* is associated with boundless duty and service. The metaphor of "sonhood" is particularly characteristic in this regard: the Vaterland is not so much the country OF one's father, as suggested in the Grimms' dictionary, as the country which IS, symbolically, one's, and one's nation's, father, a father whom one must love, revere, serve, and obey. The twin phrases *Vaterlands Söhne* and *Söhne des Vaterlandes*, 'the sons of the Vaterland', very common in German poems and songs, are particularly characteristic in this regard. For example:

Vaterlands Söhne! traute Genossen!
(A. L. Follen 1817, 85).
'Sons of the Fatherland! Beloved comrades!'

Lernt frei des Trugs, Ihr Söhne des Vaterlands
In Wort und Tat verteidigen ...
(E. C. F. Krauss 1820, H.45)
'Learn free of deceit, you sons of the Fatherland, defend, in word and deed ...'

Gruss dir, Panier voll Wunderschöne,
Dass mahnend alter deutscher Pracht
Jüngst unsres Vaterlandes Söhne ...
(T. Kellenbauer 1862, H. 205)
'Greetings to you, banner depicting the most beautiful,
Recalling old German splendour
to the youngest of our Fatherland's sons ...'

Vaterland, Vaterland, du sollst nimmer wanken:
Als deine Söhne stehen wir ...
(P. Kaiser, 60)
'Fatherland, Fatherland, you will never falter:
We stand behind you as your sons ...'

But even more revealing than the common metaphor of 'sonhood' is the ubiquitous syntactic frame "für das Vaterland" 'for the Vaterland' (or "fürs deutsche Vaterland", 'for the German Vaterland'), often in the imperative mood, or combined with modal verbs such as *soll* 'should', and often with an exclamation mark, indicating an emotive and/or 'imperative' component. For example:

> ... Dann Bruder folget mir, schwinget das Kreuzpanier.
> Fürs Vaterland!
> (Ch. v. Buri, H. 70)
> '... Then brothers follow me, wave the banner of the cross
> For the Fatherland!'

> Für Freiheit, Ehre, Vaterland
> Soll unser deutsches Schwert stets blitzen ...
> (Bunderlied 1810, H. 4)
> 'For freedom, honour, Fatherland,
> our German sword must always flash ...'

Ritual military formulae involving *Vaterland*, such as the nineteenth century Prussian formula "Für König und Vaterland", and the Nazi formula "Für Führer und Vaterland" (cf. Klemperer 1946:135) are also worth noting in this context. Their elliptical nature highlights the unspoken link between what people WANT to do for the Vaterland and what they SHOULD or HAVE TO do for it.

Similarly vague or unspecified in their modal force are imperative appeals such as the following one:

> Für Freiheit, Vaterland und Ehre
> Bleib' stets gezückt das deutsche Schwerdt!
> (G. D. Roller 1828, H. 73)
> 'For freedom, Fatherland, and honour
> Always remain poised, German sword!'

The frequent combination of the three nouns *Vaterland, Freiheit*, and *Ehre* ('Vaterland', 'freedom', and 'honour'), usually in a modal, volitional, and emotive context, highlights the status of 'Vaterland' as an ideal (something supremely good that one wants and should do something for - almost anything that might be required), rather than a descriptive term comparable to the English *native country* or *homeland*. This status of *Vaterland* is emphasized, in particular, in the common phrases such as *Tod fürs Vaterland*, 'death for the Vaterland', *sterben fürs Vaterland*, 'to die for the Vaterland', *sterben und leben fürs Vaterland*, 'to die and to live for the Vaterland', *leben und streben fürs Vaterland* 'to live and to strive for the Vaterland', and so on, always in an exalted modal context. For example:

Vaterland, dir nur ergeben
Wollen wir sterben und leben!
(E. Barbili, H. 18)
'Fatherland, devoted to you alone
We wish to die and live!'

Das höchste das wir kennen ist teutsches Vaterland,
Das schönste das wir nennen ist Tod fürs Vaterland
(K. Reh 1815, H. 67)
'The highest thing that we know is the German Fatherland,
The most beautiful thing that we can think of is death for the Fatherland'

Lass Kraft mich erwerben
In Herz und in Hand,
Zu leben und zu sterben
Fürs heilge Vaterland!
(H. F. Massman, H. 101)
'Let strength win me over
with heart and with hand,
to live and to die
for the holy Fatherland!'

Ich hab mich ergeben
Mit Herz und mit Hand
Dir, Land voll Lieb und Leben,
Mein deutsches Vaterland!
(H. F. Massmann, H. 101)
'I have yielded
with heart and with hand
to you, land full of love and life,
my German Fatherland!'

If not used in combination with the preposition *für*, the word *Vaterland* frequently occurs in the dative case, with similar implications:

Dem Vaterlande unser Gut und Blut!
(S. Höch, H. 214)
'For the Fatherland our possessions and our blood'

Among the most characteristic verbs which occur with *für* or with the dative case, with similar implications, are *(sich) opfern* 'sacrifice oneself' and *sich weihen* 'devote oneself':

> Ich bin ein Glied der heil'gen Schar,
> Die sich dir opfert, Vaterland
> (W. Flex 1914, H. 373)
> 'I am a member of the holy troop,
> who offer themselves to you, Fatherland.'

> weihte mich zu scharfer Wehre
> Für das deutsche Vaterland!
> (H. Vogt, H. 328)
> 'I devote myself to keen struggle
> for the German Fatherland!'

> Heil dir, mein Vaterland!
> Noch gibt es Herzen, welche für dich schlagen,
> Die für dich glühn in hoher Liebesglut,
> Die alles für die guten Sachen wagen,
> Die freudig opfern all ihr Gut und Blut.
> (Leipzig, H. 57)
> 'Hail to thee, my Fatherland!
> There are still hearts that beat for you,
> that glow for you with the fire of love,
> that risk everything for the noble cause,
> that sacrifice all their possessions and blood happily.'

> Die grossen Volkes Söhne all
> Sie reichen sich die Hand
> Und weihn bei unsrer Liebe Schall
> Sich neu dem Vaterland
> (W. Kleefeld 1899, H.255)
> 'The sons of the great people
> all give each other their hands
> and offer themselves afresh to the Fatherland
> at the sound of our love.'

The word *dein* 'yours', too, is often used in a sense similar to "offering oneself", for example:

Dein in Leben, dein in Sterben,
Ruhmbekranztes Vaterland!
(R. Baumbach 1878, H. 260)
'Yours in life, yours in death,
Glorious (literally: crowned with glory) Fatherland!'

Finally, one further characteristic quote which spells out quite explicitly the idea that one doesn't belong to oneself but to the Vaterland:

Du darfst dir selbst nicht angehören,
Dein Alles gilt dem Vaterland,
Nicht eh'r zu ruhen musst du schwören,
Als bis es frei und gross erstand.
(A. Börner 1926, H. 411)
'You must not belong to yourself,
Your all is deemed the Fatherland's,
You must swear not to rest
Until it is created free and great.'

In songs devoted to Vaterland, which can be regarded as a genre of its own ("Vaterlandslieder"), the loving praise of the Vaterland is often combined with promises to defend it, and with threats against its enemies. The words used most often in this connection include verbs such as *verteidigen* 'defend', *hüten* 'guard', *schützen* 'protect', *kämpfen* 'fight (for)', *streiten* 'fight for', and *retten* 'save', and the corresponding nomina agentis, especially in the plural, such as *Retter, Schützer*, or *Streiter*.

... Da stoben, wie Wetter, wie Wirbel im Meer
Des Vaterlands Retter, Teuts Söhne daher.
(1808, H. 3)
'... There raged, like the weather, like storms on the sea,
The saviours of the Fatherland, the sons of the Teuton.'

Wir stehn in des Lebens Morgenglanz,
Die kommenden Hüter des Vaterlands.
(H. F. Massman, H. 69)
'We stand in the morning-glow of life,
the coming guardians of the Fatherland.'

Doch umschlingt uns alle Ein Bruderband,
Alle Streiter dem Einen Vaterland
(H. F. Massman, H. 69)

'And still we are entwined by one brotherly tie,
All warriors for one Fatherland.'

It appears that the word *Vaterland* gradually changed its tone from purely emotional (as in Klopstock's "Vaterlandslied" quoted earlier) to moral, so that patriotic duty and obligation became absorbed from common contexts into the meaning of the word itself. Thus at some points of its history *Vaterland* came to embody a categorical moral imperative, and given the collective orientation of the word, the moral imperative had a collective character too, implicitly appealing to shared values and shared obligations.

This is highly consistent with Leo Weisgerber's (1959:262) observation (made in the context of a discussion of the formula "Volk und Vaterland", 'the people and the Vaterland') that "... im Gedanken des Vaterlandes stand nicht die ausübende Macht, sondern der Schutz vor fremdem Eingriff im Vordergrund" ('... in the idea of Vaterland it was not so much power as defense against an attack from outside that was most prominent').

The Vaterland was seen as something to be defended, protected, served, fought for, and, if need be, died for (and not only by an individual but by all its "sons"). Thus we may suggest further semantic components of *Vaterland* along the following lines:

I want to do something good for this country
I think all these people (i.e. my compatriots) want the same
I think that if this country wants me to do something I have to do it
I think all these people think the same[3]

The first two ('wanting') components are supported by explicit 'wanting' statements such as the following one:

Wahret es treu!
Vaterland, dir nur ergeben
Wollen wir sterben und leben!
Teutschland sei frei!
(E. Barbili 1820, H. 18)
'Guard it faithfully!
Fatherland, loyal to you
we wish to die and live!
Germany, be free!'

The component "if this country wants me to do something ..." is supported by very frequent mentions of the Vaterland "calling" (*rufen, Ruf*). For example:

Das ruft, das ruft mein Vaterland!
(W. Roll 1853, H. 213)
'There calls, there calls my Fatherland!'

Wir dauern aus und können mutig ringen,
Wenn es der Ruf des Vaterlands gebeut!
(K. Hinkel 1815, H. 27)
'We perservere and struggle bravely
If the call of the Fatherland demands it!'

The component "I have to do it" (and its extension: "I think all these people think the same") is supported by frequent mentions of "oaths" and "swearing", as well as references to the Vaterland's *Gebot-e* (orders, commandments).

Hier war's, in dieser Halle,
Da hoben sie fromm die Hand,
Die männlichen Burschen alle,
Zum Schwur fürs Vaterland
Zu retten, was verloren
(R. Dehe 1907, H. 270)
'It was here, in this hall,
where reverently raised their hand,
all of the manly lads,
an oath for the Fatherland,
to save what was lost ...'

Auf denn es sei: Vaterland, treu
Leb ich dir immerdar, steh ich zur frommen Schar,
Die so in Not wie Tod höret Dein laut Gebot:
Hurra juch hei!
(Ch. Buri 1819, H. 70)
'So forward, Fatherland,
I remain faithful to you forever, l stand by the reverent troops,
who, whether in need or death, clearly hear your command:
Hoorah hurray hey!'

The moral imperative may explain, to some extent, the power that this word is said to have exercised in Germany in wartime:

> ... wenn wir die Gefallenen der beiden letzten Kriege fragen würden - ihre Briefe, die ja veröffentlicht sind, erlauben uns diese Frage - wenn wir sie fragen würden, was ihnen nahe gewesen sei und ihnen die Kraft zu ihrem Opfer gegeben hat, dann antworten sie einmütig mit diesen Räumen und Gestalten, die das Wort "Vaterland" umschliesst. (Ihlenfeld 1966:55)
> '... if we were to ask the fallen soldiers of the last wars - their letters, which have been published, permit us this question - if we were to ask them, what was close to them and what gave them the strength for their sacrifice, they would unanimously answer in ways that encompass the word "Fatherland" (*Vaterland).*'

I think the proposed explication of this word makes it clear how this word could have been put to use by the Nazi propaganda and rhetoric; one doesn't need to postulate a semantic change due to "a misuse of the word and of its original meaning" ("Mißbrauch des Wortes und seines ursprüngliches Gehaltes", Ihlenfeld 1966:48). Two examples from the time of World War II illustrate this point. First, a few lines from a 1940 song by a German teacher and poet from Bessarabia evacuated (with other Bessarabian Germans) to Germany (from Greverus 1972:210):

> Es trübet sich der Blick / Doch führet uns des Schicksals Hand / Ihr Brüder, welch ein Glück / Ins grosse, deutsche Vaterland / Ins Heimatland zurück.
> 'Our countenance clouds over / But the hand of destiny leads us / Brothers, what luck (or: happiness) / to return to the great, the German Fatherland / Back to the Heimatland.'

And another example, a fragment of a World War II song from a camp for German prisoners of war (Greverus 1972:441, from a hand-written collection, hence the misspellings):

> Wir haben viele viele Freiheits Kämpfer
> sie wollen Kämfen fir ihres Treues Vaterland.
> Das Schiksal wolte Nicht das wir das Ziel erlangen
> wir sind verlassen haben keine Heimadt mehr.
> 'We have many many fighters for freedom
> they want to fight for their faithful Fatherland.
> Fate did not want us to reach our goal
> we are deserted and have no Heimat.

2.6. *Vaterland in post-war Germany*

Commentators have noted that in post-war Germany many people have avoided using the word *Vaterland* altogether, because of its Nazi associations.

As Thielike (1962, quoted in Ihlenfeld (1966:55) put it, "Wir verfügen weithin nicht über die Freiheit, unbefangen und unbekümmert ein Wort wie "Vaterland" überhaupt in den Mund zu nehmen", 'We do not feel free to say aloud a word like "Fatherland" without inhibition.' Similarly, Ihlenfled himself writes: "... für uns Deutsche (ist) dem Gedanken ans Vaterland nun auch eine kaum überwindliche Schwermut eingetan und steht gegen jeden unbefangenen, jeden unreflektierten Gebrauch des Wortes" (p. 52), 'for us Germans the thought of Fatherland is laden with a barely surmountable melancholy, and it stands against every careless, against every unreflecting usage of the word.'

It is interesting that the word *Volk* was not affected (to anything like the same degree) despite the fact that it, too, was used extensively in the Nazi propaganda. On a smaller scale, *Heimat*, too, was used by the Nazis ("In the writings of the Nazi ideologues of the 1930s, Heimat became simply one more term among many that revolved around the central themes of race, blood, and German destiny", Applegate 1990:18) - and yet, as mentioned earlier, *Heimat* survived the Nazi period unsullied. One can speculate, therefore, that if *Vaterland* became for many people in Germany an almost unusable word (especially for younger people, cf. Ihlenfeld 1966:48: "Eine so vaterlandsmüde Jugend wie die heutige hat es in Deutschland wohl noch nie gegeben." 'There has probably never been a young generation so weary of "Vaterland" as the one today in Germany.') this was due to the interaction between its use in the Nazi era and its inherent content, and not to the Nazi use alone. It seems to me that the moral-national imperative inherent in its meaning ("when this country wants me to do something I have to do it", etc.) accounts for the strong rejection of the word *Vaterland* in post-war Germany.

Nonetheless, *Vaterland* does still play an important role in public discourse; and it is important to understand what exactly it means in this discourse in Germany.[4] Thus West German president Gustav Heinemann called Germany "ein schwieriges Vaterland", 'a difficult Vaterland', in his inaugural address in 1969.

> Es gibt schwierige Vaterländer. Eins davon ist Deutschland. Aber es ist unser Vaterland. Hier leben und arbeiten wir. Darum wollen wir unseren Beitrag für die Menschheit mit diesem und durch dieses Land leisten.

> 'There are difficult Fatherlands. One of these is Germany. But it is our Fatherland. This is where we live and work. Thus we want to make our contribution to humanity with this and through this country.'

According to my German informants, one cannot speak of a "schwierige Heimat" ('difficult *Heimat*') and it would hardly make sense to speak in English of a "difficult homeland". Presumably, it is not places themselves which are difficult, but rather the obligations and responsibilities (as well as collective memories) associated with them.

2.7. *Summary: A full explication of Vaterland*

Anticipating my discussion of the Polish key concept *ojczyzna*, I have indicated the components of *Vaterland* which are also included in the explication of *ojczyzna* (marking them with the sign "= 0"), as well as the components of *Vaterland* which do not have their counterparts in the explication of *ojczyzna* (marking them with the sign "≠ 0").

I haven't similarly indicated the components shared by *Vaterland* and *Heimat*, because hardly any components included in both these concepts have exactly the same form (although there are several identical subcomponents).

(1)	a country	= 0
(2)	I am like a part of this country	= 0
(3)	when I think of this country, I feel something good	= 0
(4)	I think something like this when I think of this country:	= 0
(5)	this country is not like any other country	= 0
(6)	it is a very good country	≠ 0
(7)	other countries are not like this country	≠ 0
(8)	this country did many good things for me	= 0
(9)	if this country wants me to do something, I have to do it	≠ 0
(10)	many other people think the same when they think of this country	= 0
(11)	these people feel something good when they think of this country	= 0
(12)	these people are like one thing	= 0
(13)	I am like a part of this thing	= 0

3. Ojczyzna

3.1. Introduction

Ojczyzna (etymologically derived from *ojciec* 'father', but in meaning, roughly, 'homeland' or 'motherland') is, or at least has been for two hundred years, one of the most central concepts in Polish culture. According to the sociologist Antonina Kłoskowska (1991:52-53), it constitutes "a synthesis of the central values of this culture." As noted by the Czech linguist Damborsky (1993), the traditional "definition" of Polishness in the neighbouring Czech lands is given in the three-word slogan "Bóg, honor, i ojczyzna" ('God, honour, and *ojczyzna*').

A great deal has been written in Poland about the concept of 'ojczyzna' and its role in Polish history and literature. (For an excellent recent account of this literature, see Bartmiński 1993). What is crucial from the present point of view, however, is not so much different views about 'ojczyzna' which have been expressed (whether in literature, in public debate, or in opinion surveys) as the meaning of the word as such. As Bartmiński (1989:166) says, an explication of the concept 'ojczyzna' should show the collective consciousness articulated in the Polish language (that is, in the meaning of the word *ojczyzna* itself).

Ojczyzna is an old word, well-attested in Polish literature from the sixteenth century onwards. But it was only in the 19th century, after Poland had been partitioned between Russia, Prussia, and Austria, that the word became highly prominent in Polish literature and everyday life (as reflected in letters, diaries, memoirs, and so on); and that it developed into a veritable "sacrum narodowe", 'national sacred treasure', as Bartmiński (1989:165) put it. Throughout the nineteenth century (a century of repeated uprisings and unsuccessful attempts to regain freedom and national independence), the salience of this word steadily grew. When finally Poland did regain its independence after the First World War, this growth was apparently arrested (cf. Taborska 1993), but it received a new impetus under the Nazi occupation of World War II. During the communist era the word *ojczyzna* was the subject of political manipulation and propaganda, and in the general perception became corrupted. But when in 1982, after martial law was declared in Poland and thousands of Solidarity activists were imprisoned, Father Jerzy Popiełuszko (murdered in 1984 by the political police) introduced his famous 'msze za Ojczyzne' ('masses for the *ojczyzna*'), the word *ojczyzna* had regained a pure ring and was able to act as a rallying cry for the great majority of the nation active in, or sympathetic to, the Solidarity movement. A central feature of those masses were the homilies delivered by Father Popiełuszko, in which the key word, returning again and again, was *ojczyzna* (cf. Popiełuszko 1992).

It was only after the final demise of communism and the re-emergence of an independent Poland that the word *ojczyzna* - though still present in the political language - began to lose its central role in Polish life epitomizing Polish attitudes and Polish concerns (cf. Agnieszka Kłoskowska 1993).

What, then, does a phrase like *msze za ojczyznę* 'masses for the *ojczyzna'*, mean? Translations such as "masses for the native country", or "masses for the homeland" are inaccurate; and a German translation such as "Messen für das Vaterland" is downright dangerous, not only because of the Nazi connotations of *Vaterland*, but also because of the significant semantic differences between *ojczyzna* and even the pre-Nazi (as well as post-Nazi) *Vaterland*.

Simplifying things considerably, we could say that if one's *Vaterland* is like a wonderful father, who can demand things from one and whom one must willingly obey, *ojczyzna* is like a beloved mother, who doesn't demand anything, but who has suffered a great deal and whom one would want to protect from further misfortunes, fully expecting and accepting the need for self-sacrifice.

Before turning to a more detailed discussion of *ojczyzna*, it should be pointed out that in addition to the mainstream usage there was also a regional usage, well-known from Polish literature. Adam Mickiewicz's great classic "Pan Tadeusz" (published in Paris 1834), starts with words that every Pole knows by heart:

> Litwo, ojczyzno moja! Ty jesteś jak zdrowie!
> Ile Cię trzeba cenić, ten tylko się dowie,
> Kto Cię stracił.
> 'O Lithuania, my homeland (*ojczyzna*)! You are like good health.
> Only he can value you fully who has lost you.'

When Mickiewicz, the leading Polish political exile, writing about Poland, in Polish, and for Poles, called "Litwa" (Lithuania) his "ojczyzna", he was using this word in a sense similar to that of the German *Heimat*: he meant, roughly speaking, the places where he lived as a child, where he felt at home as a child, where his family lived, and where his life had its roots. In addition, the word has a strong emotional component (like *Heimat*).

But Mickiewicz himself used the word *ojczyzna* also in the other, broader sense, as when he dedicated his drama "Dziady" ('Forefathers'

Eve') to his friends who had similarly been exiled and who died for *ojczyzna* as "martyrs for the cause of the nation":

> Świętej pamieci Janowi Sobolewskiemu, Cyprianowi Daszkiewiczowi, Feliksowi Kółakowskiemu, spóluczniom, spółwiezniom, spółwygnancom, za miłość ku ojczyźnie prześladowanym, z tesknoty ku ojczyźnie zmarłym, w Archangielu, na Moskwie, w Petersburgu, narodowej sprawy męczennikom, poświęca autor.
> 'To the sacred memory of Jan Sobolewski, Cyprian Daszkiewicz, and Feliks Kółakowski, fellow-students, fellow-prisoners, fellow-exiles, who were persecuted for love of homeland (*ojczyzna*) and died pining for it in Archangiel, Moscow, and Petersburg, martyrs to the national cause, I dedicate this work.'

In this dedication, *ojczyzna* does not refer to beloved local places, like *Heimat*, but to a beloved country; and it is closely linked with the notion of *naród*, 'nation'. In this respect, it can be compared to *Vaterland*. It can still be compared to *Heimat*, however, in its nostalgic perspective, reflected in particular in the untranslatable phrase "z tęsknoty ku ojczyznie zmarłym", roughly, 'who died out of nostalgia for the *ojczyzna'*.

But Polish doesn't have two words which are comparable to *Heimat* and *Vaterland*; it has just one - *ojczyzna* - whose meaning differs from that of either *Heimat* or *Vaterland*, although it shares some components with both. In the mainstream modern sense *ojczyzna*, (like *Vaterland* or *homeland)*, refers to a country among other countries, that is, to a unique member of a broader category of lands viewed as separate entities. Since this word acquired its modern identity and became a key word in Polish at a time when there was no Polish state, it didn't refer to a political entity. On the other hand, it had a clear historical, as well as geographical dimension (linked with strong emotional and moral content). This historical aspect of *ojczyzna* constitutes one of its most characteristic features, (differentiating it from, for example, *homeland*, *Heimat*, *Vaterland*, or the Russian *rodina)*. The disasters which happened to Poland between the first partition (1772) and the national "resurrection" (1918) left their imprint on the very meaning of this crucial word.

3.2. Ojczyzna - the country of birth?

The nineteenth century poet Maria Konopnicka has left us the following poetical definition of *ojczyzna*:

> Ojczyzna moja - to ta ziemia droga,
> Gdziem ujrzał słońce i gdziem poznal Boga.
> 'My *ojczyzna* - is that dear land,
> where I (first) saw the sun and where I got to know God.'

In a similar vein, the "Dictionary of the Polish Language" (SJP) defines *ojczyzna* as "the country where one was born and which is the country of one's fellow countrymen (*rodacy*)". But does a person's *ojczyzna* need to be their country of birth?

The answer is not as straightforward as it seems, in view of the existence of phrases such as *"druga 'second' ojczyzna"* or "przybrana" 'adopted' *ojczyzna*". In my view, however, all uses of *ojczyzna* with respect to countries other than one's country of birth have to be regarded as metaphorical, and phrases such as *przybrana ojczyzna* should be interpreted as sui generis abbreviations along the following lines: "an adopted *ojczyzna*" is a country which is not one's *ojczyzna* but which one thinks of as if it were one's *ojczyzna*".

Personal identification "I am like a part of this country" appears to be more important for this concept than the mere fact of birth "I was born in this country"; nonetheless the idea of 'origin' is important, too. This is supported by the fact that *ojczyzna* can be used metaphorically in the sense 'country of origin of something' (e.g. China is the *ojczyzna* of silk); and also that the adjective *ojczysty* (as in the phrase *ziemia ojczysta* 'the land, earth of one's ojczyzna') can only refer to the country of origin, not to any "adopted *ojczyzna*". The very close conceptual link between *ojczyzna* (despite its etymology) and *mother* (confirmed, for example, by the common phrase *łono ojczyzny*, 'womb/bosom of *ojczyzna*') points in the same direction. (The notion of a "father figure" refers to a special kind of relationship which can extend well into a person's adulthood, but a "mother" is above all a point of origin, a "body" from which one has emerged at the beginning of one's life journey; and which, one might add, represents the archetypal security of the womb. For Poles, for nearly two centuries the nostalgia for the lost *ojczyzna* was linked symbolically with that archetypal image. To quote Mickiewicz again:

> Panno Święta, co Jasnej bronisz Częstochowy (....)
> tak nas powrócisz cudem na ojczyzny łono.
> 'Holy Virgin, who have defended the Holy Mountain of Częstochowa, (...) you will bring us back miraculously to the womb/bosom of *ojczyzna*.

In this respect, then, (the link with one's "point of origin") *ojczyzna* is closer to the German *Heimat* than to *Vaterland*; and I have posited the component 'I was born in this country' for *Heimat* and for *ojczyzna*, but not for *Vaterland* (although *Heimat* doesn't have the same strong link with 'mother' that *ojczyzna* has).

On the other hand, *ojczyzna* does not seem to have the same link with the world of childhood as *Heimat* does. Nor does it necessarily imply happy memories of a safe haven. Consequently, I have not posited for *ojczyzna* either of the two "childhood components" postulated for *Heimat*: 'when I was a child, I was like a part of these places', 'I felt something good when I was like a part of these places'.

But there are other links between *ojczyzna* and *Heimat*. In a sense, both *Heimat* and *ojczyzna* oppose one's own place to "foreign", "alien" places, places where one must feel like a stranger. In the case of *ojczyzna*, this contrast between being "at home" and being "a stranger among strangers" is highlighted by the lexical opposition between the two rhyming words: *ojczyzna* and *obczyzna* (from *obcy*, 'alien' or 'stranger'). *Obczyzna* means, roughly, 'a land of strangers, where one is a stranger oneself'; and this very contrast highlights the special quality of *ojczyzna* as a place uniquely and irreplaceably "one's own", the only place where one can truly "belong".

Two examples:

> Zmuszeni byli emigrować na obczyznę w poszukiwaniu chleba.
> (Zycie Literackie 1954, SJP)
> 'They were forced to emigrate to foreign lands in search of a livelihood.'

> Wolę wszelką nędzę znosić jak królową byc w obczyźnie.
> (Damroth, 1922; SJP)
> 'I would prefer any misery to being a queen in a foreign land.'

To portray this aspect of *ojczyzna*, I have posited the component 'I can't be like a part of any other country'. In the case of *Heimat*, the analogous components read: 'I was like a part of these places once', 'I can't be like a part of any other places'; they are therefore childhood-oriented. By implication, the uniqueness and irreplaceability of one's *Heimat* places have a great deal to do with the uniquness and unrecoverability of one's childhood. But in the case of *ojczyzna*, the uniqueness of one's link with the country where one was born lies elsewhere: it lies largely in the perceived uniqueness of this country's history and in the solidarity with the other people born in the same country and caught in the same history (with the resulting memories, feelings, and obligations). The importance and the strength of the link among the people belonging to the same *ojczyzna* is manifested in the specifically Polish word *rodacy* ('beloved countrymen'), included in the SJP definition of *ojczyzna* quoted earlier. On the surface, this word seems to correspond to the English word *fellow-countrymen*, or to the French word *compatriotes*; but in fact, it means much more; it implies that people who belong to the same *ojczyzna* share so much (through their love of that *ojczyzna* and through their participation in the same history) that they can be expected to love (or at least, feel something very good for) one another. One characteristic (and very famous) quote:

> Zwyciężonemu za pomnik grobowy zostana suche drewna szubienicy, za całą sławę krótki płacz kobiècy i długie nocne rodaków rozmowy. (Mickiewicz).
> 'The vanquished shall have as his only monument the dry wood of the gallows, as his only fame, a woman's brief lament, and the lengthy nocturnal discussions of his fellow countrymen (rodacy).'

It is interesting to note that while Russian, too, has a "loving word" for people who are not necessarily members of one's family *(rodnye)*, Polish lexically links this expectation of mutual love with belonging to the same *ojczyzna* (*rodacy*).

The link between 'country' and 'nation', which lies at the heart of *ojczyzna*, is also characteristic of *Vaterland*, but the link between *ojczyzna* and *rodacy* ('one's own people'), as well as the contrast between *ojczyzna* and *obczyzna* (alien places), are uniquely Polish.

These considerations lead us to the following partial explication:

ojczyzna
a country
I was born in this country
I am like a part of this country
I can't be like a part of any other country
many other people think the same when they think of this country
when I think of these people, I feel something good

The close links of *ojczyzna* with history and with the notion of a nation will be explored in the subsequent sections of this paper, and will be portrayed in further parts of the explication.

To account for this expectation of a strong emotional bond between people belonging to the same *ojczyzna* I have included in its explication the component 'when I think of these people, I feel something good'. While it would be hard to quote any direct evidence for including a component of this kind in the explication of the word *ojczyzna* (in contrast to *rodacy)*, it is interesting to note that in the 1991 survey of responses to the word *ojczyzna* (Agnieszka Kloskowska 1991) a large number of interviewees responded in a way linking this word with a strong bond among people belonging to the same *ojczyzna*. For example, when asked "what would you call people who have the same *ojczyzna* as you?" as many as 9% replied: *bracia* ('brothers'); and all the replies using a kinship term (including *rodzina* 'family') in connection with *ojczyzna* reach the figure of 48%.

Summing up the results of the survey, Kłoskowska (1993:11) notes that the following elements emerged in the responses as the most prominent ones: "a feeling of roots, belonging, being conscious of sharing in the history of a strongly bonded collectivity, not being a stranger in an alien place". Remarks of this kind highlight the 'solidarity' aspect of *ojczyzna* (manifested directly in the word *rodacy*), an aspect contrasting with the more individualistic character of *Heimat*.

The link between 'country' and 'nation', which lies at the heart of *ojczyzna*, is also characteristic of *Vaterland*, but the link between *ojczyzna* and *rodacy* ('one's own people'), as well as the contrast between *ojczyzna* 'one's own country' and *obczyzna* 'alien places, places of exile' is characteristically Polish.

3.3. A collective memory of the past martyrology

In modern usage, the concept *ojczyzna* is closely associated with concepts such as death, suffering, martyrdom, loss, exile. Mickiewicz's dedication linking *ojczyzna* with death, persecution, exile, nostalgia, and martyrdom, is quite characteristic in this respect. The beginning of a well-known poem by another romantic poet, Juliusz Slowacld, is also very characteristic:

> O! nieszczęśliwa! O! uciemiezona
> Ojczyzno moja.
> 'O my homeland (*ojczyzna*)! How unhappy, how oppressed!

A few more characteristic examples (quoted in Bartminski 1993):

> A ja wszędy w tej krainie Widzę jedną wielką bliznę, *jedną moję cierpiącą* Ojczyznę! (Słowacki).
> 'And everywhere in this land I see one great scar, my suffering homeland (*ojczyzna*)!'

> *Kto zostanie, niech juz nad grobem ojczyzny nie płacze*. (Norwid)
> 'Let the survivor not weep over the gravestone of the homeland (*ojczyzna*).'

czas niedaleki, W którym ojczyznę, matkę naszą biedną, z grobu wyniesiem - by żyła na wieki (Gaszynski)
'... the time is not far distant when we will raise our homeland (*ojczyzna*), our poor mother, from the grave - that she may live forever.'

Gorycz *wyssana ze krwi i łez mei ojczyzny*. (Mickiewicz)
'... a bitterness sucked from the blood and tears of my homeland (*ojczyzna*).'

Ojczyzny mojej stopy okrwawione
Włosami otrzeć na piasku upadam ... (Norwid)
'I fall to the sand to wipe the bleeding feet of my homeland (*ojczyzna*) with my hair.'

As documented by Bartmiński, in Polish literature (especially, in poetry), *ojczyzna* typically co-occurs with words such as *cierpiąca* 'suffering', *bolejąca* 'in great pain', *płacząca* 'weeping', *nieszczęsna* 'unhappy', *biedna* 'poor', or occurs in collocations such as "the blood and tears of my *ojczyzna*", "the grave of my *ojczyzna*", "my *ojczyzna* is dying", "the death of the *ojczyzna*", "the sorrow of the *ojczyzna*", and the like.

Maria Janion (1979:46-47) makes the following generalization about 'ojczyzna' in Polish romantic poetry:

> Ojczyzna pojawiła sie tu jako osoba, czy to umarła, czy to pogrążona w letargu, czy to śmiertelnie zraniona, osoba, ktorej trzeba nieść natychmiastową pomoc, dla której wszystko należy porzucić i o której nigdy nie mozna zapomnieć. ... To, ze pojawila sie ona jako osoba bezbronna, nieszczęśliwa, udręczona, niewinnie umęczona, wołająca o pomszczenie jej krzywdy, mobilizowalo u romantyków poczucie solidarności z nią oraz miłości i żądzy niesienia pomocy.
> '*Ojczyzna* was presented as a person, sometimes dead, sometimes in a coma, sometimes mortally wounded, a person who requires urgent help, for whom one must leave everything and whom one must never forget ... The fact that she (it) appeared as someone helpless, unhappy, tormented, martyred, wronged, evoked in the romantic poets a sense of solidarity and love, and a yearning to come to her rescue.'

The sorrowful, painful connotations of *ojczyzna*, so characteristic of romantic poetry, are by no means confined to the romantic period: they are detectable in most uses of the word throughout the nineteenth and twentieth century. To quote just one characteristic late twentieth century example (from a poem by Tadeusz Różewicz, quoted in Bartmiński 1993):

no początku ojczyzna
jest blisko
na wyciągnięcie ręki
dopiero póżniej rośnie
krwawi
boli
'at first the homeland (*ojczyzna*)
is near at hand
only later does it grow
bleed
ache'

The writer Marian Brandys (quoted in Bartmiński 1993), has observed that he had used the word *ojczyzna* only once in his life, in September 1939, when he was suffering an acute sense of defeat. He asked his colleagues then: "what will happen to our *ojczyzna*?" Consider also the following definition of *ojczyzna* offered in a 1989 survey of views on this subject: "Historia, wspólnota dążeń i cierpień" ('history, an awareness of shared goals and sufferings'). I doubt very much whether "sufferings" would be mentioned by anyone in a similar survey of opinions on *Vaterland* or *Heimat*.

In the eighteenth century, *ojczyzna* could still co-occur with adjectives such as *wesoła* 'merry, cheerful', as in the quote below:

> Ten sie ojczyzny zwać synem prawdziwym (...) może, który (...) Wesół z wesola, z płaczącą się smuci. (Naruszewicz, quoted in Bartmiński.)
> 'Only he can be called a true son of the motherland (*ojczyzna*) who makes merry when she makes merry, and laments when she laments.'

But in modern Polish, combinations of this kind are felt to be incongruous and are instinctively avoided. Characteristically, the typical modern collocations listed under *ojczyzna* in Skorupka's 1974 phraseological dictionary of the Polish language are *bronić ojczyzny* 'defend the ojczyzna', *polec, przelewać krew, umrzeć, walczyć, zginąć za ojczyzne, w obronie ojczyzny*, 'be killed for, shed one's blood for, die for, struggle for, perish for the *ojczyzna*'; and finally *służyć ojczyźnie* 'serve the ojczyzna' (with strong implications of self-sacrifice). This is of course similar to the phraseology of *Vaterland* - but only in its "negative" subset (see below).

Positive collocations such as *wolna ojczyzna* 'free *ojczyzna*', are possible, but they imply something like "finally liberated", "finally free", and so they, too, refer to past disasters. The following lines from a poem by Leopold Staff (written shortly after Poland regained its independence in 1918; quoted in Bartmiński 1993) are very characteristic in this regard:

Ojczyzno nasza, Matko bolesna...
Nad tobą świeci wolna Kopuła!
'O homeland (*ojczyzna*), mother of sorrows,
The dome of freedom rises above you.

Similarly, Słonimski, another 20th century poet, wrote (SJP):

Ojczyzna moja wolna, wolna ...
Wiec zrzucam z ramion plaszcz Konrada
'My *ojczyzna* is free, free ...
So I cast away [from my shoulders] the cloak of Konrad'
[Konrad is a romantic hero, a symbol of national martyrology and the struggle for national freedom, A.W.]

Admittedly, there are contexts where reference to "bad things" (past misfortunes) may seem to be entirely missing. The title of a geography textbook published in independent (recently liberated) Poland in the 1920's (*Nasza ojczyzna*, 'our *ojczyzna*') may be a case in point. I would argue, however, that even a title of this kind can be said to contain implicit allusions to past misfortunes. In this context, the implicit message can be reconstructed as follows: "this is our country; we should know it; many bad things have happened to this country; we don't want bad things to happen to this country; we want to do good things for this country; we think good things can happen to this country now".

Even the phoney, propaganda phrase "nasza socjalistyczna ojczyzna", 'our socialist *ojczyzna*', used in official language under the communist regime, sounds as if it implicitly referred to an unhappy past, overcome by the glorious present.

Many collocations characteristic of *ojczyzna* are, as we have seen, also characteristic of *Vaterland* (e.g. both frequently occur in frames such as 'to die for', 'to fight for', 'to defend'). But *Vaterland* is also frequently used in combinations with adjectives such as *großes* 'great' or *schönes* 'beautiful'; or with the verb *blühen* 'to flourish' (as in the German national anthem). By contrast, *ojczyzna* is not normally described as *wielka* 'great' or *piekna* 'beautiful'; and the optative phrases involving *ojczyzna* have typically referred to *zmartwychwstanie*, 'resurrection', rather than to blooming or flourishing.

One of the most characteristic examples in this respect is a line from a hymn, frequently sung in the past in Polish churches:

Ojczyzne wolna racz nam wrócić Panie!
'O Lord, give us back a free *Ojczyzna!*'

In the communist times, this line sounded of course as an act of political defiance (and was meant as such); and the regime demanded that it be replaced with a more bienpensant version:

> Ojczyzne wolna poblogoslaw Panie.
> 'O Lord, bless our free *ojczyzna*.'

But even in the official version the phrase *ojczyzne wolna*, literally, 'a free *ojczyzna'*, sounded like a reference to past misfortunes; in the authentic version, as normally sung in Poland, the reference was of course to present, as well as past, misfortunes.

Unlike the German word *Vaterland* or the Russian word *rodina*, *ojczyzna* is not the kind of word which could be used in vigorous, triumphant, marching songs; it is too poignant, too solemn, too pain-infused a word for this kind of context. It is also interesting to note that while the German phrase "sterben fürs Vaterland" 'to die for the Vaterland' has common counterparts in the Polish phrases *zginąć za ojczyznę polec* or *za ojczyznę*, the phrase *leben und sterben fürs Vaterland*, 'to live and to die for the Vaterland', does not. *Ojczyzna* was associated far more with dying than with living.

Similarly, there is no tradition of special songs associated with *ojczyzna*, as there was a special genre of *Vaterlandslieder* in Germany. Patriotic Polish songs, of which there are a great many, normally seem to avoid the word *ojczyzna*, common as it was in lyrical and rhetorical poetry. In particular, fighting songs typically use the word *Polska* 'Poland' rather than *ojczyzna*. All these facts suggest a unique semantic component of *ojczyzna*, which I would tentatively formulate as follows: 'I know: many bad things have happened to this country'.

A recent article on the use of the word *Vaterland* (Kleine-Brockhoff 1989) mentions a huge restaurant in the pre-war Berlin, whose name was "Das Haus Vaterland"; and one of my German informants recalls a café in Munich called "Vaterland". But according to all my Polish informants it is inconceivable that a Polish restaurant should be called "Ojczyzna". "Polska", "Polonia", "Patria", yes, but never *ojczyzna*. In fact, some older informants (World War II veterans in their seventies and eighties) got quite upset at the idea, which sounded to them like sacrilege or mockery. I believe that reactions of this kind support the references to "bad things" in the explication of *ojczyzna* proposed here.

It is worth mentioning in this connection another famous passage from a poem by the early 20th century poet Jan Kasprowicz:

Rzadko na moich wargach, niech dziś ma warga to wyzna
Jawi się krwią przepojone, najdrozsże słowo ojczyzna.
'Seldom on my lips there appears,
let my lips confess it today,
the bleeding, beloved word *ojczyzna.*'

The reticence confessed here by Kasprowicz is of course something quite different from the reluctance to use the word *ojczyzna* reported in contemporary opinion surveys. Apparently, to most young people in contemporary Poland the word *ojczyzna* is no longer relevant and doesn't correspond to their present concerns. But for Kasprowicz, the word WAS relevant; but it was too sacred and too pained ("bleeding" or "soaked in blood") to be ever used irreverently.

Discussing the concept *ojczyzna* and its closest counterparts in other European languages Bartmiński (1993:2) writes that perhaps the most characteristically Polish attitude is that

> ... which accepts as the most basic value national freedom (*wolność*) and independence (*niepodległość*) and which deduces from this a set of obligations of the individual towards the nation.

The words *wolność* 'freedom' and *niepodleglość* 'national independence' used in this passage identify Polish cultural key concepts, with no exact equivalents elsewhere. *Wolność* is not so much 'freedom' as, above all, 'national freedom', and *niepodległość* is not simply 'independence' but 'national independence' (cf. Wierzbicka, In press). Both these words reflect the historical experience of a nation for whom national freedom and independence could not be taken for granted but had to be constantly fought for. Thus, both these words carry echoes of a collective memory of national subjugation - that is, of 'bad things that happened to this country', with the concomitant protestation 'I (we) don't want bad things to happen to this country'. The concept 'ojczyzna' bears the imprint of the same concerns.

3.4. The moral aspect of 'ojczyzna'

The collective memory of "bad things" which have happened to this country leads to a desire for this country to be protected from similar "bad things" in the future:

I don't want bad things to happen to this country

This, in turn, invites an attitude of self-sacrifice:

> if something bad happens to me because of this,
> I don't want to say: "I don't want this"

In the surveys of views on *ojczyzna* reported on by Agnieszka Kłoskowska (1993), several respondents quote the great nineteenth century poet Norwid's poetic definition of this concept:

> Ojczyzna to jest wielki zbiorowy obowiązek.
> 'the homeland (*ojczyzna*) that is our great, our collective duty'.

As we have seen, the German word *Vaterland*, too, has come to have a moral dimension, which it didn't have in its earlier usage. It implies duty, as well as pride. But the duty implied by it is not so directly linked with the idea of 'sacrifice' as the duty implied by *ojczyzna* is. Rather, it is a duty to obey ('if this country wants me to do something, I have to do it'). Typically, *Vaterland* CALLS (its "sons"), whereas *ojczyzna* weeps, suffers, dies, sheds blood and tears (and silently EXPECTS her "children" to respond). Both concepts imply a moral imperative "to do good things for one's country"; but *Vaterland* suggests a "have to" modality, whereas *ojczyzna* suggests, rather, a "want to" attitude (combined with an additional element of 'I would be bad if I didn't'). Furthermore, *ojczyzna* is additionally skewed towards something like a willingness to suffer:

> if I feel something bad because of this, I don't want to say: 'I don't want this'

It is worth noting in this connection that the only proverb cited in the monumental "Dictionary of the Polish language" (SJP 1958:898) under *ojczyzna* is this: "miłe blizny dla ojczyzny", 'scars [incurred] for the *ojczyzna* gladden the heart'. Certainly, the rhyme "ojczyzna - blizna" ('ojczyzna - scar') is one of the most hackneyed rhymes in the Polish language. The link between *ojczyzna* and something like an expectation of selflessness and sacrifice is supported by the frequently expressed notion that *ojczyzna* is not necessarily a place where one can expect 'good things' to happen to one. One characteristic example is provided by the first line of Mickiewicz's satirical poem "Pan Baron":

> Gdzie dobrze tam ojczyzna.
> 'where things go well [or: where one is well off] there is (one's) *ojczyzna*'

As pointed out by Bartmiński (1993), in a different context Mickiewicz reverses this satirical statement:

> Tam ojczyzna, gdzie źle.
> '*Ojczyzna* is the place where you are not well off (where bad things happen to you).'

Furthermore, 'Ojczyzna' implies not only a moral imperative to 'do good things' for one's country (to serve it, to defend it, to fight for it), but also a moral imperative to love this country (to 'feel something good' for it). Bartmiński (1989:171) links this aspect with the symbolic identification of 'ojczyzna' with 'mother', when he writes: "The ethical requirement to love one's *ojczyzna* - like the ethical requirement to love one's mother - doesn't need any justification". Hence the need for the semantic component: 'if I didn't fccl somcthing good for this country, this would be very bad'.

The ethical requirement to love one's country and to identify with it is so strong in Polish culture that it has found its direct expression in the Polish lexicon, in the form of the special verb *wynarodowić się*. Derived from *naród* 'nation', this verb refers to the process whereby an individual loses (or sheds) his or her identification with the Polish nation. The word is strongly pejorative and implies something like treason, crime, disgrace. Frequently, this word was used with reference to persons who married a Russian or a German and as a consequence lost their Polish national consciousness and their emotional allegiance to Poland and Polish culture (and were ostracized for their "treason"). It was also frequently used of Polish emigrants who became so absorbed in the life of their new country of residence that they lost (or shed) their Polishness. For example:

> Ojcowie rodzin stwierdzali z bólem, że dzieci się wynaradawiają i że za parę lat nie beda mogli do nich po polsku przemówić.
> (Wiktor 1951, SJP)
> 'Fathers found with grief that their children were losing their nationality and that in a few years' time they wouldn't be able to speak to them in Polish.'

I know of no other European (or, for that mattcr, non-European) language which has a word like *wynarodowić się*. Clearly, this word reflects a specificially Polish historical experience, the pressure many felt to give up their Polish identity; and the unqualified condemnation of those who gave in to such pressure.

The threat to Polish national identity from neighbouring powers, especially Russia, led many Poles to political emigration or exile. Interestingly, this fact, too, found its lexical expression, leading to the emergence of a special new meaning of the word *kraj*: 1. country, 2. the country (Poland) seen from the perspective of Poles forced to live outside it. For example:

> Tesknie do kraju. (Słonimski 1951, SJP)
> 'I miss (ache for) [my] country.'
>
> I prawdziwie głosem psa takiego zawyć był gotów z tęsknoty za krajem. (Berent 1937, SJP)
> 'And he was genuinely ready to howl like a dog from nostalgia for [his] country.

(Cf. also the expression "Armia Krajowa", 'Home Army', which was the name of the Polish Army fighting against Nazi Germany on Polish soil, in contrast to the Polish forces fighting Hitler outside Poland; *krajowa* being an adjective derived from *kraj* in sense 2 of the word).

In a sense, the word *kraj*, which implicitly recognizes and legitimizes the need for many Poles to live abroad, could be said to be in semantic opposition to *ojczyzna*. It implies that Poland as the "ojczyzna" of the Polish nation extends beyond a certain geographical territory (*kraj*, the country sensu stricto), but includes also (in a spiritual sense) all those fighting, or working, or simply pining for Poland outside its geographical boundaries.

Thus, both these uniquely Polish concepts - *wynarodowić się* and *kraj* (as well as *obczyzna* and *rodacy*, discussed earlier) - closely reflect Polish historical experience, and the specifically Polish response to that experience. The concept 'ojczyzna' belongs to the same cluster of concepts.

3.5. Ojczyzna as culture and tradition

Bartmiński (1993:14) writes:

> Undoubtedly the most characteristic and unique aspect of the Polish understanding of 'ojczyzna', brought about by Poland's history in the last two centuries, consists in a special emphasis on the role of culture, stronger than elsewhere, either in the East or West. This emphasis on culture subsumes literature and art, language and customs, and also an ethical program with a strongly developed patriotic ethos. The institution of the state is seen in this context as secondary. In Poland, after the collapse of the first Republic [in 1795], the notion of 'ojczyzna-state' had no chances of continuation.

Intuitively, the idea that 'ojczyzna' gives special attention to culture and tradition, seems correct; and it can certainly be supported with numerous quotes from Polish writers and thinkers, as well as recent sociological data; but can it be supported with linguistic evidence as well?

In some measure it can. In particular, interesting light is thrown on this question by the use of the highly emotional adjective *ojczysty*, derived from *ojczyzna*. This adjective occurs in a rather limited set of collocations, which include, above all, the following: *język ojczysty* ('native language'), *mowa ojczysta* (roughly, the same, but more emotional and rhetorical), *dzieje ojczyste* ('the past history of one's native land', emotional and rhetorical), *kraj ojczysty* ('native country'), and *ziemia ojczysta* ('native land'). (SJP cites also *historia ojczysta*, 'Polish history', and *prawa ojczyste*, 'the laws of one's native land'.)

In trying to elucidate the special value of the adjective *ojczysty*, it is particularly instructive to compare the following two, roughly synonymous, expressions: *ziemia ojczysta* and *ziemia rodzinna* (both meaning roughly 'one's native land'). The difference is that *rodzinna* (derived from *rodzina* 'family') reflects an individual's point of view (like *Heimat*), whereas *ojczysta* suggests something treasured by a collectivity, that is, the nation as a whole (and by the individual as a member of that collectivity, participating in its shared values).

Thus, the collocations with the adjective *ojczysty* suggest the following further semantic components of *ojczyzna* itself:

(a) [these people are like one thing]:
(b) these people say things in the same way
(c) these people do many things in the same way
(d) these people think of many things in the same way
(e) these people often feel in the same way

Component (b) suggests a unity of language (and ways of speaking), (c) suggests a unity of customs and, more generally, way of life, (d) suggests a body of shared beliefs and attitudes, and (e) a pool of shared emotions and sentiments. Taken together, these additional components imply a high measure of cultural homogeneity, including linguistic unity.

It would be easy to adduce quotes from Polish literature which seem to undermine these postulates by linking 'ojczyzna' with cultural plurality, universal ethics, human solidarity independent of language and creed, and so on. The most famous example of this kind is furnished by Antoni Słonimski's poem entitled "Ten jest z ojczyzny mojej" ('He is from my *ojczyzna*'):

..Ten, który wszystkim serce swe otwiera
Francuzem jest, gdy Francja cierpi, Grekiem,
Gdy naród grecki z głodu obumiera,
Ten jest z ojczyzny mojej, jest człowiekiem.
'He who opens his heart to all,
Is a Frenchman when France suffers, a Greek
When the Greek nation is dying of hunger,
He is from my *ojczyzna*. He is a human being.'

It should be recognized, however, that utterances of this kind have a polemical character, and that they implicitly oppose a higher, universal ideal to the national ethos reflected in the concept 'ojczyzna' as it is. They do not seek to explicate the concept of 'ojczyzna' but to propose something that could supersede it. In fact, therefore, utterances of this kind not only do not undermine the case for including the additional components sketched above, but lend further support to them.

3.6. Ojczyzna - the country of ancestors?

In Polish literature and thought, the notion of *ojczyzna* is often explained with reference to ancestors. For example, Karol Libelt (1844) in a classic treatise on the subject says that *ojczyzna* is, first of all, one's native land, and secondly "it is one people, one stock, one tribe, from which our parents have emerged, and of which we are a part ourselves".

Characteristically, many literary and everyday definitions of *ojczyzna* include the word *groby* 'graves', apparently not only with reference to past misfortunes (uprisings, battles, etc.), but also with reference to earlier generations. To quote just one example from the 1991 survey of opinions (Agnieszka Kłoskowska 1993:11):

> *Ojczyzna* is the place where one can always find brotherly affection, perhaps it doesn't even have to be a place, what matters is the atmosphere, and in particular, the graves of the ancestors, places looking at which I become conscious of history.

It should also be pointed out that while the etymological link between *ojczyzna* and *ojciec* 'father' is no longer synchronically valid (since *ojczyzna* is certainly not thought of as "the country of one's father"), there is still a perceived link between *ojczyzna* and *ojcowie*, the plural of the word for 'father', which can also mean 'our ancestors'. If one defined *ojczyzna* as "ziemia ojców", 'the land of our ancestors', this would probably be accepted by many native speakers as intuitively quite plausible, and the morphological link between *ojczyzna* and *ojcowie* (in the sense 'ancestors') would be perceived as synchronically valid.

To account for the semantic link between *ojczyzna* and past generations, I have tentatively included in the explication of this word the following components: 'before this time, many other people were like a part of this country' and 'I am like a part of these people'.

3.7. Summary: A full explication of 'ojczyzna'

To facilitate comparison between *ojczyzna* and *Vaterland*, I have marked the components shared with *Vaterland* with the sign "≠ V", and those absent from the explication of *Vaterland*, as "= V".

(1)	a country	= V
(2)	I was born in this country	≠ V
(3)	I am like a part of this country	= V
(4)	I can't be like a part of any other country	≠ V
(5)	when I think of this country, I feel something good	= V
(6)	if I didn't, this would be very bad	≠ V
(7)	I think something like this when I think of this country:	= V
(8)	this country is not like any other country	= V
(9)	many bad things happened to this country	≠ V
(10)	I don't want bad things to happen to this country	? V
(11)	this country did many good things for me	= V
(12)	like a mother does good things for her children	≠ V
(13)	I want to do good things for this country	? V
(14)	if I feel something bad because of this I don't want to say: "I don't want this"	≠ V
(15)	many other people think the same when they think of this country	= V
(16)	these people feel something good when they think of this country	= V
(17)	these people are like one thing	= V
(18)	I am like a part of this thing	= V
(19)	these people say things in the same way	≠ V
(20)	these people do many things in the same way	≠ V
(21)	these people think of many things in the same way	≠ V

(22) these people often feel the same ≠ V

(23) when I think of these people, I feel something good ≠ V
(24) these people are like a part of this country ≠ V
(25) before this time, many other people were like a part of this country ≠ V(?)
(26) I am like a part of all these people ≠ V
(27) in many ways, I am like these people ≠ V

4. Rodina

Russian has not one but three words which can be compared with *homeland*, *Vaterland* and *Heimat*, and *ojczyzna*. These words are: *rodina*, *otečestvo*, and *otčizna*. Of the three, however, only one - *rodina* - is used frequently and can be regarded as one of the Russian key words. (For example, in Zasorina's 1977 corpus based on one million running words, *rodina* has a frequency of 172, whereas *otečestvo* has only 30, and *otčizna* 2.)

In a recent article entitled "The road to the spiritual regeneration of Russia" and published in the Russian emigré periodical *Russkaja Mysl'* the Orthodox priest Viktor Potapov (1993:7) uses all three words: *rodina*, *otečestvo*, and *otčizna*, each in a different context:

1. Tol'ko v cerkvi možno poljubit' svoju rodinu i svoj narod podlinno xristjanskoj ljubov'ju.
   'Only in the Church can one come to love one's *rodina* and one's nation with a genuinely Christian love.'

2. Pravoslavnaja cerkov' odobrjaet nacionalizm (...) esli on napravlen na zaščitu Otečestva ot vnešnej agressii.
   'The Orthodox Church approves of nationalism if it is directed towards defending the *Otečestvo* from an outside aggression.'

3. Tol'ko zabota o nebesnoj Otčizne pomožet nam obustroit' zemnuju otčiznu na xristjanskix načalax.
   'Only a concern for the heavenly *Otčizna* will help us to rebuild our earthly *otčizna* on Christian foundations.'

In another recent article published in the same periodical (cf. Russkaja Mysl' 1993/6:12) a Russian writer born in France (of emigré Russian parents), Viktor Volkov, was asked where his "rodina" was. The writer replied that he feels fully French, although he doesn't have a single drop of French blood, and fully Russian, although until very recently he had never been in Russia, and he summed up: "One could say that France is my *rodina*, but Russia - my *otčizna*".

Though obviously far from sufficient, these few examples do illuminate some of the differences between the three concepts. In particular, they highlight the "ideal" character of *otčizna* (as, so to speak, a place of one's dreams) and the "real" character of *rodina* (as a place where one was actually born); they also highlight the "personal" character of *rodina* (as a country where one was born) and the impersonal, socio-political character of *otečestvo* (not only a country but also a state). The quotes also illuminate the differences in expected attitudes: *rodina* is, roughly speaking, a country to which one is emotionally attached, *otečestvo* - a country towards which one has obligations, and *otčizna* - a mythical country that one yearns for.

In surveys conducted recently among Xar'kov university students exploring their understanding of *rodina* (cf. Antipenko & Karnaušenko 1993) the great majority (72%) defined *rodina* as the country (or territory) where one was born. In addition, many respondents mentioned the "familiar" character of *rodina*, as a place where everything is *"rodnoe, blizkoe, ponjatnoe i privyčnoe"* (that is, roughly speaking, near to one's heart, close to one's heart, understandable, and accustomed). The untranslatable adjective *rodnoj* (neuter form *rodnoe*), cognate with *rodina*, is particularly significant here: it is derived from *rodit'(sja)*, 'be born', and it implies strong emotional ties based on blood, on common origin, on "belonging together".

Like the Polish word *ojczyzna*, *rodina* is also strongly associated with the image of 'mother', and the phrase *rodina-mat'*, 'mother-*rodina*', is a common collocation.

It might be added that *rodina* has also a second meaning, referring (like *Heimat)*, to the places where one was born and where one was a child, rather than to a country as a whole. *Rodina* in that local sense, too, is semantically (as well as etymologically) linked with the adjective *rodnoj*. The two meanings (roughly, 1. native country, 2. native places) are synchronically distinct, and, for example, the collocation *rodina-mat'* can only refer to the 'native country', never to the 'native places'; but they share a number of components, and, in particular, they both imply familiarity, warmth, and a unique emotional well-being reminiscent of that associated with *Heimat*.

All these considerations lead us towards the following explication of *rodina* (as a first approximation):

rodina
(1) a country
(2) I was born in this country
(3) I am like a part of this country
(4) I couldn't be like a part of any other country
(5) when I think of this country I feel something good
(6) I think something like this when I think of this country:

(7) this country does good things for me,
(8) like a mother does good things for her children
(9) I know everything in this country
(10) I am like other people in this country
(11) when I am in this country, I feel something good
(12) I couldn't feel like this in any other country

Like *ojczyzna*, *rodina* refers to the country of one's birth. Like *ojczyzna*, it implicitly likens the country to a mother, and it implies a unique emotional bond. Unlike *ojczyzna*, however, and unlike *Vaterland*, *rodina* does not embody a moral imperative. Admittedly, phrases such as *rodina zovët*, '*rodina* is calling', have often been used in Russian public discourse (especially in Soviet propaganda)[5], but the imperative to serve, to defend or to die for, has not become embodied in the very meaning of the word *rodina*. As mentioned earlier, an imperative of this kind has become embodied in the (modern) meaning of the less common word *otečestvo* (as in *velikaja otečestvennaja vojna*, 'the great patriotic war, which everyone has to take part in'), but not in that of *rodina*.

For this reason, I suggest, *rodina* can be used much more widely than *otecestvo*; and also, more widely than either *ojczyzna* or *Vaterland*. For example, one can readily use it in Russian phrases such as *vernut'sja na rodinu* 'to return to one's *rodina*', or *pobyvat' na rodine*, 'to spend some time in one's rodina' (both listed, for example, in the Russian phraseological dictionary edited by Denisov & Morkovkin 1978). But one could hardly use *ojczyzna* or *Vaterland* (not to mention *otečestvo*) in such phrases, at least not in everyday usage. It is true, poetry does furnish some examples of such phrases, as in Słowacki's line "... Bo kiedy Zośka do ojczyzny wróci ..." ('because when you, Zośka, return to the *ojczyzna* ...'); but examples of this kind are poetic (and archaic) exceptions.

Ojczyzna and *Vaterland* do not refer to real countries with some additional emotive components; rather, they refer, in their different ways, to certain ideals, and to certain moral obligations (with the stress on something like obedience in *Vaterland* and on something like sacrifice in *ojczyzna*). This is the main reason, I suggest, why casual references to a stay in one's *Vaterland* or *ojczyzna* sound either incongruous or ironic, whereas similar references to *rodina* are fully acceptable.

The "obligation-free" character of *rodina* gives a specific tone to the "mother-image" associated with this word. If *Vaterland* evokes the image of a stern father who must be not only loved but also obeyed (by his grown-up sons, "Vaterlands Söhne"), and if *ojczyzna* evokes the image of a beloved mother, who has suffered and for whom her (grown-up) children (not necessarily sons) must be willing to make sacrifices, *rodina* evokes an image of a loving mother who does good things for her (small) children and who doesn't expect anything in return. She is a warm and indulgent mother figure, associated, so to speak, with milk rather than blood (recall the quote from Kasprowicz); and with *svoboda* (a Russian key word usually translated as 'freedom', but in fact implying a lack of all restraints), rather than with obligations. My *rodina* is a country where I can feel good (as one can feel good in one's mother's arms), rather than constrained or called upon to do something. (As mentioned earlier, there is a clear contrast in this respect between the central Russian concept of *rodina* and the more marginal concept of *otečestvo).*

As I have argued elsewhere (cf. Wierzbicka, In press), the Polish word *wolność* is strongly associated with a struggle for national independence; whereas the Russian word *svoboda* is associated with a yearning for the absence of all restraints and has a slightly anarchic ring to it. The semantic differences between *ojczyzna* and *rodina* are consistent with those between *wolność* and *svoboda*. On the other hand, the semantics of *Vaterland* is consistent with the German national ethos reflected, in a small way, in the characteristic German tautology *ein Befehl ist ein Befehl*, 'an order is an order', which, not surprisingly, has no counterpart in either Polish or Russian.

Another reason why *rodina* can be readily used in phrases such as "return to ..." or "spend some time in ..." whereas *Vaterland* and *ojczyzna* can't, is that the latter two words both refer to a nation, as well as to a country, whereas *rodina* does not seem to do so. Despite the huge differences in the German and Polish historical experience, and in the nature of German and Polish nationalisms, one could say that both *Vaterland* and *ojczyzna* are banner words of nationalism, *Vaterland* of the German nationalism, and *ojczyzna* of the Polish nationalism. But *rodina* has not been, historically, a banner word of Russian nationalism.

In some ways, then, *rodina* is more similar to *Heimat* than it is to either *Vaterland* or *ojczyzna*. It is, one might say, descriptive and sentimental; it is focussed more on biography and geography than on history or politics; and it embodies sentiment rather than pathos or appeal. It implies a love based on familiarity and "belonging", without an associated moral imperative.

Unlike *Heimat*, however, *rodina* (in its main meaning) refers to the country as a whole, and not just to one's own "native places"; it does not, therefore, imply any "local patriotism", as *Heimat* does, and it doesn't celebrate political or cultural diversity. It implies an emotional identification with either Russia or "the Russian empire" (the country of the Russian language); and perhaps even reflects a pride in the vastness of the native country. The phrase from the Soviet national anthem *neob"jatnoj rodiny svoej* 'one's vast, boundless *rodina*' does seem to ring true in this respect, despite the false, propaganda-based tone of the words as a whole.

Trying to pinpoint the differences between the Russian concept of *rodina* and the Polish concept of *ojczyzna*, it is instructive to compare the collocations of the Russian adjective *rodnoj*, cognate with (and synchronically related to) *rodina*, with those of the Polish adjective *ojczysty*, cognate with (and synchronically related to) *ojczyzna*:

English	*Russian*	*Polish*
native language	rodnoj jazyk	język ojczysty
native land	rodnaja strana	kraj ojczysty
native "earth"	rodnaja zemlja	ziemia ojczysta
one's own mother	rodnaja mat'	* matka ojczysta
history of one's country	* rodnaja istorija	dzieje ojczyste

(In older Polish usage, one could also speak of *obyczaje ojczyste* and *prawa ojczyste*, customs and laws characteristic of one's native country, whereas similar collocations including the Russian word *rodnoj* are unthinkable).

Differences of this kind support the idea that *rodina* implies an emotional identification with one's native country in terms of what is experientially given, that is, the land and the language, with no reference to history, whereas *ojczyzna* implies also a strong sense of identification with one's country's history and traditions.

The fact that in Russian the same adjective *rodnoj* can be combined with the words for land, language and mother, is consistent with the impression that *rodina* (the land where Russian language is spoken) is felt to be very much like a mother. In Polish, the emotionally-charged adjective *ojczysty*, derived from *ojczyzna*, cannot be combined with any kinship terms, and as mentioned earlier its orientation is clearly national, not personal.

These differences in collocations suggest that although both *rodina* and *ojczyzna* are somehow linked in the speakers' consciousness (or subconsciousness) with the image of a mother, in the case of *rodina* this link is more direct. *Rodina* is like a mother in an emotional sense, as something or someone in whose arms one can take refuge (no matter what life's sufferings may be); but *ojczyzna* is like a mother in a more axiological sense, someone/something of infinite value, to whom one owes one's national identity and for whom one should be ready to make sacrifices.

5. Conclusion

Every culture, every society, has its key words. Some are obviously unique, so much so that they are commonly quoted in the original: for example, *kolxoz, gulag*, *kibutz*, or *kamikaze*. Others, however, which are in fact bound to a particular culture and society, appear to have counterparts in other languages. And thus, dictionaries and translators readily equate *Vaterland, ojczyzna*, and *rodina*. Matching words which are superficially similar but in fact profoundly different, is a procedure which may seem at times unavoidable, but is nonetheless deeply misleading. In-depth cross-cultural studies can help to reveal the true individuality of a culture and society's concepts. The natural semantic metalanguage, based on universal semantic primitives, provides the necessary conceptual tools, which make it possible to describe and compare concepts across cultures in a rigorous and, I hope, truly illuminating manner.

Notes

1. The phrasing of component (d): 'when I was a child, I was like a part of these places' may be objected to, as somewhat bizarre: why not say simply that I "belonged" to that place? But "belong", though more idiomatic in English, is not a lexical universal, so it cannot be used for interpreting the notion of *Heimat* for cultural outsiders.
2. As an illustration, consider for example the following quote:

> Gestern abend traf ich Herrn R. [...] Und ich fragte Herrn R., der aus Wien war, und seit bald dreißig Jahren in New York lebte, und jetzt auf dem Wege in die DDR für einen Abend in Frankfurt Station machte, wie das denn bei ihm sei - mit dem Vaterland? Sei er nun Amerikaner? Sei er Österreicher? Oder fühle er sich vielleicht gar als Israeli? Man könne doch schließlich das Vaterland nicht einfach so wechseln - sagt man bei uns. Das feine, ironische Lächeln

> erstarb um seinen Mund, als ich das mit dem Vaterland fragte. Er richtete sich streng auf, legte die Hände flach auf den Tisch und sagte: "Was heißt denn Vaterland, lieber Freund? Bei mir war das so: Die sagten in Österreich eines Tages zu mir, daß ich kein Mensch sei, sondern irgend etwas darunter: ein Untermensch oder ein Blutsauger oder auch eine Wanze - das war 1938. Da bin ich aus diesem Lande gegangen. "Na und?" frage ich, "reicht das denn, um Amerikaner zu werden?" - "Ja", sagte er, "das reicht, es reicht vollkommen, das ist überhaupt das einzig Entscheidende. In New York nahmen sie mich auf, und die New Yorker sagten zu mir, das mit der Wanze sei falsch, ich sei ein Mensch. Sie ließen mich Mensch sein. Sehen Sie, dort ist mein Vaterland." (Krüger 1969:100).
>
> 'Last night I met Mister R. [...] And I asked Mister R., who was from Vienna, and had been living for nearly thirty years in New York, and now stopped in Frankfurt for the evening on his way to the GDR; what was the fatherland for him? Was he an American? Was he an Austrian? Or perhaps he even felt himself to be an Israeli? After all, one couldn't simply change the fatherland - as we say. (...) The fine, ironic smile faded when I asked about the fatherland. He sat up rigorously, placed his hands flatly on the table, and said: "What does fatherland mean, my friend? It was like this for me: One day they told me in Austria, that I was no longer a human being, but something else below that: a subhuman or a blood-sucker or even a bug - that was around 1938. So I left this country. - "So?" I asked, "is that enough to become American?" -"Yes", he said, "that is enough, it is completely sufficient, it is in fact the only deciding factor. They accepted me in New York, and the New Yorkers told me, the stuff about the bug was wrong, I was really a human being. They let me be a human being. So you see, that is where my fatherland is." '

3. Ulrike Mosel (personal communication) has suggested that the last line of this explication should read not 'I think that all these people think the same' but 'I think that all these people must think the same', pointing out to the existence of "Vaterlandsverräter", 'betrayers of the Vaterland'. This is an interesting suggestion, deserving further consideration; I wonder, however, whether a person who "doesn't think the same" is still considered 'a part of the same thing'. Isn't national unity and universal acceptance of the country's supreme right to dictate to the individual presupposed by the concept of 'Vaterland'? Isn't a "Vaterlandsverräter" seen as someone who breaks a certain expectation, and not only a certain rule?

   On the other hand, one must agree with Mosel's implied point that the ideologists of 'Vaterland' have often sought to impose the subordination of the individual to the state as a 'must'.

4. To see the enduring importance of the word *Vaterland* in public discourse in Germany consider, for example, the following passage from a recent magazine article (*Der Spiegel Dokument* 2/94:5):

> Ein schwieriges *Vaterland*: dabei dachte man bis 1989 an historisch teilweise weit zurückliegende deutsche Ungereimtheiten wie die Spannung zwischen vielen Staaten in einem deutschen *Vaterland*, die verspätete Nation unter Weitergeltung vordemokratischer Strukturen, die patriotischen Turbulenzen der Weimarer Republik, die blutige Diskreditierung des Begriffs *Vaterland* durch Hitler, und nach dem Krieg neue Schwierigkeiten, nicht nur mit dem Verhältnis von Staat und Nation. Unterschiedliche politische Kulturen machen es schwer, umstandslos vom deutschen *Vaterland* zu sprechen. (italics mine, A. W.)
> 'A difficult *Vaterland*: until 1989 this made one think about the abnormalities of the German past (some stretching far back in history), such as the tension between many states in one German *Vaterland*, a belatedly emergent nation still under the influence of pre-democratic structures, the patriotic turbulences of the Weimar republic, the blood-soaked discrediting of the concept *Vaterland* under Hitler, and after the war, new difficulties, and not only those involving the relationship between the state and the nation. Different political cultures make it difficult to speak of a German *Vaterland* in general.'

5. In the Soviet era, the word *rodina* (referring to the country as a whole) was frequently a subject of political manipulation, as was *ojczyzna* in "People's Poland" and as *Vaterland* was in the "German Democratic Republic", and earlier, in Nazi Germany. For this reason, today many Russians avoid using the word *rodina* just as many Poles avoid the word *ojczyzna*, and many Germans, the word *Vaterland*.

References

Antipenko, L. A. & G. N. Karnaušenko
1993 Rodina glazami xar 'kovskogo studenčestva. In: Bartmiński, J. (ed.).

Applegate, C.
1990 *A Nation of Provincials. The German Idea of Heimat*. Berkeley: University of California Press.

Bartmiński, J.
1989 "Jak biegna drogi ojczyzny?" *Ethos* 5.
1993 Ojczyzny europejskie - duze i male. In: Bartmiński, J. (ed.), pp. 5-11.

Bartmiński, J. (ed.)
1993 *Pojecie ojczyzny we wspólczesnych językach europejskich*. Lublin: Instytut Europy Wschodniej.

Damborsky, J.
1993 Discussion. In: Bartmiński, J. (ed.), pp. 62-63.

Denisov, R. A. & V. V. Morkovkin
1978 *Učebnyi slovar' sočetaemosti slov russkogo jazyka*. Moscow: Russkij Jazyk.

Der Spiegel Dokument 1992/4.

Doroszewski, W.
1958-69 SJP. *Slownik jezyka polskiego*. 11 vols. Warszawa: PWN.

Drosdowski, G. (ed.)
1980 *Duden. Das große Wörterbuch der deutschen Sprache*. 6 vols. Mannheim: Dudenverlag.
Fetscher, I.
1992 Heimatliebe - Brauch und Mißbrauch eines Begriffs. In: Görner, R. (ed.)
Fullerborn, U.
1992 "... die sich gebar im Verlust". Heimat in Rilkes Dichtung. In: Görner, R. (ed.)
Goddard, C. & A. Wierzbicka (eds.)
1994 *Semantic and Lexical Universals: Theory and Emperical Findings*. Amsterdam: Benjamins.
Görner, R. (ed.)
1992 *Heimat im Wort: die Problematik eines Begriffs im 19. und 20. Jahrhundert*. München: Iudicium.
Greverus, I.-M.
1972 *Der Territoriale Mensch. Ein literaturanthropologischer Versuch zum Heimatphänomen*. Frankfurt am Main: Athenäum.
Grimm, J.
1887 *Deutsches Wörterbuch*. Leipzig: Hirzel.
Harzmann, F.
1930 *Burschenschaftliche Dichtung von der Frühzeit bis auf unsere Tage. Eine Auslese.* Heidelberg: Carl Winters Universitätsbuchhandlung.
Ihlenfeld, K.
1966 *"Verbotene Frucht*/Gedanken zum Vaterlandsproblem. *Eckart Jahrbuch* 1966/67. Witten/Berlin: Eckart Verlag.
Janion, M. (ed.)
1979 *Reduta: romantyczna poezja niepodległościowa*. Kraków: Wydawnictwo Literackie.
Kleine-Brockhoff, T., K. Kruse & M. Sontheimer
1989 "Die Mauer". *Die Zeit*, 24th November 1989, no. 47:9.
Klemperer, V.
1946 *Die unbewältigte Sprache*. Darmstadt: Melzer.
Kłoskowska, A.
1993 "Kraj, do którego się wraca". Czym jest ojczyzna dla lubelskich studentów. In: Bartminski, J. (ed.), pp. 49-56.
1991 Kultura narodowa. *Encyklopedia kultury polskiej XX wieku*. Wroclaw.
Krüger, H.
1969 *Deutsche Augenblicke*. München: Piper & Co.
Libelt, K.
1844 [1967] *O miłości ojczyzny*. Ed. by A. Walicki. Warszawa: PWN.
Popiełuszko, J.
1992 *Kazania 1982 - 1984*. Warszawa: Wydawnictwo Archidiecezji Warszawskiej.
Potapov, V.
1993 "The road to the spiritual regeneration of Russia". *Russkaja Mysl'* 398:7.
Skorupka, S.
1974 *Slownik frazeologiczny jezyka polskiego*. Warszawa: Wiedza Powszechna.
Storck, J. W.
1992 "Meine Herkunft ist mein Schicksal." Heimat als Problem beim "zweisprachigen Grenzvogel" René Schickele. In: Görner, R. (ed.).
Taborska, H.
1993 Discussion. In: Bartmiński, J. (ed.), pp. 57-58.

Volkov, V.
1993 Interview. *Russkaja Mysl'* 1993/6 Nr. 398.

Wahrig, G., H. Krämer & H. Zimmerman (eds.)
1981 *Brockhaus' Wahrig Deutsches Wörterbuch.* 6 vols. Wiesbaden: Brockhaus.

Weisgerber, L.
1959 *Die geschichtliche Kraft der deutschen Sprache.* Düsseldorf: Pädagogischer Verlag Schwann.

Wierzbicka, A.
1991a *Cross-cultural Pragmatics: The Semantics of Human Interaction.* Berlin: Mouton de Gruyter.
1991b "Japanese key words and core cultural values". *Language in Society* 20:333-85.
1992 *Semantics, Culture, and Cognition.* New York: Oxford University Press.
In press *Freedom - libertas - svoboda - wolność*: Universal human ideals or culture-specific lexical items? In: Taylor, J. R. & R. R. MacLaury (eds.). *Language and the Construal of the World: Approaches to Cognition in Linguistics and Anthropology.* Berlin: Mouton de Gruyter.

Zasorina, L. N. (ed.).
1977 Častotnyj slovar' russkogo jazyka. Moscow: Russkij Jazyk.

On illocutions and illocutionary verbs: A cognitive perspective

Johan Vanparys

0. Introduction

Present-day semantics owes a large part of its heritage to structuralism and logical positivism (cf. Geeraerts 1988, 1992). These paradigms involved a number of commitments that pervaded scientific thinking about language and meaning for a long time and, in fact, still do to some extent. One of these commitments was a preoccupation with truth, i.e. the belief that the only interesting aspect of linguistic meaning is the expression of scientifically verifiable statements. On this account, a semantic description of a sentence consists in specifying the conditions under which it is true and an analysis of a lexical item consists in specifying its contribution to these conditions. Another commitment that has been quite pervasive is the view of language as a self-contained, autonomous system that does not require reference to its function or human cognition for an insightful description. The ramifications of these conceptions have turned out to be quite influential. As a consequence of its scientific rigour, logical positivism rejects natural language as a tool for scientific purposes, owing to its vagueness and ambiguity, and proposes instead artificial constructs such as formal logic, set theory, and mathematics. As regards the structure of categories, the model that now qualifies as the *classical* view was the predominant one. Finally, if one accepts the autonomy of language, the structure of the lexicon cannot be motivated, since extra-linguistic factors are ruled out.

The research reported on here stems from a double concern. First, the choice of the subject is inspired by the fact that illocutionary force qualifies as an integrative aspect of meaning. Second, my intellectual commitment to cognitive linguistics has led to the conviction that the way illocutions are dealt with in illocutionary theory is unsatisfactory in many respects. Let me briefly expound on this conflict.

Illocutionary theory has its roots in J. L. Austin's observation that explicit performatives are not amenable to a truth-functional analysis, since they do not state a true or false proposition. Rather, they express a proposition with a particular illocutionary force. This initial insight led to the observation that all utterances, whether explicitly performative or not, possess an illocutionary force. Therefore, it proved necessary to construct a theory of illocutionary meaning as a complement to existing theories of propositional meaning. The major contribution to such a theory has come from J. R. Searle, who has defined illocutions (in terms of felicity conditions, Searle 1969), reduced them to five basic categories (Searle 1979: Chapter 1), described indirectness (Searle 1979: Chapter 2), and sketched the role of illocutions in conversation (Searle 1992). In recent years, D. Vanderveken has developed a coherent formalization, illocutionary logic (Searle & Vanderveken [henceforward: S & V] 1985; Vanderveken 1990a, 1990b).

This article stems from my own research on the categorization of illocutions and focusses on the relationship between illocutions and the lexicon (illocutionary verbs). The categorization of illocutions constitutes the cornerstone of illocutionary logic, since all illocutions are derived from five primitives. It is my contention, however, that the categorization adhered to by Searle and Vanderveken, as well as the thirty-or-so alternatives proposed by other scholars, goes wrong in many respects. This claim has been substantiated in Vanparys (1993, 1994).

The reason for this failure, I believe, is that illocutionary logic qualifies in large part as an objectivist theory (in contrast with the subjectivism advocated by cognitive semantics) that views language as an autonomous system. One symptom of this objectivist orientation is the fact that the theory still adheres to the classical model of categorization, in spite of the overwhelming body of evidence in favour of protoype semantics. If language is viewed as a cognitive phenomenon rather than a self-contained entity, however, research results from cognitive psychology become relevant. Another symptom is the development of formal illocutionary logic, an endeavour to establish a "unification of speech act theory and of classical truth conditional semantics" (Vanderveken 1990:2). Without denying *that* formalization qualifies as a valid objective of scientific thinking, I disagree with the *how* and the *why* of illocutionary logic. Regarding the former aspect, it is clear that the formal apparatus does not incorporate any insights from prototype semantics and that it constitutes a self-contained system that isolates illocutionary force from the rest of language and human cognition.

Regarding the *why* of illocutionary logic, its *raison d'être*, I regret to see that illocutionary theory took a promising start within ordinary language philosophy but in the end returned to the principles of logical positivism. The theory owes its existence to Austin's "discovery" and subsequent scrutiny of performative verbs. The underlying motivation, shared with present-day cognitive psychology and semantics, was that natural language, including its lexicon, provides a useful entry to our "conceptual geography". On this account, metalinguistic terms such as illocutionary verbs have special relevance for linguists, since they embody the language user's conceptualization of language. Searle and Vanderveken, in contrast, consider illocutionary verbs treacherous guides to illocutions, for the lexicon is full of ambiguities and "defects" (Vanderveken 1990a:36) which make them "misleading as regards logical form" (Vanderveken 1990a:37). While Austin, together with other ordinary language philosophers considered the lexicon a useful resource for conceptual analysis, Searle and Vanderveken take the logical-positivist point of view, according to which the underlying reality to be discovered and described is obscured by natural language. Therefore, they say, we need "an ideal logically perfect unambiguous language" (Vanderveken 1990a:36), i.e. illocutionary logic.

In this controversy, I am more sympathetic to the original Austinian position. I cannot believe that the lexicon is arbitrarily structured, thus obscuring an underlying reality. My ideas on this issue were first shaped by J. Verschueren (1985). Later on, I found them confirmed by M. Johnson (1987), G. Lakoff (1987) and many other scholars. The relationship between illocutions and the vocabulary we use to talk about them will be elaborated on in the second section, where it will be argued that the semantics of illocutionary verbs *is* relevant to a proper understanding of illocutions and their categorization.

1. The objectivist orientation of illocutionary theory

In Vanparys (1993: Chapter 1, 1994), illocutionary theory has been demonstrated to be inadequate regarding its taxonomic goal and a variety of other issues. The question naturally arises why this is the case. Why does the theory fail to come up with a satisfactory taxonomy? How can the sense/force tension be accounted for? What is wrong with illocutionary theory's account of indirectness? Is the theory's disregard for perlocutions and illocutionary sequences justifiable? Crucial issues that need to be addressed are the alleged universality of illocutions and the illocution/illocutionary-verb relationship. In order to find the reasons for the theory's inadequacy, it will be necessary to uncover its implicit assumptions. I shall argue in the following paragraphs that illocutionary theory is embedded in a philosophical paradigm, referred to as *objectivism* by Lakoff and Johnson (Johnson 1987, Lakoff 1982, 1986, 1987, Lakoff & Johnson 1980), that is fundamentally misguided. An alternative will be sought in a subjectivist paradigm: cognitive semantics.

The objectivist paradigm, as described by Lakoff and Johnson, has pervaded mainstream Western thinking since the ancient Greeks and still continues to do so (see Johnson 1987:21-35 for a survey). It pertains to the nature of the world (metaphysics), human cognition (epistemology), and language. The basic tenets of objectivism can be summarized in four related doctrines:

Doctrine 1 The world consists of entities with fixed properties and relations among them. This structure is independent of human understanding. Human cognition and language reflect this objectivist world.

Doctrine 2 The entities in the world are divided up into natural kinds. Such categories are sets, determined by the essential properties shared by their members, which specify necessary and sufficient conditions on membership. Cognitive and linguistic categories reflect these categorization principles: they are definable in terms of necessary and sufficient conditions involving essential properties.

Doctrine 3 Properties of entities in the world, the mind, and language are either complex or primitive.

Doctrine 4 There are logical relations holding objectively among the entities and categories in the world. Accurate human reasoning and natural language match objectivist logic.

(abridged from Lakoff 1986)

On the objectivist account of metaphysics, reality is structured in a way that is independent of human understanding. The world is the way it is. It is made up of entities, their properties and relations holding among them. It can be given a unique correct and complete description in set-theoretical terms: entities, sets of entities (defined by the shared properties of the members), and sets of n-tuples (corresponding to relations holding of entities). The *first doctrine* makes a double claim: the world is structured in some way and this structure is objective, i.e. independent of human cognition. In objectivist epistemology, the mind functions merely as a mirror of nature: conceptual categories are symbolic representations of categories in the real world (or some possible world). Knowledge consists in correctly conceptualizing and categorizing things in the world and grasping the objectively given connections among those things and those categories. Existence and fact (metaphysics) are independent of belief, knowledge, perception, and every other human cognitive capacity (epistemology). The world is the way it is, regardless of any way people understand it. Consequently, objectivism posits the existence of a unique correct categorization of things that is independent of human perception or cognition - what might be called a God's eye view. Objectivist epistemology supports objectivist theories of language. (See Johnson 1987:xx-xxv for a survey.) In objectivist semantics, linguistic expressions get their meaning only via their capacity to correspond to the world; i.e. they are capable of referring correctly or of being true or false. Objectivist meaning is based uniquely on reference and truth.

The metaphysical part of the *second doctrine* specifies how reality is structured. It involves a commitment to three assumptions. First, it posits the existence of objective categories. That is, the entities in the world form objectively existing categories based on their shared objective properties.

Second, the doctrine relies on what is now commonly known as the classical theory of categorization, in which categories are definable in terms of necessary and sufficient conditions, i.e. properties shared by all members of the category and only them. The traditional view of categorization has become institutionalized in set theory: the objectivist world consists of entities, their properties and relations holding among them; set-theoretical models consist of entities, sets of entities (defined by shared properties of members), and sets of n-tuples (corresponding to relations among entities). On the objectivist account,

> given any property (or collection of properties), there exists a category in the world consisting of the entities that have that property. Similarly, given an n-place relation, there is a category of n-tuples of entities standing in that relation. Since categories are understood as sets, it follows that the world (which is taken to consist of entities, properties, and relations) can be accurately modeled by set-theoretical models. (Lakoff 1987:159)

Therefore, objectivism does not merely assume that there is a reality of some sort; it is much more specific:

> It additionally assumes that reality is correctly and completely structured in a way that can be modeled by set-theoretical models [...]. On the objectivist view, reality comes with a unique, correct, complete structure in terms of entities, properties, and relations. This structure exists, independent of any human understanding. (Lakoff 1987:159)

Since things in the world are definable in terms of necessary and sufficient conditions specifying essential properties of natural kinds and since the mind reflects the world, conceptual categories, too, are assumed to obey the dictates of classical categorization. Given the distinction between essential and accidental properties, one can, moreover, distinguish between definitional and encyclopedic knowledge. It follows that for each category in the world, there is one correct definition based on essential properties.

The third assumption involves a commitment to essentialism: among the properties a thing has, some are essential, others are accidental. Essential properties make the thing what it is; without them it would not be that kind of thing. Accidental properties are those characteristics a thing just happens to have; they do not capture its essence. Natural kinds, then, are classical categories consisting of entities that share essential properties. Stock examples are things found in nature, such as animals, plants, or minerals. Language is believed to fit this doctrine in all its aspects: it is claimed to work only with classical categories based on necessary and sufficient conditions involving essential features.

The *third doctrine* introduces another division concerning properties: some properties are made up of logical combinations of other properties, these are complex; those which have no internal structure are primitive (or atomic). All categories in the world, the mind, and language are either primitives or logical combinations of primitives.

Finally, the *fourth doctrine* postulates the existence in the world of mind-free logical relations among categories, such as *inclusion* and *exclusion*. Human reason is accurate when it matches objectivist logic, i.e. when the symbols used in thought correctly correspond to entities and categories in the world and when the mind reproduces the logical relations that exist objectively among the entities in the world. There are objectivist logical principles at work in language, as well. For example, the logical relation of identity surfaces as synonymy in linguistic semantics, exclusion as antonymy, and inclusion as homonymy. In sum, the objectivist world

> is extremely well-behaved. It is made up of discrete entities with discrete logical combinations of atomic properties and relations holding among these entities. Some properties are essential; others are accidental. Properties define categories, and categories defined by essential properties correspond to the kinds of things that there are. And the existence of classical categories provides logical relations that hold objectively in the world. (Lakoff 1987:162)

On the objectivist account, human cognition and language merely reflect the world as described above. Objectivist metaphysics, epistemology, and semantics have been shown to be inadequate by Lakoff and Johnson. There is no point in repeating their arguments here. Rather, I wish to demonstrate that illocutionary theory in general and its taxonomic goal in particular are objectivist in orientation, which accounts for its failure to set up an adequate taxonomy and the other deficiencies listed above. (Johnson (1987:178ff) demonstrates the objectivist orientation of Searle's theory of meaning with respect to *Intentionality* (Searle 1983). I shall not reiterate Johnson's points. My main concern is with mainstream speech-act theory, where additional objectivist elements can be found, so that my account complements Johnson's.)

Clearly, the traditional notion of *taxonomy*, as sketched in Vanparys (1993 Chapter 1, 1994), is a typical emanation of objectivism. It represents the classical theory of categorization in all its facets: necessary and sufficient conditions give rise to mutually exclusive categories without varying degrees of membership and with clear boundaries. Classical taxonomies operate with the logical, or set-theoretical notions inclusion and exclusion: subordinate classes (subsets) are included in superordinate classes, and sister categories exclude each other. In taxonomies, there is also a strong commitment to essentialism (cf. Slaughter 1982:28-29). Not just any property constitutes a valid classification criterion. Taxonomies must be based on essential characteristics that divide the world into natural kinds. Essentialism also leads to the belief that there is one unique correct taxonomy of reality. The whole tradition of attempts to construct illocutionary taxonomies can be viewed as an attempt in this direction.

Extensive research in philosophy, psychology, anthropology, and linguistics, pioneered by E. Rosch (e.g. Rosch 1977, 1978, Mervis & Rosch 1981), has undermined the viability of the classical conception of categorization, replacing it with an alternative view commonly referred to as *the prototype model* (see Corrigan *et al.* eds. 1989, Geeraerts 1985, Lakoff 1987, Smith & Medin 1981, and Taylor 1989 for comprehensive surveys.) In this model, semantic categories take the shape of clusters of interrelated senses, ranging with varying degrees of membership from one or more prototypical centres towards the periphery, where the boundaries tend to be fuzzy and overlap with those of neighbouring categories. Categories are held together, not by a checklist of necessary and sufficient conditions, but by family resemblances:

> A family resemblance relationship consists of a set of items of the form AB, BC, CD, DE. That is, each item has at least one, and probably several, elements in common with one or more other items, but no, or few, elements are common to all items" (Rosch & Mervis 1975:575).

Features may, moreover, differ in their relative weight: certain properties are more characteristic of a category than others. Regarding vertical organization, the prototype model acknowledges a basic level, where similarities between sister categories are maximal with respect to their superordinates and subordinates.

In a prototype model, the failure to construct a classical taxonomy of illocutions is predictable rather than problematic. Illocutions cannot be pigeonholed into homogeneous, neatly bounded, mutually exclusive classes. Any valid classification necessarily consists of overlapping categories with varying degrees of membership and fuzzy boundaries. In addition, indeterminacy and degrees of indirectness are normal rather than exceptional.

Granted, illocutionary theory does acknowledge the prototype model:

> One of the most important insights of recent work in the philosophy of language is that most non-technical concepts in ordinary language lack absolute strict rules. The concepts *game*, or *chair*, or *promise* do not have absolutely knockdown necessary and sufficient conditions, such that unless they are satisfied something cannot be a game or a chair or a promise, and given that they are satisfied in a given case that case must be, cannot but be, a game or a chair or a promise. But this insight into the looseness of our concepts, and its attendant jargon of "family resemblance" should not lead us into a rejection of the very enterprise of philosophical analysis; rather the conclusion to be drawn is that certain forms of analysis, especially analysis into necessary and sufficient conditions, are likely to involve (in varying degrees) idealization of the concept analyzed. In the present case, our analysis will be directed at the center of the concept of promising. I am ignoring marginal, fringe, and partially defective promises. This approach has the consequence that counter-examples can be produced [...] which do not fit our analysis. [...] Their existence does not 'refute' the analysis, rather they require an explanation of why and how they depart from the paradigm case of promise making. (Searle 1969:55)

Here I have two objections. First, an approach in terms of necessary and sufficient conditions is at odds with family-resemblance structure. Second, as Searle admits, the theory focuses on typical cases, ignoring the periphery. The result is, of course, a highly incomplete account. The strength of the prototype model lies exactly in its ability to relate marginal members of a category to its prototypical centre(s) via a chain of intermediate cases. In failing to do so, illocutionary theory commits the same sin as the classical model. In sum, it looks as if illocutionary theory pays some lip service to the prototype view in order to immunize itself against counterexamples, while refusing to accept the model's consequences.

The objectivist orientation of illocutionary theory also manifests itself in areas outside the classification issue. The classical conception of categorization permeates the theory at all levels. The seven components in terms of which illocutions are defined, are claimed to constitute a set of necessary and sufficient conditions (S & V 1985:21). They have been shown, however, to be neither necessary nor sufficient and they render illocutionary theory incapable of coping with indeterminacy. Another area where illocutionary theory's commitment to the classical view on categorization leads to erroneous conclusions is indirectness. On illocutionary theory's account of indirect illocutions (Searle 1979: Chapter 2), indirectness is an either/or matter, although psycholinguistic research (e.g. Clark & Schunk 1980, Gibbs 1983) reveals a continuum with varying degrees of indirectness.

The theory's embracement of the classical theory of categorization is accompanied by a commitment to *essentialism*. Illocutions are regarded as "natural kinds of language use", just as plants and animals are "natural biological kinds" (S & V 1985:179). The seven components of illocutions are regarded as essential properties, all other dimensions on which illocutions vary being held to be accidental. Among the essential characteristics, illocutionary point is singled out as carrying special prominence; in Searle (1969), it was even specified in a so-called "essential rule". Thus, rather than handling the binary essential/accidental distinction, illocutionary theory operates with a more complex notion of essentialism, where one essential feature receives a special status, but this does not affect its commitment to the doctrine. However, in Vanparys (1993, 1994) the primacy of illocutionary point and the possibility of characterizing illocutions in terms of a finite set of features have been seriously challenged.

The prototype model suggests a radically different view on essentialism. Though it does not deny the existence of natural kinds, it forces us to look at them from a different angle. The traditional conception in terms of necessary and sufficient conditions coupled with a bifurcation between essential and accidental characteristics needs to be replaced by an account based on prototypes, family resemblances, and features with different weights. In a prototype model, the controversy regarding the essence of illocutions noted in Vanparys (1993: Chapter 1) seems pointless. A variety of criteria has been proposed, resulting in a host of classifications. Prototype theory indicates, however, that it is pointless to look for the single feature or set of features capturing the essence of illocutions.

It is my belief, furthermore, that the theory's embracement of essentialism is also the source of its failure to deal with perlocutions, sequencing phenomena, and the sense/force relation. Illocutions as tokens are always accompanied by perlocutionary intents and usually occur in a sequence. Illocutionary theory, being concerned with natural kinds, i.e. illocutionary types, ignores these. Perlocutionary intents and discourse function are characteristics of illocutionary tokens that are accidental to types. For instance, STATEMENTS that P are not always intended to make H believe that P. In illocutionary theory, such observations are taken as reasons for disregarding perlocutionary intents altogether. But such an essentialist stance ignores the fact that in many cases STATEMENTS do aim at convincing H that P. Similar correlations exist between illocutionary force and discourse function. Although not every answer is a STATEMENT, most of them are. That is, typical QUESTIONS qualify as REQUESTS for information. The lack of a full correspondence forces an essentialist framework to disregard any partial correspondence, which impoverishes its descriptive power. The sense/force problem, too, derives from the theory's commitment to essentialism. Illocutionary theory describes illocutions without bothering about the way they are realized in practice. The form in which they appear is taken to be an accidental characteristic that can be dispensed with.

As Slaughter (1982: Chapter 2) observes, essentialism is often accompanied by *decontextualization*, i.e. the process of isolating the phenomenon under consideration from its environment and treating it as a self-contained entity. Illocutionary theory is a case in point: factors such as an illocution's formal realization, its position in a sequence, and the perlocutionary intents associated with it are placed outside the scope of analysis. The theory's essentialist orientation also comes to the fore in its recent formalization proposals (S & V 1985, Vanderveken 1985, 1990b). Formalization is a symptom of essentialism par excellence: formulas are intended to capture the essential properties of the object under study, filtering out all accidental characteristics.

Clearly, illocutionary theory is committed to the doctrine of *atomism*, which regards entities as complexes of primitive features that cannot themselves be reduced to combinations of features. Illocutions are defined as septuples of features, each of which constitutes an unanalyzed primitive. The inadequacy of such an approach is most evident in the case of the parameter "psychological state": notions such as belief, desire, intention, pleasure, regret etc. can hardly be said to be psychological primitives, as the analysis by D'Andrade & Wish (1985) reveals. Numerous specifications in the preparatory conditions of illocutions are not primitive either. A case in point is authority, which has been diagnosed as being a complex rather than monolithical phenomenon (Verschueren 1985:180ff).

Illocutionary theory deserves due credit for its role in the liberation of semantics from its objectivist preoccupation with *truth conditions*. The theory owes its existence to Austin's observation that many utterances are not amenable to a truth-functional analysis and constitutes an attempt to provide a descriptive framework that can handle constatives and (explicit and primary) performatives alike. However, what the theory chases away through the front-door slips in again through the back-door. The notion *truth* is simply replaced by fit between the words and the world, which can have different directions. For instance, assertives are successful when the state of affairs represented by the propositional content matches the world, commissives and directives succeed when S, respectively H, makes the proposition true by carrying out the future action represented by the propositional content (cf. S & V 1985:92-98). Thus, meaning in illocutionary theory is still largely reduced to matters of words-to-world correspondence (cf. Johnson 1987:xxii-xxiii).

In the foregoing paragraphs I have demonstrated the objectivist orientation of illocutionary theory. When coupled with Lakoff's and Johnson's arguments against the objectivist paradigm, this account may be said to refute the theory's basic assumptions. In order to find an alternative, I shall turn to a subjectivist conception of meaning, which can be found in cognitive linguistics. Some of its basic tenets have been formulated as follows:

> Semantic structure is nothing more than conceptualization structured in accordance with established patterns of linguistic convention; semantic description therefore requires substantive hypotheses regarding the internal structure of entities such as thoughts and concepts. Meaning is not determined in any direct way by objective reality - instead it is a matter of how we construe or structure a situation in our cognitive representation of it. (Langacker 1985:110-111)

In equating meaning with conceptualization, cognitive semantics clashes with predominant objectivist theories of the structuralist brand (e.g. Kempson 1977:15-20, Lyons 1977:113). In appealing to "hypotheses regarding the internal structure of [concepts]", it is strongly committed to the prototype model. In stating that meaning is not uniquely determined by objective reality, it rejects the God's eye view propagated by objectivism. Cognitive semantics holds, moreover, that meaning is not reducible to truth conditions. The capacity of words to refer to the world (or of trying to get the world to match the words) is only one aspect of meaning. Atomism and the possibility of describing meaning in logical or set-theoretical terms are equally discarded.

2. The empirical-conceptual approach to verbal communication

A subjectivist view of verbal communication can be found in the *empirical-conceptual approach* initiated by Verschueren (1980, 1981, 1985, 1988). The reader is referred to his work (esp. 1985: Chapter 1) for a substantive justification; in the paragraphs below I shall give only a concise sketch of its foundations. The aim of the empirical-conceptual approach is to examine the way in which verbal communication is conceptualized by the persons engaged in it. As such, it is compatible with the general programme of cognitive linguistics, where meaning is equated with conceptualization. Additional substantiation comes from social studies which point to the unity of practice and concept:

> Social action is by definition meaningful in the sense that the participants in the action perceive it in terms of a background of shared meanings. [...] Thus there is a fundamental unity between the actor's concepts and the practices they serve to conceptualize. [...] Action is always interpreted action. [...] This is because all actions have an 'understood context' (Verschueren 1985:16).

Now, aspects of the background of shared meanings, the understood context, may be hidden to an external observer. Therefore, a full understanding of social phenomena - including verbal communication - can be obtained only if we make "an attempt to penetrate the conceptual world of the participants in the action [...] to be described" (Verschueren 1985:17).

So, the aim of the empirical-conceptual approach to linguistic action is to explicate the agent's own views of what he does when he uses language. Now the question is, how can we arrive at such an understanding? Though conceptualizations do not lend themselves to direct observation, they can be studied indirectly, via language, as there is a close relationship between linguistic and conceptual structure. Various aspects of linguistic structure are relevant for this purpose, but only one will be taken into consideration in this study, namely the English lexicon. The reason for taking lexical items as a point of departure is warranted by the fact that languages tend to lexicalize those concepts that are deemed important in a particular linguistic community. Words reflect well-entrenched conceptualizations. Since illocutions are acts, the most natural items to turn to are illocutionary verbs.

It is important to emphasize that the approach advocated here is neither new nor idiosyncratic. In 1970, Osgood already wrote:

> I make the [...] assumption that in any language the words used to talk about interpersonal behaviors will be coded on the same semantic features

> as the perceived behaviors themselves. [...] This assumption [...] provides an entrée to the structure of interpersonal behavior in a culture. Appropriate analysis of the semantics of interpersonal verbs may illuminate the rules which govern the norms of interpersonal behavior in that culture. (Osgood 1970:136)

More recently, similar arguments have been adduced by Ballmer & Brennenstuhl (1984), Burkhardt (1990:108), De Raad (1985), Kay (1987), Kreckel (1981), Rosaldo (1982), Leech (1983), Rudzka-Ostyn (1990), and Wierzbicka (1985a, 1985b, 1987):

> There is likely to be a close similarity between the sorts of distinctions which are important in the analysis of speech-act verbs, and the sorts of distinctions which are important in the speech-act behaviour these verbs are used to describe. It would be perversely anti-Whorfian to suppose that [...] the verbs with which our language equips us for discussing communicative behaviour require us to draw distinctions which are not significant in the behaviour itself. (Leech 1983:198)

> I believe that one particularly fruitful way of approaching the repertoire of speech acts [...] is via their folk names [...]. This is not to say that all 'language games' [...] played in a given culture will necessarily have their own folk names. Nonetheless, those language games which do have such names are more relevant to a given culture than those which don't. (Wierzbicka 1985a:492)

The basic tenet of the empirical-conceptual approach has been conveniently summarized by Kay:

> The principal conceptual tool I will employ [...] will be that of folk theory. The term is borrowed from anthropology. In describing the system of knowledge and belief of another culture, an anthropologist speaks of that culture's folk theory of botany, the emotions, language, and so on. Anthropologists discover such folk theories by analysis of the use of words in the native language. The guiding idea is the familiar one that any natural lexicon implies a tacit, structured conceptualization of the stuff that the words of that lexicon are about. What [...] we shall be concerned with here [...] is the tacit and mostly unconscious theory of language and speech we invoke when we employ certain parts of the lexicon in English. (Kay 1987:68)

The empirical-conceptual approach derives mainly from a methodological concern. On the deductive-inductive (or, theoretical-empirical) continuum, illocutionary theory can be situated on the deductive end: "it is based on a preconceived framework of abstract and general concepts" (Verschueren 1985:14). Given the unity of practice and concept, however, it is necessary to include observable data revealing the participants' understanding of the activities they engage in. Obviously, Verschueren's position can be related to the objectivist/subjectivist opposition introduced above. Deductivity is by and large a symptom of objectivism, stemming from the belief that a God's eye view is both desirable and attainable. The empirical-conceptual approach, in contrast, is subjectively oriented, in relying on speakers' experiences. The difference between my argumentation and Verschueren's is only one of generality. The latter hinges on the unity of practice and concept in social action and is therefore restricted in applicability to such action, which includes verbal communication. The account of subjectivism and objectivism given in the previous paragraph, however, is much wider in scope, pertaining to the nature of meaning in general. In this way, the empirical-conceptual approach to linguistic action has been anchored in a more general conception of semantics.

3. On illocutions and illocutionary verbs

Ever since its inception, illocutionary theory has been beset with continuous disagreement regarding its proper object: illocutions *in abstracto* or illocutionary verbs. This debate has sometimes assumed extraordinary proportions, as in the contributions to the *Zeitschrift für Sprachwissenschaft* (Meibauer 1982, Ballmer & Brennenstuhl 1984, Strecker 1984, Dietrich 1984) following the publication of Ballmer & Brennenstuhl's (1981) *Speech Act Classification*. The issue is all too often dealt with in an either/or fashion. Advocates of a theoretical approach tend to exclude the adequacy of a verb-based account and vice versa. Not so with the empirical-conceptual approach, which advertises itself as a necessary complement and not as a substitute for deductive theories. Given the fierceness with which illocutionary-verb-based approaches have been attacked, however, I wish to go through some of the counterarguments that have been given, with a view to justify the viability of an illocutionary-verb-based analysis.

In the margin of this discussion, it is worth pointing out that Searle and other philosophers have repeatedly been "accused" of thinking of illocutions in terms of illocutionary verbs, e.g. Ballmer & Brennenstuhl (1984:252), Burkhardt (1990), Edmondson (1981a:486), Leech (1983: 176-177), Wierzbicka (1985a:493). Verschueren (1980:34-35) even argues that this is unavoidable.

The origin of the controversy can be traced back to the fact that illocutionary theory owes its existence to Austin's discovery of performative verbs. Although he abstracted from these verbs to a general theory of illocutions, his theory and its successors have never managed to liberate themselves completely from their roots. Numerous studies are based on the assumption that "the list of performative verbs will amount to the list of illocutionary forces discernible in a given language" (Vendler 1972:8), a belief that was reinforced by the performative hypothesis, which posits a performative prefix in the deep-structure of each sentence in order to account for illocutionary force in transformational grammar. Present-day illocutionary theory takes the opposite position: "the single most common mistake in speech-act theory is the confusion between features of illocutionary verbs and illocutionary acts" (Searle 1979:ix). I agree, but at the same time I wish to add that this confusion is due to a naive view of the relation between illocutions and illocutionary verbs, according to which there is a one-to-one correspondence between the two. When this view is replaced by an adequate conception of the nature of the lexicon, the counterarguments lose most of their force. They are numerous, but many are beside the point, e.g. those given by Tsui (1985:10-15). In the following discussion, I shall restrict myself to the most influential objections, namely those raised by Searle.

His first argument concerns the alleged *universality* of illocutions and the language-particularity of verbs:

> Illocutions are a part of language as opposed to particular languages. Illocutionary verbs are always part of a particular language: French, German, English, or whatnot (Searle 1979:2).

Searle's preoccupation with universality is another symptom of the objectivist commitment to a God's-eye-view. First a minor point in this connection: the quest for universals is interesting in its own right but it cannot be the only goal of linguistics. If language-specific analyses were objectionable, the greater part of linguistic studies should be discarded as uninteresting. There are, however, more detrimental problems in connection with the universality issue.

First, the non-universal character of illocutions is by now well-documented. Various studies reveal that some language-communities lack certain illocutionary classes. For instance, anthropological research reveals that "Searle's categories of commissive and expressive acts [...] lack substantial Ilongot exemplars" (Rosaldo 1982:217). Moreover, speakers of different languages distinguish between kinds of speaking on the basis of different criteria. Relevant dimensions for the Tenejapa Tzeltal include the time and place of speaking and S's bodily posture (Stross 1974), parameters that are ignored in illocutionary theory. More examples can be found in Wierzbicka (1985a:492-497). On the whole, cross-cultural research indicates that

> when philosophers of language discuss illocutionary acts such as "promising" [...], "requesting", or "commanding" [...] they are not discussing any language-independent "natural kinds". They are discussing complexes of components which have been singled out from among countless combinations of components occurring in human combination by concepts which are English-specific (Wierzbicka 1985a:493).

In other words, illocutionary theory commits the age-old sin of ethnocentricity by conferring universal status on a theory derived from introspective analysis in one language (Wierzbicka 1985b). Even if the aim is to discover universals, the empirical way is much more promising (cf. Comrie 1981: Chapter 1, Seuren 1981). The possibility of finding universals on the basis of lexical data is borne out by seminal cross-cultural studies in semantic domains such as plants and animal terms (Brown 1977, 1979) and colour terms (Berlin & Kay 1969). A wide-scale empirical study on lexical universals in the field of linguistic action is presently in progress (Verschueren 1984, 1989).

To conclude the universality issue, it is interesting to consider the position of an extreme advocate of a deductive approach to illocutions:

> An analysis of verbs always involves an individual language and cannot establish universal functions of action. At best one could attempt verbal analyses of as many individual languages as possible and then extricate from them a universal taxonomy; but such an approach would be highly uneconomical ... (Weigand 1985:4, see also Weigand 1989: Chapter 2)

It is true that the empirical approach is less economical, but this does not constitute an objection. For one, more economical deductive approaches risk committing themselves to the ethnocentric fallacy. For another, the uneconomical nature of verb-analyses in a representative sample of languages is not objectionable *per se*. The empirical way may be longer but it is definitely safer.

In illocutionary theory's second objection, "there is no *one-to-one correspondence* between illocutionary verbs and illocutionary forces" (S & V 1985:179). In this connection the following observations have been made:

> Many possible illocutionary forces do not have a corresponding verb in English (S & V 1985:179).

> ... frequently one and the same illocutionary force is named by several non-synonymous verbs (S & V 1985:179).

> Some verbs mark more than one illocutionary point (Searle 1979:28).

> Many illocutionary verbs "are not markers of illocutionary point but of some other feature of the illocutionary act" (Searle 1979: 27).

While granting the validity of these points, I intend to show that they do not constitute an impediment to a verb-based approach. The first point, that *languages do not lexicalize all possible illocutions*, has often been noted in studies of illocutionary verbs (e.g. Edmondson 1981a:490, Leech 1983:221-222, Verschueren 1985:187-204). A well-known example is the type of act for which Goffman (1971:490) has coined the term MINIMIZATION, which occurs in reply to an act of THANKING. Typical realizations in English include *Not at all, My pleasure, Don't mention it,* and *You're welcome.* Other examples of such lexical gaps are provided by Verschueren (1985). The absence of possible lexicalizations is unproblematic for a lexically oriented approach. What is more, their observation can be an asset. It is possible to detect such gaps: once the semantic dimensions on which lexical items vary have been identified, one will find possible configurations that remain unlexicalized (Lyons 1977:301-305). In this respect, a verb-based approach is not weaker than illocutionary theory. But when adding a cognitive dimension to structural analysis, one will go one step further and ask why certain slots remain unoccupied. Illocutionary theory avoids the question by attributing the existence or non-existence of certain verbs to the whims of coincidence:

> [...] there are several different continua of "illocutionary force", and the fact that the illocutionary verbs in English stop at certain points on these various continua and not at others is, in a sense, accidental. For example, we might have had an illocutionary verb "rubrify", meaning "to call something red". Thus "I hereby rubrify it" would just mean "It's red". Analogously, we happen to have an obsolete verb "macarize", meaning "to call someone happy". (Searle 1969:70)

On a cognitive account, however, lexical gaps "are due to the low cognitive salience of the corresponding acts", Verschueren says (1985:204). In a similar vein, Edmondson assumes that "the existence of distinctive illocutionary terms as a means of describing some types of illocutionary act indicates the social significance of acts of that kind" (1981b:25). In this respect, it is interesting to compare Searle's conception of the lexicon with Austin's. The latter comes much closer to the cognitive position advocated here. The lexicon is not viewed as a random collection of feature constellations. In order for a conceptualization to become lexicalized, it must have a minimal degree of salience and it must stand the test of time to persist. The verb MACARIZE is a clear case in point - although not the point Searle intends to make. Had he consulted the *Oxford English Dictionary*, he would have noticed that the verb is an artificial concoction. One of the first attestations (1864) indicates that it did not enter the English lexicon in a natural way:

> If a man possesses a genius, or a person that is admirable, he is himself admired; but not if he has an admirable horse or house; the sentiment we feel towards him is of a different nature, and we have no English word to express it [...]. I should like to introduce the word "macarise". (OED, *macarize*)

Other examples, especially under the noun MACARISM, suggest that the word may have been borrowed directly from Ancient Greek, via the Greek version of the Bible. That it is no longer used proves my point, not Searle's. Speakers of English just do not need it, just like RUBRIFY has never been needed. So, the argument concerning lexical gaps can be turned against illocutionary theory. A cognitively oriented empirical approach reveals not only the existence of such gaps but, unlike illocutionary theory, it also tries to find a motivation, and one of the possible reasons is that some illocutions have a deeper cognitive entrenchment than others.

Examples of Searle's second argument, *non-synonymous verbs referring to the same illocution*, include AFFIRM, ASSERT, CLAIM, and STATE. For illocutionary theory, the differences between them are irrelevant "because in general they come from relations between sequences in illocutionary acts in conversations and not from within the structure of each act" (S & V 1985:183). Two objections can be raised here. First, the differences between these verbs are much more numerous and subtle than illocutionary theory would like us to believe, only few of them pertaining to sequencing phenomena (see the detailed analyses in Wierzbicka 1987). By categorizing these verbs as assertives, illocutionary theory recognizes their status as illocutionary verbs, but fails to discriminate between them: they are "subject to the same feature analysis" in illocutionary theory (S & V 1985:183). So, in the case of these verbs, there are distinctions that the theory is unable to handle, although their lexicalization proves that speakers of English find them relevant. Maintaining that they bear no relevance to a theory of illocutions seems to me a symptom of unwarranted reductionism. Second, where differences related to sequencing are concerned, they reveal that speakers of English tend to conflate them with aspects of illocutionary force, which seriously undermines the possibility of keeping them apart, as illocutionary theory would like to have it.

Searle's third objection concerns the fact that *some verbs mark more than one illocutionary point.* For instance, WARN and many other verbs can be used to report assertive and directive acts. We would normally regard these cases of multiple meanings attached to one form as instances of polysemy rather than homonymy, for the different meanings associated with each verb are not unrelated. Take the two senses of WARN. Even S & V have to admit that

> the two uses are not independent. When I warn you that something is the case I am normally warning you that it is the case with a view to getting you to do something about it. Thus if I warn you (assertive) that the bull is about to charge, the aim of issuing a warning would normally be to get you to take some evasive action (directive). [...] On the other hand, when I warn you to do something, I would normally be asking you to do it (directive) while implying that if you do not do it, it would be bad for you (assertive). (1985:202-203)

This reveals that the distinctions drawn by illocutionary theory are not always conceptually relevant. The major differentiation between illocutions is stated in terms of illocutionary point and two illocutions with different points belong, by definition, to different categories. But when we look at natural-language expressions, we notice that other factors may override these differences, such as the impending danger to H in WARNINGS. This lexical item indicates that other semantic dimensions may acquire higher salience than illocutionary point. The import of the phenomenon should not be underestimated. Out of the 102 illocutionary verbs analysed in S & V (1985: Chapter 9), 28 are said to mark more than one point. If their sample is representative, between 25 and 30% of our lexical stock crosses the boundaries imposed by illocutionary theory, a number that is hard to ignore.

Finally, Searle refers to illocutionary *verbs that do not name illocutionary point* but some other illocutionary component. Examples include INSIST and SUGGEST, which can be used to refer to assertive and directive acts alike. The relevant "other" component is the intensity of the illocution, which is low in SUGGESTIONS and high in acts of INSISTING. "Paradoxical as it may sound, such verbs are illocutionary verbs, but not names of kinds of illocutionary acts", in Searle's (1979:28) opinion. This objection can be refuted on the same grounds as the previous point. The situation is paradoxical only if one accepts the primacy of the notion illocutionary point. But the verbs themselves indicate that speakers of English find it convenient to highlight other aspects, such as an illocution's intensity.

The merit of Searle's arguments resides in the fact that they undermine the naive view which posits a one-to-one correspondence between illocutions and the corresponding verbs. But, as I have shown, this does not constitute a valid objection to a lexical approach. On the contrary, Searle's observations provide us with a more adequate conception of the relation between illocutions and illocutionary verbs, which reveals that conceptualizations of illocutions differ from the distinctions drawn in illocutionary theory. Certain illocutions, such as MINIMIZATIONS, are not lexicalized at all, which is symptomatic of their low cognitive salience. Some verbs conflate illocutionary force with other dimensions, like the relation of an act to the rest of the discourse, which indicates that illocutionary force intersects with other parts of our conceptual domain relating to verbal communication. Other verbs, like WARN, INSIST, and SUGGEST bear out the inadequacy of positing illocutionary point as the only or primary dimension of categorization. On the whole, even a superficial look at a few verbs reveals a wide gap between the categories recognized in illocutionary theory and the way speakers of English categorize the same phenomena. So, it is natural to ask, who is right and who is wrong? Illocutionary theory answers in a straightforward manner:

> Illocutionary acts, are so to speak, natural conceptual kinds and we should no more suppose that our ordinary language verbs carve the conceptual field of illocutions at its semantic joints than we would suppose that our ordinary language expressions for naming and describing plants and animals correspond exactly to the natural biological kinds. (Searle 1979:ix-x)

This analogy and the conception about semantics it reveals err in various respects. Searle's pessimism regarding the fit between folk biological terms and natural reality is contradicted by seminal cross-cultural research in this field (surveyed in Berlin 1978). At a certain level of generality, known as the generic level in taxonomies of biological nomenclature and corresponding closely to Rosch's basic level, vocabularies do reflect quite successfully the discontinuities attested in nature. Moreover, mismatches between the lexicon and biological reality can often be explained on the basis of the cultural salience of the species in question. This corroborates the cognitive conception of semantics, in which meaning is not uniquely determined by objective reality alone, as objectivists tend to believe. Subjective factors, such as human interaction with nature, may play an overriding role. This is especially true for illocutions. As Searle (1969:50-53) observes, illocutions are *institutional facts*, whereas plants and animals are brute facts. Brute facts, like the solar system or the molecular structure of water, are objectively real in the sense that they exist irrespective of human experience. Institutional facts, like a wedding ceremony or a football game, derive their existence from human convention, spelled out in a set of constitutive rules. Illocutions "do not exist in the world but only in the heads of people" (Burkhardt 1990:125), while biological species live "out there". Lakoff (1987:170-172) points out that objectivists tend to treat institutional facts as if they were of the brute kind. Searle explicitly disavows any such commitment:

> In this connection, let us examine the inadequacy of the brute fact conception of knowledge to account for institutional facts. [...] To illustrate this inadequacy, imagine what it would be like to describe institutional facts in purely brute terms. Let us imagine a group of highly trained observers describing an American football game in statements of only brute facts. What could they say by way of description? [...] For example, we can imagine that after a time our observer would discover the law of periodical clustering: at statistically regular intervals organisms in like colored shirts cluster together in roughly circular fashion (the huddle). [...] But no matter how much data of this sort we imagine our observers to collect [...] they still have not described American football. What is missing from their description [...] are all those concepts which are backed by constitutive rules, concepts such as touchdown, offside, game, points, first down, time out, etc., and consequently what is missing are all the true statements one can make about a football game using those concepts. The missing statements are precisely what describes the phenomenon on the field as a game of football. The other descriptions, the descriptions of brute facts, can be explained in terms of the institutional facts. But the institutional facts can only be explained in terms of the constitutive rules which underlie them. (Searle 1969:52)

Quite ironically, in putting illocutions on a par with biological species, illocutionary theory falls into the trap it has previously laid bare. For brute facts, it is possible to construct theories that make no reference to human cognition (e.g. biology, physics). If we want to understand institutional facts, however, we have to include the participants' own experience, which we shall find reflected in the terms they use to talk about it.

Before closing this debate, one final issue needs to be addressed: could it be the case that English, as its own metalanguage, is an inadequate tool? The issue is a subtle one and cannot be resolved before enough data have been studied. This in itself already provides a sufficient reason for studying illocutions. Indeed, the empirical-conceptual approach cannot be refuted on *a priori* grounds. The lexical domain pertaining to verbal communication still remains to be explored in detail. Many misconceptions derive from the lack of a systematic empirical description (cf. Rudzka-Ostyn 1990:656, Wierzbicka 1987:7-10). On the whole, the basic rationale behind the empirical-conceptual approach is uncontroversial:

> The guiding idea is the familiar one that any natural lexicon implies a tacit, structured conceptualization of the stuff that the words of that lexicon are about (Kay 1987:68).

The vehemence with which illocutionary theory denies the relevance of a verb-based approach is therefore surprising. Why should natural language be any less successful when talking about itself than when referring to other conceptual domains? In discarding the relevance of the natural lexicon, the theory sweeps away much of present-day cognitive science.

Notice, first, that the position upheld by illocutionary theory - when pushed to its extremes - entails strange consequences. Numerous illocutionary verbs can be used performatively. If illocutions were divorced from illocutionary verbs, a speaker issuing an explicit performative would be doing something else than what he says he is doing. Thus, when saying "I PROMISE to come" I would not be doing what I mean by the verb PROMISE, which I find hard to believe.

One piece of evidence that might be cited as a case where our conceptualization of verbal communication deviates from what we actually do when we speak is the so-called conduit metaphor (Reddy 1979). According to this folk model, ideas (or meanings) are objects and words (or other linguistic expressions) are containers; when speaking, S puts ideas into words and transfers them through a kind of conduit to H, who takes the ideas out of the words and puts them into his head.

Without denying the existence of the conduit metaphor, I contend that Reddy overstates its import in claiming that "as a metalanguage [...] English is its own worst enemy" (1979:286). First, people may entertain various, sometimes conflicting, models of the same phenomenon (cf. Kay 1987). The availability of alternatives to the conduit metaphor has been established by Rudzka-Ostyn (1988). Second, folk theories are often partial in nature, each being valid with regard to a limited set of phenomena. This is corroborated when we compare various studies such as Goossens (1990), Kay (1987), Lakoff & Johnson (1980:89ff), Reddy (1979), Rudzka-Ostyn (1988), Sweetser (1987), Talmy (1985), each of which points to a different set of metaphors regarding verbal communication. As the studies by Fillmore (1977) and Sweetser (1987) indicate, each folk model represents a simplified world view that is valid to a certain extent and cancellable if need be.

4. Conclusion

In this article, I have contrasted two different approaches to illocutions: the objectivist (or, deductive) approach and the subjectivist (or, empirical) one. I would like to add that this tension already has a long history. In this context, it is useful to go back to the origin of illocutionary theory. The original Austinian conception was rooted in *ordinary language philosophy*, a reaction against logical positivism. This evolution can be seen in terms of the subjectivist/objectivist opposition. Logical positivism can be viewed as an objectivist philosophy *par excellence*. Its only preoccupation was with truth, in an extreme way. Every utterance that cannot be assessed in terms of truth and falsity was discarded as nonsense. Moreover, natural language was considered an inaccurate tool for making verifiable statements. Hence, formal languages were developed, whose structure was supposed to mirror exactly the structure of reality, which was interpreted in an atomistic way (cf. Parret 1979:39ff).

Ordinary language philosophers maintained more or less the opposite. They set themselves the task of doing "conceptual geography", which they did by analyzing natural language (cf. de Pater 1984:71ff). The subjectivist import of ordinary language philosophy also displays itself in its commitment to (a pre-theoretical conception of) the prototype model. In fact, the notion of family resemblance derives from Wittgenstein II (see also Lakoff (1987:17-21) on Austin). It is my contention that Searle's follow-up of Austin's work represents a move back in the objectivist direction. Austin was of the opinion that

> our common stock of words embodies all the distinctions men have found worth drawing, and the connections they have found worth marking, in the lifetimes of many generations: these surely are likely to be more numerous, more sound, since they have stood up to the long test of the survival of the fittest, and more subtle, at least in all ordinary and reasonably practical matters, than any that you and I are likely to think up in our armchairs of an afternoon - the most favoured alternative method. (Austin 1971:84)

Present-day illocutionary theory, on the other hand, claims that the natural-language lexicon is an imperfect instrument for representing reality. For instance, illocutionary verbs are believed to be unreliable guides to illocutions. Therefore, the theory devises a formal language, illocutionary logic (S & V 1985, Vanderveken 1990a, 1990b), which is supposed to be a better tool for talking about illocutions than the natural lexicon. The parallel with logical positivism should be apparent.

In sum, illocutionary theory originated in a subjectivist spirit (Austin) but drifted away towards objectivism (Searle, Vanderveken). The empirical-conceptual approach may be regarded as an attempt to swing the proverbial pendulum back in the opposite direction.

References

Austin, J. L.

1971 [1957] A plea for excuses. In: Lyas, C. (ed.). *Philosophy in Linguistics.* London: Macmillan, pp. 79-101.

1980 [1962] *How to Do Things with Words.* Urmson, J. O. & M. Sbisà (eds.) Oxford & New York: Oxford University Press.

Ballmer, Th. & W. Brennenstuhl
1981 *Speech Act Classification. A Study in the Lexical Analysis of Speech Activity Verbs.* Berlin, Heidelberg & New York: Springer.
1984 "Empirisch fundierte Sprechakttheorie vs. sprachphilosophische Spekulation. Eine Entgegnung auf Jörg Meibauers *Akte oder Verben oder beides?*" *Zeitschrift für Sprachwissenschaft* 3:243-260.

Berlin, B.
1978 Ethnobiological classification. In: Rosch, E. & Lloyd, B. (eds.), pp. 9-27.

Berlin, B. & P. Kay
1969 *Basic Color Terms: Their Universality and Evolution.* Berkeley & Los Angeles: University of California Press.

Brown, C. H.
1977 "Folk botanical life forms: Their universality and growth". *American Anthropologist* 79:317-342.
1979 "Folk zoological life forms: Their universality and growth". *American Anthropologist* 81:791-817.

Burkhardt, A.
1990 Speech act theory - the decline of a paradigm. In: Burkhardt, A. (ed.), pp. 91-128.

Burkhardt, A. (ed.)
1990 *Speech Acts, Meanings and Intentions: Critical Approaches to the Philosophy of John R. Searle.* Berlin & New York: de Gruyter.

Carlon, K., K. Davidse & B. Rudzka-Ostyn (eds.)
1994 *Perspectives on English: Studies in Honour of Professor Emma Vorlat.* Leuven: Peeters.

Clark, H. H. & D. H. Schunk
1980 "Polite answers to polite requests". *Cognition* 8:111-143.

Comrie, B.
1981 *Language Universals and Linguistic Typlogy. Syntax and Morphology.* Oxford: Blackwell.

Corrigan, R., F. Eckman & M. Noonan (eds.)
1989 *Linguistic Categorization.* Amsterdam & Philadelphia: Benjamins.

D'Andrade, R. G. & M. Wish
1985 "Speech act theory in quantitative research on interpersonal behavior". *Discourse Processes* 8:229-259.

de Geest, W., R. Dirven & Y. Putseys (eds.)
1981 *Twintig Facetten van de Taalwetenschap.* Leuven: Acco.

de Pater
1984 [1972] *Filosofische Taalanalyse in Engeland na 1900. Een Overzicht.* Leuven & Amersfoort: Acco.

De Raad, B.
1985 "The language of social acts". *Journal of Semantics* 4:223-236.

Dietrich, R.-A.
1984 "Sprache und Wirklichkeit. Anmerkungen zur Sprechaktklassifikation von Ballmer und Brennenstuhl". *Zeitschrift für Sprachwissenschaft* 3:265-282.

Edmondson, W. J.
1981a Illocutionary verbs, illocutionary acts, and conversational behaviour. In: Eikmeyer, H.-J. & H. Rieser (eds). *Words, Worlds and Contexts. New Approaches in Word Semantics.* Berlin, New York: Walter de Gruyter, pp. 485-499.
1981b *Spoken Discourse: A Model for Analysis.* London: Longman.

Fillmore, C. J.
1977 Topics in lexical semantics. In: Cole, R. (ed.). *Current Issues in Linguistic Theory.* Bloomington: University of Indiana Press, pp. 55-81.

Geeraerts, D.
1985 *Paradigm and Paradox. Explorations into a Paradigmatic Theory of Meaning and its Epistemological Background.* Leuven: Leuven University Press.
1988 Cognitive grammar and the history of lexical semantics. In: Rudzka-Ostyn, B. (ed.). *Topics in Cognitive Linguistics.* Amsterdam: Benjamins, pp. 647-677.
1992 The return of hermeneutics to lexical semantics. In: Pütz, M. (ed.), pp. 257-282.

Gibbs, R. W.
1983 "Do people always process the literal meanings of indirect requests?" *Journal of Experimental Psychology: Learning, Memory, Cognition* 9:524-533.

Goffman, E.
1971 *Relations in Public. Microstudies of the Public Order.* New York: Basic Books.

Goossens, L.
1990 "Metaphtonymy: the interaction of metaphor and metonymy in expressions for linguistic action." *Cognitive Linguistics* 1:323-340.

Haiman, J. (ed.)
1985 *Iconicity in Syntax.* Amsterdam: Benjamins.

Johnson, M.
1987 *The Body in the Mind. The Bodily Basis of Meaning, Imagination and Reason.* Chicago & London: The University of Chicago Press.

Kay, P.
1971 "Taxonomy and semantic contrast". *Language* 47:866-887.
1987 Linguistic competence and folk theories of language. Two English hedges. In: Holland, D. & N. Quinn (eds.). *Cultural Models in Language and Thought.* Cambridge: Cambridge University Press, pp. 67-77.

Kempson, R. M.
1977 *Semantic Theory.* Cambridge: Cambridge University Press.

Kreckel, M.
1981 *Communicative Acts and Shared Knowledge in Natural Discourse.* London: Academic Press.

Lakoff, G.
1986 Cognitive semantics. Berkeley Cognitive Science Report.
1987 *Women, Fire and Dangerous Things. What Categories Reveal About the Mind.* Chicago & London: The University of Chicago Press.

Lakoff, G. & M. Johnson
1980 *Metaphors We Live by.* Chicago & London: The University of Chicago Press.

Langacker, R. W.
1985 Observations and speculations on subjectivity. In: Haiman, J. (ed.), pp. 109-150.

Leech, G. N.
1983 *Principles of Pragmatics.* London & New York: Longman.

Lyons, J.
1977 *Semantics.* Cambridge: Cambridge University Press.

Meibauer, J.
1982 "Akten oder Verben oder beides?" (Review article of Ballmer & Brennenstuhl 1981) *Zeitschrift für Sprachwissenschaft* 1:137-148.

Mervis, C. B. & E. Rosch
1981 "Categorization of natural objects". *Annual Review of Psychology* 32:89-115.
Ortony, A. (ed.)
1979 *Metaphor and Thought*. Cambridge: Cambridge University Press.
Osgood, C. E.
1970 Interpersonal verbs and interpersonal behavior. In: Cowan, J. L. (ed.). *Studies in Thought and Language*. Tucson: University of Arizona Press, pp. 133-227.
Parret, H.
1979 *Filosofie en Taalwetenschap*. Assen: Van Gorcum.
Parret, H. & J. Verschueren (eds.)
1992 *(On) Searle on Conversation*. Amsterdam & Philadelphia: Benjamins.
Pütz, M. (ed.)
1992 *Thirty Years of Linguistic Evolution. Studies in Honour of René Dirven on the Occasion of his Sixtieth Birthday*. Amsterdam & Philadelphia: Benjamins.
Reddy, M. J.
1979 The conduit metaphor - A case of frame conflict in our language about language. In: Ortony, A. (ed.), pp. 284-324.
Rosaldo, M. Z.
1982 "The things we do with words: Ilongot speech acts and speech act theory in philosophy". *Language in society* 11: 203-237.
Rosch, E.
1977 Human categorization. In: Warren, N. (ed.). *Studies in Cross-Cultural Psychology*. Vol 1. New York: Academic Press, pp. 1-49.
1978 Principles of categorization. In: Rosch, E. & B. Lloyd (eds.), pp. 27-48.
Rosch, E. & B. Lloyd (eds.)
1978 *Cognition and Categorization*. Hillsdale: Erlbaum.
Rudzka-Ostyn, B.
1988 Semantic extensions into the domain of verbal communication. In: Rudzka-Ostyn, B. (ed.), pp. 507-553.
Rudzka-Ostyn, B. (ed.)
1988 *Topics in Cognitive Linguistics*. Amsterdam & Philadelphia: Benjamins.
1990 "Prototypes, schemas, and cross-category correspondences: The case of *ask*." *Linguistics* 27:613-661.
Searle, J. R.
1969 *Speech Acts. An Essay in the Philosophy of Language*. Cambridge: Cambridge University Press.
1979 *Expression and Meaning. Studies in the Theory of Speech Acts*. Cambridge: Cambridge University Press.
1983 *Intentionality. An Essay in the Philosophy of the Mind*. Cambridge: Cambridge University Press.
1992 Conversation. In: Parret, H. & J. Verschueren (eds.), pp. 7-29.
Searle, J. R. & D. Vanderveken
1985 *Foundations of Illocutionary Logic*. Cambridge: Cambridge University Press.
Seuren, P. A. M.
1981 Taaluniversalia. In: de Geest, W. *et al.* (eds.), pp. 112-126.
Slaughter, M. M.
1982 *Universal Languages and Scientific Taxonomy in the Seventeenth Century*. Cambridge: Cambridge University Press.
Smith, E. E. & D. L. Medin.
1981 *Categories and Concepts*. Cambridge, Mass.: Harvard University Press.

Strecker, B.
1984 "In Sachen Meibauer contra Ballmer/Brennenstuhl". *Zeitschrift für Sprachwissenschaft* 3:261-264.

Stross, B.
1974 Speaking of speaking: Tenejapa Tzeltal metalinguistics. In: Bauman, R. & J. Scherzer (eds.). *Explorations in the Ethnography of Speaking.* Cambridge: Cambridge University Press, pp. 213-239.

Sweetser, E. V.
1987 The definition of *lie*. In: Holland, D. & N. Quinn (eds.). *Cultural Models in Language and Thought.* Cambridge: Cambridge University Press, pp. 43-66.

Talmy, L.
1985 Force dynamics in language and thought. In: Eilfort, W. H. *et al.* (eds.). *Papers from the Parasession on Causatives and Agentivity at the Twenty-First Regional Meeting of the Chicago Linguistics Society.* Chicago: Chicago Linguistics Society, pp. 293-337.

Taylor, J. R.
1989 *Linguistic Categorization Prototypes in Linguistic Theory.* Oxford: Clarendon Press.

Tsui, B. M. A.
1985 Aspects of the classification of illocutionary acts and the notion of a perlocutionary act. Trier: L.A.U.T.

Vanderveken, D.
1985 What is an illocutionary force? In: Dascal, M. (ed.). *Dialogue. An Interdisciplinary Approach.* Amsterdam & Philadelphia: Benjamins, pp. 181-203.
1990a *Meaning and Speech Acts. Volume I. Principles of Language Use.* Cambridge: Cambridge University Press.
1990b *Meaning and Speech Acts. Volume II. Formal Semantics of Success and Satisfaction.* Cambridge: Cambridge University Press.

Vanparys, J.
1993 *The Categorization of Illocutionary Verbs.* Doctoral dissertation, K. U. Leuven.
1994 On illocutionary taxonomies. In: Carlon *et al.* (eds.), pp. 285-330.

Vendler, Z.
1972 *Res Cogitans. An Essay in Rational Psychology.* Ithaca: Cornell University Press.

Verschueren, J.
1980 *On Speech Act Verbs.* Amsterdam & Philadelphia: Benjamins.
1981 "De lexicalisering van taalgedrag". *Tijdschrift voor Tekst en Taal* 1:46-55.
1984 Basic linguistic action verbs: A questionnaire. *Antwerp Papers in Linguistics* 37.
1985 *What People Say They Do With Words: Prolegomena to an Empirical-Conceptual Approach to Linguistic Action.* Norwood, N. J.: Ablex.
1988 Introduction: The empirical-conceptual approach. In: Verschueren, J. (ed.), pp. 1-9.
1989 Language on language: Toward metapragmatic universals. *Papers in Pragmatics* 3.2.

Verschueren, J. (ed.)
1988 *Linguistic Action: Some Empirical-Conceptual Studies.* Norwood, N. J.: Ablex.

Weigand, E.
1985 Speech act taxonomy - an abstract or an empirical problem? Paper presented at the 1985 International Pragmatics Conference, Viareggio. Ms.
1989 *Sprache als Dialog. Sprechakttaxonomie und kommunikative Grammatik.* Tübingen: Niemeyer.

Wierzbicka, A.
1985a "A semantic metalanguage for a crosscultural comparison of speech acts and speech genres". *Language in Society* 14:491-514.
1985b "Different cultures, different languages, different speech acts. Polish vs. English". *Journal of Pragmatics* 9:145-178.
1987 *English Speech Act Verbs. A Semantic Dictionary.* Sydney: Academic Press.

The linguistic and cognitive relevance of basic emotions

Friedrich Ungerer

1. Introduction[1]

1.1. The deficiencies of the structuralist approach

Linguistic statements about emotional aspects of language, among them specialist investigations of lexical, grammatical, and intonational aspects (Charleston 1960, Stankiewicz 1964, Arndt & Janney 1987, Daneš 1987, Pohosz 1983, Hübler 1992), have been surprisingly vague in their classification of emotions. The main reason is that both lexicography and (structuralist) lexicology have never really come to grips with the description of emotion terms. Dictionary definitions are notoriously circular; sense relations can only be safely established for a few antonymic pairs, such as *happy/sad* and *love/hate,* and superordinate status can only be assigned to very general terms like *emotion, feeling,* and *mood.* Feature analysis has either been confined to very general distinctions like the positive/negative contrast (Nöth 1992) or intensity and causation (Johnson-Laird & Oatley 1989). A special case is Wierzbicka's approach of defining emotion terms on the basis of a small set of semantic primitives, i.e. "good", "bad", "do", "happen", "know", and "want" (Wierzbicka 1988:374, also Wierzbicka 1986, 1992, this volume). Though the notion of discrete semantic primitives is rooted in structuralism, Wierzbicka transcends the structuralist position by developing her definitions into "prototypical scripts" which provide very detailed descriptions of individual emotions. In doing so she primarily relies on introspection, and this is where the present study tries to take the investigation of emotion concepts one step further by tapping the additional linguistic evidence provided by cognitive linguistics and emotion psychology.

1.2. *The contribution of cognitive linguistics: Conceptual metaphors and metonymies*

As Lakoff and Kövecses have shown, emotions provide the ideal field for the application of one of the basic tenets of cognitive linguistics, i.e. that the concepts of abstract terms are to a large extent structured by metaphors and metonymies (Lakoff & Johnson 1980). Starting from this premise, Lakoff and especially Kövecses have extracted a large number of metaphors and metonymies[2] for emotion terms like *anger, fear, joy, happiness, love, pride*, and *respect* from the English language and have used them to construct conceptual scenarios for these emotions (Lakoff 1987; Kövecses 1986, 1988, 1990a, 1990b, 1991). The problem is that this research has not really been interested in a conceptual distinction of emotions. For Lakoff, the analysis of the concept ANGER has been a welcome opportunity to exemplify how the system of conceptual metaphors and metonymies works. Kövešces has been trying to prove that there is a unified emotion concept with ANGER as its most prototypical member and other emotions as not so good examples (Kövecses 1990a; see discussion below). So, on the whole he has been looking for parallels and shared characteristics rather than differences between the emotion concepts he investigated. This has led him to organize his material in a way that makes it difficult to decide whether metaphors and metonymies can, in fact, provide recognizably distinct descriptions of emotion concepts (or their prototypes), as we would wish them to do. To evaluate the "distinguishing potential" of the metaphorical and metonymic expressions collected by Kövecses we will have to analyze them more closely, and this will be one of the tasks of this paper.

1.3. *The contribution of emotion psychology: Basic emotions and reports of emotional experiences*

The third, and at the same time largest, body of research on which a description of emotion terms can be based has been accumulated by psychologists, for whom emotions have always been a major topic. More importantly, in our context, there is a long tradition in psychology and philosophy of regarding some emotions as more central or more basic than others and using them as a kind of reference system for more marginal emotions. Descartes, for instance, suggested SADNESS, JOY, DESIRE, HATE, LOVE, and ADMIRATION; William James, the important 19th century emotion psychologist, favoured FEAR, GRIEF, LOVE, and RAGE. More modern proposals, as collected by Ortony *et al.* (1988:27), range from short lists of two to detailed lists of ten or eleven basic emotions, but recent publications have shown a surprising consensus in proposing five or six basic emotions (Johnson-Laird & Oatley 1989, 1992, Shaver *et al.* 1987)[3]. The working proposal, which is presented in Figure 1, follows these suggestions, adding only compound terms where two different words are used for the interpretation of a basic emotion as occurrent states (*disgust, desire, joy*) or dispositions (*hate, love, happiness*; Ryle 1958:83ff; Lyons 1980)[4].

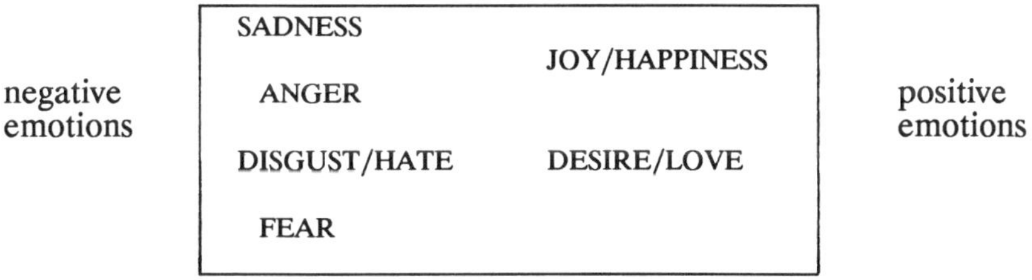

Figure 1. Basic emotions: a working proposal[5]

It is fairly obvious that this set of basic emotions can provide a good framework for the analysis of the emotional effects of language, provided these basic emotions can be adequately described and distinguished from each other, and this will also be investigated in this paper.

Yet there is a second reason why the work of emotion psychologists is attractive for linguists. Since there is no direct access to the mental phenomena of emotions, psychologists use language as one of their main sources (another favoured research field are facial expressions). Some of these psychological investigations into language could equally have been carried out by traditional linguists, notably the feature analysis of the emotion vocabulary as conducted by Johnson-Laird & Oatley (1989)[6]. More typical of the psychological approach are the use of interviews and personal reports about emotional experiences, which can either take the form of isolated statements (Davitz 1969) or story-like reports (Shaver *et al.* 1987). These methods have been regarded sceptically by linguists, and even Kövecšes makes a point of stressing their subjective character while claiming objectivity for his "conventionalized" metaphorical and metonymic expressions (Kövecšes 1990a:3). This is strange for a cognitive linguist who relies so much on psychological notions like prototype categories (and who has himself used the interview method since; Kövecšes 1993).

Seen from a more detached point of view, there is no reason why the linguistic material collected by psychologists should be less suitable for a description of emotion terms than Kövecšes' metaphorical and metonymic expressions, and this is why they will be included in the analysis.

1.4. The aim of this paper: A unified analysis of basic emotions in terms of metaphors, metonymies, and informants' statements

In our opinion, the short survey of available resources we have conducted suggests two things:

- If we look for a descriptive framework of emotional effects in language, the psychological notion of basic emotions seems to supply the most promising candidates.
- To provide a comprehensive description of these basic emotions both the conventionalized metaphors and metonymies of cognitive linguistics and the statements collected by experimental psychology should be taken into account.

Following these suggestions, the paper will examine the metaphorical and metonymic expressions of basic emotion terms provided by Kövecšes (plus some additions for SADNESS, which is not covered by Kövecšes).[7] The psychological side will be represented by the relevant data from Davitz' (1969) and Shaver *et al.*'s (1987) materials. After a general characterization of the data (Section 2), the analysis will be carried out in two stages. Section 3 will provide a content analysis which uses some of the parameters of emotion psychology; Section 4 will examine the data in terms of metaphors, i.e. it will take up Kövecšes' point of view. The concluding Section 5 will try to assess to what extent the psychological and cognitive descriptions of basic emotions meet the expectations of linguists and whether basic emotions can serve as reference points for linguistic analysis.

2. General characterization of the data

2.1. Sources of the data and selection processes

For the sake of brevity, the major facts about the sources have been assembled in Figure 2. All three sources are self-contained investigations;

COGNITIVE LINGUISTICS	EXPERIMENTAL PSYCHOLOGY	
Kövecses, Lakoff	Davitz	Shaver *et al.*
Range of investigation Intuitively selected emotion categories (*anger, love, fear, joy, happiness, pride, emotion*, etc.)	Range of investigation 50 emotion terms, selected from 400 entries in Roget's Thesaurus by judges and by author's intuition	Range of investigation 5 basic emotions selected in a typicality rating test (ANGER, SADNESS, FEAR, JOY, LOVE)
Source of material 'Conventionalized' expressions containing the emotion word or related to the emotion, based on entries in Roget's Thesaurus and on the author's linguistic intuition	Source of material 1200 statements of emotional experiences as collected from informants, reduced to 556 items; these items are attributed to the emotion terms by a second set of informants; only items approved by more than one third of informants retained.	Source of material 23 to 29 'prototypical features' for each emotion extracted from 120 story-like accounts of emotional episodes by 6 judges and rank-ordered
Contents of items - physiological phenomena (metonymies) - concrete events like fire, journey ('basic level metaphors') - general notions like container, object, person ('constitutive metaphors')	Contents of items - physical sensations - relation to external world - relations to others - relations to one's self - impulse to control behaviour - development of experience	Contents of items - antecedents - expressions - feelings - physiological reactions - behaviours
Goals 1 Assembling metaphors and metonymies into scenarios reflecting the rich category structure of emotions 2 Finding the protoype of the emotion category	Goals 1 Compiling a dictionary of emotion terms listing statements about emotional experiences 2 Compounding the statements into 12 clusters and attributing them to four scales (hedonic tone, activation, etc.)	Goals Compiling prototype scripts of the basic emotions (see Kövecses' scenarios)

Figure 2. Range and sources of data, selection processes

their goals reflect the changing research interests of the last three decades.

Davitz (1969) wants to assemble a body of material ("a dictionary of emotion terms") and to establish a classification of a large number of emotions based on a limited set of psychological features. Kövecšes (1990a, etc.; Lakoff 1987) and Shaver *et al.* (1987) use the prototype notion of cognitive psychology and the script notion of artificial intelligence to develop prototypical scripts or scenarios for (mostly basic) emotions.

All authors claim a high degree of representativity for their linguistic material. In Kövecšes' case, this claim rests on the fact that many of his metaphorical and metonymic expressions are taken from Roget's *Thesaurus* and therefore regarded as conventionalized language; examples are *cold sweat*, *gooseflesh*, *hair on end*, which are assembled under the heading of "fear" in the *Thesaurus*, and *flush with anger*, *flare up*, *fume*, *explosion*, *let off steam*, *blow one's top*, which are listed under "resentment/anger".

Davitz and Shaver *et al.* try to achieve representativity in a different way. Starting out from a large body of statements (Davitz) or stories (Shaver *et al.*) suggested by informants, they submit their material to a series of selection processes (Davitz for example uses judges' selection, selection by test subjects and a 33% agreement threshold). The result is not conventionality in the discrete, structuralist sense of the word, but a degree of acceptability which will be favourably ranked on an acceptability scale defining conventionality (Ungerer 1991:159ff). The difference between the two psychological sources is that Davitz' material reflects informants' utterances, condensed and selected as they may be, while Shaver *et al.*'s "statements" are produced by the judges who analyzed the informants' stories, and therefore tend to be more abstract and less spontaneous.

2.2. *Linguistic structure and content domains*

From a traditional linguistic point of view, the data are sentences (or sentence fragments, e.g. nominalizations) with varying clause patterns whose message can be related to a certain emotion term. This link is, of course, more obvious if the emotion term is actually contained in the statement (as in [1] and [3]); the link is more fragile where this is not the case (as in [2] and [4] - [10]):

[1] His heart pounded with fear. (Metonymy: INCREASE IN HEART RATE)
[2] She turned pale. (Metonymy: BLOOD LEAVES FACE)
[3] He was consumed by his anger. (Metaphor: ANGER IS FIRE)
[4] He has a fierce temper. (Metaphor: ANGER IS A DANGEROUS ANIMAL)

[1] - [4] from Kövečses (1990a)

[5] My teeth grind against each other. (indicating HATE)
[6] I'm jumpy, jittery. (indicating FEAR)
[7] I feel vulnerable, totally helpless. (indicating FEAR)
[8] a sense of being wanted, needed (indicating LOVE)

[5] - [8] from Davitz (1969)

[9] Sitting, lying around, inactive (indicating SADNESS)
[10] Doing nice things for other people (indicating JOY)

[9] - [10] from Shaver *et al.* (1987)

It is clear that the kind of description which can be compiled from these statements lacks the precision expected from logical definitions. Some of the links with the emotion term will be associative, there will probably be overlaps and even contradictions between statements attributed to one and the same emotion term. So one should not be disappointed if the description does not yield a well-ordered catalogue of features, but rather reflects the experiential "untidiness" which seems typical of conceptual models.

As far as the contents of the statements are concerned, the three sources converge in the domain of physiological phenomena, so these statements (including Kövecšes' metonymic expressions) offer themselves as a natural point of departure for the content analysis. For the non-physiological part of the data the proposed criteria are more divergent. While Davitz' and Shaver *et al.*'s classifications seem to expand the physiological base, Kövecšes' metaphorical categories take up quite a different perspective; their discussion will therefore be left to Section 4.

3. Content analysis

3.1. General aspects

This first part of our analysis is based on 227 items comprising all the 28 metonymies from Kövecšes' data, 115 statements from Davitz' description of basic emotion terms, and 84 items from Shaver *et al.*'s lists of what they call prototypical emotion features. After exclusion of the overlaps the remaining total is 166 items.[8] Figure 3 contains a quantitative analysis in which the data are divided up into physiological items, borderline cases and "psychological items". Another distinction is made between items specific to one basic emotion and those that are shared with other basic emotions.

3.2. *Physiological statements*

The physiological statements (see top row in Figure 3) range from observations of individual body functions (body temperature, skin colour, release of sweat, tears, and saliva, respiration, heartrate, condition of stomach and bowels, typical physical movements) to more general statements on bodily tension (tightness of body, muscular rigidity) and release of tension. In addition, two areas have to be considered which are less clearly physiological and have therefore been called borderline cases (second row in Figure 3): the functioning of the senses, which leads to behavioural responses such as the ability (or inability) to speak, and the domain of physical agitation/excitement, which, apart from obvious physiological candidates like "sexual excitement" for LOVE, also assembles more psychological items such as "sense of being keyed up", "sensation of being wide awake, more alert, bubbly" or "sensation of lightness, buoyancy, and upsurge in the body".

How much do these physiological statements contribute to the conceptual description of basic emotion terms? Without doubt, the most striking result documented in Figure 3 is the singular position of FEAR, both its total score of 24 and, even more remarkable, the number of 13 physiological items exclusively attributed to this basic emotion. Though this result may be somewhat distorted by the special attention that Kövecses seems to pay to the metonymies of FEAR, the list of specific properties makes sense (though it contains some of the expected inconsistencies like "startling" vs. "inability to move"). The items are evenly spread across the various physiological domains and provide a fair description of the concept of FEAR, as shown in Figure 4.

To provide a contrast, Figure 4 also contains the specific physiological statements for the concept of JOY & HAPPINESS, which together with DESIRE & LOVE represent the other extreme. Even if one adds the two physiological items shared with LOVE ("warmth all over", "hugging"), the conceptual structure that emerges is still very patchy. Admittedly,

Type of statement	SADNESS	ANGER	DISGUST & HATE	FEAR	JOY & HAPPINESS	DESIRE & LOVE
Physiological items	10/3*	2/12	2/10	13/11	4/3	2/4
Total	13	14	12	24	7	6
Borderline items (agitation/senses)	3/4	1/8	0/5	6/7	3/9	4/9
Total	7	9	6	13	12	13
Psychological items	9/8	4/12	3/10	14/5	8/19	9/19
Total	17	16	13	19	27	28
Overall score	37	39	31	56	48	47

* The digit before the slash refers to items which are specific to the respective basic emotion, the digit after the slash refers to items shared with other basic emotions

Figure 3. Quantitative analysis of physiological and psychological statements about basic emotions

both positive emotions put up a better performance in the borderline areas (senses, agitation); yet here it is mainly the shared statements ("I feel like smiling, singing"; "being keyed up", etc.) that add to the description but do not help to distinguish JOY from LOVE.

Of the remaining basic emotions listed in Figure 3, the score of ANGER seems to be somewhat disappointing. Though the total of 14 physiological properties makes a sizeable contribution to the description of the concept, ANGER can claim only two specific physiological and merely a single specific borderline item. Most of the items are shared with DISGUST & HATE, a fact reflected in the similar score for this basic emotion and a first indication that one of these emotions may not deserve the status of basicness after all (see below). Finally, there is SADNESS, with its medium overall score of 13, but a relatively large number of 10 specific physiological items (among them "tears well up", "lump in the throat", "heaviness in the chest", "a gnawing feeling in the pit of the stomach", and "sitting, lying around, inactive").

FEAR

Physiological items
(1) Drop in body temperature (Kö)*
(2) Hair straightens out (Kö)
(3) Skin shrinks (Kö)
(4) Blood leaves face (Kö)
(5) Dryness of mouth (Kö)
(6) I have clammy/moist hands (Da)
(7) Sweat/I'm cold, yet perspiration pours out of me (Kö, Da, Sh)
(8) Inability to breathe (Kö)
(9) Lapses of heartbeat (Kö)
(10) Unvoluntary release of bowel/bladder (Kö)
(11) Nervousness of stomach/stomach shivers and trembles (Kö, Da, Sh)
(12) Startling (Kö)
(13) Inability to move/paralyzed (Kö, Da, Sh)

Borderline items (senses/agitation)
(1) Losing ability to focus, disoriented (Sh)
(2) Specific ways of looking (Kö, Sh)
(3) Inability to speak/trembling voice (Kö, Sh)
(4) Screaming (Kö, Sh)
(5) I'm jumpy, jittery (Da, Sh)
(6) Absolute physical turmoil (Da)

JOY/HAPPINESS

Physiological items
(1) Face blushing/flushing (Kö, Sh)
(2) Jumping up an down (Kö)
(3) Breathing/moving seems easier (Da)
(4) Movements graceful, coordinated (Da,Sh)

Borderline items (senses/agitation)
(1) Senses seem to be completey open (Da)
(2) Voice enthusiastic/talking a lot (Sh)
(3) I feel like laughing (Da)

* For the sake of brevity, Kövecses' metonymies are represented by their abstract labels, not as linguistic expressions. Legend: Kö = Kövecses, Da = Davitz, Sh = Shaver et al.

Figure 4. Physiological items specific to FEAR and JOY/HAPPINESS

To sum up, basic emotion concepts are very unevenly supported by specific physiological statements. While FEAR and, more tentatively, SADNESS are well equipped, the other negative basic emotions concepts, ANGER and DISGUST & HATE, can only draw some structure, but little in terms of demarcation, from physiological items; the two positive basic emotions are definitely physiologically underspecified.

3.3. Psychological statements and the principle of compensation

Unlike physiological items, the other statements are less tangible and more difficult to classify. Loosely following Davitz (1969:127ff), one might attribute them to the categories "comfort" ("sense of harmony", "wanting to hold back time"), "attraction", ("wanting to make others happy", "sense of being wanted"), "aggression" ("keep thinking of revenge"), and "retreat" ("I become introspective, turn inside"), or to the categories "competence/control" ("being in tune with the world", "sense of sureness") and "incompetence/lack of control" ("sense of loss", "I feel vulnerable and helpless"). If this classification still leaves us with a lot of vague and overlapping items, this is perhaps not so bad in the light of the argument to be pursued in the next section. The elusiveness of psychological statements should, however, be at the back of our minds, when we now return to the quantitative analysis and take another look at Figure 3.

Starting this time with the overall scores listed in the bottom row, we find a noticeable difference between FEAR (56 items) and DISGUST & HATE (31 items), but not, as we might expect after our discussion of physiological items, between FEAR and JOY & HAPPINESS or LOVE & DESIRE (their scores are 46 and 47 items respectively). The reason is that the poor physiological scores of JOY & HAPPINESS and LOVE & DESIRE are made up for by the large number of psychological statements attracted by these emotions. Even if we make allowances for a certain pollyanna effect (informants want to show their preference for the positive aspects of life), the totals of 27 and 28 psychological (mostly shared) items listed for each of them in Figure 4 are indeed impressive and should not be regarded as a mere chance result. Rather, these scores illustrate that a principle of compensation is at work which ensures an adequate description even where there is a shortage of specific physiological statements.

Applying this principle to FEAR, with its high physiological score, one would expect a particularly small number of psychological items. Yet this is not the case. In addition to its large number of physiological statements, FEAR also assembles 14 specific psychological items (e.g. "intense concern for what will happen next", "sense of not knowing where to go") and holds a good middle position as far as the total number of these items is concerned; the result is the highest overall total of items for any basic emotion (56 items). One of the reasons why psychological items for FEAR are so numerous seems to be that they add an essential aspect to the description which cannot be properly indicated physiologically (the aspect of incompetence or lack of control; see above).

The poor performance of ANGER, especially in terms of specific items, and the even poorer results for DISGUST & HATE should not come as a surprise; they just add to our suspicion that distinctive descriptions of these basic emotions may be difficult to establish. SADNESS has the most balanced score. It is equipped with a number of specific properties in each domain, and this should facilitate description and recognition.

To sum up at this point, the quantitative analysis of the psychological statements has been reassuring in cases like JOY & HAPPINESS and DESIRE & LOVE, where the physiological description is particularly unsatisfactory. Yet as suggested above, it tends to divert attention from the vagueness and elusiveness of many of the psychological statements, and this is where the study of conceptual metaphors may prove helpful.

4. Analysis in terms of metaphors

4.1. The relationship between metaphors and informants' statements

How can metaphors, or more precisely, metaphorical expressions be integrated into the analysis? A simple and very practical approach is to juxtapose them with the statements (including Kövecšes' metonymies), using the classification into physiological, borderline, and psychological items as a grid. Figure 5 presents an excerpt from such a conceptual "profile" (the full version would have taken too much space).

As a single glance at Figure 5 shows, there are obvious links between the statements and the metaphors. Starting from the top, we find that the metaphors ANGER IS THE HEAT OF A FLUID IN A CONTAINER and ANGER IS FIRE can be related to and are probably triggered off by statements referring to increased body heat (a metonymy in Kövecšes' terminology). These metaphors (as well as the INSANITY metaphor, the next item listed in the Figure) can be seen as applications of the general principle that metaphors are generated from metonymies. In this case the metaphors tend to have a kind of intensifying, supportive function.

The picture changes when we move on to the metaphors which are juxtaposed to the psychological statements. If we look at the statements expressing aggression we find that a number of them, and certainly the more forceful ones like "I feel I'll burst or explode" or "Impulse to strike out, pound, smash, kick, strike, hurt someone" already contain a metaphorical expression, here a variant of the CONTAINER metaphor. The reason is that these feelings can only be expressed, and perhaps imagined, with the help of metaphors; in other words, they need the structuring potential of conceptual metaphors in order to work. Compared with the examples discussed above, the relationship between metaphor and statement is reversed; now it is the statements that depend on the concept-creating power of the metaphor and not vice versa.

Physiological statements	Conceptual metaphors
Increase of body heat Redness in face and neck area	ANGER AS HEAT OF A FLUID IN A CONTAINER (*seethe*, *simmer*, *make blood boil*)* ANGER AS FIRE (*flare up*, *be ablaze*, *smoulder*)
Borderline statements (agitation, senses)	
Physical agitation /excitement, keyed up Body seems to speed up, a churning inside.	ANGER AS INSANITY (*go mad*, *drive berserk*)
Aggressive visual behaviour Aggressive verbal behaviour	ANGER AS AN (ACTIVELY FOUGHT) OPPONENT (*fight*, *struggle*, *wrestle*)
Psychological statements	
Aggression: I keep thinking of getting even, of revenge	ANGER AS A DANGEROUS/AGGRESSIVE ANIMAL (*ferocious*, *fierce*, *arouse*, *awake*)
Sense as if everything inside, my stomach, etc. is expanding, almost bursting I feel that I'll burst or explode Impulse to strike out, pound, smash, kick, bite, hurt someone	AS ANGER INCREASES FLUID IN A CT RISES (*well up*, *build up*) PRESSURE INCREASES/STEAM GENERATED & LET OUT (*pent up*, *bottled up*, *steam up*, *give vent*) CT EXPLODES AS ANGER GETS TOO INTENSE (*explode*, *burst*, *flip the lid*) ....
Incompetence/lack of control Sense of being gripped/ overwhelmed by the situation	ANGER AS A NATURAL FORCE (WIND, etc) (*overwhelm*, *engulf*, *sweep over*), etc.
I feel as if I'm under a heavy burden I keep searching for an explanation	ANGER AS A BURDEN (*weigh*, *be relieved of*)

* The verbs and adjectives in brackets indicate in an exemplary way how the metaphor in question is expressed linguistically

Figure 5. Statements and metaphors for ANGER (excerpt)

Ideally, there is an almost cyclical relationship between statements and metaphors, as shown in Figure 6. In the case of the CONTAINER metaphor, which probably comes closest to this ideal, one could assume that the basic version of this metaphor (HEAT OF A FLUID IN A CONTAINER) is triggered off by a physiological metonymy ("increase in body heat", see above). This basic version of the metaphor is then elaborated or enriched by various actions which can be performed in the container and which are based on our experience of concrete actions and events. The elaborated version in turn gives conceptual support to the psychological statements ("I'll burst or explode", etc.), and the psychological statements make their contribution to the conceptual structure of the emotion concept, thus compensating for the lack of distinctive physiological statements.

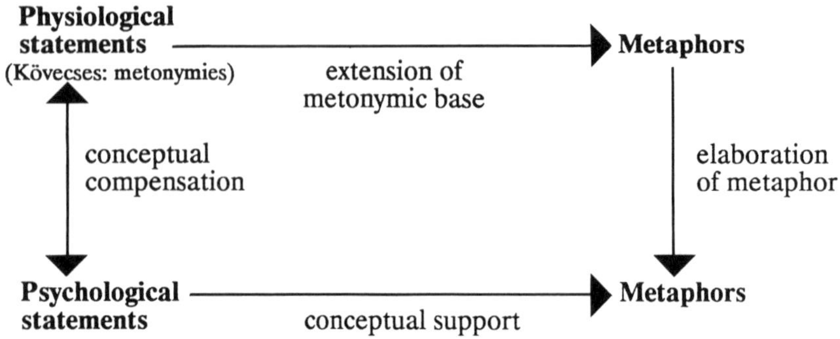

Figure 6. Relationship between statements and conceptual metaphors

Another cycle involves the metonymic statements "aggressive visual/verbal behaviour" as a base for the ACTIVE OPPONENT and DANGEROUS ANIMAL metaphors, which, after being enriched by concepts like "fight", "struggle", "ferocious", and "fierce", provide conceptual support for the psychological statement "thinking of revenge"; and this statement again complements the metonymies of aggressive visual/verbal behaviour.

On the whole, such perfect cyclical interaction will be rare; normally, the concept-creating power of the metaphors will simply arise from our knowledge of organisms, actions, and qualities, or to use cognitive terminology, from the basic level concepts which are most readily available in our minds (Ungerer, 1994). Thus the NATURAL FORCE metaphor (listed at the bottom of Figure 5) will rely on our knowledge about wind and gales, high tide and floods, and in this way help to conceptualize the psychological statements about the feeling of incompetence that is associated with ANGER. Similarly our knowledge of how heavy concrete objects are will structure the statement "I feel as if I'm under a heavy burden". Yet even with these metaphors a metonymic physiological base cannot be completely excluded. The NATURAL FORCE metaphor may be stimulated by a defensive gesture with the arm and the BURDEN metaphor by a drooping posture.

4.2. The distribution of metaphors and statements across basic emotions

To decide whether our exemplary interpretation of ANGER metaphors can be extended to other basic emotions, an analysis was made of all the metaphors for basic emotions listed in Kövecšes' publications. In addition, some metaphors were collected for SADNESS (which is not covered by Kövecšes); the total number of metaphors investigated was 61.[9] The method employed was to place metaphors in profiles according to the model of the ANGER profile. On the whole, this attempt was successful. However, there remain some metaphors which cannot be satisfactorily related to any of the statements, especially metaphors which seem to be in opposition (or mock opposition?) to the accepted characteristics of the emotion, e.g. LOVE AS WAR, LOVE AS HUNTING and LOVE AS A CAPTIVE ANIMAL.[10]

Since there is no room to present the profiles in full, some of the results have been assembled in Figure 7, where they are contrasted with the findings about statements and metonymies.

While ANGER has been included to provide the link with the exemplary analysis of Section 4.1., the findings for FEAR and DESIRE & LOVE are listed because they represent the most interesting cases. Between them these two emotions illustrate how the principle of compensation, which we found at work in the interaction of physiological and psychological statements, is also decisive for the distribution of metaphors. Quite in line with this principle, the concept of FEAR, which is already supported by numerous physiological statements, attracts relatively few metaphors (a total of 9), mainly supportive metaphors for physiological metonymies expressing pain, but also a few concept-creating metaphors for statements expressing "incompetence".

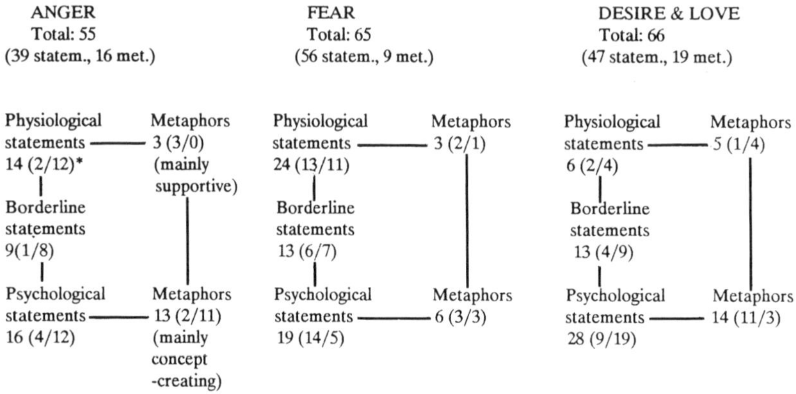

* The first digit indicates the overall number of items, the first digit in brackets indicates the number of items specific to the emotion, while the last digit indicates the number of items shared with other basic emotions.

Figure 7. Quantitative analysis of metaphors for ANGER, FEAR, and DESIRE & LOVE

In contrast, the concept of DESIRE & LOVE compensates for its low score of physiological items by having the largest number of metaphors assigned to any basic emotion (the total is 24, of which 19 can be safely placed in the profile). Among the LOVE metaphors there are many concept-creating metaphors, most of them expressing "attraction" and "comfort"; this is not surprising when we remember that LOVE has a large number of psychological statements in these domains (28), which are rather vague if taken by themselves and have to be supported by conceptual metaphors. The fact that LOVE can also muster the largest number of specific concept-creating metaphors (11) shows that metaphors are used to distinguish this concept from JOY & HAPPINESS, with which LOVE shares such a large number of statements.

The concept of ANGER, our model case, has 16 "placed" metaphors, almost as many as LOVE, among them 13 of the concept-creating kind. Yet ANGER differs from LOVE because most of its metaphors are shared with DISGUST & HATE, so the demarcation between the two concepts, which we found lacking in the content analysis of the statements, is not really improved. The results for SADNESS (not listed in Figure 7) are the least spectacular. The total number of collected metaphors is 6; four of them support and intensify the physiological statements (or metonymies) which, according to our analysis, are the dominant element in the characterization of SADNESS.

Summing up this survey of metaphors, we find that on the whole it endorses the content analysis of the statements; in fact, the distribution of metaphors and statements is as closely linked as the two sides of a coin. Besides, the analysis of metaphors is of considerable explanatory value. On the one hand, it helps to understand why certain psychological statements about emotions are preferred by informants, namely those that are sufficiently well supported by concept-creating metaphors. On the other hand, the analysis shows how physiological statements influence the choice of source domains for supportive, intensifying metaphors.

Another thing that our two analyses have in common is that they are confined to our set of basic emotions, whose saliency is taken for granted. Yet how can we be sure that ANGER, SADNESS, DISGUST & HATE, FEAR, JOY & HAPPINESS, and DESIRE & LOVE are in fact "basic" concepts of equal standing? Why, given the prototype paradigm, should they not just be seen as more or less typical exponents of a single, comprehensive concept of emotion, on which the description would naturally have to concentrate? This latter position is held by cognitive psychologists like Fehr & Russel (1984) and also by Kövecšes (1990a).

4.3. Basic emotion concepts vs. a single concept of emotion

In their study, Fehr & Russel apply the whole machinery of Rosch's typicality tests to emotions and claim the status of prototype category for the concept of emotion. However, apart from the general concept of emotion, they postulate a "middle level" (Fehr & Russel 1984:481f), the level of ANGER, FEAR, LOVE, HATE, etc., i.e. our basic emotions. This level, they find, is "basic" in the sense that it fulfils all the conditions of concrete basic level categories as listed by Rosch (short names that first come to mind, etc.). In fact one might say that Fehr & Russel, while actually favouring the superordinate concept of emotion, already attribute a strong position in the system to basic emotions. This approach is further developed by Shaver *et al.* (1987); their attention is already firmly focused on basic emotions for which they provide prototypical "features" (one of the sources for our "statements") as well as prototypical scripts. So there is nothing in this approach that would contradict our position.

Compared with Fehr & Russel and Shaver *et al.*, Kövecšes pursues the opposite course. Starting out from metonymic and metaphorical expressions for individual, mostly basic emotions like DESIRE & LOVE and ANGER, he later transfers practically all these items to the general concept EMOTION. On closer scrutiny, however, it appears that most of these metaphors and metonymies (or physiological statements) are only understood because we do not interpret Kövecšes' examples at face value, that is as statements about emotion in general. Instead, we tacitly relate the metonymies and metaphors to one of the basic emotions. In the case of of CONTAINER EXPLODES AS EMOTION GETS TOO INTENSE this may be ANGER (which Kövecšes regards as the protoypical emotion). With the metaphor EMOTION IS A TORMENTER we will fall back on the concept of FEAR, and EMOTION IS A VALUABLE COMMODITY will probably be processed via the concepts DESIRE & LOVE or JOY & HAPPINESS.

What does this mean for the status of the EMOTION concept? It seems that an alternative explanation might be based on an analogy with concepts relating to organisms and concrete objects or, more precisely, an analogy with the distinction between basic level and superordinate concepts in this field. As suggested by Brown (1990:17ff), superordinate concepts such as FRUIT, VEHICLE, or FURNITURE do not seem to have the rich conceptual structure of basic level concepts like APPLE, CAR, or CHAIR. Rather they are characterized by one or several salient attributes, e.g. "used as food" for FRUIT or "means of transportation" for VEHICLE. If someone wants to get a fuller conceptual picture of these superordinate concepts they have to fall back on the respective basic level concepts (APPLE, CAR, CHAIR etc.) - we might call this parasitic categorization (Ungerer 1994).

The question is how this notion of parasitic catagorization can be applied to emotion concepts. Which properties might be regarded as somehow equivalent to the salient attributes of concrete superordinates? Let us assume that these salient properties of the general concept of emotion (which would also have to be shared by all the basic emotion concepts) can be derived from our statements and metaphors. Figure 8 presents a list of statements and metaphors which are common to all or most basic emotions and which have intentionally been excluded from the previous analyses.

Statements	*Conceptual metaphors*
Feeling begins with a sharp sudden onset Feeling comes all involuntarily, without warning	EMOTIONAL EFFECT AS PHYSICAL CONTACT (*hit, strike, kick, stagger*) EMOTION COMES SUDDENLY FROM THE OUTSIDE (*strike, cast, blow*)
A steady, ongoing, boundless feeling	EMOTION AS LIVING ORGANISM (*grow, wilt, die*)
Lingering, lasting a long time, going slowly	PRESENCE AS EXISTENCE OF EMOTION (*stay, go away, come back*)
Feeling fills me completely	EMOTION AS FLUID IN A CONTAINER (*full, filled, empty*)
Feeling all over, nowhere special Feeling very deep inside More an "inner" than an "outer" feeling	BODY / EYES / HEART / OTHER ORGANS AS CONTAINER FOR EMOTION (*contain, be filled*)

Figure 8. Statements and metaphors shared by all or most basic emotions

According to Davitz (1969:7), the statements listed in the left-hand column refer to the length and development of the feeling. If we add that "development" may include the description of the onset and the termination it is clear that it is with these general items that Davitz' statements come closest to the notion of script and scenario as advocated by Shaver *et al.* and Kövecšes (and this is something to keep in mind for the final evaluation).

Moving from statements to metaphors (right-hand column of Figure 8) we are not only faced with some newcomers (EMOTIONAL EFFECT AS PHYSICAL CONTACT, EMOTION COMES SUDDENLY FROM THE OUTSIDE), but also with some metaphors we have already encountered in the metaphorical analysis of individual basic emotions, notably the CONTAINER metaphor. Here it is helpful to recall a distinction which is inherent in Kövecšes and Lakoff's treatment of metaphors, but is sometimes neglected. Consider the following possibilities:

- The CONTAINER metaphor may simply express that something is in a container.
- The CONTAINER metaphor may also stress various kinds of actions that may take place in the container (extension, overflowing, explosion, draining).

Of the two interpretations of the CONTAINER metaphor, the general version seems to apply to the EMOTION concept and at the same time seems to be shared by all basic emotion concepts. Similarly, the general versions of the LIVING ORGANISM and OBJECT metaphors (which are also listed in Figure 8) could be claimed for the EMOTION concept. The detailed actions (explosion, overflowing, draining) belong to the basic level concepts, i.e. our basic emotions. Their conceptual structure embraces not only the general, but also the more specific aspects of the CONTAINER metaphor, and this also applies to the LIVING ORGANISM and OBJECT metaphors. In simple words, talking about emotion, the language user tends to think in terms of basic emotions, of ANGER, SADNESS, DISGUST, FEAR, JOY, and LOVE, but may prefer to use the superordinate term *emotion* when he wants to highlight certain general properties that are common to all basic emotions.

5. Conclusion

5.1. Results

The major results of the paper may be summarized as follows:

- The combination of informants' statements, physiological metonymies, and metaphors may not provide a discrete, objective definition of basic emotion terms. However, it offers a description that is not only intersubjectively validated, but is on the whole more comprehensive than accounts based exclusively on the author's intuition. The result is a set of descriptive items ranging from 39 items (for DISGUST & HATE) to 66 items (for DESIRE & LOVE), and this can, from a cognitive perspective, be taken as proof of a rich conceptual structure.
- The distribution of statements and metaphors is governed by a principle of compensation.
- Even if one regards all basic emotion concepts as prototypically structured categories, the demarcation of basic emotions is developed in different degrees: FEAR and SADNESS are relatively well

distinguished from other basic emotions by specific items, while on the other hand the demarcation is less clear between JOY and LOVE and between ANGER and HATE; this confirms the doubts expressed by some psychologists (see note 3).

- Basic emotions are more important for the semantic description and the conceptualization of emotions than the superordinate concept EMOTION, whose function is to highlight a few common characteristics of emotions concerning the onset, development, and termination of the emotion.

5.2. *Open questions*

Again there is just room to touch on a few of the issues:

Comprehensiveness and descriptive precision
While psychological investigations are rooted in a long tradition of rigid procedure, cognitive linguistics has not yet developed a satisfactory method of processing linguistic material (Kövecšes relies on his own linguistic intuition and on Roget's *Thesaurus*, which is largely based on the authors' intuitions). The question is whether both a wider range of description and greater degree of objectivity can be achieved by making use of computerized corpora. Since many of the metonymic and metaphorical expressions do not contain the emotion word, it seems difficult to conceive a method of extracting all the relevant examples from a corpus.

Another issue is the internal or micro-analysis of the metaphors, which has been neglected in this paper. Descriptive precision could probably be improved by a careful revision of the labels used for the metaphors by Kövecšes, and further insights into the structure of the metaphors could be obtained if they were analyzed in terms of metaphtonymy (Goossens 1990).

Scripts or scenarios
This study has carefully avoided presenting the descriptions of the basic emotions in terms of scripts or scenarios, which are favoured by both Kövecšes and Shaver *et al.* The only exception was the description of the superordinate concept EMOTION, where the items seem to provide a natural sequence of onset, development, and termination (Figure 8). This does not mean that a script-like sequencing of the descriptions of the individual basic emotion should be excluded. Yet as things stand, Kövecšes' scenarios (or models) depend on his intuition, while Shaver *et al.*'s

scripts are based on pair-ratings of items by members of their team of psychologists (Shaver *et al.* 1987:1073), so both methods are not all that reliable. The proper linguistic way of deciding about the script-like qualities of emotion terms would be to study text passages describing emotions, and here again the collected corpora could provide a starting point.

Diachronic perspective
As Geeraerts & Grondelaers (1991) have rightly stressed, Kövecšes' way of looking at emotion concepts is non-historical, and we should add that this also applies to psychological investigations based on informants' statements. There can be little doubt that the choice of metaphors and their relationship with metonymies is influenced by the cultural background as it has developed over the centuries. In the case of anger Geeraerts & Grondelaers have shown that a link exists with the medieval theory of humours, and this suggests that the conceptualization of other basic emotions may also be dependent on cultural traditions.

Basic emotions as a reference framework for linguistic analysis
This final point takes us back to our initial problem. Can the emotional effects of certain grammatical features (the progressive form, the *get*-passive) or of certain intonational contours be more convincingly analyzed if we start from a limited set of basic emotions? And what is the contribution of the descriptive profiles collected from statements, metonymies, and metaphors (see Figure 5)? One thing seems to be fairly certain. By relating the emotional effects of linguistic phenonema to our set of basic emotions, it is much easier to compare and evaluate them. It is also imaginable that specific emotional effects, e.g. the expression of ANGER through the use of the progressive form coupled with an adverb of frequency (*He is always playing the piano*), can be better described if the relevant metaphors are included in the description and if their concept-creating function is stressed. However, as the example shows, we should not expect too much too soon in a domain which has so persistently evaded linguistic analysis.

Notes

1. I want to thank the editors of this volume, L. Lipka and H.-J. Schmid, for their comments on an earlier version; I am also indebted to the members of a seminar on Emotion in the English language held in the winter semester 1991/92.

2. Extending the classical definition, metonymy is here used to denote the relationship between physiological effects (or stimuli) of emotions and the emotions themselves.
3. Johnson-Laird & Oatley start out from a set of five basic emotions, which includes only one positive emotion, i.e. HAPPINESS, and only later add DESIRE (Johnson-Laird & Oatley 1989, 1992). Shaver *et al.* find that according to their goodness-rating tests HATE should not be regarded as a basic emotion, but as a subordinate category of ANGER. As our analysis will show these cautious positions are not unjustified (see final section).
4. Ryle actually distinguishes between three types of emotion; apart from "inclinations" (Lyons' "dispositions") and "moods" (Lyons' "occurrent states") he proposes the category of "feelings", which predominantly express momentary physical reactions and will therefore be neglected. The examples given in brackets in the text are partly derived from Ryle's and Lyons' classifications and only express tendencies (see also Kövecšes 1990a:26f).
5. The arrangement of the basic emotions in Figure 1 is to be seen as a first attempt to reflect the positive/negative contrast as well as the more specific antonymies SADNESS vs. JOY, DISGUST vs. DESIRE and HATE vs. LOVE. Another aim is to show the closeness of JOY/HAPPINESS and DESIRE/LOVE, and of ANGER and HATE (see discussion below); this is unfortunately only possible at the expense of SADNESS and FEAR which, of course, are not as distant from each other as they appear to be in this figure.
6. To support their hypothesis that basic emotions are (psychologically) unanalyzable, Johnson-Laird & Oatley (1989) set out to derive the meanings of all other emotion words (590 items in all) from these basic emotions plus a set of (structuralist looking) features which include degrees of intensity and causative status (as mentioned above), but also emotional goals, etc.
7. Additional material on SADNESS will be taken from an unpublished examination thesis by Susan Rosner.
8. The number of items taken from Kövecšes is so small because only the metaphorical labels, not the individual examples were considered. In addition, Kövecšes' metonymies only cover physiological properties, while Davitz' and Shaver *et al.*'s statements include psychological items. As for the total number of items given, it does not include the "general" statements about emotions presented in Figure 8.
9. This number does not include the "general" statements about emotions presented in Figure 8.
10. Kövecšes (1988) tries to solve this problem by postulating several scenarios for LOVE (the ideal or folk model of romantic love, the typical model of love leading to marriage). In addition, he assumes non-prototypical variations.

References

Arndt, H. & R. W. Janney
1987 *InterGrammar. Towards an Integrative Model of Verbal, Prosodic and Kinesic Emotions in Speech*. Berlin: Mouton de Gruyter.

Charleston, B.
1960 *Studies on the Emotional and Affective Means of Expressions in Modern English*. Bern: Francke.
Danes, F.
1987 Cognition and emotion in discourse interaction. In: *Preprints of the Plenary Session Papers. XIV International Linguistic Congress Berlin (Ost) 10-15: August 1987*, pp. 272-291.
Davitz, J.
1969 *The Language of Emotion*. New York: Academic Press.
Fehr, B. & J. A. Russel
1984 "The concept of emotion viewed from a prototype perspective". *Journal of Experimental Psychology: General* 113: 464-486.
Geeraerts, D. & S. Grondelaers
1991 *Looking Back at Anger: Cultural Traditions and Metaphorical Patterns*. Katholieke Universiteit Leuven, Preprint nr. 133.
Goossens, L.
1990 "Metaphthonymy: the interaction of metaphor and metonymy in expressions for linguistic action". *Cognitive Linguistics* 1:323-340.
Hübler, A.
1991 On the GET-Passive. In: Busse, W. G. (ed.). *Anglistentag 1991 Düsseldorf. Proceedings*, Tübingen: Niemeyer, pp. 86-101.
Johnson-Laird, P. N. & K. Oatley
1989 "The language of emotions: An analysis of a semantic field". *Cognition and Emotion* 3:81-123.
1992 "Basic emotions, rationality, and folk theory". *Cognition and Emotion* 6:201-223.
Kövecšes, Z.
1986 *Metaphors of Anger, Pride, and Love*. Amsterdam: Benjamins.
1988 *The Language of Love*. Lewisburgh: Associated University Presses.
1990a *Emotion Concepts*. New York: Springer.
1990b "Joy. An exercise in the description of emotion concepts". *Grazer Linguistische Studien* 33/34:153-164.
1991 "Happiness: A definitional effort". *Metaphor and Symbolic Activity* 6:29-46.
1993 "American Friendship". Paper delivered at the 3rd ICLA Conference at Leuven.
Lakoff, G.
1987 *Women, Fire, and Dangerous Things. What Categories Reveal about the Mind*. Chicago: Chicago University Press.
Lyons, W.
1980 *Emotion*. Cambridge: Cambridge University Press.
Nöth, W.
1992 Symmetries and asymmetries between positive and negative emotion words. In: Busse, W. G. (ed.). *Anglistentag 1991 Düsseldorf. Proceedings*, Tübingen: Niemeyer, pp.72-88.
Ortony, A., G. L. Clore & A. Collins
1988 *The Cognitive Structure of Emotions*. Cambridge: Cambridge University Press.
Pohosz, M.
1983 *Emotive Intonation. Evidence from English*. Lublin, Diss.
Ryle, G.
1958 *The Concept of Mind*. London: Hutchinson.

Shaver, P., J. Schwartz, D. Kirson & C. O'Connor (eds.)
1987 "Emotion knowledge: Further exploration of a prototype approach". *Journal of Personality and Social Psychology* 52:1061-1086.

Stankiewicz, E.
1964 Problems of emotive language. In: Sebeok, T. A. *et al.* (eds). *Approaches to Semiotics*. The Hague: Mouton, pp. 239-264.

Ungerer, F.
1991 "What makes a linguistic sign successful?" *Lingua* 83:155-181.
1994 "Basic level concepts and parasitic categorization: A cognitive alternative to conventional semantic hierarchies". *Zeitschrift für Anglistik und Amerikanistik* 42:148-162.

Wierzbicka, A.
1986 "Human emotions: universal or culture specific?" *American Anthropologist* 88:584-594.
1988 "The semantics of emotions: Fear and its relatives in English". *Australian Journal of Linguistics* 10:359-375.
1992 "Talking about emotions: Semantics, culture, and cognition". *Cognition and Emotion* 6:285-319.

Polish translation of English technical terms: Metaphor in the language of computer science

Elżbieta Tabakowska

1. Preliminary

One of the main assumptions which underlie the cognitive approach to language as developed within the theoretical framework of cognitive linguistics concerns the central status of metaphor as the governing principle of language use and development. Similarly, in the field of translation studies, it has been generally accepted that "metaphor is at the centre of all problems of translation theory" (Newmark 1980:100). It might then seem natural that the consensus about the status ascribed to metaphor by translation theory on the one hand and by cognitive linguistics on the other might provide a common ground for both empirical research and theoretical reflection. Yet, while linguists of the cognitive persuasion have much to say about metaphor, so far they have not been particularly interested in translation, and even less so in the translation of metaphor.

The present paper explores a part of the common territory on which translation theory and cognitive linguistics might profitably meet. The language of computer science seems a good choice for a case study, for two main reasons. First, when computers arrived in Poland they spoke exclusively in English, as did the narrow elite of the "initiated" who talked to or about them. Quick and dynamic development of computer science, combined with the growing popularity of personal computers among non-experts, soon made it necessary to introduce a change in the medium of communication. Even a fragmentary observation of the process - in its present *statu nascendi* - provides copious and fascinating data which illustrates various types of lingustic change. Moreover, in view of the general similarity of extralinguistic conditioning factors (political, economic, cultural, etc.), it may be legitimately claimed that phenomena observed in this particular area - if considered on an adequately generalized level - will also be found in other areas of language (one obvious example being the language of business and management).

2. Borrowing vs. translation

The following sample analysis is based on data found in popular texts (magazines and textbooks for non-professional PC users; cf. the full list of sources at the end of the paper). While it cannot claim statistical relevance, it is still illustrative of certain obvious regularities.

On the level of lexemes, direct, or modified borrowing prevails, with the transient stage on the way to full adaptation being marked by inconsistencies in spelling, or presence vs. absence of flexional and derivational morphemes. The borderline between borrowing and adaptation on the one hand and translation proper on the other is marked by different types of hybrids. Most typically these are structures in which the original English word is preceded by a Polish definition, e.g.:

(1) *urządzenia archiwizujące dane czyli streamery*
devices putting-in-archives data-ACC or streamers
'archive attribute marking devices, or streamers' (GW)[1]

(2) *sterowniki programowe (drajwery)*
drivers program-ADJ (drivers)
'program drivers'

Often a "prompt" is provided by situating a given item within a higher level conceptual category:

(3) *program typu shareware*
program of-type shareware
'shareware type of program'

The simple hybrid structure is exemplified by

(4) *środowisko graficzne Windows*
environment graphical Windows
'Windows graphical environment'

The tendency to borrow is opposed by the tendency to translate, advocated by purists who support their principled stance with appeals to authors of programs and textbooks "to make people's lives easier". The two attitudes have been clearly manifested in a recent polemics concerning Polish PC terminology, in which the proponents of the two opposing policies became engaged in a rather long and bitter argument

(Wimmer 1991, 1992, Tatarkiewicz 1991, Wimmer & Tatarkiewicz 1992).

The discussion presented further in this paper is limited to some chosen problems of translation. It will be claimed that it is the translation of metaphors that appears most illustrative of general tendencies and strategies used both by translators and original writers, and, furthermore, that the pattern which emerges out of the sample analysis corroborates the cognitive theory of metaphor.

3. Metaphor and cognitive semantics

Traditionally, metaphor was considered (by linguists and students of literature alike) as a figure of speech; it was believed to belong solely and entirely to the language of poetry and rhetoric, and consequently, it was as a rule relegated from the area of linguistic investigation. As a marginal linguistic phenomenon, it was considered to be of interest only to literary critics or philosophers of language.

Cognitive linguistics takes an opposite stance: rather than a mere figure of speech, metaphor is considered to be a mode of thought (cf. Lakoff 1990:50). Rather than a conventional linguistic expression, it is believed to be a conventional mode of thinking. As such it is ubiquitous: present in uncountable ordinary everyday expressions. The process of metaphorisation is seen as a reflection of human mental ability to understand one cognitive domain in terms of another. Thus the postulate that metaphor is regularly found in utterly "non-poetic" manifestations of language goes counter to the standard claim of "mainstream" lin-guists, who "assume that scientific or technological texts will contain mainly literal language, illustrated by an occasional simile (a more cautious form of metaphor)" (Newmark 180:93).

Naturally, source domains tend to be rooted in man's most basic, biological and bodily experience, well-known and therefore easy to grasp, while target domains present higher levels of complexity and abstraction. To quote Lakoff's famous example, the domain of love may be metaphorically understood in terms of a different domain; that of a journey, which is reflected in such English expressions as *We're at crossroads* or *We may have to go our separate ways* (Lakoff 1990:47ff, cf. also Lakoff & Johnson 1980, Johnson 1987).

Crucial for the cognitivist theory of metaphor is Lakoff's distinction between *conceptual* and *image* metaphors (Lakoff 1990). The former involve "ontological and epistemic mapping across conceptual domains" (Lakoff 1990:49); a general conceptualisation of one domain in terms of another gives rise to a number of different linguistic expressions. Thus it is the general understanding of love in terms of a *journey* that accounts for the occurrence in the language of numerous expressions which all embody and employ this common conceptualisation. And it is our understanding of the general conceptualisation that makes it possible to create - and to understand - various novel extensions of the metaphor. An image metaphor, on the other hand, only maps a single image onto another single image; to use Lakoff's (metaphorical!) definition, it is a "one-shot" metaphor, which is not "productive" in the sense of becoming a source for further extensions (Lakoff 1990:66). Thus it is assumed that, because of their "bodily" basis, linguistic realisations of conceptual metaphors prove less culture-specific, and therefore easier to translate than image metaphors.

4. Metaphor in the language of computer science

Predictably, the data provides examples of both conceptual and image metaphors. Within the first category (predictably again), various realisations of the CONDUIT METAPHOR prevail. Defined as "the principal metaphor for communication" (Lakoff 1987:108), it conceptualises meanings as objects which the speaker puts into words, which are thought of as containers. Once "wrapped up", the information is sent along a channel to the listener, who takes the meanings-objects out of the words-containers. The second highly productive conceptual metaphor is personification: COMPUTER IS A RATIONAL PERSON (in Polish additionally enhanced by the masculine grammatical gender of the noun *komputer*). These two metaphors give rise to numerous extensions; in the Polish data some of these are in all probability independent original creations rather than translations from English. On a lower level of conceptual generality, the Apple Macintosh personification COMPUTER IS A SECRETARY WORKING IN AN OFFICE is also fairly productive.

In English computer texts, image metaphors abound. Some are indeed "one-shot" ones (cf. e.g. *handshake* or *laptop*), while others prove general enough to give rise to further extensions (cf. e.g. *mouse* or *menu*). In the Polish texts, translation strategies differ. Like in the case of expressions based on conceptual metaphors, some image mataphors found in the sample are in all probability novel creations.

5. Metaphors in translation

The examples that may be nonambiguously identified as cases of translation rather than extension or creation fall into three categories:

(i) literal translation, i.e. replacing an English metaphor with a "literal" Polish equivalent. Traditionally, such instances would be classified as *calques*;
(ii) reproductions, i.e. cases in which a source language metaphor is replaced with a *different* target language metaphor;
(iii) non-metaphorical renderings of target language metaphors.

Examples falling within each of the three categories systematically coincide with Lakoff's taxonomy of metaphors, providing a unified explanation of translating strategies.

5.1. Conceptual metaphors: CONDUIT METAPHOR

Extensions of the CONDUIT METAPHOR are in most cases rendered as literal translations, resulting in fully equivalent metaphorical expressions:

(5) INFORMATION IS AN OBJECT:
a. *informacja obrobiona*
information processed
'processed information'
b. *ściągnąć informację*
fetch information
'to import information'

(6) SYSTEMS/PROGRAMS/ICONS ARE CONTAINERS:
a. *otworzyć ikonę*
open icon
'to open an icon'
b. *wyjść z Windows*
go out of Windows
'to leave Windows'
c. *włamać się do systemu*
in-break oneself to system
'to break into a system'

(7) INFORMATION TRAVELS THROUGH SPACE:
a. *program idzie*
program goes
'program runs'
b. *ścieżka (danych, krytyczna, etc.)*
footpath (of-data, critical)
'path'

Within the last extension, the word *wedrówka* (*migration*) appears systematically in such novel expressions as

(8) *ostatni z etapów wędrówki danych jest buforowany*
last of stages of-migration of-data is buffered
'The last stage of the transfer of data is moved to the buffer' (GW)

While the Polish word *wędrówka* seems fully acceptable, the synonymous borrowing *migracja* is still felt to be "foreign", and thus used as in

(9) *Wprowadzono także (...) tzw. "migrację" danych*
was introduced also the so-called migration of-data
'What has also been introduced is the so-called "migration" of data' (GW)

5.2. Conceptual metaphors: PERSONIFICATION

The general metaphor COMPUTER IS A RATIONAL BEING gives rise to numerous extensions, of which the basic one is COMPUTER AND ITS USER ENTER INTO A DIALOGUE. Thus a Polish video agency offers a teach-yourself course called

(10) *"Dialog z Wordperfektem"*
dialogue with WordPerfect
'A Dialogue with WordPerfect' (P-T)

The English metaphorical description *user-friendly* (*program*) is reflected in a chain of metaphors employed in the following description of MS-DOS:

(11) *...prompt DOS-a jest nieprzyjazny. W rzeczywistości DOS*
prompt of-DOS is unfriendly. In reality DOS
jest arogancki i zrozumie tylko pewne rzeczy. Gdy
is arrogant and will understand only some things. If
czegoś nie rozumie, wypluwa komunikat błędu.
something not [it]understands spits out message of-error
'The DOS prompt is unfriendly. In fact, DOS is arrogant and it will only understand certain things. If there is something it does not understand, it spits out an error message' (GW)

The use of inverted commas parallels that exemplified in Section 5.1. above: while the volitional verb *chcieć* (*want*) is already generally accepted, with extended uses of verbs of sensory perception and of *verba dicendi* the authors still mark their lack of confidence by providing "a translation label in inverted commas" (Newmark 1980:98):

(12) *processor "rozmawia" z pamiecia*
processor talks to memory
'the processor talks to the memory' (GW)

(13) *zaden program nie chciał skanera "zobaczyć"*
no program not wanted scanner-ACC to see
'no program wanted to see the scanner' (CH)

The same lack of confidence in metaphor use is seen in what is clearly a novel extension created by the Polish author rather than a translation:

(14) *"Samotny" komputer ma znacznie mniejszy potencjal*
Alone computer has much smaller potential
niż "żyjący w stadzie"...
than living in herd
'A computer that lives alone has a significantly lower potential than one that is a member of a herd' (GW)

The office metaphor developed by Apple Macintosh, COMPUTER IS A SECRETARY WORKING IN AN OFFICE, is systematically rendered into Polish, together with its numerous extensions, e.g.:

(15) icons: drawer: *szuflada*, envelope: *koperta*, folder: *teczka*, etc.
commands: file: *plik*, document: *dokument*, save: *przechować*, etc. (EN)

5.3. Image metaphors

Truly "one-shot" image metaphors are only exceptionally rendered in Polish translations, and even then the translator refuses to take upon himself the responsibility for using a given expression: he puts it into inverted commas, thus giving it the status of a quotation from the original author:

(16) a. *"odpluskwianie" plików*
debugging of-files
'debugging files' (GW)
b. *"sprytny sen"*
smart sleep
'smart sleep' (GW)

On the other hand, novel image metaphors are occasionally used to render original non-metaphorical expressions; even then, however, consistent use of inverted commas signals the lack of confidence on the part of the authors:

(17) a. *"plujka"*
spitter
'ink jet printer' (CH, EN, GW)
b. *"ściskacz"*
squeezer
'compressing program' (GW)

Generalized image metaphors are rendered as such when metaphorical mapping involves a high degree of iconicity between the source and the target domains. For instance, what is called a *directory tree* actually looks like a *tree*; hence its natural literal rendering into Polish as *drzewo katalogów* (*tree of directories*). But while the spatial orientation of the image in English suggests the extension *root directory*, it becomes re-oriented in Polish, with the resulting extensions:

(18) *pień główny*
main trunk
'root directory'

Consider also the following explanation (meant for general readership) of the structure of a directory tree:

(19) *Liście to nasze zbiory, gałęzie to katalogi*
leaves are our files branches are directories
(gałąź rosnaca bezpośrednio na pniu głównym)
(branch growing directly on trunk main)
i podkatalogi (gałazka odchodząca od innej
and sub-directories (little branch branching from another
gałęzi)...
branch)
'The leaves are the files, and the branches are directories (if they grow directly off the main trunk) and subdirectories (which are twigs growing on branches)' (GW)

What is perhaps most illustrative of the general translational strategy is the fate of the "mouse metaphor": SMALL PLASTIC EXTERNAL HARDWARE ATTACHED TO THE COMPUTER IS A MOUSE. As a generalized image metaphor, it was immediately accepted in Polish (probably due to the high degree of isomorphism between the domains, or - simply - the obvious perceptual similarity between the device and the rodent). The general image is "productive", and it gives rise to some obviously novel extensions (note the use of inverted commas):

(20) *mysz w pozycji "zdechła"*
mouse in position dead
'the mouse (left) in the position "dead" ' (GW)

What the mouse should do, however, soon became a bone of discontent. The literal translation of the onomatopoeic *click* (i.e. the verb *mlaskać*, with all its morphological variants) was rejected and ridiculed because of the well-established connotations with the sound produced while eating and considered as a sure symptom of a lack of table manners; the nominal *mlask* and the compound *dwumlask* (*double click*) became the target of numerous attacks (cf. e.g. "filipikę skierowaną przeciw rubasznemu 'dwumlaskowi' " (the "philippic directed against the gruff 'dwumlask' ") in Wimmer 1991). The next two proposals did no better: the Apple Macintosh *pukanie* (EN) (*knocking*), although conceptually consistent with the generalized "office metaphor", must have been still felt to be inconsistent with the "mouse metaphor" and therefore did not "take root"; *tupnięcie* (TAG) (*stamping one's foot*), although conceivable as an action of a mouse, is inherently intransitive in Polish, and thus becomes cognitively incoherent when accompanied by a noun other than *foot* in the instrumental case, cf.:

(21) *tupnąć nogą* : *tupnąć myszą (?)*
stamp foot stamp mouse
'stamp one's foot' 'stamp one's mouse' (?)

An attempt at saving the onomatopoeia of the original *click* was recently made again: the connotation-free lexeme *cyknac* appeared in the Polish version of Dan Gookin's DOS manual (Gookin 1993). But the term most frequently encountered is the borrowing *kliknac*, used as both noun and verb, and fully inflected. Although the syntactic pattern has not yet been fully established, when used as a verb, it becomes intransitive, cf.

(22) a. *kliknąć ikonę*
to click icon-ACC
'to click on an icon' (CH)
b. *kliknij na literę*
click-IMP upon letter-ACC
'to point to a letter and click the button' (GW)
c. *dwukrotne kliknięcie na nazwie*
double clicking on name-LOC
'A double-click on a name (of a prompt)' (GW)

6. Conclusions

The "mouse metaphor" is systematically undermined by those authors who chose non-metaphorical periphrases to describe the use of the device:

(23) *Po wywolaniu programu File Manager (poprzez*
After calling program F. M. (through
dwukrotne szybkie naciśnięcie lewego klawisza myszy
double quick pressing left key of-mouse
na ikonie)...
on icon-LOC
'Having started the File Manager (by pressing the left mouse button twice in rapid succession)...' (GW)

Although inconveniently long, the expression in (23) sounds "professional" enough not to raise any suspicions as to the qualifications, expertise, and scientific attitude of the writer. This, in fact, most probably provides an explanation of what is a general tendency in editing

Polish scientific texts: the fear of metaphor (which results either in non-metaphorical renderings of originally metaphorical expressions or in the use of inverted commas to mark avoidance of responsibility on the part of the translator) is conditioned by psychological rather than cognitive (linguistic) factors.

The hypothesis is corroborated by two types of evidence. First, extensions of general image metaphors are avoided when felt as novel, as opposed to such as have been long established in the general language and only later transferred to a specialist use. As an example, consider page orientation metaphors. A basic orientational metaphor (for definition and discussion, see Lakoff & Johnson 1980), it maps the dimensions of the orientation of a human body in physical space upon the spatial orientation of a sheet of paper, and appears both in English and in Polish:

(24) a. *nagłówek/główka*
on-head/little head
'header'
b. *stopka*
little foot
'footer'

When used in reference to document printing, the page orientation metaphor is extended over the domain of painting: the terms *portrait* and *landscape* refer, respectively, to vertical and horizontal orientation of a sheet of paper as it is fed to the printer. In the Polish translation these extensions are rendered as non-metaphorical descriptive phrases:

(25) a. *pionowa orientacja papieru*
vertical orientation of-paper
'portrait' (TAG)
b. *pozioma orientacja papieru*
horizontal orientation of-paper
'landscape' (TAG)

Characteristically, (25) comes from a manual for prospective users of the Polish text editor TAG. In such official texts as instructions for use or textbooks, avoidance of metaphor seems a regular strategy, as opposed to popular texts; this provides additional evidence for the hypothesis concerning possible reasons of the opposing translation strategies.

The tendency to avoid metaphor is most visible in the case of truly "one shot" metaphors, e.g.

(26) a. *połączenie łańcuchowe*
connection chain-like
'daisy chain' (EN)
b. *protokół synchronizacji*
protocol of-synchronization
'handshake' (EN)

The desire "to sound serious" in fact goes counter to the very *raison d'être* of metaphor, which is to help understand what is unknown and complicated by expressing it in terms of what is well-known and simpler to grasp. This, in turn, could be one of the reasons why manuals (computer science being just one of the many subject areas) are regularly criticised for being "illegible" and difficult to follow.

While image metaphors might be felt as sounding strange (or, God forbid, funny!), at least before they become totally assimilated in a language (cf., once again, *headers* and *footers* vs. *portrait* and *landscape*), expressions of conceptual metaphors are so deeply rooted in man's basic bodily experience that their direct rendering comes naturally, and the result is not considered as "not serious enough". Most calques (cf. examples (6) - (13), (24) above) are in fact renderings of either expressions of conceptual metaphors or their basic extensions, while novel extensions are introduced within the framework of well-established image schemas (cf. examples (14), (18), (19)).

The above analysis cannot claim statistical relevance; it only concerns a handful of randomly collected data. But it provides fairly substantial evidence for the theory of metaphor as it is formulated within the cognitivist framework. Moreover, as the emerging pattern seems fully justified by general mechanisms of metaphor formation, it might be legitimately assumed that analogous tendencies and translation strategies will also be observed in other semantic fields or areas of language use.

Note

1. For information on sources, see references. No sources are quoted for expressions found in everyday use.

Sources of examples:

CH: *Chip*. Magazyn mikrokomputerowy.
EN: *Enter*. Magazyn komputerowy.
GW: *Gazeta Wyborcza*. Supplement Komputery.
P-T: Bulletin of "Pro-Test" Co (software dealers)
TAG: Edytor tekstów *TAG*. Instrukcja obslugi. InfoService. Gdansk 1992.

References

Dagut, M. B.
1976 "Can 'metaphor' be translated?". *BABEL* XXII/1:21-33.

Gookin, D.
1933 *DOS dla opornych*. (Transl. Irasema Golebiowska.) Warszawa: Oficyna Wydawnicza Read Me.

Johnson, M.
1987 *The Body in the Mind: The Bodily Basis of Meaning, Reason, and Imagination*. Chicago: University of Chicago Press.

Lakoff, G. & M. Johnson
1980 *Metaphors We Live By*. Chicago: University of Chicago Press.

Lakoff, G.
1987 *Women, Fire, and Dangerous Things: What Categories Reveal About the Mind*. Chicago: University of Chicago Press.

Newmark, P.
1980 "The translation of metaphor". *BABEL* XXVI/2:93-100.

Tatarkiewicz, J.
1991 "Gryzienie jabłek po polsku czyli spolszczanie Macintosha". *Enter* 11:32-34.

Wimmer, P.
1991 "Kliknąć, tupnąć i dwumlasnąč". *Enter* 6:20-21.
1992 "Nomenklatura". *Enter* 4:30-31.

Wimmer, P. & J. Tatarkiewicz
1992 "Polemika". *Enter* 9:14-15.

Conditional conjunctions and conceptual companions

Angeliki Athanasiadou and René Dirven

0. Introduction

It is one of the tenets of cognitive linguistics that the strict separation of lexis and grammar is one of the many false dichotomies of structuralist and generative theories. In a cognitive-linguistic view there is a principled reluctance to draw such artificial dividing lines or to accept autonomous modules for each of the so-called levels of linguistic organisation. This non-modular position of cognitive linguistics is strongly supported by the functioning of conjunctions, which can, only very loosely speaking, be called a "closed" class and which constitute one of the clear instances of a transitional and overlapping zone between the more proto-typical cores of lexis and of grammar (see also Taylor 1989, Chapter 6). This non-closedness is perhaps best illustrated by new forms of conjunctions such as *if and only if*, which has even found a conventionalised written form as *iff*, or by the rise of new temporal conjunctions such as *once* and so on[1].

In this paper we will discuss this issue while concentrating on the semantic field of conditionality and its closest conceptual companions such as time, concession, adversativeness, etc. More specifically, the purpose of this paper is to arrive at a clear lexical and grammatical characterisation of the many conditional conjunctions in English, and of their immediately related neighbouring categories. In order to do so we will first of all give a general characterisation of the various uses of *if*, which have in common that the constructions in which they are used are in their prototypical uses non-assertive ones (Section 1). After that, we will place the conjunction *if* in a somewhat wider semantic field and contrast it with the conceptual categories of time, concession, and adversativeness. For this purpose, we will combine the three basic conjunctions *when, if*, and *though* with the four operators *only, even, all*, and *as*, yielding eight additional conjunctions (Section 2). Then finally, we will concentrate on a number of complex conjunctions of conditionality, which all make important differentiations within the more abstract conceptual category indicated by *if* (Section 3). In the conclusions, we will try to bring together all the various characterisations in one global synthesis (Section 4). Therefore, the outline of the paper will be as follows:

1. Various non-assertive *if*-constructions
2. Conceptual companions of *if*
3. New complex conjunctions of conditionality
4. Conclusions

1. Various non-assertive *if*-constructions

The conjunction *if* is not only used in the subclause of conditionals (1a), but also in other types of constructions which resemble each other to some extent. These other constructions are first of all indirect speech (1b), but also expressions denoting lack of knowledge or uncertainty (1c) or mere inquiry (1d). Compare:

(1) a. *If he knows the answer, he will tell you.*
b. *I asked him if he knew the answer.*
c. *I doubt if he knows the answer.*
d. *Can you tell me if he knows the answer.*

Although these four uses of *if* mainly differ between (1a) and (1b, c, d) and also have different equivalents in the two neighbouring Germanic languages, i.e. German and Dutch - which will be illustrated later - they all belong to a common semantic field, namely that of not committing oneself to the truth or reality of the proposition. Quirk *et al.* (1972:53ff) introduce for this semantic-syntactic group of constructions the term *non-assertive*, which for them in the first place comprises interrogative and negative constructions. But Quirk *et al.* (1972:747) also subsume under the group of non-assertives *if*-clauses "especially those expressing open conditions" (1a). Although they do not subsume *if* in (1b, c, d) under non-assertive constructions, it is clear that, both syntactically and semantically, these belong to the same semantic field. Quirk *et al.*'s main test for non-assertives is the use of the indefinite pronoun *any* in this type of context. This test applies to all the sentences of (1), which with a bit of elegant remodelling can be changed into the examples of (2):

(2) a. *If he knows any of the answers, he will tell you.*
b. *I asked him if he knew any of the answers.*
c. *I doubt if he knows any of the answers.*
d. *Can you tell me if he knows any of the answers?*

Next to the *if*-constructions in (1) or (2), which clearly all belong to the semantic field of non-assertive utterances, there is still another non-assertive category, i.e. that of the polar alternative conjunction *(either) ... or*, which somehow by nature of its polarity may include a negative element as illustrated in (3):

(3) *Either we do something about it or we don't do anything at all.*

So what becomes clear from these examples is that there is not only a common semantic element between the four *if*-constructions internally, but also between all these *if*-constructions and the *or*-construction. Now if we take a somewhat wider view and go beyond English including Dutch and German in the picture, we see a distribution of various conjunctions, which at first sight may look quite arbitrary, but which on closer inspection appears to be a highly motivated distributional network. Let us have a look at the table first, to which - for the sake of comparison - we will also add the notion of time.

	TIME	CONDITION	INDIRECT QUESTION etc.	ALTERNATIVE
E.	*when*	*if*	*if* *whether*	*(either...) or* *(whether...) or*
D.	*als* *wanneer*	*als* *indien*	*of*	*(of...) of*
G.	*wenn*	*wenn*	*ob*	*(entweder...) oder*

Table 1. Distribution of some conjunctions in English, Dutch, and German

These three very strongly related Germanic languages have a remarkably different distribution. In English we find three sets of relations. First there is a strong delimitation between time *(when)* and condition *(if)*. Secondly, there is a conflation between condition *(if)* and indirect question *(if)*. Thirdly, there is also an overlapping between an indirect question *(if/whether)* and the alternative conjunction *(whether ... or)*. Compared with the three items of English, Dutch only makes a distinction between two major subfields: on the one hand, there is a conflation between time *(als)* and condition *(als)*, and on the other hand there is overlapping between indirect question *(of)* and alternative *(of)*. Of course, Dutch can make an explicit distinction between time *(wanneer)* and condition *(indien)* if need be. But the point is that Dutch does not have to make the distinction so rigidly as English all the time. The same applies to German, but to an even stronger degree than in Dutch, since in everyday spoken language it only uses one conjunction *(wenn)* for both time and condition[2].

It is remarkable that in French (F) and its ancestor language Latin (L) and even in Modern Greek (MG) we find a picture which strongly resembles that of English. Table 2 displays these distributions:

	TIME	CONDITION	INDIRECT Q.	ALTERNATIVE
F.	*quand*	*si*	*si*	*ou/(bien)...ou (bien)*
L.	*quando/cum*	*si*	*si/ne*	*aut/vel/sive...sive*
MG.	*otan*	*(e)an*	*(e)an*	*i/ite/ite...ite*

Table 2. Distribution of some conjunctions in French, Latin, and Greek

The greater affinity between the English distribution and that of the three other languages clearly shows that English no longer follows the Germanic distributional pattern, but that it has just like in many other structural contexts experienced a very strong influence of French (see Prins 1952). This greater affinity between the uses of English *if* and the equivalents in the three non-Germanic languages allows us to characterise the schematic meaning of *if, si,* and *ean* in the same way, whereas the contrast between English and Dutch/German necessitates us to characterise Dutch *als* ("when", "if") and German *wenn* (also "when", "if") slightly differently from English *if.* In order to stress the commonalities of some semantic elements, let us repeat Table 1 as Table 3:

	TIME	CONDITIONAL	INDIRECT QUESTION etc.	ALTERNATIVE
E.	*when*	(*if*	*if*) *whether*	*(whether...) or*
D.	(*als*	*als*)	(*of*	*(of...) of*)
G.	(*wenn*	*wenn*)	*ob*	*(entweder...) oder*

Table 3. Grouping of some conjunctions in English, Dutch, and German

English *if* is clearly situated in the non-commissive area tending towards uncertainty, but *if* does not reach as far as "alternative *or*", although a synonym of *if*, viz. *whether* does. Dutch *als* and German *wenn* rather tend towards the "time" area. Consequently, the schematic meanings covering the more specified meanings of *if* vs. *als/wenn* must be different. Whereas in English the concepts of time (*when*) and condition (*if*) are expressed by "conceptual companions", in Dutch (*als*) and German (*wenn*) they belong to a family network and they exhibit a "family resemblance": the Dutch time concept and the condition concept both denoted by *als* thus stand in a very close relationship to each other. The same holds for German. Thus, concepts that in one language may be members of the same family, in other languages may be less close to each other and may just be "good" companions. This fact therefore justifies the approach adopted in this paper: in order to understand the meaning of *if* and conditionality better, it is necessary to see what family networks or companionship networks it belongs to. We cannot attempt to paraphrase the schematic meaning of *if* or the other conjunctions yet, since this would require much more insight into all the possible contexts in which *if* can be used.

2. Conceptual companions of "if"

In the first section we have been looking at the semantic field of non-assertive constructions and we have tried to position conditional *if* against its immediate neighbours within that field. Now in the second section we will systematically contrast and/or combine conditional *if* with two other semantic concepts:

(i) the two basic categories of time *(when)*, and concession *(though)*, which in English we can consider to be "conceptual companions" of conditionals, and

(ii) the four operators *only, even, all*, and *as*. The first three are quantors which together form a continuum ranging from an exclusive quantification *(only)*, via an intermediate quantification *(even)*, to a maximal quantification *(all)*. The operator *as* is of a different nature since it denotes comparison, but as an operator it will combine with two of the three basic conjunctions and yield highly specific kinds of complex conjunctions.

Given the semantic specifications of the four operators, it is clear that they will not allow being combined with each and every of the simplex conjunctions *when, if,* and *though*. In our opinion, the set of resulting forms is not an arbitrary set of combinations but rather a highly motivated one, and the challenge to a cognitive-linguistic approach is to try to account for the fact why some combinations are possible, and why others are not.

Let us now first have a look at the complete set of possibilities of these conceptual companions:

BASIC ITEMS / OPERATORS				
BASIC ITEMS:	(i)	**when**	**if**	**though**
only:	(ii)	*only when*	*only if*	–
even:	(iii)	*even when*	*even if*	*even though*
all:	(iv)	–	–	*although*
as:	(v)	–	*as if*	*as though*

Table 4. Basic and complex conjunctions of time, condition, and concession

We will discuss these conjunctions in five groups: first the basic ones, and next the complex ones in the order of the various operators.

2.1. *The basic conjunctions "when, if, though"*

These conjunctions are called basic or simplex conjunctions, since they have no operators. It may be useful to point out first of all the semantic relationship between these three "companions". The relationship between the temporal conjunction *when* and the conditional conjunction *if* was already pointed out in Section 1: in English and French the two concepts are clearly delimited, and therefore behave only like companions, but in the two Germanic languages Dutch and German the two concepts are family members and, to a certain extent, overlapping.

Although at first sight any possible relationship between conditional *if* and concessive *though* seems to be absent, the fact that we can form the same combinations *even if, even though*, and *as if, as though* clearly reveals that they have similar possibilities for compounding, which can only be due to the fact that there is also some semantic affinity or set of oppositions between these forms. But, a more direct argument for relating *if* to *though* is that conceptually the notion of concession cannot only be expressed by *though*, but also by a hypothetical sentence (*even if*) and by a seemingly conditional sentence (*if*). That is, we do not only denote concession by means of *though*, but sometimes also by means of *even if*, and even by the mere use of *if*, as illustrated in the examples in (4):

(4) a. *Though he is poor, he is (still) honest.*
b. *Even if he is poor, he is (still) honest.*
c. *If he is poor, he is still honest.*

This pragmatic use of *if* in a concessive meaning (4c) may not be the prototypical one and it may even be very heavily dependent on the context (the use of *still* seems to be indispensable here). Still, the example in (4c) shows that the meaning of *if* can be pragmatically stretched so much as to encompass the notion of contrast or, more specifically, that of concession.

This concessive use of *if* certainly is a borderline case and it does no longer represent the very notion of conditionality. As a first and still very general approximation to this notion of conditionality, we can say that the notion of conditionality presupposes the notion of dependency, that is, in conditionality one state of affairs is seen as dependent on another state of affairs. This is not the case with concessive *if*, which is even clearer in an example from the LOB-corpus:

(5) *If Ann was despondent on arrival, she very soon forgot herself in her new work.* (LOB:63)

It is remarkable that the use of *still* which carries the expression of contrast in (4c) is not necessary here, which may be due to the presence of two other contrasts in this example (viz. *despondent* vs. *forget about oneself* and *on arrival* vs. *very soon* and *in her new work*). The example in (5) therefore illustrates in a unique way how richness of lexical contrast may substitute the necessity to express grammatical contrast, e.g. by the use of *still*.

2.2. Conjunctions with "only"

The second group constructed with the operator *only* in the sense of restrictiveness can only be combined with *when* and *if*, not with *though*. In fact, there are three possibilities *only when*, *only if* and *if only*, as illustrated in (6):

(6) a. *Only when it is very hot like today, does she wear shorts.*
b. *The bystanders were attacked only if they gave an impression of favouring one side or the other* (COB: 249)
c. *If only he worked harder!*

The use of *only when* in (6a) is usually not looked upon as a compound conjunction and therefore it is not registered in dictionaries.

Semantically, *only when-* and *only if*-constructions differ in that *only when* is always fundamentally different from a mere *when*-sentence. Indeed, sentence (6a) is really restrictive and means that on no other days than on such hot days does she wear shorts. But without *only* the sentence means that she wears shorts on such days and that she may do so on many other days, too. This restrictive distinction is not necessarily present with *only if* versus *if*: when you say in (6b) that they were attacked *only if* or (just) *if* they gave a certain impression, this does make much difference and in neither of the two cases does it imply that they might be attacked on other occasions as well. Consequently, the item *only* in *only if* has a reinforcing function in (6b). Still, *only if* may also have a restrictive function in other contexts and therefore be necessary in such contexts; *only if* can then not be replaced by a mere *if*, as illustrated in (7) below:

(7) a. *Nonrenewable goods must be used only if they are indispensable.* (COB: 79)
b. **Nonrenewable goods must be used if they are indispensable.*

Obviously this difference is related to the strong negative polarity of *only*, which causes *must* to mean "it is allowed to use such goods only if" and not "it is obligatory to do so".

As is well known especially from scientific writing, a kind of complex conjunction is taking shape in the form of *if and only if*, which up till now has not occurred in the 400 examples we have randomly selected from the Cobuild corpus. (Also see Section 3.4.).

The construction with *if only* in (6c) prototypically has a hypothetical, in fact a counterfactual implication so that it can be paraphrased as follows: "He does not work hard (enough) and I regret this or I wish he did", etc. Here, we see remarkable differences with conditional *if* again: first the conditional phrase *if he worked harder* cannot stand by itself, but it can only be used as a protasis together with the apodosis; and secondly, such a conditional phrase is always ambiguous between the reading of likelihood and unreality. But the *if only* construction has only one possible reading, namely that of unreality. So *only* in *if only* clearly has a disambiguating function, viz. it deletes the conditional interpretation: in fact *if only* may have several synonyms, such as *if at least, if just, if ... but,* etc.

We thus see that the operator can only modify the meaning of a conjunction if the former precedes the latter. If the operator follows, it can only cancel possible interpretations. The synonyms of *if only*, which have the same structure as *if only*, prove that it is the first element *if* and the second element (*only, at least, just, but*) together that determine the function of these mixed types of conjunctions. This fact can be illustrated by synonymous exclamatory constructions for (6c) such as:

(8) a. *Had he only worked harder!*
b. *Had he at least worked harder!*
c. *Had he just worked (a little bit) harder!*

Finally, the impossible combination of *though* with *only* in the form of **only though* is ruled out because the notion of restrictiveness imposed by *only* is not combinable with the notion of concession. As already observed when discussing the concessive use of *if* in (4c) and (5), the notion of concession excludes the notion of dependency. Thus, whereas condition and time may be compatible with the notion of restrictiveness, the notion of concessions is not, since there is no obvious relationship between the two states of affairs in the protasis and in the apodosis. With a non-absolute (or intermediate) operator such as *even* things will be different, of course.

2.3. Conjunctions with "even"

The third group with *even* is the only group where all three basic conjunctions combine with this operator: *even when, even if, even though*, a fact which is to be explained especially when compared with the more restricted possibilities of *only* and the complete restriction of *all.*

(9) a. *Even when she is having a break like right now, she continues discussing linguistics.*
b. *Even if he loves her, he can't marry her.* (Leech:136)
c. *Even though he loves her, he can't marry her.* (Leech:136)

Just as is the case with *only when*, the expression *even when* does not change the basic meaning of *when* and therefore it does not form a canonical complex conjunction yet and it is not attested in the dictionary, whereas *even if* and *even though* are both attested as complex categories in the dictionary.

The specific function of *even* in the three complex conjunctions is to denote that an expectation raised in the subclause is not met or is even contradicted in the main clause. So, the sentence as a whole expresses something that goes counter to the expectation first raised. So, in (9a), the subclause raises the expectation that during a break you do not continue whatever work you have been doing, but this expectation is contradicted in the main clause[3].

The proper function of *even* becomes even clearer when we contrast it with *only*, as in (10), which repeats two former examples:

(10) a. *Only when it is very hot like today, does she wear shorts.*
b. *Even when it is very hot like today, she wears heavy clothes.*

With *only when* we always have a symmetrical situation in both subclause and main clause, and *only when* restricts the occurrence to a minimum of situations. But with *even when* there is an asymmetrical situation: the expectation raised in the subclause is flouted in the main clause. With *even if* there is not only an asymmetrical situation of counter-to-expectation, but this complex conjunction mainly has an intensifying hypothetical function. Thus, in (9b) we have a possible state of affairs whereby the speaker does not commit himself to the truth or falsity of the state of affairs. But this possible state of affairs is not seen in any way as being in a dependency relationship with the state of affairs in the main clause. On the contrary, the proposition of the main clause ("He can't marry her") remains true irrespective of the truth of the *even if* clause. This confirms, as already pointed out after the analysis of (4b), that *even if* is not a conditional construction, but merely an adversative one. (9b) then means "Even if it should be true that he loves her, this does not change the fact that he can't marry her". This paraphrase also shows that the use of the label "concessive" for *even if*-constructions (see König 1985, 1986) is - to say the least - very problematical[4]. Indeed, in order to make a concession, one must admit a fact, not a hypothetical situation (see Dirven to appear 1995).

The difference between *even if* (9b) and *even though* (9c) is a question of a possible state versus a state which is a fact. As Leech (1989:136) states, *even if* in (9b) implies that you do not know whether he loves her, whereas with *even though* in (9c) you present it as a fact that he loves her. What the complex conjunctions *even if* and *even though* have in common is that they both express the notion of "counter-to-expectation". Still, there is a fundamental difference between the forms *even when, even if,* and *even though. Even when* does not differ basically from *when*, whereas *even if* is completely different from *if*, and *even though* is not so strongly different from *though*, again. Let's compare the following sentences.

(11) a. *(Even) when he makes love to her, he is not in love with her.*
b. *Even if he makes love to her, he is not in love with her.*
c. *(Even) though he makes love to her, he is not in love with her.*

In the temporal sentence of (11a), both constructions with *when* and *even when* are possible: the *when* construction is a neutral statement of fact; the *even when* construction expresses the additional notion of "counter to what one would expect". But in the second example (11b), it won't make any sense to leave *even* out[5]; this would yield a conditional sentence with an apodosis depending on a contradictory protasis, which is not interpretable. This clearly reveals that *even if* differs completely from *if*. In contrast with this, *though* and *even though* do not differ strongly. Whereas *though* expresses concession, the form *even though* expresses both concession and the notion of counter-to-expectation. Since these two notions are so closely related, *even* can only have a reinforcing function in (11c).

2.4. A conjunction with "all"

Group four (*all*) has only one compound conjunction *although*, in which the phonologically reduced quantor *all* mainly has a reinforcing function, so that *though* and *although*, and even *even though*, do not differ stronly from a semantic point of view. It may also become clear from the analysis of *though*, which was given before, that the factive character of *though* easily allows such a reinforcement: something can be a fact *tout court* or it can be a very strong fact or a fact in spite of counter-to-expectation situations. It does not surprise that *all* cannot be combined with hypothetical *if* or with temporal *when*, because there is nothing to reinforce here: a condition is a condition and a time point is a time point and neither of them can be thought of in terms of "more"or "less".

Several authors (Dancygier 1988:119, König 1985:10ff) also say that there is a gradation of strength between *although* and *even though*, but the situation gets confused by assuming that all constructions with these forms have the same possibilities. Therefore, it may be desirable to make a clear delimitation between *although* and *even though*. A remarkable fact about the three forms *though, although*, and *even though* is that the former two are always interchangeable, but that *even though* - as could be expected - in many cases cannot replace *though* and *although*. This difference then would suggest that there is not simply a gradation of strength between the three conjunctions, but that they express different semantic notions. We have already pointed out that *though* and *although* express concession. Now of course, *even though* also expresses concession, but on top of that it also expresses what we have called the notion of "counter-to-expectation". Given the fact that *(al)though* expresses a single notion and that *even though* expresses two combined notions, it is not more than natural that not all instances with *(al)though* can be replaced by *even though*. For example, we can have sentences like (12a), but not normally sentences like (12b):

(12) a. *Although it is sad, that's the situation.*
b. ?*Even though it is sad, that's the situation.*

Sentence (12a) is correct, because it just expresses a concessive relation between the state of sadness and the unavoidable character of it. In (12b) the notion of concession is not sufficient to use the *even though*-conjunction: what is lacking is a contextual element that contradicts the expectation pattern created by *sad*, for instance the feeling of optimism as in the following example:

(13) *Even though life is often sad, we must always try to see the bright side of it.*

The notion "counter-to-expectation" presupposes a number of folk ideas about all kinds of expectations that go with certain expressions in given situations. Thus, for instance, the expression *to arrive somewhere first* evokes the expectation of a positive sequel, such as getting good seats, or being served first, or having the best choice for hotel rooms, etc. But *to arrive first* does not entail the notion that you are in time to catch a train or things like that. Therefore, *to arrive first* and *fail to catch your train*, may be seen in a concessive relationship, but not in a counter-to-expectation relationship. Consequently, (14a) is possible, (14b) is not, but (14c) is:

(14) a. *Although he arrived first, he was late for his train.* (= merely concessive)
b. ?*Even though he arrived first, he was late for his train.* (= in a merely concessive reading)

c. *Even though he arrived first, he had one of the worst rooms in the hotel.* (= concessive and counter-to-expectation)

What we would expect as a sufficient sequence satisfying the notion of "counter-to-expectation" is met in (14c). Similarly (14b) is alright if *first* is replaced by *early*, since then the double condition of concession and counter-to-expectation is met.

2.5. *Conjunctions with "as"*

The fifth group contains the two compound conjunctions *as if* and *as though*, which express the notion of semblance. This is again quite different from the notion of conditionality so that we are left with the conclusion that only one complex conjunction with *if*, viz. *only if* expresses conditionality, whereas the two other forms *even if* and *as if* do not[6]. Just like *even if* and *even though*, also *as if* and *as though* show up major differences. Although in many concrete instances the difference may be neutralised and/or not always be felt, it can be real, as in the following two examples:

(15) a. *She treats me as if I were her servant.* (Leech: 52)
b. *It looks as though the weather is improving.* (Leech: 52)

The construction with *as if* in (15a) has a counterfactual character, which is conditioned by the form *were*. The construction with *as though* in (15b) is not counterfactual, but rather denotes the fact that the weather is going to be the way it looks. So even here we find back something of the factive nature of *though*. Of course, in both cases *as* denotes the notion of semblance, i.e. the idea that something seems to be true or real. In the case of *as though* the semblance can be disambiguated by the factive character of *though*, but in the case of *as if* the notion of semblance remains fully intact. The total picture we get from the various combinations of *when*, *if*, and *though* with the four operators *only*, *even*, *all*, *as* is that in each single instance of a complex conjunction there is a fundamental role played by the operator, which in the case of *only* or *al(l)* may either reinforce the basic notion of *if*, *when* and *though* or else, in the case of *even if* and *as if* completely annihilates the notion of conditionality.

3. New complex conjunctions of conditionality

Up till now we have been discussing twelve simple or complex conjunctions denoting the concepts of time, condition, concession, and semblance. Whereas this relatively large number of conjunctions also covers notions different from the notion of conditionality, in the field of conditionality itself there are still very specific communicative needs which the English speech community has verbalised when facing the necessity to express various shades of conditionality itself. So it does not astonish that in English several other complex conjunctions for conditionals or conceptual companions have developed, as surveyed in the following table:

(i)	*in case, unless*
(ii)	*suppose/supposing that, assuming that*
(iii)	*on condition that, provided/providing that*
(iv)	*however much, whether... (or); in spite of/despite the fact that*

Table 5. Complex conjunctions of conditionality and conceptual companions

3.1. *in case, unless*

These two complex conjunctions are different from the simple form *if* or the negative form *if ... not* in that they pack together a great deal of pragmatic assumptions in a sentence. Thus the simplex conjunction *if* and the complex conjunction *in case* make completely different pragmatic assumptions:

(16) a. *I'll come tomorrow if Ann wants me.*
b. *I'll come tomorrow in case Ann wants me.* (TM: 204)

In the *if*-sentence of (16a), my coming depends on Ann wanting me to do so. So the *if*-clause is the trigger and the main clause is the response or the consequent, so that subclause and main clause are interdependent. The *in case*-sentence in (16b) is completely different, and expresses strong pragmatic dependency between the reason for making a statement and the statement itself. We could paraphrase it as follows: "I'll come anyway and I am telling you this, so that Ann can find me if she wants me"; so my coming is not triggered by Ann wanting me to do so, but the giving of the information of my coming takes place on behalf of Ann and the possibility that she might want me.

Whereas the semantics of *in case* is thus fairly clear, this is not so with *unless.* Most grammars (for instance Leech, 1989:492) say that *unless* can replace *if ... not*, but some grammars say the opposite, namely that *unless* is not always possible when *if ... not* is possible. We want to say that the latter is rather true and moreover that the two forms have different meanings and even when both conjunctions are possible, they still denote different relationships, as illustrated in (17):

(17) a. *I won't come tomorrow if Ann doesn't want me.*
b. *I won't come tomorrow unless Ann wants me.*

In the *if*-sentence of (17a), we again have a dependency relationship of a trigger and a consequent: my staying away is the consequent of Ann not wanting me to come. In the *unless*-sentence of (17b), the implication is rather that I won't normally come tomorrow, but in the exceptional case that Ann wants me I'll come. So, the *unless*-construction points to the area of making exceptions, and rather means "except if"[7]. Thus both constructions point to the area of causes and their consequents, but *if ... not* has a negative effect, *unless* has positive effect (if it applies).

So, we can conclude that very much more goes on when the two complex conjunctions *in case* and *unless* are used: they satisfy highly specific communicative needs, viz. to point to pragmatic conditional relationships of a special nature, in which the relationship holds between an event (or state) and the speech act as such.

3.2. suppose/supposing that, assuming that

Since the meaning of the conjunction *if* is a rather abstract and schematic one, and since it may cover various senses, such as supposition, assumption, condition, and even concession, speakers may often want to be far more specific, and this has led to the rise of many new forms of complex conjunctions, which are often derived from verbs in the *-ing* form or from complex noun phrases.

This is not only the case in the area of conditionality, but also in that of temporality (e.g. *during, pending*), concession (e.g. *notwithstanding*) and various others. The phenomenon is moreover not limited to English, but shows up in various languages, e.g. in Dutch (*gedurende* "during", *niettegenstaande* "notwithstanding"). The historical reason for the creation of these forms may be Latin or Greek influence on the creation of more unambiguous forms, especially in written language. This seems to be confirmed by the dates of the first occurrences, registered for these forms in SOED[8], which mostly stem from the 17th century.

The new *ing*-conjunctions are therefore still lexical items with a transparent meaning, but they are becoming grammaticized into a kind of new, complex grammatical morphemes. As the examples below show, the meanings of *supposing that* and *assuming that* can all be subsumed under the schematic or general meaning of *if*, the difference being that they are far more specific than *if* in that they stress the 'supposition' meaning of *if*, as the following examples may illustrate:

(18) a. *Supposing something should go wrong, what would you do then?* (CC: 1470)
b. *Keep your money or goods (assuming that you have any) separate from those of your husband.* (CC: 77)

In (18a), an unlikely supposition is expressed, which is most typically signalled by the use of the modal *should*. Still, the assertive form *something* must be used here. Of course, we could as well use the conjunction *if* instead of *supposing*, but then *if* normally requires the use of the non-assertive form *anything*. So *supposing* may in many contexts just be a bit clearer in its supposition sense although there is not such a great need for clarity in this particular context. But it is not difficult to imagine numerous other contexts, where the need for more clarity is highly desirable.

Further, it is interesting to note the difference between the more hypothetical *supposing that* and the more neutral *assuming that*. Thus in (18b), it would not be very flattering to use *supposing that you should have some*, whereas *assuming* is fully neutral and does not offend the addressee. Note by the way that just like *if* in its various non-assertive uses (see examples (2a, b, c, d)) also *assuming* is constructed with *any*. This also proves that new conjunctions follow the same syntactic-semantic patterns of the basic conjunctions. The only thing that they are adding to the latter is much more specialised lexical information and therefore they become less ambiguous.

3.3. on condition that, provided/providing that

These new conjunctions bring out the "condition" sense of polysemous *if*. The complex conjunction *on condition that* can, in most cases, be paraphrased by *if*. For instance *I will only do my share, if/on condition that you do yours*. But the fact that there are also phrasal conjunctions like *on condition that* as in (19), where the context requires the very specific use of this phrase, shows that this new complex conjunction is absolutely indispensable.

(19) *He has agreed to come on condition that there won't be any press or publicity.* (CC: 291)

The problem for the use of *if* in this example is the fact that in the main clause there are two verbs, namely *agree* and *come*. By using *if* in (19), we would create a link between the whole main clause and its main verb *agree*, on the one hand, and *there won't be any press*, on the other hand, which is clearly not what the speaker wants to express. With the lexical-grammatical complex conjunction *on condition that*, we create a link between the verb of the complement *to come* and the next subclause only. And that is precisely what the speaker wants to express: he will come on the condition that there is no press, but we cannot say that he agrees if there is no press. This seems to suggest the hypothesis that fully grammatical conjunctions like *if* are less suited to function inside embedded sentences than lexical-grammatical conjunctions like *on condition that*. This new conjunction *on condition that* is then better suited to function in reported speech, of which (19) is an instance, since unlike *if*, it is not related to the reporting speaker.

According to SOED, the English word *proviso* is a loan from Latin dating back to 1467, and was derived from the Latin phrase *proviso quod*, meaning "it being providing that". SOED also comments on the register in which the word and the expression was used, i.e. it is "a clause inserted in a legal or formal document, making some condition, stipulation, exception, or limitation". In English legal texts, the Latin form *proviso quod* was turned into the English loan translation *with the proviso that* or the more current forms *provided*, alongside which also the *-ing*-form *providing* arose. In today's English the forms *provided/providing that* probably have the same communicative function as the Latin *proviso quod*. This function is also felt and expressed in philosophical writings by the use of the form *if and only if*. The difference is that *if and only if* is very strictly limited to the scientific register, whereas *provided that* seems to have found its way from legal registers to the common core of the language, as in the example below:

(20) *You can camp here provided you leave no mess.* (TM: 203)

The difference between the use of *provided* and the use of *if* in this sentence stands out clearly: with *if* the speaker would give a rather personal permission, which could also entail the use of *may* (see Dirven *et al.* 1989: 282ff), but with *provided that* the speaker implies the existence of a whole set of restricting stipulations forbidding the leaving of mess by people camping in nature. It is the world of wild camping that is involved here. From this use with a more public background, the conjunction also has begun to be used in personal interactions in which people present the agreement they are making in the form of a deal:

(21) *She was prepared to come, provided that she might bring her daughter.* (CC: 1156)

3.4. however (much), whether... (or); in spite of/despite the fact that

These expressions are used in sentences which can be compared and related to the complex concessive conjunctions already discussed, *although* and *even though*. Just like these, they do not denote conditionality, but as conceptual companions they must be discussed here for the sake of completeness. In one respect as König (1985:3, 1986:234) claims *however (hard)* and *whether ... or* are very similar to *even if*:

(22) a. *However hard he tries, he'll never succeed.*
b. *Whether he tries hard or not, he'll never succeed.*
c. *Even if he tries hard, he'll never succeed.*

In all of these three sentences, it is not stated as an assertion, and certainly not as a fact, that a man tries hard; it is just given as a hypothesis. Still (22a, b) also differ fundamentally from (22c), since they can be used after a factual statement such as *He tries very hard* and can continue this with *but however ...* or *but whether ...* . This is excluded in (22c), because a statement of fact and a hypothesis of such a fact exclude one another. Therefore, *whether ... or* and *however (hard)*-constructions are closer to the concessive conjunctions with *though* than to *even if*.

With the forms *in spite of* or *despite* we are fully in the same factive area as with *though*:

(23) a. *In spite of the fact that he tries very hard, he'll never succeed.*
b. *Despite the fact that he tries very hard, he'll never succeed.*
c. *Though he tries very hard, he'll never succeed.*

All of these constructions presuppose the truth of his trying hard, and after the prepositions *in spite of* or *despite* this can be overtly expressed by the use of *the fact that*. We can now also better appreciate the reason why such new complex conjunctions as in the above examples in (22) and (23) arise: the non-assertive character of *even if* and the factive character of *even though* are not overtly marked, and it is this need of transparent, overt marking of the hypothetical character (see especially (22b)) or, in the opposite case, of the factive character (see (23a, b)) that is satisfied.

4. Conclusions

4.1. Characterisation of the various conjunctions

We will now try to summarise all the main characteristics of the twenty-three conjunctions that have been analysed in the previous sections. For this purpose, we shall stick to the three main conceptual categories we introduced from the beginning, i.e. time, condition, and concession. To this we will add three categories, which for lack of a better characterisation we will continue to call adversativeness, semblance, and wish. So, all of the twenty-three conjunctions will have to be allocated to one of those six major conceptual categories. We will make further differentiations within these six categories by means of more delicate semantic parameters which may apply to several of the major six categories. For instance, as we already did before, we will use a common characteristic for *even when* (TIME), *even though* (CONCESSION), and *even if* (ADVERSATIVENESS). The common semantic parameter applying to each of the three conjunctions is what we have called "counter-to-expectation". Other semantic parameters that were introduced before are: assertive, non-assertive, factive, counterfactual, exclusive, reinforcing, etc. But we will also have to introduce new semantic parameters, especially for the new complex conjunctions. Let us now first have a look at the table summarising and categorising all the conjunctions discussed in the previous sections:

CONCEPTS / Parameters	TIME	CONDITION	ADVERSAT.	CONCESS.	SEMBLANCE	WISH
assertive	*when*					
non-assertive		*if*				
factive			*though*		*as though*	
counterfactual					*as if*	*if only*
exclusive	*only when*					
counter-to-expectation	*even when*		*even though* *in spite of/* *despite*	*even if* *whether..or/* *however much*		
pragmatic		*in case*				
reinforcing		*only if*	*although*			
exceptive		*unless*				
hypothetical		*suppose/ing*				
neutral		*assuming*				
neutral		*on condition that*				
restrictive		*provided/ing*				

Table 6. Survey of conditional conjunctions and conceptual companions

It may be useful to agree first on how we intend the table to be read. We propose to combine the adjectives referring to the parameters in the left column with the nouns referring to the major conceptual categories. Thus, we propose to characterise *when* as assertive time, *if* as non-assertive condition, *though* as a factive concession.

Next, we want to emphasise that the parameters for the new complex prepositions at the bottom of the table are provisional labels which are subject to improvement. We have characterised *in case* as a pragmatic condition, and mean by this, as suggested when analysing (16b) *I'll come tomorrow in case Ann wants me*, that the speaker does not just refer to a link between a main clause and a subclause, but rather to a link between the subclause and his speech act itself, namely the reason for his coming is not Ann, but the reason for his telling that he is coming is to inform Ann that he will be available if needed. Similarly, also the other parameters for new complex conjunctions have been touched upon or analysed in the previous sections.

Although we are not fully satisfied about the characterisations offered in Table 6 (on the one hand, we would prefer to find better conceptual categories for adversativeness, semblance, and wish and on the other hand, there are far too many semantic parameters), it can serve its purposes as a first synthesis, which is certainly to be simplified, and hopefully to be deepened by further research and academic discussions. Still, the general approach is supposed to be correct in its major distinctions and we have managed to come to grips with a number of seemingly highly arbitrary uses. Most of the conjunctions that we have been discussing belong to conceptually very clearly delimited categories, and contain a number of equally well justified nuances within the conceptual category they belong to. There seems to be a very strong communicative or conceptual motivation for the use of so many different conjunctions. Now in the final sub-section we will summarise the various uses of *if* that belong to the semantic field of non-assertiveness and the compound forms using *if*.

4.2. Network of the uses of "if"

The title of this paper suggests a double area of semantic functioning: conditional conjunctions and neighbouring semantic categories. For this purpose we took a broad look at all possible forms. But now we must come back to the starting-point and summarise these findings for the conjunction *if* and its compounds. What was already vaguely implied in the discussion throughout the various sections of this paper is a kind of network of the various uses of *if* and its compounds, which is now overtly spelled out in Table 7.

This table contains a number of generalisations, which have not all been proved in this paper. But they may stimulate further research and as such they are worthwhile stating in the form of hypotheses:

1. All utterances can be attributed to two main categories, viz. assertive and non-assertive ones.
2. Non-assertive utterances consist of two syntactic categories, viz. interrogative and negative sentences on the one hand, and various types of complex sentences, one type being subclauses introduced by the conjunction *if*.
3. *If*-clauses expressing uncertainty reflect main clauses expressing interrogatives (*ask if*) or, more generally, main clauses expressing lack of knowledge (*not know if*).
4. *If*-clauses expressing supposition again fall into two different categories, viz. those functioning as conditionals (*if*-conditionals) and those functioning as different semantic categories, i.e. non-conditional categories such as counterfactual (*if only* or *as if*) or adversative propositions (*even if*).
5. Within the category of conditionals it is already now becoming clear that there is not simply a single class of hypothetical conditionals, but that various other types of conditionals, such as pragmatic conditionals (see Haegeman 1984 and Van der Auwera 1986), have to be distinguished. This question is one of our main concerns and will be given ample consideration in future research.

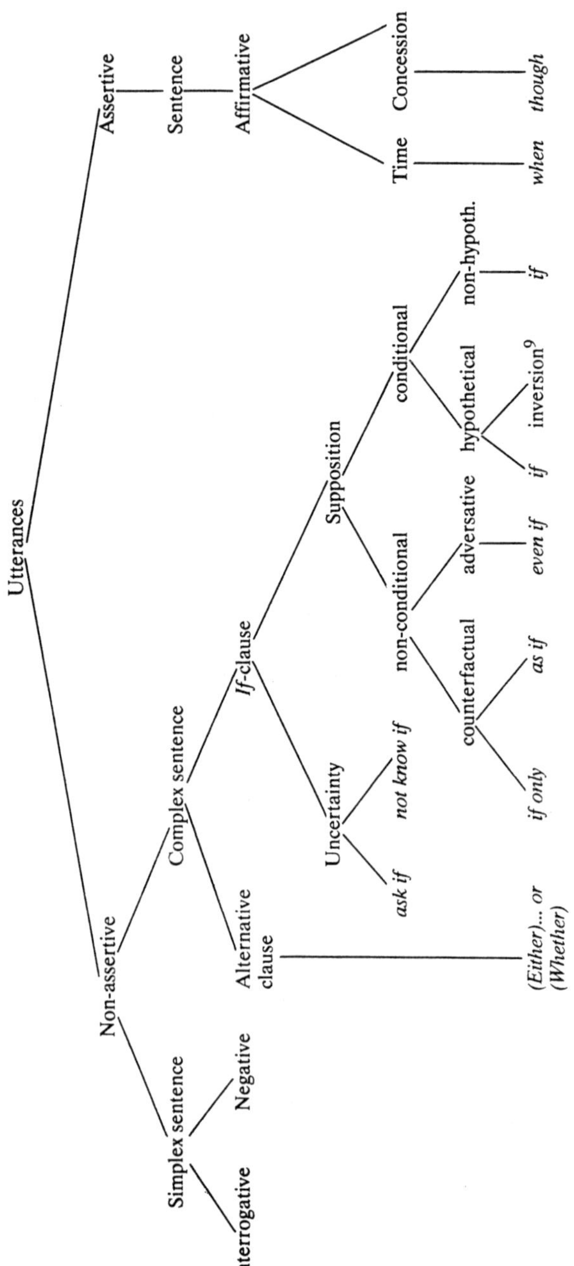

Table 7. Network of the uses of *if*

6. Conditionals seem to be covering three distinct types of dependencies: (i) a "causal" dependency, (ii) a dependency of "supposition", and (iii) a dependency of "condition".
7. There seems to be a fundamental distinction between conditionality (see its meaning relations in the previous conclusion) and hypotheticality. The former cannot only occur in *if*-constructions, but also in a number of new complex conjunctions, whereas the latter may occur both in *if*-constructions, but also in many other constructions, especially in counterfactual and adversative constructions.

Notes

1. In Sinclair (1990:345) *once* is used to talk about one event happening immediately after another: *Once environmental damage is done, it takes many years for the system to recover.* But also in the LDC *once* is met in the following way: *If this is all this boy wants from you he does not really love you and once he has had it he will quickly tire* (LDC:13).
2. German can of course express the concept of mere conditionality by means of the word *falls*, which is an old genitive of the noun *Fall/Falles* "(in) case". But the form *falls* is limited to more formal language and probably comes from judicial and legal language. The situation is similar though not identical in Dutch. The conjunction *als* is used both in a temporal and a conditional sense. Dutch also has a more formal item to express the notion of mere conditionality, i.e. *indien*, which derives from the preposition *in* and the determiner *die(n)*. The difference with German, however, is that Dutch *indien* is somewhat less marked for formal language than German *falls*.
3. In Sinclair (1987:482), *even if* and *even though* are said to "introduce a clause which appears to partly contradict the main clause in the sentence, but that does not actually affect the truth of the main clause". We have borrowed this notion of contradiction from Sinclair, but we think that the division of functions of subclause and main clause is rather distributed the other way round, i.e. that the main clause contradicts (the expectation raised in) the subclause.
4. The only work which does not mention the notion of concessiveness in connection with *even if, even though*, and *although* is Sinclair 1987, but for König 1985, 1986 there is no problem yet.
5. The way how *if* can function both in a conditional and in a hypothetical context, such as (4c) and (5) is not fully clear to us yet. But the hypothetical use of *if* certainly has a pragmatic basis and means something like, if what you say is true, i.e. that she is poor, (4c) or "that she felt despondent when she arrived" (5), I can only say that she is honest (4c) or that she very soon forgot about herself (5). What is not clear is why this mere use of *if* is ruled out in (11b).
6. The Dutch and German equivalents of *as if* are *alsof* and *als ob*, respectively. The *of/ob* forms do not belong to the area of conditionality, but only to the area of indirect questions and alternatives so that any link with condition is fully absent in Dutch or German.

7. The Dutch and German translations for (17b) are the words *behalve als/außer wenn* 'except if'.
8. The dates of first registered uses given in SOED are: *notwithstanding* 1490, *assuming* 1660, *supposing* 1660, *during* 1670.
9. By inversion we mean hypothetical conditionals of the type: *Had she been here, it would not have happened.*

References

Athanasiadou, A. & R. Dirven
to appear Typology of *if*-clauses. In: Casad, Eugene (ed.). *Cognitive Linguistics in the Redwoods.* Berlin: Mouton de Gruyter.

COB
1980 Collins Birmingham University International Language Database.

Dancygier, B.
1988 Conditionals and concessives. In: Fisiak, J. (ed.). *Papers and Studies in Contrastive Linguistics*, Vol. 24:111-121. Poznan: A. Mickiewicz University Poznan, Washington D.C.: Center for Applied Linguistics.

Dirven, R. (ed.)
1989 *A User's Grammar of English: Word, Sentence, Text, Interaction.* Frankfurt/Bern: Lang.

Dirven, R.
1995 "On so-called concessive conditionals". In: Athanasiadou, A. & R. Dirven (eds.). *Conditionals and Co.* Amsterdam: Benjamins.
1995 "The conceptual space between conditionals and concessives". In Athanasiadou, A. & R. Dirven (eds.). *Conditionals and Co.* Amsterdam: Benjamins.

Haegeman, L.
1984 "Pragmatic conditionals in English". *Folia Linguistica* 18: 485-502.

Hanks, P. (ed.)
1979 *Collins English Dictionary.* London & Glasgow: Collins.

König, E.
1985 "On the history of concessive connectives in English. Diachronic and synchronic evidence". *Lingua* 66: 1-19.
1986 Conditionals, concessive conditionals, and concessives: areas of contrast, overlap, and neutralization. In: Traugott, E. C. *et al.* (eds.), pp. 229-246.

LDC
1975 Leuven Drama Corpus.

Leech, N. G.
1989 *An A - Z of English Grammar and Usage.* London, Melbourne, Auckland: Edward Arnold.

LOB
1961 Lancaster-Oslo-Bergen Corpus

Onions, C. T. (ed.)
1973 *The Shorter Oxford English Dictionary on Historical Principles* (3rd edition). Oxford: Clarendon Press.

Prins, A. A.
1952 *French Influence in English Phrasing.* Leiden: Universitaire Pers.

Quirk, R., S. Greenbaum, G. Leech & J. Svartvik
1972 *A Grammar of Contemporary English.* London: Longman.

Sinclair, J.
1987 *Collins Cobuild English Language Dictionary*. London, Glasgow: Collins.
1990 *Collins/Cobuild English Grammar*. London, Glasgow: Collins.

SOED
1973 see Onions

Taylor, J.
1989 *Linguistic categorization: Prototypes in Linguistic Theory*. Oxford: Clarendon Press.

Thomson, A. J. & A. V. Martinet
1986 *A Practical English Grammar* (4th edition). Oxford: Oxford University Press.

Traugott, E. C., A. ter Meulen, J. S. Reilly & C. A. Ferguson (eds.)
1986 *On Conditionals*. Cambridge: Cambridge University Press.

Van der Auwera, J.
1986 Conditionals and speech acts. In: Traugott, E. C. *et al.* (eds.), pp. 197-213.

The reflection of lexical meaning relations in textual meaning concepts - a sample analysis of an English text

Beate Seidel

1. Introduction

Paradigmatic meaning relations are traditionally determined with regard to word-field analyses revealing different types of semantic contrasts, super- and subordination, and meaning identity in the lexical system of a language. Lexical research in texts often aims to describe ties between or chains of cohesive lexemes. Meaning relations and referential criteria or a combination of both are used for the subclassification of these ties (e.g. Halliday & Hasan 1976, Stotsky 1983, Hasan 1984, Hoey 1991).

With the help of a sample analysis of an English text I would like to demonstrate how one can relate the semantic systematicity of the lexicon and cohesive relations in a text to its textual meaning patterns.

A useful framework for this purpose is the text description model developed by Graustein & Thiele (cf. Graustein & Thiele 1987). It focuses on the interrelation of the textual meaning structure and its complex linguistic and non-linguistic realization forms and the dependence of both form and meaning on their text-external embedding in a specific communicative situation. Within such a comprehensive view of texts as a process and a result of human interaction it is possible to investigate a particular linguistic aspect without risking an isolated interpretation of the results, since these can easily be supplemented by research on related aspects.

For the given purpose, I will concentrate on those components of the text model which are important for the analysis of lexical relations in the sample text *Tasteful*, which was published in *The Economist* (cf. the appendix to this paper).

2. Text externals

The external communicative situation relevant to this text can be summarized as follows:

partners:	a journalist of *The Economist* and the readers of *The Economist*
temporal situation:	shortly before July 20th, 1991
local situation:	published in London
spatial situation:	partners separated
action goal:	notice the controversy over Benetton's advertisements

These externals are not a direct part of the text, but they determine text internal characteristics, thus being indispensible to text analysis and interpretation. I only want to mention a few of these dependences, which are also relevant to the selection of appropriate lexemes.

The social relation between the partners influences the stylistic level. The assessment of the recipients' knowledge of the text topic allows the producer to determine the necessary degree of explicitness and presupposed knowledge frames. In this respect, the typical readers of *The Economist* are obviously different from those of the gutter press, but also from specialists who read scientific economic journals.

The local situation accounts for the regional variety English English. The written text medium allows the spatial and temporal separation of the communication partners.

3. Internal meaning structure

The text model uses among others the categories proposition and topicalization for describing the meaning of the text as a whole and its parts.

The proposition is the statement of the specific content based mainly on referential meaning. Higher level propositions are derived by stepwise abstractions from lower levels. Newspaper headlines often reflect text propositions or at least some of their basic elements, but this does not hold for our sample text. The headline *Tasteful* gives an ironic evaluation. In connection with the picture of the priest-nun-advertisement and its ambiguous caption *heavenly* it is supposed to catch the readers' attention without naming the specific content of the text, which can be condensed in the following text proposition: *Benetton's advertisements are reflected differently by various groups of people.*

As it is hardly possible to compare texts and discover generalized meaning patterns purely on the basis of their propositions, this meaning description is complemented by a more global characterization - the topicalization. Graustein & Thiele (1987:54) define it as "the more conventionalized, socially standardized, or established part of the text content/meaning". Though there is still an open list of topicalizations, this list is definitely not endless as that of possible propositions. The text *Tasteful* is an example of the topicalization QUALITY CONTENTION because it points out attributes - mainly negative ones - of Benetton's advertisements.

Graustein & Thiele describe the internal meaning patterns below the text level in diagrams whose vertical dimension represents the super- and subordination of chunks and whose horizontal dimension indicates the relation of chunk configurations on the same level. In Figure 1 I will illustrate this only with regard to the introductory chunk. The first line on each level indicates the topicalization of the chunks (in capital letters), the relevant sentences and non-verbal parts and the meaning relation between the elements of a chunk configuration. The second line gives a short form of the proposition.

INTRODUCTION 2-5, picture -----------explicative----------- BODY 6-21
Benetton's ads are provocative ...

GENERAL 2 -------------- explicative ---------------- SPECIFIC 3-5, picture
Benetton's ads are provocative priest-nun ad

FACT 3, picture ------- evaluative --------- COMMENT 4-5
priest-nun ad assessment

VARIANT I 4 ------ adversative ------ VARIANT II 5
Benetton: human sentiment Catholics: offensive

Figure 1. The internal meaning structure of the introductory chunk

This principle can be applied to other parts of the text as well, but for the purpose of this paper it is sufficient to describe the most important meaning patterns in a less formulaic way.

The main part of the text (topicalization: BODY) starts with an outline of Benetton's aims presented by their photographer Mr. Toscani (sentences 6 and 7) and an indirect author's comment following in sentence 8.

Sentence 9 has a linking function and signals a concessive relation between the aims, which are summarized in the expression *convention-breaking*, and the actual results. Thus the scope of the coordinator *but* is not limited to adjacent sentences, but it functions as a linker in the chunk configuration

AIM 6-8 --------- concessive ----------MEANS AND RESULT 9-18.

Sentences 10-12 and 15-18 describe specific ads and people's reactions to them, with a more generalizing part in between consisting of the concessively related sentences 13 and 14. In fact, this pair of sentences is a condensed equivalent of the above mentioned chunk configuration. *Address the major social issues of our time ...* takes up and exemplifies the aims introduced in 6 and 7, *its audience ... miss the point* represents a generalization of the results and the concessive relation is explicitly marked by the connector *however.*

Sentences 19 and 20 have a summarizing function followed by the author's concluding comment.

These meaning patterns are realized by a complex of language means which were chosen and which can be understood due to knowledge of the English language system, of communicative strategies, and extra-linguistic world knowledge.

I want to have a closer look at the lexical realization forms and their contribution to the textual meaning development.

4. Lexical realization forms

4.1. Word system as a category

Graustein & Thiele use the category *word system* for the description of lexical cohesion. This term was introduced by Aphek & Tobin (1981), who discovered the occurrence of text-specific word systems and described problems of their adequate translation from the Hebrew language into English. In the framework of their text model Graustein & Thiele (1987:86) re-defined the word system as "semantically cognate items expressing configurational meaning". As far as their form is concerned, these items can be proforms, simple or complex lexemes, phrases or even clauses, which obviously goes beyond the traditional lexeme-based analysis of cohesion.

The feature "semantically cognate" allows a fairly wide interpretation, covering synonyms as well as more remote relations comparable with

Halliday & Hasan's category *collocation*, which was often criticized for including a ragbag of lexical relations. Hasan (1984) and Hoey (1991) solve this problem by restricting the cohesive ties or links to a predetermined set of semantic relations, most of them being predictable from the lexical system. Without denying the existence of other cohesive relations between lexemes, they exclude them for the sake of a higher degree of objectivity and consistency in the text analysis, which can be proved by the following revealing quotations:

> Certain relations intuitively recognized as cohesive cannot be accounted for in the revised version ... Attaching greater priority to consistency of analysis, I accepted - with regret - this shortcoming of the analytical categories.
> (Hasan 1984:203)

> [Since] complex paraphrase ..., interpreted broadly, ... will relate vast numbers of lexical items (for example, *sickness* and *doctor*, *carol* and *Christmas*) in ways that might be revealing about lexis, but are not readily controllable, we restrict its application to three situations only.
> (Hoey 1991:64)

The Graustein & Thiele model does not limit the types of connections within a word system to the traditional semantic and morphological-semantic relations of the lexicon, but it uses the relation to the overall textual meaning patterns as reference criterion for word systems, which will be demonstrated with our sample text.

4.2. *The word systems of the sample text*

With regard to the chunk characterization outlined above and the text proposition *Benetton's ads are reflected differently by various groups of people* I suggest the following main word systems:

- !Benetton company!
- !advertising! with its subsystems !advertisement!, !visual presentation! and !content!
- !Benetton's aim!
- !potential consumer! with its subsystems !groups! and !reaction!
- !temporal circumstances!

These headlines represent the basic text-semantic concepts, and it is a convention that they are formally marked by a pair of exclamation marks. A survey of the word systems and their distribution in the text is given in the appendix 2 to this paper.

I determined these word systems on the basis of my understanding of this text, which might raise the question whether this approach is purely subjective. Two arguments against this should be mentioned here. Firstly, although I cannot give statistical evidence, I have found that the analysis of various texts with my students and colleagues showed a considerable degree of agreement concerning the dominating word systems. Secondly, and more importantly, one of the reasons for this general agreement is the predictability of types of word systems from prototypical knowledge frames related to the topic, in our case *advertising.* Without reference to this specific text and without the detailed knowledge of a professional advertiser I suggest the following components for the frame *advertising:*

producer/firm --------	**advertisement** ---------------	**potential consumer**
- product/service	- type of ad (medium, size, costs ...)	- needs, consumption behaviour ...
...	- content	- money
	- persuasiveness	- reaction (buy, like, ignore, reject...)
	- aim: sale	...
	...	

Figure 2. Components of the frame *advertising*

The actual realization of these components as word systems of a text, their central or marginal character depend on the decision which parts of the frame are topicalized, which aspects are focused on. The concept !product! is one of those marginal elements in our text, just represented in sentences 2 and 8 by *jumpers* and in sentence 3 by *clothes*. In contrast to this, the !aim of advertising! is a dominating text-semantic concept in the Benetton-text, whereas it could be completely ignored in other texts about ads as long as the normal aim - i.e. to sell one's products - is taken for granted and need not be explicitly discussed.

Now I will turn to the analysis of the individual word systems and their concrete lexical representation. For easy access, a list of the elements will precede the analysis of a word system, but for a better survey of their interaction and distribution the table of word systems in appendix 2 should be consulted.

4.2.1. The word system !Benetton company!

sentence 2	Benetton's; its
sentence 3	the Italian clothes maker's
sentence 4	Benetton
sentence 6	Olivero Toscani; the photographer; who Benetton's; the firm; its
sentence 7	Mr Toscani
sentence 8	Benetton's
sentence 9	the firm
sentence 10	its
sentence 11	Mr Toscani
sentence 13	Benetton; its
sentence 14	its
sentence 15	Benetton
sentence 16	the company
sentence 19	its; Benetton
sentence 21	Benetton's

Figure 3. The elements of !Benetton company!

The word system !Benetton! runs through the whole text except for those sentences which concentrate on the reactions to the ads (5, 12, 18, 20), the evaluative headline, and sentence 17, which describes an ad whose origin has already been introduced in the preceding sentence.

This word system may be subdivided into two chains, one referring to the company, the other one referring to Mr. Toscani as Benetton's chief advertiser.They are introduced in sentences 2 and 6 respectively, but whereas the role of Toscani is explicated immediately after the first mention of his name, the knowledge of the proper noun *Benetton* seems to be presupposed. The use of the corresponding descriptive elements in sentence 3 *the Italian clothes maker* could be mainly due to stylistic reasons, i.e. avoiding the repetition of *its* or *Benetton.* However, they are also useful for those who may never have heard of Benetton, although it should be said that even those readers of *The Economist* who are not interested in fashion are certainly familiar with Benetton's commercial success and its spectacular advertising methods.

From sentence 9 onwards the two subchains are integrated, being most obvious in 13: *Benetton* is used and Toscani is quoted.

The lexical and grammatical items in this word system correspond to the subcategories of *reference* and *reiteration* in Halliday & Hasan (1976), i.e. personal reference with the possessive determiner *its,* demonstrative reference with the definite article *the*, repetition of lexemes (*Benetton, firm, Mr Toscani*), synonyms (*firm - company*), subordinate and superordinate term (*clothes maker - firm*). All these relations are predictable from the language system.

The slogan *united colours of Benetton* is so strongly fixed and well-known that even its short form *united colours* might be synonymous with *Benetton* in certain contexts. However, its occurrence in the combination *united colours global philosophy* (sentence 19) is more closely related to Benetton's aims. For that reason I did not list it as a direct element of the word system !Benetton company!, without denying the possibility of immediate associations with Benetton.

4.2.2. The word system !advertising!

The subdivision of the superordinate system !advertising! into the subsystems !advertisement!, !visual presentation!, and !content! reflects the double function of these pictures: they express a certain content in order to advertise a product. This distinction is particularly important for the given text, because Benetton's ads are famous for indirect links between the actual content and the product. This is also the basis for Toscani's attempt to disguise commercial purposes.

sentence 2	advertisements
sentence 3	campaign; an ad
sentence 6	advertising campaigns; ads
sentence 7	they
sentence 8	the ads
sentence 10	campaign
sentence 12	the ad
sentence 13	campaigns
sentence 15	an ad
sentence 16	performance
sentence 17	one ad; campaign
sentence 19	the ads
sentence 20	a campaign; that; the ad; that
sentence 21	advertising policy

Figure 4. The elements of the subsystem !advertisement!

The dominating lexical items in the subsystem !advertisement! are the lexeme *advertisement,* followed by its short form *ad,* and *campaign*. The latter is introduced in sentence 3 and should be understood as *advertising campaign*, which only occurs in sentence 6. The alternation between generalizing and exemplifying parts of the text is matched by the occurrence of plural forms in 2, 6-8, 13, and 19 and singular forms specified by temporal complements as parts of the word system !temporal circumstances!, e.g. in sentences 3, 10, 15, and 17.

The superordinate expression *advertising policy* supports the summarizing function of sentence 21, thus integrating the subsystems of !advertising!.

sentence 3	picturing
sentence 6	(photograph)
sentence 10	showed; sporting
sentence 11	full-colour image
sentence 15	showing
sentence 17	depicts
sentence 19	show

Figure 5. The elements of the subsystem !visual presentation!

All sentences that introduce particular examples of advertisements (i.e. 3, 10, 11, 15, 17) contain elements of the closely linked subsystems !visual presentation! and !content!. The lexemes belonging to !visual presentation! are predictable due to their close semantic relation in a corresponding word-field within the lexical system. The most general among these verbs is *show*, which occurs three times and is stylistically varied and semantically specified in the verbs *picture, depict, sport.* The noun *image* in sentence 11 is used in the sense of *picture* or even *photograph*.

Although sentence 6 does not include a direct reference to ways of visual presentation, this concept is hidden as a component of the suffixation *photographer* referring to Mr Toscani. In this case, the cohesive interaction of word systems is based on the incorporation of an element from another word system as a morphologically explicit determinant of a complex word. This does not imply that all determinants of complex words necessarily create cohesive relations but those which belong to the domain of the basic textually relevant concepts are very likely to be cohesive. In my lexical analyses of instruction texts this kind of cohesion proved to be quite frequent (cf. Seidel 1991:231f).

sentence 3	a kiss between a priest and a nun clad in old-fashioned habits
sentence 10	a group of tombstones; one; the Jewish star of David

sentence 11	death;
	a gunk-covered newborn baby
sentence 15	a black woman breastfeeding a white child
sentence 17	an angelic-looking white child embracing a black one whose hair has been shaped into devil's horns
sentence 19	same
sentence 20	white-baby-black-breast

Figure 6. The elements of the subsystem !content!

The only predictable semantic component shared by most of the expressions listed under !content! is *human* (e.g. in *priest, nun, Jew, baby, child, woman).* Its cohesive force does not seem to be very strong if we consider its high frequency in the lexical system. A stronger, but clearly text-bound connecting feature exists with regard to their function as specific examples of ads.

Fauconnier (1985) developed an interesting theory explaining such phenomena on the basis of mental spaces which are established in texts by explicit or pragmatically inferred space builders. Even without applying Fauconnier's formulaic description, this approach helps to interpret an expression like *a kiss between a priest and a nun* within different textually relevant spaces.

Sentence 3 introduces the existence of the kiss as a picture on an advertisement. Benetton's assessment in sentence 4 is based on its interpretation as a work of art which is to convey the symbolic message that *pure human sentiment* will overcome traditional conventions of separation. Intentionally, commercial purposes are not mentioned. The Catholics' comment *offensive* in sentence 5 seems to operate in at least two spaces. First and foremost it condemns the abuse of religious symbols for commercial ads, but in addition it shows their worry that such kisses might reflect reality.

We know that Benetton's ads are provocative and characterized by sharp contrasts. So, one could expect that their description is full of lexemes with contrasting meaning components. But, in fact, there is hardly any pair of complementary or contrary antonyms in the strict classificatory sense of these terms. Most of the contrasts are based on text- or frame-specific interpretations of meaning relations.

The pair *angel(ic)* and *devil* in sentence 17 is supposed to be associated with *good* and *bad* thus representing a contrary or - for some people - even complementary contrast. *Black* and *white* referring to races are cohyponymic. The fact that they are often used to reflect the strongest contrast of races could be partly due to their historical and present relations and partly due to the degree of contrast in the colour of their skin, which is actually neither black nor white.

The provocative character of the ads mentioned in sentence 3 (priest-nun-ad), sentence 10 (tombstones with the Jewish star) and sentence 11 (gunk-covered baby) cannot be directly inferred from lexical meanings. It requires knowledge of culture-specific frames, such as the dos and don'ts of the Catholic clergy, the history of the Jewish people and the common belief in the so-called civilized world that a human baby has to be clean and pretty. Presupposing that the readers of *The Economist* are aware of the relevant background frames the author does not need to elaborate on them.

4.2.3. The word system !Benetton's aim!

sentence 4	affirmation of pure human sentiment
sentence 6	distance from commercial considerations
sentence 7	aim; capture attention; provoke reflection; break through the barrier of indifference
sentence 8	sales grew by a healthy 24%; sell
sentence 9	convention-breaking
sentence 11	for commercial purposes
sentence 13	address the major social issues; AIDS, overpopulation, environmental problems, racial harmony
sentence 14	the point
sentence 19	united colours global philosophy

Figure 7. The elements of !Benetton's aim!

The concept !Benetton's aim! is expressed in sentences 4, 7, and 13 as an enumeration of morally positive aims given by Mr. Toscani. Supported by the verbs *distance from* and *aim to* sentences 6 and 7 establish a strong contrast between Benetton's aims and those of traditional advertising.

The author found a clever way of calling this into question without direct contradiction. In sentence 8 he mentions recent sales results, adding contrastive adjectives (*healthy* - *recessionary*) and concluding with the adverb *too*, which does not simply indicate an additive relation in this case but rather a concessive one. The doubts about the subordination of commercial purposes are substantiated in sentence 11, which includes a direct accusation against Benetton by part of its audience (*exploiting death for commercial purposes*).

Apart from these contrastive relations between Benetton's pretended and hidden aims this word system also reflects textual coherence due to anaphoric generalization of previously detailed concepts. *Convention-breaking* in sentence 9 takes up the main content of sentence 7 and the second part of sentence 6, as does *the point* in sentence 14 with regard to 13.

The summarizing part of the text (sentences 19 - 21) is introduced by the generalized expression *united colours global philosophy*, which does not only refer to the aims but indirectly integrates elements of the word systems !advertising! and !Benetton!.

4.2.4. The word system !potential consumer!

sentence 5	Catholics
sentence 7	people's
sentence 12	*Child*, an American child-care magazine
sentence 14	audience
sentence 15	American blacks
sentence 18	black groups
sentence 19	around the world
sentence 20	in one market; in others; America; in France and Italy
sentence 21	different countries'

Figure 8. The elements of the subsystem !consumer groups!

The lexical realization of the subsystem !consumer groups! again matches the alternation of generalizing and specifying parts of the text. The hyperonym *people* (7) occurs in a chunk which concentrates on Benetton's aims. The hyperonymic lexeme *audience* in sentence 14 has a twofold function. It helps to describe the general reaction to the ads and their original aims as outlined in sentence 13 and it serves as a cataphoric introduction of the following specific ads and reactions.

The occurrence and distribution of hyponyms like *Catholics* (5), *American blacks* (15) and *black groups* (18) reveal a close lexical and conceptual link between the subsystems !consumer groups! and !ad content!, because the groups obviously do not protest against the function of ads in general, but against their representation in Benetton's advertisements.

Local elements dominate in the summarizing chunk: *around the world* (19), *America, France, Italy* (20), *different countries'* (21). As they do not refer to places proper but to the consumer market there, they belong to the word system !consumer groups!.

sentence 5	offensive; outraged
sentence 11	accuse(d) of exploiting (death)
sentence 12	reject(ed)
sentence 14	miss (the point)
sentence 15	created uproar
sentence 18	starting to grumble
sentence 20	backfires; wins awards; shocked; won awards
sentence 21	sensitivities

Figure 9. The elements of the subsystem !reaction!

Most of the lexemes in the word system !reaction! express different degrees of rejection as inherent component of their denotative meaning (e.g. *grumble, backfire, reject, uproar, accuse*). Thus they provide a new level of contrast with regard to the aims outlined by Toscani and pinpoint the main conflict within this text.

Positive reactions are mentioned only in sentence 20 in the form of an antithesis supported by the intra-systemic contrast between *win awards* and *backfire* or *shock*.

4.2.5. The word system !temporal circumstances!

sentence 3	autumn 1991
sentence 6	old
sentence 8	in recessionary 1990
sentence 10	spring 1991; just as the first Iraqi Scud missiles hit Tel Aviv
sentence 11	this autumn
sentence 12	already
sentence 13	of our time
sentence 14	often
sentence 15	two years ago
sentence 16	repeat
sentence 17	in this year's autumn
sentence 18	already
sentence 20	often

Figure 10. The elements of the word system !temporal circumstances!

This word system contains expressions which function syntactically as temporal complements or noun modifiers. Unlike the other word systems it does not represent a dominating textual concept in its own right, but specifies the temporal circumstances of the other concepts, a phenomenon for which Endt (1986:87ff) introduced the term "connecting word system".

Most of the concrete temporal phrases occur in connection with the introduction of specific ads:

sentence 3	*autumn 1991*	priest and nun
sentence10	*spring 1991*	tombstones
sentence 11	*this autumn*	gunk-covered baby
sentence 15	*two years ago*	black woman and white child
sentence 17	*this year's autumn*	angel and devil

The temporal clause in sentence 11 *just as the first Iraqi Scud missiles hit Tel Aviv* elucidates why the ad with the Jewish tombstones was particularly provocative in 1991. *Already* in sentences 12 and 18 refer to the reactions to recent campaigns.

Less concrete expressions are used with regard to Benetton's aims *(old* in sentence 6, *of our time* in sentence 13) and in generalized statements about people's reactions (*often* in sentences 14 and 20).

4.2.6. The lexical analysis of sentence 21

The textual function and lexical realization of sentence 21 deserves a separate discussion. Against the background of the previous text it summarizes some basic textual concepts: *advertising policy* integrates the subsystems of !advertising!; *different countries* summarizes !consumer groups! and *sensitivities* are mentioned as reasons for !reactions!.

But the theme of this sentence *the missing link* does not properly fit into any of the described word systems. This fact can be explained by the specific communicative function of sentence 21. Whereas the main part of the text describes Benetton's aims, ads, and reactions to them, the last sentence gives a conclusion presented as the author's advice for more effective advertising. Evaluative comments by the text author also occur in the headline (*tasteful*) and the first sentence ((*not*) *soft and woolly*). Thus the predominantly objective description is framed by the more subjective initial and final sentences.

5. Conclusion

This sample analysis of the text *Tasteful* reflected on relations within a word system - as was done in the earliest descriptions of cohesive chains. Furthermore it pointed out relations that are based on the interaction of word systems - similar to what Hasan (1984) called "cohesive harmony". And most importantly, it described these relations against the background of the textual meaning development.

For the time being, this analytical method is less standardized and objective than other approaches to lexical cohesion, especially those which restrict their domain to a set of easily classifiable categories. To interpret the empirical data without such a priori limitations enables our approach to shed light on manifold sources and mechanisms that create cohesive lexical relations in texts. They comprise co-referential synonyms and proforms as well as the activation of presupposed and textually developed knowledge frames.

Although our research mainly focused on the lexical network in texts, I will suggest some hypotheses concerning the influence of these textual relations on the structure of the lexicon. In comparison with their systemic representation, lexical items in texts can be enriched by text-specific semes and semantically restructured due to textually influenced fore- and backgrounding of semes. Thus the meaning of words that is stored in the lexicon could be regarded as abstractions from concrete text occurrences.

It is not very likely that a single text notably weakens the relative stability of the lexicon, but the frequent embedding of a lexeme in similar types of text word systems certainly favours a corresponding meaning development within the lexicon. Apart from terminological neologisms, this is normally a gradual process starting with connotative associations which eventually may find their way into the domain of denotative meaning, so that the prototypical representations of existing sememes are changed or new sememes are established.

The semantic development of the lexeme *advertisement* in the course of the centuries illustrates the results of this process. It entered the English language as a French borrowing in the 15th century with the basic meanings *the action of calling the attention of others; warning, instruction* and *a (written) statement calling to anything; a notification, a notice* (OED 2). The element of *warning* did not survive the 18th century. The specification towards *public announcement* arose with the activity of town-criers who walked through the streets announcing sales and other events - a meaning which the Oxford English Dictionary (OED) traced back to 1582. The core of this meaning is still relevant today, but the medium changed from town-criers via printed placards and newspapers towards the whole range of modern media. From the mid-18th century onwards the general meaning *public announcement* was supplemented by the more specific usage as *public announcement and favourable description of products or services in order to persuade customers to buy*, which nowadays seems to be established as a separate and obviously dominating sememe.

One can only speculate on the further semantic development of this lexeme. Following the recent trend in certain types of ads, including those described in the *Tasteful*-text, one could expect the seme *description of product/service* to become less important, if not optional. On the other hand, the additional meaning element *cultural value* could gain ground in the process of semantic change, with the seme *persuade to buy* remaining fixed.

Of course, the ultimate causes of such a meaning development are the corresponding changes in the extralinguistic world. However, their subsequent reflection in the lexicon of a language is based on the actual communication practice within and about this changing world.

In order to reveal rules and guidelines of this mutual give-and-take it is necessary to complement traditional word-field analyses by methods which can discover lexical networks in texts, even if only a part of these textual relations has the chance to be stored in the lexical system. The flexibility with which lexemes enter and establish text word systems also raises the question about the sources of this flexibility within the lexicon. It cannot be exclusively based on well-defined hyponymy and opposition relations within clear-cut word-fields.

What Lipka (1992:157ff) calls "lexical sets" should be the object of further lexicological research on this problem, including the role of associative meaning elements, knowledge frames and mechanisms of foregrounding and backgrounding particular semes within those lexical sets.

As another conclusion from our textual analyses, I would favour lexicological approaches which distinguish sociologically determined subsystems of the general lexicon, because actual communication cannot primarily rely on the activation of the overall lexicon of a language but on those parts available to the communication partners.

Complementary descriptions of semantic relations in texts and the lexicon replace the old metaphor of a one-way street from the lexicon to the text by a complex system of interrelations, so aptly highlighted by Neubert and Hoey in the following quotations:

> Texts are always both trying to expand the lexicological systematicity and, at the same time, relying on the dynamic stability of the lexicon at a given period of time. (Neubert 1979:28)

The text provides the context for the creation and interpretation of lexical relations, just as the lexical relations help create the texture of the text. (Hoey 1991:8)

References

Aphek, E. & Y. Tobin
1981 "Problems in the translation of word systems", *Journal of Literary Semantics* X/1:32-45.

Endt, S.
1986 *Textwortnetze als lexikalische Realisierungsformen der Bedeutungsstruktur im englischen Fachtext.* Dissertation A, Universität Leipzig (unpublished).

Fauconnier, G.
1985 *Mental Spaces: Aspects of Meaning Construction in Natural Language.* Cambridge, Massachusetts: MIT Press.

Graustein, G. & W. Thiele
1987 *Properties of English Texts.* Leipzig: Verlag Enzyklopädie.

Halliday, M. A. K. & R. Hasan
1976 *Cohesion in English.* London, New York: Longman.

Hasan, R.
1984 Coherence and cohesive harmony. In: Flood, J. (ed.). *Understanding Reading Comprehension: Cognition, Language, and the Structure of Prose.* Newark, Delaware: International Reading Association, pp. 181-219.

Hoey, M.
1991 *Patterns of Lexis in Text.* Oxford: Oxford University Press.

Lipka, L.
1992 *An Outline of English Lexicology.* Tübingen: Niemeyer.

Neubert, A.
1979 Words and Texts. In: *Linguistische Studien* Reihe A 55. Berlin: Akademie-Verlag, pp. 16-29.

Seidel, B.
1991 Der lexikalische Beitrag der Verben zur Textkohärenz in englischen Gebrauchsanweisungen. In: Hansen, K. (ed.). *Studien zur Sprachvariation im Englischen und zur Textlinguistik.* Berlin: Humboldt-Universität, pp. 225-234.

Simpson, J. A. & E. S. C. Weiner
1989 *The Oxford English Dictionary*, Second Edition. Oxford: Oxford University Press.

Stotsky, S.
1983 "Types of lexical cohesion in expository writing: Implications for developing the vocabulary of academic discourse". *College Composition and Communication* 34/4:430-446.

Appendix 1: The sample text

The Economist, London July 1991
Note: The sentence numbers are added in brackets.

Tasteful *(1)*
BENETTON'S colourful jumpers may be soft and woolly, but its advertisements are not. *(2)* The Italian clothes maker's autumn 1991 campaign includes an ad picturing a not-so-platonic kiss between a priest and a nun clad in old-fashioned habits. *(3)* "The affirmation of pure human sentiment," says Benetton. *(4)* Offensive, say outraged Catholics. *(5)*

Olivero Toscani, the photographer who dreams up and directs Benetton's advertising campaigns, says that the firm tries to distance its ads from boring old commercial considerations. *(6)* They aim, says Mr Toscani, to capture people's attention, provoke reflection and "break through the barrier of indifference." *(7)* As Benetton's sales grew by a healthy 24 % in recessionary 1990, to 2.1 trillion lire ($1.7 billion), the ads clearly sell jumpers too. *(8)*

But the firm is finding that convention-breaking is a ticklish business. *(9)* Its spring 1991 campaign showed a group of tombstones, one sporting the Jewish star of David, just as the first Iraqi Scud missiles hit Tel Aviv. *(10)* Accused of exploiting death for commercial purposes, Mr Toscani is this autumn countering with an off-putting (and full-colour) image of a gunk-covered newborn baby. *(11)* The ad has already been rejected by *Child*, an American child-care magazine. *(12)*

Benetton reckons its campaigns "address the major social issues of our time including AIDS, overpopulation, environmental problems, and racial harmony." *(13)* Its audience, however, often seems to miss the point. *(14)* Two years ago a Benetton ad showing a black woman breast-feeding a white child created uproar among American blacks. *(15)* The company looks set for a repeat performance. *(16)* One ad in this year's autumn campaign depicts an angelic-looking white child embracing a black one whose hair has been shaped into devil's horns. *(17)* Black groups are already starting to grumble. *(18)*

In line with its "united colours" global philosophy, Benetton shows the same ads around the world. *(19)* A campaign that backfires in one market often wins awards in others: the white-baby-black-breast ad that shocked America won awards in France and Italy. *(20)* The missing link in Benetton's advertising policy may well be understanding where different countries' sensitivities lie. *(21)*

The original text is supplemented by a picture of the priest-nun-advertisement with the caption *Heavenly*.

Appendix 2: **Survey of the word systems in the text** ***Tasteful***

word system / sentence	! Benetton company !	!advertising! ! advertise-ment !	! visual pre-sentation !	! content !	! Benetton's aim !	! potential consumer ! ! groups !	! reaction !	! temporal circum-stances !
1								
2	- Benetton's - its	- advertisements						
3	- the Italian clothes maker's	- campaign - an ad	- picturing	- kiss between a priest and a nun				- autumn 1991
4	- Benetton				- affirmation of pure human sentiment			
5						- Catholics	- offensive - outraged	
6	- Olivero Toscani - the photographer - who - Benetton's - the firm - its	- advertising campaigns - ads	- (photo-graph)		- distance from commercial considerations			- old
7	- Mr Toscani	- they			- aim - capture attention - provoke reflection - break through the barrier of indifference	- people's		
8	- Benetton's	- the ads			- sales grew by a healthy 24 % - sell			- in recession-ary 1990
9	- the firm				- convention-breaking			
10	- its	- campaign	- showed - sporting	- a group of tombstones - one - Jewish star of David				- spring 1991 - just as the first Iraqi Scud missiles hit Tel Aviv
11	- Mr Toscani		- full-colour image	- death - a gunk-covered newborn baby	- for commercial purposes		- accuse(d) of exploiting (death)	- this autumn

word system / sentence	! Benetton company !	!advertising! ! advertise-ment !	! visual pre-sentation !	! content !	! Benetton's aim !	! potential consumer ! ! groups !	! reaction !	! temporal circum-stances !
12		- the ad				- *Child* - an American child-care magazine	- reject(ed)	- already
13	- Benetton - its	- campaigns			- address the major social issues - AIDS, overpop., environmental problems, racial harmony			- of our time
14	- its				- the point	- audience	- miss (the point)	- often
15	- Benetton	- an ad	- showing	- a black woman breastfeeding a white child		- American blacks	- created uproar	- two years ago
16	- the company	- performance						- repeat
17		- one ad - campaign	- depicts	- an angelic-looking white child embracing a black one ... devil's horn				- in this year's autumn
18						- black groups	- starting to grumble	- already
19	- its - Benetton	- the ads	- show	- same	- "united colours" global philosophy	- around the world		
20		- a campaign - that - the ad - that		- white-baby-black-breast		- in one market - in others - America - in France and Italy	- backfires - wins awards - shocked - won awards	- often
21	- Benetton's	- advertising policy				- different countries'	- sensitivities	

Part III

Computational approaches to the lexicon

Mental and machine-readable lexicons: What can machines learn from the mind?

Jürgen Handke

1. Introduction

In this paper an attempt is made to investigate the lexicon from two perspectives: a psycholinguistic and a computational. After a discussion of the central issues of human word processing we will evaluate the possibilities of realising the basic principles of lexicon organisation and lexical processing on machines. In some cases this leads to a gain of processing efficiency while in others it may complicate the administration and handling of lexical information.[1]

1.1. Word stores

A lexicon is a store that contains the words of a language. Three techniques of storage are available: Words can be listed in a reference book, they can be stored on storage devices connected to computers, or, they can be kept in the mind. Word stores that are primarily consulted for the reason of information retrieval are referred to as dictionaries. By contrast, word stores that constitute a component within a natural language processing system, are called lexicon. Figure 1 illustrates this typology of word stores.

Book dictionaries have been around for a long time. The most common types of book dictionaries are encyclopaedic monolingual dictionaries, bilingual dictionaries, or dictionaries for special purposes, such as synonym dictionaries, foreign word dictionaries, etc. Machine-readable dictionaries were only made available in the late 1980s, when book dictionaries such as the Oxford English Dictionary were transferred to a machine-readable format.[2] Normally, machine-readable dictionaries are delivered on special storage devices such as CD-ROM or large removable harddisks. A lexicon, by contrast, is the central module of a natural language processing system, whether human or machine. It closely interacts with the other components of the language processor and provides detailed information about the words to be produced or comprehended.

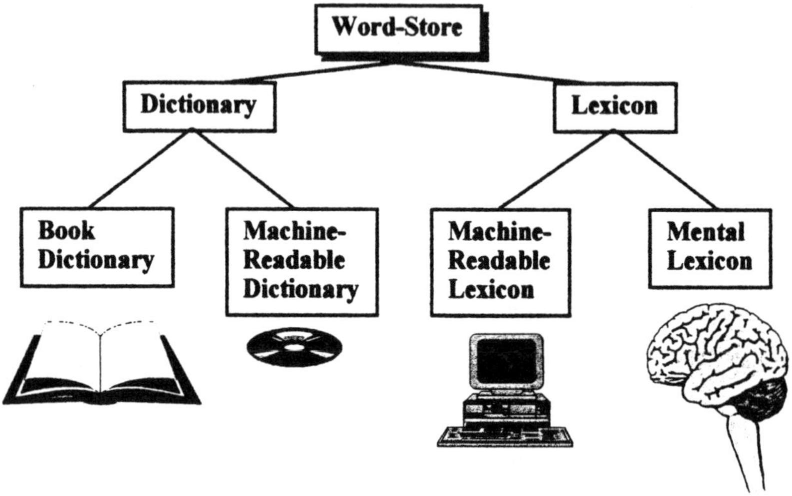

Figure 1. A typology of word stores

1.2. Lexical entries

Lexicons contain a large number of items which are defined linguistically. These items are referred to as *lexical entries*. Each lexical entry consists of a *lexical access unit*, which serves as the basis of consulting a lexicon, and its *lexical specification*, i.e. the collection of information associated with an access unit.

An essential question about the entries in the lexicon concerns the nature of the access units. Basically, there are two conceptions about the items listed in a lexicon. On the one hand, we could confine ourselves to listing only those forms in the lexicon which serve as a basis for the generation of further forms, i.e. roots or stems. Such a strategy can be referred to as *minimal listing hypothesis* (Butterworth 1983). The resulting lexicon architecture is called *root lexicon*. On the other hand, we could opt for a lexicon containing all possible word forms of a language. According to this *full listing hypothesis* all words have a lexical representation. The resulting lexicon is referred to as *full-form lexicon*.

There is even a third, somewhat hybrid position. It concerns the implementation of machine-readable lexicons. Like the mental lexicon, machine-readable lexicons have to cope with orthographical variants, such as *carry, carries, carried*, etc. In a full-form lexicon such variants would simply be listed, in a root lexicon they have to be analysed by an additional algorithm. For languages with little orthographical variation, there is a third possibility, the storing of morpho-graphemes.[3] In such a morpho-graphemic lexicon we would list morpho-graphemic roots, such as *carrI* and *carrY*, where the final elements "I" and "Y" are placeholders that stand for their own orthographical realisation in actual contexts and determine the affixational possibilities of an item. For example, the "I" in the morpho-graphemic root *carrI* is realised as "i" and combined with {-s} or {-ed} but not with {-0} or {-ing}. To illustrate that "I" and "Y" are variables they have been capitalised.

Figure 2 illustrates the three variants of organising the lexical access units on the basis of some selected orthographical access forms.

Roots	WALK	CARRY	JOG	HATE
Full Forms	WALK WALKS WALKED WALKING	CARRY CARRIES CARRIED CARRYING	JOG JOGS JOGGED JOGGING	HATE HATES HATED HATING
Morpho- Graphemes	WALK	CARRY CARRI	JOG JOGG	HATE HAT

Figure 2. Variants of lexical access units

1.3. *Processing lexical information*

The goal of processing lexical information is to retrieve the stored knowledge associated with a word in order to generate a meaningful interpretation of an utterance. There are various aspects that make the task of lexical processing particularly difficult, among which are the following:

(a) *Segmentation*
The problem here is that the input signal is not neatly segmented into words. While in written language - at least in phonographic alphabetic writing systems - individual words can be identified by spaces, punctuation marks, or upper and lower case, the segmentation of spoken language into words is a very complicated process (see McClelland and Elman 1986 for a discussion).

(b) *The nature of the contact representation*
Lexical processing begins when the fundamental perceptual properties have been extracted from the input signal to contact the lexicon. An important issue in this respect concerns the nature of representation, with which the mental lexicon is activated. The type and the internal organisation of the elements in the lexicon, it may be argued, is influenced by the nature of the contact representation. For example, if the lexicon is contacted on the basis of syllables, then it is likely that it organises its access units in terms of syllables rather than phonemes.

(c) *Lexical processing*
Two fundamental concepts of lexical processing deserve our specific attention: *lexical access* and *word recognition*. According to Tyler & Frauenfelder (1987:6ff) *lexical access* refers to the point at which the various facets of the lexical entry contacted become available, whereas *word recognition* defines the end-point of the selection phase, that is, the point at which a listener is able to decide what lexical entry he identified.

While the concept of "word recognition" is relatively unproblematic, the term "lexical access" is confusing in many ways. First, it is used fairly inconsistently throughout the relevant literature. In contrast to Tyler & Frauenfelder, Garnham (1985:43) defines "lexical access" as the retrieval of a word form from the lexicon on the basis of perceptual and contextual information, and "word recognition" as the identification of one remaining word candidate. Aitchison (1992:53, 95) views "word recognition" as a two-stage process: at the first stage, the stage of "lexical access", the input is matched against possible words, and at the second, the multiple possibilities are narrowed down to one candidate. Thus, we are confronted with two completely different interpretations of the term "lexical access". On the one hand, it is viewed as the initial stage of the more general process of word recognition (Aitchison, Garnham), on the other hand, it is defined as the retrieval of lexical information (Tyler & Frauenfelder). In both cases, the term "access" seems to be interpreted too narrowly. To "access something" means to "reach" or "make use of something". Thus, the process of "lexical access" should not be confined to the retrieval of the information associated with a lexical entry; rather, it should be interpreted as "making use of the lexicon" or "preparing the lexicon for use" just like we open a dictionary before we actually start reading in it. Such a generalised interpretation is much more plausible if we consider the computational interpretation of "access" in the sense of "file access", which is normally read as "making use of a file" or "preparing a file for read/write operations". Thus, it seems reasonable to extend the term "lexical access" and consider it synonymous with lexical processing henceforth. The process of making available lexical information, i.e. "lexical access" in Tyler and Frauenfelder's sense, will be referred to as *lexical retrieval* instead.[4]

The relationship between word recognition and lexical retrieval is assumed to be sequential. Most theories of lexical processing claim that word recognition precedes lexical retrieval. This in turn raises the question whether either of the two stages can be by-passed. Put dif-

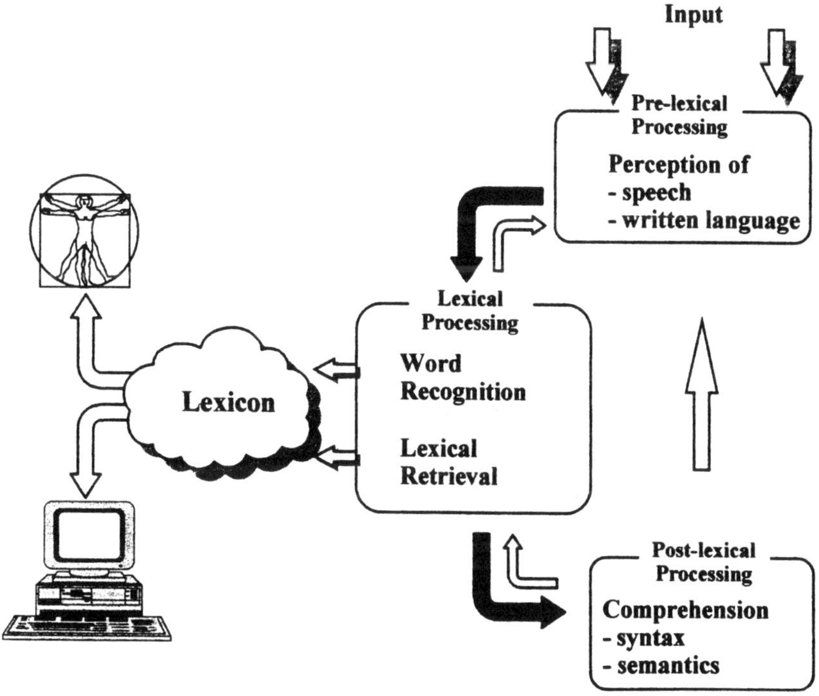

Figure 3. The central stages of processing lexical information

ferently, is it possible to retrieve information from the mental lexicon without recognising what was heard, or, vice versa, is it possible to perceive a sensory input, i.e. hear or read a word, without understanding it? The answer to these issues places some very important constraints on models of lexical processing.

Figure 3 summarises the various stages of processing lexical information irrespective of the lexicon type, i.e. mental or machine-readable lexicon.

In the following sections we will outline the central principles of human word processing and the fundamental principles of organising the mental lexicon. Subsequently, we will investigate the possibilities of implementing a machine-readable lexicon in such a way that it not only realises as many human principles as possible but also profits in terms of processing speed and memory management.

2. The mental lexicon

The investigation of the mental lexicon seeks to solve the following basic issues:

- On the basis of what units do we consult the mental lexicon?
- How are the access units in the mental lexicon organised?
- How are the various parts of an entry's lexical specification organised?
- What variables influence word recognition and lexical retrieval?
- How can we model the stages of lexical processing?

These and other aspects have been in the centre of psycholinguistic research for more than 25 years. Even though a great deal of progress has been made, there are numerous issues that are still speculative and beyond our judgement. The following sections summarise the basic insights.

2.1. Lexical entries

In order to retrieve a lexical entry from the mental lexicon its access unit has to be recognised first. This evokes two major questions. The first concerns the unit on the basis of which we consult the lexicon, the second deals with the internal structure of the access units in the lexicon, i.e. do humans employ a root or a full-form lexicon?[5]

2.1.1. Lexical contact units

To identify words from the input stream they have to be isolated. While in visual processing words can in most cases be relatively easily separated from each other, auditory processing involves numerous segmentation problems. One such problem is that the acoustic input string is not neatly divided into linguistic units. Neither individual phonemes nor words can be separately identified from the acoustic input. One essential problem for this lack of segmentation is the high degree of encodedness of speech sounds: The overlap of acoustic cues and the lack of a one-to-one correspondence between acoustic cues and phonemes make the acoustic segmentation process an almost insurmountable problem. Nevertheless, words can be identified from the input. Hence, we must be able to overcome the segmentation problem. How can this be achieved?

Altmann (1990:3ff) discusses two central lines of reasoning. One says that segmentation primarily employs phonetic/phonological strategies, while the other asserts a high-level segmentation strategy based on syntactic and semantic aspects. According to recent suggestions (Mehler *et al.* 1990:237ff), the segmentation problem can only be lifted in terms of a pre-lexical unit which is based on phonetic principles. Studies into language acquisition, especially into infant speech processing, suggest that this unit corresponds roughly to the syllable. The significance of the syllable in written language has been experimentally supported by Taft (1986:298), who put forward the idea of a syllable based on orthographic and morphological considerations. He referred to this unit as BOSS (*B*asic *O*rthographic *S*yllable *S*tructure). Essentially, the BOSS is defined as the first syllable of a word's root which includes all consonants following the first vowel. Taft illustrates the structure of the BOSS on the basis of *blemish* whose BOSS is *blem-*, and *blend* whose BOSS is not *blen-* but *blend*.

2.1.2. Lexical access units

From a linguistic point of view, a root lexicon architecture seems highly economical and efficient. Unfortunately, experimental data suggests that the story is not as simple as that.

Butterworth (1983) evaluated the possibilities of organising the basic forms and their morphological variants in the lexicon. Despite the high degree of economy in a minimal listing hypothesis, which only lists base forms (roots) and generates the variants by a system of morpho-phonological rules, disappointingly little experimental evidence was found to support this position. In discussing experimental data from speech perception, speech production, and reading, Butterworth outlined the possibility of an alternative view, the full listing hypothesis, where all words have a lexical representation. A somewhat weaker hypothesis says that the morphological variants of a root are related within a lexical entry, that is, that forms such as *flies, flying, flew, flown,* and *fly* can be found under the same lexical entry or address. The phonological or graphemic structure in language comprehension and morphological features such as tense, number, etc. in language production would then take care of triggering the relevant item within a lexical entry. Such a hypothesis was not rejected, however, no evidence could be collected that such a group of related words has a common base form or some sort of abstract heading. Thus, a full listing hypothesis seems much more likely than previously thought.

Henderson (1985) rejected the full listing hypothesis and concluded on the basis of production experiments and speech errors that morphological regularities are conceived of as rules which permit a reduction in the amount of information to be stored. Further arguments against the full listing hypothesis come from Hankamer (1989). On the basis of agglutinative languages such as Turkish he argued that the lexical entry includes representations of morphological structure so that affixes are processed via the root.

Sproat (1992:110ff) also argues for a minimal listing hypothesis. The fact that speakers are able to coin as well as to comprehend new words, such as *giraffishness*, indicates that they have some knowledge about roots and affixes and are thus aware of the morphological structure of their language. Further arguments involve evidence from specific cases of aphasia where the generation and comprehension of prefixes is impaired (Sproat 1992:111).

Despite many arguments in favour of a minimal listing hypothesis, we are still confronted with two opposing views, a full listing hypothesis, which stores all morphological variants in a full-form lexicon, and a weaker position, which excludes morphological variants from the lexicon and generates them using morphological rules. As the previous discussion has indicated, it may be the case that the strategy of storing entries in the lexicon is language-specific. While non-agglutinative languages tend to favour a full listing hypothesis, agglutinative languages seem to be in line with a somewhat weaker position.

2.1.2. Partitioning

Levelt (1990:182ff) suggested a subdivision of lexical entries into form-related features and content-related features or *lemmas*. Both are linked by a pointer which activates the lemma after the recognition of the formal aspects. The picture shown in Figure 4 illustrates this conception of lexical entries from the view of language comprehension.

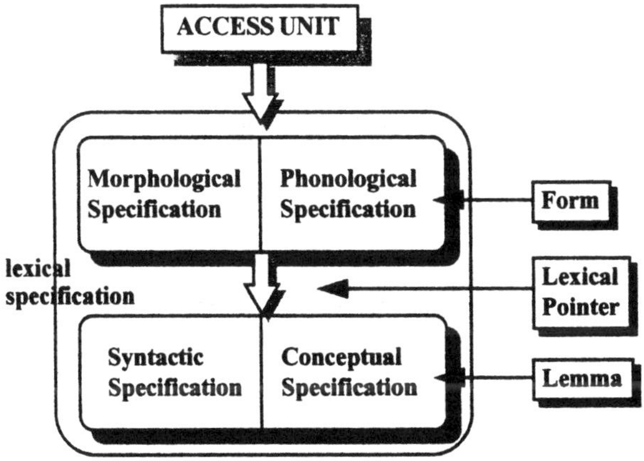

Figure 4. Partitioned lexical entries

Even though this partitioning of a lexical entry into morpho-phonological form and lemma (the specification of meaning and syntax) is still very much an open issue (Levelt 1990:187ff), language production phenomena, such as the *tip-of-the-tongue phenomenon* or speech errors provide evidence that the retrieval of formal aspects from the lexicon can be independent of lemma-related aspects.[6]

2.1.3. Lexical entries: A summary

Even though evidence is not conclusive, the following basic findings about the organisation of the mental lexicon have emerged:

- the mental lexicon seems to be consulted on the basis of syllables
- lexical entries are subdivided into access unit and lexical specification
- the lexical specification is subdivided into form and lemma

Whether the mental lexicon is organised in terms of roots or fullforms is not clear. Factors, such as the degree of synthesis of a language, or general aspects of structuring information seem to favour a root lexicon; however, there is evidence that fullforms are also employed.

2.2. *Lexical processing*

Lexical processing can be subdivided into two stages. At stage one, the input, regardless of whether it is visually or orally presented, is matched against the collection of access units contained in the lexicon, until there is only one remaining candidate, and the input has been identified. This process is called *word recognition*. At stage two, the stage of *lexical retrieval*, the various properties associated with the access unit identified are made available.

In order to study the phases and strategies of lexical processing, a variety of experimental techniques, such as lexical decision tasks, naming tasks, shadowing techniques, priming techniques, masking techniques, etc. have been used. On the basis of real word and non-word stimuli psycholinguists have established a number of effects that influence lexical processing:[7]

- the frequency effect	(high-frequency words are recognised faster)
- the length effect	(word-length does not affect word recognition)
- the regularity effect	("irregular" words, such as *sew*, are recognised slowly)
- the lexicality effect	(regular non-words, e.g. **mav*, are processed slowly)
- the homophone effect	(homophones and pseudo-homophones are problematic)
- the word superiority effect	(words are superior to individual letters)
- the contextual effect	(the context facilitates word recognition)

All these experimental findings cannot be dealt with in isolation. They influence each other, they are often a matter of degree, and they are affected by various processing levels, ranging from low-level to high-level processing. Also, by and large, a number of experimental findings are irrelevant for auditory lexical processing and are confined to the processing of written phonographic information. Figure 5 illustrates the relevance of the experimental findings for visual and auditory lexical processing.

Even though we have to be careful about putting too much emphasis on certain experimental effects, any model of lexical processing has to explain at least those effects relevant for the auditory processing mode and has to be modelled accordingly.

	Visual Lexical Processing	Auditory Lexical Processing
the frequency and recency effect	*	*
the length effect	(x)	(x)
the regularity effect	*	x
the lexicality effect	*	*
the homophone effect	*	x
the word superiority effect	*	x
the contextual effect	*	*

Figure 5. Experimental effects in word recognition
Annotations: * = relevant, x = irrelevant

2.2.1. Modelling word recognition

There are two influential models of word recognition: the *Cohort model of spoken word recognition* (Marslen-Wilson 1987) and *TRACE* (McClelland & Elman 1986). While the Cohort model was shaped to account for psychological data on language comprehension, TRACE grew out of computational, more particularly, connectionist efforts to model human speech understanding. On the theoretical side, the connectionist approach is based on an abstraction of our current understanding of the information properties of neurons; on the technological side, it relies on the feasibility of building parallel computers (Feldman & Ballard 1982:

Type of Knowledge/Effect	Cohort Model	TRACE
phonotactic knowledge	implicit	implicit
lexical knowledge	via elements in the cohort	via word detectors
sentence context	via higher level knowledge	via higher level knowledge
length effect	via recognition point	not represented
lexicality effect	via cohort structure	via activation levels
- regular non-words	- long search	- reduced activation level
- impossible non-words	- no or short search	- reduced activation level
frequency effect	via internal cohort structure	not represented
categorical perception	not represented	via activation levels
handling of distorted input	via parallel cohort	via activation across levels
phoneme as processing unit	implicit, in terms of abstract phonological representation	explicit, in terms of phoneme detectors
syllable as processing unit	implicit in initial cohort	not represented

Figure 6. The Cohort model and TRACE compared

205, 206). Essentially, a connectionist model consists of two primitives, *units* and *connections*. Units, also referred to as nodes, are simple processing devices with associated *activation values*. These values result from a weighted sum of the inputs to a unit and from other units. The interaction between the units is based on connections. Connections, also called links, may have positive weights, so that an input may excite or inhibit the processing unit that receives the input. The total set of processing units and connections is normally referred to as *network*. A fundamental premise of connectionism is that the individual units do not transmit large amounts of information. Instead, they compute information on the basis of a set of appropriate connections to a large number of similar units (Feldman & Ballard 1982:208).

Both the Cohort model and TRACE belong to the class of interactive models of comprehension allowing the top-down flow of information, where higher processing levels influence lower levels (Cutler *et al.* 1987:142). Figure 6 summarises the realisation of various knowledge sources in the Cohort model and in TRACE and the possibility of integrating experimental observations and structures.

The primary advantage of the Cohort model can be seen in its excellent account of the length effect and its elegant technique of narrowing down the set of possible word candidates. Furthermore, it makes an attempt to incorporate as many theoretical linguistic and psycholinguistic insights and theories as possible. The disadvantage of this model lies in the fact that some aspects are fairly abstract in character. For example, the frequency effect and the possibility of coping with distorted input have been solved via abstract activation thresholds. This is not surprising, since Marslen-Wilson's (1987) innovations were primarily a reaction towards McClelland & Elman's (1986) connectionist TRACE, where activation thresholds are essential.

Due to the activation levels and the multitude of connections across the network, TRACE has no problems in handling distorted input. Furthermore, it provides the possibility of provisional input identification, it is capable of changing preliminary guesses, etc. Also, the integration of the temporal factor of speech processing enables TRACE to incorporate aspects such as the phonetic context or categorical perception. Thus, viewed as a coherent theory from pre-lexical to lexical processing TRACE seems to be well equipped to cope with natural language input.

One aspect which neither of the two models has been able to solve is the problem of segmenting the input stream into processing units. Above we argued that some sort of syllable structure is central to pre-lexical processing. Since both models incorporate the stage of pre-lexical processing (TRACE more explicitly than the Cohort model), they should be able to use syllabic structures to some extent. TRACE certainly does not; as far as the Cohort model is concerned, it builds the initial cohort around some sort of syllabic structure, i.e. around the initial CV-cluster.

Over and above the Cohort model and TRACE, there are further models of word recognition. Norris (1986) subsumes Morton's Logogen model, Forster's Search model, Becker's Verification model, and his own alternative, the Checking model under models of word recognition. However, as we have outlined above terminology is not straight in this field. These models should be treated as more general models of lexical access rather than as isolated word recognition models.

2.2.2. The mental lexicon: A summary

At present, we are confronted with numerous approaches towards the lexicon and word processing. In modelling word recognition, conventional symbolic and connectionist models compete for predominance; with regard to lexical retrieval we can choose from interactive and non-interactive architectures.[8] Nevertheless, more and more parallels emerge between all these frameworks. They concern the reliance on a recognition system that operates with activation values. Irrespective of the processing mode, the selection of a word from a set of alternative candidates can be best defined by associating a value with each item. These values can be affected by other levels of processing, such as lexical knowledge or contextual integration.

The second parallel within all the models is the availability of a set of alternative candidates at an early stage of lexical processing. While the Cohort model defines word recognition as a process of narrowing down an initially large set of possible candidates until only one remaining element is left, TRACE constantly establishes and rebuilds hypotheses about the input on the basis of the strength of the connections between the processing units. This strategy of building sets of alternatives distinguishes the mental lexicon from ordinary databases, where search does not narrow down existing sets but examines individual candidates sequentially.

To sum up, word processing can be subdivided into three general levels: the level of pre-lexical processing, the level of word recognition, and the level of lexical retrieval. Figure 7 illustrates the contribution of each of these levels to the overall process.

Today, many researchers argue for a realisation of pre-lexical processes by a system of feature detectors. These feature detectors are an integral part of connectionism and can thus easily be combined with the connectionist approaches to word recognition, e.g. with the TRACE model or the Word Detector model, and merge the pre-lexical level and the level

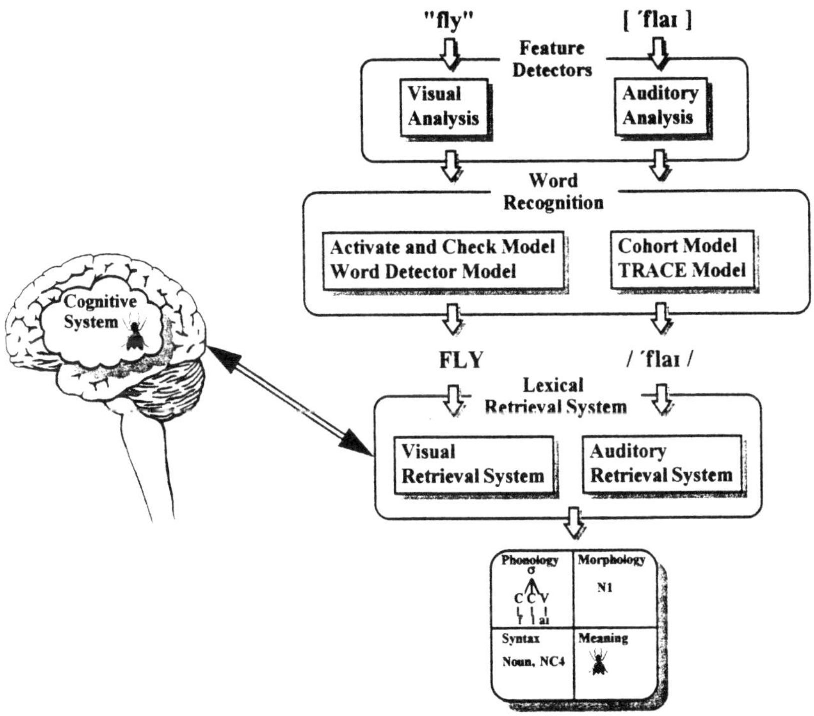

Figure 7. A general conception of word processing[9]

of word recognition into one general level. Conventional symbolic models, by contrast, are less specific about low-level processes and maintain a separate level of feature detectors. Whether the level of word recognition has access to the cognitive system is not clear. The question boils down to the debate about the interaction between the components of lexical processing. The lexical retrieval system, however, interacts with the cognitive system. In Figure 7 no specific claim about the internal nature of the retrieval system has been made, though Morton's (1979) differentiation between a visual and an auditory system has been maintained to account for the lack of cross-modal priming effects, i.e. the possibility of mutual influences between, and top-down influences on, the input channels.

3. Machine-readable lexicons

The following computational sections are based on an actual implementation of a machine-readable lexicon by the author and his colleagues. This system is called LexEcon.[10] It runs under Microsoft-Windows ® and can be used as an on-line translation tool for economy vocabulary in English and German or as a lexical component of a natural language processing system. The heart of the program is the machine-readable lexicon which contains 25,000 English root entries and 4,000 German root entries (German is still in the build-up phase). To handle orthographical and morphological alternation LexEcon makes use of an affix lexicon, a morphological component, and an orthographical rule system.

(a) *Pre-lexical processing*
LexEcon neither accepts spoken input nor does it handle written information. It analyses textual data solely in terms of ASCII-code. There are two ways to initiate analysis. In the direct mode, words are simply typed using the keyboard. In the indirect mode, words are forwarded to LexEcon from standard software applications, such as word processors or graphics applications. In this mode a word is marked first and then - together with its environment - transferred to LexEcon for further analysis. While in the direct mode no preparation of the incoming data is necessary, each word is directly analysed in terms of its ASCII-code, the indirect mode requires some sort of pre-lexical processing. Whenever a word is forwarded to LexEcon in the indirect mode, it is not just one word that is analysed but also its context. The maximum context that is prepared for one analysis is a sentence. Sentences are defined as units between two punctuation marks, such as full-stops, colons, exclamation marks, question marks, and semi-colons. Alternatively, sentences can start or end with two or more blanks, with one or several empty line feeds, for example, at the beginning or the end of a paragraph or the entire document. In other words, in the indirect mode LexEcon analyses the information to the left and to the right of the item marked, until a sentence can be isolated. By the application of a filtering mechanism this sentence is converted

into the ASCII-format and passed on to the central analysis component of LexEcon.

(b) *Lexical processing*
LexEcon has two lexicons, one for English and one for German. Both lexicons contain roots as access units and are coupled with an additional affix lexicon for each language. Hence, the lexical look-up process involves morphological and orthographical rules that handle affixation and orthographical alternation at root boundaries.

(c) *Post-lexical processing*
In order to disambiguate words in context LexEcon uses a strategy of context analysis that inspects the local context of the item marked. This strategy is based on the syntactic information about the neighbouring words drawn from the lexicon. By analogy with the machine translation system SYSTRAN, LexEcon looks both to the left and to the right (Wheeler 1987:198).

Figure 8 illustrates the analysis result of the items *materials* and *flies* by LexEcon.

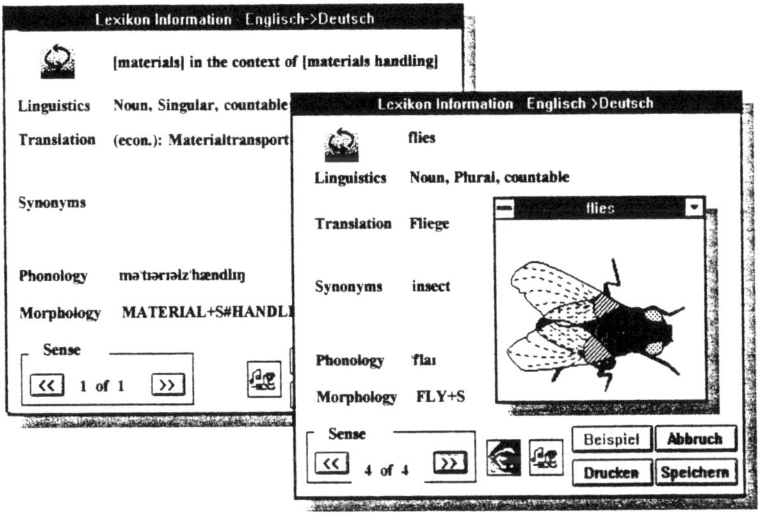

Figure 8. Word processing in LexEcon

The analysis of *flies* illustrates the direct mode where one word is forwarded to LexEcon as an individual context-independent item.[11] The analysis of *materials*, by contrast, shows the indirect mode, i.e. the analysis of a word in its context, here in the context of "materials handling". Note that materials has only one meaning (Bedeutung/meaning 1 von/of 1), whereas LexEcon provides four (4 von/of 4) interpretations of *fly*. Note that FLY is also coupled with a picture, which has been optionally retrieved via the eye-button.

Including pre-lexical processing, morphological and contextual analysis, and the preparation of the information as a user-friendly output, the entire process lasts roughly a second. The linguistic analysis alone, i.e. word recognition and the retrieval of an item's lexical specification, takes less than 150 msec.

3.1. Lexical entries

The entries in machine-readable lexicons can be constructed by analogy with the mental lexicon where each entry consists of an access unit coupled with its lexical specification (see Figure 4). For reasons of system performance and memory management the subdivision of lexical entries into several parts is even more important for a machine-readable lexicon. An essential demand on the implementation of a machine-readable lexicon is the most economical use of a machine's working memory. Should we not segregate the access units from their lexical specification in a large-scale machine-readable lexicon, we will have to load the entire lexicon into the machine's working memory and will soon reach the limits of memory capacity. A split of each lexical entry into access unit and lexical specification is much more economical. Now only the access units are loaded into working memory, whereas the lexical specifications are stored in a separate file on an external storage device. The link between each access unit and its lexical specification is established by means of a pointer.[12] Hence, such a split is not only psychologically motivated as suggested above, but it is also an important organisational principle for a machine-readable lexicon.

An entry's lexical specification is not only amazingly complex but also requires a certain amount of memory. In order to recognise whether an item is a word or not, only the phonological and morphological, i.e. the form-related aspects are required. Hence, a subdivision of an entry's lexical specification into form and lemma is highly recommendable. Depending on the word type (i.e. does it allow orthographical alternation or not?) and on the application area of the lexicon (machine-translation, tutorial system, simple word retrieval, etc.) additional facets of information may have to be included in an entry's lexical specification.[13] Since all these additional aspects are not constantly needed in a natural language processing system, they do not have to be available in working memory but should be loaded at request via additional readpointers. Figure 9 illustrates the highly-pointered structure of a lexical entry in a machine-readable lexicon, where the pointers have been drawn as arrows.

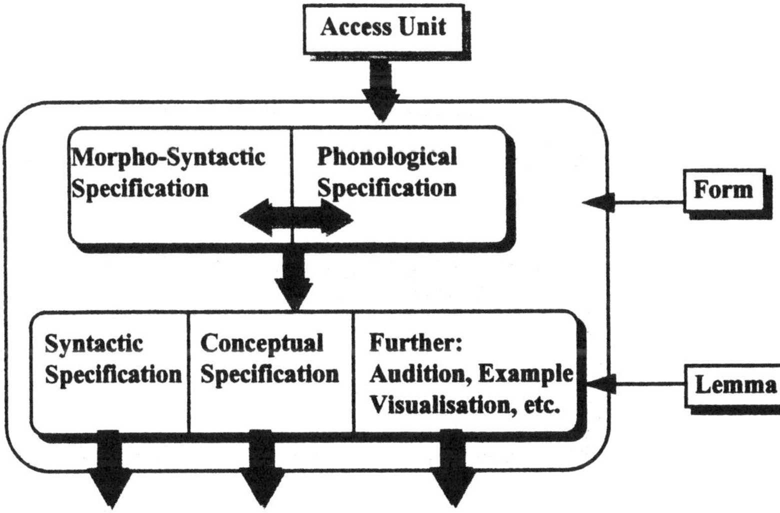

Figure 9. The structure of an entry in a machine-readable lexicon

To sum up, each lexical entry can be subdivided into an access unit and its lexical specification which in turn is subdivided into various aspects. Hence, a machine-readable lexicon ideally consists of two general file systems: the access file that contains the set of all access units and the data files with the lexical specification for each access unit. The connection between both file systems is established by a system of pointers associated with each access unit. The various aspects of lexical specification can also be externalised on the basis of additional file and pointer systems (see Section 3.4.).

3.3. *Lexical processing*

It has been argued elsewhere (Charniak *et al.* 1987:149ff, Smith 1991:106ff, Karttunen 1987:177) that there are good reasons to implement all lexical access units in terms of a discrimination network.[14]

Such a structure has at least two advantages. First, it allows extremely fast data access, since search is no longer a function of the position of an element in the database but depends on the number of branching nodes on the search path. Secondly, a discrimination network can easily be converted into an adequate code for an AI programming language. Figure 10 illustrates such a structure.

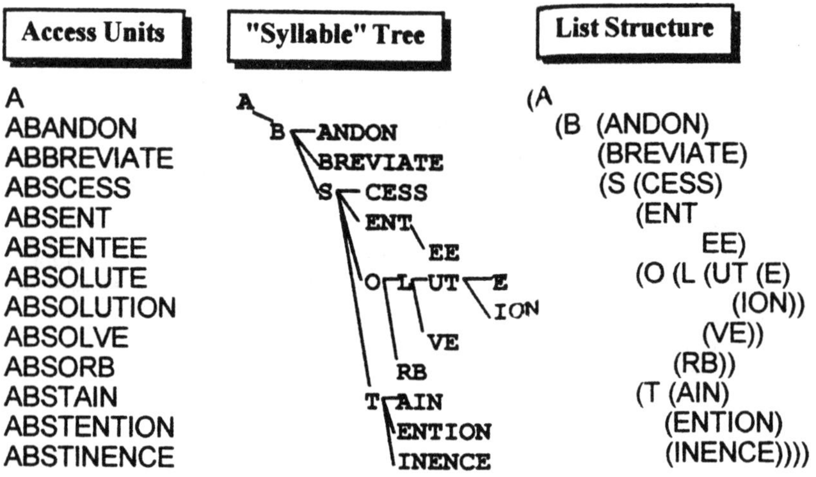

Figure 10. Access units as cohort network

Furthermore, the discrimination network permits the simulation of some of the psycholinguistic effects of word recognition. Regular non-words, such as **mav*, for example, are rejected very slowly, while irregular non-words, such as ***sjimf*, are rejected very fast. Furthermore, long words, such as *hallucination*, do not necessarily slow down processing but are recognised as soon as their recognition point (in this case HALLU-) is reached. In other words, just like in Marslen-Wilson's cohort model, word recognition depends on the word's recognition/rejection point and the number of candidates in the remaining cohort.

The simulation of the frequency effect in the access algorithm of a machine-readable lexicon, by contrast, unnecessarily complicates lexical processing. Since frequent words are generally easier to get at than infrequent ones and infrequent words can be redefined as frequent words as soon as they are used often enough (the recency effect), the incorporation of these aspects would require a constant regrouping of a machine-readable lexicon. This would complicate lexicon administration to a considerable extent.

An alternative to simulate the frequency effect is to split the lexical access file into a system of "weighted" subfiles. For example, in SYSTRAN, one of the most well-known machine translation systems, the lexicon is subdivided into two basic components: a stem "dictionary" and a high-frequency "dictionary" (Wheeler 1987:194).[15] While the stem "dictionary" contains all standard words, the high-frequency "dictionary" contains unambiguous entries such as AND, BUT, OR, as well as numbers or punctuation marks and idioms. Such a lexical split leads to a speeding up of the overall system since the access algorithm can now be programmed in such a way that high-frequency words are examined first. Smith (1991:109ff) suggests an even more advanced strategy of organising the access units to incorporate the frequency effect. Instead of one general access file he proposes a stratified organisation of the lexicon. At the first level, the most common high-frequency words are represented in terms of weighted, i.e. pre-arranged, binary trees. This initial part of the lexicon contains only a few dozen items which are organised according to frequency of occurrence.[16] If the target word does not occur in the high-frequency lexicon, search continues in a "circular queue" that contains several dozen words used most recently. This second level is not realised by a binary tree but as a mere list which is restricted in length and constantly updated. Failing to find an item in either the high-frequency tree or the recency queue the general lexicon, which contains all other access units, is approached.

Another method of simulating the frequency effect makes use of activation levels, where high-frequency words would be associated with a lower activation threshold than low-frequency words. In a machine-readable lexicon activation levels could be realised in terms of numerical values. However, for the partitioned cohort network this would imply a waste of search potential. If we were to couple all branching nodes that represent word candidates with an activation value and tried first to access those with a low value, then those with a higher value, and so on, we might have to look up the same access unit more than once. This is certainly an undesirable option that would drastically slow down word recognition. Hence, the introduction of activation values to simulate the word frequency effect does not lead to an acceleration but to a delay of word recognition.

Another very reliable finding in the word recognition literature is that the context may facilitate word recognition. However, this facilitatory influence is exerted at higher levels than word recognition and can thus only be simulated via the interaction with the other components of a natural language processing system.

3.4. Externalisation

One fundamental disadvantage of a network as introduced in Figure 10 is its enormous size. Machine-readable lexicons that are operative in natural language processing systems beyond the experimental phase contain several thousand lexical entries. A network representing such a large number of access units, however, is too large to be held in a standard machine's working memory. With every new entry inserted into the net, the situation becomes worse. In other words, we are likely to lose control over the size of the lexicon.

One possibility of regaining control is a method of *partitioning*. In a *partitioned network* the access file is split into a main network and a number of subordinate networks. Whereas the main network contains the first three letters of all access units, the subnets contain the respective remainders.[17] Due to graphotactic restrictions the main network is limited in size, because the combinatorial possibilities of the first three letters decrease with increasing word length. While word-initially all 26 letters of the English alphabet can occur, clusters of two letters, and even more so triplets, are combinatorily heavily restricted. For example, the Z-branch does not allow a continuation with any consonant, *ZB, *ZC, *ZD, etc., are all impossible word-initially in English. These combinatorial possibilities are even more constrained if three characters are concerned. Hence, if a sufficient number of access units is collected, the main network will soon reach its limits. In terms of size this limit is roughly 20 KB. Such a file can easily be loaded into working memory.

The number of subnets depends on the number of letters in the alphabet of a language, i.e. 26 in English, 29 in German (26 plus Ä, Ö, and Ü). While the main network is now constantly available in working memory, the subnet files can be reached via a subsidiary pointer system. In other words, items that consist of three letters only can be directly found in the main network, whereas longer words lead to an activation of a subnet.

The system of partitioning requires a modified overall structure of the machine-readable lexicon. This structure is represented in Figure 11. (The sizes of the main net and the subnet files are actual values from LexEcon's lexicon).

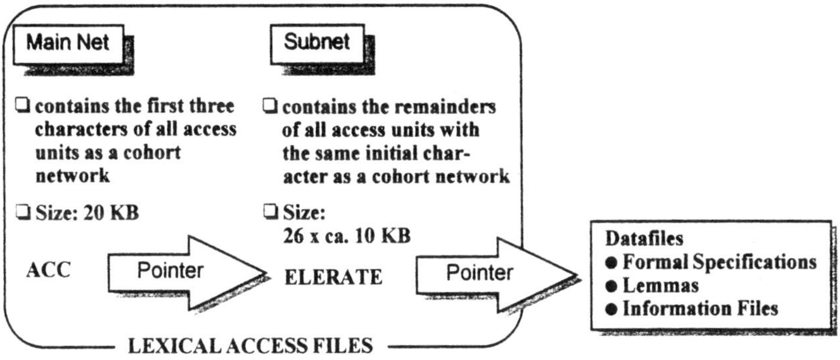

Figure 11. Access files in a partitioned network

This file structure is generated by a compiler (see Deiß *et al.* 1990:109ff) that integrates all access units into the discrimination network and transforms the raw format of each lexical specification into an abstract representation. The lexical access unit BOOK, for example, will eventually be associated with the lexical information in Figure 12.

Phonology	Morph.	Syntax	Semantics	Translation	Synonyms	Example	Picture
/buk/	N1	N4	BOOK1.	2368	45682	-	BOOK.
/buk/	V1	V2	ATR9.	2468	45975	783	-

Figure 12. The lexical entry BOOK in LexEcon (a fragment)

Now most lexical aspects have been externalised and are represented by pointer-values or in terms of filenames (e.g. BOOK. or ATR9.). Only the phonological, morphological, and syntactic information, i.e. those aspects that are required for word recognition, is represented explicitly. This guarantees extremely fast lexical processing.

4. Summary: Man vs. machine

Ideally, the implementation of a machine-readable lexicon and a powerful lexicon access algorithm would be a straightforward transfer of the insights of pre-lexical and lexical processing to a computer program, i.e. a simulation of the strategies of human processing by the machine. Yet, there is absolutely no guarantee that human processing strategies are the most efficient ones. Even though human language processing is more robust than anything that we can currently build (Sproat 1992:110), a direct conversion of natural techniques to develop an artificial mechanism may turn out to be impossible, on the one hand, and undesirable, on the other. Nevertheless, the realisation of human principles of lexical processing and lexicon organisation may considerably improve machine-readable lexicons. For example, the insights into the internal structure and the organisation of the entries in the mental lexicon, that is, the network structure of the access file and the pointered structure of lexical entries, may lead to an enormous gain in processing speed and data management. On the other hand, there are aspects that have been attributed to the mental lexicon but do not make sense for today's machine-readable lexicons. The integration of contextual influences and the simulation of the frequency/recency effect are good cases in point.

In summary, there are advantages and disadvantages in realising human processing strategies on machines. To make use of the advantages and to go round the disadvantages must be an essential aim of computational linguistics.

Notes

1. The terminology in this field is very fluid. For this reason, we will define a number of terms and concepts as we proceed.
2. Alternatively, machine-readable dictionaries are often referred to as *electronic dictionaries* or *electronic lexical databases*.
3. The term *morpho-grapheme* has been chosen by analogy with the *morpho-phoneme*. Morpho-phonemes are abstract phonemic symbols. They are normally represented as capital letters and serve as place-holders for the members of a set of related variants, for example, the morpho-phoneme /S/ may stand for all plural realisations in English, or the morpho-phoneme /D/ for all past tense forms.

4. In Section 4.5. we will reconsider the term "lexical access" in relationship with general models of word processing that comprise word recognition and lexical retrieval.
5. Morpho-graphemes need not be considered as the basic access units of the mental lexicon. They are confined to machine-readable lexicons, and make only sense in a such cases where orthographic or phonological alternation occurs.
6. One major research area concerns the description and formalisation of the specification of lexical entries. Due to the complexity of these aspects we dispense with a description of the lexical specification of lexical entries and refer the reader to Handke 1994, Chapter 2.
7. We cannot elaborate on these issues here. A detailed description of the experimental techniques, the stimuli used and the major findings can be found in Handke 1994, Chapter 4.
8. We cannot discuss the basic insights into lexical access here. Again, the reader is referred to Handke 1994, Section 4.5.ff.
9. The Activate and Check model and the Word Detector model have not been discussed in this essay, since the process of written word recognition, which they seek to model, has not been considered in this paper.
10. *LexEcon* stands for *Machine-Readable lexicon for Economy vocabulary*. It is a commercial product by Kwintus Teachware and Data Consulting, Sternstr. 5, Wuppertal, Germany and was developed by Klaus Deiß, Jürgen Handke and Lothar Otto. LexEcon is programmed in LISP and C.
11. The comments in LexEcon depend on the target language. Thus, the menu-buttons are labelled in the target language. Here is an explanation: "Abbruch" = "quit", "Beispiel" = "example", "Drucken" = "print", and "Speichern" = "save".
12. In terms of computer programs "pointers" are digits that determine the location of an item on an external storage device, such as a harddisk. They are generated and retrieved using the relevant commands of the programming language employed. For example, most LISP-dialects include the primitives WRITEPTR, for the generation, and READPTR, for the retrieval of pointers.
13. In Handke 1994 (Section 5.2.1.) numerous arguments for the subdivision into form and lemma and into additional subdivisions are provided.
14. The term *discrimination network* is primarily used in computational linguistics and artificial intelligence. Computer scientists alternatively refer to this data structure as *trie*, a term that represents the affinity with trees but is derived from re-*trie*-val. However, in order to distinguish it from *tree* it is pronounced as /'traɪ/ (Smith 1991:111).
15. According to our classification (Figure 1), SYSTRAN's word store should not be referred to as "dictionary" but as "lexicon".
16. In fact, Smith only lists thirty-one items for the binary tree with OF being the top node, THE and FOR the next level, and so on.
17. The number three has proved to be very efficient for English: many words are fairly short and can thus be reached without accessing any subnet file, and, moreover, the main network remains relatively small in size. Nevertheless, this figure is arbitrary and has been chosen purely for practical reasons. Psychologically, there is nothing special about this value.

References

Altmann, G.
1990 Cognitive models of speech processing: An introduction. In: Altmann, G. T. (ed.). *Cognitive Models of Speech Processing.* Cambridge, Mass.: MIT Press, pp. 1-23.

Butterworth, B.
1983 Lexical representation. In: Butterworth, B. (ed.). *Language Production Volume 2: Development, Writing, and Other Language Processes.* London: Academic Press, pp. 257-294.

Charniak, E., C. Riesbeck, R. McDermott & J. R. Meehan
1987 *Artificial Intelligence Programming.* Hillsdale, New Jersey: Lawrence Erlbaum.

Cutler, A., J. Mehler, D. Norris & J. Segui
1987 "Phoneme identification and the lexicon". *Cognitive Psychology* 19:141-177.

Deiß, K., J. Handke & B. Meyer
1990 *Professionelles Programmieren mit LISP.* Hamburg: McGraw-Hill.

Feldman, J. A. & D. H. Ballard
1982 "Connectionist models and their properties". *Cognitive Science* 6:205-254.

Handke, J.
1994 *The Structure of the Lexicon: Human versus Machine.* [In preparation].

Hankamer, J.
1989 Morphological parsing and the lexicon. In: Marslen-Wilson, W. D. (ed.). *Lexical Representation and Process.* Cambridge, Mass.: MIT Press, pp. 392-408.

Henderson, L.
1985 Toward a psychology of morphemes. In: Ellis, A. (ed.). *Progress in the Psychology of Language.* London: Lawrence Erlbaum, pp. 15-72.

Karttunen, L.
1983 "KIMMO: A general morphological analyzer". *Texas Linguistics Forum* 22:165-186.

Levelt, W. J. M.
1990 *Speaking.* Cambridge, Mass.: MIT Press.

Marslen-Wilson, W. D.
1987 Functional parallelism in spoken word recognition. In: Frauenfelder, U. & L. K. Tyler (eds.). *Spoken Word Recognition.* Cambridge, Mass.: MIT Press, pp. 71-102.

McClelland, J. L. & J. L. Elman
1986 "The TRACE model of speech perception". *Cognitive Psychology* 18:1-86.

Mehler, J., E. Dupoux & J. Segui
1990 Constraining models of lexical access. In: Altmann, G. T. (ed.). *Cognitive Models of Speech Processing.* Cambridge, Mass.: MIT Press, pp. 236-262.

Morton, J.
1979 Word recognition. In: Morton, J. & J. C. Marshall (eds.). *Psycholinguistics 2: Structures and Processes.* Cambridge, Mass.: MIT Press, pp. 107-156.

Myers-Scotton, C.
1994 Language processing and the lexicon in bilinguals. (This volume).

Norris, D.
1986 "Word recognition: Context effects without priming". *Cognition* 22:93-136.

Smith, G. W.
1991 *Computers and Human Language.* Oxford: Oxford University Press.

Sproat, R.
1992 *Morphology and Computation.* Cambridge, Mass.: MIT Press.

Taft, M.
1986 "Lexical access codes in visual and auditory word recognition". *Language and Cognitive Processes* 1:297-308.

Tyler, L. K. & U. H. Frauenfelder
1987 The process of spoken word recognition: An introduction. In: Frauenfelder, U. & L. K. Tyler (eds.). *Spoken Word Recognition.* Cambridge, Mass.: MIT Press, pp. 1-20.

Wheeler, P.
1987 SYSTRAN. In: King, M. (ed.). *Machine Translation: The State of the Art.* Edinburgh: Edinburgh University Press, pp. 193-208.

Automatic acquisition of lexical-semantic relations from machine-readable dictionaries

Stephan Mehl

0. Introduction

One of the main bottlenecks of computational linguistics is the large-scale acquisition of lexical knowledge. Whereas small hand-coded dictionaries have served as a basis for research work in computational linguistics and artificial intelligence for decades, the need for extensive knowledge bases has become more and more pressing in recent years. On the one hand, many people suspect that small dictionaries may not be representative of the entire vocabulary and that accounting for more lexical items may make a qualitative rather than a mere quantitative difference. On the other hand, computational linguistics strives to cross the threshold between academic research and commercial development, and dictionaries covering the entire vocabulary are an indispensible prerequisite for this step.

There are two possible ways of automatic lexical acquisition: statistical corpus analysis and exploitation of traditional monolingual dictionaries supplied in machine-readable form. Most probably, a combination of both methods will be optimal; neither method alone can provide for unambiguous results, and the other may serve to check alternative proposals. This paper will be restricted to the analysis of dictionaries, however; Zernik (1991) gives an overview of methods for lexical acquisition based on corpus analysis.

Section 1 will introduce the subject by giving a survey of recent projects on the automatic extraction of information from machine-readable dictionaries. Up to now, similar investigations in Germany have been impeded by the fact that no acknowledged German dictionary is commercially available in machine-readable form. In Sections 2 and 3, I will report on my own work with an excerpt from *Duden - Deutsches Universalwörterbuch* (DDUW, 1989), namely, all entries beginning with the letter "A" (graciously provided by the publisher in machine-readable form).[1]

A dictionary contains information on various levels (phonetic, morphological, syntactic, semantic, stylistic, etc.). Some aspects are already given in a formal code (e.g. syllabification, valency patterns) and may therefore be extracted quite easily; others, namely the semantic information, have to be converted into a formal representation. I have concentrated on the acquisition of lexical semantic relations by analysing the meaning paraphrases and examples commonly given in a monolingual lexical entry. Most research work previously done in this area has focussed on the extraction of hyperonyms; these relations are most easily identified since most entries follow the pattern of definition by *genus proximum* and *differentia specifica*. The results to be documented here point out some additional problems of analysis and show the advantages of taking syntagmatic relations into account, too.

An outlook on tasks of further investigation will be given in conclusion.

1. State of the art: Extracting hyperonyms

Entries in monolingual dictionaries contain two components that are relevant for semantic analysis: the lexical definition as well as examples for the use of a word. In terms of semantic relations, the definition is usually based on paradigmatic relations, the examples consist of syntagmatic ones. Since most previous investigations have dealt exclusively with paradigmatic relations, the analysis of example texts will be postponed till Section 2; for the moment, I will focus on the definitions. The term "definition" may not, of course, be understood in a strictly logical sense but rather as a colloquial abbreviation of more precise terms such as "account of meaning paraphrase" (German *Bedeutungsparaphrasenangabe*, cf. Wiegand 1989) etc.

Since definitions are usually phrases, not sentences, their interpretation is guided by their phrasal heads, which may be one of the following:

- a synonym:
  abattoir: *slaughterhouse*[2]
- a *genus* term modified by the *differentia specifica*:
  lapdog: *a small pet dog*
- an indicator of some other kind of semantic relation, such as *part* for partonymy:
  stomach: *the front part of the body below the chest*

A dictionary entry may consist of a sequence of several definitions, possibly of different types.

The analysis of the definitions is usually based on the following assumptions:

A1. A complex entry can be easily cut up into its component definitions.
A2. The head may be found by simple parsing techniques.
A3. The three kinds of heads can be easily distinguished: if there is only one term, it is supposed to be a synonym; relations other than hyponymy can be recognized by keywords such as *part, member, act* etc.; any other construction is taken to contain a hyperonym.
A4. Since the aim is to extract a relation of synonymy or hyponymy between the headword and its *genus* term, the *differentia* may be neglected.

Let us first look at the technical realization of assumptions A2 and A3; the validity of these hypotheses will be discussed later, in Section 3.

The following questions have to be answered first:

Q1. How can the head of a definition be found?
Q2. What exactly are the indicators that judge a head to be something other than a *genus* term?

To answer the first question, we have to distinguish between entries for different parts of speech. First results on the extraction of *genus* terms for nouns and verbs have already been presented by Chodorow *et al.* (1985, see also Byrd *et al.* 1987). In the case of verb definitions the case was simple because Chodorow *et al.* used a dictionary (Webster's Seventh) rendering infinitives preceded by *to:*

winter: (v) *to pass the winter*

Therefore, the head simply is the verb following the word *to.*

As with nouns, the case is more complex because of the greater variety of noun definitions. Since the head may be surrounded by pre- and post-modifiers, a syntactic analysis has to be carried out to identify the head. However, to cut down processing time Chodorow *et al.* (1985) simply check for words like prepositions, relative pronouns or past participles that indicate the beginning of the post-modifier, choosing the noun before that word as a head of the definition. Note that all procedures discussed in this section require that the words of a definition be tagged according to their part of speech.

Question Q2 has been far more interesting for most authors than Q1. Chodorow *et al.* (1985) maintain that in case of heads like *kind, class, manner, family, race, group, complex* etc. followed by *of*, the noun following that *of* could still be used as a *genus* term.

More detailed work concerning this point has been carried out at the university of Amsterdam, mainly in the framework of the ACQUILEX project sponsored by the European Community (cf. Vossen *et al.* 1989, Meijs 1990). Besides synonyms and hyperonyms ("links"), the Amsterdam group distinguishes between the following syntactic heads of noun definitions:

> LINKERS are definitions in which the syntactic kernel is taken from a restricted set of "relator words" mediating and labelling the relation between the entry-word and the semantic head of the definition (often contained in a post-modifying "*of*-phrase"). Thus *candy* is defined as a "**type** of sweet", *stomach* as "a **part** of the body", *waste* as "a **stretch** of land", *band* as "a **group** of musicians", etc.
>
> SHUNTERS are cases in which the syntactic head of the definition is again a general "relator-word", and in which the semantic burden is carried by an element from a different part of speech (Verb or Adjective in the case of nominal meaning definitions). Thus *actor* is defined as "a **person** who acts ..."; *gasp* as "an **act** of gasping"; *ambiguity* as "a **condition** of being ambiguous", etc.
>
> SHIFTERS, finally, are definitions in which the syntactic head of the definition is itself a transform of some kind of a word from a different part of speech. Thus *advent* is defined as "the **coming** of Christ", *apiculture* as "the **keeping** of bees", etc. (Meijs 1990:5f)

Obviously, the class to which the Chodorow examples belong and which is most relevant for the extraction of hyperonyms is the class of linkers. Meijs notes that many linkers serve to specify attributes like quantity, structure, shape, membership, etc. This might mean that linkers have a similar function as the *differentiae specificae*, namely, to add additional features to a hyperonym and thus create hyponyms. Nevertheless, a stomach definitely is not a kind of body but a part of the body; the nouns connected by linkers should certainly be included in the lexical acquisition process, but be carefully distinguished from hyperonyms.

Shifters and shunters, on the other hand, are less easily interpreted in terms of semantic relations; they will therefore be excluded from further analysis for the moment. Shifters might be recognized by analysing their morphological structure (verb + *-ing*) and by the fact that they do not correspond to a lexical entry (in contrast to *evening*, for example). In the case of shunters, an exclusion would require that the number of keywords like *person, condition* etc. were limited. Vossen *et al.* (1989: 180) point out, however, that some words form a transition between hyperonyms and shunters because their semantic impact on the definition is too strong for a shunter and too weak for a hyperonym. Examples:

angling: *the sport of catching fish with a hook and line*
beatification: *the ceremony of beatifying*
admixture: *a substance that is added to another in a mixture*

Vossen *et al.* assign these examples to the class of hyperonyms rather than shunters. This might be a prerequisite for setting up the required list of shunters, although it will be difficult to draw a line.

Thus, answers to questions Q1 and Q2 seem to be straightforward. Vossen *et al.* (1989:187) only mention one single obstacle: due to part-of-speech ambiguity, the head of a noun definition may not be clear, as in:

drink: *a liquid suitable for swallowing*
embrocation: *a liquid medicine used for ...*

However, this is not the only ambiguity that may impede the analysis. The following two sections will describe an attempt to tailor the methods documented above to German definitional texts. It will not only turn out that German syntax may cause different problems for the analysis than English, but also that some other problems which also pertain to English have not been discussed yet. The emphasis, however, will be on the additional investigation of syntagmatic relations that have been widely neglected up to now.

2. Evidence from the analysis of a German dictionary

This section describes my own work on the analysis of a German monolingual dictionary, the *Duden - Deutsches Universalwörterbuch* (DDUW, 1989). Unfortunately, I have only the entries beginning with "A" at my disposal (and fortunately, at least those); the sample consists of 4,505 lexical entries for nouns, with a total of 5,430 readings, and 2,758 verb entries totalling 5,654 readings. Other parts of speech have not been considered up to now.

Whereas the lexical entries include a part of speech label, I have not yet tried to tag the entire definitional texts according to their part of speech. In contrast to the LDOCE, the DDUW definitions are not based on a restricted vocabulary; the lemmatization and dictionary look-up procedures would therefore have left many gaps and ambiguities. For that reason, I had to confine myself to using a partial parsing. Since noun and verb entries required different analyses, I will give details on the parsing procedures separately for nouns (2.1.) and verbs (2.2.).

2.1. Nouns

2.1.1. Scope of analysis

In the case of nouns, only the head of the definition was retrieved. The *differentia* (i.e. adjectives or post-modifying nouns and relative clauses) was neglected for two reasons:

(i) since lexical entries for adjectives have not been analysed yet, there was no further semantic information on adjectives; and (ii) the post-modifying noun phrases and relative clauses often have too complex and ambiguous a structure to yield satisfactory results without employing in-depth semantic information. In (a), for example, the second prepositional phrase is attached to the first, in (b) it is attached to the head:

(a) **Anakonda:** ... *Riesenschlange mit runden schwarzen Flecken auf dem gelbbraunen Rücken*
'boa with round black blotches on its yellowish-brown back'[3]
(b) **Arbeitsverteilung:** *Verteilung von Arbeit an verschiedene Personen*
'distribution of work onto different persons'

The examples included in noun entries were not considered, either. Lacking syntactic information, sentences could not be safely distinguished from sentence fragments, let alone parsed properly:

(c) *ein erfreulicher, trostloser* **Anblick** *bot sich ihm dar;*
(sentence with discontinuous form of the verb *sich darbieten*)
(d) *man wollte ihm den traurigen* **Anblick** *ersparen;*
(sentence with infinitive in final position)
(e) *sich in einen* **Anblick** *vertiefen;*
(fragment with infinitive in final position)

2.1.2. Method of analysis

German nouns can be easily identified by the fact that they begin with a capital letter. In most cases, the first noun will be the head of the definition. However, in German nouns are frequently included in the pre-modifier as part of phrases that are attached to participial adjectives:

(a) **Aal:** *in Süßwasser u. Meer lebender, schlangenförmiger Fisch mit schlüpfriger Haut* '**eel:** *snake-like fish living in fresh water or in the sea, with slippery skin*'

Most of these constructions were recognized by a morphosyntactical analysis based on information about the closed word classes (prepositions, articles, conjunctions) and possible inflectional endings for the different parts of speech. For example, adjectives derived from present participles end with *-ende, -endem, -endes, -ender* or *-enden*, depending on case, number, and gender.

However, noun phrases can only be identified as part of the pre-modifier if the latter begins with a preposition or an article that is clearly discernable as non-nominative. For example, the article *dem* in (b) indicates a dative, so *Kommandeur* must be an imbedded noun (modifying the adjective *beigegebener*) instead of the *genus* term:

(b) **Adjutant:** *dem Kommandeur einer militärischen Einheit zur Unterstützung beigegebener* <u>*Offizier*</u>

Since other articles (like *der*) may indicate a nominative as well as other cases, embedded nouns preceded by such an article or by no article or preposition at all are falsely regarded as representing the *genus* term, as is *Ameisen* in (c):

(c) **Ameisenbär:** *in Mittel- und Südamerika beheimatetes, Ameisen und Termiten fressendes* <u>*Säugetier*</u> ...

This is an example for an ambiguity leading to a false interpretation that was deliberately ignored because of its rare occurrence. A similar case is the systematic word-class ambiguity between articles and pronouns in German. For example, *eine* in (d) could be used as a pronoun; this would render *für eine* into a complete noun phrase attached to the participial adjective *festgelegte*, which in turn would proclaim *Zeit* to be the *genus* term (instead of *Vertreter*):

(d) **Abgeordnete:** *vom Volk für eine festgelegte Zeit in eine parlamentarische Institution gewählter* <u>*Vertreter*</u>

Because such an interpretation is highly improbable, it was automatically rejected.

Another class of ambiguities cannot be handled as easily, however: enumerations. If two or more paraphrases are given in a DDUW entry, they may be separated either by a semicolon or simply by a comma:

(e) **Allmacht:** *Macht über alle und alles, grenzenlose Machtfülle, uneingeschränkte Macht; Allgewalt*

A comma, however, may also indicate subordinate clauses or conjunctions within one paraphrase:

(f) **Affe:** *menschenähnliches Säugetier, das in den Tropen ... lebt*
(g) **Alligator:** *in tropischen Flüssen ... lebendes, zu den Krokodilen gehörendes Reptil*
(h) **Azalee:** *als Strauch wachsende Pflanze mit großen, weißen, rosa oder roten, trichterförmigen Blüten und kleinen, dunkelgrünen Blättern*

Can enumerations within one paraphrase, as in (f) - (h), be distinguished from enumerations of several paraphrases, as in (e)?

The easiest case is an enumeration within the pre-modifier, as in (a) and (g): since no head noun has been isolated yet, the comma cannot conjoin paraphrases. Subordinate clauses (f) start with a relative pronoun or a subordinate conjunction and end with a verb; they are thus quite easily discernable from enumerations of paraphrases. A problem arises, however, if they are combined with a post-modifier enumeration that causes the verb to disappear behind further commas, as in (i):

(i) **Abgesandte:** *Person, die mit einem bestimmten Auftrag, mit einer (offiziellen) Botschaft zu jmdm. geschickt wird*

Since relative pronouns and definite articles are largely identical in German and the final verb is hidden, both criteria for a relative clause fail in (i); other syntactic cues cannot be exploited (e.g., the gender of nouns is not available), and therefore *Auftrag* might falsely be considered to be a second head noun.

Post-modifiers are the hardest case with respect to enumeration: Even with a full-fledged syntactic analysis, they may not be discernable from an enumeration of paraphrases. Compare (j) and (k):

(j) **Abbau:** *Zerlegung komplizierter Moleküle, Strukturen in einfachere* (**disintegration:** *decomposition of complex molecules, structures into simpler ones;* one paraphrase)
(k) **Aktualität:** *Bedeutsamkeit für die unmittelbare Gegenwart, Gegenwartsbezogenheit*
(**topicality:** *relevance for the immediate present, condition of being of present interest;* two paraphrases)

The structural ambiguity involved in (j) and (k) cannot be resolved with the information available. Having to choose between ignoring additional head nouns (e.g. *Gegenwartsbezogenheit* in (k)) and including false ones (e.g. *Strukturen* in (j), *Auftrag* in (i)), the safer alternative was selected - which still yields at least one head term per entry.

2.1.3. Results

The procedure described in 2.1.2. results in a total of 1,656 synonyms and 4,828 head nouns - somewhat less than the number of readings given above because many definitions contain *jmd. (somebody)* or *etw. (something)* as a head; both have not been counted.

Applying the distinction between synonyms, hyperonyms, linkers, shifters, and shunters described in Section 1 to the German data, it turned out that most linkers and shunters, i.e. stopwords indicating something different from a hyponymy relation, appeared in different functions. Consider the example of *Art* which can be used as a linker, as in

(i) **Almandin:** *dunkelrote Art des Granats*
'almandin: *dark-red kind of garnet'*

or as a shunter, as in

(ii) **Arroganz:** *arrogante Art*
'arrogance: *way of being arrogant'*

or as a true hyperonym, as in

(iii) **Abart:** *ähnliche, sich nur durch wenige Merkmale unterscheidende Art*
'variety: *similar kind, differing only in few features'*

The difference between (i) and (ii) can be explained as a lexical ambiguity, namely, the difference between the readings "a kind of" and "way of doing something". It should be noted, however, that by way of its lexical meaning, even a linker or shunter can serve as a hyperonym. This is especially true since there is a gradual transition between hyperonyms and shunters, no sharp distinction.

As far as the head nouns can be interpreted as hyperonyms, they form a hierarchy that can be inspected in two directions: vertically and horizontally.

In the vertical dimension, it is interesting to examine the topmost elements of the hierarchy as well as the length and circularity of the definitional chains; this may contribute on one hand to discussions about semantic primitives and measures of abstractness (cf. the analysis of the DDUW by Schierholz 1991), on the other hand to an evaluation of the dictionary itself: Are there gaps in the hierarchy, have similar words been described in a similar way, has circularity been minimized, etc.?

In the horizontal dimension, words with common hyperonyms can be compared: Which aspect of the hyperonym's meaning is further specified by its various hyponyms? At this point, an analysis of the *differentia specifica* comes in; because of the importance of this subject, it will be discussed in greater detail in Section 3.

Both investigations suffer from the fact that the *genus* terms usually are not disambiguated. It would be interesting to test whether similarities in the definitions of cohyponyms can indicate that they refer to the same reading of their hyperonym; e.g. all of the following verbs are hyponyms of the same out of 14 readings of *abgehen*, namely, *"ein Gerät mit einem Schwung, Sprung o.ä. verlassen und damit eine Übung beenden"* *'to leave a piece of gymnastic apparatus in order to finish an exercise'*:

abbücken: mit einer Bücke vom Gerät abgehen
abflanken: mit einer Flanke vom Gerät abgehen
abgrätschen: mit einer Grätsche vom Gerät abgehen
abhechten: mit einem Hecht vom Gerät abgehen
abhocken: mit einer Hocke vom Gerät abgehen
etc.

Due to the restrictions of the sample investigated, an examination of the vertical dimension of the hierarchy was hardly possible. Results concerning the horizontal dimension will be presented in Section 3.

2.2. *Verbs*

2.2.1. Scope of analysis

Since both definitions and examples in verb entries have a simpler structure than those for nouns, the analysis was broader here. Definitions consist of a head verb in the infinitive form modified and complemented by adverbs, noun phrases or prepositional phrases. The same structure applies to many examples, except for the fact that the lemma takes the position of the *genus* term. The remaining examples consist of full sentences; these have to be discarded for lack of tagging and parsing facilities. Sentences and infinitival fragments can be distinguished by the fact that the infinitive is abbreviated and located at the end, whereas finite verbs are in the second position.

In addition to the acquisition of synonyms and hyperonyms, syntagmatic relations could therefore be extracted both for the lemmata (derived from examples) and the hyperonyms (derived from definitions). Because additional semantic relations are available for nouns, but not for adverbs, the latter were ignored.

Unfortunately, no specification of the nature of the syntagmatic relations beyond their surface realization was possible. The DDUW does not contain any information on the valency frame of a verb, and even if this information was taken from other sources, it would be difficult to assign complements to the respective valency slots because the infinitive constructions leave out obligatory complements.

2.2.2. Method of analysis

The extraction of synonyms and hyperonyms from verb definitions is quite simple because the *genus* verb usually stands at the end of the definitional phrase. In this respect, even enumerations are no problem:

(a) **abbrennen:** *durch Brand zerstören, niederbrennen*

The main exception are verb phrases that contain auxiliaries or modal verbs which can be recognized easily (b); they are dropped, and the verb preceding them is taken to be a hyperonym.

(b) **abkriegen:** *etwas Festhaftendes, -sitzendes mit Mühe lösen können*

The hardest problems in the analysis of verb entries arise from the extraction of syntagmatic relations. First, there is the standard case of structural ambiguity: Should prepositional phrases be interpreted as adjuncts to the verb, as in (c), or as attributes to some other noun phrase, as in (d)?

(c) **abhorchen:** *mit dem Ohr auf Geräusche prüfen*

(d) **akademisieren:** *nur mit Leuten mit akademischer Ausbildung besetzen*

Without further knowledge on a verb's valency, many genitive attributes in German could be interpreted as dative complements, too:

(e) *um die Hand der Tochter anhalten*

Ambiguities such as (c) - (e) can only be solved with additional syntactic, semantic or encyclopedic knowledge. While the complement interpretation of constructions like (e) is very rare, there is no statistical bias for either (c) or (d). Therefore, the safest way of handling this case consists of ignoring phrases with ambiguous attachment.

Two other kinds of structural ambiguities are due to enumerations. The first is caused by the fact that prepositions need not be repeated in conjoined phrases, as in (f); however, the second phrase may as well form a noun phrase on its own, without any connection to the preposition (g):

(f) *den Gegner mit Panzern, Geschützen angreifen*
'to attack the enemy with tanks, cannons'; i.e. one direct object, scope of preposition includes two nouns

(g) *die Wäsche zum Trocknen, Gardinen aufhängen*
'to hang the washing out for drying, [to hang out] curtains'; i.e. two direct objects, scope of preposition includes only one noun)

The choice here is either to attach a preposition to the second noun in all cases, or to interpret it as a direct object, or to drop it entirely. Although dropping would be safer, the first interpretation was chosen because it turned out to be much more frequent than the second.

The last type of ambiguity occurs within enumerations of paraphrases that may share complements (h), or not (i):

(h) *mit Beifall* <u>*bedenken, aufnehmen*</u>
'to greet, receive with applause'; i.e. PP belongs to both verbs
(i) *auf dem laufenden* <u>*halten, aktualisieren*</u>
'to update, keep up to date'; i.e. PP belongs to one verb only

An interesting impact of this structural ambiguity is that verbs like *aufnehmen* in (h) would be considered to be synonyms for lack of a *differentia specifica* if the prepositional phrase was not attached to it, too. To avoid this effect, phrases were generally attached to both verbs, taking the risk of falsely interpreting a synonym as a hyponym. When evaluating the results, it turned out that in many cases it could hardly be decided how to resolve the ambiguity, anyway.

2.2.3. Results

The analysis of verb entries yielded 4,412 synonyms, 3,836 head verbs (most of which are hyperonyms), 7,213 syntagmatic relations for the hyperonyms, extracted from definitions, and another 2,991 syntagmatic relations for the lemmata themselves, extracted from examples.

Unfortunately, a number of the head verbs extracted can hardly be interpreted as hyperonyms. However, the distinction of linkers, shifters, and shunters proposed for nouns by the Amsterdam ACQUILEX group cannot be applied to verbs. Apart from the use of modal verbs and auxiliaries mentioned above, there are two types of constructions which are not correctly interpreted:

(i) The *genus* term consists of several elements ("Funktionsverbgefüge"), namely empty verbs with one complement:

abschließen: *seinen Abschluß finden*

(ii) The meaning of a headword is explained by describing a sequence of events, none of which can properly be regarded as a hyperonym:

aufreißen: *die gegnerische Deckung durch geschicktes Spiel auseinanderziehen und so Platz für einen Durchbruch schaffen*
(to rip up: *to break up the opponents' coverage by playing skillfully in order to make room for a breakthrough)*

The first case could only be handled if an exhaustive list of empty verbs were established; however, most of them have non-empty readings which cannot be automatically distinguished from the empty ones. - In the second case only the last verb will be detected at all, due to the lack of information for parsing.

3. Discussion

In Section 1, four assumptions were given that are often taken to hold for the automatic extraction of semantic relations from dictionaries.

These assumptions shall now be reconsidered in the light of the results reported in Section 2.

Assumption A1 requires that paraphrases be separated clearly if a lexical entry contains more than one of them. Yet, ellipses, i.e. enumerations sharing common parts, are indispensible for printed dictionaries where the need to save space is extremely urgent. Since ellipses almost invariably lead to ambiguities, A1 will rarely hold.

A2 expects simple parsing techniques to be sufficient. At least for languages admitting complex syntactic structures, like German, there are again a number of ambiguities that cannot be resolved with the kind of knowledge that can be employed in a large-scale lexical acquisition process.

A3 states that different types of lexical definitions (by hyperonyms, linkers, shunters, etc.) can be distinguished automatically. There are three types of problems here:

- it may be difficult to establish exhaustive lists of the stopwords needed because of borderline cases (cf. Section 1),
- the stopwords are ambiguous, as was shown in Section 2.1.3. using the example of the German *Art*, which may serve as a linker, as a shunter, or simply as a hyperonym,
- constructions may differ from the *genus-et-differentia*-approach without using any stopwords at all, as is the case with verb definitions describing steps of some kind of action (Section 2.2.3.).

A4 stresses the importance of extracting hyperonyms, neglecting an analysis of the *differentiae*. Comparing words with the same hyperonym shows a high degree of variance, however. For example, both *abschminken (to remove the make-up)* and *ablecken (to lick off)* are hyponyms of *säubern (to clean)*, but it is important to know that *abschminken* means *"säubern <u>von</u> Schminke"* and not *"<u>durch</u> Schminken"* (*to clean the make-up off*, not *to clean by applying make-up*). Similar to the disambiguation of hyperonyms described in 2.1.3., hyponyms that serve as a further specification of the same aspect of their hyperonym's meaning might be automatically grouped together:

abbürsten: durch Bürsten säubern
abbaden: durch Baden säubern
abkehren: durch Kehren säubern
abklopfen: durch Klopfen säubern
ablecken: durch Lecken säubern
etc.

This leads to the question whether the various aspects of the meaning of a word can automatically be determined by investigating the *differentiae* of its hyponyms - for *säubern* that it is applied to some kind of surface, with some kind of method, to clean off some kind of substance, etc. If such a procedure worked well, linguists as well as researchers in artificial intelligence would have found a panacea to overcome the famous "knowledge acquisition bottleneck". No wonder that ACQUILEX has considered this question, too.

Vossen (1991:21) gives a list of 35 features for *food and drinks* that has been established manually on the basis of lexical entries from the LDOCE and the Dutch van Dale dictionary, including:

age: *young, old, from the year*
telic: *as food, eatable, to soften, to preserve, tranquilizing, to hide smell*
colour: *yellow, pale in colour*
constituents: *including marrows, without bones, boneless, bony, with flesh, with cream, alcoholic*
evaluative: *nice, splendid, delicious, heavenly, good, fine, nutritious, bad*
(...)
taste: *bitter, bitter-sweet, peppermint-flavoured*
temperature: *cold, hot, cool*
texture: *fine, hard, juicy, set (become solid), dry, thick*
transport: *served, supplied, give, pour*
weight: *heavy*

The intention of ACQUILEX was to turn the lexical database that was built from relations extracted from dictionaries into a "knowledge base" in which features could be inherited along the semantic hierarchy. To achieve this goal, the following two questions have to be answered:

- Which features should be attributed to a given word (or category)?
- How can the values of the *differentia specifica* be automatically assigned to a feature?

If one accepts that the list of features can be restricted to those properties for which there are values in some lexical entry, a good guiding principle might be found that is less likely to suffer from idiosyncrasies and gaps than a "top-down" approach that starts with fixing a schema and then tries to fill it. On the other hand, it is still left to the judgement of the lexicographer to combine items to form values of one property.

Given a list of features, the information from a lexical entry can be assigned to it only if there is another list of possible values for those features, or if the words in the lexical entry can be semantically interpreted. The only way of arriving automatically at a list of values would be again to use semantic relations: *cold, cool, hot* are co-hyponyms (sharing a pseudo-hyperonym *"of (low, high ,...) temperature"*) that might be extracted from a dictionary; and an analysis of syntagmatic relations might yield further data (cf. the various instruments of *säubern* mentioned above).

Taken together, extracting semantic relations promises to lead to interesting results, both for the analysis of the semantic system of a language and as a means for knowledge acquisition for a natural language processing system (not to mention the possibility of evaluating the dictionary used as a source). The difficulties in lexical acquisition should not be underestimated, however.

Notes

1. The computer programs for the dictionary analysis were written by a group of students at the University of Koblenz in 1991, under the guidance of Sonja Kowalewski and me. The evaluation of the results was done by me at the University of Duisburg, in 1992/93.
2. Examples from LDOCE (taken from Vossen *et al.* 1989). Head words are underlined.
3. Examples are translated only if the point to be demonstrated is preserved; otherwise the purpose of the example is explained.

References

Byrd, R. J., N. Calzolari, M. S. Chodorow, J. L. Klavans, M. S. Neff & O. A. Rizk
1987 Tools and methods for computational lexicology. *Computational Linguistics* 13, 3-4:219-240.

Chodorow, M. S., R. J. Byrd & G. E. Heidorn
1985 Extracting semantic hierarchies from a large on-line dictionary. In: *Proceedings of the Conference of the Association for Computational Linguistics*, pp. 299-304.

Duden
1989 *Duden - Deutsches Universalwörterbuch.* 2nd ed. Mannheim: Dudenverlag.

Meijs, W.
1990 The expanding lexical universe: Extracting taxonomies from machine-readable dictionaries. IVth International Euralex Congress, Benalmádena; also published as ESPRIT ACQUILEX report.

Schierholz, S.
1991 *Lexikologische Analysen zur Abstraktheit, Häufigkeit und Polysemie deutscher Substantive.* Tübingen: Niemeyer.

Vossen, P.
1991 Converting data from a lexical database to a knowledge base. ESPRIT ACQUILEX report No. 27.

Vossen, P., W. Meijs & M. den Broeder
1989 Meaning and structure in dictionary definitions. In: Boguraev, B. T. Briscoe (eds.). *Computational Lexicography for Natural Language Processing.* London: Longman, pp. 171-192.

Wiegand, H. E.
1989 Die lexikographische Definition im allgemeinen einsprachigen Wörterbuch. In: Hausmann, F. J. *et al.* (eds.). *Wörterbücher. Ein internationales Handbuch zur Lexikographie.* Berlin: Mouton de Gruyter, pp. 530-588.

Zernik, U. (ed.)
1991 *Lexical Acquisition.* Hillsdale: Erlbaum.

GOLD: An object-oriented lexical tool for German

Nils Lenke, Stefan Dreckmann and Rolf Heinze

0. Introduction and overview

An interesting new direction of research in computational linguistics is the use of inheritance as a means of lexicon and/or grammar representation. Besides this, there is also the more practically oriented trend to use object-oriented software/database systems for use with natural language systems. This paper deals with work belonging to this latter area of research. It describes the GOLD lexical browser, which allows access to the data of the Bonnlex WDB. The motivation for GOLD is presented in Section 1; Section 2 discusses the question of relational data model vs. object-oriented data model and gives an overview of the GOLD system. The functionality of GOLD is briefly described in Section 3, whereas Sections 4 and 5 discuss the question of querying an object-oriented system and the solution adopted in GOLD and the morphological component of GOLD, respectively. Section 6 reports on some results achieved during the project and Section 7 is dedicated to open questions and future work.

1. The 'Bonnlex WDB', a machine-readable lexical resource for German

Machine-readable lexical resources of considerable size for German are rather rare. In comparison to the situation for English there is a certain backlog as for example Bläsius & Wermke (1990) acknowledge. One of the available lexical resources for German is the "Bonnlex WDB" (Wortdatenbank = word data base), a lexicon of approximately 300,000 entries compiled from different machine-readable dictionaries in the early 80s (Brustkern & Schulze 1982, Lenders 1991).

It suffers from two major drawbacks:

(a) The range of information contained in the entries is rather limited (syntactic and morphological information; further syntactic and semantic information exists only for a subset of entries and this is not available outside the two sites of the Bonnlex project due to copyright problems). Even the included types of information are not available for all entries (incomplete knowledge) or are inconsistent with information in other entries (inconsistent knowledge), cf. Section 7 below.

(b) It is only available on mainframes in Bonn and Mannheim (access systems for PCs and workstations are being developed, (Hornung 1990, Winter 1990), or as transfer files, coded in a rather awkward fashion, cf. Table 1 with some example entries.

Both, the mainframe and the PC version under development, are based on the relational data model.

ABASTEN	,CAT='VRB',FKL='S5',MSB='00000000'
ABATTIERT	,LEMMA='',CAT='VRB',MSI='0100000000010000010000000'
A POSTERIORI	,CAT='QAV',MS='0000000000000000001000000'
ABBAUENDEM ,	LEMMA='ABBAUEND',CAT='QAN',MS='0100000000000000011000000'
AALFAENGE	,LEMMA='AALFANG',CAT='NOM',MSI='0111010000000000011000000'
AALFANG	,CAT='NOM',FKL='71',MSB='01000000'

Table 1. Example entries of the Bonnlex WDB in the transfer file format

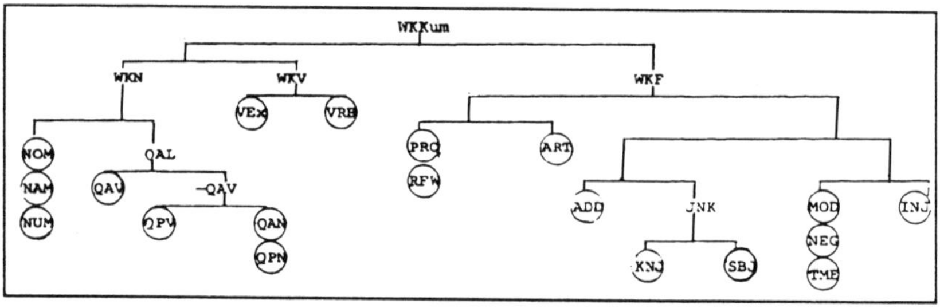

Figure 1. The system of word classes in the Bonnlex project from Brustkern & Schulze (1982)

2. An object-oriented approach

Of course, problem (a) cannot be remedied without compiling a completely new dictionary, but we have tried to work on a solution for (b) in order to explore the usability of the object-oriented paradigm for computer based lexicography. So we built an access system to the data of the Bonnlex WDB, named GOLD (Great Object-oriented Lexicon of Duisburg).

The relational data model is widely recognized as not being ideal for the representation of complex objects of variable form like dictionary entries (Hötker & Ludewig 1991:12). Some of the problems can be seen when looking once again at Table 1: The entries for base forms and full forms and for the different grammatical categories are attributed with quite different features. They were only partially brought into a similar format by coding the information in these ugly bit strings, the bits meaning different things for different categories.

As a consequence, we have chosen the object-oriented approach drawing from ideas of similar approaches bundled under the name "inheritance in grammar/lexicon", cf. e.g. Daelemans (1992). There are also similarities to the approach of the Project Aquilex, cf. Boguraev & Briscoe (1989), Briscoe (1991), Copestake (1992). The well-known advantages of the object-oriented approach are:

- possibility to store complex objects
- possibility to store objects in different formats
- integration of procedural knowledge (methods)
- inheritance of features and methods
- polymorphy of methods.

(Inheritance and polymorphy will be discussed below, in Section 5.)

Ideally, one would use an object-oriented DBMS (data base management system) as a platform and we are planning to do so in the future (cf. Section 7). But due to restriction of resources we had to build our own object-oriented file system for GOLD. We implemented an efficient data structure (B-tree, cf. Sedgewick 1988) allowing fast access to single entries.

We then designed a hierarchy of around 55 word classes using the inheritance mechanism of the used implementation language (Object Pascal). This hierarchy is based on the system of word classes already used in the Bonnlex project, cf. Figure 1, and takes into account that some word classes exist as full forms and as base forms and some only in one of these forms, cf. Figure 2 below.

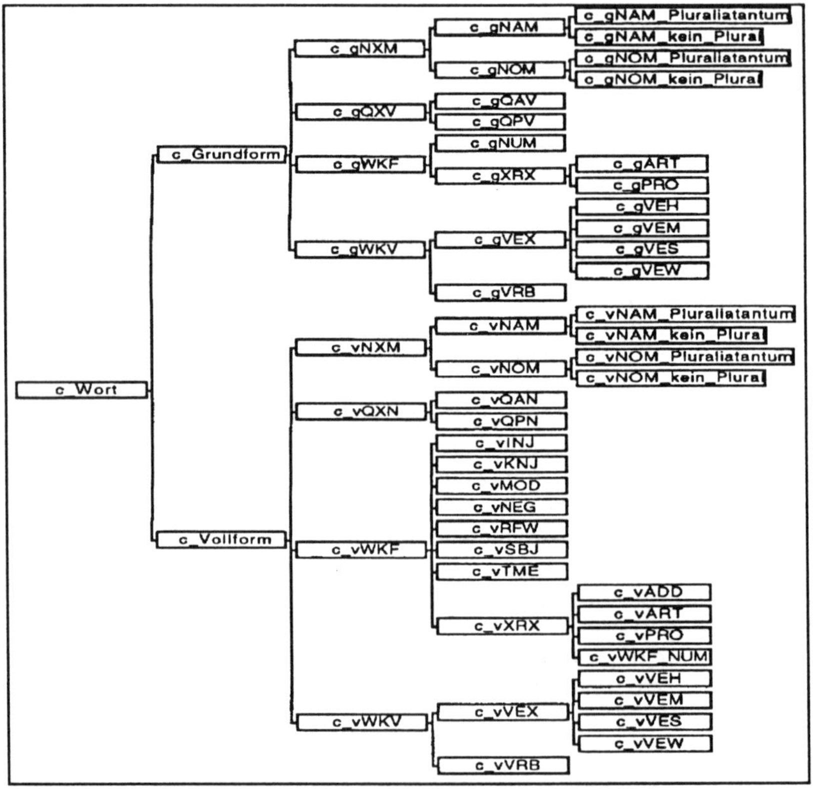

Figure 2. The class hierarchy of GOLD

We then converted the 300,000 entries of the Bonnlex WDB from the transfer files to objects of the appropriate classes and stored them in the data structure. Figure 3 shows the overall architecture of the system.

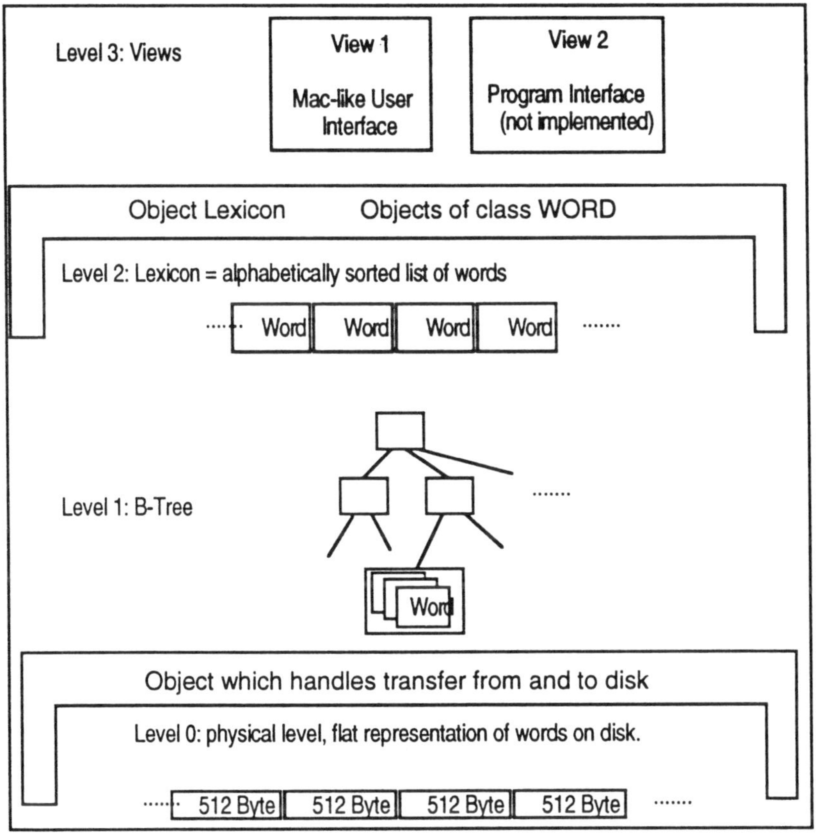

Figure 3. Four-level architecture of GOLD

The implementation is running on Macintosh Computers. A Mac-like user interface allows access to the levels below. Its functionality is reviewed in the following section.

3. A short overview of the GOLD Lexical Browser

The browser allows using two ways of navigation in the database: serially and by searching for specific entries. Thus, you can scroll through the database, but this is of course quite tedious due to the size of the database. A better way is to search for a string; the system then sets a pointer to the first appropriate entry. This operation is very fast due to the efficient data structure. A user-defined number of entries is displayed on the screen at each moment, one entry with some of its features per line, cf. Figures 4 and 5, background.

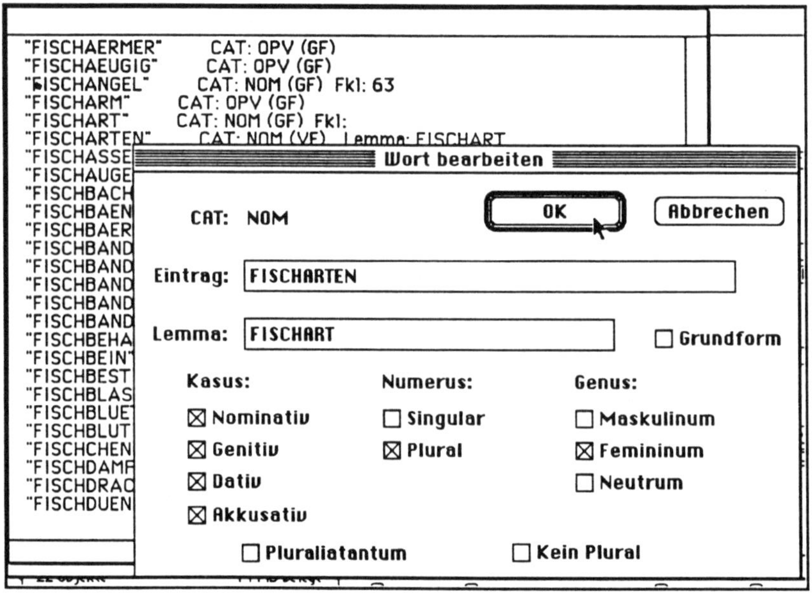

Figure 4. Two example screen shots from GOLD

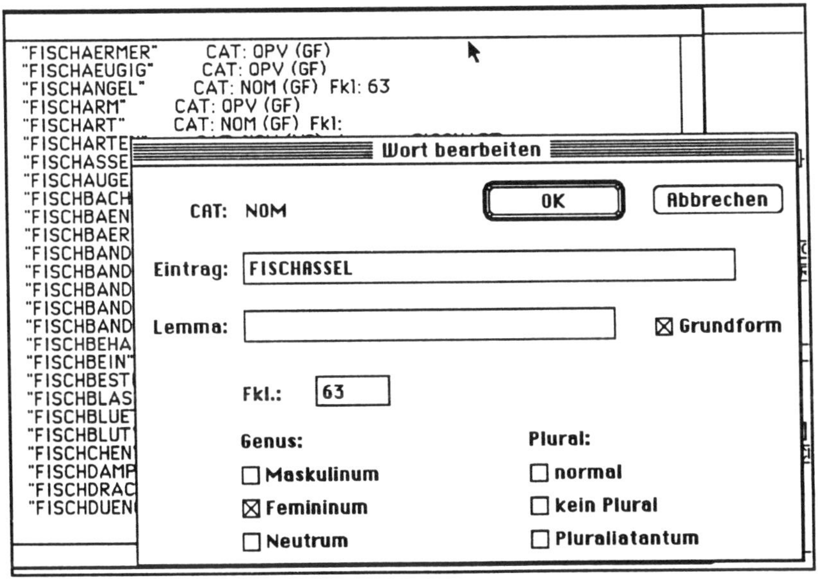

Figure 5. Two example screen shots from GOLD

Scrolling can then take place from this location in the database. But the user can also decide to view one entry in a more detailed fashion. The display methods of the different classes then display only the relevant features of each class. Figure 4 shows a NOM full form, Figure 5 a NOM base form. The user can also choose to have base forms inflected, cf. Section 5; Figure 6 shows the produced inflection forms of the entry displayed in Figure 5.

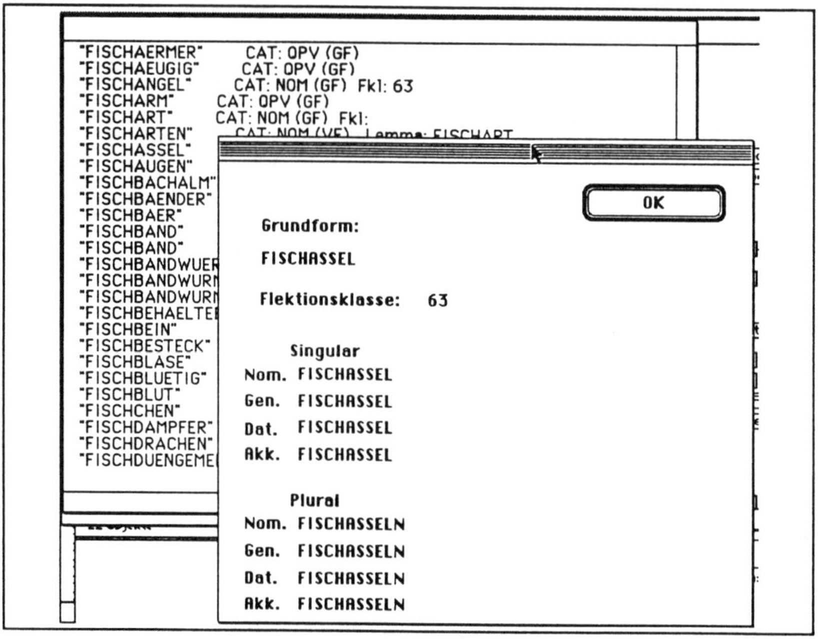

Figure 6. Yet another screen shot from GOLD

Displaying of entries can further be modified by using a filter that only lets pass those entries fulfilling certain conditions. This is described in the section below.

4. Querying an object-oriented database

One of the advantages of DBMS based on the relational data model is their simple querying facility. Given their construction from tables with rows of equal form, the SQL-like form of querying expressions "select from ... where ..." is quite obvious and simple. It is part of the price you have to pay when changing to the object-oriented data model that you loose this nice feature. In the object-oriented paradigm, you are dealing with complex objects of variant forms connected by links, so the general form of querying languages is still a question of research, cf. Bancilhon (1989).

In our approach we "solved" the problem in a rather pragmatic and *ad hoc* way. We decided not to introduce a new separate query language but to use the objects and classes themselves for that purpose. So, in order to query the lexicon, the user interactively builds an object with only partially specified information. Then, this (partial) object is compared to all the entries in the lexicon. The user is allowed to use all classes, even the abstract ones. He first has to decide on the class of the object and whether he is to construct a full form or base form. The system will then create an object of the appropriate class and present it to the user so that he can add the information he wants. If, for example, the user wants to see all nouns and proper names with inflection type "62", he would create an object of the (abstract) class NXM with "baseform" checked and would then enter the information FKL = "62" interactively, leaving all other information fields unspecified (cf. Figure 7).

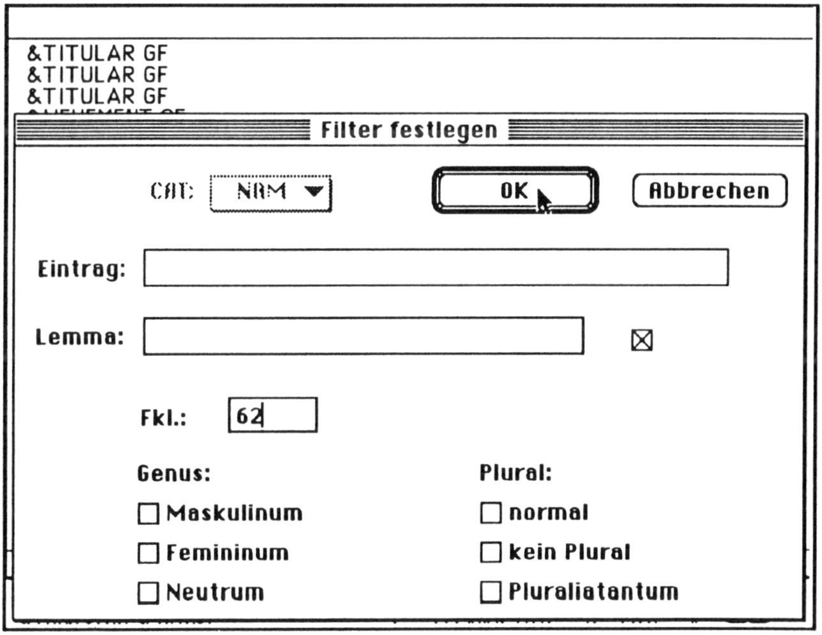

Figure 7. Searching for base form NAMs with FKL = "62"

In this way, the system will not scan the whole lexicon for appropriate entries and store them away in a separate "selection", but will instead use the partially specified object as a filter when browsing through the database. This has a certain advantage when constructing a non-restrictive query, e.g. "all nouns and proper names". The alternative procedure would first have to scan the lexicon completely (which might cost considerable time) resulting in a selection of, say, 200,000 entries. The user could only then start to browse through the selection. In our approach, browsing would start immediately with the system (within seconds) presenting the first 20 or so entries complying with the query object. With restrictive queries of, say, 15 hits, the time problem of course remains since the user will have to wait for the next hit to be displayed while browsing through the lexicon (for 15 entries he won't have to "browse", of course, since they can be diplayed on the same screen).

The comparison of the query object to the lexicon entries itself is a kind of "liberal unification", defined as follows:

> a query object q and a lexical entry e unify *iff*
>
> e is of the same class as q or of a descendant class of q's class *and*
> all the attributes of q unify to the corresponding attributes of e
>
> an attribute unifies with another attribute *iff*
>
> the values are equal *or*
> at least one attribute has a "nil" value (is not specified) *or*
> the attributes are of set-type and the value of one is included in the other's value

Displayed are the original lexical entries, though, not the results of the unification process.

5. An object-oriented morphological component

Among the few linguistic attributes included in the entries of the Bonnlex WDB are inflection types for the base forms. It should therefore be possible to use the WDB as a component in a natural language generation system. To test and demonstrate this we included a facility to generate and display all surface forms of a base form. This can, of course, also be used to inform oneself about the inflection behavior of a word, since the inflection type itself, eg. "62", is not very informative for the casual user.

The generation component consists of several methods distributed over the class hierarchy of GOLD and thus demonstrates the typical features of object-oriented systems: polymorphism, inheritance, and overriding, and also some of the problems with current object-oriented systems.

Polymorphism means that different classes can own methods with the same name but different behavior. That is, the method "inflect" for verbs does other things than the same method for nouns. In our system, all classes own an "inflect" method but the full form classes just own a default method which produces an error message and the base form classes of the different types (adjectives, verbs, nouns) each own an appropriate method. So, inflectional knowledge is distributed over all classes and can be updated or changed locally.

Inflectional knowledge that is common to more than one class is attached to an abstract superclass of these classes (cf. the picture in Figure 8, which is a detail of Figure 2). Here, the inflection method for NOM and NAM is identical and thus attached to NXM; NOM and NAM inherit the method from there.

Of course, according to the same diagram "pluralia tantum" and "singularia tantum" would inherit the same method, which of course is utterly wrong. So, these classes have their own inflection methods which override the inherited method. Thus the inherited method is modified in the following way: the methods "inflect" for "pluralia tantum" and "singularia tantum" call the inherited method and then cancel the forms for singular or plural, respectively. In other words, there is no new inflection mechanism for "pluralia tantum" but only the knowledge that no singular forms exists is added - and that is as it should be. (This could be described as a kind of default inheritance for methods; for features it is not possible in our approach.)

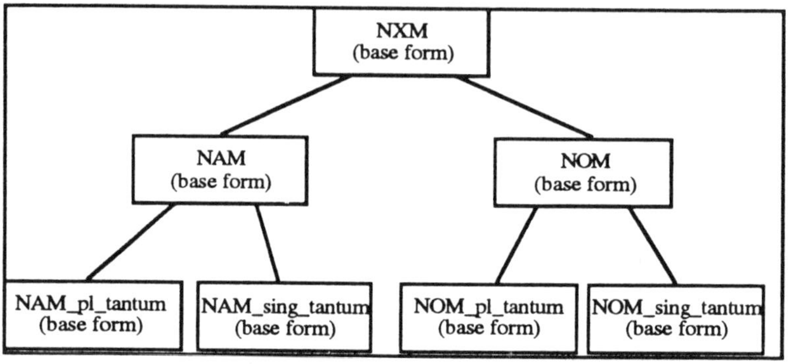

Figure 8. Detail of the class hierarchy

Regarding Figure 8 once again, one of the problems with our approach and with object-oriented systems as they are today in general becomes obvious. Since we used single inheritance, two classes had to be designed for "pluralia tantum" (the same holds for "singularia tantum") one stemming from NOM and one from NAM. This is, of course, not very satisfying and becomes intolerable if more orthogonal distinctions are relevant (e.g. for German verbs: reflexive/non-reflexive, strong/weak, perfect tense with "haben"/perfect tense with "sein", passive yes/no and so on) since it leads to a combinatorial explosion of classes. But even if multiple inheritance was allowed, this would not solve the problem as can easily be seen in Figure 9.

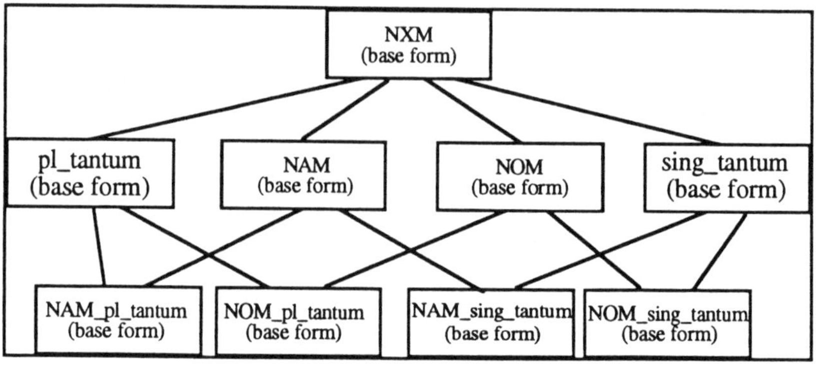

Figure 9. Possible solution with multiple inheritance

You would have to introduce a class for each combination of yes/no decisions involved. This can lead to a quite awkward inflation of exotic, sparsely populated classes, like: "reflexive - weak - verbs - with - perfect - with - *haben* - and - passive". This problem is well known to exist not only for our domain of application but for other domains as well, cf. Vossen (1992b). One solution would be to allow for not only multiple inheritance but multiple class-membership as well. That is, an object could then be a member of more than one class, a thing strictly forbidden in current object-oriented systems. A lexical entry could then be a member in the classes "reflexive verbs", "weak verbs", "verbs with passive" and so on and could inherit features and methods from all of them without introducing a special class for it.

6. Some results

As has already been stated, one of the main results of this work was that the object-oriented data model is in principle well suited for computer-based lexicons. But it also became clear that multiple inheritance or, better, multiple membership is a necessary feature of such systems.

Further results concern our idea to use the Bonnlex WDB as a basis for the realization component of a NL generation system. When implementing the morphological component of GOLD and using it, it became obvious that there are severe problems with this idea. We had already found out that the data of the Bonnlex WDB are partially incomplete and inconsistent, but we had to learn that the coding system of the Bonnlex WDB is *a priori* inadequate for a full morphological component.

Example I: Nouns

Inflections classes for "normal" German words work rather well. But for special word classes, mostly of foreign heritage, this is not the case. The information for these words, e.g. *Atlas - Atlanten, Kaktus - Kakteen*, does not allow unambiguous formation of plural forms.

Example II: Verbs

Here, the situation is even worse. It is well known that for many German verbs inflection includes vocalic alterations (Umlaut, Ablaut). This is reflected in the inflection classes of the Bonnlex WDB. But for some words there is also a consonantic alteration, especially in the past tense forms and the past participle, e.g. *ziehen - zog - gezogen, gehen - ging - gegangen.*

And this is not coded in the WDB. Using the information included there, the forms should be: **ziehen - zoh - gezohen*, **gehen, gih, gegahen*. With past participles there is an additional problem: Some words take a *ge*-prefix, some incorporate the *ge*-affix between prefixes and stem, others take no such affix. Example: *sehen - gesehen* vs. *abfahren - abgefahren* vs. *eliminieren - eliminiert*. Which of the alternatives applies depends on two factors: whether prefixes are detachable and where primary word stress is. And whereas the first factor is coded, the second is not. All in all, past tense forms, forms based on past tense forms, and forms based on the past participle cannot be generated in a reliable way with the data from the Bonnlex WDB.

To test the overall quality of the data we examined some samples of it:

- 300 verbs (base forms) chosen randomly from the Bonnlex WDB
- 300 nouns (no proper names, base forms), chosen randomly from the Bonnlex WDB
- 300 verbs (tokens = 215 types, base forms) found in newspaper articles[1] (forms of *sein* and *haben* excluded)
- 300 nouns (tokens = 233 types, no proper names, base forms, found in the same newspaper articles)
- 300 nouns (= the stems of the compound nouns of the 300 nouns of the last sample; 189 types)

The last three samples were meant to test which percentage of naturally occurring forms you could expect to be able to generate using the Bonnlex WDB as a lexicon. The results are shown in the following tables:

entries with missing inflection class	21
entries with incorrect inflection class	21
entries with correct inflection class	236
total	278*

* 22 found entries were nonsense (= no words of German)

Table 2. 300 verbs from the Bonnlex WDB ("correct" only means present tense forms, cf. above)

entries with missing inflection class	124
entries with incorrect inflection class	6
entries with correct inflection class	170
total	300

Table 3. 300 nouns from the Bonnlex WDB

	types	tokens
missing entries	1	1
entries with missing inflection class	29	57
entries with incorrect inflection class	33	44
entries with correct inflection class	152	198
total	215	300

Table 4. 300 verbs from running text

	types	tokens
missing entries	58	61
entries with missing inflection class	61	84
entries with incorrect inflection class	21	33
entries with correct inflection class	93	122
total	233	300

Table 5. 300 nouns from running text

	types	tokens
missing entries	8	12
entries with missing inflection class	69	119
entries with incorrect inflection class	15	29
entries with correct inflection class	97	140
total	189	300

Table 6. 300 nouns from running text; composite nouns reduced to stems

7. Future work

In the future, we are planning to further investigate the usability of the object-oriented paradigm for computer-based lexicograpy. It is planned (a) to use a commercially available object-oriented database system running on an IBM RS 6000 workstation, and (b) to implement the structure of more complex dictionaries like the *Duden Deutsches Universal Wörterbuch* as a hierarchy using the multiple inheritance facility of the new platform and modelling links between entries (e.g. semantic relations) as well.

(a) Object-oriented Data Base Management Systems (OODBMS), like all database systems, have features which make them seem appropriate for computer-based lexicography. Among them are:

- high performance
- user-friendly query facility (but cf. Section 4, above)
- client-server architecture
- recovery facility

You get all this "for free", which is an advantage over approaches which build their own retrieval/access system, e.g. the approach described in this paper and the LDB/LKB system of the Acquilex project (Briscoe 1991, Copestake 1992).

You only have to add the linguistic knowledge which forms the difference between a machine-readable lexicon and, say, a CAD system. But in this regard the object-oriented paradigm helps a lot as should have become clear in this paper.

An interesting question will be the comparison between systems based on feature structures as advocated in the linguistic approach and systems based on objects as in object-oriented databases. At a first glance there seems to be a huge difference, but a closer look reveals that typed feature structures (as used e.g. in the Acquilex project) are not so different from classes (with the exception, perhaps, of negation and disjunction in the formation of values).

This kind of research will also be interesting the other way round: machine-readable lexicons are used as new applications for OODBMS since these are still a topic of research themselves. Valuable insights into the design of OODBMS could be drawn from this new type of application with its very special needs.

Nevertheless, the number of available OODBMS has risen sharply in the last few years. Vossen (1992a) counts 8 commercial and 20 experimental systems.

(b) The *Duden Deutsches Universal Wörterbuch* is quite interesting in this context for several reasons:

- it offers a wealth of information including definitions and semantic information;
- there has been an attempt to use the relational data model for a computer version of the dictionary, which proved to be problematic (Bläser & Wermke 1990);

- the structure of the dictionary raises problems which can be solved by features of object-oriented systems that were not used in the work described in this paper, e.g. the formation of complex objects (for example several readings within one entry) and links between objects.

Note

1. "General-Anzeiger", Bonn, March 13th, 1993, p. 1 - 2.

References

Bancilhon, F.
1989 Query languages for object-oriented database systems: Analysis and a proposal. In: Härder, T. (ed.): *Datenbanksysteme in Büro, Technik und Wissenschaft* (= IFB 204). Berlin: Springer, pp. 1 - 18.

Bläser, B. & M. Wermke
1990 Projekt "Elektronische Wörterbücher/Lexika": Abschlußbericht der Definitionsphase. *IWBS Report* 145, IBM.

Boguraev, B. & T. Briscoe
1989 *Computational Lexicography for Natural Language Processing*. London: Longman.

Briscoe, T.
1991 *Lexical Issues in Natural Language Processing*. ACQUILEX Working Paper No. 41.

Brustkern, J. & W. Schulze:
1982 "Aufbau einer Wortdatenbank für das Deutsche". *Sprache und Datenverarbeitung* 2.

Copestake, A.
1992 The ACQUILEX LKB: Representation issues in semi-automatic acquisition of large lexicons. In: ACL. *Proceedings of ANLP 92*, Trento, pp. 88 - 96.

Daelemans, W., K. De Smedt,& G. Gazdar
1992 "Inheritance in natural language processing". *Computational Linguistics*, Vol. 18,2:205-218.

Hötker, W. & P. Ludewig
1991 *Ein neuer Ansatz zur Integration unterschiedlicher lexikalischer Ressourcen*. IWBS Report 196, IBM.

Hornung, E.
1990 Entwurf und Implementierung einer betriebssystemunabhängigen Benutzeroberfläche für die Verwaltung lexikalischer Informationen. *IKP-Arbeitsberichte, Abt. LDV No. 8*. Bonn: IKP.

Lenders, W. (ed.)
1991 Studien zur maschinellem Lexikographie. *IKP-Arbeitsberichte, Abt. LDV No. 11*. Bonn: IKP.

Sedgewick, R.
1988 *Algorithms*, 2nd edition. Reading (Mass.): Addison Wesley.

Vossen, G.
1992a Bibiography on object-oriented database management (2nd edition). *Bericht No. 9202 der Arbeitsgruppe Informatik*. University of Giessen.

1992b On formal models for object-oriented databases. *Bericht No. 9203 der Arbeitsgruppe Informatik*. Universität Giessen.

Winter, A.

1990 Entwurf und Implementierung eines abstrakten, dynamisch modifizierbaren Datenmodells für die Speicherung und Wiedergewinnung lexikalischer Information. In: *IKP-Arbeitsberichte, Abt. LDV No. 8*. Bonn: IKP

Syntagmatic context information for computer assisted (human) translation

Dieter Seelbach

0. Introduction

Only very few studies in the fields of Computer Assisted Translation (CAT), Computer Assisted Language Learning (CALL), bi- or multilingual Data Banks and Comparative Linguistics have simultaneously been concerned with two apparently separated phenomena, which are, however, connected with one another: phraseology and terminology.

The importance of syntagmatic context for translation is outstanding. There are essentially three relatively new linguistic facts with regard to the comparative study of grammars and lexicons of living languages that form the basis for the development of bilingual or multilingual data banks as well as for CAT and CALL systems. These new facts "explain" why verbs like German *tragen* or French *prendre* are each time differently rendered in either English or German. The facts are:

(1) Contrastive typologies for multi-word expressions or compound words (in a very wide and new sense of the word): nouns, adverbs, and verbs

einer Sache Rechnung *tragen*	to take sth. into account
prendre le large	das Weite suchen

(2) Predicative nouns and their support verbs

Verantwortung *tragen*	to bear responsibility
prendre une décision	eine Entscheidung fällen/treffen

(3) Object classes with their specific predicators

einen Hut *tragen*	to wear a hat
prendre des insultes	Beleidigungen einstecken.

The examples give a first orientation for the understanding of these three phenomena, which must be distinguished clearly, and show their importance for translation. Just consider the equivalents of the German verb *tragen* in English and of the French verb *prendre* in German, which differ according to their contexts. Obviously, the English verb *carry* could not be used in order to translate *tragen* in these contexts or the German verb *nehmen* for the translation of *prendre*.

In the following, we confine ourselves to a contrastive study of German and French. Let us first go on motivating our work.

There is hardly ever a unique equivalent, or "le mot juste", in terms of translation, for isolated words. And this is important from the computational-linguistic point of view, where "words" are sequences of graphemes separated by blanks. Just take a simple noun like *raison* in the verbal multi-word expressions or compound verbs:

avoir raison	Recht haben
(avoir une raison	einen Grund haben)
perdre la raison	den Verstand verlieren
se faire une raison	sich ins Unvermeidliche fügen

Or let's take *raison* as an element of another category of multi-word expressions, namely compound nouns, and look at the equivalents we get:

de mauvaises raisons	vorgeschobene Gründe
l'âge de raison	urteilsfähiges Alter
la raison d'être	Daseinsberechtigung
la raison d'Etat	Staatsraison
un mariage de raison	Vernunftheirat

This leads the linguist who is interested in CAT and CALL to elaborate typologies of compound words and to integrate them in his data bank to facilitate their identification in the texts, thanks to their belonging to classes, and finally their translation, thanks to the attribution of their equivalents.

I suppose that there really are equivalents, at least in special or technical languages, but also to a large extent in the common core of the language, especially when we consider compound words, predicative nouns and their support verbs and collocations.

1. Contrastive typologies of compound words

Concerning language use, what poses the most serious problems is, of course, the high number of compound nouns in the texts, often technical or semi-technical terms. But compound verbs and adverbs are not negligible, either in quantity or in complexity, and sometimes they also belong to special or technical languages , that means to the field of terminology.

As a starting point we take a global structure for the free and fixed adverbials proposed by M. Gross (1986), which we have slightly modified. It is a good candidate for being the basis for the contrastive typologies of free and fixed adverbials of several languages:

Prep Det Adj N Modif

In French the modifiers (Modif) of the head of the phrase (N) are:

Modif_F: Adj, Rel, de N, Prep N

(Il est parti) après un long repas improvisé
que nous avons tous apprécié
de trois heures
sur la terrasse

Modifiers of the postponed *Adj* and *de N* type do not exist in German:

(Er ist gegangen) nach einem langen Essen
Essen, das uns gefiel
Essen auf Geschäftskosten

In Table 1 you will find the first sketch of a comparative German and French typology of *compound adverbs*, i.e. of fixed and half-fixed expressions (where C designates the *constrained* or fixed elements of the adverbial expression; in most cases this is a noun and often even the head of the construction. C will serve to identify compound adverbs in the texts).

About five to six thousand compound adverbs have been shown to exist in French, divided up into sixteen classes (M. Gross 1986). I have found about 160 compound *time* adverbs in French weather reports (Seelbach 1990). Concerning the contrastive aspect that we are especially interested in, we observe *formal equivalence classes* as well as *formal affinity classes* to fill the gaps in the typologies, where there are no structurally equivalent multi-word expressions in the target language.

E.g. starting from the German class that is marked PAC, we find first a formal equivalence class in French (PAC); we then have PCA as a representative of what we call *affinity classes* and finally we find other "affinity

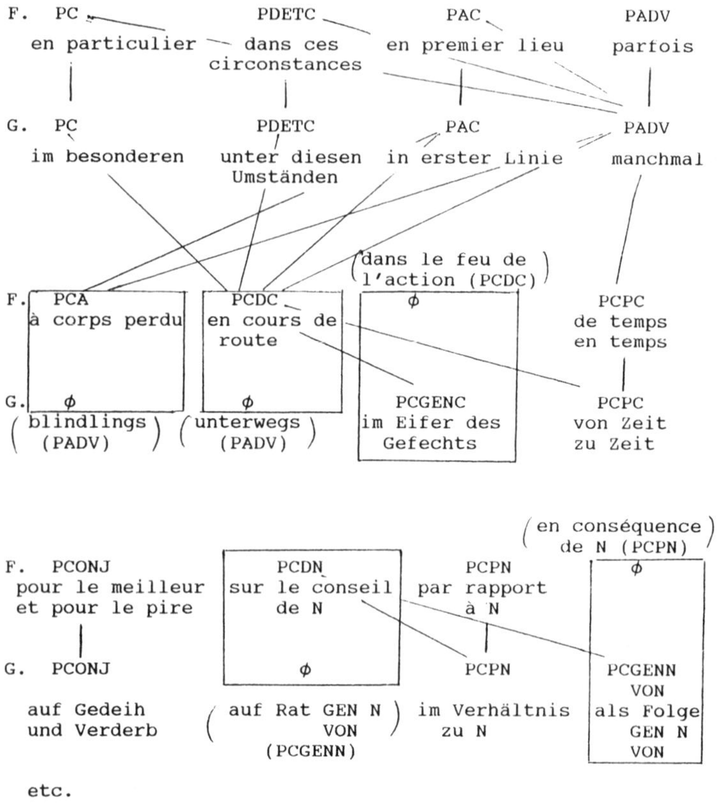

Table 1. Typology of compound adverbs in French (F) and German (G) C = Constrained or fixed elements, P = Preposition, Det = Determiner, A = Adjective, GEN = Genitive marker (determiner)

classes" whose structure is a little further away from the prototypical formal affinity class PCA, but which are still more or less close to the German class PAC, if we take into account all the formal classes of compound adverbs:

am frühen Morgen	PAC	au petit matin	PAC
zum gegenwärtigen Zeitpunkt	PAC	à l'heure actuelle	PCA
von ganzem Herzen	PAC	du fond du coeur	PCDC
im tiefsten Herzen	PAC	au fond du coeur	PCDC
auf weite Sicht	PAC	à la longue	PDETC

If we start from the PCDC class in French, we do not find any formal equivalence class in German. This gap is filled by formal affinity classes:

sous le sceau du secret	PCDC	unter dem Siegel der Verschwiegenheit	PCGENC
au lever du jour	PCDC	bei Tagesanbruch	PC
pour cause de maladie	PCDC	wegen Krankheit	PC
à la tombée du jour	PCDC	in der Dämmerung	PDETC
à titre de comparaison	PCDC	zum Vergleich	PDETC
à peu de distance	PCDC	in geringer Entfernung	PAC
sans espoir de retour	PCDC	ohne Hoffnung auf Rückkehr	PCPC

A few remarks on the notations are in order here: in German the elements that C stands for can also coin genuine compounds as in *Tagesanbruch*. Simple adverbs are given the notation PADV, just like the other classes with a P in the initial position, due to the fact that paraphrases like the following are possible:

apparamment	(≡ *en* apparence):	PADV
nuitamment	(≡ *de* nuit):	PADV
instamment	(≡ *avec* instance):	PADV
mensuellement	(≡ *au* mois):	PADV
gestern	(≡ *am* gestrigen Tag):	PADV
abends	(≡ *am* Abend):	PADV

and, indeed, a strong affinity can be realized between PADV and the PC, PDETC, PCDC, PCA and PAC classes respectively, if the contrastive aspect is taken into consideration.

With the exception of the first two classes (PC and PDETC), which differ by the existence of a determiner (de jour, de nos jours; sans doute, sans aucun doute), the determiner is allowed or not according to the nature of C and/or the preposition (à long terme, sur le long terme; de prime abord, à (la) première vue; en cours de semaine, dans le courant de la semaine). The preposition is optional in some cases ((dans) l'après-midi, (pour) la plupart du temps)), or is completely absent:

Il a gagné	les yeux fermés	(mit geschlossenen Augen)
	dimanche dernier	(letzten Sonntag)

Here are some German examples and French compound adverbs with *raison* as the head of the phrase (C).

Er arbeitet	manchmal		PADV
	wider Erwarten		PC
	über die Maßen		PDETC
	auf gut Glück		PAC
	in den Grenzen seiner Möglichkeiten		PCGENC
	aus Spaß an der Freud'		PCPC
	für'n Appel und 'n Ei		PCONJ
	auf Kosten	seiner Gesundheit	PCGENN
		von Max	VONN
	im Gegensatz zu Luc		PCPN

Il est parti sans raison	(ohne Grund)	PC
(à + avec) raison	(mit Recht)	PC
à tort ou à raison	(zu Recht oder zu Unrecht)	PCONJ
pour (des) raison(s) de santé	(aus Gesundheitsgründen)	PCDC
en raison du mauvais temps	(wegen des schlechten Wetters)	PCDN

Remember that the identification of these groups can be carried out through their C element. This makes it possible to look them up in the dictionary and to translate them by passing through the indicated classes.

Compound verbs in our sense of multi-word expressions have as yet been very little investigated in descriptive linguistics and even less in contrastive linguistics. Their importance for CAT has been underestimated up to now. We present a contrastive description of such verbs in German and French, keeping within the same theoretical framework that we have adopted for compound adverbs. We again propose *formal equivalence classes* and *formal affinity classes*.

Let us take as a starting point the basic distributional structures of simple sentences, also called "Satzbaupläne" in a different framework:

N_0 V N_1	Luc sucht das Buch Luc cherche le livre
N_0 V Prep N_1	Max lacht über Luc Max rit de Luc
N_0 V DAT N_1	Das Buch gehört dem Lehrer Le livre appartient au professeur

N_0 V N_1 Prep N_2	Max legt das Buch auf den Tisch Max dépose le livre sur la table
N_0 V N_1 DAT N_2	Max schenkt das Buch dem Lehrer Max donne le livre au professeur
N_0 V (Prep) N_1 GEN N VON N	Luc liest das Buch des Lehrers pfeift auf von Max
N_0 V (Prep) N_1 de N	Luc lit le livre de Max se moque du
N_0 V ADV	Max arbeitet nachts Max gesticule longuement

We might characterize the compound verbs or verbal multi-word expressions in the following way: in every simple sentence there are at least two fixed elements one of which is the verb. Either we have the verb and one (or two) of its objects being fixed or we have the constellation "fixed verb + fixed adverb". Often, especially in metaphorical expressions, it is possible for one of the two fixed elements to be translated by an equivalent simple lexeme, while the other cannot:

Max *prend* le large	(*Max nimmt das Weite)
Max *sucht* das Weite	(literal translation)
N_0 V N_1	

N_0 V N_1	
Luc jette *l'éponge*	(?Luc wirft den Schwamm)
Luc wirft *das Handtuch*	(literal translation)

Even more frequently, neither of the two elements can receive a literal translation but the type of construction remains the same:

N_0	V	N_1		N_0	V	N_1
Max	*décroche*	la *timbale*	=	Max	schießt	den Vogel ab
Max	*schwimmt*	im *Geld*	=	Max	*roule*	sur l'*or*
N_0	V	Prep N_1		N_0	V	Prep N_1

Yet in the comparable metaphorical expression

Max nage dans l'*abondance* (variant)
(Max schwimmt im *Geld*)

one of the fixed elements is translated literally again. - About fifteen thousand compound verbs have been shown to exist in French (M. Gross 1989).

Some formal equivalence classes as well as some formal affinity classes are given in Table 2, where C denotes the fixed verb, the number(s) the fixed object(s) and N the "free" or variable elements (different object types or noun modifiers); DAT denotes the dative marker (determiner):

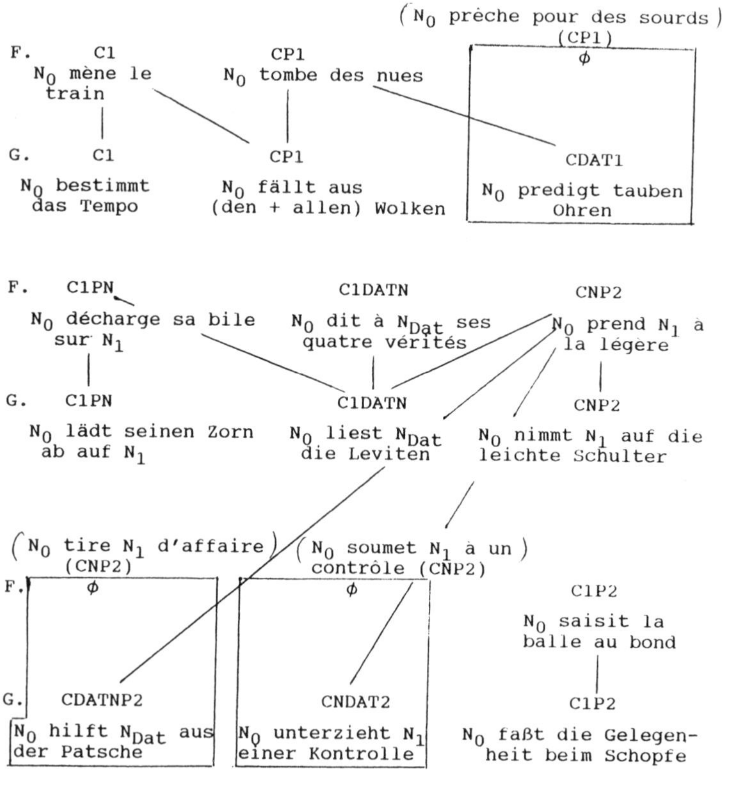

etc.

Table 2. Typology of compound verbs in French (F) and German (G)

The class names can be decoded as follows:

class names:	fixed elements:
C1	N_0 *V* N_1
CP1	N_0 *V* *Prep* N_1
C1PN	N_0 *V* N_1 Prep N_2
C1P2	N_0 *V* N_1 *Prep* N_2
CNP2	N_0 *V* N_1 *Prep* N_2
C1DATN	N_0 *V* N_1 DAT N_2
etc.	

The French compound verb *entendre raison* is classified and notated the same way as its German equivalent *Vernunft annehmen*: *C1* (the verb and the direct object are fixed).

N_0 entend raison C1 N_0 nimmt Vernunft an C1

In

Max a eu raison de ses difficultés
= Max hat seine Schwierigkeiten überwunden

the notation is N_0 avoir raison de N_1 A1PN

which is brought into a semantic equivalence relation to the German simple lexeme *überwinden* (*to overcome*).

Similar cases rather frequently occur in the two directions of the translation

N_0 a raison de N_1 A1PN
N_0 überwindet N_1 (verb)

N_0 rebrousse chemin C1
N_0 kehrt um (verb)

N_0 faßt N_1 ins Auge CNP2
N_0 envisage N_1 (verb)

Daß S liegt auf der Hand CP1
Que S est évident (adjective)

More frequently compound verbs are rendered by compound verbs in the target language, too, but they may be members of formally different classes.

N_0 trägt N_{Dat} Rechnung	C1DATN
= N_0 tient compte de N	C1PN
(= N_0 takes N into account	CNP2)
N_0 fait le plein	F1
= N_0 tankt voll	CADV

N_0 respire la santé	C1
N_0 strotzt vor Gesundheit	CP1
N_0 mord la poussière	C1
N_0 beißt ins Gras	CP1

N_0 schneidet sich in den Finger	CP1
N_0 se fourre le doigt dans l'oeil	C1P2

Fortunately however, in the vast majority, we have cases of formal equivalence as we have seen above.

Even if we keep within the limits of the description of one given language, we can easily find out that synonymous expressions or paraphrases may belong to formally different classes:

N_0 schmiert N_{Dat} Brei um den Mund	C1DATNP2
N_0 geht N_{Dat} um den Bart	CDATNP2
N_0 küßt die Füße GEN N	C1GENN
N_0 redet N_{Dat} nach dem Mund	CDATNP2
N_0 macht N_{Dat} die Cour	F1DATN
N_0 schmeichelt N_{Dat}	(verb)

Here we are confronted with the very principle of our method of analysis and translation: the semantic equivalence relations between formally different classes that we observe in a few cases while passing from one language to another are also to be found in the paraphrases formed by differently structured expressions of one and the same language. For a good translation, paraphrases, often in the form of expansion or reduction, ought to be accounted for. This holds for the grammar and the lexicon, which are intimately connected.

The theoretical framework that aims to describe paraphrasal relations explicitly or, what amounts to the same, to describe syntactically and semantically related structures, is *Lexicon Grammar*, which was proposed on the basis of Distributional and Transformational Grammar by Z. S. Harris 1957 and further developed and founded empirically above all for French by M. Gross and his collaborators. We place our present work in this theoretical framework and we plan to use the results of our contrastive analyses for CAT and CALL as well as for Computer Assisted Human Translation (CAHT).

By the way, we here observe a phenomenon that generally concerns compound words: absolutely fixed cases are rare, fixation shows a gradation or cline:

(mit der Faust) auf den Tisch (jemandem) ins Gesicht über die Stränge	schlagen hauen

versus

auf die Pauke	hauen *schlagen

aus der Art	schlagen *hauen

Honig ums Maul Brei um den Mund Honig um den Bart	schmieren streichen

versus

um den Bart gehen
nach dem Mund reden

manquer rater louper	le coche	(die Gelegenheit	verpassen versäumen)

versus

casser *briser	sa pipe	(den Löffel	abgeben wegwerfen)

das Tempo	bestimmen / angeben	(mener le train)
den Ton	*bestimmen / angeben	(donner le ton)

As a rule, considering the internal syntax of compound verbs, the nouns and determiners are more fixed than the verbs.

Now what particularly needs to be recorded in the electronic lexicon are all those very numerous expressions - compound nouns, verbs and adverbs - *that are only half-fixed*, according to our conception, in order to help the human translator or to execute a Computer Assisted Translation with human pre-editing and post-editing.

There is not enough space in this article to include a complete contrastive description of *compound nouns* or nominal multi-word expressions. Yet we should mention that, just as is the case with compound verbs and adverbs, formal equivalence classes and formal affinity classes can be detected (cf. Table 3):

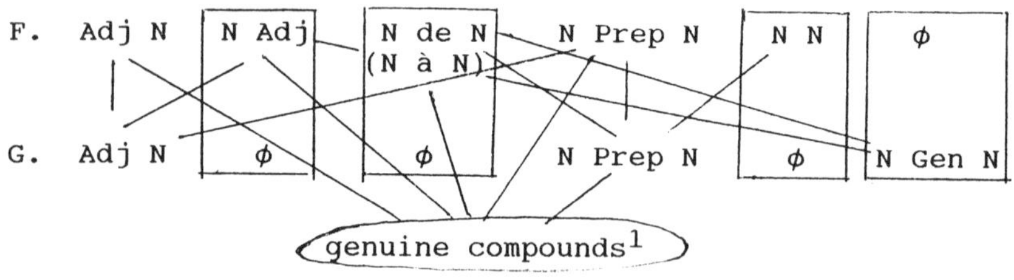

etc.

Table 3. Typology of compound nouns of French (F) and German (G).

Examples:

F. *N Adj*:

un carton rouge	un pont aérien	la pierre philosophale
eine rote Karte	eine Luftbrücke	der Stein der Weisen
(Adj N)	(N_N)	(N Gen N)

G. *Adj N*:

ein alter Bekannter	die romanischen Sprachen	eine fahrlässige Tötung
une vieille connaissance	les langues romanes	un homicide par imprudence
(Adj N)	(N Adj)	(N Prep N)

F. *N de N*:

banque de données	l'homme de la rue	pierre d'achoppement
Datenbank	der Mann auf der Straße	Stein des Anstoßes
(N_N)	(N Prep N)	(N GEN N)

Here are other examples of formal equivalence and affinity classes:

F.	Numeral N	N à V_{Inf}
	les dix commandements	un terrain à construire
	die zehn Gebote	ein Baugelände
G.	Numeral N	$V_{stem\_}N$
F.	N1 N2	Prep-N
	un mètre cube	l'arrière-pays
	ein Kubikmeter	das Hinterland
G.	N2_N1	Prep_N
F.	V-N	N Rel
	un ouvre-boîtes	le singe qui parle
	ein Dosenöffner	der sprechende Affe
G.	N_VN_{er}	Part N

We can observe an affinity between German genuine compounds and compound nouns of the *N Prep N*-type in French, where the preposition often reveals the kind of semantic relation existing between the elements of the German genuine compound:

nourriture pour enfants	Kindernahrung N_VN[2]
fuite hors du monde	Weltflucht N_VN
course contre la montre	Zeitfahren N_VN

steak dans le filet	Filetsteak N_N
voie sur berge	Uferstraße N_N
lotion avant rasage après	Rasierwasser V_N
diapositive en couleurs	Farbdia N_Abkürzung
voie sans issue	Sackgasse N_N
table avec rallonge	Ausziehtisch V_N
service après vente	Kundendienst N_VN
montée au filet	Netzattacke N_VN

French complex compound nouns (three elements), which are mostly extensions of the four binary classes *N Adj*, *N de N*, *N à N*, and *N en N*, have a formal affinity class of the *Adj N*-type in German, where the adjective or the noun are often genuine compounds themselves:

la politique agricole commune N Adj / Adj	die gemeinsame Agrarpolitik Adj N
une heure de grande écoute N de / Adj N	eine hohe Einschaltzeit Adj N
un emprunt à long terme N / à Adj N	eine langfristige Anleihe Adj N
une agression à main armée N / à N Adj	ein bewaffneter Überfall Adj N
la non-assistance à personne en danger N / à N en N	die unterlassene Hilfeleistung Adj N
un médicament en vente libre N / en N Adj	ein freiverkäufliches Medikament Adj N

un couteau à cran d'arrêt	ein feststehendes Messer
N / à N de N	Adj N

According to what we have seen with compound verbs and adverbs, the binary compound nouns and German genuine compounds also have simple lexemes as target language equivalents or the other way round:

jeune fille	Mädchen	Pilotenkanzel	carlingue
cheval blanc	Schimmel	Telefonhörer	écouteur
doigt de pied	Zehe	Tischtuch	nappe
chaise à porteurs	Sänfte	Ehebruch	adultère
mise en scène	Inszenierung	Graupelschauer	giboulées
histoire pour rire	Witz	Rechtsstreit	litige
		Kostenvoranschlag	devis

In a similar way we can very often find, taking again French as source language, binary German genuine compounds as equivalents of expanded or complex compound nouns (three and more elements)

F.	N/en Adj N	N/de N Adj
	un enfant en bas âge	un incendie d'origine criminelle
	ein Kleinkind	eine Brandstiftung
G.	Adj_N	VN_VN
F.	N/de N de N	N/à N Adj
	la bande d'arrêt d'urgence	une association à but terminé
	die Standspur	ein Zweckverband
G.	VN_N	N_VN
F.	N Adj Prep N	
	les organes chargés de l'exécution	
	Vollzugsorgane	
G.	VN_N	

as well as expanded or complex German genuine compounds (three elements) as equivalents of binary compound nouns:

une collection de timbres	eine Briefmarkensammlung
N de N	N_N_VN
le prix de gros	der Großhandelspreis
N de N	Adj_VN_N

un mot composé N Adj	ein Mehrwortausdruck Adv_N_VN
un trois pièces Numeral N	eine Dreizimmerwohnung Numeral_N_VN

The types of formal equivalence and affinity classes we have presented in this section can be and have been found in parallel texts (e.g. weather reports, cf. Seelbach 1990 and 1991) as well as in translated texts (e.g. legal texts on water protection, cf. Section 3). They can be confirmed by studying, from a descriptive and quantitative point of view, corresponding or equivalent multi-word expressions in different bi- or multilingual text corpora. Therefore our contrastive typologies are also motivated by corpus-oriented investigations. In this sense we may speak of prototypical formal equivalence and affinity classes expressing semantic correspondence between expressions of different languages and being described in terms of a theoretically and empirically well-founded, lexicon-oriented grammar conception.

The formal equivalences and affinities are helpful not only in the course of a translation assisted by computer in the sense of CAT or CAHT in order to make the access to equivalents more economical and quicker or even possible, it is also useful for human translators to be aware of such equivalence and affinity classes. Awareness of the gaps existing in the target language is also important.

2. Definition of predicative nouns with their support verbs and of object classes with their specific predicators

As opposed to compound verbs where the relation between the verb and its object is (half-)fixed (cf. the examples under (1) in the Introduction), we now deal with two other types of relations between a verb and its object which, although being of a different nature, still cannot be considered as free combinations (cf. the examples under (2) and (3) in the Introduction). Traditionally and roughly speaking, we were concerned, in the preceding section, with "idioms" and we will examine, in this section, "collocations".

Let us start from the following examples:

(1)	Er fällt eine Entscheidung	E. to make a decision F. prendre une décision I. prendere una decisione

(2) Er fällt eine Tanne

E. to fell a fir
F. abattre un sapin
I. abbattere un abete

There are good reasons for analyzing *fällen* in (1) as a *support verb* or for supposing that (1) contains a *support verb construction* consisting of a support verb and a predicative noun. In contrast to *fällen* in (1), the same form in (2) is a "semantic" verb. The following can be adduced for the analysis supported here:

1. A nominal group can be formed (by way of deleting the support verb):

Seine Entscheidung [= Die Entscheidung, die er (trifft + fällt)]

2. There are restrictions on the determiner:

?* Er fällt meine Entscheidung
unsere

but: Er fällt meine Tanne
unsere

3. A standard support verb and/or support verb variants exist:

treffen/fällen

4. An argument structure for the predicative noun exists:

ÜBER-OBJ
Entscheidung (SUBJ, SATZ-OBJ)

The first argument is grammatically represented by the subject, the second one either by a sentential complement or by a prepositional object with *über*.

5. It is possible to express the predicate by an equivalent single lexeme (simple verb or adjective) in the language under investigation or in a foreign language:

Er hat entschieden He has decided

As opposed to the situation in (1), *two* arguments come into play in (2). *Fällen* is a semantic predicate. *Tanne* and *fällen* form a collocation. However, the relations between predicative nouns and their support verbs as in (1) *are also called collocations* by most linguists and lexicographers, e.g. in the BBI Dictionary and in *Langenscheidts Kontextwörterbuch* (Ilgenfritz/Stephan-Gabinel/Schneider 1989), which goes back to Hausmann. The rather vague collocation concept which is presented by Hausmann (Hausmann 1985), Mel'cuk (Mel'cuk 1989) and the authors of the BBI dictionary (Benson/Benson/Ilson 1986) is to be made more precise in the following way: *Tanne* is an element of an *object class* (<trees>), which can simultaneously be defined syntactically and semantically by means of a limited set of *specific predicators* (namely *pflanzen* and *fällen*). In order to find out object classes and their specific predicators, we must try to define the arguments through their predicators instead of defining the predicators through their arguments, as it is done when the analysis starting from the verb characterizes its arguments by semantic features and thematic roles. To this end the start must be from the noun in an argument position and then a combination of predicators must be looked for so as to define on this basis the arguments or more generally the object classes.

As we can say that *pflanzen* and *fällen* define their second arguments not only as concrete and as theme/patient but as being members of a certain well-defined subclass of the set of concrete things, namely of the object class <trees>, we call them specific predicators as opposed to generic predicators like *betrachten, lieben* etc.

Specific predicators are generally harder to translate than general predicators. A detailed description of the collocation concept based on object classes and specific predicators can be found in Seelbach 1992.

The importance of support verbs for translation becomes obvious in the subsequent examples:

E. to have/take a walk
F. faire une promenade
S. dar un paseo

E. to make preparations for
F. prendre des dispositions pour
G. Vorbereitungen treffen für
Dispositionen

E. to have/take a shower
F. prendre sa douche
I. fare la doccia etc.

These support verb constructions must not be confused with collocations defined above as the relation between (an element of) an object class and its specific predicators.

Object class membership of nouns, the specific predicators of an object class as well as the support verbs of the predicative nouns are to be represented in lexical and terminological data banks. In the perspective of *bilingual* data banks and of CAT and CALL are to be taken into account correspondences between the specific predicators for the same object class of one language and those of another language, between support verbs and their target language counterparts depending on the equivalent predicative nouns, between support verb constructions and simple verbs or adjectives (category switching) as well as correspondences between support verb constructions with compound predicative nouns and compound verbs. Examples of the last type of correspondence where category switching is also involved, are:

vollen Erfolg haben	réussir pleinement	CADV
die freie Auswahl haben	choisir librement	CADV

Some of these correspondences can be described in the form of matrix-tables, a typical *Lexicon Grammar* description that has turned out to be useful for contrastive linguistics as well (cf. Böhmer 1993).

Here are two examples of lexical entries of a data bank design, with some syntagmatic context information being integrated:

cours de tennis	M	:	N de N
	G	:	nm
	FL	:	N2 /--/
	V	:	ø
	T	:	ina, comptable
	C	:	< Unterricht >
	W	:	- (Sujet, Dat-obj) V_{sup}: donner <Lerner>
			- (Sujet, Avec-obj) V_{sup}: prendre <Lerner>
	S	:	Sport, Tennis
	D	:	Tennisstunde
	W_D	:	- (Sujet, Dat-obj) V_{sup}: geben <Lerner>
			- (Sujet, Von-obj) V_{sup}: bekommen <Lerner>

		- (Sujet, Bei-obj) <Lerner>	V_{sup}:	nehmen
	SP	: (ne pas) aller à	SP_D :	hingehen; schwänzen
		préparer		vorbereiten
		manquer		versäumen
		- (ne pas) avoir lieu		- stattfinden; ausfallen

court de tennis	M	: N de N		
	G	: nms		
	FL	: N1 / + - /		
	V	: court		
	T	: inc, locatif, comptable		
	C	: < Sportgelände >		
	W	: ø		
	S	: Sport, Tennis		
	D	: Tennisplatz		
	SP	: entrer ⌉ aller ⎥ sur jouer ⌋	SP_D:	betreten gehen ⌉ auf spielen ⌋
		quitter		verlassen, runtergehen von

For predicative nouns, the support verbs and the predicate argument structure are noted in field W; for nouns in general, the object class is noted in C and the specific predicators in SP. For a detailed description of all the fields of this design of lexical entries see Seelbach 1992.

3. Application to the development of a CAT-System in the domain of water protection

The appendix contains extracts from a legislative text on water protection in Switzerland (Bundesgesetz 1988). Moreover it contains some compound nouns, adverbs, and verbs from the extracts, which are given together with the code of the classes and types they belong to. Attention should particularly be paid to the fact that compound verbs are frequently equivalent to simple verb lexemes: *X untersteht dem Schutz von Y = Y concerne X = Y protegge X.*

In addition you will find some lexical entries specified according to our data bank design. The most important fields for translation are C, SP of C, SP-X, and C-X (X = F, D, I). E.g. you may learn from the entry *eaux usées* what you can do with this kind of water: *produire*, *assainir* or *épurer*, *évacuer*, *éliminer* or *supprimer*, *traiter* and *recevoir*, and you may also learn the German and Italian equivalents of these verbs having as arguments *Abwässer* and *acque di rifiuto* respectively. For a translator of German into French it is not only necessary to know the equivalents of the technical term *Abwässer*, it is equally useful to know that *ableiten* must be rendered in this context and in the context of each element of the object class <Abwässer> by *évacuer* and not by *dériver*, and *reinigen* by *épurer* or *assainir* and not by *nettoyer*. In the entry *police de la protection des eaux*, the following specific predicators are given: on peut *alerter* ou *appeler* la <police>, *signaler* qch. à la <police>, la <police> *intervient*, elle *interpelle* quelqu'un ou *contrôle* quelqu'un et *arrête* quelqu'un. The equivalents *alarmieren* or *rufen* or *holen*, *melden*, *eingreifen*, *überprüfen* or *kontrollieren*, and *festnehmen*, respectively *avvertire*, *notificare*, *intervenire*, *controllare*, *fermare* sometimes do not come to the translator's mind as quickly as he might wish.

In our extract Art. 24,3 there is an example of corresponding support verb constructions:

G. Vorkehrungen treffen
F. prendre des dispositions
I. prendere i provvedimenti

But in 24,4 the support verb constructions of French and Italian are used as equivalents of a simple verb in German: *vorkehren* (Swiss regional variant).

Let us finally demonstrate the usefulness of the entry of the predicative noun *Instruktion* (in the sense of its Swiss regional variant) and the mechanism of deletion and addition of the support verb (cf. Section 2.1.):

Instruktion

M : N
G : nfs
FL : \
V : Ausbildung
T : ina, non comptable
C : \
W : - (Sujet, Dat-obj) V_{sup}: geben
<Lerner>

		- (Sujet, Von-obj) <Lerner>	V_{sup}: bekommen
			Det: INDEF
S	:	\	
R	:	Schweiz	
F	:	instruction	
W_F	:	- (Sujet, Dat-obj) <Lerner>	V_{sup}: donner
		- (Sujet, De-obj) <Lerner>	V_{sup}: recevoir
I	:	istruzione	
W_I	:	- (Sujet, Dat-obj) <Lerner>	V_{sup}: dare
		- (Sujet, Dat-obj) <Lerner>	V_{sup}: ricevere

On the basis of the information given as well as on the basis of the semantic equivalence relation between a support verb construction and a nominal group (which is described in syntax by the deletion of the support verb), it is possible to "explain" the translations of a German sentence in Art. 24,3 into French and Italian:

G: Sie sind zu einer hinreichenden Instruktion ihres Personals verpflichtet

F: Ils feront en sorte que leur personnel *reçoive* une instruction suffisante

I: Essi sono pure tenuti a *dare* al personale una sufficiente istruzione

Remember first the semantic equivalence relation we have already alluded to in Section 2, which can be described in the following way:

$$N_0 \quad V_{sup} \, N_{pred} \quad = N_{pred} \quad \begin{matrix} \text{GEN} \\ \text{de} \\ \text{di} \end{matrix} \quad N_0$$

die Polizei trifft Vorkehrungen = die Vorkehrungen der Polizei
la police prend des dispositions = les dispositions de la police
la polizia prende i provvedimenti = i provvedimenti della polizia

We now recognize that the nominal group in the original German text (G) is to be put in relation with a support verb construction:

ihr Personal bekommt eine hinreichende Instruktion = eine hinreichende Instruktion ihres Personals

In the French version the support verb has been "added", it is the result of the translation of a German paraphrase that contains the support verb *bekommen*:

(Sie sind verpflichtet, dafür zu sorgen, daß ihr Personal eine hinreichende Instruktion *bekommt*) = > F

In order to get to the Italian version, the translation must start from a German paraphrase containing the support verb *geben*:

(Sie sind gehalten, ihrem Personal eine hinreichende Instruktion zu *geben*) = > I

In this case G. Gross (1989) speaks of a *converse* support verb and a *converse* support verb construction. Here we have two fine examples of translation by expansive paraphrases.

4. Application to a CALL project

We are about to apply the contrastive linguistic background knowledge we have gained so far to the development of a CALL system aiming at the perfection of language skills of *foreign language learners* and *translation trainees*. This system is supposed to help them to overcome the difficulties in translating lexical and terminological units together with or within their syntagmatic contexts. To this end, we propose translation exercises concerning the three aforementioned types of *lexicon-grammatical* phenomena. The user has to translate short sentences from French into German and the other way round. Starting from the following information in a bilingual data bank containing above all support verb constructions, compound words, and object class memberships for the arguments of simple verb lexemes, we can conceive such exercises.

Verbs:

Pol avance	sa chaise <Möbel>	vorrücken
Max avance	sa voiture <Fahrzeug>	vorfahren

Luc avance	son départ <Termin, Ereignis>	vorverlegen, verschieben
Max avance	mille francs à Luc <Geldsumme>	vorlegen, vorschießen
Luc avance	la pendule <Chronometer>	vorstellen
Pol avance	la thèse de doctorat de Max <Arbeit>	voranbringen, dem Ziel näherbringen
Sa thèse de doctorat avance <Arbeit>		vorankommen, dem Ziel näherkommen
Le balcon avance légèrement <lieu>		(her)vorspringen
La nuit avance <temps>		voranschreiten
La montre avance (de n minutes) <Chronometer>		(n Minuten) vorgehen

Support verb constructions (predicative nouns):

Max a une avance (de n minutes) sur Luc	einen Vorsprung haben
Luc fait une avance (de n francs) à Luc	einen Vorschuß geben
Pol donne de l'avancement à Luc <fonctionnaire>	befördern
Max fait des avances à Marie	Annäherungsversuche machen

Compound verbs:

être en avance	EP1	zu früh da sein
avancer en âge	CP1	älter werden
avancer sur Poss-O âge	CP1	seinem Alter voraus sein
avancer à grands pas	CP1	schnell vorankommen
avancer des gages à qn	C1	jdm. eine Lohnvorauszahlung gewähren
avancer un pion (sur l'échiquier)	C1P2	in den Angriff gehen die Offensive
avancer sur Poss-O temps	CP1	seiner Zeit voraus sein
avancer en grade	CP1	befördert werden
avancer prudemment	CADV	mit Bedacht vorgehen
s'avancer trop (+beaucoup)	CADV	zu optimistisch sein, zu weit gehen
être en avance sur son temps	EP1P2	seiner Zeit voraus sein

payer d'avance	CP1	im voraus bezahlen

Simulation of a dialog with the system

S: Traduisez s'il vous plaît: — S: System
(1) Max rückt seinen Stuhl vor — U: User
(2) Luc verlegt seine Abreise vor
(3) Pol ist zu früh da
(4) Max hat 10 Minuten Vorsprung vor Luc
(5) Seine Uhr geht eine Stunde vor
(6) Der Chef gibt Luc einen Vorschuß
(7) Der Minister befördert diesen Lehrer
(8) Pol macht einen Annäherungsversuch bei Marie
(9) Max ist seinem Alter voraus
(10) Luc ist seiner Zeit voraus
(11) Pol avance à grands pas
(12) Max avance prudemment
(13) Pol avancera cette somme à Luc
(14) Luc avance en grade
(15) Sa thèse de doctorat avance
(16) Le patron avance des gages à Luc
(17) Max avance de deux mètres
(18) Luc fait une avance à Marie
(19) Pol n'aurait pas dû avancer ça
(20) Il avait avancé que Luc refuserait de payer d'avance

U:
(19 Max avance sa chaise
(2) Luc avance son départ
(3) Pol est en avance
(4) Max a dix minutes d'avance sur Luc
(5) Sa montre avance d'une heure
(6) Le patron fait une avance à Luc
(7) Le ministre donne de l'avancement à ce professeur
(8) Pol fait des avances à Marie
(9) Max avance sur son âge
(10) Luc est en avance sur son temps (Luc avance sur son temps)
(11) Pol kommt schnell (mit Riesenschritten) voran
(12) Max geht mit Bedacht vor
(13) Pol wird diese Summe Luc vorlegen
(14) Luc wird befördert
(15) Seine Doktorarbeit kommt voran

(16) Der Chef gewährte Luc eine Lohnvorauszahlung
(17) Max fährt den Wagen zwei Meter vor
(18) Luc gibt Marie einen Vorschuß
(19) Pol hätte das nicht vorbringen sollen
(20) Er hatte vorgebracht, daß Luc sich weigern würde, im voraus zu bezahlen

S: Toutes les traductions sont OK.

S: Traduisez s'il vous plaît:
(1) Der Kundendienst ist ausgezeichnet
(2) Il viendra le samedi suivant
(3) Das spricht zu seinen Gunsten
(4) Sie sind in den roten Zahlen
(5) Luc a fait ses excuses à Marie
(6) Max hat die Vorlage gegeben
(7) Il a emprunté le vélo

U:
(1') Le service pour le client est excellent
(2') Er wird am nächsten Samstag kommen
(3') Ça parle en sa faveur
(4') Vous êtes dans les chiffres rouges
(5') Luc hat sich bei Marie entschuldigt
(6') Max a donné la passe
(7') Er ist mit dem Fahrrad gefahren.

S: La traduction de la phrase 5 est OK. Les phrases (1'), (3'), (4') und (6') ne sont pas acceptables en français. Les traductions de (2) et (7) sont des faux sens.
U: Pourquoi?
S: [lexical entries as well as trees resulting from the parsing and generation of the source and target sentences are shown]

Solution:
(1) Le service après vente est excellent
(2) Er wird am Samstag drauf kommen
(3) Ça milite en sa faveur
(4) Vous êtes dans le rouge
(5) Luc hat sich bei Marie entschuldigt
(6) Max a fait la passe
(7) Er hat das Fahrrad geliehen.

S: Traduisez s.v.p.:
(1) ein blaues Auge
(2) ohne Zweifel
(3) en premier lieu
(4) unter diesen Umständen
(5) auf diesem Gebiet
(6) auf der Straße
(7) il a examiné son malade
(8) il a enlevé son chapeau
(9) er gab das Versprechen zu kommen
(10) il a touché un chèque
(11) l'avertissement de Luc à Max
(12) il nous a augmenté
(13) er schwimmt im Geld
(14) er hat (die Nummer) gewählt

U:
(1) un oeil bleu
(2) sans doute
(3) in erster Stelle
(4) sous ces circonstances
(5) sur ce domaine
(6) sur la rue
(7) er hat seinen Patienten geprüft
(8) er hat seinen Hut ausgezogen
(9) il a donné la promesse de venir
(10) er hat einen Scheck angefaßt
(11) Lucs Nachricht an Max
(12) er hat uns erhöht
(13) il nage dans l'argent
(14) il a choisi (le numéro)

S: Les traductions sont ou bien inacceptables ou bien des faux sens.

Solution:
(1) un oeil au beurre noir
(2) sans aucun doute
(3) in erster Linie, an erster Stelle
(4) dans ces circonstances
(5) dans ce domaine, sur ce terrain
(6) dans la rue
(7) er hat seinen Patienten untersucht

(8) er hat seinen Hut abgesetzt
(9) il a promis de venir
(10) er hat einen Scheck abgehoben
(11) Lucs Warnung an Max
(12) er hat uns das Gehalt erhöht
(13) il roule sur l'or (il nage dans l'abondance)
(14) il a composé le numéro
fait

5. Conclusion

From the theoretical and methodological points of view, the following conclusion may be drawn: If you are aiming at (computer assisted) translation, you need lexicon-oriented grammatical knowledge represented in the empirically and theoretically well-founded *Lexicon Grammar* framework. Especially when you are working on authentic text corpora, you can find out that this formal syntactic approach is absolutely compatible on the semantic side with stereotype semantics (Putnam 1975) and with Wittgenstein's theory of language use (Wittgenstein 1953). Our specific predicators are not so far away from the stereotypical semantic properties of (compound) nouns proposed by Putnam, cf. his semantic description of *water*: thirst quenching etc. Moreover we can learn a lot about the meaning of (compound) nouns and technical terms if we detect how they are used in texts, i.e. if we look at their co-occurrences, because, as Wittgenstein puts it: "For a large class of cases - though not for all - in which we imply the word "meaning" it can be defined thus: the meaning of a word is its use in the language".

These complementary semantic theories also play an important role in Foreign Language Learning, Information Retrieval, and other fields of Applied Linguistics. They find, so to speak, their grammatical (and lexical) counterpart in *Lexicon Grammar*, which started around forty years ago with the famous slogan "Difference of meaning correlates with difference of distribution" (Harris).

Note

1. By "genuine compounds" we understand 'Komposita' or compounds in their traditional and structural sense (e.g. Fleischer 1971). From the computational-linguistic point of view they are isolated units (sequences of graphemes between two blancs) consisting of two or more bases.

2. The notation VN is equivalent to Harris' notation of deverbal nominals: V-n.

References

Benson, M., E. Benson & R. Ilson
1986 *The BBI Combinatory Dictionary of English: A Guide to Word Combinations.* Amsterdam/Philadelphia: Benjamins.

Böhmer, H.
1993 Komplexe Prädikatsausdrücke im Deutschen und Französischen - Theoretische Aspekte, kontrastive Aspekte und Aspekte der Anwendung. Diss. Uni Mainz. Frankfurt: Lang.

Bundesgesetz
1988 *Bundesgesetz über den Schutz der Gewässer gegen Verunreinigung (Gewässerschutzgesetz) vom 8. Oktober 1971, Stand am 1. Januar 1988 (Schweiz).*

Fleischer, W.
1975 *Wortbildung der deutschen Gegenwartssprache.* Tübingen: Niemeyer.

Gross, M.
1986 *Grammaire transformationnelle du français, 3 - Syntaxe de l'adverbe.* Paris: ASSTRIL.
1989 Les expressions figées. Une description des expressions françaises et ses conséquences théoriques. Rapport technique du L.A.D.L. Paris.

Gross, G.
1989 *Les Constructions Converses du Français.* Genève: Librairie Droz.

Harris, Z. S.
1957 "Co-occurrence and transformation in linguistic structure". *Language* 33:283-340.

Hausmann, F. J.
1985 Kollokationen im deutschen Wörterbuch. Ein Beitrag zur Theorie des lexikographischen Beispiels. In: Bergenholtz, H. & J. Mugdan (eds.). *Lexikographie und Grammatik. Akten des Essener Kolloquiums zur Grammatik im Wörterbuch, 28. bis 30.6.1984.* Tübingen: Niemeyer, pp. 118-129.

Ilgenfritz, P., N. Stephan-Gabinel & G. Schneider
1989 Langenscheidts Kontextwörterbuch Französisch-Deutsch. In: *Neues Wörterbuch zum Schreiben, Lernen, Formulieren.* Berlin: Langenscheidt.

Mel'cuk, I. A. *et al.*
1988 *Dictionnaire Explicatif et Combinatoire du Français Contemporain. Recherches Lexico-Sémantiques II.* Montréal: Les Presses de l'Université de Montréal.

Putnam, H.
1975 The meaning of "meaning". In: Gunderson, K. (ed.). *Language, Mind, and Knowledge.* Minneapolis: Minnesota Studies in the Philosophy of Science. Vol. VII, pp. 131-193.

Seelbach, D.
1990 Zur Entwicklung von bilingualen Mehrwortlexika Frz.-Dtsch.: Stützverbkonstruktionen und adverbiale Ausdrücke. In: Rieger, L. B. S. & L. B. R. Schaeder (eds.). *Lexikon und Lexikographie, (Sprache und Computer, Band 11).* Hildesheim: Georg Olms, pp. 179-207.

1991 Nominale Mehrwortausdrücke und prädikative Nomina im Französischen. In: Rolshoven, J. & D. Seelbach (eds.). *Linguistische Arbeiten: Romanistische Computerlinguistik.* Tübingen: Niemeyer, pp. 159-193.

1992 Zur Entwicklung von zwei- und mehrsprachigen lexikalischen Datenbanken und Terminologiedatenbanken. In: Kuhlen, R. (ed.). *Experimentelles und praktisches Information Retrieval. Festschrift für Gerhard Lustig.* Konstanz: Universitäts-Verlag, pp. 225-253.

Wittgenstein, L.

1953 *Philosophical Investigations*. Oxford: Basil Blackwell and Mott.

Appendix

Art. 1

Dem Schutze dieses Gesetzes unterstehen die ober- und unterirdischen, natürlichen und künstlichen, öffentlichen und privaten Gewässer mit Einschluß der Quellen.

Art. 17

Für die Ableitung und Reinigung der Abwässer sind die erforderlichen öffentlichen Kanalisationssysteme und zentralen Abwasserreinigungsanlagen zu erstellen. Der Bau der öffentlichen Kanalisationen hat gestützt auf generelle Projekte zu erfolgen, deren Ausdehnung und technische Ausgestaltung der zu erwartenden baulichen Entwicklung in angemessener Weise Rechnung tragen. In abgelegenen Gebieten oder solchen mit geringer Bevölkerungsdichte sind die Abwässer, wenn es die tatsächliche Gefährdung der ober- und unterirdischen Gewässer erlaubt, statt durch zentrale Abwasserreinigungsanlagen durch andere Systeme zu beseitigen.

Art. 24

1. Für die Herstellung, die Verarbeitung, den Umschlag, die Beförderung und die Lagerung von wassergefährdenden Stoffen, insbesondere von flüssigen Brenn- und Treibstoffen, sind die zum Schutze von Gewässern nötigen baulichen und technischen Vorrichtungen zu erstellen und regelmäßig zu kontrollieren.

2. Beim Umgang mit Straßen- und Schienenfahrzeugen, Motorschiffen, Flugzeugen, Maschinen u. dgl. sind alle erforderlichen Vorkehrungen zur Verhütung von Gewässerverunreinigungen zu treffen. Es ist verboten, im Bereiche von Gewässern Motorfahrzeuge, Maschinen u. dgl. zu reinigen und zu warten.

3. Die Eigentümer oder Inhaber von Einrichtungen zur Lagerung, zur Beförderung und zum Umschlag wassergefährdender Stoffe haben für deren einwandfreies Funktionieren, die Instandhaltung und die richtige Bedienung zu sorgen. Sie sind zu einer hinreichenden Instruktion ihres Personals verpflichtet. Die Einrichtungen sind in angemessenen Zeitabständen sachgemäß zu revidieren.

4. Die Eigentümer oder Inhaber von Einrichtungen im Sinne von Absatz 3 und die mit der Bedienung oder Wartung dieser Einrichtungen betrauten Personen haben allfällige Stoffverluste sowie die erkennbare Gefahr von Verlusten unverzüglich der Gewässerschutzpolizei zu melden. Sie haben vorbehältlich der Anordnungen der zuständigen kantonalen Behörde von sich aus alles Zumutbare vorzukehren, um eine mögliche Gewässerverunreinigung zu verhindern. Die an den Einrichtungen festgestellten Mängel sind sofort zu beheben.

Art. 1

La présente loi concerne les eaux superficielles et souterraines, naturelles et artificielles, publiques et privées, y compris les sources.

Art. 17

Pour assurer l'évacuation et l'épuration des eaux usées, il y a lieu d'établir les réseaux de canalisations publiques et les stations centrales nécessaires à cet effet. Les canalisations publiques seront aménagées selon des plans directeurs d'égouts tenant compte d'une manière convenable de l'extension du réseau et de l'équipement technique qu'exigera l'évolution prévisible de la construction. Dans les régions retirées ou dans celles qui ont une faible densité de population et si les dangers qui menacent effectivement les eaux souterraines et superficielles le justifient, on utilisera pour les eaux usées, en lieu et place de stations centrales d'épuration, d'autres systèmes d'élimination.

Art. 24

1. Pour la fabrication, le traitement, le transvasement, le transport et l'entreposage de matières pouvant altérer les eaux, notamment de combustibles et de carburants liquides, il faut disposer de constructions et d'installations de sécurité permettant d'assurer la protection des eaux, constructions et installations seront régulièrement contrôlées.

2. Ceux qui utilisent des véhicules routiers, du matériel ferroviaire roulant, des bateaux à moteur, des aéronefs, des machines et d'autres engins similaires doivent prendre toutes les dispositions nécessaires pour prévenir la pollution des eaux. Il est interdit de nettoyer des véhicules à moteur, des machines et d'autres engins similaires ou d'assurer leur entretien à proximité des eaux.

3. Les propriétaires ou exploitants d'installations servant à l'entreposage, au transport et au transvasement de liquides altérant les eaux veilleront à ce qu'elles fonctionnent convenablement, soient maintenues en bon état et soient utilisées selon les règles. Ils feront en sorte que leur personnel reçoive une instruction suffisante. Les installations seront revisées à des intervalles convenables par du personnel spécialisé.

4. Les propriétaires ou exploitants d'installations au sens du 3e alinéa ainsi que les personnes chargées d'assurer l'exploitation, l'entretien et la surveillance de ces installations devront signaler immédiatement à la police de la protection des eaux toute fuite ou tout risque décelable de fuite de matières liquides. Ils prendront de leur propre chef, avant que la police des eaux n'intervienne, toutes les dispositions qu'on est en droit d'attendre d'eux pour prévenir une pollution des eaux. Il sera immédiatement remédié aux défauts constatés.

Art. 1

La presente legge protegge le acque superficiali e sotterranee, naturali e artificiali, pubbliche e private, comprese le sorgenti.

Art. 17

Per l'evacuazione e la depurazione delle acque di rifiuto devono essere costruite le necessarie canalizzazioni pubbliche e stazioni centrali di depurazione. Le canalizzazioni pubbliche devono essere costruite secondo progetti generali che tengano convenientemente conto dell'ampliamento e del perfezionamento tecnico correlativi al presumibile sviluppo edilizio. Nelle zone discoste o in quelle di debole densità demografica, le acque di rifiuto devono essere eliminate con sistemi diversi dalle stazioni centrali di depurazione, purchè lo giustifichi la pericolosità effettiva per le acque superficiali o sotterranee.

Art. 24

1. Per la fabbricazione, il trattamento, il travaso, il trasporto e il deposito di sostanze nocive per le acque, segnatamente di combustibili e carburanti liquidi, si devono attuare e controllare periodicamente le strutture e i dispositivi tecnici necessari alla protezione delle acque.

2. Nell'impiego di veicoli stradali e ferroviari, natanti a motore, aeromobili, macchine e simili, si devono prendere tutti i provvedimenti necessari per prevenire l'inquinamento delle acque. In prossimità delle acque è proibito provvedere alla pulizia e alla manutenzione di veicoli a motore, macchine e simili.

3. I proprietari o esercenti di impianti di deposito, trasporto e travaso di sostanze nocive per le acque devono attendere all'ineccepibile funzionamento, alla manutenzione e alla confacente utilizzazione degli stessi. Essi sono pure tenuti a dare al personale una sufficiente istruzione. Gli impianti vanno, ad intervalli opportuni, sottoposti ad adeguate verifiche.

4. I proprietari o esercenti di impianti a tenore del capoverso 3 come anche le persone adibite all'esercizio o alla manutenzione degli stessi devono notificare immediatamente alla polizia di protezione delle acque tutti i casi di perdite o di pericolo ravvisabile di perdite di sostanze. Riservate le disposizioni dell'autorità cantonale competente, essi devono prendere di moto proprio tutti i provvedimenti che si possono pretendere da loro per prevenire un eventuale inquinamento delle acque. Ai difetti costatati negli impianti dev'essere posto immediatamente rimedio.

Compound Nouns

die ober- und unterirdischen Gewässer	Adj und Adj N
les eaux superficielles et souterraines	N Adj et Adj
le acque superficiali e sotterranee	N Adj e Adj
die natürlichen und künstlichen Gewässer	Adj und Adj N
les eaux naturelles et artificielles	N Adj et Adj
le acque naturali e artificiali	N Adj e Adj
die öffentlichen und privaten Gewässer	Adj und Adj N
les eaux publiques et privées	N Adj et Adj
le acque publiche e private	N Adj e Adj
Abwässer	Prep_N
les eaux usées	N Adj
le acque di rifiuto	N di N
öffentliche Kanalisationssysteme	Adj N
des réseaux de canalisations publiques	N de N/Adj
le canalizzazioni publiche	N Adj
zentrale Abwasserreinigungsanlagen	Adj N
des stations centrales d'épuration	N Adj/de N
stazioni centrali di depurazione	N Adj/di N
öffentliche Kanalisationen	Adj N
les canalisations publiques	N Adj
le canalizzazioni publiche	N Adj
abgelegene Gebiete	Adj N
des régions retirées	N Adj
le zone discoste	N Adj
Gebiete mit geringer Bevölkerungsdichte	N/Prep Adj N
des régions à faible densité de population	N/à Adj N de N
(des régions qui ont une faible densité de population)	
zone di debole densità demografica	N/di Adj N Adj

wassergefährdende Stoffe	Adj N
des matières altérant les eaux	N V-ant W
(des matières qui peuvent altérer les eaux	
des matières pouvant altérer les eaux)	
le sostanze nocive per le acque	N Adj Prep N
flüssige Brenn- und Treibstoffe	Adj V-und V N
des combustibles et carburants liquides	N et N Adj
combustibili e carburanti liquidi	N e N Adj
Straßen- und Schienenfahrzeuge	N- und N_N
des véhicules routiers et des	N Adj et N̄ Prep N
véhicules sur rail	
veicoli stradali e ferroviari	N Adj e Adj
Motorschiffe	N_N
des bateaux à moteur	N‾à N
natanti a motore	N a N
Motorfahrzeuge	N_N
véhicules à moteur	N‾à N
veicoli a motore	N a N
Gewässerschutzpolizei	N_VN_N
la police de la protection des eaux	N‾/de N̄ de N
la polizia di protezione delle acque	N/di N di N
Sammelstellen	V_N
centres de ramassage	N‾de N
i servizi necessari per la racolta	N/Adj Prep N
bauliche und technische Vorrichtungen	Adj und Adj N
constructions et installations	N et N Adj
strutture e i dispositivi tecnici	N et N Adj
Gewässerschutz	N_VN
la protection des eaux	N‾de N
la protezione delle acque	N di N
Gewässerverunreinigung	N_VN
la pollution des eaux	N‾de N
l'inquinamento delle acque	N di N

generelle Abwasserprojekte	Adj N
des plans directeurs d'égout	N Adj de N
progetti generali di depurazione	N Adj di N
die zu erwartende bauliche Entwicklung	zu V-end Adj N
l'évolution prévisible de la construction	N Adj de N
il presumibile sviluppo edilizio	Adj N Adj
Flüssigkeitsverlust	Adj N_VN
fuites de matières liquides	N de N̄ Adj
perdite di sostanze	N di N
wassergefährdende Flüssigkeiten	N Adj
liquides altérant les eaux	N V-ant W
sostanze nocive per le acque	N Adj Prep N
technische Vorrichtungen	Adj N
installations techniques	N Adj
dispostivi technici	N Adj
die zuständige kantonale Behörde	Adj Adj N
l'autorité cantonale compétente	N Adj Adj
l'autorità cantonale competente	N Adj Adj

Compound Adverbs

mit Einschluß GEN N	PCGENN
y compris N	
compreso N	
in angemessener Weise	PAC
d'une manière convenable	PCA
convenientemente	PADV
en lieu et place de N	PCONJN
beim Umgang mit N	PCPN
nell'impiego di N	PCDN
en utilisant N	(gérondif)

in der Nähe GEN N von		PCGENN
à proximité de N		PCDN
in prossimità di N		PCDN
in angemessenen Zeitabständen		PAC
à des intervalles convenables		PCA
ad intervalli opportuni		PCA
vorbehaltlich N		PADVN
sous réserve de N		PCDN
riservato N		PADVN
von sich aus		PCP
de leur propre chef		PAC
di moto proprio		PCA

Compound Verbs

N_0	untersteht dem Schutz GEN N von	CDAT1GENN
N	concerne N_0	(verb)
N	protegge N_0	(verb)
N_0	trägt N_{Dat} Rechnung	C1DATN
N_0	tient compte de N	C1PN
N_{D0}	tiene conto di N	C1PN
(N_0	takes N_1 into account	CNP2)
N_0	assure l'entretien de N_1	C1DN
N_0	maintient N_1 en bon éta t	CNP2
N_0	provedde alla manutenzione di N	CP1DN
N_0	wartet N_1	(verb)
N_0	sottopone N_1 a verifiche	CNP2
N_0	verifica N_1	(verb)
N_0	unterzieht N_1 einer Kontrolle Prüfung	CNDAT2

N_0	kontrolliert	N_1	
	überprüft		(verb)
	revidiert		
N_0	soumet N_1 à une vérification		CNP2
N_0	revise	N_1	(verb)
	vérifie		
N_0	pone rimedio a N_1		C1PN
N_0	remédie à N_1		(verb)
N_0	behebt N_1		(verb)
N_0	bedient N_1 richtig		CADVN
N_0	utilise N_1 selon les règles		CNP2
N_0	utilizza N_1 confacentemente		CADVN
N_0	funktioniert einwandfrei		CADV
N_0	fonctionne convenablement		CADV
N_0	funziona ineccepibilmente		CADV

Support verb constructions (predicative nouns)

N_0	prend des	mesures		pour N_1
		dispositions		
N_0	trifft	Maßnahmen		zu N_1
	ergreift	Vorkehrungen		
N_0	prende	le misure		
		i provvedimenti		per N_1
N_0	dà	una istruzione	a	N_1
	riceve		da	
N_0	donne	une instruction	à	N_1
	reçoit		de	
N_0	gibt	eine Instruktion (Ausbildung)	DAT	N_1
	bekommt		von	

eaux_souterraines/M: N Adj/G: nfp, les/F:/S:Hydr./SP: capter-; faire le captage de-; enrichir-/C: <eaux superficielles et souterraines>/SP von C: polluer-; protéger-; déposer qch. dans-; introduire qch dans-/
D: unterirdisches Gewässer/M-D: Adj N/
G-D: nn/F:/V-D: unterirdisches Wasser; Grundwasser/SP-D: fassen-, Fassungen (vornehmen) von-; anreichern-/C-D: <ober- und unterirdische Gewässer>/SP von C-D: verunreinigen-; schützen-; ablagern in-; hineinschütten, (versickern lassen) in-/
...I: acqua sotterranea/G-I: nf/F:/V-I: acqua profonda/SP-I: prendere-, (fare) le prese di-; rialimentare-/C-I:<acque superficiali e sotterranee> /SP von C-I: inquinare-; proteggere-; depositare in-; immettere in-/

eaux_superficielles/M: N Adj/G: nfp, les/F:/S: Hydr./SP: préparer-; exploiter du gravier (+ sable) dans-/C: <eaux superficielles et souterraines>/SP von C: polluer-; protéger-; déposer qch. dans-; introduire qch. dans-/
D: oberirdisches Gewässer/M-D: Adj N/G-D: nn/F-D:/V-D:/
SP-D: aufbereiten-, Kies (+ Sand) gewinnen aus-/C-D und SP von C-D wie oben/
...I: acque superficiali/M-I: N Adj/G-I: nfp/F-I:/V-I:/
SP-I: preparare-, fare l'estrazione di ghiaia (+ sabbia) di-/C-I und SP von C-I wie oben/

eaux_publiques/M: N Adj/G: nfp, des/F:/S: Jur./SP: faire du ski nautique sur-; faire du bateau à moteur sur-/C: <eaux publiques et privées>/
D: öffentliche Gewässer/M-D: Adj N/SP-D: Wasserski fahren auf-, Motorboot fahren auf-/
...I: acque pubblicche/M-I: N Adj

eaux_privées/M: N Adj/G: nfp, des/F:/S:Jur./SP: faire du ski nautique sur; faire du bateau à moteur sur/C:<eaux publiques et privées>/
D: private Gewässer/M-D: Adj N/
...I: acque private/M-I: N Adj

eaux_usées/M: N Adj/G: nfp, les/F:/S:/SP: produire; assainir, épurer; déverser; évacuer; éliminer, supprimer; traiter; recevoir/D: Abwässer/M-D: Prep_N/G-D: nnp/F:/S:/V-D: Abwasser/
SP-D: produzieren; reinigen; einleiten; ableiten; beseitigen; behandeln; sammeln/
.../I: acque di rifiuto/M-I: N di N/F:/S:/SP-I: produrre; depurare; immettere; evacuare; eliminare; trattare; raccogliere/

Haushaltsabwasser (acque di rifiuto provenienti da abitazioni; les eaux usées qui proviennent d'habitations), *Industrieabwässer* (acque di rifiuto da aziende industriali; les eaux usées d'entreprises industrielles), *Kühlwasser* (acqua di raffreddamento; eaux de refroidissement), *Abwässer von Werkstätten, Landwirtschaft, Baustellen, Schiffen* etc. (acque di rifiuto da aziende artigianali, agricole, da cantieri, da imbarcazioni; les eaux usées d'entreprises artisanales, d'exploitations agricoles, de chantiers, de bateaux).

matières altérant les eaux/M: N V-ant N/G: nfp/F:/V: matières pouvant altérer les eaux/V: matières qui peuvent altérer les eaux/V: liquides altérant les eaux/SP: fabriquer-; traiter-; transvaser-; transporter-; entreposer-/D: wassergefährdende Stoffe/M-D: Adj N/G-D: nfp/F:/SP-D: herstellen-; verarbeiten-; umschlagen-; befördern-; lagern-/I: sostanze nocive per le acque/M: N Adj Prep N/G-I: nfp/F:/SP-I: fabbricare-; trattare-; travasare-; trasportare-; depositare-/

combustibles et carburants liquides/M:N et N Adj/G: nmp/F:/D: flüssige Brenn- und Treibstoffe/M-D: Adj V- und V_N/G-D: nfp/I: combustibili e carburanti liquidi/M-I: N e N Adj/ G-D: nmp/C:<matières altérant les eaux>/C-D:<wassergefährdende Stoffe>/C-I:<sostanze nocive per le acque>/SP von C: fabriquer-; traiter-; transvaser-; transporter-; entreposer-/SP von C-D: *wie oben*/SP von C-I: *wie oben*

véhicule à moteur/M: N à N/G: nm/F:/S:/D: Motorfahrzeug/M-D: N_N/G-D: nn/F:/S:/I: veicolo a motore/M-I: N a N/G-I: nm/F:/S:/SP: utiliser-; nettoyer-; assurer l'entretien de-/ SP-D: umgehen mit-; reinigen-; warten-/SP-I: utilizzare-; provvedere alla pulizia di-; provvedere alla manutenzione di-/

bateau à moteur/M: N à N/G: nm/F:/S:/D:Motorschiff/M-D: N_N/G-D: nn/F:/S:/I: natante a motore/M-I: N a N/G-I:nm/F:/S:/C:<véhicule à moteur>/C-D: <Motorfahrzeug>/C-I: <veicolo a motore>/SP von C: utiliser-; nettoyer-; assurer l'entretien de -/SP von C-D:*wie oben*/ SP von C-I: *wie oben*

véhicule routier/M: N Adj/G: nm/F:/S:/D:Straßenfahrzeug/M-D: N_N/ G-D: nn/I: veicolo stradale/M-I: N Adj/G-I: nm/C:<véhicule à moteur>/C-D: <Motorfahrzeug>/C-I: <veicolo a motore>/SP von C: utiliser-; nettoyer-; assurer l'entretien de -/SP von C-D:wie oben/SP von C-I: *wie oben véhicule sur rail*/M: N Prep N/G: nm/F:/S:/V: matériel ferroviaire roulant/D: Schienenfahrzeug/M-D: N_N/G-D: nn/I: veicolo ferroviario/M-I: N Adj/G-D: nm/C: <véhicule à moteur> /C-D: <Motorfahrzeug> /C-I: <veicolo a motore> /SP von C: utiliser-; nettoyer-; assurer l'entretien de -/SP von C-D:*wie oben*/SP von C-I: *wie oben*

Einrichtungen zur Lagerung, zur Beförderung und zum Umschlag wassergefährdender Stoffe/M:/G:/F:/I: impianti di deposito, trasporto e travaso di sostanze nocive per le acque/F: installation servant à l'entreposage, au transport et au transvasement de liquides altérant les eaux/SP: betreiben-; warten-; wachen über-; richtig bedienen-; - einwandfrei funktionieren/SP-I: esercire-; provvedere alla manutenzione di -; sottoporre- a verifiche; utilizzare confacentemente-; - funzionare ineccepibilmente/ SP-F: exploiter-; assurer l'entretien de-; reviser-, vérifier-; utiliser - selon les règles; -fonctionner convenablement/

police de la protection des eaux/M: N de N de N/G: nfs/V:/T:/C: <police> /D: Gewässerschutzpolizei/M-D: N_VN_N/G-D: nfs/I: polizia di protezione delle acque/M-I: N di N di N/_G-I: nfs/SP: alerter-, appeler-; signaler qch à -; -intervenir; -interpeller, -contrôler; -arrêter/SP-D: holen-, rufen-; etwas DAT - melden; -eingreifen; -überprüfen, -kontrollieren; - festnehmen/SP-I: avvertire-; notificare qc a -; - intervenire; -controllare; - fermare

Abwasseranlage /M: Prep_N_N/G: nf/V: Abwasserreinigungsanlage/ F: installation dépuration/I: impianto di depurazione/SP: bauen -; betreiben -; unterhalten - (warten -); periodisch untersuchen - (regelmäßig kontrollieren -)/ SP-F: construire -; exploiter -; entretenir - (maintenir en bon état -); vérifier périodiquement le bon fonctionnement de - (contrôler régulièrement -)/SP-I: costruire -; esercire - (provvedere all'esercizio di -); provvedere alla manutenzione di _;sottoporre periodicamente a verifica il buon funzionamento di - (controllare periodicamente -)/

öffentliche Abwasseranlage /M: Adj N/G: nf/F: installation d'épuration publique/I: Impianto di depurazione pubblico/C: <Abwasseranlage> /C-F: <installation d'épuration> /C-I: <impianto di depurazione> /SP von C: wie oben/SP-F von C: wie oben/SP-I von C: wie oben/

zentrale Abwasseranlage /M: Adj N/G: nf/F: station centrale d'épuration/I: stazione centrale di depurazione/C: <Abwasseranlage> /C-F:

<installation d’épuration>/C-I: <impianto di depurazione>/SP von C: wie oben/SP-F von C: wie oben/SP-I von C: wie oben/

private Abwasseranlage /M:Adj N/G: nf/F: installation d’épuration privée/I: impianto di depurazione privato/C: <Abwasseranlag>/C-F: <installation d’épuration>/C-I: <impianto di depurazione>/SP von C: wie oben/SP-F von C: wie oben/SP-I von C: wie oben/

pollution des eaux/M: N de N/G: nf/F:/V: pollution/D: Gewässerverunreinigung/M-D: N_VN//G-D: nf/F:/V: Verunreinigung/I: inquinamento delle acque/M-I: N di N/G-D: nm/V: inquinamento/SP: empêcher-, prévenir-, remédier à-; déterminer l’existence de -; être la cause de-, occasionner-; - exister/ SP-D: verhindern-, abwehren-, zuvorkommen DAT-, beheben-; feststellen-; verursachen-; - vorliegen/SP-I: prevenire -, rimediare a- (porre rimedio a -); accertare-; essere cagione di (cagionare-); - esistere;

Part IV

Lexicography and the lexicon

Lexicology and lexicography: Poor relations, competition, or co-operation?

Leonhard Lipka

1. Introduction

In the eighth edition of the *Concise Oxford Dictionary of Current English* (1990) *poor relation* is defined as "an inferior or subordinate member of a family or any other group". Is lexicography the poor relation of lexicology or linguistics in general, since the latter provides the theoretical foundations for lexicography? Is it merely applied lexicology? What are the relations between these two disciplines concerned with words?

In the dictionary mentioned, *lexicography* is defined as "the compiling of dictionaries", while *lexicology* is said to be "the study of the form, history, and meaning of words". Obviously, the first definition sounds very practical, while the second one seems far more interesting, and both appear unrelated. Nevertheless, the subject matter of both disciplines is the same, namely words, lexis, or the lexicon - the topic of our conference.

This will come as a surprise to no one. But the extent to which the theoretical linguist/lexicologist and the practising lexicographer compete or cooperate is certainly a legitimate question to discuss. As we all know, long before the advent of linguistics and the coining of the term *lexicology*, lexicographers were busily writing dictionaries. Lexicography is no Cinderella or merely the applied stepchild of lexicology, but rather a brother or sister with some degree of family resemblance.

1.1.

Let us, therefore, have a closer look at the complex *relationship* between the two. To begin with, we will sketch briefly the general contributions linguistics has made to lexicography, before going on to consider in detail the nature and status of definitions and their function in dictionary entries. This includes purely verbal definitions, as well as ostensive definitions by means of illustrations. A number of concrete cases will then be studied in detail and, finally, we will draw some conclusions concerning the status of the two lexical disciplines and the extent to which they co-operate.

1.2.1.

If we now consider the influence of linguistics on lexicographic practice in general, we can claim that the internal development of linguistic theory is reflected, with some delay, in the work of the lexicographer. Thus, during the time of structuralism, language was seen as an abstract system of signs, neatly separated from extralinguistic reality, and the two were not to be confused. Consequently, dictionaries proper were clearly distinguished from encyclopedias. A prototypical case in point is the *Oxford English Dictionary*, the OED, and all the dictionaries which are derived from it, especially the *Concise Oxford Dictionary,* the COD, up to its seventh edition (1982).[1] In structural semantics, Coseriu made out a case for a strict separation of *Bedeutung* "sense" and *Bezeichnung* "reference".

1.2.2.

The later development, away from a purely language-immanent approach, can be characterized by the catchword *pragmatization*. The existence of language variation was already recognized in lexicography before the dawning of this new perspective, and an ever more refined system of labels for user-related and use-related varieties of English was produced by most dictionary makers. As early as 1979, the *Collins Dictionary of the English Language* listed special consultants and contributors for Scottish, Caribbean, Indian, Canadian, Irish, East, West, and South African, and Australian Englishes, and 14 urban dialects. Chomsky's abstraction of an ideal speaker/hearer in a perfectly homogenous speech community has clearly disappeared by this time. Both British and American dictionaries of practically any size (except for those from Oxford mentioned earlier) had also long given up the strict separation of linguistic and encyclopedic knowledge and included all sorts of biographical, geographical, technical, and other information.

Perhaps the most striking end-point of this line of change can be seen in the latest editions of two famous learners' dictionaries which came out last year: *The Oxford Advanced Learner's Dictionary. Encyclopedic Edition* and the *Longman Dictionary of English Language and Culture*, which replaces the second edition of the *Longman Dictionary of Contemporary English*, or LDCE. The former, the encyclopedic edition, now contains 4,500 encyclopedic entries covering people and places, politics and current affairs, history and the arts and also special articles on British and American life and institutions. So-called *Mini-Notes* outline special connotations, e.g. of the verb *to queue*. *The Longman Dictionary of English Language and Culture* claims 15,000 new cultural and encyclopedic entries on British and American people, organizations, life, literature, and cultural associations, e.g. with the word *flag* in America and with *garden party* in England, explained in so-called *Cultural Notes*.

1.2.3.

It all started in 1978, when the first edition of the *LDCE* was in several ways a pioneering trendsetter. It introduced so-called *Usage Notes* to show the connection of words with others (eg *rent* and *hire*, *tennis*, *racket*, *court*), to show fine differences of meaning (*lonely*, *solitary*, *alone*) and to show unacceptable sentences marked by an asterisk. The dictionary also used a computer-controlled defining vocabulary of 2,000 words.

The second edition of the *LDCE* (1987) showed pragmatization proper in two ways: 1. by the addition of a system of so-called *Language Notes*, dealing with topics such as: addressing people, apologies, criticism and praise, invitations and offers, politeness, thanks, which are treated at great length, and 2. by an introductory essay on "Pragmatics and the Dictionary" by Geoffrey Leech & Jenny Thomas.

1.3.

A similar development can be seen in non-alphabetical, or thematic, lexicography. Its history is discussed in great detail in McArthur (1986). Here, words are described in an arrangement not dictated by the coincidence of the alphabet, but organized in groups dealing with the same themes, representing the internal coherence of the vocabulary.

1.3.1.

According to McArthur (1986:119), for most people "the only serious example of a thematic wordbook" is Peter Mark Roget's *Thesaurus of English Words and Phrases*, published in 1852. In this pioneering work the English lexicon was classified into six classes: (1) abstract relations, (2) space, (3) matter, (4) intellect, (5) volition, and (6) emotion, religion, and morality, with further subclassification into sections like: existence, relation, quantity etc, and finally into so-called heads. This taxonomy is highly abstract, with a largely Latinate superstructure, where hard facts like birds, beasts, and animals almost vanish from sight. Since its first appearance, Roget's *Thesaurus* has gone through many editions, reflecting the expansion of the vocabulary and scientific, cultural, and social changes. However, the basic structure grouping items according to logical connection, association, and semantic likeness, has remained unaltered. The *Thesaurus* also presupposes a user who knows the meanings of words, their differences, and the principles of derivation and compounding. It therefore neither provides productive rules of word-formation, nor even definitions of words.

1.3.2.

A completely new kind of non-alphabetical vocabulary reference book is the *Longman Lexicon of Contemporary English* (1981), the LLCE. As its author Tom McArthur (1981:vi) puts it in the preface, it has "fourteen "semantic fields" of a pragmatic, everyday nature", e.g. A: Life and Living Things, B: The Body: Its Functions and Welfare, C: People and the Family etc, which provide the macrostructure of the *Lexicon*. These 14 themes, or major topics, each contain a range of sub-themes, such as: living creatures, animals/mammals, birds etc., with further subclassification into so-called "sets", which form the microstructure. Thus the lexical set A 73, *waterbirds*, contains the words *heron, stork, pelican, swan*, and *kingfisher*, together with illustrations of these birds, and a definition of *waterbird* as "any bird which lives mainly or generally in and around esp. fresh water". The meanings of the other nouns are not specified, but defined by means of a visual image, by showing. Such a demonstration can be called an "ostensive definition". In the next word set in the *Lexicon*, A 74, *common wild birds,* the same procedure is used for *finch, wren, pigeon, blackbird, sparrow, thrush, starling, robin, swallow, swift*, but verbal definitions are given for *magpie, lark, cuckoo, titmouse*, and *dove*. Further sets for classes of birds include A 76, *unusual birds,* which contains ostensive definitions for *cockatoo* (an Australian type of parrot with a crest), *toucan, peacock*, and *ostrich*. Verbal definitions are clearly judged unnecessary for the intended user of the *Lexicon*, the foreign learner.

With other kinds of words, e.g. adjectives like *funny*, defining by using pictorial material is obviously not appropriate. *Funny* may belong to the lexical set B 111, *showing poor bodily condition*, which also contains other words like *ill, unhealthy, unwell, unfit, sick, bad, dizzy* etc. In this case only verbal definitions can show the differences between the synonymous words, but McArthur here also uses style labels (like *infml*, *AmE*, *ScotE* etc.) and examples of usage in context. *Funny* in B 111 has two senses:

(1) "slightly unwell" and (2) "slightly mad", of which only the first bears the label *infml*. The index to the *Lexicon*, however, reveals that *funny* has two additional meanings, besides those in B 111, namely "amusing" (K 3) and "peculiar" (N 68). In the lexical set K 3 it is grouped together with *entertaining, amusing, diverting, comic* etc., in N 68 with *strange, odd, peculiar, queer* etc.

The *LLCE* provides a compact description of the central vocabulary of the English language. It contains some 15,000 items, with definitions based on the 2,000-word defining vocabulary introduced in the *LDCE* (1978) and does not pretend to be exhaustive. It is firmly rooted in the view that language and the world cannot be interpreted independently of each other, and that our linguistic and encyclopedic knowledge is stored as a network of associations in a conceptual framework. As McArthur (1981:vi) puts it: "The alphabet ... places animals and zoos, uncles and aunts far apart ... whereas in the human mind such words go close together".

2. The nature and status of definitions

Let us now turn to the nature and status of definitions in lexicographic practice and lexicological theory. We have just seen that in certain kinds of thematic wordbooks definitions may be missing altogether, as in Roget's *Thesaurus* and partly also in the *Longman Lexicon*. Clearly, this has to do with the type of user and use, namely the native speaker on the one hand and the advanced learner with a considerable body of encyclopedic knowledge on the other. As regards the theoretical status of definitions in lexicology, with the exception of some comments on the topic in the 1960s by Uriel Weinreich and the proposals made in Wierzbicka (1985) - also in her earlier work - there is not much to report.

2.1.

Having used repeatedly, in connection with lexical sets in *LLCE*, the verb *contain*, and keeping in mind also the importance of the CONTAINER schema in Cognitive Linguistics, I will now pick out this verb and its derivatives to illustrate the defining practice in dictionaries and its function. We will compare the following definitions of *contain* from the *LDCE* 2 (1987), *COD* 8 (1990), and *COBUILD* (1987):

(1a)
LDCE 2:
1. to hold; have within itself or as a part ...
2. to hold back; keep under control or within limits ...
3. *tech* to surround (esp. an angle) ...

(1b)
COD 8:
1. hold or be capable of holding within itself; include, comprise
2. (of measures) consist of or be equal to (*a gallon contains eight pints*)
3. prevent (an enemy, difficulty, etc.) from moving or extending
4. control or restrain (oneself, one's feelings, etc.)
5. (of a number) be divisible by (a factor) without a remainder

(1c)
COBUILD:
1. If something such as a box, bag, room, or place *contains* a particular thing, it has that thing inside it ...
2. If something *contains* something else, it has the other thing amongst its parts or ingredients ...
3. If a piece of writing, speech, or painting *contains* a statement, idea, or image, it has that statement, idea, or image in it ...
4. If an account, idea, system etc. *contains* ...
5. To *contain* something means
   5.1 to prevent it from spreading ...
   5.2 to keep it within a particular area ...
   5.3 to enclose or form the boundary of an area ...
6. If you *contain* a feeling such as excitement or anger, or if you *contain* yourself, you prevent yourself from showing your feelings ...

In all three dictionaries, the verb *contain* is treated as a case of polysemy with up to six different senses. The controlled defining vocabulary of the *LDCE* 2 accounts for a certain simplicity of the definitions, but some of the illustrative examples left out in (1a) for sense 2, namely *Try to contain your enthusiasm/anger, Doctors are struggling to contain the epidemic,* show the equivalent to the *COD's* senses 3 and 4. The possible subjects and objects of *contain* are given in brackets in the *COD* and as open lists in the *COBUILD*. The definitions in this dictionary, with their extraordinary length, result from the *COBUILD's* policy of using complete sentences, in order to show the word in natural English.

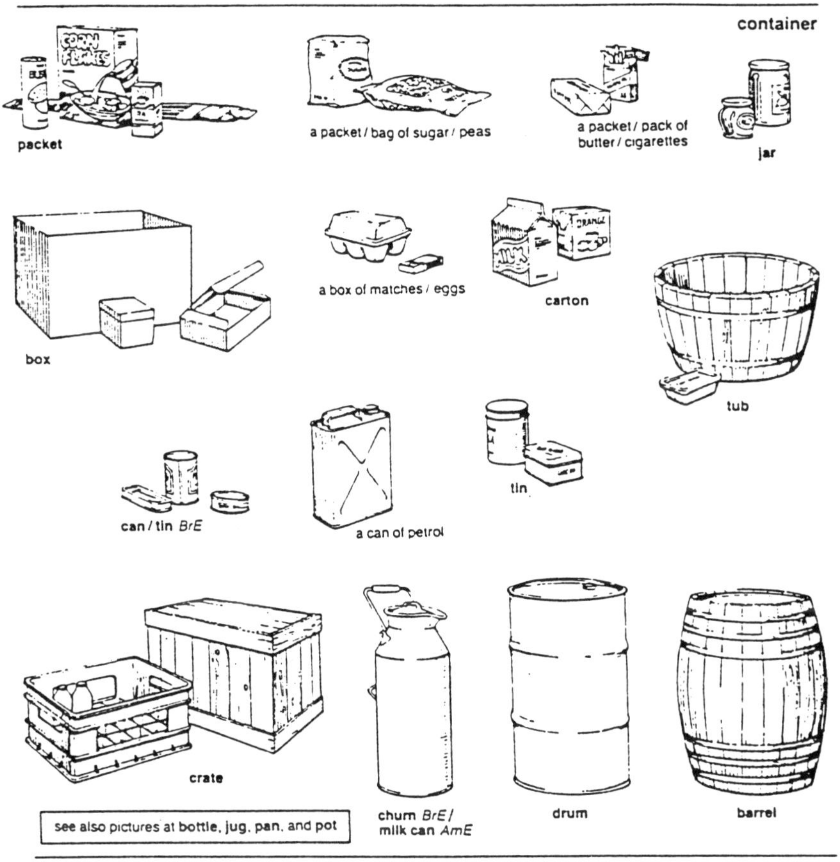

Figure 1. Container in LDCE 2

With regard to derivatives, all three dictionaries give very similar two senses for *container*, but only LDCE 2 and COD 8 also mention *containerize*, as a main entry, and *containerization*, within this headword, because of its predictable meaning.

The illustration *Figure 1* gives a visual representation of the range of objects which make up the complex functional category *container*.

As can be seen from the illustrations, there is considerable variation and fuzziness within some subcategories such as *packet*, *pack*, *bag*, and *can*. This also holds for various containers for liquids, as the next group of pictures with definitions, Figure 2 and Figure 3, show i.e. the denotata for *bottle, carafe, decanter*, and *flask*.

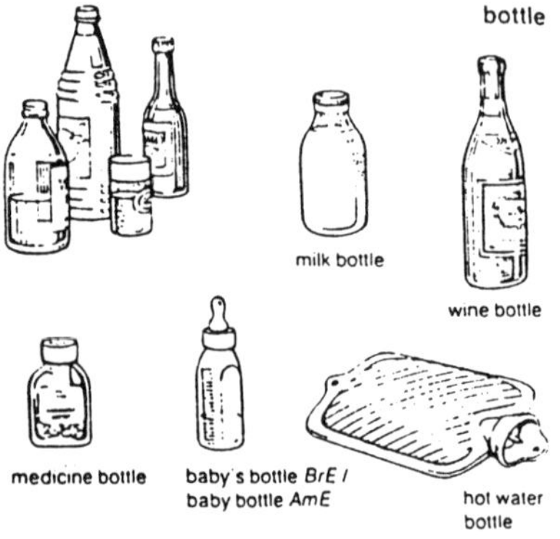

see also pictures at decanter and flask

bot·tle[1] /'bɒtl‖'bɑːtl/ *n* **1** [C] a container for liquids, usu. made of glass or plastic, with a rather narrow neck or mouth, and usu. no handle: *an empty milk bottle|to unscrew the top of a bottle|to uncork a wine bottle|(infml) Why don't we crack open another bottle of champagne?* **2** [C (of)] also **bot·tle·ful** /-fʊl/— the quantity held by a bottle: *We drank a whole bottle/two bottlefuls of wine!* **3** [*the*+S] alcoholic drink: *He* **hit the bottle** *when he lost his job.|She gave up for a while, but she's back* **on the bottle** *again now.* **4** [C *usu. sing.*] milk in bottles used in place of mother's milk: *to give the baby its bottle* **5** [U] *BrE sl* courage; daring; NERVE: *You have to hand it to her — she's got (a lot of) bottle.*

de·cant·er /dɪ'kæntəʳ/ *n* a container (usu. of glass and decorated) for holding alcoholic drinks, esp. wine

flask

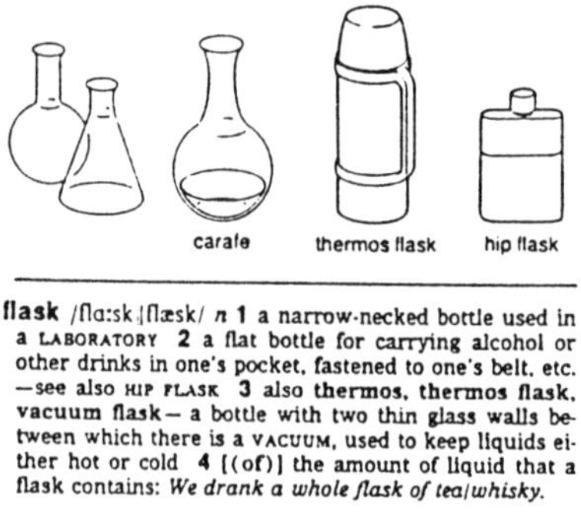

flask /flɑːsk‖flæsk/ *n* **1** a narrow-necked bottle used in a LABORATORY **2** a flat bottle for carrying alcohol or other drinks in one's pocket, fastened to one's belt, etc. —see also HIP FLASK **3** also **thermos, thermos flask, vacuum flask**— a bottle with two thin glass walls between which there is a VACUUM, used to keep liquids either hot or cold **4** [(of)] the amount of liquid that a flask contains: *We drank a whole flask of tea/whisky.*

Figure 2. Bottle, decanter, flask in *LDCE 2*

ca·rafe /kəˈræf/ *n* ⇨illus at BOTTLE. **1** glass container in which wine or water are served at meals. **2** amount contained in this: *I can't drink more than half a carafe.*

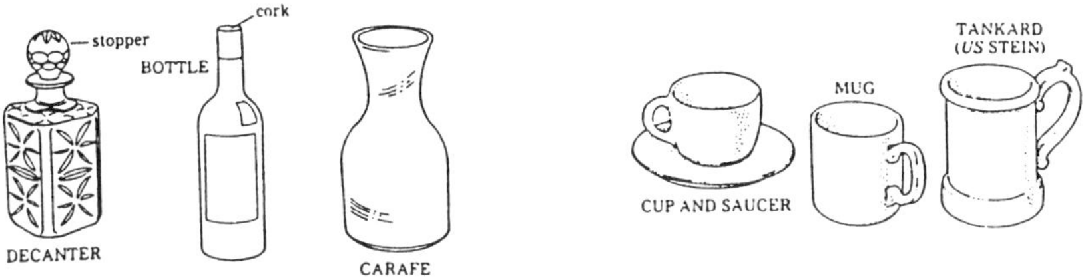

Figure 3. Bottle, carafe, cup etc. in *OALD 4*

The *hot water bottle,* clearly, does not belong to the prototypical kernel of the category. *Carafes* have particular shapes and proportions, while *decanters* are usually decorated and have a glass stopper as a necessary attribute. Although definitions are given for *bottle*, *carafe*, *decanter*, *flask* in the dictionaries, accompanying the illustrations, pictures might also stand alone, as ostensive definitions, similar to the other container terms in Figure 1.

2.2.

Extreme cases of purely verbal definitions of concepts are to be found in Wierzbicka (1985). She argues (1985:83) in her extensive discussion of *cup* and *mug*, in the first chapter of her book, that the need for a picture of such concrete objects is "a misconception". She also admits that the most controversial feature of her definitions "will be their gargantuan length" (1985:37). The following schema (2) from Wierzbicka (1985:164) shows the shortest definition in the whole book, namely that for *tiger*.[2]

It also contains, besides complete sentences, parameters like HABITAT, SIZE, and APPEARANCE.[3] The metalanguage used by Wierzbicka is derived exclusively from natural language and belongs to a postulated set of universal semantic primitives. There is, however, no procedure for verification and Wierzbicka's introspective method is often felt to be subjective and even questionable.

(2)

TIGERS

A KIND OF ANIMAL
IMAGINING ANIMALS OF THIS KIND PEOPLE COULD SAY THESE THINGS ABOUT THEM:

they live in the jungle in places which are away from places where people live in parts of the Earth where they don't live people can see them in a zoo	*HABITAT*
they are similar to cats in the way they look and in the way they move but they are much bigger than cats being more like people in size than like cats	*SIZE*
they have black stripes on a yellowish body they have big sharp claws and big sharp teeth	*APPEARANCE*
they attack other animals and people and kill and eat them they can move quickly and without noise like cats and they can move easily in places where other big animals can't so that they can come close to people without people noticing them, and attack people	*BEHAVIOR*
people are afraid of them, and think of them as fierce animals [people also think of them as animals who know what they want and who know how to get it, and whom one can't help admiring for that]	*RELATION TO PEOPLE*

2.3.

As opposed to any type of componential analysis, or lexical decomposition, there is a tradition in linguistics which stresses the holistic nature of words and concepts. This has recently been strengthened in Prototype Theories and Cognitive Semantics, under the influence of gestalt psychology. Clearly, there is a relation here between the use of illustrations in wordbooks and the theory that visual images play an important role in linguistic categorization and in perception. The former subject, illustrations in dictionaries, is discussed very lucidly and competently in Stein (1991), while the latter, the importance of visual images for the mental lexicon, is stressed in Lipka (1989:256ff).

In this context, the so-called "dual-coding hypothesis", originally introduced by the psychologist Paivio (1971) and adopted in Hörmann (1986:161), must be mentioned. In Hörmann's words it means that:

> concrete words and sentences are stored as images AND as words, whereas abstract words and sentences are stored only in verbal form.

According to Hörmann (1986:159), the word *car*, for example, would not be represented in the consciousness or memory of a speaker as a list of semantic features, but as a visual image of a car[4]. Further support for such a psycholinguistic theory can be found in Cognitive Linguistics in the notion of mental imagery. I would just like to quote the following statement from Lakoff (1987:126):

> SEEING TYPICALLY INVOLVES CATEGORIZING. For example, seeing a tree involves categorizing and an aspect of your visual experience as a *tree*. Such categorization in the visual realm generally depends on conventional mental images.

This idea has been further pursued by Gibbs & O'Brien (1990) and applied to English idioms and their metaphorical motivation. Their article describes three experiments in which well-known idioms, such as *spill the beans* and *let the cat out of the bag* where used. The mental images formed by the subjects showed a high degree of consistency and similarity.

3. Some examples of English nouns and verbs

Let us now look at some English nouns and verbs and the treatment of these categories in learners' dictionaries. A comparison with other languages and their different categorization may be implied, but cannot be dealt with explicitly. Thus, for example, as in my next set of illustrations, both *pin* and *needle* together correspond to the German simple lexeme *Nadel*.

The examples of the nouns all denote concrete objects, so that the dual-coding hypothesis may apply, and the use of illustrations in dictionaries is appropriate.

needle

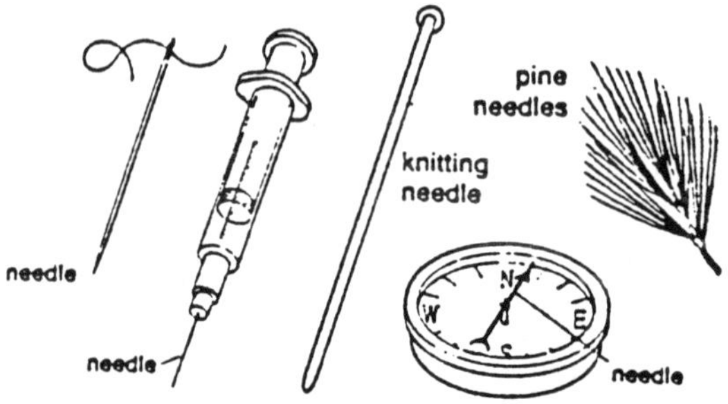

nee·dle[1] /'ni:dl/ *n* **1** [C] a long pointed metal pin with a hole in one end through which a piece of thread is passed, used in sewing **2** [C] a thin pointed object that looks like this: *a pine needle* (= a thin leaf of this tree) **3** [C] a thin pointed rod used in knitting (KNIT) **4** [C] a very small pointed jewel or piece of metal used in a RECORD PLAYER to pick up sound from records; STYLUS **5** [C] a very thin hollow pointed tube, at the end of a HYPODERMIC, which is pushed into someone's skin to put a liquid (esp. medicine) into the body **6** [C] a long thin moving pointer in a scientific instrument: *the needle of a compass* **7** [U] strong dislike or bad feeling between people, teams, etc., esp. as a result of competition **8** **needle in a haystack** *infml* something very small which is hard to find in a big place —see also PINS AND NEEDLES

Figure 4. Pin, needle, and their compounds in *LDCE 2*

3.1.

For both *pin* and *needle* the *LDCE* distinguishes several senses, which may be interpreted as metaphorical and metonymic extensions of the prototype. The prototype is represented in both cases in the upper left-hand corner of the illustration. Obviously, resemblance of SHAPE plays an overriding role, more important than MATERIAL.[5] American English *pin* in the sense of British English *brooch*, is not explained by the definitions, but becomes immediately motivated, if we assume a metonymic HAVE-relation. This also holds for the complex lexemes *safety pin* and *tie pin*. From all the dictionaries used here, only the *COBUILD* has a subcategory 4.1 of *pin* defined as "a small brooch or badge with a pin attached to the bottom of it". Sense 5 of *needle*, defined as "a very thin pointed tube, at the end of a hypodermic", is motivated by SHAPE, but the hole of the prototypical *needle* may be claimed to have been converted to the hollowness of the tube. In general, there is a considerable degree of family resemblance between the senses of *pin* and *needle*.

It must be noted in passing that the subcategories in the two illustrations contain a remarkable number of complex lexemes, such as *safety pin, tie pin, drawing pin, hairpin, knitting needle, pine needles*. This phenomenon and its implications have not attracted a great deal of a attention in Cognitive Linguistics. The *COBUILD*, again as the only dictionary, refers implicitly to the textlinguistic and pragmatic implications of the relationship between simple and complex lexemes. Sense 2 of *pin* is defined as:

> 2. You can also refer to a safety pin, a hairpin, a hatpin, or a panel pin as a *pin* when you have already mentioned it using its full name or when it is obvious what you are referring too.

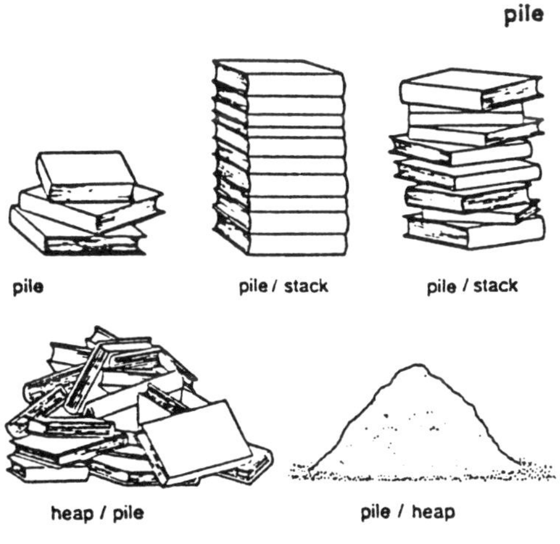

---

pile[1] /paɪl/ *n* **1** [(of)] a tidy collection of objects, esp. when made of a number of things of the same kind placed on top of each other: *a pile of books/plates | We put the newspapers in piles on the floor.* —see USAGE **2** a PYRE **3** [(of)] also piles *pl.*— *infml* a lot: *I've got piles of work to do today.* **4** [*usu. sing.*] *infml* a very large amount of money; fortune: *He* **made a/his pile** *and retired to the Bahamas.* **5** *pomp* a large tall building or group of buildings: *They live in a rambling Victorian pile.* —see also PILES, ATOMIC PILE

Figure 5. Pile, stack, heap in *LDCE 2*

3.2.

My next example, Figure 5 (see previous page), is again from the area of concrete nouns, but concerns simple lexemes only, namely *pile, stack,* and *heap* and the categories denoted by these words. The *LDCE 2* uses the illustrations in Figure 5, which clearly demonstrate the fuzzy borders between the three categories.

The first definition of *pile* "a tidy collection of objects" seems to be at variance with the pictorial representation. But if we look at the following *Usage Note* for the three lexemes, we can see that *stack* is described as "a carefully arranged *pile*", and *heap* as a "largely disorderly *pile* of things".

> ▪ USAGE Compare **pile, stack** and **heap**, which can all mean "a mass of things placed one on top of he other". A **pile** is a usually tidy collection of objects, usually of the same kind: *a pile of books/papers/leaves*. A **stack** is a carefully arranged pile usually made up of a lot of things of the same shape and size: *a stack of books/coins/cassettes*. A **heap** is a large disorderly pile of things, not necessarily of the same kind: *a heap of toys/books/dirty washing*. Both **pile** and **heap** can also be used with uncountable nouns: *a pile/heap of sand/straw/manure*.

The *COBUILD* has a so-called *Extra Column*, in which superordinate words, antonyms and synonyms are indicated with special symbols (⬆ for superordinate terms, ≠ for antonyms, = for synonyms). It distinguishes several senses of *pile*, inter alia 1.1 "a quantity of things which ... form a mass which is high in the middle and has sloping sides... "and 1.2 "the quantity of things which have been put neatly ... on top of the one below". The synonym for 1.1 is given as *heap* and for 1.2 as *stack*, at the same time referring to a superordinate category *group*.

3.3.

The biological categories *bird, cat, dog, tiger* are my next brief case studies. Figure 6 from Aitchison (1987:54) illustrates the meaning of the category *bird*, with different *birdiness* rankings, and the *robin* in the centre as the prototypical *bird*.[6]

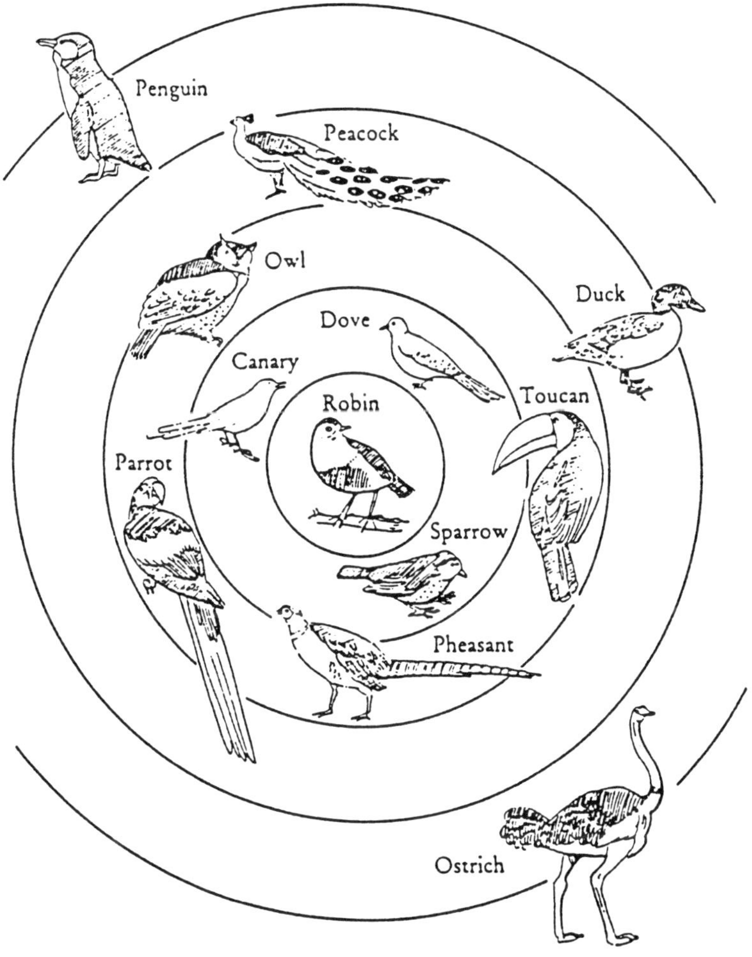

Figure 6. Experimental birdiness rankings

The periphery contains McArthur's group of *unusual birds.* Figure 7, varieties of large non-domestic cats, is taken from the *Longman Lexicon* as part of the lexical set A 53, *The cat and similar animals.*

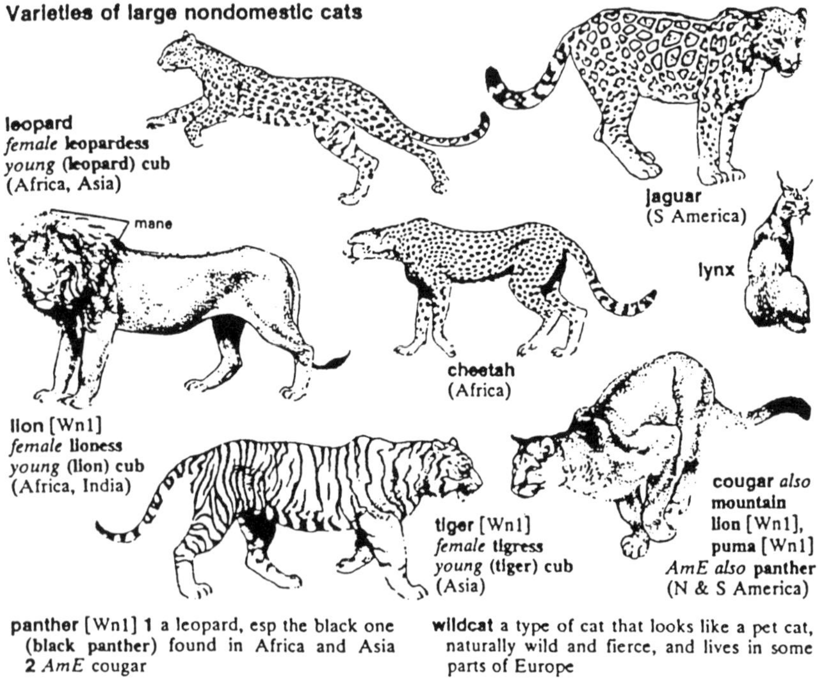

Figure 7. Nondomestic cats in *LLCE*

It contains an ostensive definition of *tiger*. Three definitions for *cat* are given in the *Lexicon*: 1 "a small domestic animal with fur", 2 "any animal of a group which includes the domestic cat and the lion", 3 a metaphorical extension with the labels *fig* and *deprec*, "a woman who says unkind things about other woman."[7] The habitual collocation *rain cats and dogs* cannot be discussed here, but a few words should be said about the category *dog* and related complex metaphorical derivatives. To take up the latter first, *dog-eared* is illustrated by the *OALD* as in Figure 8:

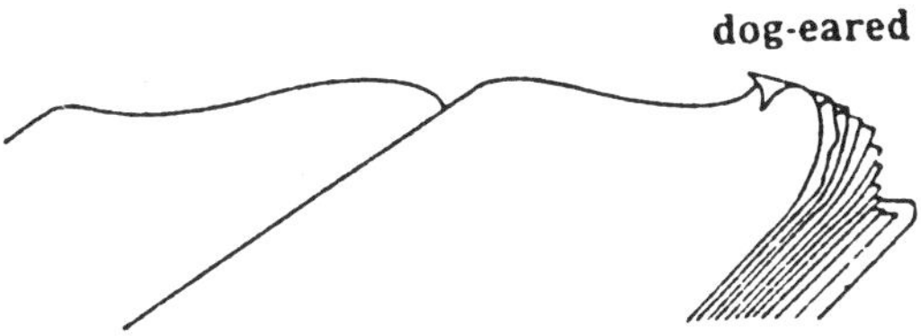

'**dog-eared** *adj* (of a book) having the corners of many pages turned down through use.

Figure 8. Metaphorical derivative in *OALD 4*

BREEDS OF DOG

All the drawings are to scale and represent the average size reached.

Figure 9. Breeds of dog and their size in *OALD 4*

It might be argued that this is a more appropriate metaphor than the German equivalent *Eselsohren*. In my opinion, the experience of language users and visual images would play a crucial role in such an argument. Other *dog*-related metaphors listed in *OALD 4* are *dog-collar*, sense 2 (*infml*) "stiff white collar worn by a clergyman", *dog-fight* 1 "close combat between fighter aircraft", *dog-leg* "sharp bend, esp. on a golf course" and the idiom *in the doghouse* "in disgrace; out of favour".

Figure 9 shows ostensive definitions of *breeds of dog* which are, I believe, highly superior to any verbal definition. Again, shape, size, and holistic gestalt perception play an enormous role in the finer, internal categorization of *dog*.

3.4.

There isn't much room left for the other matters that I would have liked to present here in more detail. The following two figures for the verbs *damage* and *walk* can only give a hint. I would claim that they are instances of the application of linguistic field-theory to lexicography. If we

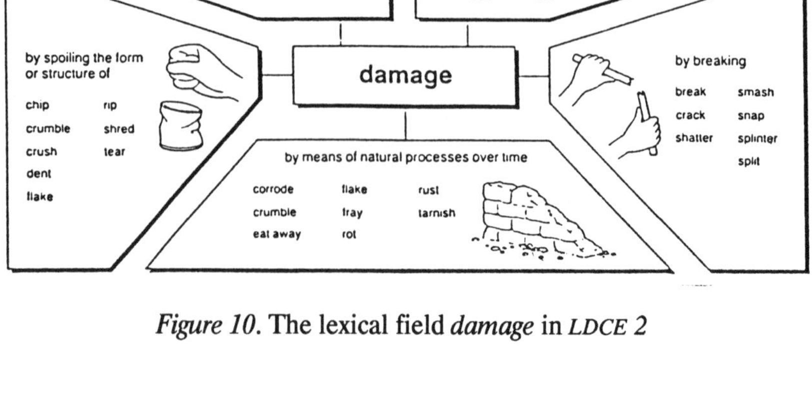

Figure 10. The lexical field *damage* in *LDCE 2*

first look at *Figure 10* for *damage*, five subcategories of this superordinate archilexeme, all concerning the semantic dimension MANNER, are distinguished: (1) by spoiling the form or structure of, (2) by spoiling the appearance of, (3) with a weapon, tool, etc., (4) by breaking, (5) by means of natural processes over time.

For the meaning of the respective hyponyms *chip, crumble, deface, discolour* etc., the dictionary gives cross-references.

A similar procedure is used for the field of human locomotion covered by the superordinate verb *walk* as represented in Figure 11:

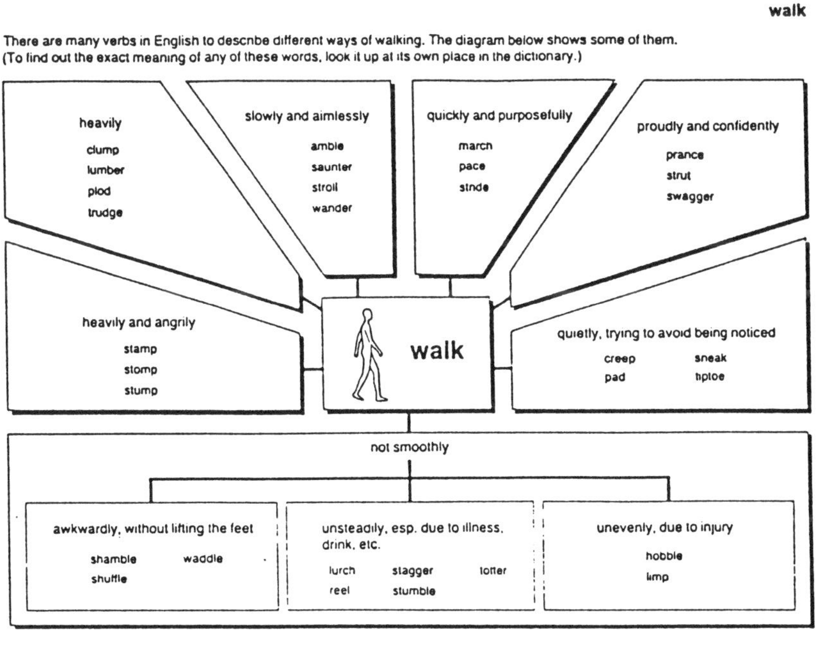

Figure 11. The field of human locomotion in *LDCE 2*

Here, the dimension MANNER provides the criterion for subcategorization on the first level as: 1 heavily and angrily, 2 heavily, 3 slowly and aimlessly, 4 quickly and purposefuly, 5 proudly and confidently, 6 quietly, trying to avoid being noticed, and 7 not smoothly. The last group is then further subclassified again according to MANNER: (a) awkwardly, without lifting the feet, (b) unsteadily, esp. due to illness, and (c) unevenly, due to injury.

Unfortunately, this very happy application of linguistic theory to lexicographic practice has disappeared in the latest edition of the dictionary, mentioned at the beginning of my talk, namely the *Longman Dictionary of English Language and Culture*. The diagrams for *damage* and *walk* obviously had to give way to more or less useful *Cultural Notes,* encyclopedic entries, maps, and photos.

3.5.

Not much can be said at this point about another field of lexicology and lexicography, besides concrete nouns, namely abstract verbs of linguistic action. *Speak, talk, say*, and *tell* were investigated in great detail, on the basis of a corpus consisting of sixty modern British stage plays, in Dirven *et al.* (1982). The analysis resulted in postulating several subcategories for the individual verbs, for example three different *speaks*. An interesting contrast between *speak* and *talk* is set up in the part contributed by Dirven (1982:56), dealing with *talk*, in the following way:

> *speak* sees linguistic action mainly from the point of view of the *speaker*, whereas *talk* sees both partners, implicitly or explicitly, equally essential to the discourse.

The lexicographers, for example in *OALD* or *LDCE*, have to deal with such aspects in *Usage Notes*. Let me quote from the latter dictionary, the *LDCE 2* (s.v. *talk*):

> *Speak* and *talk* are very close in meaning, but *talk* usually gives the idea of a conversation rather than a single person making statements.

The verb *agree* is not precisely a linguistic action verb. In Dirven (1991), the lexical structure of this verb is analysed and described in terms of the notions *schema* and *subschemata*, on the basis of impressive corpus data and introspection. It is explicitly intended as a contribution to the Cognitive Perspective in linguistics. What is most remarkable and unusual about this study, in our context, is that in the Conclusion a proposal for a dictionary entry for *agree* is made. Dirven (1991:40) states:

> Another question is whether such descriptive data can be incorporated into the daily practice of lexicographers and dictionary makers. Not being a lexicographer myself, the following attempt to write a dictionary entry can only be judged by workers in the field.

4. Conclusion

Perhaps I can adopt this statement as a fitting conclusion to my talk, since I myself am no lexicographer either. I think that Dirven's statement can be interpreted as a plea for more co-operation between linguists, lexicologists, and lexicographers. The examples I have discussed were meant to show that in the majority of concrete cases, lexicographic practice is unrelated to lexicological theory. Nevertheless, it produces most impressive descriptions of the language in the form of alphabetical and thematic lexicography. I have tried to show that a stronger consideration for the visual aspect of our daily experience may contribute both to greater lexicological insight into linguistic categorization and to more fruitful lexicographic practice, especially from a pedagogical point of view.

Notes

1. Cf. Lipka (1992:30), where it is pointed out that the neat distinction between linguistic and encyclopedic information is no longer made in the eighth edition (1990).
2. Aitchison (1987:45) quotes other (much shorter) definitions of *tiger*, in her discussion of the difficulties of a checklist theory of meaning and mentions non-prototypical exemplars such as three-legged, lame, toothless, and albino tigers.
3. These parameters are equivalent to the semantic *dimensions* used in certain theories of meaning, such as AGE, COLOUR, MATERIAL, PLACE, PURPOSE, SEX, SHAPE, SIZE (cf. Lipka 1992:124, 145f).
4. For the further development of Paivio's dual-coding theory, containing *imagens* and *logogens* as nonverbal and verbal representational units, cf. Paivio (1990:53ff, esp. 59, 67). Visual images also play a great role in certain writing systems, such as the Egyptian hieroglyphs, or the Chinese ideograms, which have been taken over into Japanese as *kanji*. They originally evolved from iconic pictograms.
5. Cf. note 3 for semantic dimensions.
6. The highest ranking for *robin* seems surprising, as the original experiments were carried out with psychology students at Berkeley, and the robin is probably not a very common bird in California. Did the stereotypical robin in English and American Christmas cards play a role here?
7. Senses 1 and 2 of *cat* could be regarded as two lexemes differentiated by the distinctive features [±Domestic], [±Large] but also as two *lexical units* (in the sense of Lipka 1992:130ff) belonging to a single polysemous lexeme.

References

Aitchison, J.
1987 *Words in the Mind. An Introduction to the Mental Lexicon*. Oxford: Basil Blackwell.

Cowie, A. P.
1988 Language as words: lexicography. In: Collinge, N. E. (ed.). *An Encyclopaedia of Language*. London: Routledge, pp. 671-700.

Dirven, R.
1991 Schema and subschemata in the lexical structure of the verb *agree*. In: Granger, S. (ed.). *Perspectives on the English Lexicon*. Louvain: Peeters, pp. 25-42.

Dirven, R., L. Goosens, Y. Putseys & E. Vorlat
1982 *The Scene of Linguistic Action and its Perspectivization by SPEAK, TALK, SAY, and TELL*. Amsterdam/Philadelphia: Benjamins.

Gibbs, R. & J. O'Brien
1990 "Idioms and mental imagery: The metaphorical motivation for idiomatic meaning". *Cognition* 36:35-68.

Hörmann, H.
1981 [1986] *Meaning and Context. An Introduction to the Psychology of Language*, ed. by Robert Innis. New York/London: Plenum.

Lakoff, G.
1987 *Women, Fire, and Dangerous Things*. Chicago/London: University of Chicago Press.

Lipka, L.
1982 "Causatives and inchoatives in English and their treatment in recent lexicographic practice". *Studia Anglica Posnaniensia* 14:3-16.
1989 The state of the art in lexicology. In: Müllenbrock, H.-J. & R. Noll-Wiemann (eds.). *Anglistentag 1988 Göttingen*. Tübingen: Niemeyer, pp. 250-263.
1990 [1992] *An Outline of English Lexicology. Lexical Structure, Word Semantics, and Word-Formation*, 2nd edition. Tübingen: Niemeyer.

McArthur, T.
1986 *Worlds of Reference*. Cambridge: Cambridge University Press.

Nuccorini, S.
1993 Lexicology and lexicography revisited. In: Hart, D. (ed.). *Aspects of English and Italian lexicography. [Aspetti della lessicologia Italiana e Inglese.]* Rome: Bagatto Libri, pp. 127-139.

Paivio, A.
1971 *Imagery and Verbal Processes*. New York: Holt, Rinehart and Winston.
1990 *Mental Representation. A Dual Coding Approach*. New York, Oxford: Oxford University Press.

Stein, G.
1991 "Illustrations in dictionaries". *International Journal of Lexicography* 4:99-127.

Wierzbicka, A.
1985 *Lexicography and Conceptual Analysis*. Ann Arbor: Karoma.

Zgusta, L.
1988 *Lexicography Today*. Tübingen: Niemeyer.

Dictionaries

1987 *Collins COBUILD English Language Dictionary.* Collins.
1979 *Collins Dictionary of the English Language.* Collins.
1990 *Concise Oxford Dictionary*, 8th edition. OUP. (COD)
1987 *Longman Dictionary of Contemporary English,* 2nd edition. Longman. (LDCE)
1992 *Longman Dictionary of English Language and Culture*, Longman.
1981 *Longman Lexicon of Contemporary English*, Longman. (LLCE)
1989 *Oxford Advanced Learner's Dictionary*, 4th edition. OUP. (OALD)
1992 *Oxford Advanced Learner's Dictionary. Encyclopedic Edition.* OUP.
1989 *Oxford English Dictionary,* 2nd edition. OUP. (OED)
1987 *Roget's Thesaurus of English Words and Phrases.* Longman (1852ff).

Pedagogical lexicography: Some desiderata

Reinhard R. K. Hartmann

1. Introduction

Both inside and outside language teaching, the dictionary is one of the most important sources of linguistic information available. For most languages, there is a wide range of reference works that offer useful information on points of pronunciation, grammar, and other aspects of vocabulary in context. However, the potentially close interaction between language teaching on the one hand and lexicography on the other hand has only recently come into open view, thanks to such publications as Cowie (1987) and Tickoo (1989). The international encyclopedia of lexicography, *Wörterbücher/Dictionaries/Dictionnaires*, has also devoted several articles to this topic, e.g. Herbst (1990).

It has become apparent that language teachers, lexicographers, linguists, and languager learners have much to gain from an increased awareness of the role of dictionaries in the language-learning process. Teachers, rather than distrusting the dictionary as a competitor, should explore its possibilities as an aid to independent learning and provide deliberate instruction to improve their learners' reference skills. Lexicographers should take an interest in what happens to their products when they are handled by learners, and be willing to experiment with new formats. Linguists should consider the dictionary not as a repository of stale and static data about language, but as an instrument of codifying usage and a means towards communicative action.

All this would require a degree of willingness to collaborate in an interdisciplinary and problem-solving spirit of the kind very much in evidence at this symposium. One of the overriding desiderata then would be to address the double fact that the dictionary is still an underused tool in language learning and an underresearched topic in applied linguistics, in spite of centuries of parallel development of lexicography and foreign-language teaching.

2. Dictionary research

As the success of the so-called "learner's dictionary" during the last few years has demonstrated, the time is now ripe for a reassessment of the role of various dictionaries in the classroom and in self-tuition. I have myself made a modest contribution to the debate by looking at some issues of vocabulary teaching, dictionary use, the English learner's dictionary, and the reconcilability of the monolingual and the interlingual approaches (Hartmann 1989, 1991, 1992a, 1992b) in their relation to "metalexicography" or "dictionary research".

I find it useful to distinguish four aspects or branches of dictionary research, i.e. dictionary history, dictionary typology, dictionary criticism, and dictionary use. I intend to show that these can help to lay a proper foundation for pedagogical lexicography.

We now know much more than ever before about the lexicographical traditions of various countries and languages. While a full history of the learner's dictionary has still to be written, we do have some evidence that learners' concerns (or at least their assumed potential reference needs) figure prominently throughout lexicographic history. What is also becoming clear is that the interlingual format is just as important as the unilingual.

A similar picture emerges when we consider dictionary typology, or the attempt to bring order into the enormous diversity of existing dictionaries by classifying them into genres. We find a range of types, from monolingual ones like the famous *Oxford Advanced Learner's Dictionary* through bilingualised or translated adaptations right through to bilingual dictionaries and even polyglot ones; other distinctions we can make are between general and specialised ones, or between alphabetic-semasiological and thematic-onomasiological ones.

Dictionary criticism, or the principled evaluation of particular dictionaries, also has a contribution to make in our understanding of pedagogically motivated reference works. All the great language teachers and lexicographers have spotted faults and suggested improvements in the dictionaries of their day, like Hornby, who argued that the traditional native-speaker dictionaries need to be modified to meet the needs of foreign learners, especially with regard to grammatical information, and by Šcerba who questioned the very foundations of bilingual lexicography by insisting that factors such as the mother tongue of the user, the directionality of the activity engaged in, and the learner's proficiency level all have a bearing on the design of dictionaries for language teaching.

This leads us on to the fourth branch of dictionary research, which is concerned with the special needs of learners as dictionary users. Such research into dictionary use is of relatively recent vintage, and is certainly capable of refinement in terms of the various observational methods used, but most authorities seem to agree that bilingual dictionaries, in spite of their obvious shortcomings, still outnumber monolingual learners' dictionaries by a sizeable margin, something perhaps like 2 to 1.

3. Monolingual or interlingual?

So we come away from this exercise with a widened perspective: all sorts of dictionaries are used by language learners, and they can be monolingual as well as interlingual. Seen in this light, the definition of learners' dictionaries by Thomas Herbst (1990:1379) rings a little hollow: "A learner's dictionary is a synchronic monolingual dictionary intended to meet the demands of the foreign user."

Herbst is right to stress the demands (or reference needs) of the foreign user, but to restrict the notion of the learner's dictionary to the monolingual type is misleading. Even John Battenburg, in his book *English Monolingual Learners' Dictionaries* (1991) is more realistic than that. He describes the various prototypes from Hornby's *Advanced Learner's Dictionary* to LDOCE and COBUILD and extracts their essential design features, but he also devotes two of the 31 sections of the book on bridging and combining the features of the monolingual and the bilingual dictionary.

We should not forget the important fact that for many languages other than English, monolingual learners' dictionaries have not yet been developed (the first German dictionary for foreign learners of German has just been published: *Langenscheidts Großwörterbuch Deutsch als Fremdsprache*). Hence this quotation from Jerzy Tomaszczyk (1983:45) is particularly appropriate: "People use bilingual dictionaries whether language teaching methodologists like it or not. Indeed, to many people the word *dictionary* means *a bilingual dictionary*."

And it is also true, certainly for the language pair that I know best, German and English, that the quality of bilingual dictionaries has dramatically improved over the last few years, so much so that one critic (Zimmer 1986) has claimed, in a review that reads like a product test, that truly bad examples of this genre are hard to find nowadays. This view is echoed by others who have admitted that while there is still room for improvement and experimentation, the general bilingual dictionary does serve foreign learners well for most of their reference needs.

So the question whether learners' dictionaries should be monolingual or interlingual cannot be answered by a simple one-way choice, since such choices do not exist for all language pairs, and since the issue is complicated by the presence of dictionary types other than the general alphabetic format.

Ekkehard Zöfgen, in his excellent article (1991) in the *International Encyclopedia of Lexicography*, draws our attention to the fact that at least for the major languages of Europe (English/French/German), learners can choose from a wide range of reference works, including thesauruses, basic-core vocabularies, pictorial dictionaries, faux-amis dictionaries, and LSP compilations, some for several graded proficiency levels. I will just specifically exemplify four of these dictionary types because they may not be widely known, although they have broken new ground.

- *Sinnverwandte Wörter der englischen Sprache* compiled by Rudolf Meldau & Ralph Whitling. München: Hueber (1956/64/81), a bilingual synonym dictionary with example sentences for German learners of English;
- *Words you can use* compiled by Klaus Berold, Berlin: Cornelsen (1987), a thematically organised vocabulary book, with collocational information and warnings about false friends;
- *Oxford Grundwörterbuch* compiled by Shirley Burridge & Helga Holtkamp. Oxford U.P. [& Berlin: Cornelsen] (1990), a bilingualisation or German translation of the *Oxford Elementary Learner's Dictionary* (1980);
- *Falsche Freunde. Ein vergleichendes Wörterbuch* compiled by Klaus-Dieter Barnickel, Heidelberg: J. Groos (1992), a comprehensive list of false cognates in English and German.

4. Desiderata

I now come to the final part of my presentation, in which I list some desiderata for pedagogical lexicography. I concentrate on dictionaries for foreign learners and deliberately exclude native-speaker dictionaries for school use.

(1) We have some sketchy outlines of the history of learners' dictionaries, but what is needed is a more comprehensive account of particular traditions, e.g. that for English and German.

(2) Even if we did possess histories of learners' dictionaries for a particular language or language pair, it may be helpful to compare parallel developments elsewhere, e.g. for French or Russian, in order to find out similarities and contrasts, and perhaps adapt patterns that have worked successfully there.

(3) All this entails a fuller documentation than is currently available for each language or language pair. Even for German and English,

we do not have complete bibliographies of all types of pedagogically oriented dictionaries.

(4) The argument that dictionaries for foreign learners should be different from dictionaries for native speakers sounds plausible, but it needs to be supported by evidence of which features would make a positive difference.

(5) The same is true about differences between ordinary general bilingual dictionaries and those specifically designed for learners (see also (9) below.)

(6) It has been found that there is an uneasy tension between learners' use of monolingual and interlingual dictionaries, but we need to know more about what their relative advantages and disadvantages are and at what point learners should move from one to the other.

(7) There is at present no consensus on which information categories are essential or redundant for which (groups of) learners, and more user studies are required to settle this issue.

(8) One crucial criterion for the selection of the wordlist of learners' dictionaries is frequency, combined with utility, but more work needs to be done to find out what is most appropriate for specific types of learners at specific levels of proficiency.

(9) It is taken for granted that learners' dictionaries are useful for all sorts of tasks (encoding, decoding, translation, vocabulary acquisition, cultural reference), but there is at present no agreement on how to assess relative priorities.

(10) The textual structure of learners' dictionaries (as of other dictionary types) is complex and often dense, e.g. definitions as one means of explaining meanings of words, so we need to experiment with different styles of presentation to measure relative effectiveness and to improve intelligibility.

(11) More information is needed on how dictionaries should fit into the overall pattern of teaching materials, learning styles, and examination syllabuses.

(12) We are all aware that dictionary reference skills are important, but we are not really sure about how they can best be taught.

(13) Many information categories in dictionaries, and indeed some dictionary types, for learners are not yet available, or are only inadequately covered today. Examples: encyclopedic and cultural information, pictorial illustration, technical terminology.

(14) Formats other than traditional alphabetic dictionaries may be appropriate for learners, such as computer-based reference tools, and experimentation should be encouraged.

(15) In dictionary research, more training facilities are needed, supported by a collaborative interdisciplinary spirit (see also Section 1 above).

(16) In dictionary-making, more training should be provided, supported by a greater openness to alternative formats.

5. Conclusion

My conclusion is that the field of pedagogical lexicography is there to be developed, and this development is likely to succeed better if we can encourage intensive interaction between language teachers, teacher trainers, dictionary makers, publishers, and academic dictionary researchers. This in turn demands a greater awareness of the resources that already exist for this purpose: conferences (like this one on "The Lexicon"), societies (like EURALEX), publications (like the ones mentioned below), and academic courses (like the ones offered at Exeter).

References

Battenburg, J. D.
1991 *English Monolingual Learners' Dictionaries. A User-oriented Study* (Lexicographica Series Maior 39). Tübingen: Niemeyer.

Cowie, A. P. (ed.)
1987 *The Dictionary and the Language Learner.* (Lexicographica Series Maior 17). Tübingen: Niemeyer.

Hartmann, R. R. K.
1989 Sociology of the dictionary user: Hypotheses and empirical studies [Art. 12]. In: Hausmann, F. J., O. Reichmann, H. E. Wiegand & L. Zgusta (eds). *Wörterbücher/Dictionaries/Dictionnaires. An International Encyclopedia of Lexicography.* Vol. 1. Berlin: de Gruyter, pp. 102-111.

1991 "What's the use of learners' dictionaries?" *Institute of Language in Education Journal* 8:73-83.

1992a Learner's references: from the monolingual to the bilingual dictionary. In: Tommola, H., K. Varantola, T. Salmi-Tolonen & J. Schopp (eds.). *EURALEX '92 Proceedings.* Tampere: Yliopisto, pp. 63-70.

1992b "Lexicography, with particular reference to English learners' dictionaries". *Language Teaching [Abstracts]* 25:151-159.

Herbst, T.
1990 Dictionaries for foreign language teaching: English [Art. 151]. In: Hausmann, F. J., O. Reichmann, H. E. Wiegand & L. Zgusta (eds.). *Wörterbücher, Dictionaries, Dictionnaires. An International Encyclopedia of Lexicography.* Vol. 2. Berlin: de Gruyter, pp. 1379-1385.

Tickoo, M. L. (ed.)
1989 *Learners' Dictionaries: State of the Art* (RELC Anthology Series 23). Singapore: SEAMEO Regional Language Centre.

Tomaszczyk, J.
1983 On bilingual dictionaries: The case for bilingual dictionaries for foreign language learners. In: Hartmann, R. R. K. (ed.). *Lexicography. Principles and Practice*. London: Academic Press, pp. 41-51.

Zimmer, D. E.
1986 "Wörterbuchtest". *Die Zeit* 21 (16.5.1986):47-48.

Zöfgen, E.
1991 Bilingual learners' dictionaries [Art. 305]. In: Hausmann, F. J., O. Reichmann, H. E. Wiegand & L. Zgusta (eds.). *Wörterbücher/Dictionaries/Dictionnaires. An International Encyclopedia of Lexicography*. Vol. 3. Berlin: de Gruyter, pp. 2888-2903.

The special lexicon and problems of EST/ESP - course design or the box of the Pandora

Winfried Lange

In Greek mythology Pandora was the first woman made by Hephaestus. The name means "all gifts". Pandora was adorned by the gods with special qualities. Zeus gave her a box from which all the evils which plague mankind came out. The myth seems to be a good simile to describe the problems of the special lexicon.

The sciences and technology have considerable influence upon language in general and special languages in particular. The fast development requires new words for new concepts and their relationships make demands upon language unprecedented in history. We are witnessing a change from isolated subject studies to interdisciplinary studies. Completely new processes are introduced often via a foreign language. Polysemy, metaphor, metonymy, and other forms of extending meaning have to be used with much greater care since the subject label no longer serves as a clear differentiating mark between areas of meaning. The danger of imperfect communication is real as the confusing diversities of vocabulary items in technology and engineering show. Linguistic variation and innovation are fundamental to the generation of new thought. Better knowledge of the means available in language can help to formulate new thought in a more easily comprehensible manner. In engineering the need for guidance is very great. To formulate and to teach a multidisciplinary language seems to be a very appealing conclusion.

1. Analysis and classification of the special lexicon

1.1. General problems

1.1.1. Special languages of science and technology

Science proceeds from observation to discovery and formulation of laws. The task of technology and engineering is to apply this knowledge, through the construction of equipment and machines. Philosophers and linguists stress the rationality of the approach and the associated rationalisation of linguistic expression. A detailed linguistic investigation of all special languages of English would need to be of encyclopedic proportions and point to lexical differentiation as the main distinction of the subject fields. Discussing the subsystems of special languages the term "Special English of Science and Technology" is preferable to the more widely used notations of "English for Special Purposes" and "English of Science and Technology" (Sager & Dungworth 1980:182) because it comprises a number of particular special languages.

A study based on subject fields would reveal significant differences in the varieties of English of more specific areas selected under the broad headings of mechanical engineering and chemical engineering. The main distinction would point to lexical differentiation. An investigation of traditional text types would yield certain predominances of sentence patterns. The division proposed by Hoffmann according to text levels seems to be the most promising approach (Hoffmann 1984:65):

(a) the language of the theoretical basic sciences
(b) the language of the experimental and technical sciences
(c) the language of applied sciences and technology
(d) the language of material production
(e) the language of consumption

Scientists and technologists communicate with each other chiefly through the medium of "technical literature". The term "covers a wide variety of publications, all of which have as their object the conveying of information from one person to another. This information .to be of greatest use. must be conveyed as efficiently and as clearly as possible and herein lies the whole art of technical writing" (Godfrey & Parr 1959: 7). The special languages only exist as subsystems of natural languages. The lexicon is their most obvious distinguishing characteristic. A high density of nominal groups is statistically a very significant property.

1.1.2. Lexical characteristics of special texts

The question of lexicalisation is fundamental to the description of special languages. The lexicon of a special subject code reflects the organisational characteristics of the subject. The items which are characterised by special reference within a discipline are the "terms". Collectively they form the terminology. Those which function in general reference over some codes are "words" and their totality the vocabulary. Terms and words are supplemented by standards.

Innovation in science and technology is dependent upon the ability to question the validity of certain concepts while keeping others fixed. We have to accept that there are degrees of terminologisation. A term may have several expression forms according to the number of text types and forms.

Text forms are characterised by the frequency and type of special designation they contain. Patents and contracts contain fully terminologised designations and must define all terms which do not have an acknowledged designation and definition. Production memoranda or discussions contain many shortened designations, *ad hoc* abbreviations and popular synonyms, reports on new development many tentative and established terms. "The diversity of text forms required in any special language community therefore determines the range of designations necessary for a special text." (Sager & Dungworth 1980:232).

1.1.3. Frequency of special vocabulary

Statistical methods determining the frequency of occurrence of terms are important for the compilation of glossaries, for information processing, and for the development of teaching materials.

Frequency counts show that the nominal character of scientific and technological texts is confirmed by a 40% coverage of texts by nouns and adjectives and by a 70% coverage of the lexicon. Special texts have a use rate of function words of about 50% (Buchholz 1978). The main burden of information therefore clearly falls on a small number of two-item nominal groups, although the function of the individual elements varies considerably. In special languages modifiers usually offer a greater chance of predicting the combination than the head nouns.

Statistical methods assist in the attribution of special texts to particular subject fields. A comparison of frequency dictionaries leads to a number of conclusions:

- the five most frequent words permit a clear identification of the broad subject area
- general scientific and technological vocabulary appears in many fields
- function words have a high frequency in many sublanguages
- modal verbs represent a significant part of the basic vocabulary (Hoffmann 1970, 1973, 1976, Alekseev 1973, Buchholz 1978).

Statistical data confirm that special languages have a higher rate of repetition of lexical items, avoid synonyms, and heavily rely on compounds or extended terms.

1.2. The form of the special lexicon

1.2.1. Content forms

In fields like engineering it is not easy to establish regular patterns of designation. Through habit and repeated acts of agreements about the definition of concepts a certain consistency is achieved. The special language and the special knowledge structure are indivisable.

In engineering and technology categorial statements are predominating. These require names for apparatus, plants, and equipment, for operations, for the measurement of processes and properties. They alone render the observations susceptible to further analysis, repetition, and use. The tendency to identify things and their functions leads to designation based on the function of the concept. The function as the primary concept, is then supplemented by verbal concepts to describe the operation performed and by concrete nominal concepts naming the tools, equipments and plants involved.

Concepts based on verifiable phenomena are fixed by means of standards which describe methods and circumstances of demonstration. Material objects, equally, permit the formation of precise concepts, but abstractions, which rely entirely on linguistic definition and the acceptance of other concepts, are more flexible. The method of designation is influenced by the ease with which a concept can be firmly placed within the knowledge structure. New concepts are often rather vague and can be named only tentatively by means of sometimes erroneous analogies, metaphor or transferred meaning. This process is vital for the formulation of new concepts and the creation of terminological systems. This phenomenon is increasingly common with the growing interrelation of sciences, e.g. the term *morphology* in chemical engineering, mathematics, biology.

The lexicon of special subjects consists of several major groups of words:

- general language words used in all disciplines,
- general language words appropriate to a particular discipline, e.g. *freeze*, *boil*, *stir* in chemistry and chemical engineering

- general language words used specifically with some modification or restriction of meaning, e.g. *precipitate*, *segregate* in chemistry, chemical engineering, biotechnology,
- the terms specific to a discipline. These are created for a particular subject or are general language words redefined for the purpose and thus terminologised.

All these words also have a high frequency and would justify their being declared part of the common vocabulary of science and engineering (Barber 1962, Hoffmann 1984).

Generally the objects of scientific observation are named systematically by nomenclatures ("observation terms"). Apparatus and processes involved, abstractions made, properties observed ("disposition terms") and measurements taken ("quantity terms") are named according to means also available to general language. The three terms go back to Hempel (1952).

In technology, the objects are named according to existing nomenclatures as in chemistry, often with simplifications. Materials and products are named according to principles of nomenclature or other precise methods of description, according to general reference and usage, e.g. metals, minerals and advertising. The equipment, processes, and operations of technology are named according to general principles. The designation of units of measurements follows a separate code.

1.2.2. Expression forms

Special languages strive to systematise principles of designation to achieve transparency and consistency. Related terms have a comparable expression form e.g. *ball valve oiler, sight gravity feed oiler*. Analytic and synthetic means of word formation are used extensively in special languages. Of interest are those affixes borrowed from Greak and Latin, e.g. *ocul-*, *odont-*, *ops-*, *opt-*, *oro-* or abbreviations of independent words, e.g. *al* in *alcohol*.

In special reference the classificatory use of language is highly developed. Designation is made by consistent criteria. The essential relationships that operate among concepts are reflected in the term. Logical relationships supplemented by quasi-empirical considerations provide useful guiding principles.

Determination is the most common mode of term formation. It works both by means of word composition and by derivation. It uses as a starting point a hyperonym and creates on this basis a more specific term. The shortest specification becomes generally accepted, e.g. *box for tools - tool box - toolbox*. Determination by simple juxtaposition of nouns may be misleading according to specifications of object and function, e.g. *diamond drilling* vs. *concrete drilling*.

Pre-modification can be carried out by any word category, e.g. *form sheet, fast feed, T-iron* etc. The determining modifier usually precedes the concept modified. Difficulties of interpretation occur when more modifiers are used or the determined element is omitted, e.g. *high-tension wire, chief(engineer)*. In complex compounds of three or four elements one is sometimes omitted in order to shorten the expression, e.g. *oil bath lubrication - bath lubrication*.

Many compounds reveal their constituents by conjunction, e.g. *gas and air mixture*. Dual purpose devices are often named by conjunction of functions, e.g. *lifting and forcing pump*. Disjunction joins the extensions of concepts into a new hyperonym and presents "either - or" or "and/or" relationships, e.g. *left-right indicator, on-off valve*.

1.3. Modes of designation

1.3.1. Use of existing designations

By exploiting general language, meanings can be widened (polysemy), narrowed (redefinition) and transferred.

Simile is the most common way of designation, highlighting a pertinent feature of concept in a striking way. Comparisons are particularly useful in introductory material to a subject and in textbooks. Overt simile occurs in compounds with *-style, -like*, or *-type*, e.g. *portal-type frame, knee-type milling machine*. Similarity of form can be indicated specifically by compounds with *-shape(d)*, e.g. *c-shaped column*. These comparisons narrow the meaning of the head words which in the process become generic.

Many items are designated metaphorically. The metaphors are based on form, function, and position. These criteria are often difficult to distinguish. Metaphoric use can be names of animals, e.g. *gripping jaw, worm gear*. Many other metaphors are less easily groupable, but their inspiration also lies in physical characteristics or similarities, e.g. *drum cylinder*.

In special reference there are also other transfers of meaning: the use of proper names to designate objects and measurements in nomenclatures and terminological systems, e.g. *Reynold number*, the name of the material for the object made of it, e.g. *iron, glass*, the genus for the species or the form of the object for another object of the form, e.g. *spiral, ball, ring*.

General notions are often the basis for scientific investigation. But the process of developing special reference requires the definition of the concepts that have been developed. Such a definition usually entails reducing the extension of the word. So *speed* and *velocity* are often used synonymously in general reference. In special reference the former is usually reserved for the rate at which a body moves, whereas the latter includes the direction of the movement.

1.3.2. Modification of resisting resources

The principal method of designation in special reference is modification by means of derivation and compounding.

(i) *Derivation.* Affixation is of particular importance because it can contribute to precision of expression. The number of affixes is considerably greater than in general language, largely because of the borrowing or adaptation of Latin or Greek words and methods of word formation. Certain affixes are used with limited meanings or functions in different special languages. So the suffix *-ity* is used in chemical engineering to describe a property, e.g. *density, viscosity*. English freely admits and assimilates words and elements from other languages. The various lists describing the functions and meanings of the most productive affixes are quite useful for technical writing, syllabus design, language teaching and learning (Sager & Dungworth 1980:295-300). However, these affixes have become thoroughly assimilated into English. Therefore they are subject to redefinition, extension, and narrowing of meaning.

Prefixes assist considerably in the structuring of special vocabularies. Contrasting sets of terms can be created easily by the negatives *un-, in-, dis-* or *a-*, the privatives *un-, de-, dis-*, the prefixes of degree or size *super-, sur-, sub-, hyper-, ultra-, mini-*, the locatives *super-, sub-, inter-, trans-*, the temporal or sequential *pre-, post-, re-* and the numerals *uni-, bi-, di-* etc. Usually such sets maintain terminological unity. A number of prefixed words take on special meanings in the process of terminologisation, e.g. *solvent, dissolvent*. Certain neoclassical stems are so frequently used that they can be considered prefixes from the functional and structural point of view, e.g. *auto-, equi-, macro-, mega-, meta-, micro-, para-*. Stems like *carb-, cycle-, electr-, ferr-, petr-* develop prefix character by adding "o" to the stem, e.g. *petrochemical*.

Like prefixes many suffixes are borrowed from Greek and Latin. For the naming of objects the suffix *-ing* is highly used in the expression of processes and in the conversion of countable nouns to mass nouns, e.g. *fitting, tubing, sleeving*. Other concrete nouns, mainly tools and machines, are derived by means of *-er/-or*, e.g. *dryer, connector*. This terminological agreement can be established between the action and the instrument of action.

Extended in special language designations is the use of the causative *-fy, -fier, -fication*, which produces verbs, agents, instruments, and processes, e.g. *gasify, gasifier, gasification*. Agent nouns can also be formed by *-ant*, e.g. *lubricant*. Most process nouns end in *-ation*, e.g. *saturation* or simply in *-ion*, e.g. *suction, fission*. The process-describing suffixes *-ment, -al* are not productive in special languages.

Property terms are nouns derived from adjectives ending mainly in *-al, -ent, -ic, -ous*, e.g. *solvency, elasticity*. Other property nouns end in *-ance* and *-ivity*, e.g. *reluctance, conductivity*. Many of them designate measurable properties. In chemical engineering *-ity* often designates properties of substances, e.g. *permeability, resistivity of heat*, while *-ance* refers to properties of bodies, e.g. *resistance of a conductor*. Measuring devices are usually designated by suffix-like expressions indicating the method of measurement, e.g. *oscillograph, microscope*. Certain suffixes are restricted to one field exclusively or with a special meaning in foodstuff engineering and biotechnology to designate enzymes, salts from acids, two-element compounds, salts from acids in *-ous* and metals, alcohols or phenols, carbohydrates e.g. *oxidase, nitrate, chloride, nitrite, bauxite, glycerol, glucose*. However, even within a single field suffixes may have more than one function.

The antonym of affixation is backformation or back-derivation. This process occurs principally in the formation of verbs, e.g. *evaporate, absorb*. In special languages backformation is closely linked to verb-compound terminologising verbs. The first elements may designate the instrument or agent, the purpose, the method or the place, e.g. *gravity-feed, stress-relieve, dry-lubricate, site-construct*.

(ii) *Compounding*. Usually a compound is the combination of two or more words into a new syntagmatic unit with a new meaning. Compounds are formed on the principle that normally the first element determines the other. In special reference most compounds are fully lexicalised or terminologised units developed from regularly occurring collocations and phrases. Two methods of analysis are frequently applied, paraphrasing and interpretation of compounds as shortened sentences. The *-ing* form compounds are particularly difficult to identify. On the other hand the interpretation of compounds is assisted by the relatively high frequency of neoclassical words with clear word category indicators.

In special languages the majority of compounds are nouns. Compounds with names of persons or places are very frequent to designate materials, objects, instruments, methods, measurements, and processes. Unique differentiation possibilities support the creation of terminological systems. According to the nucleus three types of compounds can be distinguished, those which designate objects (materials, substances, products, apparatus), those which designate properties, those which designate operations and processes. The determinant specifies the distinctive feature of the new concept.

Compounds designating objects form the largest group:

1. The determinant compares the nucleus to another object. This method is also used in nomenclatures. When similarity is not apparent, a more complex-type compound may be formed, e.g. *ring nut, ethane-type interaction*.
2. The determinant specifies the material. In chemical engineering a past participle indicating the relationship of the substance to the object is frequently inserted, e.g. *oil film, rubber-sheathed cable.*
3. The determinant expresses an inherent property of the new concept. It may be an adjective or a past participle, the former specifying the colour, dimension, taste, e.g. *packed bed, low octane*.
4. Many determinants specify the use of the nucleus. Frequently the determinant is a verbal noun, e.g. *grinding machine*. This method is an approximation to a new term, e.g. *grinder*. The reversal of the relationship is a special type of this compound. The nucleus serves against what is specified, e.g. *insect spray*.
5. The determinant may express the product which is regularly associated with the nucleus. It serves as a means of differentiation, e.g. *air vessel, oil-well*. Alternatively, the determinant may indicate the origin of the nucleus by specifying the primary product, the place of origin, the instrument or object which is the cause of the nucleus, e.g. *Canadian spruce, malt beer*.
6. The nucleus expresses the instrument which operates on the determinant. The determinant therefore specifies the object on which the nucleus operates, e.g. *oil filter, water pump*.
7. The determinant specifies the mode of operation of the nucleus. The insertion of a part participle makes the relationship more overt, e.g. *splash lubrication, power-operated feed*.
8. The determinant is the whole of which the nucleus is a part, e.g. *tracer finger, spindle nose.*

9. The determinant asserts identity with the nucleus, e.g. *fuel oil, carrier gas.*

The description of methods of term formation is not exhaustive. Property or disposition terms are frequently formed by the determinant specifying the concept to which the property term is related. A new property concept is this created, e.g. *speed ratio, heat transfer.*

In terminology the determinant is often an adjective, e.g. *tensile strength, buckling strength.* Process and operation noun compounds are usually created from phrases linked by "of" or "by means of", specifying the subject, the object or the instrument of the verbal action, e.g. *temperature change, probe sampling.* Process noun compounds are usually created from verbs, e.g. *dust collection.* Compounds designating operation are created from the verbal noun, e.g. *point coating, tensile testing.* Compounds with particles form a considerable number of specialised terms, e.g. *back-mixing, off-line.* In terminology there are also many phrasal compounds linked by prepositions, e.g. *out-of-balance, out-of-band pulse ringing.*

(iii) *Multiple compounding.* Compounds can be made of two, three or more separate elements. The frequency of occurrence is inverse with the increased number of constituents for the language of chemical engineering. The data are similar to those of the language of chemistry (Gläser & Winter 1975, Weise 1982:54).

Three- and more element compounds usually contain one or two-element compounds and permit formally transparent hierarchies. The basic patterns are:

(1) (X + (Y + Z)), e.g. *taper roller bearing*

(2) ((X + Y) + Z), e.g. *box-section column*

Multiple compounds of five - or six-element compounds are rare and usually consist of compound groupings, e.g. *(step-by-step) (variable speed) transmission.*

It is common practice of employing long compounds for classificatory purposes, but in texts one element is frequently omitted, e.g. *fluid power transmission (system).* The conclusion seems to be justified that longer terminological units are text specific and individually motivated.

Special language compound adjectives serve to describe production processes, to specify operations, to identify new units. Important patterns are:

- concrete noun + adjective, e.g. *heat-resistant*
- adverb + adjective or present participle, e.g. *liquid-state, high boiling*
- noun + past participle. The noun fulfills instrumental or locative functions, e.g. *diffusion-controlled, centre-mounted*. The instrumental function is very productive and important for term creation (Gerbert 1977)
- adverb + past participle, e.g. *thermostatically controlled*.

Compound verbs in special languages are frequently formed by back-formation, conversion, or with particles. The possibility of ambiguity can often be avoided by the use of *hyper-, supra-, hypo-* and *sub-*, e.g. *over-cure, superheat, hypercharge, superheat*.

(iv) *Conversion.* Conversions are constantly being created. Conversion considerably increases the range of designation, since it can co-exist with grammatical or semantic derivation. However, in biotechnology it seems to be less productive because of the many terms derived from Latin and Greek word elements with identifiable noun endings. When conversion occurs with a noun in *-ion*, it usually expresses a concrete noun, while the latter designates a process, e.g. *aggregate-aggregation, hydrate-hydration*.

(v) *Compression.* Special languages are able to compress information both syntactically and lexically. In the vocabulary this process is carried out by abbreviation, by the omission of compound elements, by symbols, by the combination of letters and numbers and by pictograms.

Abbreviations (letter words, shortenings, clippings, Latin abbreviations) are common in written language, in commercial correspondence, laboratory and experimental reports, in minutes and in-factory notes, but are avoided in patents, contracts, and other formal modes of writing.

Acronyms are constantly being created in special languages to designate products, processes, institutions, e.g. *ABS-resins, CAD, CAM*. The use of abbreviations in the designation of measurable properties and units of measurement is widespread in chemical engineering, e.g. *rpm, a* for *revolutions per minute, acceleration*.

Another method of compression is to use single letter symbols to represent numerical values or complex concepts, e.g. *A-battery, X-ray*. There are also combinations of letters and numbers, e.g. *A6-Format, &-resin*.

In chemical engineering pictograms are a highly developed symbol system mainly used in drawings and plans, symbols for values, tubes, transformers, measuring instruments.

(vi) *Neologisms*. Special languages need new designations. Fairly widespread are the processes of creating new words by blending, by the use of eponyms, by the use of letters, and by loan-translation.

Neologisms in technology result from the need for the naming of new concepts. Eponyms, for example, are widely used in technology and engineering for processes, apparatus, tools, and products, e.g. *Hindley worm gear*. The use of letters and of the Greek alphabet also occur, e.g. *K-filter, gamma cellulose*.

(vii) *Borrowing*. English has a strong tradition of borrowing. Many Latin and Greek words have been taken over unmodified. In most borrowings the endings are slightly adjusted. Borrowed elements serve to create neologisms. In nomenclatures Latin word-formation patterns are strictly followed, or inflections are omitted and changed, respectively, e.g. *suffocate, lenient, aperture*. In chemical engineering many French and German borrowings occur, e.g. *machine, technique*. Borrowing has the advantage that the highly specific nature of reference is maintained. Most borrowings are concerned with concrete objects, apparatus, and processes. In general, however, borrowing and loan-translation in special languages are neglected areas of study.

2. The special lexicon, course design, materials development

Technical language teaching stands at the crossroads. In view of the special lexicon the pressing issue is not whether to reverse the process but rather to look at what one is doing, to suggest ways to cope with the lexical problem areas more efficiently, especially the integration of the rules of term formation, the conscious use of "sub-technical vocabulary", i.e. "context-independent words which occur with high frequency across disciplines", "words that occur with special meanings in specific scientific and technical fields" (Cowan 1974:391), and the analysis and translation of compounds.

Compounding is itself "a kind of shorthand" (Trimble 1985:131) with a growing "illegibility factor". The longer and more technical the compound, the less chance any but the most knowledgeable specialist has of "deciphering" it.

Irrespective of the character of the subject area, the register and the "different varieties of usage" in language materials (Widdowson 1986: 195), applicable lexical problem solving strategies (Trimble 1985:162, Lange 1983:17) are required in practical language teaching.

Demand is high. Its "realization" is utopian for the time being, the means are not there. There are no mandatory study/training programmes for the foreseen "functional training programme", in which the "planning of material and teaching methods are linked to one another in a meaningful way" and the "acquisition of a communicative system of training", "based upon classes of communicative exercises" (Weise 1984: 58), which this implies, is even further away. Teaching plans emerge *ad hoc* being born out of need, and shape the "pressing needs" of individual language teachers or institutions. "An indication that language programs are failing to meet learners' objectives", which characterized the situation met by Dubin & Olshtain, "is often signaled by the existence of flourishing schools and courses outside the official educational system" (Dubin & Olshtain 1990:11). The incessant discussion about "syllabus design" and "curriculum development" bears out this view and creates more confusion than clarity.

In general, one understands the term *curriculum* to be "all aspects of planning, implementing, and evaluating and managing an educational programme" (Nunan 1989:14) "to describe the broadest contexts in which planning for language instruction takes place, either on the national level or for a community's school" (Dubin & Olshtain 1990:3) and under "syllabus" "the selecting and grading of content" (Nunan 1989:14), "a statement of content which is used as the basis of planning courses of various kinds"; and "which is concerned with the 'what' of a language programme" (Nunan 1988:6).

Programme planning and organization presupposes a grasp and an objective view of facts: "...where adults are concerned, there are generally two kinds of needs: (a) objective (foreseeable), those that can be deduced from a job analysis, or from a study of a person engaging in the duties of his profession and (b) subjective (partly or not at all foreseeable), depending upon the people one meets or the events that occur in an unexpected situation." (Finocchiaro & Brumfit 1983:60).

"Needs analysis" can be used to evaluate such situations. Under this term one understands all the techniques and processes for obtaining information which is required for the organization of teaching programmes. Originally the processes were taken from the sphere of education and developments in technology and industry. The analysis of the requirements must, however, start from the analysis of needs and/or arise from that. In that way the decisions that are made on the basis of the data obtained also have a socio-linguistic dimension.

The specification and varying emphases of the contents leads to many "syllabuses", which Widdowson considers to lead to two archetypes: the "structural" and the "functional-notional" syllabus.

The structural syllabus "will tend to promote activities which serve to internalize the formal properties of language" (Widdowson 1987:71). In contrast, the functional-notional syllabus supports activities which replicate "real" language communication in the language lesson and are a "dress rehearsal" for the real world. In technical language courses, which cater for special requirements and which aim for a "restricted competence", this is true to a large extent (Widdowson 1983:6).

Therefore the taxonomy for ESP courses, which Peter Strevens has produced, is still of the greatest interest (Strevens 1983:92). The taxonomy can be amended for EAP courses and in-company language training, which all have an underlying modular structure (Dubin & Olshtain 1990:53).

The development of technical language and/or subject-specific elements within the desired subject-specific foreign language training, as well as in integrated degree courses, post-graduate courses etc., opens perspectives and opportunities for the establishment of a technical language education. New effective possibilities emerge from that, however, always bearing in mind that technical language training is placed close to the end of a continuum that stretches from ESL-EFL-ESP to ESP "at the tertiary level" (Nunan 1983:50). The basic problem results from the difficulty of finding an answer to the question of how the subject-related aspect of the language training can be increased and how to increase both linguistic and specialist ability.

The controversy lies in whether the field of the topic or theme corresponds to actual specialist communication and if it succeeds in exploiting permissible possibilites. If one begins with the discourse character of specialist texts, then the obvious consequence suggests itself, i.e. to harmonize the methodology of the language lesson and the specialist training. This procedure offers the "didactic break" (Boeck 1987:10), in order to integrate those fields of language lessons which constitute "relevant English use", in which "usage into use" is transformed "by reference to the student's existing communicative competence in his own language" (Widdowson 1979:43-44).

The discourse orientation favours thematic and linguistic suitability and communicative strategies in order to fully complete the language tasks involved. The possibilities of solving the problem presented here have been considerably increased by the recognition, above all, of communicative-functional language provision.

In practice, the tailoring of language teaching material is of central importance, along with the linguistic description. An important key concept for the scope and description of functional effective language material is the concept of the "language means complex". The language means complex is differentiated between those where content and specialist treatment are centred on a communication object and those where the intention and communicative-pragmatic aspects are centred on a communication design. As a result peripheral types such as relational/ activated, subjective-modal, expressive-modal and auxilliary language material complexes have been derived (Boeck 1985:10).

The concept of language means complexes forms a suitable framework for the communicative-functional selection and tailoring of language material for such heterogeneous fields as engineering and technology because they allow a functional-semantic description of language "in a wider sense" and this will include the special perspective of the language lesson and the way the language material used is regarded (Boeck 1987:14). The selection of language materials for technical language training is dependent upon many factors. For example: upon previous knowledge, the aims of the training, the practical support, and upon the demands made by the individual and by specialists. As concrete expressions are always realised on the basis of particular themes or topics, these themes, along with the desired career, the communication design and language handling, form a second important selection principle: "Themes and the demand for communication ... are indispensable assumptions for the realisation of communication exercises and within the framework of the selection of the communication process." (Thesen 1986:5). That is an important premise for the organization of technical language teaching material. Without themes, texts are unthinkable. Texts with communicative themes have a higher value. Such themes "provoke" communicative responses, "thus acting as the central generator of the lexical items that the speaker or writer has to be able to understand or produce" (Munby 1988:38). In this way the underlying texts play the role "of implementing correct conceptual representations of the language material" (Lademann 1986:10, 1990:9). For specific technical language training and further training the field of the topic/theme and themes and the referential vocabulary categories pertaining to it are of primary importance (Lange 1989:62).

An important source of the theme is the specialist text. The specialist text is the result of linguistic-communicative activity in relation to the work being done. Therefore it is not only communicatively and structurally functional but is also socially determined and, in a specialist topic, is organised linearly-sequentially and hierarchically (Baumann 1987:3). The specialist text "actualizes" technical language and is the result of an "intellectual-linguistic process of a specialist nature in a particular communication situation, which is determined by the respective sphere of work, the specialist competence of the reader, the intention of the writer, and the correspondingly targeted linguistic and visual material." (Gläser 1985:4). In the language lesson it is necessary to reconstruct the processing of the specialist content and to prepare for the communicative task. This is the way to clear the hurdle of specialism and technical language.

The specialism of texts can be determined on the basis of the non-linguistic field, of the level of development of the technical language, of the communication conditions and of the level of specialism of the representation. The degree of specialism also depends upon the specialist knowledge of the writer and reader, upon the function of the specialist text, and upon the intention of the author (Baumann 1987:13). The resort to further criteria for differentiation such as semantic structure, degree of abstraction of the linguistic representation, relevant logic, macrostructure, and their subdivision signals and stylistic specialities (Baumann 1987:13) allows one to characterize a sufficient level of difficulty and to delimit varying types of text. Specialism in language is put into effect, however, through "the entirety of all the linguistic means that are used within a communication field limited by the specialism concerned, in order to guarantee communication between people occupied in that field of work" (Hoffmann 1984:64). With regard to technical language teaching, this implies selecting relevant specialist communication and language materials and examples of how to produce such texts, taking into consideration the actual requirements of the students, with the aim of clarifying how the two are functionally combined. The one can succeed, with the help of levels of relationship, e.g. factual knowledge vs. language knowledge, concepts vs. linguistic terms, cognitive structures vs. construction principles, typical specialist facts vs. typical specialist jargon, typical specialist situations and methods of representation vs. technical language means of expression (Blei 1988:80). The concept of binary semantic relationships, which Crombie proposed, proves to be very appropriate for technical language teaching (Crombie 1986).

Language description and didactic-methodological conversion have a close correlation. Similar areas covered are: the situation, the communication conditions, the intent, the communication object, and the means of communication. The "realization" of these similarities leads to "loss of friction". Under institutionalized training, along with the demand, there is the desire to express a known content in a particular situation, the intention to be able to express what was learnt, and the fulfilment "of the unrenouncable grammar", which forms "a major difficulty on the way to effective speech". In the language means complex, i.e. "the complex functional concentration of language material above the structural level" this is only modelled linguistically "according to whether the speaker in the communicative situation consciously puts what he knows into words" (Boeck 1987:4). In their entirety they link "into a new didactic unit", "the language material complex" (Boeck

1987:11). Language material complexes are determined by lesson/units according to Norbert Lademann. Their object is language acquisition. In contrast to the language means complex they are more comprehensive: "language material complexes are ... bundles of language material which by their mastery place learners in the position within the framework of a theme and under the conditions of a specific communication situation, to take part in a discourse and thereby to bring their own thoughts, standpoints, and values as well as to react to the contributions of other participants" (Lademann 1990:9). The "language material complexes", as with the "language means complexes", consist of items determined according to substance and intention. Their acquisition accentuates success and takes place in a complex manner, and enables the mastery of communicative language tasks.

For the organization of the material complexes/units made up of individual specialist elements, a structural scheme is recommended that commencing from relevant topics, fixes themes and the related texts selected according to the target task, and establishes systems of practice which are integrated with the language material and with the ability to communicate and individualised into work phases (Lange 1987:34). The impetus which starts with the communicative-functional language viewpoint, is not only confined to the choice of language material and the organization of the teaching material but is effected by the organization of the learning and teaching process. The language means complexes form an important interface. They build the bridges in foreign language work.

The acquisition process is carried out in general with models, patterns, and prototypes. The student undertakes the individal language implementations only through speaking tasks and the kinds of text typical for that subject. Such texts contain samples of good practice, which can be taken as models, expecially when in the process they lead to more complex facts. That is why they are excellent as examples for technical/subject-specific language teaching, learning, and pratice units (Weise 1982:206, Gläser 1985:5).

The rapid scientific and technical-technological developments are "taken on board" with the help of both traditional and new kinds of texts and specialist texts. As a result technical/subject-specific language training is also in a constant process of updating its training content or otherwise it would lose its essence. It maintains a suitable character of its own if it is involved in the specialist degree course, whilst creating scope for the insertion of variable subject-specific materials and for the inclusion of special problem situations. These lead to corresponding differences in the training and, finally, they have as a consequence an individualizing effect on the degree course.

This aim is achievable with the help of a phase model which is oriented towards specialist discourse, the difficulties of which gradually increase and with the help of which the desired target tasks are developed with varying emphases. The way shown fulfils the requirement, i.e. the aim of interweaving specialist and language degree courses, and takes genuinely communicative-functional language teaching into account in which "the dynamic process of meaning creation" (Widdowson 1979:129) by way of a "genre-specific approach" (Swales 1990) has become a reality.

The technical-content centred, thematic-oriented strategy helps to bring concordance between the selected communication items and themes and the actual communications which are demanded, and also helps to solve the problem of a rigid object or process relationship. As in specialist degree courses, it is the use of language which is paramount. This occurs, for example, in specialist communication, in naming and determining, evaluating and describing objects, stating the characteristic features, classifying and describing processes, cycles and equipment, and in discussing problems, thus generating the lexicon. So not only the evils come out of the box of the Pandora, but also hope which was left in the bottom of the box.

References

Alekseev, P. M.
1975 *Statistíceskaja leksiografija.* Leningrad.

Barber, C. L.
1962 "Some measurable characteristics of modern English scientific prose". *Gothenburg Studies in English* 14:21-43.

Baumann, K. D.
1986 "Der Versuch einer integrativen Betrachtung des linguistischen Phänomens 'Fachtext' ". *Deutsch als Fremdsprache* 2:96-102.
1987 Ein Versuch der ganzheitlichen Betrachtung von Fachtexten. In: Hoffmann (ed.). *Fachsprachen. Instrument und Objekt.* Leipzig: VEB Verlag Enzyklopädie, pp. 10-22.

Blei, D.
1988 "Zur Fachlichkeit der Fachtextsorten - Dilemma oder Vorzug für den Fremdsprachenlehrer?". *Deutsch als Fremdsprache* 2:78-83.

Boeck, W.
1985 Kommunikativitätsstufen bei der Darstellung der Sprachmittel funktional-semantischer Felder des Russischen. In: *Arbeitsberichte und wissenschaftliche Studien/KFS*, 106/1. MLU Halle, pp. 9-30.
1987 Funktional-semantische Sprachbeschreibung im Dienst des allgemein- und fachsprachlichen Fremdsprachenunterrichts. In: *Arbeitsberichte und wissenschaftliche Studien/KFS*, 122. MLU Halle, pp. 3-22.

Buchholz, E.
1978 Zum Wortschatz der englischen Fachsprache der Seewirtschaft. In: Hoffmann, Lothar (ed.). *Sprache in Wissenschaft und Technik.* Leipzig: VEB Verlag Enzyklopädie.

Cowan, J. R.
1974 "Lexical and syntactic research for the design of EFL reading materials". *TESOL Quarterly* 8.

Crombie, W.
1986 *Discourse and Language Learning: A Relational Approach to Syllabus Design.* Oxford: Oxford University Press.

Dubin, F. & E. Olshtain
1990 *Course Design, Developing Programms and Materials for Language Learning.* Cambridge: Cambridge University Press.

Finocchiaro, M. & C. Brumfit
1983 *The Functional-Notional Approach: From Theory to Practice.* Oxford: Oxford University Press.

Gerbert, M. & P. Zimmermann
1977 "Englische Adjektivkomposita vom Typ man-made". *Zeitschrift für Anglistik und Amerikanistik* 25,4:307-316.

Gläser, R. & H. Winter
1975 "Name und terminologische Wortgruppe in der chemischen Fachsprache des Englischen." *Wissenschaftliche Zeitschrift der Friedrich-Schiller-Universität Jena.* (Gesellschafts- und Sprachwissenschaftliche Reihe 24) 5,6:735-754.

Gläser, R.
1985 "Standortbestimmung einer Fachtextlinguistik". *Linguistische Studien,* Reihe A/133. Berlin: Akademie-Verlag.

Godfrey, J. W. & G. Parr
1959 *The Technical Writer, a Guide to the Presentation and Production of Technical Literature.* London.

Hempel, C. G.
1952 *Fundamentals of Concept Formation in Empirical Sciences.* Chicago.

Hoffmann, L.
1970 *Fachwortschatz Physik. Häufigkeitswörterbuch Russisch, Englisch, Französisch.* Leipzig: VEB Verlag Enzyklopädie.
1973 *Fachwortschatz Chemie. Häufigkeitswörterbuch Russisch, Englisch, Französisch.* Leipzig: VEB Verlag Enzyklopädie.
1976 *Fachwortschatz Bauwesen. Häufigkeitswörterbuch Russisch, Englisch, Französisch.* Leipzig: VEB Verlag Enzyklopädie.
1984 *Kommunikationsmittel Fachsprache. Eine Einführung.* Berlin: Akademie-Verlag.

Lademann, N.
1986 Kommunikativ-funktional orientierter Fremdsprachenunterricht - eine Betrachtung relevanter Aspekte aus fremdsprachenmethodischer Sicht. In: *Arbeitsberichte und wissenschaftliche Studien/KFS, 119.* MLU Halle, pp. 6-24.
1990 Sprachstoffkomplex im Fremdsprachenunterricht - Determination und Bestandteile. In: *Arbeitsberichte und wissenschaftliche Studien/KFS, 136.* MLU Halle, pp. 1-19.

Lange, W.
1983 Erfassung von Sinnstrukturen und Segmentierung von Texten - Wege zur Erarbeitung von Fachtexten mit Hilfe der Übersetzung. In: *Ausgewählte Probleme der Effektivierung der Fremsprachenausbildung.* Köthen: Ingenieurhochschule, pp. 1-20.

1987 Entwicklungstendenzen auf dem Gebiet der Stoffwandlung und Stoffwirtschaft und kommunikativ-orientierter Fremdsprachenunterricht. In: *Arbeitsberichte und wissenschaftliche Studien/KFS,* 123. MLU Halle, pp. 29-37.
1989 Überlegungen zur funktionalen, kommunikativ-orientierten Sprachstoffauswahl in Englisch für die Aus- und Weiterbildung von Biotechnologen. In: *Arbeitsberichte und wissenschaftliche Studien/KFS,* 134. MLU Halle, pp. 38-44.

Munby, J.
1988 *Communicative Syllabus Design. A Sociolinguistic Model for Defining the Content of Purpose-Specific Language Programmes.* Cambridge: Cambridge University Press.

Nunan, D.
1988 *Syllabus Design*. Oxford: Oxford University Press.
1989 *Designing Tasks for the Communicative Classroom.* Cambridge: Cambridge University Press.

Sager, J. C., D. Dungworth & P. F. Mc Donald
1980 *English Special Languages. Principles and Practice in Science and Technology.* Wiesbaden: Brandstetter.

Strevens, P.
1983 *New Orientations in the Teaching of English.* Oxford: Oxford University Press.

Swales, J. M.
1990 *Genre Analysis. English in Academic and Research Settings*. Cambridge: Cambridge University Press.

Thesen
1987 2. Wissenschaftliche Konferenz "Kommunikativ-funktional orientierter Fremdsprachenunterricht". In: *Arbeitsberichte und wissenschaftliche Studien/KFS,* 119. MLU Halle, pp. 1-5.

Trimble, L.
1985 *English for Science and Technology. A Discourse Approach.* Cambridge: Cambridge University Press.

Weise, G.
1982 *Systemaspekt und Tätigkeitsaspekt in der Wissenschaftssprache. Untersuchungen an englischen Fachtexten der Chemie.* Halle (Diss. B).
1984 Zur kommunikativen Orientierung des fachbezogenen Fremdsprachenunterrichts. In: *Arbeitsberichte und wissenschaftliche Studien/KFS,* 100. MLU Halle, pp. 58-69.

Widdowson, H. G.
1979 *Exploration in Applied Linguistics.* Oxford: Oxford University Press.
1983 *Learning Purpose and Language Use.* Oxford: Oxford University Press.
1986 *Explorations in Applied Linguistics 2.* Oxford: Oxford University Press.
1987 Aspects of syllabus design. In: Tickoo, M. (ed.). *Syllabus Design: The State of the Art.* Singapore: SEAMEO Regional Language Centre.

The lexicon of metaphor models as a mental tool for analogical problem-solving in science

Wolf-Andreas Liebert

1. Introduction

Cognitive Linguistics has shown the ubiquitous character of metaphor, but, of course, metaphorically structured coherence is not limited to ordinary language, it is a phenomenon which can be shown in all kinds of discourse. Metaphor models are natural kinds of thinking, but they are not fixed or "untouchable", they are accessible and changeable by human reflection, which is itself a natural process of (meta)cognition. This view connects Cognitive Linguistics with the tradition of problem-solving, especially problem-solving by analogical reasoning. Using the power of both disciplines the TLMSF-project[1] works with virologists in the field of AIDS-research detecting established metaphor models in their thinking, accumulating them in a hypertext-lexicon, and finally letting the virologists reflect their own models in a game-like manner in order to gain new perspectives for their current research.

2. General idea of the project

The general idea of the project can be formulated in two theses:

First thesis:

The reflection of one's own cognitive models is an effective problem-solving method for research teams.

Second thesis:

The lexicon of metaphor models is an appropriate tool for the reflection of cognitive models.

How can we get evidence for these theses? Let us begin with the discussion of the first thesis.

2.1. Metaphors, analogy, and innovation in the sciences

It is a consensus in the research of analogy and creativity in science that analogy and metaphors play an important role in the construction and innovation of theories in science. Let me mention the studies of Kompa (1989), Falkenhainer (1987), Gentner & Gentner (1983), Gick (1990), Gilhooly, Keane, Logie & Erdos (1990), Holyoak & Thagard (1990), Keane (1990a, 1990b), Walsh (1990), Dörner (1979), Knorr-Cetina (1991), and Hesse (1991).

Some historical examples are:

- Kékulé's discovery of the cyclic structure of the benzene is connected with his legendary dream of a snake biting its own tail. By introducing the image schema of a circle he laid the foundations for aromatic chemistry (1865).
- Rutherford's model of the atom rests on an analogy of the model of the solar system.
- The discovery of the structure of the DNA by Watson and Crick was preceded by the introduction of a new image schema: Linus Pauling postulated the helix as a structural model for proteins. This triggered research looking for such helix stuctures in the DNA, which was finally found as the double helix structure of the DNA (see Watson 1990:41ff).

As a final example let me present the discovery of the reverse transcriptase.

2.1.1. The discovery of the reverse transcriptase

In the late sixties there was a problem puzzling molecular biologists. At this time an assumption was believed to be valid, the so-called "dogma of molecular biology" (according to Watson and Crick (see Watson 1990)):

> The genetic information is always *transcribed from* the DNA *to* the RNA, which *produces* the proteins.

This dogma presupposes a model of a process of genetic transformation (see Figure 1).

Figure 1. Model of the *Genetic Transformation Process*

But there was a virus which was disturbing this central dogma, because this virus contained only RNA outside of the infected cell, but in the infected cell one found DNA of this virus. Of course this could not be true according to the assumed dogma and several discussions followed whether this was a fact at all. In this discussion a molecular biologist, Howard Temin, postulated a new enzyme: If the DNA of the cell doesn't *understand* the viral RNA, he argued, there must be an enzyme that *transcribes* RNA *reverse* in DNA, which can be *understood* by the human cell and then integrated[2]. The first reactions to Temin's hypothesis were not very friendly, but this hypothesis was then proved by experiments, the enzyme was found, and was therefore called "*reverse transcriptase*", whereas the type of virus was called "*retrovirus*" (Klingholz 1988:13).

2.1.2. The reconstruction of the discovery of the reverse transcriptase with the ICM-Theory

Let us now try to reconstruct this discovery by means of the ICM-theory (Lakoff 1987). First one can discover the well-known image schema FROM-TO resp. PATH (Johnson 1987, Lakoff 1987), which is used metaphorically for a transformation process (see Figure 2).

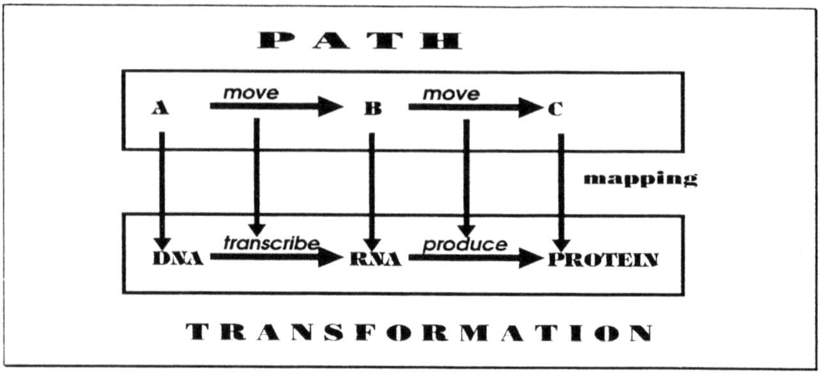

Figure 2. Model of the *Genetic Transformation Process* structured by the PATH model

A main source domain for the understanding of molecular structures is COMMUNICATION / WRITING / READING in terms of information theory. So you can construct concepts like "genetic code", "decode", "code", "transcribe", "character", and others (see Figure 3). According to Blumenberg (1986) there is a general metaphor THE WORLD IS A BOOK involved here. In his historical study of this metaphor in Western thought, he showed the old tradition of looking at the world as a book and human beings as reading the "book of nature" so as to get at the "hidden" truth. This metaphor can be shown in old Greek and Christian thought throughout all the history of Western philosophy. Arthur Schopenhauer, who states that life and the dreams are the pages of one and the same book and reading these pages together is real life (quoted in Blumenberg 1986:331), has been viewed as the pioneer of Freud's theory of dreams. The metaphor "Reading the book of nature" thus provided emerging modern biology at the beginning of the 20th century with a powerful concept of what is going on in the reproduction of the cell. Thus, at the dawning of the age of modern genetics, Erwin Schrödinger suggests the model of agents communicating within the same language code as a model for what is going on in the cell (Blumenberg 1986:374/375). The researchers become the "readers of the genetic code"

(Blumenberg 1986:372). The development of information theory (Shannon 1948) provided genetics with a more schematic model of communication than the old metaphor THE WORLD IS A BOOK. Therefore if you look at texts of modern genetics or molecular biology you will find that terms and concepts of this metaphor model mostly refer to the communication model of the information theory.

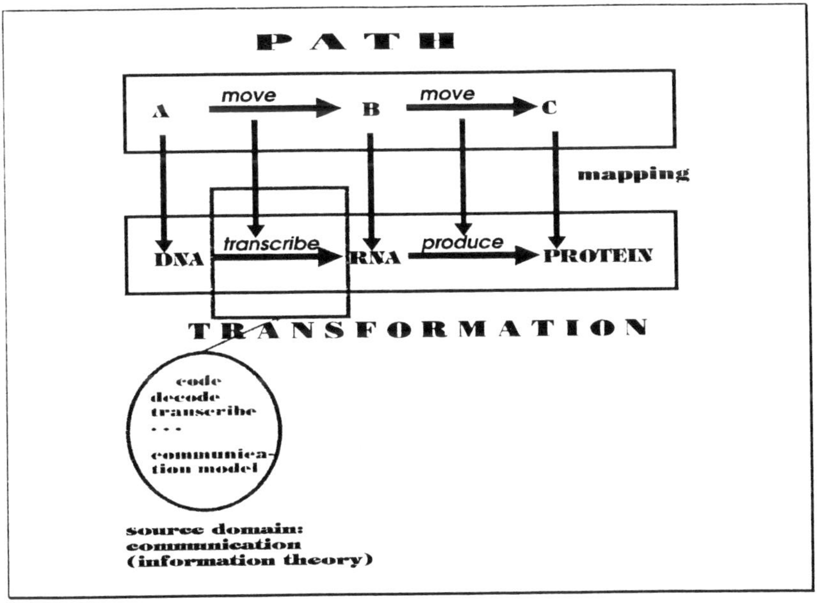

Figure 3. Model of the *Genetic Transformation Process* structured by the PATH and by the COMMUNICATION model

A second source domain for the understanding of the structure and functioning of the cell is the model of a FACTORY. You can construct metaphorical concepts like "blueprint" (The RNA is a blueprint for the protein) or "produce" for the RNA-protein-relation (The RNA produces proteins.), (see Figure 4).

One can demonstrate that the model of FACTORY is conceptualised as a specific model of a COMPUTER CONTROLED FACTORY with the DNA as the PROGRAM of the COMPUTER (Liebert 1992c). The history of this metaphor has not yet been written but it can be assumed that the metaphor of the Newtonian era, NATURE IS A CLOCK, was dropped at the beginning of the age of cybernetics and computers, and COMPUTER itself became the major source domain for many sciences (see Liebert 1992a:103), whereas biological disciplines remained the prominent scientific field which conceptualised cellular processes in terms of a COMPUTER CONTROLLED FACTORY[3].

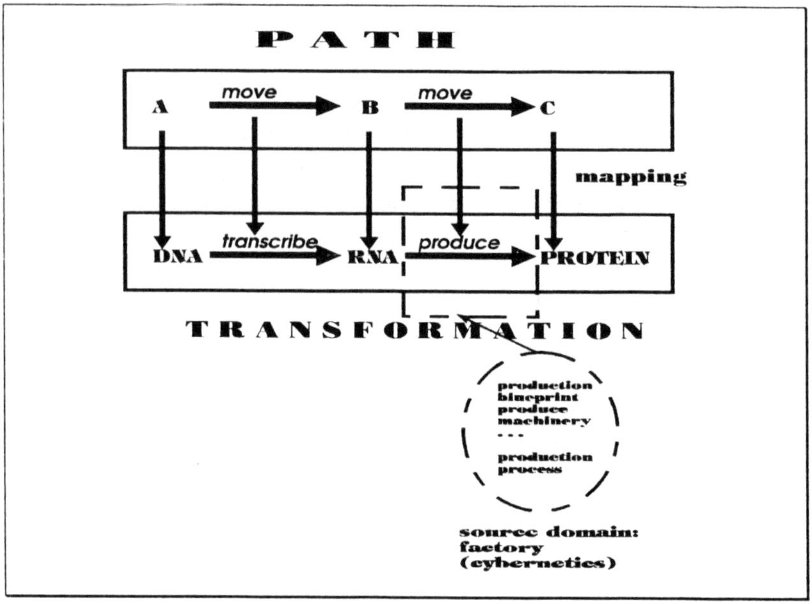

Figure 4. Model of the *Genetic Transformation Process* structured by the PATH model and by the FACTORY model

All three metaphor models,

- THE GENETIC TRANSFORMATION PROCESS IS AN OBJECT MOVING ALONG A PATH,
- THE GENETIC TRANSFORMATION PROCESS IS TRANSCRIBING INFORMATION,
- THE GENETIC TRANSFORMATION PROCESS FROM RNA TO THE PROTEINS IS PRODUCING ACCORDING TO A BLUEPRINT

can be combined into a metaphorically structured complex cognitive model, which is coherent in such a multifarious way that it resembles a holographically constructed picture (see Figure 5).

The PATH model reappears in the domain of COMMUNICATION / WRITING / READING as the COMMUNICATION model as well as the model of INFORMATIONAL FLOW (of the genetic information from the DNA to the proteins). Similarly in the domain FACTORY, the PATH model can be seen as the PRODUCTION PROCESS (of proteins by the "blueprint" RNA), which itself is controlled by the PROGRAM of the DNA, which suggests the COMPUTER CONTROLLED FACTORY as discussed above.

The model of what this enzyme does, "transcribing reverse", can now be reconstructed within the COMMUNICATION model as part of the more complex metaphorically structured model of the GENETIC TRANSFORMATION PROCESS. This reconstruction shows that the discovery of the reverse transcriptase is consistent with the common metaphor models of molecular biology (THE GENETIC TRANSFORMATION PROCESS IS AN OBJECT MOVING ALONG A PATH, THE GENETIC TRANSFORMATION PROCESS IS TRANSCRIBING INFORMATION, THE GENETIC TRANSFORMATION PROCESS FROM RNA TO THE PROTEINS IS PRODUCING ACCORDING TO A BLUEPRINT).

This means that the dogma of the "one way" was wrong, but the presupposed cognitive models of the dogma are still working and they are working in an effective way:

It was the PATH model and the model of COMMUNICATION/WRITING/READING, which were used to infer via analogical reasoning that when the transcription of genetic information is possible, then the reverse transcription must be possible as well.

Therefore if we gave researchers access to their own cognitive models, making them conscious of the metaphors they live by, then we could perhaps stimulate research processes, helping them play within and outside their shared metaphors.

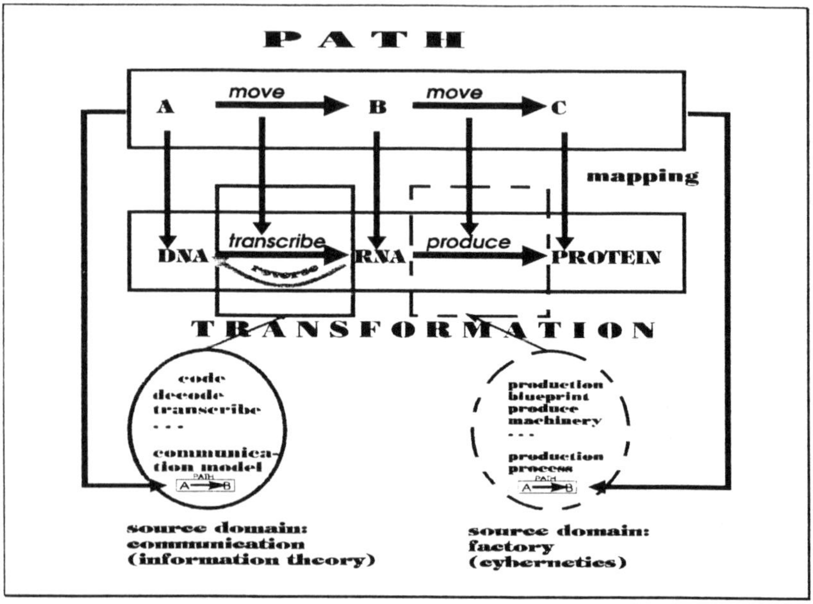

Figure 5. The discovery of the reverse transcriptase as part of a complex, metaphorically structured model of the *Genetic Transformation Process*

This should be sufficient evidence for the first thesis and we can now turn to the second thesis.

2.2. *The lexicon of metaphor models as a mental tool*

The second thesis was formulated as:

The lexicon of metaphor models is an appropriate tool for the reflection of cognitive models.

How can we get evidence for this second thesis? I propose a procedure containing eight steps:

1st step:	Choose a real science team.
2nd step:	Go and experience this team's everyday life.
3rd step:	Analyse the metaphors they live by.
4th step:	Relate the metaphors they live by to the problems they have in their research.
5th step:	Construct a lexicon as a tool which enables them to reflect their own models.
6th step:	Let the team interact with this tool and actually reflect their own models.
7th step:	Observe what reflections and reorganisation processes are taking place.
8th step:	Evaluate the possibilities of the reflection of one's own cognitive models by such a tool.

According to these eight steps I have chosen a team from the field of applied tumorvirology, which is researching the inhibition of replication of the AIDS-virus HIV. This science team serves as a test case in order to get more evidence as to whether such a lexicon of metaphor models is an effective tool in reflection processes and might, therefore, be helpful in scientific problem-solving.

3. Procedure

3.1. Data acquisition, data analysis, and the construction of the lexicon of metaphor models

3.1.1. First data acquisition: Developing the basic corpus

In order to get at the metaphors and problem-specific knowledge of the research team, which may be regarded as metaphors they live by, a basic corpus was developed. This corpus contains:

- 10 meetings (weekly, 20-25 persons, 90 minutes, 2 speakers and discussion)
- Guided group discussion in order to diagnose the problem-understanding of the research team

- Interviews with every researcher in order to diagnose the background knowledge and promote the task of related problem-understanding and the metaphorically structured concepts

The next step is the analysis of the metaphors emerging from the corpus.

3.1.2. Data analysis of the basic corpus

The analysis of the basic corpus went as follows:

- Coding source domains with a content analysis program
- Reconstructing the metaphor ICMs the research team lives by in the way described above
- Analysing and structuring their tasks and problems

Until now we have analysed the metaphors the research team lives by and have combined them into a complex metaphorically structured cognitive model as discussed above.

3.1.3. Cognitive lexicography: Constructing the basic lexicon

Therefore, the next step is to construct a lexicon of these metaphor models as a mental tool, so that the scientists can reflect their own cognitive models. The implementation of complex ICMs as discussed above requires a new approach in lexicography, cognitive lexicography, which can be defined as "constructing a lexicon by describing lexical meaning relative to cognitive models" (Liebert 1992a:203)[4].

Of course this kind of lexicon cannot have an alphabetical structure. It should give fast access to the problems occurring in the ongoing research process and the metaphor models which are involved there. Therefore we will implement the problems and tasks we have got from the group discussions and the interviews as an index of contents of the lexicon. After this the metaphor models have to be related to tasks and problems, and finally these problem-specific metaphor models will be implemented in a hypertext system running on a PC.

3.1.4. Second data acquisition: Developing the expanded corpus

The next step is the acquisition of texts which contain metaphors that are coherent with the analysed source domains or which establish other source domains cited by the scientists. This selection is determined by the three main strategies of metaphorical projections: new metaphors within an established source domain, outside an established source domain, and situationally emerging source domains from the daily life of the scientists (for a more detailed view see Martin 1990, Liebert 1992a:140-155). These texts stem from the textual environment of the researchers:

- Lexicons, dictionaries, and monographs which contain additional knowledge according to the observed metaphorical lines of thinking (e.g. supplementing the WAR-metaphor)
- Articles, textbooks, and monographs, normally read by the researchers in order to get "unseen" metaphor models

3.1.5. Data analysis of the expanded corpus

The next step is the search for models fitting the outlined, hitherto fragmental metaphor ICMs of the basic lexicon and analysing new metaphor concepts and new metaphor domains from the textual environment.

3.1.6. Constructing the expanded lexicon

Now the expanded lexicon can be finished by completing the outlined, fragmental metaphor ICMs and implementing new metaphor concepts and new metaphor domains from the textual environment.

3.2. Using the lexicon as a mental tool in an innovation workshop

How can such a lexicon be used by the scientists for innovation processes?

Let us assume that some researchers are living by the WAR metaphor. This means that the complex SCENARIO-ICM of WAR is mapped onto the SCENARIO-ICM of the HIV INFECTION. The mapping includes the projection of the parts of the whole WAR SCENARIO which has typical PARTICIPANTS (COMBATANTS) with typical ROLES (AGGRESSOR, AG-

GRESSED, and DEFENDER[5]) who have STRATEGIES in order to reach their GOALS (WIN THE WAR) and which furthermore has the typical stages of a BATTLE with a typical BEGINNING and END (WIN / LOOSE THE WAR). Thus the HIV becomes the AGGRESSOR, the T4-CELLS[6] become the AGGRESSED and the HUMAN PROTECTION SYSTEM becomes the DEFENDER (see Figure 6).

SCENARIO-ICM WAR

PARTICIPANTS (COMBATANTS)
ROLES (*AGGRESSOR, AGGRESSED, DEFENDER*)
STRATEGIES
GOALS (WIN THE WAR)
TYPICAL STAGES OF A BATTLE
BEGINNING
END (WIN/LOOSE THE WAR, DEAD/SURVIVING COMBATANTS)
HIV INFECTION IS WAR
AGGRESSOR: HIV
AGGRESSED: T4-CELLS
DEFENDER: HUMAN PROTECTION SYSTEM

Figure 6. HIV INFECTION IS WAR

Let us further assume that a certain researcher is concerned with the problem of how the HIV ENTERS the CELL.

Now the WAR metaphor is highlighting the active role of the virus (HIV = AGGRESSOR) and the passive role of the cell (T4-CELLS = AGGRESSED) while it is hiding any possible aspects of an active role of the cell itself which therefore may remain unseen in the observations.

A different metaphor, for example a metaphor which refers to a kind of cooperation like TRADE or something of this kind, would highlight other aspects of the cell-virus interaction and would, therefore, lead to another focus of observation - say activities of the cell.

4. Conclusion

There is sufficient evidence from cognitive semantics and research in analogical reasoning that the reflection and changing of metaphors can help in scientific problem-solving. For the implementation of complex ICMs as discussed above, a new lexicographic approach, cognitive lexicography, is needed. Hypertext environments provide cognitive lexicography with the possibility of dealing with non-alphabetical, holistic structures in the lexicon. Cognitive lexicography seen as applied cognitive semantics may therefore produce mental tools for creative problem-solving in science.

Notes

1. TLMSF is an acronym for "Das Theoriesprachliche Lexikon der Metaphern-Modelle als Sprachreflexionsmittel im Forschungsprozeß" (The lexicon of metaphor models as a language reflector in research processes) which is sponsored by the German Research Foundation (DFG).
2. A non-metaphorical formulation could be: Is there an enzyme that can catalyze RNA in DNA?
3. Note that cybernetics itself suggests a communication theory which is assumed to apply to animal and machines in an equal way (Wiener 1948).
4. For a detailed discussion of cognitive lexicography, see Liebert (1992a:203-227).
5. If the WAR SCENARIO is perspectivated then the ME/WE perspective is typically the AGGRESSED and the ENEMY perspective is typically the AGGRESSOR. It is not unusual that the AGGRESSED is the DEFENDER. This is also important for the target domain where T4-cells are part of the human protection system.
6. There are also other cells which are infected by HIV for example the macrophages, but this is not important here.

References

Blumenberg, H.
1986 *Die Lesbarkeit der Welt.* Frankfurt/Main: Suhrkamp.

Dörner, D.
1979 *Problemlösen als Informationsverarbeitung.* Stuttgart, Berlin, Mainz etc.: Kohlhammer-Standards Psychologie.

Falkenhainer, B.
1987 Scientific theory formation through analogical inference. In: Langley, P. (ed.). *Proceedings of the Fourth International Workshop on Machine Learning.* June 22-25, 1987, University of California, Irvine. Los Altos: Morgan Kaufmann, pp. 218-229.

Gentner, D. & D. Gentner
1983 Flowing water or teeming crowds: Mental models of electricity. In: Gentner, D. & A. Stevens (eds.). *Mental Models*. Hillsdale, N.J.

Gick, M. I.
1990 Transfer in insight problems. The effects of different types of similarity. In: Gilhooly, K. J., M. T. G. Keane, R. H. Logie & G. Erdos (eds.). *Lines of Thinking: Reflections on the Psychology of Thought. Volume 1: Representation, Reasoning, Analogy, and Decision Making.* Chichester, New York etc.: John Wiley & Sons, pp. 251-266.

Gilhooly, K. J., M. T. G. Keane, R. H. Logie & G. Erdos (eds.)
1990 *Lines of Thinking: Reflections on the Psychology of Thought. Volume 1: Representation, Reasoning, Analogy, and Decision Making.* Chichester, New York etc.: John Wiley & Sons.

Hahn, A.
1991 Paradoxien in der Kommunikation über AIDS. In: Gumbrecht, H. U. & K. L. Pfeiffer (eds.). *Paradoxien, Dissonanzen, Zusammenbrüche. Situationen offener Epistemologie.* Frankfurt/Main: Suhrkamp, pp. 696-618.

Hesse, F. W.
1991 *Analoges Problemlösen: Eine Analyse kognitiver Prozesse beim analogen Problemlösen.* Weinheim: Psychologie Verl. Union.

Holyoak, K. J. & P. Thagard
1990 A constraint-satisfaction approach to analogue retrieval and mapping. In: Gilhooly, K. J. , M. T. G. Keane, R. H. Logie & G. Erdos (eds.). *Lines of Thinking: Reflections on the Psychology of Thought. Volume 1: Representation, Reasoning, Analogy, and Decision Making.* Chichester, New York etc.: John Wiley & Sons, pp. 205-220.

Johnson, M.
1987 *The Body in the Mind. The Bodily Basis of Reason and Imagination.* Chicago, London: University of Chicago Press.

Keane, M. T. G.
1990a Analogy, metaphor, and transfer. In: Gilhooly, K. J., M. T. G. Keane, R. H. Logie & G. Erdos (eds.). *Lines of Thinking: Reflections on the Psychology of Thought. Volume 1: Representation, Reasoning, Analogy, and Decision Making.* Chichester, New York etc.: John Wiley & Sons, pp. 210-203.
1990b Incremental analogizing: Theory and model. In: Gilhooly, K. J., M. T. G. Keane, R. H. Logie & G. Erdos (eds.). *Lines of Thinking: Reflections on the Psychology of Thought. Volume 1: Representation, Reasoning, Analogy, and Decision Making.* Chichester, New York etc.: John Wiley and Sons, pp. 221-236.

Klingholz, R.
1988 Aids: Immunologie und Evolution. In: Burkel, E. (ed.). *Der AIDS-Komplex. Dimensionen einer Bedrohung.* Frankfurt/Main: Ullstein, pp. 13-37.

Knorr-Cetina, K.
1991 *Die Fabrikation von Erkenntnis. Zur Anthropologie der Naturwissenschaft.* Frankfurt/Main: Suhrkamp.

Kompa, A.
1989 Kreativität. In: Brander, S., A. Kompa & U. Peltzer. *Denken und Problemlösen. Einführung in die kognitive Psychologie.* Opladen: Westdeutscher Verlag, pp. 58-107.

Lakoff, G.
1987 *Women, Fire, and Dangerous Things. What Categories Reveal About the Mind.* Chicago: University of Chicago Press.

1991a *Metaphor and War. The Metaphor System Used to Justify War in the Gulf.* Network message. 14 pp. Again in: Pütz, M. (ed.). *Thirty Years of Linguistic Evolution*. Philadelphia, Amsterdam: Benjamins, pp. 463-481.

1991b Krieg und Metapher. Die Rechtfertigung eines Krieges am Golf: ein Metaphernsystem. In: *Why SPEZIAL*. Hannover: AStA d. Uni Hannover, pp. 30-43. (partly reprinted in: Brie, M. (ed.): *Let's Play Golf. Die Welt im Widerstreit*. Berlin, pp. 249-251.)

Lakoff, G. & M. Johnson
1980 *Metaphors we Live by.* Chicago, London: University of Chicago Press.

Langacker, R. W.
1987 *Foundations of Cognitive Grammar, Vol. 1. Theoretical Prerequisites.* Stanford: Stanford University Press.
1990 *Concept, Image, and Symbol. The Cognitive Basis of Grammar.* Berlin, New York: Mouton de Gruyter.

Langley, P., H. Simon, G. Bradhaw & J. Zytkow
1987 *The Process of Scientific Research.* Cambridge, Mass.: MIT Press.

Liebert, W.-A.
1990 Zu einem Wörterbuch der festen Metaphern der deutschen Alltagssprache im Spannungsfeld zwischen Kognitiver Linguistik und onomasiologischer, lexikographischer Datenbank. In: Rieger, B. & B. Schaeder (eds.). *Lexikon und Lexikographie. Maschinell - maschinell gestützt. Grundlagen - Entwicklungen - Produkte.* Hildesheim, Zürich, New York: Olms, pp. 11-28.
1992a *Metaphernbereiche der deutschen Alltagssprache. Kognitive Linguistik und die Perspektiven einer Kognitiven Lexikographie.* Frankfurt/Main, Berlin, Bern etc.: Lang.
1992b *Das theoriesprachliche Lexikon der Metaphern-Modelle als Sprachreflexionsmittel im Forschungsprozeß. Eine exemplarische Studie am Beispiel der AIDS-Forschung. Projektvorstellung* (TLMSF Working Paper 1). Mannheim: IDS Mannheim.
1992c *AIDS-Forscher und ihre Metaphern. Eine kognitiv-linguistische Textanalyse einiger Modelldeterminanten der AIDS-Forschung.* (TLMSF Working Paper 3). Mannheim: IDS Mannheim.
1993a *Das theoriesprachliche Lexikon der Metaphern-Modelle als Sprachreflexionsmittel im Forschungsprozeß. Theoretische und methodische Grundlagen.* (TLMSF Working Paper 2). Mannheim: IDS Mannheim.
1993b *Metapher und Innovation. Ein Trainingsprogramm zur Sprachreflexion und Kreativität im Forschungsprozeß.* (TLMSF Working Paper 4). Mannheim: IDS Mannheim.
1993c *The Lexicon of Metaphor Models of Theoretical Language as a Language Reflector in Research Processes. A Study in the Language of AIDS Research. Project Presentation* (TLMSF Working Paper 6). Mannheim: IDS Mannheim.

Link, J. & R. Parr
1989 Militarisierung der "Sprache"? Zum Verhältnis von elementarer Literatur, Mediendiskursen und subjektiver Aufrüstung. In: Förster, J., E. Neuland & G. Rupp (eds.). *Wozu noch Germanistik? Wissenschaft - Beruf - Kulturelle Praxis.* Stuttgart: Metzler, pp. 224-238.

Martin, J. H.
1990 *A Computational Model of Metaphor Interpretation. (Perspectives in Artificial Intelligence 8.)* Boston, San Diego etc: Academic Press.

Reddy, M.
1979 The conduit metaphor - A case of frame conflict in our language about language. In: Orthony, A. (ed.). *Metaphor and Thought.* Cambridge, London, New York etc.: Cambridge University Press, pp. 284-324.

Schön, D. A.
1979 Generative metaphor: A perspective on problem-setting in social policy. In: Orthony, A. (ed.). *Metaphor and Thought.* Cambridge, London, New York etc.: Cambridge University Press, pp. 254-283.

Shannon, C. E.
1948 "A mathematical theory of information". *Bell Systems Technical Journal* 27:379-423, 623-656.

Sontag, S.
1989 *AIDS und seine Metaphern.* München, Wien: Hanser.

Varela, F. J.
1990 *Kognitionswissenschaft - Kognitionstechnik. Eine Skizze aktueller Perspektiven.* Frankfurt/Main: Suhrkamp.
1991 Der Körper denkt. Das Immunsystem und der Prozeß der Körper-Individuierung. In: Gumbrecht, H. U. & K. L. Pfeiffer (eds.). *Paradoxien, Dissonanzen, Zusammenbrüche. Situationen offener Epistemologie.* Frankfurt/Main: Suhrkamp, pp. 727-743.

Vosniadou, S. & A. Orthony (eds.)
1989 *Similarity and Analogical Reasoning.* Cambridge, New York etc.: Cambridge University Press.

Walsh, P.
1990 Imagery as a heuristic in the comprehension of metaphorical analogies. In: Gilhooly, K. J., M. T. G. Keane, R. H. Logie & G. Erdos (eds.). *Lines of Thinking: Reflections on the Psychology of Thought. Volume 1: Representation, Reasoning, Analogy, and Decision Making.* Chichester, New York etc.: John Wiley & Sons, pp. 237-250.

Watson, J. D.
1990 *Die Doppel-Helix. Ein persönlicher Bericht über die Entdeckung der DNS-Struktur.* Reinbek bei Hamburg: Rowohlt.

Wiener, N.
1948 *Cybernetics, or Control and Communication in the Machine.* Cambridge, Mass.

Part V

Pedagogical approaches to the lexicon

WIC ("Words in Context"): An assessment

Lut Baten and Johan Vanparys

In this article we will briefly introduce a computer program for vocabulary learning called WIC ("Woorden in Context") and then assess it. It is used with adult students of Dutch as a foreign language, pre-intermediate, after 150 hours of Dutch, at university level. It exists for IBM compatibles and Apple Macintosh. It was developed by J. Vanparys (DOS version), L. Baten, and Y. Wullaert (Mac version).

This assessment is based on observation during the computer activities and on two questionnaires, one devised by the National Confederation of Belgian Banks for independent testees acquainted with both DOS and Mac and our own questionnaire given to the students of Dutch FL at the end of the course. As the teacher, who was one of the developers, invited the students to comment on the program while working with it in order to improve it, oral reactions already popped up from the very beginning. These have also been incorporated in the assessment. 40 students completed the questionnaire.

1. WIC: Awareness of how to learn a foreign language

WIC is an authoring tool, geared at learners of Dutch as a foreign language who need to deepen and practise their vocabulary. The version described here is a Macintosh version with a database of about 2,000 Dutch headwords, each used in contexts. For retrieval purposes the words are categorized in themes. Translations and grammatical feedback are available as well as an interface for an electronic dictionary, if present.

The theoretical basis of WIC has been described before (Baten *et al.* 1992). It applies insights from frequency analysis, the Threshold Level (thematic ordering), learning psychology, and studies on autonomous learning. As a result, language learning strategies are built in and room is left for finding out about one's own learning strategy. The method of practising is hypothesis formation: Students are offered sentences with a gap, they try to infer the meaning of the missing word, then insert the corresponding word, and finally check their solution.

On the basis of several specially written contexts for one word, all appearing on screen in the shape of a card the learner has to find which word fits in best Only one answer is accepted. This is the dictionary entry of the word. If this is correct, the different forms in the sentences may be completed. The different types of feed-back and help can be selected by the learner himself and put in default. Hence, the most preferred device can be put first. The learner can choose among translations in two different languages, the length of the word, letter by letter, and scrambled order. The preferred selection appears first, but the other help can be called up as well. This helps to develop one's own learning strategy.

Before moving on to a next word, more lexical information can be activated at the consultative level: about gender, plurals, main tenses, spelling, thus enabling the learner to further deepen his insight in the language, rather than to punish him for looking up information.

There is also an *auto-referential system* to help the learner. The contexts contain only words included in the database of words-to-be-learned. As a result, this database qualifies as its own dictionary, which can be consulted on-line: If the learner does not understand a word other than the target one, doubleclicking that word calls forth the card of that word. It is the morphological analyser that provides for the automatic analysis of a token. Upon consultation, the learner presses a return arrow and simply proceeds with words of his selected theme. Also verbs may be practised separately.

Some students attach more importance to the competitive aspect. Therefore, a scoring system is operational. One may either consult a list of words and then practise in the order given, or one may ask for a random selection. The known words appear in bold print in the thematic list. They are automatically substracted from the target list until the user initializes the database. The scores can be stored on a smart card for further use on another computer.

As such WIC sustains the user in various ways: (i) hypothesis formation on the semantic field of a word by means of the pregnant contexts, (ii) customizing by means of adjustable modes of selection, consultation, help, pace, and scoring, (iii) management, self testing, and initiative (i.e. autonomous learning), (iv) learning facilitation by means of a familiar user-friendliness: browsing, cutting, pasting, copying, note taking, and interfacing with CD applications. On an experimental basis, a pronunciation dictionary was devised for Dutch. In this way students can call up the pronunciation of a word either before doing the exercise, or as a help function within the exercise.

WIC was originally developed with a Dutch database. But it is conceived as an authoring system. The editing function allows for a very easy feeding of new themes, words, sentences, feedback. In this respect, an existing database can be adjusted, or a new database made e.g. for special purposes. A good frequency analysis, a Kwic index on a well selected corpus, and the necessary rules for context building are the basic tools to start with. No programming experience is needed. Even a secondary school pupil can devise his own WIC (e.g. of Latin). All words should be organised such that they belong to a theme and one of the two levels of difficulty. The themes for Dutch have been composed on the basis of the functional-notional research of the Council of Europe. The division into two levels has been inspired by the availability of institutionalized target lists for Dutch vocabulary (Beheydt 1991, de Kleijn & Nieuwborg 1983).

As schools use different hardware systems, the Dutch version of WIC is also available on DOS. And as not all students do have access to hardware at all times, we have published a printed out version of the Dutch database, in the form of a textbook, *Woorden in Context.* Students who would rather study on paper can do so.

2. Assessment

2.1. Overall impression

Students state that working with WIC is more fun than studying the exercise book on their own. It is more challenging. The program is very user-friendly. It helps in becoming more accurate as it allows self-testing. It is appreciated that one can practise with and without writing.

2.2. Effort

2.2.1. Time spent

Good students need about one hour to finish 30 words. In order to cover the whole program, at least 40 hours are required.

Weaker students state that they first have a look at the list of words within the theme. If they don't know more than half of the words, they take the book, look up, and study the words. They often use their own dictionary and the textbook (with texts and groups of related words in the shape of semantic networks) to study the words. Apparently, adjoining texts should be available on computer.

All students confirm that one 50-minute computer session per week is not enough. However, spending more class time is not welcome either.

As students need extra time at their convenience, the computer lab is reserved three afternoons per week. They can freely use the room for practising.

2.2.2. Price

There is no charge for using the computer room, neither during class time nor afterwards. On the whole, students consider 3,000 BEF for the package too high. They argue that if they register for a course, the software should be given free or at a very low expense (e.g. 500 BEF, covering copying expenses). Only few students buy the software as there is a very flexible arrangement for them to come and work freely in the afternoons in the lab.

2.2.3. Stress and discontentment

The words are classified in themes. There are about 20 themes for each of the two levels, each containing quite a long list of words (as lengthy as 80 words in some cases.) The acquired words appear in bold type and are not elicited when the student reactivates the theme of those words. The developers conceived of this system because they thought it was motivating for the students to actually see which words they already knew and which were thus substracted from the (long) list. But most students show discouragement when they see such a long list of words per theme for the first time. As only a maximum of 30 words (known and new words) can be covered in one hour, it is better to subdivide the themes in subthemes. In this way the learner has the satisfactory feeling of having achieved a unit at the end of his hour when most of his words appear in bold type. Students make quite a lot of annotations and they make print-outs of the themes and the lists. Hence a sort of notepad on computer or access to textbook is advisable.

Most students ask for the pronunciation when they look at the target theme for the first time. Hence, a tape with pronunciation circulates. We are technically too limited to provide pronunciation on computer, e.g. by CD-Rom.

2.3. *Help*

2.3.1. Access

A general introduction is given at the beginning of the course as most students have never worked on a computer before. It needs further investigation to find out why students have personal preferences. Some always work on the Mac and some always on the DOS PC, even though they have never operated either machine before at all. One reason may be that they were all introduced to the DOS system first as the Mac lab was installed when the course had already started. In both versions all help is available on line. It takes longer than expected for students to find out about all the possibilities of the feedback. In the DOS version, students apparently do not want to lose on their scores. Each time they press the return key for more help, their scores are lowered. As such they refrain from asking information. The Apple version is menu driven. As such all options can be perceived at the same time. Here it is rather a question of getting adjusted to the system. After three sessions with teacher help, all students work on their own and only ask information on language items.

2.3.2. Flexibility

Students prefer flexibility in the feedback. In the DOS version the first hint is a scramble version of the word, then a translation and only then the first letter. In the mean time the score goes down. In the Mac version they can set their own default: their preferred help comes first. They all appreciate that a theme need not be finished before moving on to another one or leaving the lab. They also appreciate the flexibility in the concept: if they want to test themselves, they merely start with the theme without looking at the list first. If they want to see the list, they can do so at all times.

2.3.3. List and auto-referential function

In the DOS version the auto-referential function (cf. Section 1) is not immediately available: students have to type in the word they do not understand in the form of a dictionary entry (i.e. the infinitive form of verbs, the singular form of nouns, ...). This causes problems e.g. with conjugated verbs. The Apple version implements this function in a more user-friendly way. By clicking on the difficult word, WIC automatically selects the cards in which that word is a possible key word.

2.4. Scoring

The scoring system is more primitive in Apple version: if the student makes a spelling or typing error, the system assumes he gave a wrong word and rejects it as a mistake. The DOS version, on the other hand, analyzes the user's input, tells the student that he made a spelling or typing error and gives him the opportunity to correct it. The student also sees his score drop whenever he asks for more hints. Hence, they tend to look longer for a solution before typing in the answer.

2.5. Content

2.5.1. Number of words/theme

As mentioned above there is a discrepancy between the length of themes, which is not so very well received by the learners.

2.5.2. Link with textbook

WIC is conceived of as an autonomous program. But students ask to have the words available in other forms as well, e.g. in class, in texts, in networks, practice in conversation before and after the computer session. This request is only fair: one needs to learn words in semantic contexts, but also in their communicative and cultural settings. With CD applications, more opportunities can be offered.

2.5.3. Number of sentences

Two contexts per word are not enough for setting up hypotheses; three is the minimum requirement.

2.5.4. Different meanings

The contexts were written in view of polysemy. All students, weaker and good ones, express their surprise about the fact that so many words have another meaning than the one they have keyed words down to. Not only different meanings but also different collocations are much appreciated. They argue it is not confusing at all, but rather suggest providing them with the necessary information they need about the words.

However, students express the wish to have more lexical information per word. For instance, if they want to consult the semantic field of a word, words with similar meanings could appear in a list (synonyms, antonyms, false friends). Clicking on the word would highlight the card with that word. Students want to have the required information readily available at any time, without leaving the item they are dealing with. Hence, a hypertext-like environment would be advisable, where clicking on an item on screen triggers a search in the database for information on that item.

2.5.6. Translations

Students can ask translations as a hint to the solution, but this reduces the score. Consequently, they are not inclined to rely on the translation as the first hint. Still, they often consult the translation, even upon completion of the headword, especially because the meaning of the words changes with the different contexts. Hence, more than one translation per word is required, which is provided by the package. Suggestions were made to link the exact translations to the specific context instead of giving all translations at the same time.

2.5.7. Grammar

Every word is morphologically annotated. This information includes irregular plurals and diminutives of nouns, verb conjugations, etc. Students can consult this when the headword has been filled in correctly. As such, the information can still be processed in order to find the right form of the word according to the context. Students often use this function, also because it does not affect their score and because the information appears on screen together with the contexts.

Some students even suggest forcing the students' attention to the grammar before moving on to the next word. They would like to have *de/het* (article choice), irregular plurals, main tenses, separable verbs to be shown automatically before moving on to the next word. In this way the lexical features of the word are enforced. An option could appear in default: practice with grammar or without.

In the Mac version verbs may be accessed from two angles: within the thematic fields or separately for consultation purposes.

2.6. General organisation of the program

2.6.1. Gearing system

Students can adapt the speed of the exercise themselves. There are four possibilities ranging from typing in all forms per context, which is the slowest and consequently the first speed, to not typing at all and merely press the return key for the solutions which all appear at once on screen (cf. Baten 1991, Baten *et al.* 1992). In this "fourth gear" no scores can be obtained. The exercise is meant for mere consultation. In the DOS version students have to set the default at the beginning. In the Mac version they can adapt the speed while working, which they apparently like better. In this way they can speed up or slow down as they please.

2.6.2. Inaccuracies and bugs

Both versions are bug-free. There are limitations due to the system, e.g. the 2,000 cards had to be split up in two units (WIC 1 and WIC 2) which is not so user-friendly as to the referential function interface of WIC 2 with WIC 1. As HyperCard has different working languages (French, Dutch, English...) the instructions had to be put in these languages as well. WIC was originally designed on an English HyperCard. This is still best fitting.

2.6.3. System

The user needs a hard disk to store the programs. The DOS version works at a good speed, irrespective of the machine. As HyperCard operates on quite a lot of cards, it works slower on small machines. The new edition of HyperCard has solved this problem. It is now being delivered with the smaller machines.

2.6.4. Keeping track of one's activities

WIC is personalized as the student has to type in his name at the beginning of a working session. All scores are saved on disk under that label. The Mac version goes a step further. If the student wants to continue the exercise at home, or on another machine, he saves his scores on a separate diskette. When he loads this diskette on any other Mac, any WIC will automatically take these data into account.

We noticed that students are so used to working with one machine that they don't even look at the name appearing on the screen. Hence, for class use, a message should appear with the opening screen warning the student that he hasn't changed the name and asking him whether he wants to continue with the present name.

2.6.5. Ergonomics

The DOS version does not support the mouse and consequently the interface does not involve any buttons, which is encompassing to a mouse user. It is not so obvious for a beginner to select the options from a pull-down menu. It takes a bit of experience to make selections with the arrow keys and the return key.

The Mac version is easier to use, because of the mouse, but it could be more systematically implemented in view of suggestions made above: e.g. one click would display the solution, a doubleclick the extra-information e.g. on grammar, on word meaning (referential function).

The Macintosh still has a smaller screen than other computers. With small machines (e.g. the SE) this might cause an overlap in the right corner of the menu bar. Also good care should be taken as to the operations of the students: e.g. the Grammar button should stand under Solution button, all indicators in the same right corner. A developer has to be very strict with the icons of HyperCard if he wants to be user-friendly. Spending one hour of introduction to the system (DOS or Mac) is mandatory and in fact only polite to the user.

2.8. Consultation and control

The facilities of (i) being able to go back to the original themes and word lists at all times; (ii) the referential function to look up words one does not know and which are in the contexts; (iii) the filter to keep track of the words one does not know; (iv) the random selection for a testing situation: these are all frequently used and appreciated by the students. It is very motivating for a learner to get the right information at the right time and to actually see that one is progressing well.

But as mentioned above, the number of words to be learned is demotivating even though students realize that they have to clear the job if they want to participate in standardized tests (e.g. the "Certificaat Nederlands" uses the same word list) and if they wanted to pursue their studies in Dutch. But if a student does not have this external motivation, neither a classroom to provide him with contact hours, he might drop out on WIC. Hence, the program should be subdivided into smaller units better equipped to achievable targets.

WIC should also be combined with texts, dictionaries, pictorial and audio information etc. An interface should be available (with a textprocessor, an electronic dictionary etc.). HyperCard facilitates this. But it will still take some time for school workstations to be equipped with the required hardware and software.

2.9. Cooperation

Due to a limited number of machines available at the beginning of the course, we asked students to work together. They were mostly two, sometimes three persons working on one machine. Three is definitely too many, two is very good in the early stages to overcome manipulation problems. When the Macs arrived, a number of students preferred to work alone. They stayed away from the reserved time during class hours (with the teacher present) to reserve for a longer session at the dead hours (without the teacher). This proves that students can work perfectly on their own with WIC. Those students who continued to work in pairs did so because on average they showed about the same level of acquisition. Most pairs who split up did so because they preferred to work at their own pace.

3. Conclusion

The authors of WIC have taken the comments of the users in careful consideration not only because of their intrinsic value but also and primarily because they wanted to put an apparently good tool to the benefit of more learners. A Lingua project has been set up in which the achievements and improvements of WIC are being incorporated. The practical adjustments as to the load of words per theme, translations per context etc. are easily made. However, more encompassing efforts have been made as well: all contexts are rewritten with tighter guidelines in a more systematic way as to better sustain the inferential competence of the learner and facilitate memorizing. The single lexemes are thematically more narrowly traced. Students' hypotheses about the meaning of a headword do not involve incidental guessing but are guided into encoding the language and hence learn how to make meaning. There is more micro-structural information than in WIC, but also macro-structurally the words are contextualized as a database of texts is linked to the words so that a larger setting is available. A grammar programme will be interfaced in due course. Above all, the audio input is ensured as a CD-based system will be provided.

Note

The Lingua Project in progress is called *EuroLing*. It is a joint undertaking of several European universities of which the Universities of Duisburg, Tilburg, Namur, and Leuven form the core (see Dirven *et al.* 1993).

References

Beheydt, L.
1991 *Elementair Woordenboek Nederlands*. Lier, Brussel: Van In.
Baten, L.
1991 Wic-hy: een oefenpakket op computer. In: Verlinde (ed.).
Baten, L., J. Vanparys, Y. Wullaert & L. Dieltjens
1992 "WIC: Woorden in Context". In: *School en Computer* 92/5.
de Kleijn, P. & Nieuwborg, E.
1983 *Basiswoordenboek Nederlands*. Leuven: Wolters.
Dirven, R., A. Albrecht & W. Waumans
1993 *Foreign Language Vocabulary Learning by Computer: Principles, Fundamentals and Instructions for the Setting up of a Database*. Duisburg: L.A.U.D., Series B 245. (Again in this volume.)
Verlinde, S. (ed.)
1991 *Proceedings of the Symposium on Differentiation in LSP, Learning and Teaching*. Leuven: Instituut voor Levende Talen.

Foreign language vocabulary learning by computer: Principles, fundamentals, and instructions for the setting up of a database

René Dirven, Angela Albrecht and Wim Waumans

1. Preliminaries

1.1. An overall view of the EuroLing project

The lexical database which is described in this paper is part of a larger project called EuroLing, which is a foreign language learning program sponsored by the LINGUA office of the European Union. The purpose of the EuroLing project is:

(i) to promote communication among the inhabitants of the EC countries in less frequently taught or less widespread languages both for participants in Erasmus student mobility programmes and more generally for all interested Europeans, and
(ii) to develop computer-assisted learning programs for the lexicon, grammar, and intercultural aspects of the less taught or less widespread EU languages.

Dutch is taken as a pilot program: Dutch will be the target language for the speakers of the other EU languages; the first source language, i.e. the learners' mother tongue, is English, but in a later phase French and German and the five other languages will be added as source languages.

The partners of the EuroLing project are, besides the University of Duisburg: the University of Leuven (Prof. Dr. Lut Baten), the University of Namur (Dr. Johan Vanparys), the University of Brabant at Tilburg (Dr. Guust Meijers) and Drs. Per van de Wijst (coordinator), and the division ESCAPE of the educational centre OMO (Ons Middelbaar Onderwijs) at Tilburg (Drs. Bas Cartigny). The opinions expressed in the present paper are, in fact, the outcome of one year's work for the lexicon program EuroLex Dutch. This is not only a program for 3,500 basic lexical items of Dutch, but it also constitutes the pilot framework for five other European languages (see below). The three Duisburg authors of this report of the pilot group's work thank all the participants for their inspiring spirit of cooperativeness.

The components of the global program will be developed in two phases:

In the first phase, the lexicon (EuroLex) and grammar (EuroGram) for each of the six languages will be dealt with. In the second phase, intercultural programs will be developed. The first phase (lexicon, grammar) is planned like this:

First year: A lexicon of 3,500 items based on frequency lists and on a familiarity list will be developed. Each item is presented in three or four different contexts taking account of the item's polysemy and each time translations for the learner's source language are added; the items are grouped in thematic fields and in three blocks of about 1,000 items. The diversification of the translation into other languages is carried out in the second year, or depending on funding, in a later phase.

Second year: Grammar and exercises; a basic grammar containing the very basic rules of morphology and syntax is provided both graphically and in an internationally accepted metalanguage, e.g. English; depending on funding, the more advanced grammar could be presented in the target language itself in a later phase.

In the second phase programs aiming at developing a European intercultural competence (EuroLink) will be taken up. For this purpose, the data bases for the lexicon and the grammar are linked to various up-to-date texts and provide an automatic basic analysis of the texts, and new lexical items are to be explained. The purpose is to build up an intercultural understanding of the foreign and one's own cultures.

Following the principles of the pilot program and limiting ourselves to six target languages, we envisage the long-term program as in Table 1:

Components	EuroLex	EuroGram	Finalising year	EuroLink
Pilot program: Dutch	1992	1993	1994	1995
Further programs: Italian Spanish Greek Portuguese Greek	 1993 1993 1994 1994 1994	 1994 1994 1995 1995 1995	 1995 1995 1996 1996 1996	 1996 1996 1997 1997 1997

Table 1. EuroLing's long-term program

Extension of EuroLing to Finnish, Swedish, and Norwegian is now being considered, too.

The programs do not aim to impose any order of learning or even methodology; on the contrary, the learner can choose his own order and methods. The programs are made in such a way that the components of EuroLing for each of the six target languages can be worked through separately or cumulatively. Consequently, learners can also aim at different levels of competence: a survival or pidgin-like competence (various blocks of the EuroLex), a minimum communicative competence (EuroGram), and/or an intercultural competence (EuroLink). Moreover, the programs do not compete with group instruction, but can render this more intensive and communicative by providing for the individual prepa-ration of lexical, grammatical, and intercultural materials.

1.2. The primacy of the text in foreign language learning

EuroLing starts from the assumption that learning can be most successful if it starts from texts. So whatever order and method learners may follow, they will as much as possible be confronted with texts. This holds for the two phases of the project, viz. the lexico-grammatical one and the intercultural one. Consequently, learners will have the choice between two or even three approaches also for the lexicon: the thematic approach to words by means of three or four contexts for each word, or a running text or a combination of both. The lexicon is presented in texts for various reasons. First and very generally, all communication takes place within specific texts, and consequently any kind of language acquisition program should similarly operate via the text level (cf. e.g. McCarthy 1984). The term "text" refers to any form of communication, i.e. all forms of discourse whether spoken (as a monologue, dialogue or multilogue) or written. Secondly, the use of texts is the best way to deeply impregnate words in memory. Thirdly, the ultimate purpose of vocabulary (and even of grammar) learning is to come to grips with whatever forms of text one may encounter or want to produce. In other words, it has to be the purpose of foreign language teaching (FLT) to prepare the learner for the understanding and production of written and spoken communication, i.e. texts. So in the ideal situation, computerised vocabulary and grammar programs have as their ultimate learning objective the mastery of intercultural communication, which occurs in the form of texts. Therefore they are suitable to preface the programs for intercultural analysis. Thus, while it remains possible to aim at one level of competence only, it is also possible to use the three programs cumulatively and aim at the highest level of competence. If working exclusively on one of these three levels, a student would merely acquire partial communicative skills. Limiting oneself to vocabulary training, for instance, one would acquire a pidgin-like mastery of the language. Using words in combination with a lot of gesticulation would allow the learner restricted communication in certain very specific situations such as shopping, giving directions, asking for the way etc. Combined with a knowledge of grammar, higher level communication would become possible. However, this still leaves the dimension of culture-specific competence unexplained. Only contact with authentic, or at least semi-authentic texts - as suggested by Geddes & White (1978) - can facilitate actual intercultural communicative competence. Of course there is no proof as yet that the use of computers can successfully support learning at the third level, i.e. that of intercultural competence, but neither can we rule out the possibility of such a positive effect. In any case, computer application to the two previous levels is very likely to prove much more efficient than teaching in the classical classroom scenario, as it takes individual learning speeds into account. The time and energy thus saved can then be reallocated to really communicative group learning via the classroom discourse.

The remainder of this paper will concentrate on lexical learning.

2. The selection and structuring of vocabulary

2.1. The use of frequency lists

Traditionally, at least since the *General Service List* first published by Michael West in 1925, most foreign language vocabulary has been selected on the basis of frequency lists. But it was also admitted fairly soon that the frequency of words is strongly dependent on the kind of source materials used to compute the frequency: different figures are obtained for written and spoken materials, for literature and non-fiction, for newspapers, and more general texts. That is, most larger corpora of texts exhibit a word frequency which may correspond up to the level of the first 2,000 words, but once beyond 2,000 words there is very great variation or divergence. If one aims at a minimum of 3,500 words as one's learning objective (as the EuroLing vocabulary programs do), one has still to select 1,500 words. How can these be selected in a scientifically reliable and didactically sound way? Several possibilities arise:

(i) One can compare all the existing frequency lists for a given language and then compute a new, common list of 3,500 words.
(ii) Another possibility is to take all the vocabulary lists of existing foreign language textbooks and to add all the words, or the common words of these textbooks, to the 2,000 first items of a frequency list. In this way not only new words can be added to the list of 2,000 but also the relative position of these 2,000 words may be changed fundamentally.
(iii) A third possibility is to give absolute priority to the vocabulary as it has already been selected by the authors of one given textbook (see 2.4), which is chosen as the accompanying work for the computer vocabulary program.

Let us illustrate this, by referring to a program for German vocabulary called *Wortmeister*, elaborated by a Duisburg team in collaboration with the University of Antwerp and K. V. H (Katholieke Vlaamse Hogeschool, Antwerp).

By means of a computer program, the four already existing but greatly divergent frequency lists for German were combined and compared. After examining which words occurred in more than one list, new frequencies were established on a much broader basis, which led to a final list of the 5,000 most frequent words.

For greater accuracy, the word lists of existing teaching materials, such as textbooks for German as a foreign language, were further added to the corpus in order to arrive at a more reliable list. This did not only add words, but it also changed the position of a number of items in the final frequency list. Although the choice of a corpus of basic vocabulary for FLT remains problematic, and although *Wortmeister* does not claim to have solved this problem, it has nevertheless arrived at a pragmatic working solution.

2.2. *Comparison with Richards' familiarity list*

Any frequency list (even one that has been improved by the intuition of FL textbook authors) remains a limited instrument because of its sources. Everyday language, and especially spoken language, is not taken into account sufficiently by the majority of those lists. Therefore, another type of correction becomes necessary. Although the project *Le Français Fondamental* has tried to tackle this problem for the French language (Gougenheim *et al.* 1967), it arises again and again for every language, even for the French language as it is spoken in the nineties, the reason for this being the very quick changes in the spoken language.

Gougenheim *et al.* introduced the "principle of disposability". They realised that in spoken language we need a large number of concrete words such as, for instance, the words *matches, alarm-clock, purse*, which may not occur very frequently in written materials. However, the problem is that such words may very quickly come and go, together with the artefacts they denote. Thus, *matches* may be far less important now and be replaced by *lighter*.

A different approach was followed by Richards (1971, 1974). Instead of subjectively compiling an additional list of disposability items, he asked large numbers of informants how "familiar" a certain word was to them. He asked his informants to estimate how often they read, heard or used a given word, and based his list on this data.

The question of how familiar a word appears to the user can become an important criterion: if we add up the results of the subjective assessment of many single speakers we obtain a result which reflects an intersubjective, common tendency. This subjective assessment is vital, since many words possessing a high familiarity index are missing in the quantity-oriented frequency lists. The familiarity index by Richards (1971) would necessitate serious amendments to the frequency lists if those are to be used for teaching purposes.

For the *Wortmeister* program already referred to, approximately 800 items from Richards' familiarity list were chosen, some of which had a low frequency index but nevertheless appeared to be vital for everyday communication. By means of the computer it was possible to combine the already improved frequency list with Richards' familiarity list.

Working with familiarity lists one must bear in mind, however, that such lists are highly culture-specific, so that e.g. an English list cannot be transferred into other languages directly, such as the six European target languages, four of which belong to non-Anglo and non-Germanic cultures. Consequently, the English list has to be translated "culture-specifically" for each individual language. For German this has been done by Am Zehnhoff (1991).

Conclusion: Theoretically it is possible to compose a good, user-oriented basic vocabulary list of 3,500 vocabulary items from frequency lists, vocabulary lists in textbooks, results of research on spoken language, and familiarity lists put together. However, in actual practice this stage has not been reached yet. On the one hand, the spoken language aspect, which should not be underestimated, is still largely missing. On the other hand, lists that extend beyond the 3,500 word limit pose a problem, because important differentiations as regards frequency and relevance to everyday life become close to impossible to verify.

2.3. *The Threshold Level*

Word frequency lists and familiarity lists are based on language facts and try to make a selection from them. The Threshold Level also contains a list of 2,000 basic words, but it does not start from the language side, but from the side of the communicative needs of the learner, viz. from the language he needs in order to cope with a number of situations he may be in when abroad.

In 1971 the Council of Europe initiated a project called "Modern Languages", which aimed at developing teaching systems, i.e. materials for learners of the project's target languages, the overall goal being the promotion of foreign language skills among adults. Currently such systems have been developed, viz. are in their final stages for the following languages: Basque, Catalan, *Danish, Dutch,* German, English, French, Galician, *Italian, Norwegian, Portuguese* and *Spanish* (italicised languages are possible EuroLing target languages).

Such teaching systems are always the product of a time-consuming deductive development. As a first step, the target group has to be defined. This decision is highly significant because efficient language teaching first has to assess the learner's communicative needs. When this is done, the individual learning objectives have to be described as precisely and explicitly as possible so that the teaching material can be divided into units in the following step. This division takes place on the basis of a pragmatic analysis of all the situations in which the learner will be required to use the new language. In other words, the important question is not "What does the learner have to be able to say?", but "How does he need to communicate?", i.e. which linguistic means does he require?

However, different learners have different needs, so that it is not possible to devise a uniform system. On the contrary, a system should aim at maximum flexibility and versatility if a large variety of learner types is to apply it to a number of different cultures. Moreover, the system should be able to cater for various learning situations. In other words, it should be applicable in the classroom as well as in private one-to-one tuition. This consideration led to the creation of the so-called "unit-credit-system", in which you collect credits as you pass through the units.

The Threshold Level for English (Danish *Taerskelniveau,* Dutch *Drempelniveau,* French *Niveau seuil,* German *Kontaktschwelle,* Italian *Li-*

vello soglia, Portuguese *Nivel limiar*, Spanish *Nivel umbral*), which was developed in 1975, was meant as an example of the lowest unit. On the one hand, it is intended as a specification of those learning objectives which have to be reached in order to achieve a minimal competence in a language. On the other hand, the Threshold Level constitutes a point of reference for further systems which will be built up on this basic level. Thus, the Threshold Level serves as a point of departure for the development of a series of teaching materials in two respects:

(i) The vocabulary put down in the Threshold Level will create a sound basis for the creation of teaching materials which will then enable the learner to cope with the elementary situations he will encounter in everyday communication in the foreign language. For this purpose, the Threshold Level proceeds as follows: it takes a given situation e.g. buying a newspaper or reading it, and investigates intuitively and deductively what a speaker might want to say and which words he needs in order to achieve this goal. Buying a newspaper for instance belongs to Section *4. Free time, entertainment,* and the subcategory 4.8. *Press*. Words like *newspaper, paper, magazine, article, picture, advertisement, page, reporter/journalist, to read* and the phrase *Let's buy some magazines* can be found under this heading (van Ek & Trim 1991:75).

(ii) Furthermore, the Threshold Level marks a stage in the learning process from where more advanced teaching materials can be employed and upon which basis such materials can be designed.

Contrary to the various versions of the Threshold Level for other languages, the Threshold Level for English, as van Ek & Trim (1991:2) point out in their Introduction, has been developed for genuine beginners or also for "false beginners". The notion of "false beginners" is being used to describe a group of learners who in the (near) past have already acquired some familiarity with the foreign language but nevertheless feel that they need a fresh start. While learning or after having learned according to the Threshold Level they should be enabled to communicate in normal situations.

2.4. Choice (or elaboration) of a textbook

First of all, it may be useful to begin the discussion of the use of the textbooks in vocabulary programs by pointing out some possible shortcomings. These shortcomings are also a very good reason for not simply basing the whole of the vocabulary selection for vocabulary practice programs such as EuroLing on an existing textbook alone.

On the one hand, most textbooks do not include all the basic vocabulary from frequency lists, familiarity lists ot intuitive lists such as the Threshold list. So a number of words will tend to be overlooked. On the other hand, most textbooks offer a fairly large number of words which are not part of the basic vocabulary but which are useful or even necessary for that particular text sample. Therefore, it remains a very good strategy to keep a clear distinction between these two components of a database (the texts of a textbook and the three or four contexts for each of the 3,500 words) and to realise their different potential.

Second, it is important to understand what a basic vocabulary list is in comparison with the vocabulary list of a textbook and what function a textbook can have with respect to foreign language vocabulary learning.

The basic vocabulary (list) is the statement (and in the case of EuroLing also presentation - see next Section) of the learning objectives in the lexical component of a foreign language learning curriculum. It is a goal to be achieved, not a method of learning. In contrast to this "descriptive" function of the basic vocabulary list, the texts of a textbook constitute one of various methods of mastering a "given" set of words. A text is the richest and most natural "context" in which to learn foreign language words, since the words appear in a double context: the context of situation (or "context" proper) and the sentential context (or "cotext").

But since both types of context have a specific role to play, also the sentential context has its function. Here the notion of a "pregnant context" comes in. The isolated contexts for each lexical item can, in fact, be made much richer than the sentences of a text: the former create their own "context of situation" and can be "manipulated" in many different ways (see Section 3.3.) so that it is fully justified to speak of "pregnant contexts" as Baten (1991) does. These pregnant contexts can make the meaning(s) of a given item much clearer than a text can do. In a text, there will usually be one meaning for a word only, and it will be very rare that the full meaning of a word is learnt in that one text only. Words in a text very often have a "situational" meaning, only valid for that specific text. But the systematic set of meanings and their relationships and differences may be much better grasped by means of pregnant contexts.

What then is the specific didactic value of the text for learning foreign language vocabulary? The text evokes a full chain of mental images, which together constitute a "script" or the chain of successive steps in a global event. Thanks to this script any single word denoting a step in the chain of events is highly activated. Thus the text can lodge words (forms and meanings) very strongly in the mind and memory of the learner. This is a consequence of the gestalt character (such as e.g. a script for events) of any text and the need for gestalts in the learning of anything.

Consequently, any program for foreign lexical learning must ideally exploit the textual approach, but it can enrich and intensify this textual approach further by the "pregnant context" approach.

In the EuroLing project both of these approaches are exploited, but in such a way that there is a priority of the textual approach over the other. This implies that the "pregnant contexts" must at least always contain the meaning of the word as it is used in the text of the textbook. But theoretically it must remain possible to work through a set of words without starting from a text. Learners, especially adult ones, must be trained to become "autonomous learners" (see Roos 1993), who are aware of their learning process, decide themselves what they want to do (and what first and what next), which requires a very great amount of flexibility in the database.

2.5. Division of basic vocabulary in larger blocks

Since Michael West's (1925) pioneering work, foreign language teaching has witnessed a very long tradition of gradation in the foreign language acquisition process. Although this tradition is now somewhat threatened by recent attempts to create "physical" contextual learning such as the "Total Physical Response Approach" or "Silent Way", the principle of "graded" learning as such is still firmly believed in and practised.

There are various ways of dividing the vocabulary into blocks. One possibility is to take blocks of 500 words, as has been done in the lexical program *Wortmeister*, which contains ten blocks of 500 words. The Euro-Ling project, which only contains 3,500 words, has opted for bigger blocks, viz. from 1 to 1,000, from 1,001 to 2,000, and from 2,001 to 3,500. The principle of gradation not only implies that one sticks to a given block in a given period of learning (e.g. 1,000 words in one schoolyear), but also and more importantly, that the texts and explanations offered remain within the limits of a given block. For *Wortmeister*, the words in each of the ten blocks of 500 words are used in contexts that do not contain words beyond the upper limit of the block in question (e.g. the third block - 1,001 - 1,500 - has in its example contexts no words beyond the 1,500 limit).

Obviously, there are different orientations behind such apparently arbitrary looking numbers. The smaller-block option shows an orientation towards greater control of the learner's progress, and it is certainly not apriori wrong for younger learners. The bigger-block option contains more challenges for the learner, who in the EuroLing project's target group is the adult learner (see 1.1.). An important consequence of the bigger-block option is that the pregnant contexts may contain many more new learning difficulties than in the smaller-block option. The learner is called upon to "guess" the meanings of these words, to make hypotheses, to venture down possible avenues of testing the possible relationships between meanings and words.

In conclusion, it is more important to stress the principle and the fact that in any learning process the learner goes about things in smaller units of the total skill, be it swimming, driving, or the more complex "language" or "communication" skill. The necessity to make manageable steps or "blocks" is the major truth; the minor truth is, then, a question of variability according to age, developmental level, learning situation (regular school curriculum vs. autonomous computer learning), the time available, the presence or absence of teachers, etc.

2.6. Assigning the vocabulary and the texts to thematic fields

As just stated, in order to acquire a certain skill such as driving one must learn to master a series of consecutive smaller steps. This law of learning the global skill by gradually mastering the smaller components of the complex whole also applies to vocabulary learning.

One way to do this is the use of texts in a textbook. The other way is the use of a smaller set of words that somehow forms an experiential unit in human interaction or categorisation. Theoretically, there are many possibilities of building up such units.

A very typical example of an attempt to build up a taxonomy of human experience is the famous *Thesaurus* by Roget, which is a kind of conceptual dictionary, viz. a classification of the words and phrases of English according to their meaning (and not according to orthography). Such an endeavour is in fact a taxonomy of all the meanings or concepts in a language. This would presuppose that there are very basic main classes. Indeed, Roget came up with six main classes:

(i) abstract relations
(ii) space
(iii) matter
(iv) intellect
(v) volition
(vi) sentient and moral powers.

But its overall division and its subdivisions are too complex to be useful in teaching/learning situations. This also applies to most other attempts in various languages and the constructs which try to organise the whole taxonomy of human experience in structured networks. (For a brief survey, see Lyons 1977:300f).

A far less ambitious, but pedagogically attractive taxonomy is the Threshold Level, developed by van Ek for the Council of Europe (see e.g. Van Els *et al.* 1977). Although the structure and division of the Threshold Level were not conceived of as a taxonomy of human experience, but as a minimal set of learning objectives for foreign language courses, the list is multifunctional and can, with some adaptations, also be used for dividing the whole of the 3,500 vocabulary items into a number of thematic fields. The great usefulness of the Threshold list of thematic fields is that there are not just static units, viz. things to talk about, but that there is also a whole section with things to do by means of language, viz. the various types of speech acts. Thus the Threshold Level consists of three major sections: (1) speech acts, (2) general notions, (3) specific notions. Since many of the categories of the first section (speech acts) have not merely lexical items, but whole phrases and sentences as members, it is necessary to adapt the category somewhat, so that we propose the following adaptation of van Ek's system:

Thematic units for vocabulary learning:

1. Speech acts, emotions, thinking
   - 1.1. Imparting and seeking factual information
   - 1.2. Expressing and finding out attitudes and emotions
   - 1.3. Deciding on courses of action
   - 1.4. Socialising
   - 1.5. Structuring discourse
   - 1.6. Communication repair

2. General notions
   - 2.1. Existential
   - 2.2. Spatial
   - 2.3. Temporal
   - 2.4. Quantitative
   - 2.5. Qualitative
     - 2.5.1. Physical
     - 2.5.2. Evaluative
   - 2.6. Mental
   - 2.7. Relational

2.7.1. Spatial relations
2.7.2. Temporal relations
2.7.3. Action/event relations
2.7.4. Contrastive relations
2.7.5. Possessive relations
2.7.6. Logical relations
2.8. Deixis

3. Specific notions
3.1. Personal identification
3.2. House and home, environment
3.3. Daily life
3.4. Free time, entertainment
3.5. Travel
3.6. Relations with other people
3.7. Health and bodycare
3.8. Education
3.9. Shopping
3.10. Food and drink
3.11. Services
3.12. Places
3.13. Language
3.14. Weather

Such a taxonomy allows us to divide the whole of the EuroLing lexicon into about 30 thematic units. If all had the same number of lexical items, we would have about 100 items per thematic unit. But this is, of course, not the case. Some will only consist of a handful, others of a couple of hundred items. But since we have another division of the 3,500 words in blocks of three sets (two sets of 1,000 and one of 1,500 words) we can split up the larger thematic units into three levels. But the above major categories are and have to be further subdivided into still more refined categories. (For the full list of categories, see the publications by the Council of Europe.)

2.7. Compatibility of textbook and thematic fields

The textbook that has been selected for the pilot program (Dutch) is *Code Nederlands* by F. Kuiken & A. van Kalsbeek (1990). Amongst other things, this textbook offers the advantage that for each unit not only the thematic field, but also the (communicative) functions (speech acts in the Treshold Level) and notions are explicitly stated in the table of contents. Let's take its Lesson 9 as an example, with the title "What's in the newspaper" and the thematic field *Newspapers and journals*. It contains the following characterisations (in translation):

	Text situation	*Functions*	*Notions*
1.	At breakfast	Urging sb.	Reading matter
2.	Newspapers and journals	Doubting sb.	The press
3.	In a newspaper shop	Enumerating	General events
4.	Immigrants and the media	Giving an example	Quantity/number
5.	Newspaper headlines	Agreeing with sb.	
6.	Newspaper stand		

(These three columns should be read from top to bottom, not from left to right).

Even if this type of analysis is not explicitly mentioned in the textbook, it is possible for the project team to carry out such an analysis on the textbook of their choice, or to elaborate a textbook along these criteria.

The combination between textbook and thematic fields that can be built up now is that a given unit (or lesson) of the textbook can be enriched or made more attractive by "hanging up" the vocabulary items (and their pregnant contexts) marked for a given thematic field or subfield to this unit or lesson. This means that learners can choose, on the computer menu, additional vocabulary and vocabulary exercises in the thematic field they encounter in the text of a given unit.

But also the opposite combination is possible and offers a great, potential enrichment for the learning process that learners organise for themselves.

If learners choose to work on a given thematic (sub)field, e.g. the press, and have worked through a certain number of words by means of the "pregnant contexts" approach, they may want to find a text in which these words occur in a natural and (semi)authentic context. Technically speaking, it is a great challenge to try to "hang up" so many different thematic fields to the various, more limited set of units/lessons of the textbook. This presupposes that each of the units and texts in these units gets a code of their own, which, however, is fairly simply. In the example of Lesson 9, this code could range from 9.1. *At breakfast* to 9.6. *Newspaper stand*; but then the difficulty begins. How can one determine the main thematic field of a text? Usually, a text covers and refers to different thematic fields and the moot question is: what is the dominant theme in a given text?

As with all language teaching situations, one must not look for principled solutions to such problems but rather for pragmatic ones. Indeed, it may not be so important how well the thematic fields and the textbook lessons can be matched to each other, but it may be much more important that learners get the feeling of an intellectual and emotional motivation to go through a set of exercising materials.

3. Presentation and explanation of vocabulary

3.1. Basic assumptions

For the presentation and explanation of the vocabulary, EuroLing starts from a major assumption, which also underlies most work in cognitive linguistics. This is the principle that language use and language learning is part of conceptualisation and that both can be realised only in salient cognitive contexts or domains. Domains are units of experience which can be said to coincide to a large extent with the more refined subcategories of thematic fields alluded to in the previous section. So domains can be thought of as the further experiential subcategories of the categories summed up in Section 2.6.

These domains structure our experiences and our world knowledge. Even though they may be strongly culturally defined, they also reflect a number of universal basic needs (e.g. the four F's: family, feeding, fighting, and fleeing), which offers the basis and common ground for very general categorisation processes.

Vocabulary learning, especially when computerised and hence isolated from social and communicative classroom learning, can only succeed if it takes contextual learning (or learning within a given domain) as its most central principle. This means, first of all, that for each of the meanings of a polysemous word these meanings are linked to their domains. This is done by means of "pregnant contexts", which not only explain the meaning but do this by referring to the domain to which each meaning belongs. This also means using all the tracks along which we may remember the form and the meaning(s) of words. Many-track learning comprises words used in a running text, many different "pregnant contexts" for each word, auditive support, translation of each contextual meaning, reading texts etc. All of these requirements and still others will be gone into in more detail in the following sections.

3.2. The principle of polysemy

The notion that many forms of language are polysemous is not only a subjective conviction of many linguists, but has also been proved quantitatively more than once, at least as far as the English language is concerned. Shuanfan Huang (1991) analysed the polysemy of the words on the first 1,000 pages of the English learner's dictionary *Longman Dictionary of Contemporary English* (LDOCE), which has a total of 56,000 entries. He came to the conclusions displayed in Table 2 (results divided into nouns (N), verbs (V), and adjectives (A)):

	N	V	A
(a) Number of words	14,041	4,565	4,966
(b) Number of polysemes	4,678	2,068	1,694
(c) Number of polysemous meanings	13,697	6,894	4,531
(d) Level of ambiguity	0,33	0,45	0,33
(e) Level of polysemy	2,93	3,33	2,75

Table 2. Polysemy of words in LDOCE

As can be seen, one third of all nouns and adjectives and almost half of the verbs analysed were polysemous; these nouns and adjectives had an average of three different meanings while the verbs had slightly more than three meanings. In addition, it must be taken into account that the LDOCE is a learner's dictionary and consequently does not list all the existing meanings of a word. For the word *cup*, for instance, LDOCE only gives ten different meanings whereas other dictionaries list twice as many under the same entry, i.e. over twenty different meanings. Thus it may be inferred that the true level of polysemy is even considerably higher than that established by Huang. Gentner (1981) had already demonstrated this for a fairly small sample from an American English frequency list (Kucera & Francis 1969). Although we do not know of comparable studies for other languages, it can be safely assumed that polysemy is as strongly developed in those languages as in English.

These findings throw up the following two questions:

(i) What exactly is polysemy, particularly when seen against the background of the paradigmatic relationship between meaning and domain?, and
(ii) How can FLT, and computer programs in particular, take this into account?

Polysemy develops when a word and its meaning, which is directed at one specific domain, is extended or transferred to another domain. The German adjective *schief* "leaning, lopsided, crooked", for instance, is linked to the "vertical dimension" domain, as e.g. in *Das Bild hängt schief* "the picture is crooked".

This spatial relation can now be metaphorically extended to other domains such as psychological experience, e.g. *eine schiefe Lage* "a sticky situation", facial expression, e.g. *jemanden schief ansehen* "to look askance at sb", *ein schiefes Maul ziehen* "to pull a wry face", moral judgement *eine schiefe Ansicht* "an inappropriate opinion" or logical evaluation *ein schiefer Vergleich* "an inappropriate comparison" etc. With regard to polysemy, it is of particular importance to include the figurative meanings systematically into the lexicon entry in order to establish the figurative potential of a foreign language in FLT. Here, it cannot be the aim to demonstrate as many meanings as possible, but to make the learner aware of the basically polysemous nature of language. In those cases where it is possible to employ graphics to depict these meanings, as for example *schiefer Blick* or *schiefes Maul*, it would seem advisable to do so. Such illustrations should contrast the focused figure against the unfocused background.

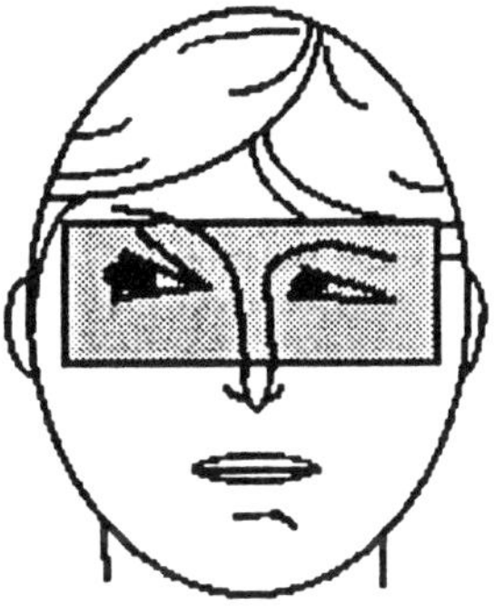

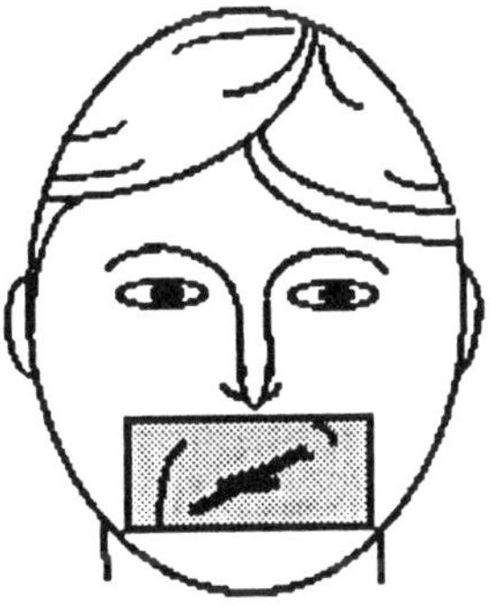

(1) *jmd schief ansehen* (to look askance at sb) — *ein schiefes Maul ziehen* (to pull a wry face)

But although technically speaking it is not a problem to provide for storage space in the computer program, EuroLing has not yet decided, whether the use of graphics is to be applied systematically or only very occasionally.

3.3. What is a pregnant context?

The fact that a given word cannot have a meaning outside a (most often linguistic) context is a fundamental fact of language. Another piece of well-established knowledge is the fact that a word can only be learnt in a specific context. What a context actually is, however, has not yet been established. As a matter of fact, there are a number of alternative definitions, some of which claim supremacy over others. Contexts may be understood in various ways: they might either be paradigmatic or syntagmatic, linguistic or psycholinguistic, speech-internal or contrastive, verbal or non-verbal. An attempt will be made to take all these aspects into consideration as far as this is possible.

If, for the time being, we only look at linguistic contexts, one of the first questions to arise is whether a paradigmatic or a syntagmatic context is the more suitable one.

In a paradigmatic context, we define words e.g. *a knuckle is part of a finger.* In a syntagmatic context, we use the word in a natural collocation, e.g. *He knocked on the table with his knuckles*. When choosing a paradigmatic context such as *A knuckle is part of a finger, i.e. the place where its parts are joined*, we assume that, firstly, a word denotes a concept which belongs to a specific domain, and, secondly, that it can only be understood within this domain. Since the word *knuckle* belongs to the domain "finger" it follows that without any reference to this domain, *knuckle* cannot be understood and cannot even be explained. The same holds for *finger*: this word belongs to the domain "hand", *hand* in turn belongs to the domain "arm", *arm* to the domain "body" etc. A domain can also be an abstract category; the German adjectives *schief* and *schräg*, for example, belong to the domain "vertical dimension" which can be indicated by contexts containing words such as *Turm* "tower" or *Decke* "ceiling". Paradigmatic pregnant contexts for *schief* and *schräg* could be the following:

(2) *schief* "leaning"
Der Turm von Pisa ist schief.
'The Pisa tower is leaning.'

(3) *schräg* "sloping"
Die Decke meines Zimmers ist nicht gerade, sondern schräg.
'The ceiling of my room is not straight, but sloping.'

Since no expression can be understood without simultaneously looking at its domain, it follows that one of the pregnant contexts of a word ought to be a paradigmatic one.

A syntagmatic context, on the other hand, would present a word together with a more or less randomly chosen collocation. The following set of examples will further illustrate the difference between paradigmatic (4) and syntagmatic (5) contexts for the word *finger*:

(4) There are five fingers on each hand.

(5) He has cut his finger.

Although paradigmatic contexts as in (4) are necessary to explain the meaning of a word, it is also true that paradigmatic pregnant contexts such as in (4) do not occur very frequently in natural language. Consequently, programs should aim at a vocabulary presentation with more than just one context, so that words can be seen in a paradigmatic context as well as in a number of syntagmatic collocations such as, for instance, *to point one's finger at sb, to cut one's finger*, etc. The latter would then demonstrate the actual usage of the word. Further types of pregnant contexts are example sentences giving metaphorical and/or idiomatic uses of a word, a subject which is to be discussed in Section 3.5. But let us first point out that the notion of presenting vocabulary in a variety of contexts finds additional support in psycholinguistics and semantics. Before going into this, let's illustrate the notion of pregnant contexts by means of an example for the word *shape*.

(6) *shape*

a. *At Ascot most ladies wore pink round hats.*
But some hats also had a different colour or shape.

b. *We want to make round biscuits.*
Have you got a round shape for us?

c. *I cannot see if it's a man or a rock, it's too far away.*
I can only see a vague shape in the distance.

d. *Manchester's goalkeeper hasn't done any training for two months. He was injured and now he's in very bad shape for the game.*

3.4. Multi-track learning

There is now general agreement among language teaching experts that efficient learning largely depends on a rich learning context. Unfortunately, the Anglo-Saxon literature in favour of rich learning contexts (Carter 1987, Carter & McCarthy 1988, McArthy 1984, Meara 1980) has not taken van Parreren's "track theory" (1967) into account at all. According to this theory, the learning of a new language builds up a new system of tracks in the mind. Later Schouten-van Parreren (1985) demonstrated that a word can be recalled more easily, the more attributes of it are stored in memory. In other and simpler words, it could be claimed that the more tracks there are towards a word in memory, the more easily it will be accessible. Generally speaking, every new item of vocabulary therefore has to be offered in a variety of contexts, so that the learner can memorise one or several contexts which suit his learning style and personality. Varying between paradigmatic and syntagmatic contexts hereby has to be considered as a first possible enrichment. Also a number of other tracks, such as auditive, visual or further conceptual contexts will supply even more support.

If a vocabulary item is not only presented in written form but also acoustically, then long-term-memory has double access to this word through both these tracks. Technological progress has now made this possible. Computers can now be equipped with CD-ROM, an additional appliance which has to be added to the computer. It makes it possible to store and digitalise language that has been spoken onto the CD via a microphone. This system is already available on the market and will soon become easily accessible for the general consumer.

The area of semiotics provides one more perspective for the expansion of contexts. The doubly stored word form (orthographic and auditive) can not only be connected with a paradigmatic verbal context (e.g. *finger-hand*), but this paradigmatic relationship can also be further consolidated by a visual-conceptual illustrations. The Apple computer is particularly suited for working with detailed graphic images. Such conceptual illustrations should highlight that part of the picture which represents the figure or focused part of the concept. The ground or unfocused part of the picture represents the domain which paradigmatically belongs to the word, as can be seen in the illustation for *finger* below:

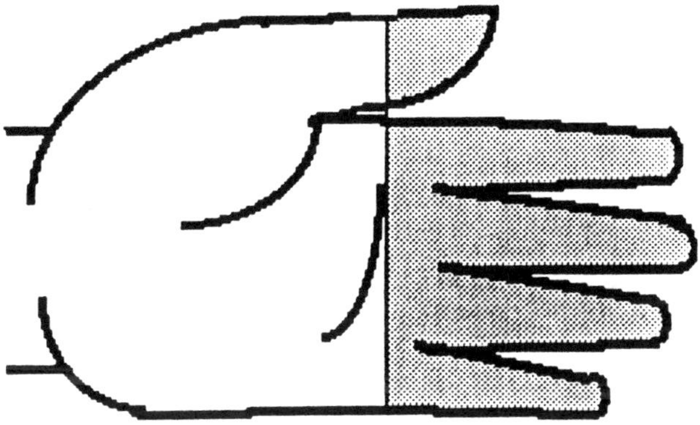

Psychologically speaking, such a way of visual representation corresponds to the way we actually perceive the world, since we basically always distinguish between an emphasised "figure" and a supporting "ground".

To sum up, it can be said that ten possible tracks are available for each word as represented in the Table 3 below. We can group these possibilities into three fundamentally different sets of tracks which can be used for vocabulary presentation, namely the four tracks for the pregnant contexts (paradigmatic, syntagmatic, figurative and idiomatic contexts), orthographic and auditive tracks, and conceptual and visual ones. A question that arises here is, of course, the abundance of possibilities. Moreover, there is not just a neat, simple array of four pregnant contexts, but another criterion has to be added to the list, namely that of polysemy discussed in Section 3.2. All these possibilities, therefore raise completely new linguistic and pedagogical challenges, viz. how can we possibly decide upon which meanings of a word we are going to present and what tracks can be used to do so? Here the discussion of prototypes and prototypical instances of a given category may be helpful to make decisions.

	(1) Graphic			(2) Acoustic
		Word		
(3) in running text	(4) - (7) pregnant contexts 1. paradigm 2. syntagm 3. figurative 4. idiomatic	(8) picture figure/ ground	(9) translation	(10) exercises

Table 3. Multi-track learning: The 10 possible tracks in vocabulary programs

3.5. Prototype semantics

Obviously, it is necessary to select only a small number of contexts from the vast amount which is, semantically seen, possible for each vocabulary item. According to fundamentally new insights in cognitive psychology (Rosch 1977), this choice does not have to be taken at random any more. One can base one's selection on the principle of categorisation according to prototypes. Rosch has demonstrated that concepts and terms are not categorised according to so-called "necessary" or "sufficient" semantic features. Thus in classical theories, a word, e.g. *bachelor* is said to be a unit of meaning composed of the three features "human", "male", and "unmarried". This classical view had been supported by philosophers ever since Aristotle and has so far been the working hypothesis in traditional and even in generative linguistics. Rosch found, however, that conceptual categorisation always takes place by means of keeping a prototypical member of a category in mind. Also linguists such as Fillmore (1982) and Lakoff (1987) pointed out that the "feature" definition of *bachelor* does not work since it does not apply to persons such as the Pope, Roman Catholic priests, Robinson Crusoe or all lonely people in an isolated place. These persons all possess the three features, but are not bachelors in the every-day use of that term. Indeed, the prototypical, culture-biased image of a bachelor is someone between 30 and 50, who is of marriageable age, could marry, but for some hedonistic or private reasons prefers not to do so, although he lives in a society where marriage is traditionally valued highly. It is such a man who is the prototypical example of a bachelor. All the other cases are very marginal. But things are even more subtle. Rosch found that we have a whole range of gradations in categories: Prototypical representatives of the category *furniture* are for example *bed, chair, cupboard* and *table*; other good examples of the category *furniture* such as *bench* or *desk* are already somewhat less prototypical; items like *bar, mirror* and *lamp* are considered peripheral, and *piano* is ranked fully marginal to the concept of *furniture*.

Since our concepts are structured around prototypes, there should not be a problem when concentrating on prototypical examples for vocabulary contexts. Still, it has to be noted that adjectives refer to much more abstract categories, i.e. that they do not denote objects but properties. However, even properties are prototypically linked with certain categories of objects.

Schief for instance prototypically describes aspects of an object with two or three dimensions, as for example *eine Fläche* 'a plane' or *ein Turm* 'a tower'. *Schräg*, on the other hand, prototypically links up with a one-dimensional object, such as *eine Linie* 'a line'. This difference is illustrated below:

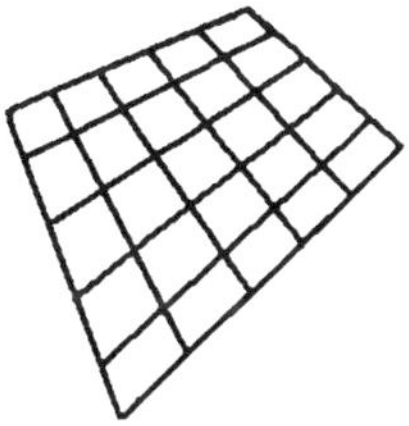

(7) *eine schiefe Fläche* 'inclined plane' — *eine schräge Linie* 'diagonal line'

Thus, the difference between *schief* and *schräg* lies in the fact that *schief* does not only have the "vertical dimension" as a background domain, but also the domain of "deviation from what is normal", whereas *schräg* does not imply such a judgement. Compare for example:

(8) *ein schiefer Turm* 'a leaning tower' — *das Schiff liegt schräg* 'the ship lies at an angle'

(9)	*ein schiefer Schrank* 'a crooked wardrobe'	*eine schräge Decke/ein schräges Dach* 'a sloping ceiling/roof'
(10)	*eine schiefe Tür* 'a crooked door'	*Schrägstrich* 'oblique'

As can be seen, *schräg* only denotes a direction or orientation in the vertical dimension, whether it is the line of a roof or of a ceiling. It follows that there are few problems involved in choosing the first context. The real difficulty lies in the selection of the following two or three contexts for which it is necessary to bridge the gap between the more prototypical and the less prototypical or even peripheral meanings and in particular for the more figurative meanings of the word. Provided such a balanced composition of contexts can be made, the common features of the meanings and the communicative sense and functioning of a word's polysemy in the target language becomes accessible for the learner. Without such a sufficient number of contexts, the learners would not be able to understand the prototypical character of one single context. The contrast between the contexts offered, however, allows them to grasp this characteristic instinctively.

3.6. The use of translations

Although the direct method has rightfully rejected an approach to foreign language learning, based on systematic translation, it cannot be denied that the translation of a specific meaning of a word in a pregnant context is a great help for the exact shade of meaning that is at stake.

We will illustrate the necessity for such translations by contrasting some German and Dutch lexical items. The German language has three different words for the polysemous Dutch word *wortel(en)* 'carrot(s)', which denotes a type of vegetable and can be translated into German as *Karotte(n)*, *Möhre(n)* or even *Rübe(n)* in this domain. A native speaker of German learning Dutch and also a Dutch learner of German will need a translation in order to understand this phenomenon. Moreover, the German word *Rübe* can also be translated into Dutch as *gele peen* 'turnip'. In such cases, translations are the most effective help a learner can get.

However, generally, a word should not be translated on its own. Normally, only a contextual translation makes sense. Although the Dutch translation for the German *schief* as in *schiefer Blick* and *schiefes Maul* is the related word *scheef* 'lopsided, crooked, slanting', in the context of the moral judgement domain, e.g. *schiefe Ansicht*, *schief* would have to be translated more generally by the evaluating adjective *verkeerd* 'wrong' as *een verkeerde visie* 'an inappropriate view'. *Ein schiefer Vergleich* would even have to be translated by the anthropomorphic metaphor *mank gaan* 'to limp'.

Thus a translation can have various functions: firstly, it can add to a clearer understanding of the meaning of a word; secondly, it has a feedback function and gives the learner an opportunity to verify his hypotheses about the meaning of a word (for this important learning strategy see de Haan *et al.* 1991); thirdly, a translation can emphasise the fact that two languages make certain lexical distinctions (e.g. German: *Karotten, Möhren*) or do not do so (e.g. Dutch: *wortelen*). The example of German *schief/schräg* 'leaning, sloping' is significant in this respect, too: whereas German distinguishes between the two conditions described by the adjectives, Dutch does not, so that the difference does not become immediately understandable. The Dutch expression *een scheve toren* 'a leaning tower' in German is *ein schiefer Turm*, but the expression *het schip ligt scheef* 'the ship lies at an angle' has to be translated into German as *Das Schiff liegt schräg im Wasser* (cf. illustration below):

(11) D *een scheve toren* — *Het schip ligt scheef*
G *ein schiefer Turm* — *Das Schiff liegt schräg im Wasser*
E (a leaning tower) — (the ship is lying at an angle)

Dutch does not distinguish between these cases. It only uses one word, namely *scheef* for both dimensions. For other meanings of *schräg*, however, such as *ein schräges Dach* (a sloping roof) or *er wohnt schräg gegenüber* (he lives across the road) the Dutch language has a different adjective, namely *schuin*. A translation can therefore demonstrate how words structure our perception of the world in a culture-specific way and it will show that such a structuring may be, and in fact often is, different in different languages. Nevertheless, a translation cannot illuminate why such differences occur, i.e. for example why the Dutch *scheef* partly covers the same aspects of meaning as the German *schief* and partly those of *schräg*, and why other meanings of *schräg* correspond to the Dutch *schuin*. But as was shown in Section 3.5., the insights of prototype semantics can shed some light on such problems nevertheless.

4. Conclusion

Thanks to the computer, especially the one with the additional appliance of CD-ROM, foreign language learning finds itself confronted with challenging new possibilities. The old audio-visual dream can to a large extent be realised now: graphic, written and spoken representations of the language can now all be combined in one medium. Instead of a multimedia approach FLT now has at its disposal a single medium as a multichannel carrier.

This medium offers the best guarantees for a variety of learning strategies that may indeed differ strongly from learner to learner: some tend to rely more strongly on the visualised context surrounding speech events and on graphic representations; others tend to rely predominantly on what they hear; still, others tend to rely on the written presentation of words and texts; most will tend to use a combination of these modes of representation but with varying emphases. These will now all be given opportunities. Moreover, it is not a cumbersome and time-consuming process to call up whatever graphics, single text, phrase, word, thematic unit etc. the user may want, but this can be achieved in a minimum of time. In one word, multi-track learning now becomes increasingly possible.

But not only the technological innovations offer bright prospects for FLT, also the didactic and linguistic insights in the processes of language acquisition and semantic structuring have changed fundamentally.

The concept of thematic fields proved to be a simple, but realisable and even fertile basis to structure the enormous panoply of linguistic signs, be it words or expressions, into conceptually plausible and didactically manageable learning units. The fact that both basic word lists and FL textbooks have been based on thematic fields is ample proof of the attractiveness of this principle.

Also semantically, FLT now has a new stronghold thanks to prototype semantics. The ideas of frequency lists, disposability lists or familiarity lists were all very interesting, but only yielded lexical forms, hardly or not at all their most important aspect, i.e. their meanings. Thanks to the distinction between prototypical, peripheral, and marginal meanings in a polysemous item, we can now give priority to some meanings over others and structure the relation between the lexical units to be learned much more adequately. In one word, many new opportunities are there; it is now up to FLT theory and practice to grasp them.

References

Baten, L.
1991 *Nieuwe Trends in Didactiek, Dus Ook in Software.* Leuven: Vlieberg-Senciecentrum.

Carter, R.
1987 *Vocabulary. Applied Linguistic Perspectives.* London: Allen and Unwin.

Carter, R. & M. McCarthy (eds.)
1988 *Vocabulary and Language Teaching.* London: Longman.

Decoo, W. & M. Goethals
1991 Een computer in het talenonderwijs. In: *Computer in Het Onderwijs.* Brussels: Ministerie van de Vlaamse Gemeenschap.

van Ek, J. A.
1991 *The Threshold Level for Modern Language Learning in Schools.* 8th Edition. Strasbourg (Groningen): The Council of Europe (Longman).

van Ek, J. A., & J. L. M. Trim
1991 *Threshold Level 1990.* Strasbourg: Council of Europe Press, Council for Cultural Co-operation.

van Els, T., G. Extra, Ch. van Os & Th. Bongaerts
1977 *Handboek voor de Toegepaste Taalkunde. Het leren en Onderwijzen van Vreemde Talen.* Groningen: Wolters-Noordhof.

Fillmore, C.
1982 Towards a descriptive framework for spacial deixis. In: Jarvella, R. J. & W. Klein (eds.). *Speech, Place and Action.* London: John Wiley, pp. 31-59.

Geddes, M. & R. White
1978 "The use of semi-scripted simulated authentic speech and listening comprehension". *Audio-Visual Language Journal* 16: 137-143.

Gentner, D.
1981 "Some interesting differences between verbs and nouns". *On Cognition and Brain Theory* 4(2): 161-178.

Gougenheim, G., R. Michéa, R. Rivenc & A. Sauvageot
1967 *L'Élaboration du Français Fondamental.* Paris:

de Haan, H., M. Kat, C. Schouten-van Parreren *et al.*
1991 "Het trainen van raadvaardigheid met de computer". *Levende Talen* 458.

Halliday, M. A. K.
1973 *Explorations in the Functions of Language.* London: Arnold.

Hatch, E. M.
1983 *Psycholinguistics: A Second Language Perspective.* Cambridge, Mass.: Newbury House.

Huang, S.
1991 *On the Nature of Lexical Ambiguity*. Paper read at the Second International Cognitive Linguistics Conference. Santa Cruz, California.
Kucera, H. & W. N. Francis
1969 *Computational Analysis of Present-day American English*. Washington: Brown University Press.
Kuiken, F. & A. van Kalsbeek
1990 *Code Nederlands*. Vol. 1 & vol. 2 (textbooks and exercise books). Amsterdam: Meulenhof Educatief.
Lakoff, G.
1987 *Women, Fire, and Dangerous Things: What Categories Reveal about the Mind*. Chicago, London: The University of Chicago Press.
Lyons, J.
1977 *Semantics*. Vol. 1. Cambridge: Cambridge University Press.
McArthy, M. J.
1984 "A New Look at Vocabulary in EFL". *Applied Linguistics* 5/1:12-22.
Meara, P.
1980 "Vocabulary acquisition: A neglected aspect of language learning". *Language Teaching and Linguistic Abstracts* 13:221-226.
Nation, P. & R. Carter
1988 *Vocabulary Acquisition*. Amsterdam: University Press.
Nattinger, J.
1989 Some current trends in vocabulary teaching. In: Carter, R. & M. McArthy (eds.), pp. 62-80.
van Parreren, C.
1967 "Psychologische faktoren bij het verwerven van de woordenschat van een vreemde taal". *Levende Talen* 239:159-169.
van Parreren, C. & C. Schouten-van Parreren
1979 Erwerb eines fremdsprachlichen Wortschatzes. In: Detering & R. Högel (eds.). *Englisch auf der Sekundarstufe*. Hannover: Schrödel, pp. 22-36.
Richards, J. C.
1971 *Word Familiarity as an Index of Vocabulary Selection with Indices for 4495 Words*. PhD Dissertation. Canada: Université de Laval.
1974 "Word lists: Problems and prospects". *RELC Journal* 5/2:69-84.
Roget, P. M.
1852 *Thesaurus of English Word and Phrases*. London (Abridged and revised, with additions by J. L. Roget & S. R. Roget). Harmondsworth 1953: Penguin.
Roos, R.
1993 *Lexical Acquisition and Language Awareness*. Duisburg: L.A.U.D., Series B 248.
Rosch, E.
1977 Human categorization. In: Warren, N. (ed.). *Studies in Crosscultural Psychology*. Vol. 1. London: Academic Press, pp. 1-49.
Schouten-van Parreren, C.
1985 *Woorden Leren in het Vreemdetalenonderwijs*. PhD Dissertation. University of Utrecht.
Am Zehnhoff, H. W.
1991 *Familiaritätsliste Deutsch*. Unpublished Manuscript.

Computer programs for vocabulary training in foreign language learning

Agnieszka Leńko

1. Introduction

The topic of this article is a presentation of various computer programs which may be used for vocabulary training in class and at home. However, the paper is not a description of specific vocabulary software currently on the market. Instead, it concentrates on a broader perspective and presents certain categories of programs, their characteristic patterns and the way they can contribute to enriching the student's vocabulary. The specific programs cited hereafter are only supposed to illustrate certain points which are raised in the paper.

1.1. Introductory assumptions

Before describing different types of software it is worthwhile to spend a little time on the role of the computer in the process of vocabulary training. Actually, it does not differ from the role of the computer in language teaching in general, so some assumptions which are mentioned may seem obvious; nevertheless, they are sketched briefly to present a full picture of the role of the computer for vocabulary teaching.

The first crucial assumption is that the computer's role in the lexical training process is that of a medium. Within the familiar type of classroom teaching[1], the computer is a tool like any other media used in language learning such as the video, the tape recorder, the overhead projector, the textbook, or even the blackboard. The computer is not supposed to replace the teacher in teaching vocabulary, nor is it supposed to replace any other medium mentioned above in this task. It is meant to act only as another teaching aid, perhaps a more powerful and valuable one, but always subservient to the teacher's needs.

In order for it to be effective, the computer has to be integrated into the whole educational process. It should not serve as a provider of end-of-the-week vocabulary activities, when the syllabus requirements have already been satisfied and there is nothing to do for the remaining 20 minutes. On the contrary, computer activities should constitute a part of regular classwork or even homework during which the student is given an opportunity to learn and acquire new vocabulary, to practise it, and to test his[2] knowledge.

The integration of the computer into the process of teaching and learning means also that the vocabulary which is learnt, acquired, practised, and tested with the help of the computer stays in tune with the syllabus. There is no point in making the student learn and practise words connected with travelling at the computer, if travelling is not what is currently being studied and if there are no other classroom activities using this vocabulary.

Another important assumption is that the computer has no inherent methodology of its own. It is not like the language laboratory in the 60's which was strictly connected with the audio-lingual approach. The computer serves any teaching principles and the methodological background of a particular program depends entirely on its designers and on what the teacher chooses to do with it. The popular stereotype that the vocabulary software is only of the drill-and-practice type is not valid. The computer has much more to offer, as this paper endeavours to demonstrate.

The teaching principles which are currently dominant in language education belong to the communicative methodology. However, the categories of programs which are presented and discussed are based on various methodologies ranging from grammar-translation and audio-lingual approaches to the communicative method. This presentation has not been limited only to communicative software because most teachers are eclectic in their choices of appropriate methods and they use whatever works for their students.

2. The categories of vocabulary programs

In their book entitled *Something to Do on Monday*, Macey Taylor and Laura Perez (1989) divided language software into three categories, which they named "knower of the right answer", "workhorse", and "stimulus". Although the book deals with all kinds of language programs, the same classification may be applied specifically to vocabulary-training software. The major part of this paper presents each of the three categories of programs, describes their characteristics, points out their advantages and their limitations, and illustrates them with specific examples.

2.1. *Computer as the knower of the right answer*

The first category of programs according to Taylor and Perez's classification is the one in which the computer is the knower of the right answer or, in other words, it acts as a referee judging the student's performance. This is the oldest and the most popular role of the computer in education. The vocabulary programs belonging to this category may appear in three modes: the presentation mode in which the student is presented with new vocabulary items to learn, the practice mode which lets the student practise the words he has learned giving feedback at each answer, and the test mode which tests the student's knowledge delivering the score at the end of the activity. Most programs contain a combination of two or three of these modes. Perhaps it would be best to start by describing how new vocabulary can be presented to the student.

The simplest programs of this first category present the student with stimuli in the form of graphics and deliver words which correspond to the pictures. The scope of application of such programs is very limited as only objects can be illustrated by simple graphics. This program can be recommended for children at the beginning stages of learning a language.

In other programs of this category target language vocabulary is presented together with their equivalents in the student's native tongue. The range of application of such programs is much wider than of the ones mentioned before, but they have significant drawbacks. They may create in the student the notion of one-to-one correspondence between the words of two languages and moreover, the vocabulary the student learns is taken out of context. Only a limited use of these programs can be advised, and then only for the vocabulary items which correspond between the two languages on a one-to-one basis. The program can be recommended for students at early stages of learning when they are still very dependent on their native tongue for understanding and learning a foreign language.

More sophisticated programs present a word in its context which not only refines the word's meaning to the student but also gives him additional information on its collocations. For example, there is a very good and ambitious English-French program called *Wordchip*, which belongs to a series of vocabulary programs published by a Belgian group *Didascalia* (1991). This software contains 5,000 English words in context. The words are divided into 10 difficulty levels on the basis of frequency lists. In the presentation mode the student is given an English word and its context. The French equivalent is also given and it is assigned the role of helping the student to grasp the meaning of the word before it is refined by the context. It is also very interesting that the contexts for the words from a certain difficulty level are taken from the vocabulary belonging to lower levels, which makes it sure that the context is comprehensible to the student. This program and other programs based on the same principle may be used with students at all proficiency levels.

The same approach has been taken by Jones (1988a) in his program called *Wordstore*. However, the author replaces the target language equivalent with a hint or a definition of a word. Again this program can be used by students at any level of proficiency with the exception of early beginners who may be intimidated by such an extensive exposure to the foreign language and who may find working with definitions and hints in a foreign language too difficult.

So far I have discussed how lexical software may present the vocabulary to the student. Now we should concentrate on various forms of lexical exercises offered on the computer. When talking about vocabulary training in general, exercises which immediately come to mind are translation, gap filling, and multiple choice. They are the most popular and widely-used forms of lexical exercises on the computer as well. They differ from the traditional paper-and-pencil methods in that they give immediate feedback and point out incorrect answers. If the student's answer is wrong he may be given another try and the computer may give him hints in the form of a beginning letter or a word definition.

A lexical exercise may contain elements of a game. The simplest kind of a game is exactly the same translation, multiple choice, or gap-filling exercise but with an elaborate scoring incorporated into it. For instance, the student may get 200 points for a correct answer, 100 points for a correct answer at a second try, and 50 points if he asked for a hint. The computer may also ask the student to gamble some points before it gives the feedback.

However, the computer programs may also offer games which do not take the form of regular classroom exercises but the form of popular entertainment games such as the wheel of fortune. The programs called *Vocab* by Jones (1988b) and *Matchmaster* by Jones and Higgins (1989) offer a variety of such vocabulary games. One of them named *Skullman* is a version of a popular game called *Hangman*. The student chooses a semantic category of the vocabulary such as "travelling" and he is shown the first word in the form of dashes each standing for one letter. The instructions are obvious - the student has to reconstruct the word by guessing letters. Each time he guesses incorrectly another part of a skull appears on the screen. The student has only seven lifes. At the seventh unsuccessful attempt the whole skull appears on the screen along with the correct answer and the student may proceed to another word. If the student guesses all the letters successfully he wins.

Another game called *Mindword* is a vocabulary version of *Mastermind*. A word is replaced by dashes one for each letter and the student has to decipher it. The computer gives the feedback in the form of information on how many correct letters the student used in his guess and if they are in the right places. In another game, which is called *Matchit*, the program takes advantage of the time factor. Two words appear on the screen changing every few seconds and the student has to press a key if they match a certain pattern. If the student misses a match, he loses points, if he presses a key and the words do not match, he loses points as well.

Games have all the characteristics of a regular computer vocabulary exercise and in addition, they are much more exciting for the student. His desire to perform a task correctly is replaced by the desire to beat his peer or the computer, which increases his motivation considerably.

All the programs belonging to the knower of the right answer category focus on developing accuracy in the student. The computer knows the correct answer (or a few possible answers) and it will accept nothing but the correct input. Very few programs offer error analysis so even a slight spelling mistake makes the computer answer "wrong". Some critics consider it a serious drawback, but I personally regard it as a virtue that the computer forces the student to be as accurate as possible.

2.2. *Computer as a workhorse*

The second category of programs distinguished by Taylor and Perez is the one in which the computer acts as a workhorse or, in other words, as an instrument for dealing with large amounts of text or data. This group includes powerful professional software packages designed for other purposes than language learning or learning in general. They are primarily meant for use in an office or as a tool for linguistic research. The programs include concordancers, electronic dictionaries, databases, word-processors, and multimedia.

Although these programs are designed for other purposes than language learning, it appears that they lend themselves very well to vocabulary training. However, their application for that purpose is not as obvious as in the case of programs belonging to the previous category. They do not contain any prepared activities and the way they are used in the classroom depends mainly on the teacher and his imagination.

(i) *Concordancers* seem to be among the most valuable programs for vocabulary training. They come from the field of linguistic and literary research where they have been used for such purposes as word frequency studies or authorship studies. When used in vocabulary training, they promote working with authentic language and discovery learning. Instead of getting the lexical information on the meaning of a word or its collocations from the teacher, a textbook, or a dictionary, the student has to discover it on his own using an authentic text. The student is no more a passive recipient of the knowledge but he becomes an active researcher. Concordancers facilitate a variety of searches and may be used for a variety of activities. For example, the student may try to establish the meaning of a word by looking at its context. He may also look for compounds with a word, for the distribution of different forms of a word, its collocations and its frequency in the text.

Unfortunately, concordancers have their drawbacks which are connected with the technical and organisational side. If the use of a concordancer has to make real sense a large corpus of texts is necessary. It can either be created by a teacher, which is rather time-consuming, or else be bought, which is rather costly. Another problem is that concordancers need powerful equipment to be really effective. In any case the possibilities concordancers offer are worth the effort and the money.

(ii) *Electronic dictionaries* constitute another kind of software belonging to the workhorse group. They have all the characteristics of a traditional dictionary except that information is presented on the computer screen instead on the page of a book. However, electronic dictionaries have some advantages over traditional dictionaries. The first and the most important one is the speed of access. Looking up a word in a book dictionary usually takes some time and when the student is confronted with several new vocabulary items he may get discouraged very easily. Electronic dictionaries deliver the answer instantaneously. Another advantage of an electronic dictionary is the variety of searches it can execute. If the student knows the word but he is not sure of its spelling he may type in just the first, the middle or the last part of it or even type some of the letters replacing the rest with variable characters. The computer finds all the words that match the pattern and the student may simply choose from the list. Moreover, electronic dictionaries are usually resident, which means that they can be accessed practically from any other program in the computer. For example, when the student is writing a text on a word-processor or playing a language game he can call up the dictionary at any moment, and find the word he needs. Unfortunately, computer dictionaries are not always so convenient to use. For example, it is hard to use them when reading a book in a target language unless someone chooses to read this book in front of a working computer.

(iii) Commercial *databases* such as *dBASE* also lend themselves very well for vocabulary learning. The student can use them for writing his own mini-dictionary. The structure and the contents of such a dictionary depend entirely on the student so the dictionary will contain only the information which the student finds useful to himself. A database is particularly good when the student is working on a new text containing a lot of unknown vocabulary items. Instead of writing the meanings of new words on a piece of paper, which is very difficult to consult and which will soon be lost, the student can type these words into his personal dictionary and they will stay there for later reference. Afterwards the student can easily create his own vocabulary exercises using the words included in his database. In the course of time the personal database expands and it is good for revising one's vocabulary, especially before a test.

(iv) *Multimedia* are a fairly new kind of computer software. As the very name suggests, they integrate different media of presenting information, that is text, sound, graphics, and animation. Unfortunately, they enter the field of teaching and learning very slowly as they require really powerful computers and additional equipment such as CD-ROM or a sound card, which very few educational establishments can afford. The main application for multimedia in vocabulary teaching is to create very attractive vocabulary programs in which the definition, translation and the context of a word will be supported by longer texts, by graphics, presenting the object in question such as *a computer* for example, by animation illustrating the action such as *swim*, and by sound illustrating such words as *whistle* or *loud*. Multimedia also give the pronunciation of a word much better than any phonetic transcription can. They also offer a possibility of branching, which makes cross-referencing very easy. Multimedia can be used to create not only excellent lexical exercises but also electronic encyclopedic dictionaries, which have been proven to be very effective in language learning. I have seen an encyclopedia of animals created by two teenagers with the help of a very simple program called *IBM LinkWay*. In addition to the name and the definition of an animal, the user of this encyclopedia can get a text about this animal, a map showing where it lives, its picture or a short film and he may even listen to the sound it makes, all this at the click of a mouse button. I am sure that after studying all this information the language student will remember what an elephant is.

(v) The possibilities of using professional *word-processors* in vocabulary training are rather limited even though word-processors themselves constitute a very good educational tool for other purposes. The most powerful ones such as *WordPerfect* or *Microsoft Word* offer spell-checkers and thesauruses which may be useful when the student is working on his writing assignments. If the student has a problem with a certain word which appears too often in the text he may call up the thesaurus to find synonyms of that word. There is no need to browse through dictionaries as the answer appears instantaneously on the screen. The student may also check the spelling of a particular word or make the spell-checker proof-read the entire text.

The scope of applications of the programs of the workhorse category to vocabulary training is wide and it depends, as has already been mentioned, on the equipment available to the teacher and his imagination. The activities can focus on accuracy as well as on fluency. Although the programs can in principle be used with learners at all levels, concordancers and word-processors seem to be more appropriate for intermediate and advanced students.

2.3. Computer as a stimulus

The third and the last category of programs discussed is the one in which the computer acts as a stimulus for students. This group of programs includes simulations, adventures, action mazes, etc. Their main characteristic is that in contrast to games mentioned in the first group the computer does not know the answers and its aim is not to judge the student's performance but to supply him with opportunities for language acquisition. In this group of programs the focus is not on the language but on a task, and the language acts only as a tool to achieve this task. Therefore, it is very often hard to pinpoint how these programs contribute specifically to vocabulary training, but it is certain that vocabulary is acquired together with other language factors such as grammar and discourse strategies.

(i) The most useful programs of the stimulus category in terms of vocabulary acquisition are *simulations*. They make the student perform activities which would be too dangerous, too expensive, or simply impossible to perform in the real world. For example, a simulation program may make the student run a factory, conduct a difficult chemical experiment, or let him be a pilot of a plane. There are two types of simulations: move-based and real-time simulations.

The progression of the program in *move-based simulations* depends entirely on the student's decisions and the computer will wait until the student enters chosen data. These simulations are particularly good for language learning. Unfortunately, there are very few simulation programs which have been designed specifically for language learners. The only one I know of, called *Granville*, offers the student a free holiday in a French holiday resort. The student makes his decisions about how he wants to spend his time, making his choice among such activities as visiting a museum, going for an excursion, or going shopping. While having a good time organising his activities, the student acquires vocabulary connected with holiday-making.

Although there is a shortage of simulations designed specifically for language learning there are quite a number of move-based simulations which have been created for teaching other subjects and which may be very well used for language and vocabulary acquisition. Business, chemical, or medical simulations are very good for teaching English or other languages for special purposes. For example, while making decisions about how to run a factory the student is confronted with a range of words such as *taxes, wages, income*, etc., and has an opportunity to practise them in a meaningful activity.

In a simulation called *Crime Lab* the student is told a story of a theft in a museum. Luckily, the thief got cut when breaking in to the building and left some blood speckles on the shattered glass. The student acts the part of a lab assistant who has to determine the thief's blood type and choose him from a list of suspects. However, before the student starts his analysis the computer explains how blood typing tests are performed. Students have to read the instructions in order to conduct a test correctly. They do not very often realise that when reading the blood typing briefing they acquire a good deal of specialist vocabulary. If the activity is done in groups the student has a chance to reinforce this vocabulary when discussing with his peers the results of the test and determining the blood type. The game is an excellent activity for students of English for medicine, chemistry, or biology.

Real-time simulations have less to offer for language and vocabulary acquisition. The progression of action in these programs is continuous and the student has no time to think and discuss his decisions with his peers. Real-time simulations include such software as flight or race simulators. Apart from instructions at the beginning of a program, there is usually very little language involved in them. That is why these programs are only suitable at the beginner's level as the programs let them practise very simple words and expressions as left, right, west, north, turn, stop, forward, etc.

(ii) *Adventures* constitute another kind of software belonging to the stimulus category. There is no clear-cut division between adventures and simulations, the only difference being their setting. Whereas simulations are set in quite realistic situations, adventures tend to take place in a fantastic world of fairies, goblins, captive princesses, and abandoned castles. The student is always presented with a difficult task such as rescuing a princess or finding a treasure and he encounters many dangers such as dragons or traps in his way. Actually, if these games are handled well by the teacher, that is, if there is some pre-computer briefing and post-computer debriefing done, the student may acquire quite a lot of vocabulary from them. The problem is that most of that vocabulary will not be very useful to him. In addition, the adventures are often very complicated and time-consuming to solve, and that is why they may be very difficult to use for in-class or homework activities. However, students enjoy playing them tremendously, so if the teacher adapts them for use in class by revealing some information to students in advance, an adventure may turn into an interesting and instructive activity for students at all levels, even though they will mostly acquire some fairy-tale vocabulary.

The stimulus category of language programs includes also other types of software such as *text mazes*, in which the student is posed with a problem and its alternative solutions, *exploratory programs*, which let the student experiment with the language, *"chatting" programs*, in which the student can have a chat with the computer or play a game of 20 questions with it, and others. However, as has already been mentioned, it is really hard to subtract vocabulary acquisition from the whole-language acquisition which these programs accommodate. That is why these types of software are not dealt with in detail in this paper.

The last comment to be made about all the programs belonging to the stimulus category is that they develop fluency but are not very good for accuracy training.

3. Conclusions

As I have tried to show in this paper there are a large variety of vocabulary programs available. They are based on different methodologies, they offer a range of interesting activities and they accommodate different learning styles. We can now hope that thanks to computers vocabulary learning will cease to be a painful and tedious task and that it will become an enjoyable activity which will keep students interested and will make them ask for more.

Notes

1. This paper does not discuss the potential role of the computer for teacher-independent or autonomous learning. (Editors' note).
2. For simplification I will refer to the student and the teacher as "he" throughout my paper.

Trademark acknowledgments

- *dBASE* is a trademark of Ashton-Tate.
- *IBM LinkWay* is a trademark of International Business Machines Corporation.
- *Microsoft Word* is a registered trademark of Microsoft Corporation.
- *WordPerfect* is a registered trademark of WordPerfect Corporation

References

Bumblebee Enterprises
1989 *Crime Lab*. Bumblebee Enterprises (Shareware).
Didascalia
1991 *Wordchip*. Antwerp: Universiteit Antwerpen.
Jones, C.
1988a *Wordstore*. Zürich: Eurocenters, and London: Wida Software Ltd.
1988b *Vocab*. Zürich: Eurocenters, and London: Wida Software Ltd.
Jones, C. & J. Higgins
1989 *Matchmaster*. Zürich: Eurocenters, and London: Wida Software Ltd.
Taylor, M. & L. Perez
1989 *Something to Do on Monday*. La Jolla: Athelstan.

Fast forward: Electronic acceleration and improving comprehension and speaking in foreign language learning

Ulrike A. Kaunzner

In this article I intend to present a project which is being cosponsored by the Commission of the European Union under the LINGUA program. This project, which was begun in January 1993 and will be completed in 1995, falls under action, V, B: "Diversification of foreign language provision through the development of teaching materials".[1]

I shall introduce a method for improving listening ability which may have revolutionary implications in various areas of language learning. Improved listening ability is instrumental in overcoming pronunciation and intonation difficulties, which are often a major stumbling block and sometimes an unsurmountable barrier for language learners. This method may provide an answer to the often unsuccessful attempts to produce the right sound. Moreover, listening difficulties affect the acquisition of the lexicon. Words may not be heard correctly, therefore not be understood correctly, and consequently not be produced correctly either. Improved auditory input and sound perception means improved word recognition and can therefore be of enormous assistance to the learner in his/her approach to the lexicon. The instrument presented here, the so-called "Electronic Ear", may, especially for adult learners of a foreign language, become such a "liberating" instrument that it also deserves attention in a section that concentrates on lexical learning.

1. Listening and foreign language learning

When we want to learn a new language, there are various components which all have to be considered: grammar (morphology and syntax), lexicon, and phonetics. Whereas in grammar and lexicon considerable progress can be made through the study of texts and memorization, this is not the case with sound discrimination ability and consequently, pronunciation and intonation.[2] Here adult learners often see themselves in front of an insuperable barrier.

The importance of listening in language teaching and its role in helping the learner overcome this barrier, has long been recognized. There is hardly an institution without a language laboratory and tape-recorders. But this is not what I mean by "electronic acceleration and improving comprehension and speaking". What we are focusing on in this project has to take place before or in addition to other, more conventional aspects of foreign language learning.

1.1. Language-specific auditory patterns

The neuro-muscular system of the hearing and speaking apparatus is clearly adapted to the ethnic auditory pattern of the language one is brought up with, one's mother tongue. By collecting various sound bands from one language group (audiograms which show the grade of auditory sensitivity), we are able to determine the "standard band" of that particular group. Alfred A. Tomatis, the French otolaryngologist who started doing studies on these bands in 1947, talks about *envelope curves*. Envelope curves are obtained from voice recordings and listening tests, and show characteristic mean spectra of Hz-frequencies in the overtones for different languages. This is because not every language group uses the same sounds, phonemes and phoneme combinations. (See Figure 1).

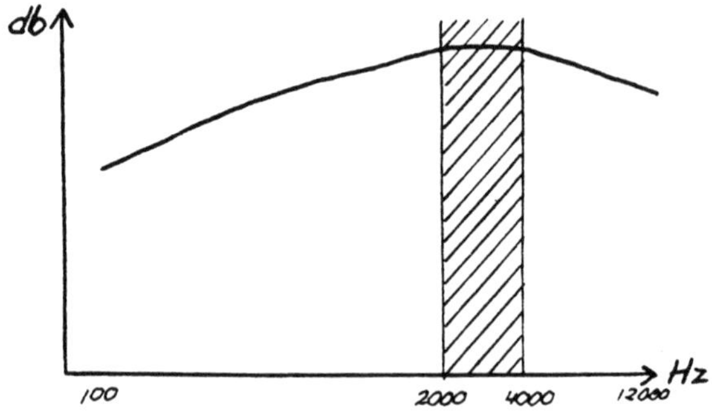

Italian

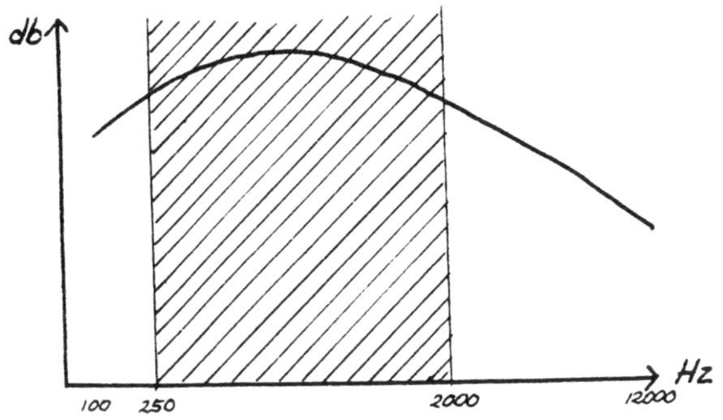

German

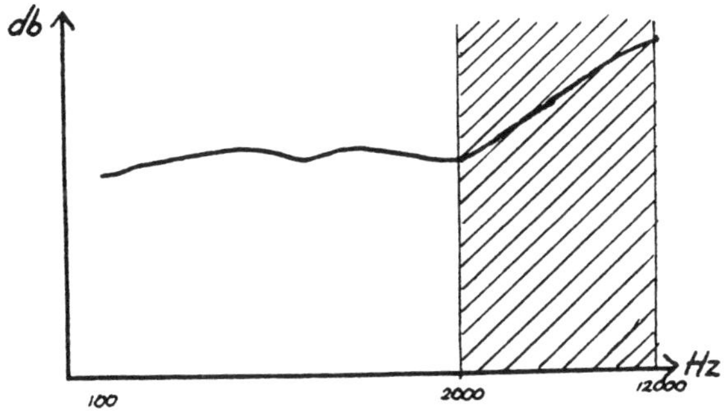

English

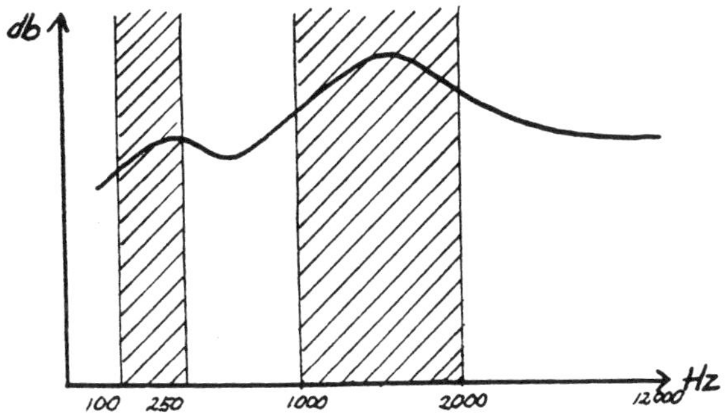

French

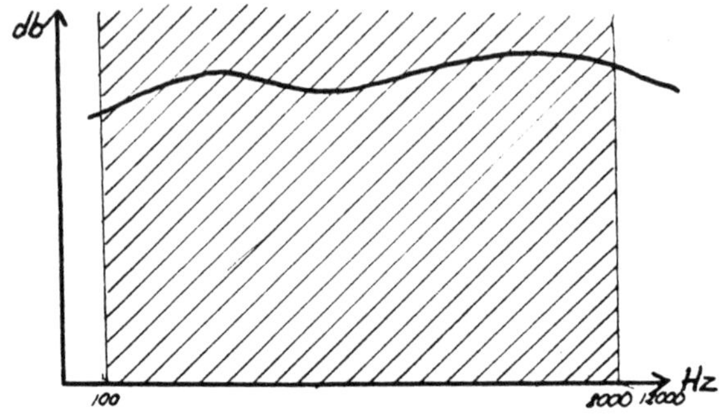

Slavic languages

Figure 1. Envelope curves for Italian, German, English, French and Slavic languages (see Tomatis 1991:129-37)

1.2. *Age and phonological development*

Whereas the ear of a newborn child is still open to perceiving the whole spectrum of whatever language the child is exposed to, an adult on the other hand, especially one who has lived exclusively in the environment of his mother tongue, shows a vocal curve as well as a listening curve which are typical of that language group. This explains why children, when they learn more than one language at a time, have no "foreign accent" in either or any of them - and, vice versa, why adult learners have great difficulties with new sound systems. It has nothing to do with intelligence. It is the result of a listening habit which has focused on one sound system only and closed itself off to new ones.

In fact, in the area of the grammar and the lexicon, it has been proved that older learners do better because of the use of cognitive skills; only in terms of phonological development do younger children show much better results. Whereas conscious attention and correction can improve grammar skills for example, this hardly helps with fossilized listening patterns which are due to subconscious blocks (see McLaughlin 1987:29, 46).

Stephen D. Krashen, however, claims that children are generally superior in all areas of second-language acquisition in the long run. He sees a main reason for adult learners' poorer language acquisition ability in a high affective filter which works as a barrier against acquisition. This happens when the learner is for example not motivated, lacks self-confidence, or is anxious. The application of this theory to phonological performance has been questioned by other researchers (see Krashen 1985:3, 13, and McLaughlin 1987:51-55).

1.3. Auditory selectivity

Apart from the fact that someone who does not hear certain sounds will naturally fail to reproduce them, there are also sounds which a person might be able to hear but still be unable to produce. This is due to the ear's tendency to concentrate on certain sound ranges, regions of high sensitivity which again are typical of a specific language group. Tomatis (1981) calls this the *auditory selectivity* of the various ethnic ears. For a typical Italian ear for example, sensitivity is greatest between 2,000 and 4,000 Hz (see Figure 1), while for a German ear the area of greatest sensitivity is between 250 and 2,000 Hz with the high point at 500 to 1,000 Hz and a reduced sensitivity in the high frequencies. An English ear is very sensitive in the high frequencies, between 2,000 and 12,000 Hz. (One of the reasons for this is its richness in sibilants). The high sensitivity of a French ear is shown in two areas, the major one between 1,000 and 2,000 Hz. Finally, a typical Slavic ear shows great sensitivity in the entire frequency-range, and consequently is more likely to hear other languages correctly (see Figure 1).

It is not surprising that people who are exposed to a new language and are asked to repeat what they hear cannot easily reproduce the sounds correctly. They will repeat the new sounds as they hear and interpret them, i.e. the closest they can come to hearing this sound in their own inventory. To give an example: A large number of my Italian students cannot hear the difference between the German /ü/ and /u/. When I ask them to repeat the word "drücken" they say "drucken", thinking this is the correct pronunciation.

2. Theoretical background: Tomatis's theory of the functioning of the ear and his conclusions

Alfred A. Tomatis was a pioneer in researching the functioning of the ear, and was able to produce evidence to counter the traditional theories

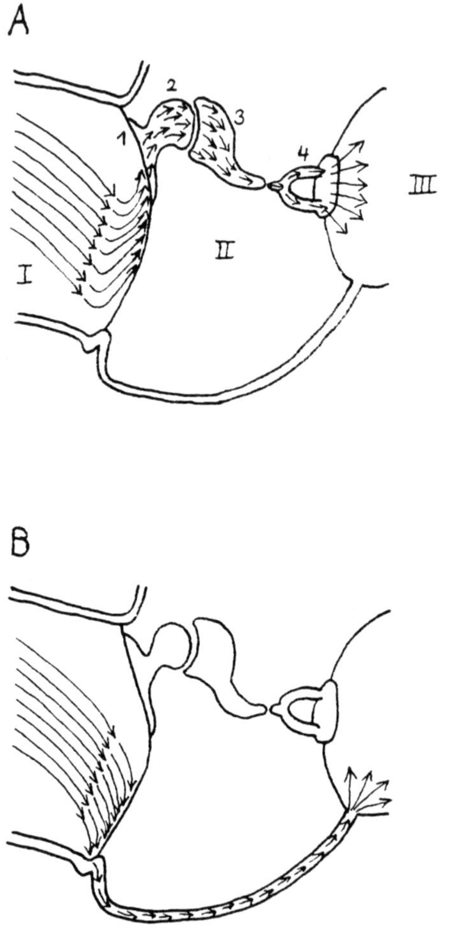

1. tympanum
2. hammer \
3. anvil ossicular chain
4. stirrup /

I = auditory canal, II = middle ear, III = inner ear

Figure 2. Transmission of the sound to the inner ear: A - traditional theory; B - Tomatis's version (see Tomatis 1981:138) which have been presented by von Békésy and others in this century. According to their theories, sound enters the ear through the tympanum and then passes on through the ossicular chain (hammer - anvil - stirrup) before reaching the inner ear (see Figure 2). One of Tomatis's discoveries was that a sound of, say, 100 decibels would cause a minute amplitude of vibration in the tympanum and would require the ossicular chain to be in such tension that the gap which exists between the anvil and the stirrup (about 1 mm) is unlikely to be crossed.

The passage of a sound occurs in three ways which can be explained by physics: Through air, bone and, to a lesser degree, through muscle. This is also Tomatis's theory of the auditory process; it is a combination of air and bone conduction. According to Tomatis, the three ossicles, which are linked by tiny muscles, have the function of controlling the transmission of sound. Thus you can hear yourself perfectly without any sound waves having passed into your ears (when you put your fingers in your ears and speak for example).

The fundamental innovation in Tomatis's approach is the dimension of the psyche. Because there is no automatic chain reaction in the transmission of sound through the middle ear, but rather a control by the muscles of the ossicles, auditory integration is performed by the brain.

Motivation has been proved to be the main factor in learning, and this also applies to the auditory process. While 90% of auditory nerve fibers go from the brain to the ear, only 10% go from the ear to the brain. This means we hear only what we want to hear or (and this is essential for foreign language acquisition) what we are used to hearing. The symptoms of many autistic children illustrate this principle: even if their cochlea (spiral tube in the inner ear with nerve endings necessary for hearing) is perfectly intact, if they decide not to hear, you can have a bomb explode next to them and they will show no reaction. Or take the phenomenon of people who live next to the Niagara Falls: after seven years they no longer consciously hear the noise of the water. Without this mechanism of self-protection we could not carry on a conversation in a noisy environment.

Based on his research on the functioning of the ear, Tomatis claims that three principles underlie the relationship between hearing and phonation (see Gilmor 1989:12-13).

(i) Tomatis discovered that defective hearing is always accompanied by vocal deficiency. More precisely, those frequencies which an individual does not hear do not appear in his voice spectrum either. This also means that the auditory curve and the vocal emission curve show great similarity. This first conclusion, also known as *The Tomatis Effect*, is stated as follows:

The voice can only reproduce those sounds which the ear can hear.

(ii) The logical consequence of the first theory is stated as follows:

If the lost frequencies are restored to the ear, they are automatically reintegrated into the voice.

(iii) The third principle focuses on the possibility of modification of phonation, i.e. the conditioning of the self-listening faculty. This hypothesis is based on the retention effect:

Auditory stimulation administered over a certain time produces lasting effects on audition and phonation.

It should be added that the muscles of the ossicles in the middle ear and all the muscles which are at work in the phonatory system (e.g. larynx, tongue, lips, and jaw) are under the command of the same neuron (the *nervus vagus*) and are thus closely linked.

3. The 'Tomatis method' and foreign language learning

3.1. The "electronic ear"

It becomes clear after studying Tomatis's theory that the best language laboratory is of little use if the student's ear is not able to hear correctly, i.e. if he/she is not able to discern the new sounds. Tomatis has developed an electronic apparatus called the *Electronic Ear*, which he describes as follows:

> This is a "model" that seems not only to obey the laws governing the mechanics of the ear but one which also has the ability to lead any human ear that has not, perchance, attained it, towards reaching its optimum listening potential. This model has progressively developed into an educator of the labyrinth, one which accords both vestibular aptitude and the full range of cochlear perceptiveness. (Tomatis 1980:15)

In short, the electronic ear modifies one's way of hearing and hence one's way of speaking. With this instrument the individual listens through headsets to electronically modified sounds (modified in terms of timbre and the content of frequencies). The headsets, which are part of the apparatus, have an additional transmitter for bone conduction. What the users of the electronic ear listen to can be either music, someone else's voice, or their own voices (in the latter case an immediate playback enables them to hear themselves in a modified and filtered way, which will be explained later).

This listening training, which is called *Audio-Psycho-Phonology* and is known as the *Tomatis Method*, has been used successfully for many years in various, mainly pedagogical fields including voice, speech and listening education, learning problems, concentration and communication improvement, and medical therapy dealing with psychological and neurological illnesses. The use of the electronic ear has also shown positive results in foreign language acquisition in tests made with school children mainly in France, with English as a foreign language.

Listening training with the electronic ear in foreign language acquisition does not change the learner's hearing potential, but rather integrates into his/her own familiar inventory the new sounds of the target language, i.e. unfamiliar frequencies which the learner is not used to and therefore ignores. The learner's mental blocks and rigidified listening patterns are loosened; the ear "opens up" and becomes receptive to the unfamiliar.

3.2. Training program

The listening program will precede or accompany conventional language study. It is not meant to be a competitive or substitute approach, but rather a remedial or complementary one aimed at overcoming certain barriers, an additional door to the new world of the target language. The electronic ear is not an instrument which has to be used constantly in order to have the required effect. After a certain number of listening sessions, the training is completed and should not loose its effects over time. It should be seen as an instrument for the correction of rigid listening habits, which provides a "shortcut for learners" (McLaughlin 1987:48).

The listening training is subdivided into various steps and adapted to the language learning program in the specific fields where the method is being applied. First, a diagnostic listening test is administered in order to establish the learners' range of listening in both air and bone conduction. This is followed by a certain number of sessions starting with a receptive or *passive phase* and proceeding to a productive or *active phase*. During the passive phase the students listen to tapes with texts in the language they want to learn. Frequencies are gradually filtered from lower to higher ones (i.e. from 0 to 12,000 Hz), so that the ear is forced to listen to the entire frequency range which includes, of course, those which are less frequent in the learners' mother tongue. In addition to filtering, the instrument also creates quick shifts between modifications of the sound wave in two different channels, and abrupt, almost imperceptible separations between bone and air conduction. Learners are not always consciously aware of these modifications, but the ossicular muscles are forced to perform a kind of "earobics", which helps them adapt to unfamiliar sounds.

During the active phase, the students listen to words and phrases in the target language, repeat them, and then read a text aloud themselves. While they are reading, the electronic ear is constantly adapting their ears and thus their voices to the typical frequency spectrum of the new language, so that the training has a double effect: it affects both listening and speaking. The students learn to experience how a native speaker of the language they are studying hears the language, and this gives them an advantage over someone who confronts the foreign language with only his/her own ethnic sound frame to rely on. During and after the training students are more likely to speak with a correct pronunciation, rhythm, and intonation.

Training with the electronic ear has to be discontinued once or twice in order to achieve lasting results; this gives the ear time to "rest". Regular listening tests will show progress in the listening curve.

3.3. *Expected results*

If training with the electronic ear is done with absolute beginners who are learning a new language, it will make them familiar with the basic parameters of the target language, such as an overall feel for its rhythm, sound, timbre, and pronunciation. The students will integrate the new sounds into their sound inventory and learn to distinguish and recognize them before they get used to false interpretations and pronunciations. As a result, they should show greater confidence in using the new language, have less of a foreign accent, and achieve a clearer pronunciation. The students' auditory capability and voice spectrum will be measured before, during, and after the training. By means of a comparison with a control group, we hope to obtain evidence of the progress made.

Following the listening training, we would also expect a better understanding of the target language in general, and therefore a faster acquisition of its lexis. This can be easily explained by the fact that only those sounds identified as a carrier of a message can be received and memorized. When a previously unfamiliar sequence of sounds can be recognized, a meaning will be attached to it, and it is no longer undistinguishable "noise" in the learner's ears. (Because of their difficulty in distinguishing aspirated sounds, many of my Italian students could not grasp the difference between "hoffen" and "offen" until they could actually hear it.)

If what learners hear starts making sense, their attention will increase automatically. When students overcome the barrier of the unfamiliar they can use these new elements for making connections and transfers within word groups, thus memorizing new expressions more easily. As a result, this process should help them to enlarge their vocabularies more fluently and more quickly.

Finally, we expect the students using this method to get a feel for the use of lexical variants right away. They are not confronted with the target language piece by piece, as if they were putting together a puzzle made up of isolated lexemes; they listen to the whole text with a variety of lexical items in different surroundings, contractions, coarticulations, and intonation patterns right from the beginning. The result should be a noticeable decrease in the "staccato" speaking which is typical of beginners.

3.4. Applications

As mentioned in the previous section, this method is *not* meant to substitute conventional language teaching or even other listening training. What it in fact does is to add an important component to any listening comprehension program: the physical and psychological disposition of receiving a message by sound. It should therefore be introduced prior or in addition to listening exercises. In Meuleman's description of a "Listening Comprehension Approach", he refers to the major components of listening comprehension, described by J. R. Anderson (see Meuleman 1993:63-64). These consist of the following parts: perceptual processing, parsing, and utilization.

During *perceptual processing*, the learners concentrate on sounds, chunks or word sequences, and nonverbal parts of the spoken language (e.g. pauses or melody), using mainly their echoic memory. This way they are trying to grasp key words and skip messages which appear to contain irrelevant information. In order to be successful in this, the learners have to be able to recognize auditory input and to distinguish relevant parts from noise, a skill which the electronic ear will help to develop. Only after this prerequisite has been fulfilled, is the learner able to listen effectively in the sense of perceptual processing.

During *parsing*, the listeners store chunks of word sequences in their short term memory and concentrate more on semantics than on syntax.

This top-down approach is only possible if the learner can identify the words without difficulty. If the process is stopped at the identification of meaningful sound sequences, they will remain in a bottom-up listening situation, not grasping the meaning of the whole. Here again, the training with the electronic ear can make an enormous difference in acquiring this technique.

The third component of listening comprehension, *utilization*, is the logical consequence of the first two: the storage of the new meaning in the long-term memory and the connection with previous knowledge.

It becomes clear how important a part training with the electronic ear can play in language learning. It prepares the learner to listen effectively to the new sound system and recognize the message with more efficiency and less effort, and to get ready for further listening comprehension exercises. Only then can these be fully satisfactory. For Meuleman for example, listening comprehension exercises are the only way to teach metacognitive strategy (which for him is the basis of language teaching). Shouldn't the preparation with the electronic ear become step one in the training?

3.5. Work plan of the LINGUA-project

It is estimated that the project will take at least three years to be completed. During the first year, 1993, the pilot project was initiated at the University of Bologna (with Italian students learning German as a foreign language):

In the first half of the year, audio tapes were prepared with pronunciation exercises based on predicted "problem" sounds for this specific language group. We compiled exercises with words, phrases, and texts, each emphasizing a particular "problem" sound or intonation.

During the second half of 1993, the didactic plan for the pilot project in Italy was prepared. Experiences and reports from teachers and participants in the training sessions which had been carried out in France and Italy (obtained from interviews and questionnaires) were taken into consideration.

The testing procedure was scheduled for the end of 1993 and included the following components:

- the completion of questionnaires (language background, attitude towards the new language, etc.)
- a listening test (focusing on both air and bone conduction)

- a tape recording of the student reading, speaking, and repeating words or phrases in the foreign language
- a listening comprehension test
- differentiation tests.

After the installation of the electronic instruments at the University of Bologna (the Institute of Interpreting and Translation) the work with the students started in November 1993: According to the results of the initial tests, a group of around 60 persons was divided into an experimental and a control group, with 30 students in each group. Only the experimental group was given the listening sessions with the electronic ear in ad-dition to general language instruction, which was held for both groups. The control group did pronunciation exercises with the same cassettes in a standard language laboratory. Interim tests were given to each student of the experimental group in order to assess his or her progress. The sessions were scheduled to finish in February 1994, after the suggested one-month discontinuation of the work with the electronic ear over the Christmas period. Again, each student in the experimental as well as the control group was tested to ascertain final results. Results of these tests are being evaluated.

The initial, interim, and final tests will provide evidence of the progress made in listening comprehension, pronunciation, and intonation. Changes in the voice and listening curves, frequency spectra, the quality and quantity of vowels, aspiration, melody, etc. will be shown by an analysis with electronic instruments. A statistical and systematic comparison of the tests and of the two groups will indicate to what extent the method could be applied to groups in institutions like schools, universities, firms, etc.

In autumn of 1994, during the analysis of the results, we will develop a similar program at the University of Duisburg and the Università Sapienza in Rome for German and Dutch speakers who are learning Italian as a foreign language. After the experiment has been carried out in Duisburg and Antwerp, we will apply the knowledge and results obtained from the first two tests to the program at the KVH in Antwerp, working with native Dutch speakers who want to learn Italian or German.

4. Conclusion

This method, which is not bound to the learning of any specific language, can be applied in all cases where the aim is the improvement and development of comprehension and production of the spoken language. The goal is to improve the student's ability to recognize the characteristic frequencies and rhythms of the target language. The listening training can be integrated with all standard didactic methods which involve the teaching of spoken language (pronunciation, rhythm, and intonation).

In this project we do not want to develop a new method, but rather apply one which is already in existence (although up till now it has mainly been used in other, especially medical fields). Our pedagogical aims are:

1. to develop the possibility of using the method with groups rather than in individual sessions alone;
2. to examine the practicability of combining the method with foreign language instruction for adults;
3. to develop a way of integrating the method into standard foreign language instruction programs (e.g. at universities);
4. to enable adult learners in particular to overcome the barriers which prevent htem from achieving correct comprehension and fluent speaking, especially pronunciation, and prosodic competence;
5. to establish, from the experience and results obtained in the pilot project, a basis from which programs for other languages can be derived.

Notes

1. Besides the coordinating establishment, the Department of Interpreting and Translation at the University of Bologna (Scuola Superiore di Lingue Moderne per Interpreti e Traduttori), other participants in the project are: 1. Diapason Ltd. in Milan, a company which specializes in listening and communication training; 2. the University of Duisburg, 3. the Katholieke Vlaamse Hogeschool of Antwerp which, like our institute, trains interpreters and translators, 4. the Università Sapienza in Rome, and 5. the Università Cattolica in Milan.
2. According to H. H. Stern, the three separate abilities which have to be considered in a language teaching program are 1. sound discrimination ability, 2. short-term and long-term lexical memory, and 3. grammatical sensitivity (see Meuleman 1993:60).

References

Gilmor, T. M.
1989 "The Tomatis method and the genesis of listening". *Pre- and Peri-Natal Psychology* 4,1:9-24.

Kaunzner, U. A.
1994 "Neue Wege zur Verbesserung des Hörverstehens und der Aussprache im Fremdsprachenunterricht". *Zielsprache Deutsch 2.*

Krashen, S. D.
1985 *The Input Hypothesis: Issues and Implications.* New York: Longman.

McLaughlin, B.
1987 *Theories of Second-Language Learning.* London: Arnold.

Meuleman, C.
1993 "A case for metacognitive strategy teaching: The listening comprehension approach." *INTERFACE. Journal of Applied Linguistcs* 7,2:55-70.

Tomatis, A. A.
1972 The Electronic ear and new theories on auditory physiology. (Congress of Audio-Psycho-Phonology in Paris).
1974 *Vers l'Écoute Humaine*. Vol. 1 and 2. Paris: ESF éditeur.
1980 *Audio-Psycho-Phonology: A New Challenge.* Potchefstroom University.
1981 *La Nuit Utérine*. Paris: Stock. (German version: *Der Klang des Lebens*. Hamburg: Rowohlt 1990.)
1986 Apprendre une langue étrangère avec une nouvelle oreille. (Speech at the Northeast Conference, Washington D.C.).
1987 *L'Oreille et la Voix*. Paris: Laffont.
1991a *L'Oreille et le Langage*. Paris: Seuil.
1991b *Nous Sommes Tous Nés Polyglottes*. Paris: Fixot.

Subject Index

DUISBURGER ARBEITEN ZUR SPRACH- UND KULTURWISSENSCHAFT
DUISBURG PAPERS ON RESEARCH IN LANGUAGE AND CULTURE

Herausgegeben von Prof. Dr. René Dirven, Dr. Martin Pütz und Prof. Dr. Siegfried Jäger

Band 1 René Dirven / Yvan Putseys (Eds.): A User's Grammar of English: Word, Sentence, Text, Interaction - Part A. The Structure of Words and Phrases. 1989.

Band 2 René Dirven / Richard A. Geiger (Eds.): A User's Grammar of English: Word, Sentence, Text, Interaction - Part B. The Structure of Sentences. 1989.

Band 3 René Dirven / Wolfgang Zydatiß / Willis J. Edmondson (Eds.): A User's Grammar of English: Word, Sentence, Text, Interaction - Parts C & D. The Structure of Texts / The Structure of Interaction. 1989.

Band 4 René Dirven: (Ed.): A User's Grammar of English: Word, Sentence, Text, Interaction - Compact Edition. 1989.

Band 5 Martin Pütz / René Dirven (Eds.): Wheels within Wheels. Papers of the Duisburg Symposium on Pidgin and Creole Languages. 1989.

Band 6 Ulrich Schmitz / Rüdiger Schütz / Andreas Kunz (Eds.): Linguistic Approaches to Artificial Intelligence. 1990.

Band 7 Friedrich Lenz: Organisationsprinzipien in mündlicher Fachkommunikation. 1989.

Band 8 Luc Van Doorslaer (Hrsg.): Niederländische Literatur im Spiegel niederländischer Kultur. Aufsätze zur Gastprofessur von Prof. Dr. Marcel Janssens (Universität Löwen) in Duisburg, Sommersemester 1988. 1990.

Band 9 Frank Lüschow / Marita Pabst-Weinschenk (Hrsg.): Mündliche Kommunikation als kooperativer Prozeß. Sprechwissenschaftliche Arbeitsfelder. Festschrift für Elmar Bartsch. 1991.

Band 10 Susanne Niemeier: Ein Fall im Medienvergleich: Film- und Fernsehversion von "A Streetcar Named Desire". Beitrag zur Annäherung an eine Mediensemiotik. 1990.

Band 11 Paul Kent Andersen: A new look at the passive. 1991.

Band 12 Richard Kremer: The efficiency of English language teaching in smaller countries: Denmark. Basic English language teaching in Denmark and its wider context. 1991.

Band 13 Frank Lüschow: Sprache und Kommunikation in der technischen Arbeit. 1992.

Band 14 Günter Kellermann / Michael D. Morrissey (Eds.): Diachrony within Synchrony: Language History and Cognition. Papers from the International Symposium at the University of Duisburg 26-28 March 1990. 1992.

Band 15 Wim Waumans (Hrsg.): Mit fremden Augen. Niederländisch: eine Sprache, verschiedene Kulturgemeinschaften. 1993.

Band 16 Eberhard Klein: Konditionalität in didaktischen und pädagogischen Grammatiken des Englischen. Prinzipien zur Erstellung von Lehr- und Lerngrammatiken. 1993.

Band 17 Xiaoan Zhu: "Wenn sich das Gras bewegt, dann muß auch der Wind blasen!" Studien zur Metapher in der deutschen politischen Pressesprache – unter besonderer Berücksichtigung der China-Berichterstattung. 1993.

Band 18 Fritz Ponelis: The Development of Afrikaans. 1993.

Band 19 Martin Pütz: Sprachökologie und Sprachwechsel. Die deutsch-australische Sprechgemeinschaft in Canberra. 1994.

Band 20 Heiner Pürschel (Ed.); Co-Editors: Elmar Bartsch, Peter Franklin, Ulrich Schmitz, Sonja Vandermeeren: : Intercultural Communication. Proceedings of the 17th International L.A.U.D. Symposium. Duisburg, 23-27 March 1992. 1994.

Band 21 Dominiek Sandra: Morphology in the reader's mental lexicon. 1994.

Band 22 René Dirven: Metaphor and Nation. Metaphors Afrikaners live by. 1994.

Band 23 Ralph Bisschops: Die Metapher als Wertsetzung. Novalis, Ezechiel, Beckett. 1994.

Band 24 René Dirven / Johan Vanparys (Eds.): Current Approaches to the Lexicon. A Selection of Papers Presented at the 18th LAUD Symposium, Duisburg, March 1993. 1995.

Dominiek Sandra

Morphology in the reader's mental lexicon

Frankfurt/M., Berlin, Bern, New York, Paris, Wien, 1994. II, 144 pp., 2 tab.
Duisburg Papers on Research in Language and Culture.
Edited by René Dirven, Martin Pütz and Siegfried Jäger. Vol. 21
ISBN 3-631-44251-3 pb. DM 54.--*

The work addresses the question whether morphemes play a role in lexical representation and processing. Three hypotheses can be entertained: (i) morphemes (or a particular morpheme like the root) might be needed to access a representation of the whole word, or (ii) be used to express morphological relatedness at a postaccess level, or (iii) be used to determine the meaning of the word. These hypotheses are tested against experimental data on inflectional, derivational and compound morphology. The emerging picture is of a lexical architecture with two parallel access routes: one making use of whole-word access representations and postaccess connections between morphosemantically related words and another one in which the meaning of the whole word is computed from its morphemes.

Contents: Polymorphemic words · Mental lexicon · Visual word recognition · Ways of lexically representing/processing morphology · Motivations for morphological involvement in the mental lexicon · Inflectional morphology · Derivational morphology · Evaluation of Taft & Forster's prefix stripping model · Compound words